MODERN POLITICAL IDEOLOGIES

Modern
Political
Ideologies

ALAN P. GRIMES

and ROBERT H. HORWITZ

Department of Political Science, Michigan State University

New York   OXFORD UNIVERSITY PRESS   1959

ACKNOWLEDGMENTS

THE All-University Research Committee of Michigan State University has generously supported the preparation of this volume during the past two years with several grants through which much onerous labor has been accomplished. To Mr. James Wresinski we are indebted for extensive and careful research and to Miss Barbara Guthrie for her extraordinary expertise in typing. Mrs. Louise M. Horwitz assumed the responsibility of preparing the manuscript for publication, for which we are indeed grateful.

CONTENTS

IV: COMMUNISM

V: ELITISM

VI: NATIONALISM

GENERAL INTRODUCTION

Ours is an age of competing ideologies, an age which has been increasingly dominated by the sharp clash of differing political perspectives. Hardly a day passes in which we are not reminded of these ideological struggles: headlines, newscasts, popular and even scholarly literature keep these conflicts in the forefront of attention. So accustomed has our generation become to an apparently unending political crisis that a state of "cold war" has come to be accepted as normal. The college student of today is therefore prone to assume that this is the natural state of political affairs. It is little wonder, for he may well have been born in the decade of the 1930's — that politically turbulent decade which marked the rise of National Socialism in Germany, the brutal consolidation of Stalinism in the Soviet Union, and the attempts of Fascist Italy and a militaristic Japan to embark upon the road of imperial power.

These and many other catastrophies sounded the death knell for that facile political optimism of an earlier generation whose hopes and expectations were most poignantly expressed in President Wilson's prediction that democracy is "about universally to prevail . . ." Far from prevailing in the second quarter of the twentieth century, the Western democracies have instead found themselves engaged in a desperate struggle for survival. Between 1933 and 1939, democratic regimes were destroyed in Germany, Austria, Spain, and Czechoslovakia, and, with the outbreak of the Second World War, Europe's remaining democracies, with the notable exception of Britain, were subverted or conquered by anti-democratic regimes.

The world-wide ideological struggle was by no means diminished by the temporary dominance of the forces of Germany, Italy, Japan, and the other conquerors. Military defeat led rather to a heightening of ideological considerations as Partisans struggled valiantly against the Axis forces to recover their national freedom. It was within these fierce and heroic — yet often confused — struggles that the stage was set for the ideological battles of the post-war period, the difficult period in which we now find ourselves.

The present dominance of Communism in Eastern Europe, the domestic political struggles within the countries of Western Europe, and the rapid march of Nationalism in both the Middle and Far East have, in fact, roots which must be traced back to the wartime ideological conflicts and alliances — and beyond.

For the young person whose political awareness has developed during these past two decades of ideological strife, there are perhaps no more pressing tasks than the acquisition of that understanding which will enable him to comprehend the major political forces operative in the modern world and the development of the political wisdom which is required if our nation is to survive and prosper in the perilous times ahead. But, beset as he is by the claims and counterclaims of competing ideologies, how is the student to acquire a sound political orientation? How can he begin to find some clarity amidst the clamor and confusion of myriad doctrines?

The editors of this volume have, like countless other college instructors, faced this problem with numerous classes in modern political thought, the "isms," and related courses. Their experience, and seemingly that of many others, points to two basic conclusions. The first is the growing conviction that students best begin to acquire — and retain — a basic understanding of political thought through a direct and sustained consideration of the major political ideologies themselves, rather than through exclusive reliance on textbooks and other secondary sources. If the student is to develop his personal capacity to weigh and judge competing political arguments, he must early learn to confront them in their original and unadulterated form, that is to say, in the words that were meant to carry conviction, challenge the reason, and influence the passions.

While many instructors would agree with this view, they, like us, have found that the presentation of courses based on original sources has raised overwhelming practical problems. Many of the basic works are out of print or can be secured only in limited quantities and with considerable effort, if at all. Many of the contemporary documents have not been published in an accessible form. Few college libraries and fewer students can afford to secure an adequate supply of such original readings. We have made an attempt to meet the problem in this volume by bringing together a substantial number of such basic, original readings in a convenient but inexpensive format. These selections are not mere bits or samples of a particular ideology or writer; rather, the attempt has been made to present substantial statements, sometimes in their entirety, or in any event, abridged in such a way that the full structure of the argument has been retained.

But this very approach has, in turn, given rise to two other practical problems, for considerations of space could not be neglected. Thus we have been forced to limit both the number of topics covered in the present volume as well as the number of selections contained in each. In meeting these space limitations we have been guided by two considerations. In the first place, we have concerned ourselves with political ideologies, both in their historic and in their contemporary statements, rather than with attempting to cover the larger and more indeterminate domain of modern political thought. By ideologies we have understood in this context primarily those politically consequential belief systems which have determinate spokesmen and leaders and a politically consequential following. It has not been possible to provide selections illustrative of every currently significant ideology; nor should the six major categories which have been utilized be considered mutually exclusive. Selections included under one rubric oftentimes have a bearing on other ideologies. For example, while Rousseau has been placed in Part I under Democracy, it is recognized that he has been instrumental in the development of modern nationalism and in other areas as well. Or again, the very term "national Communism" indicates the convergence of two major ideological currents. Ideological hybrids, rather than pure strains, will be discovered in the analysis of almost any given political movement of our day — the disentangling of the threads in any given instance is a complex and challenging task.

Considerations of space have, in the second place, led us to make sacrifices in the total number of authors represented in the interests of providing more adequate statements for those who were included. Needless to say, this has involved the dropping of many useful selections; yet we have felt, on the basis of classroom experience, that this is sounder than the attractive alternative of strengthening the table of contents with a variety of titles which would prove, in the body of the text, to be mere "snippets." It is our hope that the application of this general approach has resulted in a volume which will prove to be genuinely enlightening to the serious student.

By way of a final comment on the contents of this volume, it may be noted that brief introductory essays precede each of the six major sections. In these essays we have not summarized the contents of the selections which follow or attempted to explicate them. The essays are rather background statements, in part historical, in part analytical, and it cannot be emphasized too strongly that they are in no way intended to provide a substitute for the student's own analysis of the selections. In fact, the authors know from their own classroom experience that these essays often provoke disagreement, and that thoughtful students will soon come to recognize that in the interpretation of these selections there is room for great divergence of views. It is our hope that the selections which follow will increase the readers' understanding of the rapidly changing world of ideologies.

A.P.G.

R.H.H.

Michigan State University
East Lansing, Michigan
February, 1959

MODERN POLITICAL IDEOLOGIES

I. DEMOCRACY

FEW words in modern political usage possess the emotional appeal contained in the term "democracy." Two costly world wars were fought — and a cold war continues — in its name; yet the meaning of democracy remains in dispute.[1] Perhaps as some have remarked it is the imprecision of the term that has given rise to its popularity as an ideological label. For certainly today in spite of the conflicting interpretations, the word democracy has almost universal appeal; even the Communist countries prefer to identify themselves as "peoples' democracies."

The current prestige of democracy is distinctly a modern phenomenon. In Russia and the satellite countries, the vogue for democracy as a label did not come about until the Second World War; in the West the current ideological significance of "democracy" is probably only as recent as the First World War. Certainly democracy as a label was not ideologically significant in world politics prior to the twentieth century. Yet, curiously, democracy is one of the oldest terms in man's political vocabulary. And from the beginning there has been disagreement over its usage.

Pericles, in his famous funeral oration (431 B.C.) early in the Peloponnesian War is reported by the historian Thucydides to have declared in his panegyric on Athenian greatness:

> It is true that we are called a democracy, for the administration is in the hands of the many and not of the few. But while the law secures equal justice to all alike in their private disputes, the claim of excellence is also recognized; and when a citizen is in any way distinguished, he is preferred to the public service, not as a matter of privilege, but as the reward of merit. Neither is poverty a bar, but a man may benefit his country whatever be the obscurity of his condition. There is no exclusiveness in our public life, and in our private intercourse we are not suspicious of one another, nor angry with our neighbor if he does what he likes; we do not put on sour looks at

[1] Over three hundred definitions of democracy are offered in Arne Naess and Associates, *Democracy, Ideology and Objectivity* (Oslo University Press, 1956), pp. 277–329.

him which, though harmless, are not pleasant. While we are thus unconstrained in our private intercourse, a spirit of reverence pervades our public acts; we are prevented from doing wrong by respect for the authorities and for the laws, having an especial regard to those which are ordained for the protection of the injured as well as to those unwritten laws which bring upon the transgressor of them the reprobation of the general sentiment.[2]

From an etymological point of view the word democracy presents no difficulty; it is derived from the Greek *demos* and *krateo,* meaning rule of the "people." The difficulty appears however, when one asks what democracy means taxonomically. Did Pericles consider Athens a democracy because the government was "in the hands of the many and not of the few," or because of the characteristics of the society he noted in the paragraph quoted above, or because of both considerations?

When the philosopher Plato classified governments he described democracy as "the form of government in which the magistrates are commonly elected by lot." It was also a city-state controlled by the "poor"; a "city full of freedom and frankness," in which there was the "greatest variety of human natures." Democracy was "a charming form of government, full of variety and disorder, and dispensing a sort of equality to equals and unequals alike." "Freedom," in a democracy was "the glory of the State . . . therefore, in a democracy alone will the freeman of nature deign to dwell." [3] It was a characteristic of democracy, Plato thought, for freedom to degenerate into license and anarchy, and thus democracy would tend to give way to tyranny. Plato in his *Republic* clearly assumes that in a democracy the government will be in the hands of the many, who are poor, and that the characteristic features of the society will be liberty and equality. Thus he considered democracy both a form of government and a way of life.

Aristotle, Plato's pupil, used the term "polity" to describe that system of government in which the "citizens at large administer the state for the common interest." He considered "polity," which was a fusion of the principles of democracy and oligarchy, to be a "just" form of government. But this was not democracy in the usual sense of the word today. Like Plato, Aristotle considered pure democracy to be a perverted or inferior form of government. It was not concerned with the common good, but looked rather to the interests of the poor. For, he noted, "the real difference between democracy and oligarchy is poverty and wealth. Whenever

[2] Benjamin Jowett, *Thucydides* (Boston: D. Lothrop & Co., 1883), pp. 117–18.
[3] *The Republic,* translated by Benjamin Jowett (New York: The Modern Library), pp. 312, 318.

men rule by reason of their wealth, whether they be few or many, that is an oligarchy, and where the poor rule, that is a democracy. But, as a fact the rich are few and the poor many." If number was not the major criterion for classification of governments ("it is only an accident that the free are the many and the rich are the few"), nevertheless it was not to be omitted from a sound scheme of classification. Thus he further observed that "the form of government is a democracy when the free, who are also poor and the majority, govern, and an oligarchy when the rich and the noble govern, they being at the same time few in number." [4] Aristotle's analysis of democracy is so penetrating, especially in the light of its modern manifestation, that it is worth quoting at some length.

> The basis of a democratic state is liberty; which, according to the common opinion of men, can only be enjoyed in such a state; — this they affirm to be the great end of every democracy. One principle of liberty is for all to rule and to be ruled in turn, and indeed democratic justice is the application of numerical not proportionate equality; whence it follows that the majority must be supreme, and that whatever the majority approve must be the end and the just. Every citizen, it is said, must have equality, and therefore in a democracy the poor have more power than the rich, because there are more of them, and the will of the majority is supreme. This, then, is one note of liberty which all democrats affirm to be the principle of their state. Another is that a man should live as he likes. This, they say, is the privilege of a freeman, since, on the other hand, not to live as a man likes is the mark of a slave. This is the second characteristic of democracy, whence has arisen the claim of men to be ruled by none, if possible, or, if this is impossible, to rule and be ruled in turns; and so it contributes to the freedom based upon equality.[5]

After developing the institutional implementation of these democratic principles, Aristotle observed:

> These are the points common to all democracies; but democracy and demos in their truest form are based upon the recognized principle of democratic justice, that all should count equally; for equality implies that the poor should have no more share in the government than the rich, and should not be the only rulers, but that all should rule equally according to their numbers. And in this way men think that they will secure equality and freedom in their state.[6]

[4] *Aristotle's Politics*, translated by Benjamin Jowett (New York: The Modern Library, 1943), pp. 174, 175.
[5] *Ibid.*, p. 260.
[6] *Ibid.*, pp. 261–62.

Thus in Greek thought there was a conflicting evaluation of democracy. Pericles extolled its virtues; Plato and Aristotle were each critical of democracy, believing it to be an inferior political system, subject to instability and injustice. In the intervening centuries between the Greek and modern usage of democracy both the ideology and its associated institutions have undergone modifications. Institutionally the concept of representative institutions, which made bold beginnings under the Romans, experienced only faltering progress for centuries elsewhere. World history, with few exceptions, such as in Switzerland, was rather the repetitious chronicling of various forms of absolutism. Gradually, after the seventeenth century, and at first only in the West, the consolidated and absolute power of monarchs passed into the hands of the rising industrial and commerical classes. This extension of political power from the one to the few to the many, coupled with a distinctive ideology, proceeded for the next three centuries. This transference of power was first characteristically described as republicanism, after the Latin *res publica,* a public thing. Late in the eighteenth century in America the Founding Fathers clearly thought they were establishing a republican form of government; in France was established the first French Republic. Yet the Declaration of Independence (1776) and the French Declaration of the Rights of Man (1791) are usually considered two of the basic public documents in the record of democratic ideology. The spread of republicanism continued apace throughout the nineteenth and early twentieth centuries. Kingdoms and empires became known as republics as their institutions and their ideologies changed. Germany, Russia, and China, for instance, along with many smaller states, took on the appellation "republics." Not until after the Second World War did "democracy" become the more fashionable title; and now, more than ever before, democracy is subjected to a variety of interpretations.

Only a little over a century ago Alexis de Tocqueville, believing equality to be the principle ingredient of democracy, foresaw the spread of democracy as though ordained by God. In his *Democracy in America* he observed:

> The various occurrences of national existence have everywhere turned to the advantage of democracy; all men have aided it by their exertions: those who have intentionally labored in its cause, and those who have served it unwittingly; those who have fought for it and those who have declared themselves its opponents, have all been driven along in the same track, have all labored to one end, some ignorantly and some unwillingly; all have been blind instruments in the hands of God.

The gradual development of the equality of conditions is therefore a providential fact, and it possesses all the characteristics of a Divine decree: it is universal, it is durable, it constantly eludes all human interference, and all events as well as all men contribute to its progress.[7]

Tocqueville used the term democracy in its broadest sense; it encompassed not only equality but freedom, individualism, and popular sovereignty as well. Another noted foreign observer of American politics, James Bryce, in his comparative study *Modern Democracies* (1921), gave the term a much more limited connotation.

The term democracy has in recent years been loosely used to denote sometimes a state of society, sometimes a state of mind, sometimes a quality in manners. It has become encrusted with all sorts of associations attractive or repulsive, ethical or political, or even religious. But democracy really means nothing more nor less than the rule of the whole people expressing their sovereign will by their votes.[8]

Furthermore, in analyzing the forces that had brought forth the rise of democracy, Bryce was led to some interesting conclusions. He doubted that the ideological statement of democratic principles had been the decisive factor in bringing about democratic institutions. For, he noted, "neither the conviction that power is better entrusted to the people than to a ruling One or Few, nor the desire of the average man to share in the government of his own community, has in fact been a strong force inducing political change. Popular government has been usually sought and won and valued not as a good thing in itself, but as a means of getting rid of tangible grievances or securing tangible benefits, and when those objects have been attained, the interest in it has generally tended to decline." [9]

At the time Bryce wrote, no major country which had instituted popular government (other than France under Napoleon) had abandoned democracy. Subsequent history suggested a less promising future for democracy. Indeed, when Carl Becker wrote *Modern Democracy* in 1941 he observed, "the most obvious political fact of our time is that democracy . . . has suffered an astounding decline in prestige." [10] He attributed this decline to

[7] Alexis de Tocqueville, *Democracy in America*, translated by Henry Reeve (New York: Oxford University Press, 1947), pp. 6–7.

[8] James Bryce, *Modern Democracies* (New York: The Macmillan Company, 1921), vol. 1, pp. vii–viii.

[9] *Ibid.*, p. 41.

[10] Carl Becker, *Modern Democracy* (New Haven: Yale University Press, 1941), p. 7.

the lack of an adequate economic or material base to support democracy, which he characterized "an economic luxury." With the decline of prosperity following the First World War, democracy declined as well. For the many who were also poor, as the Greeks had anticipated, were often blocked by the constitutional processes from giving political and economic effect to their interpretations of liberty and equality. Political liberty thus suffered the aggravated effects of economic inequality. Thus, to Becker, writing at the conclusion of a world economic depression terminated only by a world war, the basic dilemma which confronted democratic societies was "to solve the economic problem by the democratic method, or to cease to be democratic societies." [11]

Democracy, even in definition, poses a problem that is infinitely complex, for different theorists have seen in democracy different things. Is democracy simply the rule of the majority, without regard to the policies they adopt? Is democracy a political system which guarantees individual rights? Or is it both? In cases of conflict between majority rule and minority rights, which is the more basic attribute of democracy? Does democracy require certain institutional, that is, constitutional, arrangements of the political order, and if so, what are these? Are certain economic and sociological conditions necessary prerequisites for the realization of democracy? What is the significance of the word "liberal" so frequently used in conjunction with democracy? And what is "neo-conservative" in liberal-democratic thought?

Democracy survives today in an increasingly precarious setting. The ideology of democracy as it has been articulated by some of its most notable and representative and diverse adherents in other periods of crisis in world history is peculiarly appropriate for study today. The readings below were first published as follows:

John Locke, *Two Treatises of Government* (1690)
Jean Jacques Rousseau, *The Social Contract* (1762)
John Stuart Mill, *On Liberty* (1859)
John Dewey, *Freedom and Culture* (1939)
George Gallup and Saul Forbes Rae, *The Pulse of Democracy* (1940)
A. D. Lindsay, *The Modern Democratic State* (1943)
Walter Lippmann, *The Public Philosophy* (1955)

[11] *Ibid.*, p. 67.

OF CIVIL GOVERNMENT

by John Locke *

OF THE STATE OF NATURE

To understand political power aright, and derive it from its original, we must consider what state all men are naturally in, and that is, a state of perfect freedom to order their actions and dispose of their possessions and persons as they think fit, within the bounds of the law of nature, without asking leave, or depending upon the will of any other man.

A state also of equality, wherein all the power and jurisdiction is reciprocal, no one having more than another; there being nothing more evident than that creatures of the same species and rank, promiscuously born to all the same advantages of nature, and the use of the same faculties, should also be equal one amongst another without subordination or subjection, unless the lord and master of them all should, by any manifest declaration of his will set one above another, and confer on him, by an evident and clear appointment, an undoubted right to dominion and sovereignty. . . .

But though this be a state of liberty, yet it is not a state of licence; though man in that state have an uncontrollable liberty to dispose of his person or possessions, yet he has not liberty to destroy himself, or so much as any creature in his possession, but where some nobler use than its bare preservation calls for it. The state of nature has a law of nature to govern it, which obliges every one, and reason, which is that law, teaches all mankind who will but consult it, that being all equal and independent, no one ought to harm another in his life, health, liberty, or possessions: for men being all the workmanship of one omnipotent and infinitely wise maker; all the servants of one sovereign master, sent into the world by his order, and about his business they are his property, whose workmanship

---

* John Locke, "An Essay Concerning the True Original, Extent and End of Civil Government," *Social Contract: Essays by Locke, Hume and Rousseau* (New York: 1948). By permission of Oxford University Press.

they are, made to last during his, not one another's pleasure: and being furnished with like faculties, sharing all in one community of nature, there cannot be supposed any such subordination among us, that may authorize us to destroy one another, as if we were made for one another's uses, as the inferior ranks of creatures are for ours. Every one, as he is bound to preserve himself, and not to quit his station wilfully, so, by the like reason, when his own preservation comes not in competition, ought he as much as he can to preserve the rest of mankind, and not unless it be to do justice on an offender, take away, or impair the life, or what tends to the preservation of the life, the liberty, health, limb or goods of another.

And that all men may be restrained from invading others' rights, and from doing hurt to one another, and the law of nature be observed, which willeth the peace and preservation of all mankind, the execution of the law of nature is, in that state, put into every man's hands, whereby every one has a right to punish the transgressors of that law to such a degree, as may hinder its violation. For the law of nature would, as all other laws that concern men in this world, be in vain, if there were nobody that in the state of nature had a power to execute that law, and thereby preserve the innocent and restrain offenders. And if any one in the state of nature may punish another for any evil he has done, every one may do so: for in that state of perfect equality where naturally there is no superiority or jurisdiction of one over another, what any may do in prosecution of that law, every one must needs have a right to do. . . .

'Tis often asked as a mighty objection, where are, or ever were there any men in such a state of nature? To which it may suffice as an answer at present, that since all princes and rulers of *independent* governments all through the world, are in a state of nature, 'tis plain the world never was, nor never will be, without numbers of men in that state. I have named all governors of *independent* communities, whether they are, or are not, in league with others: for 'tis not every compact that puts an end to the state of nature between men, but only this one of agreeing together mutually to enter into one community, and make one body politic; other promises, and compacts, men may make one with another, and yet still be in the state of nature. . . .

OF PROPERTY

God, who hath given the world to men in common, hath also given them reason to make use of it to the best advantage of life and convenience. The earth and all that is therein is given to men for the support and comfort of their being. And though all the fruits it naturally produces, and beasts it feeds, belong to mankind in common, as they are produced by the spontaneous hand of nature, and no body has originally a private dominion exclusive of the rest of mankind in any of them, as they are thus in their natural state, yet being given for the use of men, there must of necessity be a means to appropriate them some way or other before they can be of any use, or at all beneficial, to any particular man. The fruit or venison which nourishes the wild Indian, who knows no enclosure, and is still a tenant in common, must be his, and so his — *i.e.*, a part of him, that another can no longer have any right to it before it can do any good for the support of his life.

Though the earth and all inferior creatures be common to all men, yet every man has a *property* in his own person. This nobody has any right to but himself. The *labour* of his body and the *work* of his hands, we may say, are properly his. Whatsoever, then, he removes out of the state that nature hath provided and left it in, he hath mixed his labour with it, and joined to it something that is his own, and thereby makes it his property. It being by him removed from the common state nature placed it in, it hath by this labour something annexed to it that excludes the common right of other men. For this labour being the unquestionable property of the labourer, no man but he can have a right to what that is once joined to, at least where there is enough, and as good left in common for others.

He that is nourished by the acorns he picked up under an oak, or the apples he gathered from the trees in the wood, has certainly appropriated them to himself. Nobody can deny but the nourishment is his. I ask, then, when did they begin to be his? when he digested? or when he ate? or when he boiled? or when he brought them home? or when he picked them up? And 'tis plain, if the first gathering made them not his, nothing else could. That labour put a distinction between them and common. That added something to them more than Nature, the common mother of all, had done, and so they became his private right. And will any one say he had no right to those acorns or apples he thus appropriated because he had not the consent of all mankind to make them his? Was it a robbery thus to assume to himself what belonged to all in common? If such a consent as that was necessary, man had starved, notwithstanding the plenty God had given him. We see in commons, which remain so by compact, that 'tis the taking any part of what is common, and removing it out of the state Nature leaves it in, which begins the property, without which the common is of no use. And the taking of this or that part does not depend on the express consent of all the commoners. Thus, the grass my horse has bit, the turfs my servant has cut, and the ore I have digged in any place, where I have a right to them in common with others, become my property without the assignation or consent of anybody. The labour that was mine, removing them out of that common state they were in, hath fixed my property in them. . . .

It will perhaps be objected to this, that if gathering the acorns or other fruits of the earth, etc., makes a right to them, then any one may engross as much as he will. To which I answer, Not so. The same law of nature that does by this means give us property, does also bound that property too. *God has given us all things richly,* I *Tim.* vi. 17. Is the voice of reason confirmed by inspiration? But how far has he given it us, *to enjoy?* As much as any one can make use of to any advantage of life before it spoils, so much he may by his labour fix a property in. Whatever is beyond this is more than his share, and belongs to others. Nothing was made by God for man to spoil or destroy. And thus considering the plenty of natural provisions there was a long time in the world, and the few spenders, and to how small a part of that provision the industry of one man could extend itself and engross it to the prejudice of others, especially keeping within the bonds set by reason of what might serve for his use, there could be then little room for quarrels or contentions about property so established.

But the chief matter of property being now not the fruits of the earth and the beasts that subsist on it, but the earth itself, as that which takes in and carries with it all the rest, I think it is plain that property in that too is acquired as the former. As much land as a man tills, plants, improves, cultivates, and can use the product of, so much is his property. He by his labour does, as it were, enclose it from the common. Nor will it invalidate his right to say, Every body else has an equal title to it, and therefore he cannot appropriate, he cannot enclose, without the consent of all his fellow-commoners, all mankind. God, when he gave the world in common to all mankind, commanded man also to labour, and the penury of his condition required it of him. God and his reason commanded him to subdue the earth — *i.e.,* improve it for the benefit of life and therein lay out something upon it that was his own, his labour. He that, in obedience to this command of God, subdued, tilled, and sowed any part of it, thereby annexed to it something that was his property, which another had no title to, nor could without injury take from him.

Nor was this appropriation of any parcel of land, by improving it, any prejudice to any other man, since there was still enough and as good left, and more than the yet unprovided could use. So that, in effect, there was never the less left for others because of his enclosure for himself. For he that leaves as much as another can make use of does as good as take nothing at all. Nobody could think himself injured by the drinking of another man, though he took a good draught, who had a whole river of the same water left him to quench his thirst. And the case of land and water, where there is enough of both, is perfectly the same.

God gave the world to men in common, but since he gave it them for their benefit and the greatest conveniences of life they were capable to draw from it, it cannot be supposed he meant it should always remain common and uncultivated. He gave it to the use of the industrious and rational (and labour was to be his title to it); not to the fancy or covetousness of the quarrelsome and contentious. He that had as good left for his improvement as was already taken up needed not complain, ought not to meddle with what was already improved by another's labour; if he did 'tis plain he desired the benefit of another's pains, which he had no right to, and not the ground which God had given him, in common with others, to labour on, and whereof there was as good left as that already possessed, and more than he knew what to do with, or his industry could reach to.

'Tis true, in land that is common in England or any other country, where there are plenty of people under government who have money and commerce, no one can enclose or appropriate any part without the consent of all his fellow-commoners; because this is left common by compact, *i.e.*, by the law of the land, which is not to be violated. And, though it be common in respect of some men, it is not so to all mankind, but is the joint property of this country, or this parish. Besides, the remainder, after such enclosure, would not be as good to the rest of the commoners as the whole was, when they could all make use of the whole; whereas in the beginning and first peopling of the great common of the world it was quite otherwise. The law man was under was rather for appropriating. God commanded, and his wants forced him to labour. That was his property, which could not be taken from him wherever he had fixed it. And hence subduing or cultivating the earth and having dominion, we see, are joined together. The one gave title to the other. So that God, by commanding to subdue, gave authority so far to appropriate. And the condition of human life, which requires labour and materials to work on, necessarily introduce private possessions. . . .

From all which it is evident, that though the things of nature are given in common, man (by being master of himself, and proprietor of his own person, and the actions or labour of it) had still in himself the great foundation of property; and that which made up the great part of what he applied to the support or comfort of his being, when invention and arts had improved the conveniences of life, was perfectly his own, and did not belong in common to others.

Thus labour, in the beginning, gave a right of property, wherever any one was pleased to employ it, upon what was common, which remained a long while, the far greater part, and is yet more than mankind makes use of. Men at first, for the most part, contented themselves with what unassisted nature offered to their necessities; and though afterwards, in some parts of the world, where the increase of people and stock, with the use of money, had made land scarce, and so of some value, the several communities settled the bounds of their distinct territories, and, by laws, within themselves, regulated the properties of the private men of their society, and so, by compact and agreement, settled the property which labour and industry began; and the leagues that have been made between several states and kingdoms, either expressly or tacitly disowning all claim and right to the land in the other's possession, have, by common consent, given up their pretences to their natural common right, which originally they had to those countries; and so have, by positive agreement, settled a property amongst themselves in distinct parts of the world; yet there are still great tracts of ground to be found, which the inhabitants thereof, not having joined with the rest of mankind in the consent of the use of their common money, lie waste, and are more than the people who dwell on it do, or can make use of, and so still lie in common; though this can scarce happen amongst that part of mankind that have consented to the use of money.

The greatest part of things really useful to the life of man, and such as the necessity of subsisting made the first commoners of the world look after, as it doth the Americans now, are generally things of short duration, such as, if they are not consumed by use, will decay and perish of themselves. Gold, silver, and diamonds are things that fancy or agreement have put the value on, more than real use and the necessary support of life. Now of those good things which nature hath provided in common, every one had a right (as hath been said) to as much as he could use, and had a property in all he could effect with his labour; all that his industry could extend to, to alter from the state nature had put it in, was his. He that gathered a hundred bushels of acorns or apples had thereby a property in them, they were his goods as soon as gathered. He was only to look that he used them before they spoiled, else he took more than his share, and robbed others. And, indeed, it was a foolish thing, as well as dishonest, to hoard up more than he could make use of. If he gave away a part to any body else, so that it perished not uselessly in his possession, these he also made use of. And if he also bartered away plums that would have rotted in a week, for nuts that would last good for his eating a whole year, he did no injury; he wasted not the common stock; destroyed no part of the portion of goods that belonged to others, so long as nothing perished uselessly in his hands. Again, if he would give his nuts for a piece of metal, pleased with its colour, or exchange his sheep for shells, or wool for a sparkling pebble or a diamond, and keep those by him all his life, he invaded not the right of others; he might heap up as much of these durable things as he pleased; the exceeding of the bounds of his just property not lying in the largeness of his possessions, but the perishing of anything uselessly in it.

And thus came in the use of money, some lasting thing that men might keep without spoiling, and that, by mutual consent, men would take in exchange for the truly useful but perishable supports of life. . . .

But since gold and silver, being little useful to the life of man, in proportion to food, raiment, and carriage, has its value only from the consent of men, whereof labour yet makes in great part the measure, it is plain that the consent of men have agreed to a disproportionate and unequal possession of the earth, I mean out of the bounds of society and compact; for in governments the laws regulate it; they having, by consent, found out and agreed in a way how a man may rightfully, and without injury, possess more than he himself can make use of by receiving gold and silver, which may continue long in a man's possession without decaying for the overplus, and agreeing those metals should have a value.

And thus, I think, it is very easy to conceive, without any difficulty, how labour could at first begin a title of property in the common things of nature, and how the spending it upon our uses bounded it; so that there could then be no reason of quarrelling about title, nor any doubt about the largeness of possession it gave. Right and conveniency went together. For as a man had a right to all he could employ his labour upon, so he had no temptation to labour for more than he could make use of. This left no room for controversy about the title, nor for encroachment on the right of others. What portion a man carved to himself was easily seen; and it was useless as well as dishonest to carve himself too much, or take more than he needed. . . .

Of Political or Civil Society

Man being born, as has been proved, with a title to perfect freedom and an uncontrolled enjoyment of all the rights and privileges of the law of nature, equally with any other man, or number of men in the world, hath by nature a power not only to preserve his property, that is, his life, liberty, and estate, against the injuries and attempts of other men, but to judge of and punish the breaches of that law in others, as he is persuaded the offence deserves, even with death itself, in crimes where the heinousness of the fact, in his opinion, requires it. But because no political society can be, nor subsist, without having in itself the power to preserve the property, and in order thereunto punish the offences of all those of that society; there, and there only, is political society, where every one of the members hath quitted this natural power, resigned it up into the hands of the community in all cases that exclude him not from appealing for protection to the law established by it. And thus all private judgement of every particular member being excluded, the community comes to be umpire, by settled standing rules; indifferent, and the same to all parties: And by men having authority from the community for the execution of those rules, decides all the differences that may happen between any members of that society concerning any matter of right, and punishes those offences which any member hath committed against the society with such penalties as the law has established; whereby it is easy to discern who are, and who are not, in political society together. Those who are united into one body, and have a common established law and judicature to appeal to, with authority to decide controversies between them and punish offenders, are in civil society one with another; but those who have no such common appeal, I mean on earth, are still in the state of nature, each being, where there is no other, judge for himself and executioner; which is, as I have before showed it, the perfect state of nature.

And thus the commonwealth comes by a power to set down what punishment shall belong to the several transgressions they think worthy of it, committed amongst the members of that society (which is the power of making laws) as well as it has the power to punish any injury done unto any of its members by any one that is not of it (which is the power of war and peace); and all this for the preservation of property of all the members of that society, as far as is possible. But though every man entered into society has quitted his power to punish offences against the law of nature in prosecution of his own private judgement, yet with the judgement of offences which he has given up to the legislative in all cases where he can appeal to the magistrate, he has given up a right to the commonwealth to employ his force for the execution of the judgements of the commonwealth whenever he shall be called to it, which, indeed, are his own judgements, they being made by himself or his representative. And herein we have the original of the legislative and executive power of civil society, which is to judge by standing laws how far offences are to be punished when committed within the commonwealth; and also by occasional judgements founded on the present circumstances of the fact, how far injuries from without are to be vindicated, and in both these to employ all the force of all the members when there shall be need.

Wherever therefore any number of men are so united into one society as to quit every one his executive power of the law of nature, and to resign it to the public, there and there only is a political or civil society. And this is done wherever any number of men, in the state of nature, enter into society to make one people, one body politic under one supreme government: or else when any one joins himself to and incorporates with any government already made. For hereby he authorises the society, or which is all one, the legislative thereof, to make laws for him as the public good of the society shall require, to the execution whereof his own assistance (as to his own decrees) is due. And this puts men out of a state of nature into that of a commonwealth, by setting up a judge on earth with authority to determine all the controversies and redress the injuries that may happen to any member of the commonwealth; which judge is the legislative or magistrates appointed by it. And wherever there are any number of men, however associated, that have no such decisive power to appeal to, there they are still in the state of nature. . . .

Of the Beginning of Political Societies

Men being, as has been said, by nature all free, equal, and independent, no one can be put out of this estate and subjected to the political power of another without his own consent, which is done by agreeing with other men to join and unite into a community for their comfortable, safe, and peaceable living one amongst another, in a secure enjoyment of their properties, and a greater security against any that are not of it. This any number of men may do, because it injures not the freedom of the rest; they are left, as they were, in the liberty of the state of nature. When any number of men have so consented to make one community or government, they are thereby presently incorporated, and make one body politic, wherein the majority have a right to act and conclude the rest.

For, when any number of men have, by the consent of every individual, made a community, they have thereby made that community one body, with a power to act as one body, which is only by the will and determination of the majority. For that which acts any community, being only the consent of the individuals of it, and it being one body, must move one way, it is necessary the body should move that way whither the greater force carries it, which is the consent of the majority, or else it is impossible it should act or continue one body, one community, which the consent of every individual that united into it agreed that it should; and so every one is bound by that consent to be concluded by the majority. And therefore we see that in assemblies empowered to act by positive laws where no number is set by that positive law which empowers them, the act of the majority passes for the act of the whole, and of course determines as having, by the law of nature and reason, the power of the whole.

And thus every man, by consenting with others to make one body politic under one government, puts himself under an obligation to every one of that society to submit to the determination of the majority, and to be concluded by it; or else this original compact, whereby he with others incorporates into one society, would signify nothing, and be no compact if he be left free and under no other ties than he was in before in the state of nature. For what appearance would there be of any compact? What new engagement if he were no farther tied by any decrees of the society than he himself thought fit and did actually consent to? This would be still as great a liberty as he himself had before his compact, or any one else in the state of nature hath, who may submit himself and consent to any acts of it if he thinks fit.

For if the consent of the majority shall not in reason be received as the act of the whole, and conclude every individual, nothing but the consent of every individual can make anything to be the act of the whole, which, considering the infirmities of health and avocations of business, which in a number though much less than that of a commonwealth, will necessarily keep many away from the public assembly, and the variety of opinions and contrariety of interests which unavoidably happen in all collections of men, 'tis next impossible ever to be had. . . . For where the majority cannot conclude the rest, there they cannot act as one body, and consequently will be immediately dissolved again.

Whosoever therefore out of a state of nature unite into a community, must be understood to give up all the power necessary to the ends for which they unite into society to the majority of the community, unless they expressly agreed in any number greater than the majority. And this is done by barely agreeing to unite into one political society, which is all the compact that is, or needs be, between the individuals that enter into or make up a commonwealth. And thus, that which begins and actually constitutes any political society is nothing but the consent of any number of freemen capable of a majority, to unite and incorporate into such a society. And this is that, and that only, which did or could give beginning to any lawful government in the world. . . .

Of the Ends of Political Society and Government

If man in the state of nature be so free as has been said; if he be absolute lord of his own person and possessions; equal to the greatest and subject to no body, why will he part with his freedom? Why will he give up this empire, and subject himself to the dominion and control of any other power? To which 'tis obvious to answer, that though in the state of nature he hath such a right, yet the enjoyment of it is very uncertain, and constantly exposed to the invasion of others: for all being kings as much as he, every man his equal, and the greater part no strict observers of equity and justice, the enjoyment of the property he has in this state is very unsafe, very unsecure. This makes him willing to quit this condition which, however free, is full of fears and continual dangers; and 'tis not without reason that he seeks out and is willing to join in society with others who are already united, or have a mind to unite for the mutual preservation of their lives, liberties, and estates, which I call by the general name, property.

The great and chief end therefore, of men's uniting into commonwealths, and putting themselves under government, is the preservation of their property; to which in the state of nature there are many things wanting.

First, There wants an established, settled, known law, received and allowed by common consent to be the standard of right and wrong, and the common measure to decide all controversies between them. For though the law of nature be plain and intelligible to all rational creatures, yet men, being biased by their interest, as well as ignorant for want of study of it, are not apt to allow of it as a law binding to them in the application of it to their particular cases.

Secondly, In the state of nature there wants a known and indifferent judge, with authority to determine all differences according to the established law. For every one in that state being both judge and executioner of the law of nature, men being partial to themselves, passion and revenge is very apt to carry them too far, and with too much heat in their own cases, as well as negligence and unconcernedness, to make them too remiss in other men's.

Thirdly, In the state of nature there often wants power to back and support the sentence when right, and to give it due execution. They who by any injustice offended, will seldom fail where they are able by force to make good their injustice. Such resistance many times makes the punishment dangerous, and frequently destructive to those who attempt it.

Thus mankind, notwithstanding all the privileges of the state of nature, being but in an ill condition while they remain in it, are quickly driven into society. Hence it comes to pass, that we seldom find any number of men live any time together in this state. The inconveniences that they are therein exposed to by the irregular and uncertain exercise of the power every man has of punishing the transgressions of others, make them take sanctuary under the established laws of government, and therein seek the preservation of their property. 'Tis this makes them so willingly give up every one his single power of punishing to be exercised by such alone as shall be appointed to it amongst them, and by such rules as the community, or those authorised by them to that purpose, shall agree on. And in this we have the original right and rise of both the legislative and executive power as well as of the governments and societies themselves. . . .

But though men when they enter into society give up the equality, liberty, and executive power they had in the state of nature into the hands of the society, to be so far disposed of by the legislative as the good of the society shall require, yet it being only with an intention in every one the better to preserve himself, his liberty and property (for no rational creature can be supposed to change his condition with an intention to be worse), the power of the society, or legislative constituted by them, can never be supposed to extend farther than the common good, but is obliged to secure every one's property by providing against those three defects above-mentioned that made the state of nature so unsafe and uneasy. And so, whoever has the legislative or supreme power of any commonwealth, is bound to govern by established standing laws, promulgated and known to the people, and not by extemporary decrees, by indifferent and upright judges, who are to decide controversies by those laws; and to employ the force of the community at home only in the execution of such laws, or abroad to prevent or redress foreign injuries and secure the community from inroads and invasion. And all this to be directed to no other end but the peace, safety, and public good of the people. . . .

Of the Dissolution of Government

Here 'tis like the common question will be made. Who shall be judge whether the prince or legislative act contrary to their trust? This, perhaps, ill-affected and factious men may spread amongst the people, when the prince only makes use of his due prerogative. To this I reply, The people shall be judge; for who shall be judge whether his trustee or deputy acts well and according to the trust reposed in him, but he who deputes him and must, by having deputed him, have still a power to discard him when he fails in his trust? If this be reasonable in particular cases of private men, why should it be otherwise in that of the greatest moment, where the welfare of millions is concerned and also where the evil, if not prevented, is greater, and the redress very difficult, dear, and dangerous?

But, farther, this question, (Who shall be judge?) cannot mean that there is no judge at all. For where there is no judicature on earth to decide controversies amongst men, God in heaven is judge. He alone, 'tis true, is judge of the right. But every man is judge for himself, as in all other cases so in this, whether another hath put himself into a state of war with him, and whether he should appeal to the supreme Judge, as *Jephtha* did.

If a controversy arise betwixt a prince and some of the people in a matter where the law is silent or doubtful, and the thing be of great consequence, I should think the proper umpire, in such a case, should be the body of the people. For in such cases where the prince hath a trust reposed in him, and is dispensed from the common, ordinary rules of the law; there, if any men find themselves aggrieved, and think the prince acts contrary to, or beyond that trust, who so proper to judge as the body of the people (who at first lodged that trust in him) how far they meant it should extend? But if the prince, or whoever they be in the administration, decline that way of determination, the appeal then lies nowhere but to Heaven. Force between either persons, who have no known superior on earth, or which permits no appeal to a judge on earth, being properly a state of war, wherein the appeal lies only to Heaven; and in that state the injured party must judge for himself when he will think fit to make use of that appeal and put himself upon it.

To conclude, The power that every individual gave the society when he entered into it, can never revert to the individuals again, as long as the society lasts, but will always remain in the community; because without this there can be no community, no commonwealth, which is contrary to the original agreement; so also when the society hath placed the legislative in any assembly of men, to continue in them and their successors, with direction and authority for providing such successors, the legislative can never revert to the people whilst that government lasts; because, having provided a legislative with power to continue for ever, they have given up their political power to the legislative, and cannot resume it. But if they have set limits to the duration of their legislative, and made this supreme power in any person or assembly only temporary; or else when, by the miscarriages of those in authority, it is forfeited; upon the forfeiture of their rulers, or at the determination of the time set, it reverts to the society, and the people have a right to act as supreme, and continue the legislative in themselves or place it in a new form, or new hands, as they think good.

THE SOCIAL CONTRACT

by J. J. Rousseau *

OF THE SOCIAL PACT

I assume, for the sake of argument, that a point was reached in the history of mankind when the obstacles to continuing in a state of Nature were stronger than the forces which each individual could employ to the end of continuing in it. The original state of Nature, therefore, could no longer endure, and the human race would have perished had it not changed its manner of existence.

Now, since men can by no means engender new powers, but can only unite and control those of which they are already possessed, there is no way in which they can maintain themselves save by coming together and pooling their strength in a way that will enable them to withstand any resistance exerted upon them from without. They must develop some sort of central direction and learn to act in concert.

Such a concentration of powers can be brought about only as the consequence of an agreement reached between individuals. But the self-preservation of each single man derives primarily from his own strength and from his own freedom. How, then, can he limit these without, at the same time, doing himself an injury and neglecting that care which it is his duty to devote to his own concerns? This difficulty, in so far as it is relevant to my subject, can be expressed as follows:

"Some form of association must be found as a result of which the whole strength of the community will be enlisted for the protection of the person

* J. J. Rousseau, "The Social Contract," *Social Contract: Essays by Locke, Hume and Rousseau* (New York: 1948). By permission of Oxford University Press.

and property of each constituent member, in such a way that each, when united to his fellows, renders obedience to his own will, and remains as free as he was before." That is the basic problem of which the Social Contract provides the solution.

The clauses of this Contract are determined by the Act of Association in such a way that the least modification must render them null and void. Even though they may never have been formally enunciated, they must be everywhere the same, and everywhere tacitly admitted and recognized. So completely must this be the case that, should the social compact be violated, each associated individual would at once resume all the rights which once were his, and regain his natural liberty, by the mere fact of losing the agreed liberty for which he renounced it.

It must be clearly understood that the clauses in question can be reduced, in the last analysis, to one only, to wit, the complete alienation by each associate member to the community of *all his rights*. For, in the first place, since each has made surrender of himself without reservation, the resultant conditions are the same for all: and, because they are the same for all, it is in the interest of none to make them onerous to his fellows.

Furthermore, this alienation having been made unreservedly, the union of individuals is as perfect as it well can be, none of the associated members having any claim against the community. For should there be any rights left to individuals, and no common authority be empowered to pronounce as between them and the public, then each, being in some things his own judge, would soon claim to be so in all. Were that so, a state of Nature would still remain in being, the conditions of association becoming either despotic or ineffective.

In short, whoso gives himself to all gives himself to none. And, since there is no member of the social group over whom we do not acquire precisely the same rights as those over ourselves which we have surrendered to him, it follows that we gain the exact equivalent of what we lose, as well as an added power to conserve what we already have.

If, then, we take from the social pact everything which is not essential to it, we shall find it to be reduced to the following terms: "each of us contributes to the group his person and the powers which he wields as a person, and we receive into the body politic each individual as forming an indivisible part of the whole."

As soon as the act of association becomes a reality, it substitutes for the person of each of the contracting parties a moral and collective body made up of as many members as the constituting assembly has votes, which body receives from this very act of constitution its unity, its dispersed *self*, and its will. The public person thus formed by the union of individuals was known in the old days as a *City*, but now as the *Republic* or *Body Politic*.* This, when it fulfils a passive role, is known by its members as *The State*, when an active one, as *The Sovereign People*, and, in contrast to other similar bodies, as a *Power*. In respect of the constituent associates, it enjoys the collective name of *The People*, the individuals who compose it being known as Citizens in so far as they share in the sovereign authority, as *Subjects* in so far as they owe obedience to the laws of the State. But these different terms frequently overlap, and are used indiscriminately one for the other. It is enough that we should realize the difference between them when they are employed in a precise sense.

OF THE SOVEREIGN

It is clear from the above formula that the act of association implies a mutual undertaking between the body politic and its constituent members. Each individual comprising the former contracts, so to speak, with himself and has a twofold function. As a member of the sovereign people he owes a duty to each of his neighbours, and, as a Citizen, to the sovereign people as a whole. But we cannot here apply that maxim of Civil Law according to which no man can be held to an undertaking entered into with himself, because there is a great difference between a man's duty to himself and to a whole of which he forms a part.

Here it should be pointed out that a public decision which can enjoin obedience on all subjects to their Sovereign, by reason of the double aspect under which each is seen, cannot, on the contrary, bind the sovereign in his dealings with himself. Consequently, it is against the nature of the

---

* The true meaning of the word "City" has been almost entirely lost by the moderns, most of whom think that a Town and a City are identical, and that to be a Burgess is the same thing as to be a Citizen. They do not know that houses may make a town, but that only citizens can make a City. This same error cost the people of Carthage dear in the past. I have never anywhere read that the title *"cives"* could be conferred on the subject of a Prince, not even upon the Macedonians of ancient times, nor upon the English in our own day, though the latter are more nearly in the enjoyment of freedom than any other people. Only the French use *citizens* as a familiar word, the reason for this being that they have no true apprehension of its meaning, as may be seen by anyone who consults a French dictionary. Were it otherwise, they would fall, by adopting it, into the crime of *lèse-majesté*. In their mouths it is held to express not so much legal standing as quality. When Bodin speaks of "our citizens and burgesses" he commits a grave blunder in giving the same meaning to the two words. Not so deceived is M. d'Alembert, who, in his article on GENEVA, properly distinguishes between the four Orders (five, if foreigners be counted) which go to make up our city, of which two only constitute the Republic. No French author known to me understands the meaning of the word "Citizen."

body politic that the sovereign should impose upon himself a law which he cannot infringe. For, since he can regard himself under one aspect only, he is in the position of an individual entering into a contract with himself. Whence it follows that there is not, nor can be, any fundamental law which is obligatory for the whole body of the people, not even the social contract itself. This does not mean that the body politic is unable to enter into engagements with some other Power, provided always that such engagements do not derogate from the nature of the Contract; for the relation of the body politic to a foreign Power is that of a simple individual.

But the body politic, or Sovereign, in that it derives its being simply and solely from the sanctity of the said Contract, can never bind itself, even in its relations with a foreign Power, by any decision which might derogate from the validity of the original act. It may not, for instance, alienate any portion of itself, nor make submission to any other sovereign. To violate the act by reason of which it exists would be tantamount to destroying itself, and that which is nothing can produce nothing.

As soon as a mob has become united into a body politic, any attack upon one of its members is an attack upon itself. Still more important is the fact that, should any offence be committed against the body politic as a whole, the effect must be felt by each of its members. Both duty and interest, therefore, oblige the two contracting parties to render one another mutual assistance. The same individuals should seek to unite under this double aspect all the advantages which flow from it.

Now, the Sovereign People, having no existence outside that of the individuals who compose it, has, and can have, no interest at variance with theirs. Consequently, the sovereign power need give no guarantee to its subjects, since the body is incapable of injuring its members; nor, as we shall see later, can it injure any single individual. The Sovereign, by merely existing, is always what it should be.

But the same does not hold true of the relation of subject to sovereign. In spite of common interest, there can be no guarantee that the subject will observe his duty to the sovereign unless means are found to ensure his loyalty.

Each individual, indeed, may, as a man, exercise a will at variance with, or different from, that general will to which, as citizen, he contributes. His personal interest may dictate a line of action quite other than that demanded by the interest of all. The fact that his own existence as an individual has an absolute value, and that he is, by nature, an independent being, may lead him to conclude that what he owes to the common cause is something that he renders of his own free will; and he may decide that by leaving the debt unpaid he does less harm to his fellows than he would to himself should he make the necessary surrender. Regarding the moral entity constituting the State as a rational abstraction because it is not a man, he might enjoy his rights as a citizen without, at the same time, fulfilling his duties as a subject, and the resultant injustice might grow until it brought ruin upon the whole body politic.

In order, then, that the social compact may not be but a vain formula, it must contain, though unexpressed, the single undertaking which can alone give force to the whole, namely, that whoever shall refuse to obey the general will must be constrained by the whole body of his fellow citizens to do so: which is no more than to say that it may be necessary to compel a man to be free — freedom being that condition which, by giving each citizen to his country, guarantees him from all personal dependence and is the foundation upon which the whole political machine rests, and supplies the power which works it. Only the recognition by the individual of the rights of the community can give legal force to undertakings entered into between citizens, which, otherwise, would become absurd, tyrannical, and exposed to vast abuses.

Of the Civil State

The passage from the state of nature to the civil state produces a truly remarkable change in the individual. It substitutes justice for instinct in his behaviour, and gives to his actions a moral basis which formerly was lacking. Only when the voice of duty replaces physical impulse and the cravings of appetite does the man who, till then, was concerned solely with himself, realize that he is under compulsion to obey quite different principles, and that he must now consult his reason and not merely respond to the promptings of desire. Although he may find himself deprived of many advantages which were his in a state of nature, he will recognize that he has gained others which are of far greater value. By dint of being exercised, his faculties will develop, his ideas take on a wider scope, his sentiments become ennobled, and his whole soul be so elevated, that, but for the fact that misuse of the new conditions still, at times, degrades him to a point below that from which he has emerged, he would unceasingly bless the day which freed him for ever from his ancient state, and turned him from a limited and stupid animal into an intelligent being and a Man.

Let us reduce all this to terms which can be easily comprehended. What a man loses as a result of the Social Contract is his natural liberty and his unqualified right to lay hands on all that tempts him, provided only that he can compass its possession. What he gains is civil liberty and the ownership of what belongs to him. That we may labour under no illusion concerning these compensations, it is well that we distinguish between natural liberty which the individual enjoys so long as he is strong enough to maintain it, and civil liberty which is curtailed by the general will. Between possessions which derive from physical strength and the right of the first-comer, and ownership which can be based only on a positive title.

To the benefits conferred by the status of citizenship might be added that of Moral Freedom, which alone makes a man his own master. For to be subject to appetite is to be a slave, while to obey the laws laid down by society is to be free. But I have already said enough on this point, and am not concerned here with the philosophical meaning of the word *liberty*. . . .

That Sovereignty Is Inalienable

The first, and most important, consequence of the principle so far established is that only the general will can direct the powers of the State in such a way that its true purpose, which is the good of all, will be achieved. For, while it may be true that the antagonism which exists between the divergent interests of different individuals makes it necessary to establish a social order, yet, it is no less true that only because those interests are, at bottom, identical, is a social order of this kind possible. The bond of society is that identity of interests which all feel who compose it. In the absence of such an identity no society would be possible. Now, it is solely on the basis of this common interest that society must be governed.

I maintain, therefore, that sovereignty, being no more than the exercise of the general will, can never be alienated, and that the sovereign, who is a collective being only, can be represented by no one but himself. Power can be transmitted, but not will. And though, in fact, it is possible that the will of the individual may, on some point, accord with the general will, what is impossible is that any such agreement should be durable and constant. For the will of the individual tends naturally to privilege, the general will to equality. Still more impossible is it that there should be any guarantee of such a harmony of interests, even where it exists, since chance only, and not contrivance, is the foundation upon which it rests. It is certainly open to the sovereign to say — "What I wish at this moment agrees with what this or that individual wishes or says that he wishes": but he cannot say, "What he may wish to-morrow will conform in every respect to my wish," it being absurd to think that will can bind itself in respect of the future, and it being no part of the function of will to consent to any action contrary to the will of him who wills. If, therefore, the People undertake simply and solely to obey, they, by that very act, dissolve the social bond, and so lose their character as a People. Once the Master appears upon the scene, the sovereign vanishes, and the body politic suffers destruction. . . .

Whether the General Will Can Err

It follows from what has been said above that the general will is always right and ever tends to the public advantage. But it does not follow that the deliberations of the People are always equally beyond question. It is ever the way of men to wish their own good, but they do not at all times see where that good lies. The People are never corrupted though often deceived, and it is only when they are deceived that they appear to will what is evil.

There is often considerable difference between the will of all and the general will. The latter is concerned only with the common interest, the former with interests that are partial, being itself but the sum of individual wills. But take from the expression of these separate wills the pluses and minuses — which cancel out, the sum of the differences is left, and that is the general will.*

If the People, engaged in deliberation, were adequately informed, and if no means existed by which the citizens could communicate one with another, from the great number of small differences the general will would result, and the decisions reached would always be good. But when intriguing groups and partial associations are formed to the disadvantage of the whole, then the will of each of such groups is general only in respect of its own members, but partial in respect of the State. When such a situation arises it may be said that there are no longer as many votes as men, but only as many votes as there are groups. Differences of interest are fewer in number, and the result is less general. Finally, when one of these

---

* "Every interest," says the Marquis d'Argenson, "has different principles. An identity of interests between any two given persons is established by reason of their opposition to the interests of a third." He might have added that the identity of the interests of all is established by reason of their opposition to the interests of each. Did individual interests not exist, the idea of a common interest could scarcely be entertained, for there would be nothing to oppose it. Society would become automatic, and politics would cease to be an art.

groups becomes so large as to swamp all the others, the result is not the sum of small differences, but one single difference. The general will does not then come into play at all, and the prevailing opinion has no more validity than that of an individual man. . . .

Of the Limits of the Sovereign Power

If the State or the City is nothing but a moral person the life of which consists in the union of its members, and if the most important of its concerns is the maintenance of its own being, then it follows that it must have at its disposition a power of compulsion covering the whole field of its operations in order that it may be in a position to shift and adjust each single part in a way that shall be most beneficial to the whole. As nature gives to each man complete power over his limbs, so, too, the social compact gives to the body politic complete power over its members: and it is this power, directed by the general will, which, as I have already pointed out, bears the name of sovereignty.

But we have to consider not only the State as a public person, but those individual persons, too, who compose it, and whose lives and liberties are, in nature, independent of it. It is important, therefore, that we carefully distinguish between the rights of the citizens and the rights of the sovereign, between the duties which the former owe as subjects, and the natural rights which, as men, they are entitled to enjoy.*

It is agreed that what, as a result of the social compact, each man alienates of power, property, and liberty is only so much as concerns the well-being of the community. But, further, it must be admitted that the sovereign alone can determine how much, precisely, this is.

Such services as the citizen owes to the State must be rendered by him whenever the sovereign demands. But the sovereign cannot lay upon its subjects any burden not necessitated by the well-being of the community. It cannot even wish to do so, for in the realm of reason, as of nature, nothing is ever done without cause.

The undertakings which bind us to the Commonwealth are obligatory only because they are mutual: their nature being such that we cannot labour for others without, at the same time, labouring for ourselves. For how can the general will be always right, and how can all constantly will

---

* I must beg the attentive reader not hurriedly to accuse me of contradiction. The terms of which I have made use might give some colour to such a charge, but that is owing to the poverty of human language. But wait.

the happiness of each, if every single individual does not include himself
in that word *each*, so that in voting for the general interest he may feel
that he is voting for his own? Which goes to show that the equality of
rights and the idea of justice which it produces derive from the preference
which each man has for his own concerns — in other words, from human
nature: that the general will, if it be deserving of its name, must be general, not in its origins only, but in its objects, applicable to all as well as
operated *by* all, and that it loses its natural validity as soon as it is concerned to achieve a merely individual and limited end, since, in that
case, we, pronouncing judgment on something outside ourselves, cease to
be possessed of that true principle of equity which is our guide.

    In fact, as soon as issue is joined on some *particular* point, on some
specific right arising out of a situation which has not previously been
regulated by some form of general agreement, we are in the realm of debate. The matter becomes a trial in which certain interested individuals
are ranged against the public, but where there is no certainty about what
law is applicable nor about who can rightly act as judge. It would be
absurd in such a case to demand an *ad hoc* decision of the general will,
since the general will would then be the decision of one of the parties
only. To the other it would appear in the guise of a pronouncement made
by some outside power, sectarian in its nature, tending to injustice in
the particular instance, and subject to error. Thus, just as the will of the
individual cannot represent the general will, so, too, the general will
changes its nature when called upon to pronounce upon a particular object. In so far as it is general, it cannot judge of an individual person or
an isolated fact. When, for instance, the people of Athens appointed or
removed their leaders, according honours to one and penalties to another:
when, in other words, using the machinery supplied by a multiplicity of
specific decrees, they exercised, in a muddled sort of way, all the functions
of government, they ceased, strictly speaking, to have any general will at
all, and behaved not as sovereign so much as magistrate. This statement
may seem to be at variance with generally accepted ideas. I ask only
that I may be granted time in which to develop my own. What makes the
will general is not the number of citizens concerned but the common
interest by which they are united. For in the sort of community with
which I am dealing, each citizen necessarily submits to the conditions
which he imposes on his neighbours. Whence comes that admirable
identity of interest and justice which gives to the common deliberations
of the People a complexion of equity. When, however, discussion turns
on specific issues, this complexion vanishes, because there is no longer

any common interest uniting and identifying the pronouncement of the judge with that of the interested party.

No matter by what way we return to our general principle, the conclusion must always be the same, to wit, that the social compact establishes between all the citizens of a State a degree of equality such that all undertake to observe the same obligations and to claim the same rights. Consequently, by the very nature of the pact, every act of sovereignty — that is to say, every authentic act of the general will — lays the same obligations and confers the same benefits on all. The sovereign knows only the nation as a whole and does not distinguish between the individuals who compose it.

What, then, is a true act of sovereignty? It is not a convention established between a superior and an inferior, but between the body politic and each of its members: a convention having the force of law because it is based upon the social contract: equitable, because it affects all alike: useful because its sole object is the general good: firm, because it is backed by public force and the supreme power. So long as the subjects of a State observe only conventions of this kind, they are obeying not a single person, but the decision of their own wills. To ask what are the limits of the respective rights of sovereign and citizens is merely to ask to what extent the latter can enter into an undertaking with themselves, each in relation to all, and all in relation to each.

From which it becomes clear that the sovereign power, albeit absolute, sacrosanct, and inviolable, does not, and cannot, trespass beyond the limits laid down by general agreement, and that every man has full title to enjoy whatever of property and freedom is left to him by that agreement. The sovereign is never entitled to lay a heavier burden on any one of its subjects than on others, for, should it do so, the matter would at once become particular rather than general, and, consequently, the sovereign power would no longer be competent to deal with it.

These distinctions once admitted, it becomes abundantly clear that to say that the individual, by entering into the social contract, makes an act of renunciation is utterly false. So far from that being the case, his situation within the contract is definitely preferable to what it was before. Instead of giving anything away, he makes a profitable bargain, exchanging peril and uncertainty for security, natural independence for true liberty, the power of injuring others for his own safety, the strength of his own right arm — which others might always overcome — for a right which corporate solidity renders invincible. The life which he devotes to the State is, by the State continually protected, and, when he offers it in the State's defence, what else is he doing than giving back the very boon which he has received at its hands? What, in such circumstances, does he do that he has not done more often and more perilously in a state of nature when, inevitably involved in mortal combat, he defended at the risk of his life what served him to maintain it? All citizens, it is true, may, should the need arise, have to fight for their country, but no one of them has ever to fight singly for himself. Is it not preferable, in the interest of what makes for our security, to run some part of the risks which we should have to face in our own defence, were the boon of forming one of a society taken from us? . . .

That the General Will Is Indestructible

So long as a number of men assembled together regard themselves as forming a single body, they have but one will, which is concerned with their common preservation and with the well-being of all. When this is so, the springs of the State are vigorous and simple, its principles plain and clear-cut. It is not encumbered with confused or conflicting interests. The common good is everywhere plainly in evidence and needs only good sense to be perceived. Peace, unity and equality are the foes of political subtlety. Upright and simple men are hard to deceive by the very reason of their simplicity. Lures and plausible sophistries have no effect upon them, nor are they even sufficiently subtle to become dupes. When one sees, in the happiest country in all the world, groups of peasants deciding the affairs of State beneath an oak-tree, and behaving with a constancy of wisdom, can one help but despise the refinements of other nations which, at so great an expense of skill and mystification, make themselves at once illustrious and wretched?

A State thus governed has need of very few laws, and when it *is* found necessary to promulgate new ones, the necessity will be obvious to all. He who actually voices the proposal does but put into words what all have felt, and neither intrigue nor eloquence are needed to ensure the passing into law of what each has already determined to do so soon as he can be assured that his fellows will follow suit.

What sets theorists on the wrong tack is that, seeing only those States which have been badly constituted from the beginning, they are struck by the impossibility of applying such a system to *them*. The thought of all the follies which a clever knave with an insinuating tongue could persuade the people of Paris or of London to commit, makes them laugh. What they do not know is that Cromwell would have been put in irons by the people of Berne, and the Duc de Beaufort sent to hard labor by the Genevese.

But when the social bond begins to grow slack, and the State to become weaker; when the interests of individuals begin to make themselves felt, and lesser groups within the State to influence the State as a whole, then the common interest suffers a change for the worse and breeds opposition. No longer do men speak with a single voice, no longer is the general will the will of all. Contradictions appear, discussions arise, and even the best advice is not allowed to pass unchallenged.

Last stage of all, when the State, now near its ruin, lives on only in a vain and deceptive form, when the bond of society is broken in all men's hearts, when the vilest self-interest bears insolently the sacred name of Common-Weal, then does the general will fall dumb. All, moved by motives unavowed, express their views as though such a thing as the State had never existed, and they were not citizens at all. In such circumstances, unjust decrees, aiming only at the satisfaction of private interests, can be passed under the guise of laws.

Does it follow from this that the general will is destroyed or corrupted? No; it remains constant, unalterable and pure, but it becomes subordinated to other wills which encroach upon it. Each, separating his interest from the interest of all, sees that such separation cannot be complete, yet the part he plays in the general damage seems to him as nothing compared with the exclusive good which he seeks to appropriate. With the single exception of the particular private benefit at which he aims, he still desires the public good, realizing that it is likely to benefit him every whit as much as his neighbours. Even when he sells his vote for money, he does not extinguish the general will in himself, but merely eludes it. The fault that he commits is to change the form of the question, and to answer something which he was not asked. Thus, instead of saying, through the medium of his vote, "This is of advantage to the State," he says, "It is to the advantage of this or that individual that such and such a proposition become law." And so the law of public order in assemblies is not so much the maintenance of the general will, as the guarantee that it shall always be asked to express itself and shall always respond.

I might say much at this point on the simple right of voting in every act of sovereignty, a right of which nothing can deprive the citizen — and on that of speaking, proposing, dividing and discussing; a right which the government is always very careful to leave only to its members: but this important matter would require a whole treatise to itself, and I cannot cover the whole ground in this one.

Of Voting

It is clear, from what has just been said, that the manner in which public affairs are conducted can give a pretty good indication of the state of a society's morale and general health. The greater the harmony when the citizens are assembled, the more predominant is the general will. But long debates, dissension and uproar all point to the fact that private interests are in the ascendant and that the State as a whole has entered on a period of decline.

This seems less evident when two or more social orders are involved, as, in Rome, the Patricians and the Plebs, whose quarrels so often troubled the *comitia* even in the best days of the Republic. But this exception is more apparent than real. For, in such circumstances, there are, so to speak, because of a vice inherent in political bodies, two States in one. What is not true of the two together is true of each separately. Indeed, even in the most stormy times, the *plebiscita* of the Roman people, when the Senate did not interefere, were always passed quietly and by a large majority of votes. The citizens having but one interest, the people had but a single will.

At the other extremity of the scale unanimity returns; when, that is to say, the citizens, having fallen into servitude, have no longer either liberty or will. When that happens, fear and flattery transform votes into acclamations. Men no longer deliberate, they worship or they curse. In this base manner did the Senate express its views under the Emperors, sometimes with absurd precautions. Tacitus relates that, in the reign of Otho, the Senators, in heaping execrations on Vitellius, were careful to make so great a din that, should he chance to become their master, he would not be able to tell what any one of them had said.

From these various considerations spring those general rules which should regulate the manner of counting votes and comparing opinions, according as whether the general will is more or less easily to be discerned, and the State more or less in a condition of decline.

There is one law only which, by its very nature, demands unanimous consent, and that is the social pact. For civil association is, of all acts, the most deliberately willed. Since every man is born free and his own master, none, under any pretext whatsoever, can enslave him without his consent. To decide that the son of a slave is born a slave is tantamount to saying that he is not born a man.

If, then, when the social pact is made, voices are raised in opposition, such opposition does not invalidate the contract, but merely excludes from it those who voice it, so that they become foreigners among the general body of the citizens. When the State is instituted, residence implies consent. To live in a country means to submit to its sovereignty.*

In all matters other than this fundamental contract, a majority vote is always binding on all. This is a consequence of the contract itself. But, it may be asked, how can a man be free and yet constrained to conform to a will which is not his own? How comes it that the members of the opposition can be at the same time free and yet subject to laws which they have not voted?

My reply to this is that the question is wrongly put. The citizen consents to all the laws, even to those which have been passed in spite of him, even to those which will visit punishment upon him should he dare to violate any of them. The constant will of all the members of a State is the general will, and by virtue of it they are citizens and free men.† When a law is proposed in the assembly of the People, what they are asked is not whether they approve or reject the proposal in question, but whether it is or is not in conformity with the general will, which is *their* will. It is on this point that the citizen expresses his opinon when he records his vote, and from the counting of the votes proceeds the declaration of the general will. When, therefore, a view which is at odds with my own wins the day, it proves only that I was deceived, and that what I took to be the general will was no such thing. Had my own opinion won, I should have done something quite other than I wished to do, and in that case I should not have been free. True, this assumes that all the characteristics of the general will are still in the majority. When that ceases to be the case, no matter what side we are on, liberty has ceased to exist.

When I showed above how the wills of individuals come to be substituted for the general will in public deliberations, I made sufficiently clear what practical means existed for preventing this abuse. . . . In regard to the proportional number of votes needed to declare this will, I have

---

* This must always be understood to relate to a free State, for elsewhere family interests, property, the impossibility of finding a refuge abroad, necessity or violence, may all keep a man resident in a country in spite of his wish to leave it. When this is so, the mere fact of his living there does not imply his consent to the contract or to the violation of it.

† At Genoa one can see written on the walls of the prisons and engraved on the irons of the Galley-slaves, the word *Libertas*. The use of such a device is excellent and just. In all States it is the malefactors only who prevent the citizens from being free. If all such folk were one and all confined to the galleys, it would be possible to enjoy perfect freedom.

also stated the principles on which it can be determined. The difference of a single vote destroys equality: one voice raised in opposition makes unanimity impossible. But between unanimity and equality there are many unequal divisions, at each of which this number can be fixed as the State and the needs of the body politic may demand.

Two general rules may serve to regulate this proportion: one, that the more important and solemn the matters under discussion, the nearer to unanimity should the voting be: two, that the more it is necessary to settle the matter speedily, the less should be the difference permitted in balancing the votes for and against. Where a verdict must be obtained at a single sitting, a majority of one should be held to be sufficient. The first of these rules seems to be more suited to the passing of laws, the second to the transaction of business. Be that as it may, only a combination of them can give the best proportion for the determining of majorities. . . .

ON LIBERTY

by John Stuart Mill *

INTRODUCTORY

The subject of this Essay is not the so-called Liberty of the Will, so unfortunately opposed to the misnamed doctrine of Philosophical Necessity; but Civil, or Social Liberty: the nature and limits of the power which can be legitimately exercised by society over the individual. A question seldom stated, and hardly ever discussed, in general terms, but which profoundly influences the practical controversies of the age by its latent presence, and is likely soon to make itself recognised as the vital question of the future. It is so far from being new, that, in a certain sense, it has divided mankind, almost from the remotest ages; but in the stage of

* John Stuart Mill, "On Liberty," *Utilitarianism, Liberty and Representative Government* (New York: 1940). Everyman's Library, reprinted by permission of E. P. Dutton and Co., Inc.

progress into which the more civilised portions of the species have now entered, it presents itself under new conditions, and requires a different and more fundamental treatment.

The struggle between Liberty and Authority is the most conspicuous feature in the portions of history with which we are earliest familiar, particularly in that of Greece, Rome, and England. But in old times this contest was between subjects, or some classes of subjects, and the Government. By liberty, was meant protection against the tyranny of the political rulers. The rulers were conceived (except in some of the popular governments of Greece) as in a necessarily antagonistic position to the people whom they ruled. They consisted of a governing One, or a governing tribe or caste, who derived their authority from inheritance or conquest, who, at all events, did not hold it at the pleasure of the governed, and whose supremacy men did not venture, perhaps did not desire, to contest, whatever precautions might be taken against its oppressive exercise. Their power was regarded as necessary, but also as highly dangerous; as a weapon which they would attempt to use against their subjects, no less than against external enemies. To prevent the weaker members of the community from being preyed upon by innumerable vultures, it was needful that there should be an animal of prey stronger than the rest, commissioned to keep them down. But as the king of the vultures would be no less bent upon preying on the flock than any of the minor harpies, it was indispensable to be in a perpetual attitude of defence against his beak and claws. The aim, therefore, of patriots was to set limits to the power which the ruler should be suffered to exercise over the community; and this limitation was what they meant by liberty. It was attempted in two ways. First, by obtaining a recognition of certain immunities, called political liberties or rights, which it was to be regarded as a breach of duty in the ruler to infringe, and which if he did infringe, specific resistance, or general rebellion, was held to be justifiable. A second, and generally a later expedient, was the establishment of constitutional checks, by which the consent of the community, or of a body of some sort, supposed to represent its interests, was made a necessary condition to some of the more important acts of the governing power. To the first of these modes of limitation, the ruling power, in most European countries, was compelled, more or less, to submit. It was not so with the second; and, to attain this, or when already in some degree possessed, to attain it more completely, became everywhere the principal object of the lovers of liberty. And so long as mankind were content to combat one enemy by another, and to

be ruled by a master, on condition of being guaranteed more or less effi-
caciously against his tyranny, they did not carry their aspirations beyond
this point.

A time, however, came in the progress of human affairs, when men
ceased to think it a necessity of nature that their governors should be
an independent power, opposed in interest to themselves. It appeared
to them much better that the various magistrates of the State should be
their tenants or delegates, revocable at their pleasure. In that way alone,
it seemed, could they have complete security that the powers of government would never be abused to their disadvantage. By degrees this new
demand for elective and temporary rulers became the prominent object
of the exertions of the popular party, wherever any such party existed;
and superseded, to a considerable extent, the previous efforts to limit the
power of rulers. As the struggle proceeded for making the ruling power
emanate from the periodical choice of the ruled, some persons began to
think that too much importance had been attached to the limitation of
the power itself. *That* (it might seem) was a resource against rulers whose
interests were habitually opposed to those of the people. What was now
wanted was, that the rulers should be identified with the people; that their
interest and will should be the interest and will of the nation. The nation
did not need to be protected against its own will. There was no fear of its
tyrannising over itself. Let the rulers be effectually responsible to it,
promptly removable by it, and it could afford to trust them with power
of which it could itself dictate the use to be made. Their power was but
the nation's own power, concentrated, and in a form convenient for
exercise. This mode of thought, or rather perhaps of feeling, was common
among the last generation of European liberalism, in the Continental
section of which it still apparently predominates. Those who admit any
limit to what a government may do, except in the case of such governments as they think ought not to exist, stand out as brilliant exceptions
among the political thinkers of the Continent. A similar tone of sentiment
might by this time have been prevalent in our own country, if the circumstances which for a time encouraged it, had continued unaltered.

But, in political and philosophical theories, as well as in persons, success discloses faults and infirmities which failure might have concealed
from observation. The notion, that the people have no need to limit their
power over themselves, might seem axiomatic, when popular government
was a thing only dreamed about, or read of as having existed at some
distant period of the past. Neither was that notion necessarily disturbed
by such temporary aberrations as those of the French Revolution, the worst

of which were the work of a usurping few, and which, in any case, belonged, not to the permanent working of popular institutions, but to a sudden and convulsive outbreak against monarchical and aristocratic despotism. In time, however, a democratic republic came to occupy a large portion of the earth's surface, and made itself felt as one of the most powerful members of the community of nations; and elective and responsible government became subject to the observations and criticisms which wait upon a great existing fact. It was now perceived that such phrases as "self-government," and "the power of the people over themselves," do not express the true state of the case. The "people" who exercise the power are not always the same people with those over whom it is exercised; and the "self-government" spoken of is not the government of each by himself, but of each by all the rest. The will of the people, moreover, practically means the will of the most numerous or the most active *part* of the people; the majority, or those who succeed in making themselves accepted as the majority; the people, consequently *may* desire to oppress a part of their number; and precautions are as much needed against this as against any other abuse of power. The limitation, therefore, of the power of government over individuals loses none of its importance when the holders of power are regularly accountable to the community, that is, to the strongest party therein. This view of things, recommending itself equally to the intelligence of thinkers and to the inclination of those important classes in European society to whose real or supposed interests democracy is adverse, has had no difficulty in establishing itself; and in political speculations "the tyranny of the majority" is now generally included among the evils against which society requires to be on its guard.

Like other tyrannies, the tyranny of the majority was at first, and is still vulgarly, held in dread, chiefly as operating through the acts of the public authorities. But reflecting persons perceived that when society is itself the tyrant—society collectively over the separate individuals who compose it—its means of tyrannising are not restricted to the acts which it may do by the hands of its political functionaries. Society can and does execute its own mandates: and if it issues wrong mandates instead of right, or any mandates at all in things with which it ought not to meddle, it practises a social tyranny more formidable than many kinds of political oppression, since, though not usually upheld by such extreme penalties, it leaves fewer means of escape, penetrating much more deeply into the details of life, and enslaving the soul itself. Protection, therefore, against the tyranny of the magistrate is not enough; there needs protection also against the tyranny of the prevailing opinion and feeling; against the tendency of society to impose, by other means than civil penalties, its own ideas and practices as rules of conduct on those who dissent from them; to fetter the development, and, if possible, prevent the formation, of any individuality not in harmony with its ways, and compels all characters to fashion themselves upon the model of its own. There is a limit to the legitimate interference of collective opinion with individual independence: and to find that limit, and maintain it against encroachment, is as indispensable to a good condition of human affairs, as protection against political despotism. . . .

The object of this Essay is to assert one very simple principle, as entitled to govern absolutely the dealings of society with the individual in the way of compulsion and control, whether the means used be physical force in the form of legal penalties, or the moral coercion of public opinion. That principle is, that the sole end for which mankind are warranted, individually or collectively, in interfering with the liberty of action of any of their number, is self-protection. That the only purpose for which power can be rightfully exercised over any members of a civilised community, against his will, is to prevent harm to others. His own good, either physical or moral, is not a sufficient warrant. He cannot rightfully be compelled to do or forbear because it will be better for him to do so, because it will make him happier, because, in the opinions of others, to do so would be wise, or even right. These are good reasons for remonstrating with him, or reasoning with him, or persuading him, or entreating him, but not for compelling him, or visiting him with any evil in case he do otherwise. To justify that, the conduct from which it is desired to deter him must be calculated to produce evil to some one else. The only part of the conduct of any one, for which he is amenable to society, is that which concerns others. In the part which merely concerns himself, his independence is, of right, absolute. Over himself, over his own body and mind, the individual is sovereign. . . .

It is proper to state that I forego any advantage which could be derived to my argument from the idea of abstract right, as a thing independent of utility. I regard utility as the ultimate appeal on all ethical questions; but it must be utility in the largest sense, grounded on the permanent interests of a man as a progressive being. Those interests, I contend, authorise the subjection of individual spontaneity to external control, only in respect to those actions of each, which concern the interest of other people. If any one does an act hurtful to others, there is a *prima facie* case for punishing him, by law, or, where legal penalties are not safely applicable, by general disapprobation. There are also many positive acts for the benefit of others, which he may rightfully be compelled to perform; such as to give evidence in a court of justice; to bear his fair share in the common defence, or in any other joint work necessary to the interest of the society of which he enjoys the protection; and to perform certain acts of individual beneficence, such as saving a fellow-creature's life, or interposing to protect the defenceless against ill-usage, things which whenever it is obviously a man's duty to do, he may rightfully be made responsible to society for not doing. A person may cause evil to others not only by his actions but by his inaction, and in either case he is justly accountable to them for the injury. The latter case, it is true, requires a much more cautious exercise of compulsion than the former. To make any one answerable for doing evil to others is the rule; to make him answerable for not preventing evil is, comparatively speaking, the exception. Yet there are many cases clear enough and grave enough to justify that exception. In all things which regard the external relations of the individual, he is *de jure* amenable to those whose interests are concerned, and, if need be, to society as their protector. There are often good reasons for not holding him to the responsibility; but these reasons must arise from the special expediencies of the case: either because it is a kind of case in which he is on the whole likely to act better, when left to his own discretion, than when controlled in any way in which society have it in their power to control him; or because the attempt to exercise control would produce other evils, greater than those which it would prevent. When such reasons as these preclude the enforcement of responsibility, the conscience of the agent himself should step into the vacant judgment seat, and protect those interests of others which have no external protection; judging himself all the more rigidly, because the case does not admit of his being made accountable to the judgment of his fellow-creatures.

But there is a sphere of action in which society, as distinguished from the individual, has, if any, only an indirect interest; comprehending all that portion of a person's life and conduct which affects only himself, or if it also affects others, only with their free, voluntary, and undeceived consent and participation. When I say only himself, I mean directly, and in the first instance; for whatever affects himself, may affect others through himself; and the objection which may be grounded on this contingency, will receive consideration in the sequel. This, then, is the appropriate region of human liberty. It comprises, first, the inward domain of consciousness; demanding liberty of conscience in the most comprehensive sense; liberty of thought and feeling; absolute freedom of opinion and sentiment on all subjects, practical or speculative, scientific, moral, or theological.

The liberty of expressing and publishing opinions may seem to fall under a different principle, since it belongs to that part of the conduct of an individual which concerns other people; but, being almost of as much importance as the liberty of thought itself, and resting in great part on the same reasons, is practically inseparable from it. Secondly, the principle requires liberty of tastes and pursuits; of framing the plan of our life to suit our own character; of doing as we like, subject to such consequences as may follow: without impediment from our fellow-creatures, so long as what we do does not harm them, even though they should think our conduct foolish, perverse, or wrong. Thirdly, from this liberty of each individual, follows the liberty, within the same limits, of combination among individuals; freedom to unite, for any purpose not involving harm to others: the persons combining being supposed to be of full age, and not forced or deceived.

No society in which these liberties are not, on the whole, respected, is free, whatever may be its form of government; and none is completely free in which they do not exist absolute and unqualified. The only freedom which deserves the name, is that of pursuing our own good in our own way, so long as we do not attempt to deprive others of theirs, or impede their efforts to obtain it. Each is the proper guardian of his own health, whether bodily, *or* mental and spiritual. Mankind are greater gainers by suffering each other to live as seems good to themselves, than by compelling each to live as seems good to the rest. . . .

It will be convenient for the argument, if, instead of at once entering upon the general thesis, we confine ourselves in the first instance to a single branch of it, on which the principle here stated is, if not fully, yet to a certain point, recognised by the current opinions. This one branch is the Liberty of Thought: from which it is impossible to separate the cognate liberty of speaking and of writing. Although these liberties, to some considerable amount, form part of the political morality of all countries which profess religious toleration and free institutions, the grounds, both philosophical and practical, on which they rest, are perhaps not so familiar to the general mind, nor so thoroughly appreciated by many even of the leaders of opinion, as might have been expected. Those grounds, when rightly understood, are of much wider application than to only one division of the subject, and a thorough consideration of this part of the question will be found the best introduction to the remainder. Those to whom nothing which I am about to say will be new, may therefore, I hope, excuse me, if on a subject which for now three centuries has been so often discussed, I venture on one discussion more.

Of the Liberty of Thought and Discussion

The time, it is to be hoped, is gone by, when any defence would be necessary of the "liberty of the press" as one of the securities against corrupt or tyrannical government. No argument, we may suppose, can now be needed, against permitting a legislature or an executive, not identified in interest with the people, to prescribe opinions to them, and determine what doctrines or what arguments they shall be allowed to hear. This aspect of the question, besides, has been so often and so triumphantly enforced by preceding writers, that it needs not be specially insisted on in this place. . . . Let us suppose, therefore, that the government is entirely at one with the people, and never thinks of exerting any power of coercion unless in agreement with what it conceives to be their voice. But I deny the right of the people to exercise such coercion, either by themselves or by their government. The power itself is illegitimate. The best government has no more title to it than the worst. It is as noxious, or more noxious, when exerted in accordance with public opinion, than when in opposition to it. If all mankind minus one were of one opinion, and only one person were of the contrary opinion, mankind would be no more justified in silencing that one person, than he, if he had the power, would be justified in silencing mankind. Were an opinion a personal possession of no value except to the owner; if to be obstructed in the enjoyment of it were simply a private injury, it would make some difference whether the injury was inflicted only on a few persons or on many. But the peculiar evil of silencing the expression of an opinion is, that it is robbing the human race; posterity as well as the existing generation; those who dissent from the opinion, still more than those who hold it. If the opinion is right, they are deprived of the opportunity of exchanging error for truth: if wrong, they lose, what is almost as great a benefit, the clearer perception and livelier impression of truth, produced by its collision with error. . . .

In politics, again, it is almost a commonplace, that a party of order or stability, and a party of progress or reform, are both necessary elements of a healthy state of political life; until the one or the other shall have so enlarged its mental grasp as to be a party equally of order and of progress, knowing and distinguishing what is fit to be preserved from what ought to be swept away. Each of these modes of thinking derives its utility from the deficiencies of the other; but it is in a great measure the opposition of the other that keeps each within the limits of reason and sanity. Unless opinions favourable to democracy and to aristocracy, to property and to equality, to co-operation and to competition, to luxury and to abstinence, to sociality and individuality, to liberty and discipline, and all the other standing antagonisms of practical life, are expressed with equal freedom, and enforced and defended with equal talent and energy, there is no chance of both elements obtaining their due; one scale is sure to go up, and the other down. Truth, in the great practical concerns of life, is so much a question of the reconciling and combining of opposites, that very few have minds sufficiently capacious and impartial to make the adjustment with an approach to correctness, and it has to be made by the rough process of a struggle between combatants fighting under hostile banners. On any of the great open questions just enumerated, if either of the two opinions has a better claim than the other, not merely to be tolerated, but to be encouraged and countenanced, it is the one which happens at the particular time and place to be in a minority. That is the opinion which, for the time being, represents the neglected interests, the side of human well-being which is in danger of obtaining less than its share. I am aware that there is not, in this country, any intolerance of differences of opinion on most of these topics. They are adduced to show, by admitted and multiplied examples, the universality of the fact, that only through diversity of opinion is there, in the existing state of human intellect, a chance of fair play to all sides of the truth. When there are persons to be found who form an exception to the apparent unanimity of the world on any subject, even if the world is in the right, it is always probable that dissentients have something worth hearing to say for themselves, and that truth would lose something by their silence. . . .

We have now recognised the necessity to the mental well-being of mankind (on which all their other well-being depends) of freedom of opinion, and freedom of the expression of opinion, on four distinct grounds; which we will now briefly recapitulate.

First, if any opinion is compelled to silence, that opinion may, for aught we can certainly know, be true. To deny this is to assume our own infallibility.

Secondly, though the silenced opinion be an error, it may, and very commonly does, contain a portion of truth; and since the general or prevailing opinion on any subject is rarely or never the whole truth, it is only by the collision of adverse opinions that the remainder of the truth has any chance of being supplied.

Thirdly, even if the received opinion be not only true, but the whole truth; unless it is suffered to be, and actually is, vigorously and earnestly contested, it will, by most of those who receive it, be held in the manner of a prejudice, with little comprehension or feeling of its rational grounds. And not only this, but, fourthly, the meaning of the doctrine itself will be in danger of being lost, or enfeebled, and deprived of its vital effect on the character and conduct: the dogma becoming a mere formal profession, inefficacious for good, but cumbering the ground, and preventing the growth of any real and heartfelt conviction, from reason or personal experience. . . .

Of Individuality, As One of the Elements of Well-Being

Such being the reasons which make it imperative that human beings should be free to form opinions, and to express their opinions without reserve; and such the baneful consequences to the intellectual, and through that to the moral nature of man, unless this liberty is either conceded, or asserted in spite of prohibition; let us next examine whether the same reasons do not require that men should be free to act upon their opinions — to carry these out in their lives, without hindrance, either physical or moral, from their fellow-men, so long as it is at their own risk and peril. This last proviso is of course indispensable. No one pretends that actions should be as free as opinions. On the contrary, even opinions lose their immunity when the circumstances in which they are expressed are such as to constitute their expression a positive instigation to some mischievous act. An opinion that corn-dealers are starvers of the poor, or that private property is robbery, ought to be unmolested when simply circulated through the press, but may justly incur punishment when delivered orally to an excited mob assembled before the house of a corn-dealer, or when handed about among the same mob in the form of a placard. Acts, of whatever kind, which, without justifiable cause, do harm to others, may be, and in the more important cases absolutely require to be, controlled by the unfavourable sentiments, and, when needful, by the active interference of mankind. The liberty of the individual must be thus far limited; he must not make himself a nuisance to other people. But if he refrains from molesting others in what concerns them, and merely acts according to his own inclination and judgment in things which concern himself, the same reasons which show that opinion should be free, prove also that he should be allowed, without molestation, to carry his opinions into practice at his own cost. That mankind are not infallible; that their truths, for the most part, are only half-truths; that unity of opinion, unless resulting from the fullest and freest comparison of opposite opinions, is not desirable, and diversity not an evil, but a good, until mankind are much more capable than at present of recognising all sides of the truth, are principles applicable to men's modes of action, not less than to their opinions. As it is useful that while mankind are imperfect there should be different opinions, so it is that there should be different experiments of living; that free scope should be given to varieties of character, short of injury to others; and that the worth of different modes of life should be proved practically, when any one thinks fit to try them. It is desirable, in short, that in things which do not primarily concern others, individuality should assert itself. Where, not the person's own character, but the traditions or customs of other people are the rule of conduct, there is wanting one of the principal ingredients of human happiness, and quite the chief ingredient of individual and social progress. . . .

He who lets the world, or his own portion of it, choose his plan of life for him, has no need of any other faculty than the ape-like one of imitation. He who chooses his plan for himself, employs all his faculties. He must use observation to see, reasoning and judgment to foresee, activity to gather materials for decision, discrimination to decide, and when he has decided, firmness and self-control to hold to his deliberate decision. And these qualities he requires and exercises exactly in proportion as the part of his conduct which he determines according to his own judgment and feelings is a large one. It is possible that he might be guided in some good path, and kept out of harm's way, without any of these things. But what will be his comparative worth as a human being? It really is of importance, not only what men do, but also what manner of men they are that do it. Among the works of man, which human life is rightly employed in perfecting and beautifying, the first in importance surely is man himself. Supposing it were possible to get houses built, corn grown, battles fought, causes tried, and even churches erected and prayers said, by machinery — by automatons in human form — it would be a considerable loss to exchange for these automatons even the men and women who at present inhabit the more civilised parts of the world, and who assuredly are but starved specimens of what nature can and will produce. Human nature is not a machine to be built after a model, and set to do exactly the work prescribed for it, but a tree, which requires to grow and develop itself on all sides, according to the tendency of the inward forces which make it a living thing.

It will probably be conceded that it is desirable people should exercise their understandings, and that an intelligent following of custom, or even occasionally an intelligent deviation from custom, is better than a blind and simply mechanical adhesion to it. To a certain extent it is admitted that our understanding should be our own: but there is not the same willingness to admit that our desires and impulses should be our own likewise; or that to possess impulses of our own, and of any strength, is anything but a peril and a snare. Yet desires and impulses are as much a part of a perfect human being as beliefs and restraints: and strong impulses are only perilous when not properly balanced; when one set of aims and inclinations is developed into strength, while others, which ought to co-exist with them, remain weak and inactive. It is not because men's desires are strong that they act ill; it is because their consciences are weak. There is no natural connection between strong impulses and a weak conscience. The natural connection is the other way. To say that one person's desires and feelings are stronger and more various than those of another, is merely to say that he has more of the raw material of human nature, and is therefore capable, perhaps of more evil, but certainly of more good. Strong impulses are but another name for energy. Energy may be turned to bad uses; but more good may always be made of an energetic nature, than of an indolent and impassive one. Those who have most natural feeling are always those whose cultivated feelings may be made the strongest. The same strong susceptibilities which make the personal impulses vivid and powerful, are also the source from whence are generated the most passionate love of virtue, and the sternest self-control. It is through the cultivation of these that society both does its duty and protects its interests: not by rejecting the stuff of which heroes are made, because it knows not how to make them. A person whose desires and impulses are his own — are the expression of his own nature, as it has been developed and modified by his own culture — is said to have a character. One whose desires and impulses are not his own, has no character, no more than a steam-engine has a character. If, in addition to being his own, his impulses are strong, and are under the government of a strong will, he has an energetic character. Whoever thinks that individuality of desires and impulses should not be encouraged to unfold itself, must maintain that society has no need of strong natures — is not the better for containing many persons who have much character — and that a high general average of energy is not desirable. . . .

Of the Limits to the Authority of Society over the Individual

What, then, is the rightful limit to the sovereignty of the individual over himself? Where does the authority of society begin? How much of human life should be assigned to individuality, and how much to society?

Each will receive its proper share, if each has that which more particularly concerns it. To individuality should belong the part of life in which it is chiefly the individual that is interested; to society, the part which chiefly interests society.

Though society is not founded on a contract, and though no good purpose is answered by inventing a contract in order to deduce social obligations from it, every one who receives the protection of society owes a return for the benefit, and the fact of living in society renders it indispensable that each should be bound to observe a certain line of conduct towards the rest. This conduct consists, first, in not injuring the interests of one another; or rather certain interests, which, either by express legal provision or by tacit understanding, ought to be considered as rights; and secondly, in each person's bearing his share (to be fixed on some equitable principle) of the labours and sacrifices incurred for defending the society or its members from injury and molestation. These conditions society is justified in enforcing, at all costs to those who endeavour to withhold fulfilment. Nor is this all that society may do. The acts of an individual may be hurtful to others, or wanting in due consideration for their welfare, without going to the length of violating any of their constituted rights. The offender may then be justly punished by opinion, though not by law. As soon as any part of a person's conduct affects prejudicially the interests of others, society has jurisdiction over it, and the question whether the general welfare will or will not be promoted by interfering with it, becomes open to discussion. But there is no room for entertaining any such question when a person's conduct affects the interests of no persons besides himself, or needs not affect them unless they like (all the persons concerned being of full age, and the ordinary amount of understanding). In all such cases, there should be perfect freedom, legal and social, to do the action and stand the consequences. . . .

APPLICATIONS

I have reserved for the last place a large class of questions respecting the limits of government interference, which, though closely connected with the subject of this Essay, do not, in strictness, belong to it. These are cases in which the reasons against interference do not turn upon the principle of liberty: the question is not about restraining the actions of individuals, but about helping them; it is asked whether the government should do, or cause to be done, something for their benefit, instead of leaving it to be done by themselves, individually or in voluntary combination.

The objections to government interference, when it is not such as to involve infringement of liberty, may be of three kinds.

The first is, when the thing to be done is likely to be better done by individuals than by the government. Speaking generally, there is no one so fit to conduct any business, or to determine how or by whom it shall be conducted, as those who are personally interested in it. This principle condemns the interferences, once so common, of the legislature, or the officers of government, with the ordinary processes of industry. But this part of the subject has been sufficiently enlarged upon by political economists, and is not particularly related to the principles of this Essay.

The second objection is more nearly allied to our subject. In many cases, though individuals may not do the particular thing so well, on the average, as the officers of government, it is nevertheless desirable that it should be done by them, rather than by the government, as a means to their own mental education — a mode of strengthening their active faculties, exercising their judgment, and giving them a familiar knowledge of the subjects with which they are thus left to deal. This is a principal, though not the sole, recommendation of jury trial (in cases not political); of free and popular local and municipal institutions; of the conduct of industrial and philanthropic enterprises by voluntary associations. These are not questions of liberty, and are connected with that subject only by remote tendencies; but they are questions of development. It belongs to a different occasion from the present to dwell on these things as parts of national education; as being, in truth, the peculiar training of a citizen, the practical part of the political education of a free people, taking them out of the narrow circle of personal and family selfishness, and accustoming them to the comprehension of joint interests, the management of joint concerns — habituating them to act from public or semi-public motives, and guide their conduct by aims which unite instead of isolating them from one another. Without these habits and powers, a free constitution can neither be worked nor preserved; as is exemplified by the too-often transitory nature of political freedom in countries where it does not rest upon a sufficient basis of local liberties. The management of purely local business by the localities, and of the great enterprises of industry by the union of those who voluntarily supply the pecuniary means, is further recommended by all the advantages which have been set forth in this Essay as belonging to individuality of development, and diversity of modes of action. Government operations tend to be everywhere alike. With individuals and voluntary associations, on the contrary, there are varied experiments, and endless diversity of experience. What the State can usefully do is to make itself a central depository, and active circulator and diffuser, of the experience resulting from many trials. Its business is to enable each experimentalist to benefit by the experiments of others; instead of tolerating no experiments but its own.

The third and most cogent reason for restricting the interference of government is the great evil of adding unnecessarily to its power. Every function superadded to those already exercised by the government causes its influence over hopes and fears to be more widely diffused, and converts, more and more, the active and ambitious part of the public into hangers-on of the government, or of some party which aims at becoming the government. If the roads, the railways, the banks, the insurance offices, the great joint-stock companies, the universities, and the public charities, were all of them branches of the government; if, in addition, the municipal corporations and local boards, with all that now devolves on them, became departments of the central administration; if the employés of all these different enterprises were appointed and paid by the government, and looked to the government for every rise in life; not all the freedom of the press and popular constitution of the legislature would make this or any other country free otherwise than in name. . . .

FREEDOM AND CULTURE

by John Dewey *

DEMOCRACY AND HUMAN NATURE

The present predicament may be stated as follows: Democracy does involve a belief that political institutions and law be such as to take fundamental account of human nature. They must give it freer play than any non-democratic institutions. At the same time, the theory, legalistic

* John Dewey, *Freedom and Culture* (New York: 1939). Copyright 1939 by John Dewey. Reprinted by permission of G. P. Putnam's Sons.

and moralistic, about human nature that has been used to expound and justify this reliance upon human nature has proved inadequate. Upon the legal and political side, during the nineteenth century it was progressively overloaded with ideas and practices which have more to do with business carried on for profit than with democracy. On the moralistic side, it has tended to substitute emotional exhortation to act in accord with the Golden Rule for the discipline and the control afforded by incorporation of democratic ideals into *all* the relations of life. Because of lack of an adequate theory of human nature in its relations to democracy, attachment to democratic ends and methods has tended to become a matter of tradition and habit — an excellent thing as far as it goes, but when it becomes routine is easily undermined when change of conditions changes other habits.

Were I to say that democracy needs a new psychology of human nature, one adequate to the heavy demands put upon it by foreign and domestic conditions, I might be taken to utter an academic irrelevancy. But if the remark is understood to mean that democracy has always been allied with humanism, with faith in the potentialities of human nature, and that the present need is vigorous reassertion of this faith, developed in relevant ideas and manifested in practical attitudes, it but continues the American tradition. For belief in the "common man" has no significance save as an expression of belief in the intimate and vital connection of democracy and human nature.

We cannot continue the idea that human nature when left to itself, when freed from external arbitrary restrictions, will tend to the production of democratic institutions that work successfully. We have now to state the issue from the other side. We have to see that democracy means the belief that humanistic culture *should* prevail; we should be frank and open in our recognition that the proposition is a moral one — like any idea that concerns what *should* be.

Strange as it seems to us, democracy is challenged by totalitarian states of the Fascist variety on moral grounds just as it is challenged by totalitarianisms of the left on economic grounds. We may be able to defend democracy on the latter score, as far as comparative conditions are involved, since up to the present at least the Union of Socialist Republics has not "caught up" with us, much less "surpassed" us, in material affairs. But defense against the other type of totalitarianism (and perhaps in the end against also the Marxist type) requires a positive and courageous constructive awakening to the significance of faith in human nature for development of every phase of our culture: — science, art, education, morals and religion, as well as politics and economics. No matter how uniform and constant human nature is in the abstract, the conditions within which and upon which it operates have changed so greatly since political democracy was established among us, that democracy cannot now depend upon or be expressed in political institutions alone. We cannot even be certain that they and their legal accompaniments are actually democratic at the present time — for democracy is expressed in the attitudes of human beings and is measured by consequences produced in their lives.

The impact of the humanist view of democracy upon all forms of culture, upon education, science and art, morals and religion, as well as upon industry and politics, saves it from the criticism passed upon moralistic exhortation. For it tells us that we need to examine every one of the phases of human activity to ascertain what effects it has in release, maturing and fruition of the potentialities of human nature. It does not tell us to "re-arm morally" and all social problems will be solved. It says, Find out how all the constituents of our existing culture are operating and then see to it that whenever and wherever needed they be modified in order that their workings may release and fulfill the possibilities of human nature.

It used to be said (and the statement has not gone completely out of fashion) that democracy is a by-product of Christianity, since the latter teaches the infinite worth of the individual human soul. We are now told by some persons that since belief in the soul has been discredited by science, the moral basis for democracy supposed to exist must go into the discard. We are told that if there are reasons for preferring it to other arrangements of the relations of human beings to one another, they must be found in specialized external advantages which outweigh the advantages of other social forms. From a very different quarter, we are told that weakening of the older theological doctrine of the soul is one of the reasons for the eclipse of faith in democracy. These two views at opposite poles give depth and urgency to the question whether there are adequate grounds for faith in the potentialities of human nature and whether they can be accompanied by the intensity and ardor once awakened by religious ideas upon a theological basis. Is human nature intrinsically such a poor thing that the idea is *absurd?* I do not attempt to give any answer, but the word *faith* is intentionally used. For in the long run democracy will stand or fall with the possibility of maintaining the faith and justifying it by works.

Take, for example, the question of intolerance. Systematic hatred and suspicion of any human group, "racial," sectarian, political, denotes deep-seated scepticism about the qualities of human nature. From the stand-point of a faith in the possibilities of human nature possessing religious quality it is blasphemous. It may start by being directed at a particular group, and be supported in name by assigning special reasons why that group is not worthy of confidence, respect, and decent human treatment. But the underlying attitude is one of fundamental distrust of human nature. Hence it spreads from distrust and hatred of a particular group until it may undermine the conviction that any group of persons has any intrinsic right for esteem or recognition — which, then, if it be given, is for some special and external grounds, such as usefulness to our particular interests and ambitions. There is no physical acid which has the corrosive power possessed by intolerance directed against persons because they belong to a group that bears a certain name. Its corrosive potency gains with what it feeds on. An anti-humanist attitude is the essence of every form of intolerance. Movements that begin by stirring up hostility against a group of people end by denying to them all human qualities. . . .

Democracy and America

I make no apology for linking what is said in this chapter with the name of Thomas Jefferson. For he was the first modern to state in human terms the principles of democracy. Were I to make an apology, it would be that in the past I have concerned myself unduly, if a comparison has to be made, with the English writers who have attempted to state the ideals of self-governing communities and the methods appropriate to their realization. If I now prefer to refer to Jefferson it is not, I hope, because of American provincialism, even though I believe that only one who was attached to American soil and who took a consciously alert part in the struggles of the country to attain its independence, could possibly have stated as thoroughly and intimately as did Jefferson the aims em-bodied in the American tradition: "the definitions and axioms of a free government," as Lincoln called them. Nor is the chief reason for going to him, rather than to Locke or Bentham or Mill, his greater sobriety of judgment due to that constant tempering of theory with practical experi-ence which also kept his democratic doctrine within human bounds.

The chief reason is that Jefferson's formulation is moral through and through: in its foundations, its methods, its ends. The heart of his faith is expressed in his words "Nothing is unchangeable but inherent and inalienable rights of man." The words in which he stated the moral basis of free institutions have gone out of vogue. We repeat the opening words of the Declaration of Independence, but unless we translate them they are couched in a language that, even when it comes readily to our tongue, does not penetrate today to the brain. He wrote: "These truths are self-evident: that all men are created equal; that they are endowed by their Creator with inherent and unalienable rights; that among these are life, liberty and the pursuit of happiness." Today we are wary of anything purporting to be self-evident truths; we are not given to associating politics with the plans of the Creator; the doctrine of natural rights which governed his style of expression has been weakened by historic and by philosophic criticism.

To put ourselves in touch with Jefferson's position we have therefore to translate the word "natural" into *moral*. Jefferson was under the influence of the Deism of his time. Nature and the plans of a benevolent and wise Creator were never far apart in his reflections. But his fundamental beliefs remain unchanged in substance if we forget all special associations with the word *Nature* and speak instead of ideal aims and values to be realized — aims which, although ideal, are not located in the clouds but are backed by something deep and indestructible in the needs and demands of humankind.

Were I to try to connect in any detail what I have to say with the details of Jefferson's speeches and letters — he wrote no theoretical treatises — I should probably seem to be engaged in a partisan undertaking; I should at times be compelled to indulge in verbal exegesis so as to attribute to him ideas not present in his mind. Nevertheless, there are three points contained in what has to be said about American democracy that I shall here explicitly connect with his name. In the first place, in the quotation made, it was the *ends* of democracy, the rights of *man* — not of men in the plural — which are unchangeable. It was not the forms and mechanisms through which inherent moral claims are realized that are to persist without change. Professed Jeffersonians have often not even followed the words of the one whose disciples they say they are, much less his spirit. For he said: "I know that laws and institutions must go hand in hand with the progress of the human mind. . . . As new discoveries are made, new truths disclosed, and manners and opinions change with the change of circumstances, institutions must change also and keep pace with the times. We might as well require a man to wear the coat which fitted him when a boy, as civilized society to remain ever under the regime of their barbarous ancestors."

Because of the last sentence his idea might be interpreted to be a justification of the particular change in government he was championing against earlier institutions. But he goes on to say: "Each generation has a right to choose for itself the form of government it believes the most promotive of its own happiness." Hence he also said: "The idea that institutions established for the use of a nation cannot be touched or modified, even to make them answer their end . . . may perhaps be a salutary provision against the abuses of a monarch, but is most absurd against the nation itself." "A generation holds all the rights and powers their predecessors once held and may change their laws and institutions to suit themselves." He engaged in certain calculations based on Buffon, more ingenious than convincing, to settle upon a period of eighteen years and eight months that fixed the natural span of the life of a generation; thereby indicating the frequency with which it is desirable to overhaul "laws and institutions" to bring them into accord with "new discoveries, new truths, change of manners and opinions." The word *culture* is not used; Jefferson's statement would have been weakened by its use. But it is not only professed followers of Jefferson who have failed to act upon his teaching. It is true of all of us so far as we have set undue store by established mechanisms. The most flagrantly obvious violation of Jefferson's democratic point of view is found in the idolatry of the Constitution as it stands that has been sedulously cultivated. But it goes beyond this instance. As believers in democracy we have not only the right but the duty to question existing mechanisms of, say, suffrage and to inquire whether some functional organization would not serve to formulate and manifest public opinion better than the existing methods. It is not irrelevant to the point that a score of passages could be cited in which Jefferson refers to the American Government as an *experiment*.

The second point of which I would speak is closely bound up with an issue which has become controversial and partisan, namely, states rights versus federal power. There is no question of where Jefferson stood on that issue, nor as to his fear in general of governmental encroachment on liberty — inevitable in his case, since it was the cause of the Rebellion against British domination and was also the ground of his struggle against Hamiltonianism. But any one who stops with this particular aspect of Jefferson's doctrine misses an underlying principle of utmost importance. For while he stood for state action as a barrier against excessive power at Washington, and while on the *practical side* his concern with it was most direct, in his theoretical writings chief importance is attached to local self-governing units on something like the New England town-meeting plan. His project for general political organization on the basis of small units, small enough so that all its members could have direct communication with one another and take care of all community affairs was never acted upon. It never received much attention in the press of immediate practical problems.

But without forcing the significance of this plan, we may find in it an indication of one of the most serious of present problems regarding democracy. I spoke earlier of the way in which individuals at present find themselves in the grip of immense forces whose workings and consequences they have no power of affecting. The situation calls emphatic attention to the need for face-to-face associations, whose interactions with one another may offset if not control the dread impersonality of the sweep of present forces. There is a difference between a society, in the sense of an association, and a community. Electrons, atoms and molecules are in association with one another. Nothing exists in isolation anywhere throughout nature. Natural associations are conditions for the existence of a community, but a community adds the function of communication in which emotions and ideas are shared as well as joint undertakings engaged in. Economic forces have immensely widened the scope of associational activities. But it has done so largely at the expense of the intimacy and directness of communal group interests and activities. The American habit of "joining" is a tribute to the reality of the problem but has not gone far in solving it. The power of the rabblerouser, especially in the totalitarian direction, is mainly due to his power to create a factitious sense of direct union and communal solidarity — if only by arousing the emotion of common intolerance and hate.

I venture to quote words written some years ago: "Evils which are uncritically and indiscriminately laid at the door of industrialism and democracy might, with greater intelligence, be referred to the dislocation and unsettlement of local communities. Vital and thorough attachments are bred only in the intimacy of an intercourse which is of necessity restricted in range. . . . Is it possible to restore the reality of the less communal organizations and to penetrate and saturate their members with a sense of local community life? . . . Democracy must begin at home, and its home is the neighborly community."* On account of the vast extension of the field of association, produced by elimination of distance and lengthening of temporal spans, it is obvious that social agencies, political and non-political, cannot be confined to localities. But the problem of harmonious adjustment between extensive activities, precluding direct contacts, and the intensive activities of community intercourse is a pressing one for democracy. It involves even more than apprenticeship in the

* The Public and Its Problems, pp. 212–13.

practical processes of self-government, important as that is, which Jefferson had in mind. It involves development of local agencies of communication and cooperation, creating stable loyal attachments, to militate against the centrifugal forces of present culture, while at the same time they are of a kind to respond flexibly to the demands of the larger unseen and indefinite public. To a very considerable extent, groups having a functional basis will probably have to replace those based on physical contiguity. In the family both factors combine.

The third point of which I would make express mention as to Jefferson and democracy has to do with his ideas about property. It would be absurd to hold that his personal views were "radical" beyond fear of concentrated wealth and a positive desire for general distribution of wealth without great extremes in either direction. However, it is sometimes suggested that his phrase "pursuit of happiness" stood for economic activity, so that life, liberty, and property were the rights he thought organized society should maintain. But just here is where he broke most completely with Locke. In connection with property, especially property in land, he makes his most positive statements about the inability of any generation to bind its successors. Jefferson held that property rights are created by the "social pact" instead of representing inherent individual moral claims which government is morally bound to maintain.

The right to pursue happiness stood with Jefferson for nothing less than the claim of every human being to choose his own career and to act upon his own choice and judgment free from restraints and constraints imposed by the arbitrary will of other human beings — whether these others are officials of government, of whom Jefferson was especially afraid, or are persons whose command of capital and control of the opportunities for engaging in useful work limits the ability of others to "pursue happiness." The Jeffersonian principle of equality of rights without special favor to any one justifies giving supremacy to personal rights when they come into conflict with property rights. While his views are properly enough cited against ill-considered attacks upon the economic relations that exist at a given time, it is sheer perversion to hold that there is anything in Jeffersonian democracy that forbids political action to bring about equalization of economic conditions in order that the equal right of all to free choice and free action be maintained.

I have referred with some particularity to Jefferson's ideas upon special points because of the proof they afford that the source of the American democratic tradition is moral — not technical, abstract, narrowly political nor materially utilitarian. It is moral because based on faith in the ability of human nature to achieve freedom for individuals accompanied with respect and regard for other persons and with social stability built on cohesion instead of coercion. Since the tradition is a moral one, attacks upon it, however they are made, wherever they come from, from within or from without, involve moral issues and can be settled only upon moral grounds. In as far as the democratic ideal has undergone eclipse among us, the obscuration is moral in source and effect. The dimming is both a product and a manifestation of the confusion that accompanies transition from an old order to a new one for the arrival of the latter was heralded only as conditions plunged it into an economic regime so novel that there was no adequate preparation for it and which dislocated the established relations of persons with one another.

Nothing is gained by attempts to minimize the novelty of the democratic order, nor the scope of the change it requires in old and long cherished traditions. We have not even as yet a common and accepted vocabulary in which to set forth the order of moral values involved in realization of democracy. The language of Natural Law was once all but universal in educated Christendom. The conditions which gave it force disappeared. Then there was an appeal to natural rights, supposed by some to center in isolated individuals — although not in the original American formulation. At present, appeal to the individual is dulled by our inability to locate the individual with any assurance. While we are compelled to note that his freedom can be maintained only through the working together toward a single end of a large number of different and complex factors, we do not know how to coordinate them on the basis of voluntary purpose.

The intimate association that was held to exist between individualism and business activity for private profit gave, on one side, a distorted meaning to individualism. Then the weakening, even among persons who nominally retain older theological beliefs, of the imaginative ideas and emotions connected with the sanctity of the individual, disturbed democratic individualism on the positive moral side. The moving energy once associated with things called spiritual has lessened; we use the word *ideal* reluctantly, and have difficulty in giving the word *moral* much force beyond, say, a limited field of mutually kindly relations among individuals. That such a syllogism as the following once had a vital meaning to a man of affairs like Jefferson today seems almost incredible: "Man was created for social intercourse, but social intercourse cannot be maintained without a sense of justice; then man must have been created with a sense of justice."

Even if we have an abiding faith in democracy, we are not likely to express it as Jefferson expressed his faith: "I have no fear but that the result of our experiment will be that men may be trusted to govern themselves without a master. Could the contrary of this be proved, I should conclude either there is no God or that he is a malevolent being." The belief of Jefferson that the sole legitimate object of government among men "is to secure the greatest degree of happiness possible to the general mass of those associated under it" was connected with his belief that Nature — or God — benevolent in intent, had created men for happiness on condition they attained knowledge of natural order and observed the demands of that knowledge in their actions. The obsolescence of the language for many persons makes it the more imperative for all who would maintain and advance the ideals of democracy to face the issue of the moral ground of political institutions and the moral principles by which men acting together may attain freedom of individuals which will amount to fraternal associations with one another. The weaker our faith in Nature, in its laws and rights and its benevolent intentions for human welfare, the more urgent is the need for a faith based on ideas that are now intellectually credible and that are consonant with present economic conditions, which will inspire and direct action with something of the ardor once attached to things religious.

Human power over the physical energies of nature has immensely increased. In moral ideal, power of man over physical nature should be employed to reduce, to eliminate progressively, the power of man over man. By what means shall we prevent its use to effect new, more subtle, more powerful agencies of subjection of men to other men? Both the issue of war or peace between nations, and the future of economic relations for years and generations to come in contribution either to human freedom or human subjection are involved. An increase of power undreamed of a century ago, one to whose further increase no limits can be put as long as scientific inquiry goes on, is an established fact. The thing still uncertain is what we are going to do with it. That it is power signifies of itself it is electrical, thermic, chemical. What will be done with it is a moral issue. . . .

Individuals can find the security and protection that are prerequisites for freedom only in association with others — and then the organization these associations take on, as a measure of securing their efficiency, limits the freedom of those who have entered into them. The importance of organization has increased so much in the last hundred years that the word is now quite commonly used as a synonym for association and society. Since at the very best organization is but the mechanism through which association operates, the identification is evidence of the extent in which a servant has become a master; in which means have usurped the place of the end for which they are called into existence. The predicament is that individuality demands association to develop and sustain it and association requires arrangement and coordination of its elements, or organization — since otherwise it is formless and void of power. But we have now a kind of molluscan organization, soft individuals within and a hard constrictive shell without. Individuals voluntarily enter associations which have become practically nothing but organizations; and then conditions under which they act take control of what they do whether they want it or not.

Persons acutely aware of the dangers of regimentation when it is imposed by government remain oblivious of the millions of persons whose behavior is regimented by an economic system through whose intervention alone they obtain a livelihood. The contradiction is the more striking because the new organizations were for the most part created in the name of freedom, and, at least at the outset, by exercise of voluntary choice. But the kind of working-together which has resulted is too much like that of the parts of a machine to represent a co-operation which expresses freedom and also contributes to it. No small part of the democratic problem is to achieve associations whose ordering of parts provides the strength that comes from stability, while they promote flexibility of response to change. . . .

I have stated in bare outline some of the outstanding phases of the problem of culture in the service of democratic freedom. Difficulties and obstacles have been emphasized. This emphasis is a result of the fact that a *problem* is presented. Emphasis upon the problem is due to belief that many weaknesses which events have disclosed are connected with failure to see the immensity of the task involved in setting mankind upon the democratic road. That with a background of millennia of non-democratic societies behind them, the earlier advocates of democracy tremendously simplified the issue is natural. For a time the simplification was an undoubted asset. Too long continued it became a liability.

Recognition of the scope and depth of the problem is neither depressing nor discouraging when the democratic movement is placed in historic perspective. The ideas by which it formulated itself have a long history behind them. We can trace their source in Hellenic humanism and in Christian beliefs; and we can also find recurrent efforts to realize this or that special aspect of these ideas in some special struggle against a particular form of oppression. By proper selection and arrangement, we can even make out a case for the idea that all past history has been a movement, at first unconscious and then conscious, to attain freedom. A more sober view of history discloses that it took a very fortunate conjunction of events to bring about the rapid spread and seemingly complete victory of democracy during the nineteenth century. The conclusion to be drawn is not the depressing one that it is now in danger of destruction because of an unfavorable conjunction of events. The conclusion is that what was won in a more or less external and accidental manner must now be achieved and sustained by deliberate and intelligent endeavor. . . .

If there is one conclusion to which human experience unmistakably points it is that democratic ends demand democratic methods for their realization. Authoritarian methods now offer themselves to us in new guises. They come to us claiming to serve the ultimate ends of freedom and equity in a classless society. Or they recommend adoption of a totalitarian regime in order to fight totalitarianism. In whatever form they offer themselves, they owe their seductive power to their claim to serve ideal ends. Our first defense is to realize that democracy can be served only by the slow day by day adoption and contagious diffusion in every phase of our common life of methods that are identical with the ends to be reached and that recourse to monistic, wholesale, absolutist procedures is a betrayal of human freedom no matter in what guise it presents itself. An American democracy can serve the world only as it demonstrates in the conduct of its own life the efficacy of plural, partial, and experimental methods in securing and maintaining an ever-increasing release of the powers of human nature, in service of a freedom which is co-operative and a co-operation which is voluntary.

We have no right to appeal to time to justify complacency about the ultimate result. We have every right to point to the long non-democratic and anti-democratic course of human history and to the recentness of democracy in order to enforce the immensity of the task confronting us. The very novelty of the experiment explains the impossibility of restricting the problem to any one element, aspect, or phase of our common everyday life. We have every right to appeal to the long and slow process of time to protect ourselves from the pessimism that comes from taking a short-span temporal view of events — under one condition. We must know that the dependence of ends upon means is such that the only *ultimate* result is the result that is attained today, tomorrow, the next day, and day after day, in the succession of years and generations. Only thus can we be sure that we face our problems in detail one by one as they arise, with all the resources provided by collective intelligence operating in co-operative action. At the end as at the beginning the democratic method is as fundamentally simple and as immensely difficult as is the energetic, un-flagging, unceasing creation of an ever-present new road upon which we can walk together.

THE PULSE OF DEMOCRACY

by George Gallup and Saul Forbes Rae *

WILL THE POLLS DESTROY REPRESENTATIVE DEMOCRACY?

Another accusation leveled at the modern polls is based on the assumption that they intensify the "band-wagon" instinct in legislators and undermine the American system of representative government. "Ours is a representative democracy," a newspaper editorial suggested soon after the polls had become prominent in 1936, "in which it is properly assumed that those who are chosen to be representatives will think for themselves, use their best judgment individually, and take the unpopular side of an argument whenever they are sincerely convinced that the unpopular side is in the long run in the best interests of the country."

The point has been made more recently by a student of public opinion. "If our representatives were told," it has been written, "that 62% of the people favored payment of the soldier's bonus or 65% favored killing the World Court Treaty, the desire of many of them to be re-elected would lead them to respond to such statistics by voting for or against a measure not because they considered it wise or stupid but because they wanted to be in accord with what was pictured to them as the will of the electorate." †

Beyond such criticisms, and at the root of many objections to the polls of public opinion, lies a fundamental conflict between two opposed views of the democratic process and what it means. This conflict is not new — it is older than American political theory itself. It concerns the relation-

* George Gallup and Saul Forbes Rae, *The Pulse of Democracy: The Public-Opinion Poll and How It Works* (New York: 1940) Copyright © 1940 by George Gallup and Saul Rae. Reprinted by permission of Simon and Schuster, Inc.
† Smith, C. W., *Public Opinion in a Democracy* (New York: 1939), p. 411.

ship between representative government and direct democracy, between the judgments of small exclusive groups and the opinions of the great mass of the people. Many theorists who criticize the polls do so because they fear that giving too much power to the people will reduce the representative to the role of rubber stamp. A modern restatement of this attitude may be found in an article written by Colonel O. R. Maguire in the November, 1939, issue of the *United States Law Review*.*

Colonel Maguire quotes James Madison: ". . . pure democracies . . . have ever been spectacles of turbulence and contention; have ever been found incompatible with personal security or the rights of property; and have in general been as short in their lives as they have been violent in their deaths."

To support these statements made by an eighteenth-century conservative who feared the dangers of "too much democracy," Maguire insists that the ordinary man is incapable of being a responsible citizen, and leans heavily on the antidemocratic psychological generalizations of Ross, Tarde, and Le Bon. He follows James Madison and the English Conservative, Edmund Burke, in upholding the conception of representative government under which a body of carefully chosen, disinterested public representatives "whose wisdom may best discern the true interest of their country, and whose patriotism and love of justice will be least likely to sacrifice it to temporary or partial considerations," interpret the real will of the people. Under such conditions, it is argued, "it may well happen that the public voice, pronounced by the representatives of the people, will be more consonant to the public good than if pronounced by the people themselves, convened for that purpose." The polls are condemned because, in his view, they invite judgments on which the people are ignorant and ill-informed, on which discussion must be left to representatives and specialists. Finally, a grim picture is drawn of the excesses that will follow the growth of "direct democracy": ". . . the straw ballot will undermine and discourage the influence of able and conscientious public men and elevate to power the demagogue who will go to the greatest extremes in taking from those who have and giving to those who have not, until there has been realized the prophecy of Thomas Babington Macaulay that America will be as fearfully plundered from within by her own people in the twentieth century as Rome was plundered from without by the Gauls and Vandals."

This case against government by public opinion reveals suspicion not

* Maguire, O. R., "The Republican Form of Government and the Straw Poll — an Examination," *U. S. Law Review*, November, 1939.

only of the public-opinion surveys, but also of the mass of the people. By and large, the thesis that the people are unfit to rule, and that they must be led by their natural superiors — the legislators and the experts — differs only in degree, and not in essence, from the view urged by Mussolini and Hitler that the people are mere "ballot cattle," whose votes are useful not because they represent a valuable guide to policy, but merely because they provide "proof" of the mass support on which the superior regime is based. It must not be forgotten that the dictators, too, urge that the common people, because of their numbers, their lack of training, their stupidity and gullibility, must be kept as far away as possible from the elite whose task it is to formulate laws for the mass blindly to obey.

Many previous statements and charges of just this kind can be found throughout history. Every despot has claimed that the people were incapable of ruling themselves, and by implication decided that only certain privileged leaders were fit for the legislative task. They have argued that "the best" should rule — but at different times and in different places the judgments as to who constituted "the best" have been completely contradictory. In Burke's England or Madison's America, it was the peerage or the stable wealthier classes — "the good, the wise, and the rich." In Soviet Russia, the representatives of the proletariat constitute "the best."

But the history of autocracy has paid eloquent testimony to the truth of Lord Acton's conclusion that "Power corrupts — absolute power corrupts absolutely." The possible danger of what has been called "the never-ending audacity of elected persons" emphasizes the need for modifying executive power by the contribution of the needs and aspirations of the common people. This is the essence of the democratic conception: political societies are most secure when deeply rooted in the political activity and interest of the mass of the people and least secure when social judgment is the prerogative of the chosen few.

The American tradition of political thought has tried to reconcile these two points of view. Since the beginning of the country's history, political theorists have disagreed on the extent to which the people and their opinions could play a part in the political decision.

"Men by their constitutions," wrote Jefferson, "are naturally divided into two parties: 1. – Those who fear and distrust the people and wish to draw all powers from them into the hands of the higher classes; 2. – Those who identify themselves with the people, have confidence in them, cherish and consider them as the most wise depository of the public interests."* Jefferson himself believed that the people were less likely to misgovern themselves than any small exclusive group, and for this reason urged that public opinion should be the decisive and ultimate force in American politics.

His opponents have followed Alexander Hamilton, whose antidemocratic ideas provide an armory for present-day conservatives. "All communities divide themselves into the few and the many," Hamilton declared. "The first are the rich and well-born, the others are the mass of the people. The voice of the people has been said to be the Voice of God; and however generally this maxim has been quoted and believed, it is not true in fact. The people seldom judge or determine right." Those who have followed the Federalist philosophy have largely been concerned with the liberties and property of the minority and have continually urged the necessity of building checks against the people's power.

Those who favor rule of "the best," through the gifted representative, and those who desire to give the common people more power are frequently at loggerheads because their arguments do not meet each other. The need exists to find the right balance between the kind of mass judgments and comments obtained by the public-opinion polls and the opinions of legislators. Both extreme views contain a kernel of truth. No one would deny that we need the best and the wisest in the key positions of our political life. But the democrat is right in demanding that these leaders be subject to check by the opinions of the mass of the people. He is right in refusing to let these persons rule irresponsibly. For in its most extreme form, the criticism that opposes any effort, like the modern polls, to make the people more articulate, that inveighs against the perils of a "direct democracy," leads directly to antidemocratic government. If it is argued that legislators understand better than the people what the people want, it is but a short step to give legislators the power to decree what the people *ought* to want. Few tendencies could be more dangerous. When a special group is entrusted with the task of determining the values for a whole community, we have gone a long way from democracy, representative or any other kind.

The debate hinges to some extent on which particular theory of the representatives' role is accepted. There is the view which the English Conservative, Edmund Burke, advanced in the eighteenth century to the electors of Bristol: "His unbiased opinion, his mature judgment, his enlightened conscience, he ought not to sacrifice to you; to any man, or to

* Agar, Herbert, *Pursuit of Happiness*, p. 42.

any set of men living. These he does not derive from your pleasure. They are a trust from Providence, for the abuse of which he is deeply answerable. Your representative owes you, not his industry only, but his judgment; and he betrays instead of serving you, if he sacrifices it to your opinion." This view has been restated more sharply in the words of the Southern Senator who is reported to have told a state delegation: "Not for hell and a brown mule will I bind myself to your wishes." But, on the other hand, it must be remembered that the electors of Bristol rejected Burke after his address, and that there are many in our own day who take the view that one of the legislator's chief tasks in a democracy must be to "represent."

Unless he is to be the easy prey of special interests and antisocial pressure, he must have access to the expression of a truly "public" opinion, containing the views of all the groups in our complex society. For free expression of public opinion is not merely a right which the masses are fortunate to possess — it is as vital for the leaders as for the people. In no other way can the legislators know what the people they represent want, what kinds of legislation are possible, what the people think about existing laws, or how serious the opposition may be to a particular political proposal. A rigid dictatorship, or any organization of political society which forbids the people to express their own attitudes, is dangerous not only to the people, but also to the leaders themselves, since they never know whether they are sitting in an easy chair or on top of a volcano. *People who live differently think differently.* In order that their experience be incorporated into political rules under which they are to live, their thinking must be included in the main body of ideas involved in the process of final decisions. That is why the surveys take care to include those on relief as well as those who draw their income from investments, young as well as old, men and women of all sorts from every section of the country, in the sample public.

Another form which the case against the people takes is the argument that we are living today in a society so complex and so technical that its problems cannot be trusted to the people or their representatives, but must be turned over to experts. It has been urged that only those who know *how* to legislate should have the power of decreeing what type of legislation *ought* to exist. The Technocracy movement put this view squarely before the American public. If it is true, it means that the kind of mass value judgments secured by the polls and surveys is quite useless in political life. It means that the people and their representatives must abdicate before the trained economist, the social worker, the expert in public finance, in tariffs, in rural problems, in foreign affairs. These learned persons, the argument runs, are the only ones who know and understand the facts and, therefore, they alone are competent to decide on matters of policy.

There is something tempting about the view that the people should be led by an aristocracy of specialists. But Americans have learned something from the experience of the past decade. They have learned, in the first place, that experts do not always agree about the solutions for the ills of our times. "Ask six economists their opinion on unemployment," an English wag has suggested, "and you will get seven different answers — two from Mr. John Maynard Keynes."

The point is obviously exaggerated. Certainly today a vast body of useful, applicable knowledge has been built up by economists and other specialists — knowledge which is sorely needed to remedy the ills of our time. But all that experts can do, even assuming we can get them to agree about what need be done, is to tell *how* we can act.

The objectives, the ends, the basic values of policy must still be decided. The economists can suggest what action is to be taken if a certain goal is to be reached. He, speaking purely as an economist, cannot say what final goal *should* be reached. The lawyer can administer and interpret the country's laws. He cannot say what those laws should be. The social worker can suggest ways of aiding the aged. He cannot say that aiding aged persons is desirable. The expert's function is invaluable, but its value lies in judging the means — not the ends — of public policy.

Thus the expert and his techniques are sorely needed. Perhaps Great Britain has gone even further than the United States in relating expert opinion to democratic government. The technique of the Royal Commission, and the other methods of organizing special knowledge, are extremely valuable ways of focusing the attention of the general public on specific evils and on solutions of them. In these Commissions, expert opinion is brought to bear, and opportunities for collective deliberation are created for those with special knowledge of political and economic questions. But even these Royal Commissions must remain ineffective until the general public has passed judgment on whether or not their recommendations should be implemented into legislation.

As a corollary of this view that expert opinion can bear only on specific questions of means, on the technical methods by which solutions are to be achieved, we must agree that most people do not and, in the nature of things, cannot have the necessary knowledge to judge the intimate details of policy. Repeated testing by means of the poll technique reveals that they cannot be expected to have opinions or intelligent judgments about details of monetary policy, of treaty making, or on other questions involving highly specialized knowledge. There are things which cannot be done by public opinion, just as there are things which can only be done by public opinion. "The people who are the power entitled to say what they want," Bryce wrote, "are less qualified to say how, and in what form, they are to obtain it; or in other words, public opinion can determine ends, but is less fit to examine and select means to those ends." *

All this may be granted to the critics. But having urged the need for representatives and experts, we still need to keep these legislators and experts in touch with the public and its opinions. We still have need of declarations of attitudes from those who live under the laws and regulations administered by the experts. For only the man on relief can tell the administrator how it feels to be on relief. Only the small businessman can express his attitude on the economic questions which complicate his existence. Only women voters can explain their views on marriage and divorce. Only all these groups, taken together, can formulate the general objectives and tendencies which their experience makes them feel would be best for the common welfare. For the ultimate values of politics and economics, the judgments on which public policy is based, do not come from special knowledge or from intelligence alone. *They are compounded from the day-to-day experience of the men and women who together make up the society we live in.*

That is why public-opinion polls are important today. Instead of being attempts to sabotage representative government, kidnap the members of Congress, and substitute the taxi driver for the expert in politics, as some critics insist, public-opinion research is a necessary and valuable aid to truly representative government. The continuous studies of public opinion will merely *supplement*, not destroy, the work of representatives. What is evident here is that representatives will be better able to represent if they have an accurate measure of the wishes, aspirations, and needs of different groups within the general public, rather than the kind of distorted picture sent them by telegram enthusiasts and overzealous pressure groups who claim to speak for all the people, but actually speak only for themselves. Public-opinion surveys will provide legislators with a new instrument for estimating trends of opinion, and minimize the chances of their being fooled by clamoring minorities. For the alternative to these surveys, it must be remembered, is not a perfect and still silence in which the Ideal Legislator and the Perfect Expert can commune on desirable policies. It

* Bryce, James, *The American Commonwealth*, p. 347.

is the real world of competing pressures, vociferous demonstrations, and the stale cries of party politics.

Does this mean that constant soundings of public opinion will inevitably substitute demagogery for statesmanship? The contrary is more likely. The demagogue is no unfamiliar object. He was not created by the modern opinion surveys. He thrives, not when the people have power, facts, information, but when the people are insecure, gullible, see and hear only one side of the case. The demagogue, like any propagandist of untruths, finds his natural habitat where there is no method of checking on the truth or falsity of his case. To distinguish demagogues from democratic leaders, the people must know the facts, and must act upon them.

Is this element secured by having no measurement of public opinion, or by having frequent, accurate measurement? When local Caesars rise to claim a large popular support for their plans and schemes, is it not better to be able to refer to some more tangible index of their true status than their own claims and speeches? The poll measurements have, more than once, served in the past to expose the claims of false prophets.

As the polls develop in accuracy, and as their returns become more widely accepted, public officials and the people themselves will probably become more critical in distinguishing between the currents of opinion which command the genuine support of a large section of the public and the spurious claims of the pressure groups. The new methods of estimating public opinion are not revolutionary — they merely supplement the various intuitive and haphazard indices available to the legislator with a direct, systematic description of public opinion. Politicians who introduced the technique of political canvassing and door-to-door surveys on the eve of elections, to discover the voting intentions and opinions of the public in their own districts, can hardly fail to acknowledge the value of canvassing the people to hear their opinions, not only on candidates, but on issues as well. It is simply a question of substituting more precise methods for methods based on impressions. Certainly people knew it was cold long before the invention of the thermometer, but the thermometer has helped them to know exactly how cold it is, and how the temperature varies at different points of time. In the same way, politicians and legislators employed methods for measuring the attitudes of the public in the past, but the introduction of the sampling referendum allows their estimates to be made against the background of tested knowledge.

Will the polls of the future become so accurate that legislators will automatically follow their dictates? If this happened would it mean rule by a kind of "mobocracy"? To the first point, it may be suggested that although great accuracy can be achieved through careful polling, no poll can be completely accurate in every single instance over a long period of time. In every sampling result there is a small margin of error which must never be overlooked in interpreting the results. The answer to the second question depends essentially on the nature of the judgments which people make, and on the competence of the majority to act as a directive force in politics.

There has always been a fear of the majority at the back of the minds of many intelligent critics of the polls. Ever since the time of Alexis de Tocqueville, the phrase, "tyranny of the majority," has been used widely by critics of democratic procedure, fearful lest the sheer weight of numbers should crush intelligent minorities and suppress the criticism that comes from small associations which refuse to conform to the majority view. It has been asserted that the same tendencies to a wanton use of power which exist in a despotism may also exist in a society where the will of the majority is the supreme sovereign power.

What protection exists against this abuse of power by a majority scornful of its weaker critics and intolerant of dissenting opinions? The sages of 1787 were fully aware of the danger, and accordingly created in the Bill of Rights provisions whereby specific guarantees — free speech, free association, and open debate — were laid down to ensure the protection of the rights of dissident minorities.

Obviously, such legal provisions cannot guarantee that a self-governing community will never make mistakes, or that the majority will always urge right policies. No democratic state can ever be *certain* of these things. Our own history provides abundant evidence pointing to the conclusion that the majority can commit blunders, and can become intolerant of intelligent minority points of view. But popular government has never rested on the belief that such things *cannot* happen. On the contrary, it rests on the sure knowledge that they *can* and *do* happen, and further, that they can and do happen in autocracies — with infinitely more disastrous consequences. The democratic idea implies awareness that the people *can* be wrong — but it attempts to build conditions within which error may be discovered and through which truth may become more widely available. It recognizes that people can make crucial mistakes when they do not have access to the facts, when the facts to which they have access are so distorted through the spread of propaganda and half-truths as to be useless, or when their lives are so insecure as to provide a breeding ground for violence and extremes.

It is important to remember that while the seismograph does not create earthquakes, this instrument may one day help to alleviate such catastrophes by charting the place of their occurrence, their strength, and so enabling those interested in controlling the effects of such disasters to obtain more knowledge of their causes. Similarly, the polls do not create the sources of irrationalism and potential chaos in our society. What they can do is to give the people and the legislators a picture of existing tendencies, knowledge of which may save democracy from rushing over the edge of the precipice.

The antidote for "mobocracy" is not the suppression of public opinion, but the maintenance of a free tribunal of public opinion to which rival protagonists can make their appeals. Only in this atmosphere of give-and-take of rival points of view can democratic methods produce intelligent results. "The clash and conflict of argument bring out the strength and weakness of every case," it has been truly said, "and that which is sound tends to prevail. Let the cynic say what he will. Man is not an irrational animal. Truth usually wins in the long run, though the obsessions of self-interest or prejudice or ignorance may long delay its victory."

There is a powerful incentive to expose the forces which prevent the victory of truth, for there is real value in the social judgments that are reached through widespread discussion and debate. Although democratic solutions may not be the "ideally best," yet they have the fundamental merit of being solutions which the people and their representatives have worked out in co-operation. There is value in the method of trial and error, for the only way people will ever learn to govern themselves is by governing themselves.

Thus the faith to which the democrat holds is not found so much in the inherent wisdom of majorities as in the value of rule by the majority principle. The democrat need not depend upon a mystic "general will" continually operating to direct society toward the "good life." He merely has to agree that the best way of settling conflicts in political life is by some settled rule of action, and that, empirically, this lies in the majority principle. For when the majority is finally convinced, the laws are immeasurably more stable than they would be were they carried out in flagrant opposition to its wishes. In the long run, only laws which are backed by public opinion can command obedience.

"The risk of the majority principle," it has been said, "is the least dangerous, and the stakes the highest, of all forms of political organization. It is the risk least separable from the process of government itself. When you have made the commonwealth reasonably safe against raids by oligarchies or depredations by individual megalomaniacs; when you have provided the best mechanisms you can contrive for the succession to power, and have hedged both majorities and minorities about with con-

stitutional safeguards of their own devising, then you have done all that
the art of politics can ever do. For the rest, insurance against majority
tyranny will depend on the health of your economic institutions, the
wisdom of your educational process, the whole ethos and vitality of your
culture." * In short, the democrat does not have to believe that man is
infinitely perfectible, or that he is infinitely a fool. He merely has to
realize that under some conditions men judge wisely and act decently,
while under other conditions they act blindly and cruelly. His job is to see
that the second set of conditions never develops, and to maximize the
conditions which enable men to govern themselves peacefully and wisely.

The "tyranny of the majority" has never been America's biggest problem. It is as great a danger to contemplate the "tyranny of the minority,"
who operate under cover of the Bill of Rights to secure ends in the
interests of a small group. The real tyranny in America will not come
from a better knowledge of how majorities feel about the questions of the
day which press for solution. Tyranny comes from ignorance of the power
and wants of the opposition. Tyranny arises when the media of information are closed, not when they are open for all to use.

The best guarantee for the maintenance of a vigorous democratic life
lies not in concealing what people think, but in trying to find out what
their ultimate purposes are, and in seeking to incorporate these purposes
in legislation. It demands exposing the weakness of democracy as well as
its values. Above all, it is posited on the belief that political institutions
are not perfect, that they must be modified to meet changing conditions,
and that a new age demands new political techniques.

THE MODERN DEMOCRATIC STATE

by A. D. Lindsay †

Democracy is a revolutionary form of government. For its aim is to
find a place for continual change within government. Its law exists to

---

* Lerner, Max, *It Is Later Than You Think*, 1938, p. 111.
† A. D. Lindsay, *The Modern Democratic State* (New York & London: 1947). By
permission of Oxford University Press.

foster freedom: its force exists to protect law. It is an organization to preserve, leave room for, these precious things of the spirit which in their nature cannot be organized. This may seem a high-flown statement of democracies as we know them. No doubt men and women abuse liberty and we must all be prevented from using our own liberty to destroy the liberty of others. Nevertheless the steady insistence in democratic government that there is always a strong *prima facie* case against interference with free association, that there ought to be spheres of life which government does not control, is based on the conviction of the value of change and experiment and initiative.

If equality and liberty, so conceived, are the marks of a democratic community, it will be the task of the government of such a community to be sensitively aware of the conditions which are making equality and liberty hard to maintain. There are of course certain elementary minimum conditions which will have to be laid down and provided. These are the kind which can at least be defined in a list of rights — minimum legal rights and a minimum standard of economic security. . . . There are some obvious and outstanding evils like widespread unemployment which can so poison the life of a community that they make equality and liberty and true democratic life impossible. The diagnosis of such evils is not difficult. But just because true equality and liberty are not mechanical conceptions and not standardized articles, a successful democratic government will . . . have to be sensitively aware of the conditions in society which prevent the community from being a community.

It will never be its business to construct a complete plan for society, nor to run and dominate or plan the community. A democratic government has to take the community for granted, to recognize . . . that there are activities essential for the health of the community which cannot be the state's activities — must be done by independent and free organizations or not done at all. The democratic state may support such activities but it cannot perform them.

DEMOCRATIC SOCIETY AND DEMOCRATIC GOVERNMENT

If this, then, is the task set before the government of a democratic state, we have now to face the rather unexpected question . . . can this complex, delicate, and difficult job be done by what we ordinarily call democratic machinery? Of course the government of any large modern state differs immensely from the governments of those simple societies which first got the name, but "democratic" governments have at least this in common that they profess to give the final power to the mass of the people, expressed somehow or other by their votes.

The task of the government of a democratic society implies a wisdom and understanding of the complicated life of modern societies very far removed from the simple "horse sense" which is sufficient for the running of small and simple democracies. It is clear that a modern state can do its job only with a lot of expert help, expert statesmen, expert administrators. We must nowadays go on and say "expert economists and expert scientists." Perhaps we must go further and say "expert sociologists."

That is clear enough. What is not so clear is where the ordinary plain man comes in. What is the justification of submitting the expert work of all these superior people to the control of the ordinary voter? We recognize that the man in the street cannot, in the strict sense of the word, govern a modern state. The ordinary person has not the knowledge, the judgement, or the skill to deal with the intricate problems which modern government involves. The primitive democracy of a Swiss commune or of a New England township in the eighteenth century was quite different. The things which the community had to get done in those simple societies were within the competence of most members of the community and open to the judgement of all. Readers of *Coniston*, that admirable political novel in which the American Winston Churchill describes the corruption of simple New Hampshire democracy by the coming of the boss, will remember the society he depicts — hard-headed, sensible, decent farmers, good judges of men and of horses. The select men whom they elect to govern them are well known to them all. They have nothing to do about which their electors cannot form a sound and shrewd judgement.

To ignore the immense difference between such a society and the society of the modern democratic state is to court disaster. Where are the simple and familiar issues on which shrewd if unlearned men may judge? Where, perhaps it may be asked, in our great urban populations are the hard-headed, shrewd, independent men to judge soundly on any issues?

We all recognize that expert and technical knowledge must come from specialists — that the ordinary man or woman is not capable of judging the detail of legislative proposals. We say that the public decides upon broad issues. That is what the working of modern democracy is supposed to imply. An election makes clear that the public insists, for example, that something pretty drastic must be done about unemployment, or that the United States should support Great Britain by all measures "short of war," and so on. One party rather than another gets into power because the public broadly approves of its programme more than the programme of its rivals, and judges well of its capacity to carry out its programme. The public is not supposed to have any views as to how that programme should be carried out but it is supposed to have decided that it prefers the main lines of one party's programme to another's.

What does this imply? Does democracy assume that ordinary men and women are better judges on broad issues than experts or than educated people? We can only take this line if we hold that "broad issues" demand not knowledge or skill or special training but "common sense" or sound judgement and that "common sense" is the possession of the ordinary man.

This is the stumbling-stone of democratic theory. On this subject men seem to hold opposing views which cannot be reconciled. Think of the way in which some people talk with conviction of the mob or the herd or the vulgar. Think of the long tradition of denunciation from Thucydides downwards of the folly and fickleness and weakness of the masses. Think, on the other hand, of the continual appreciation in democratic litera-ture of the good sense and sound judgement of the common man — the often expressed conviction that there is something in the "plain man" or in "the man in the street" which makes his judgement often more worth while than that of many superior persons.

There must be something to be said for both sides in such a contro-versy. It is worth while to attempt some disentangling.

Let us begin by noting that there are arguments for democratic control which do not assume that men and women are or ought to be given votes only because of the soundness of their judgement. We may summarize the two arguments in the two statements: "Only the wearer knows where the shoe pinches" and "We count heads to save the trouble of breaking them."

The "Shoes Pinching" Argument

Let us begin with the argument about shoes pinching. If we start with the statement I have described as the authentic note of democracy, "The poorest he that is in England has a life to live as the richest he," if we remember that the end of democratic government is to minister to the common life of society, to remove the disharmonies that trouble it, then clearly a knowledge and understanding of that common life is a large part of the knowledge essential to the statesman. But the common life is the life lived by all members of the society. It cannot be fully known and appreciated from outside. It can only be known by those who live it. Its disharmonies are suffered and felt by individuals. It is their shoes that pinch and they only who can tell where they pinch. No doubt the ordinary voter has the vaguest ideas as to what legislative or administrative reform will stop the pinching of his shoes. That is no more his business and no more within his capacity than it is the ordinary customer's business to make shoes. He may think, and often does think, that his shoes are pinching only because of the gross ignorance or perhaps because of the corrupt and evil intentions of his government; he may think the making of governmental shoes which ease his feet to be a much simpler business than it is; he may listen too easily to charlatans who promise to make the most beautiful shoes for the lowest possible price. But for all that, only he, the ordinary man, can tell whether the shoes pinch and where; and without that knowledge the wisest statesman cannot make good laws. It is sadly instructive to find what a gap there always is between the account even the best administrations give of the effect of their regulations and the account you get from those to whom the regulations apply. The official account tells what ought to happen if men and women behaved and felt as decent respectable officials assume that they think and feel. What is actually happening is often quite different.

The argument about shoes pinching is the argument which justifies adult suffrage. If government needs for its task an understanding of the common life it exists to serve, it must have access to all the aspects of that common life. All classes in society must be able to express their grievances. The qualification for voting is not wisdom or good sense but enough independence of mind to be able to state grievances. This does not seem a difficult qualification, but oppressed people are not always prepared to stand up for themselves or even always to think that there is anything wrong in what happens to them. They do not always accept the teaching of "certain revolutionary maniacs" referred to by the Rev. Mr. Twist "who teach the people that the convenience of man, and not the will of God, has consigned them to labour and privation." They vote as "their betters" or their employers or their bosses tell them. To give more of them votes in a society where these conditions exist is to give more power into the hands of those who can manage and exploit them. So in some societies to give votes to women would only mean to give more power into the hands of the men who could deliver their votes. To be an independent person, to be ready to stand up for your rights, to be able to express your grievances and demand that something should be done about them, demand qualities of character and mind which are not always forthcoming, as organizers and defenders of the downtrodden and oppressed often learn sadly to their cost.

LIMITATIONS OF THIS ARGUMENT

However weighty this argument about "shoes pinching" may be, it does not seem necessarily to involve the control of government by public opinion. It does involve that government should be sensitive and accessible to public opinion, but that is not necessarily the same thing. The safeguarding of the right of petition has little to do with democracy. It is an old tradition of kingly rule that the humblest member of the public should have access to the king to state his grievances. That is the mark of the good Eastern king from Solomon to Haroun al Rashid. The administration of government always gives opportunities for petty tyranny. The member of parliament who asks a question on behalf of one of his constituents who has a complaint against the administration is fulfilling a very old function which existed in undemocratic days. Why should the argument about shoes pinching imply the control of government by the ordinary voter?

The answer is that experts do not like being told that the shoes they so beautifully make do not fit. They are apt to blame it on the distorted and misshapen toes of the people who have to wear their shoes. Unless there is power behind the expression of grievances, the grievances are apt to be neglected. The very way in which the stories talk about the good king who takes pains to find out what his subjects really think implies that most kings do not do so. Solomons or Harouns al Rashid do not grow on every bush. Contrast the very great care which is officially taken in the army to encourage and listen to complaints with what the men say about it. There may be the most regular machinery by which men can express their grievances, the most frequent opportunities to respond to the question "Any complaints?"; but the rank and file will remain convinced that, if they complain, nothing will be done, but the sergeant-major will have it out of them somehow. Men will continue to talk and think quite differently about getting their grievances redressed through their member of parliament who wants their votes on the one hand and through their superior officer over whom they have no power on the other.

On this theory what happens in parliamentary democracy is that the people vote for a government on the understanding that it will remedy their grievances, deal with what is most manifestly wrong, and that they judge and they alone can judge whether the grievances are remedied. The vote at a general election is primarily a judgement on results: the people say, "Our shoes are still pinching and we shall try another shoemaker, thank you": or, "Yes, you have made our feet so much more comfortable that we shall let you go on and see if you can do still better." Of course what happens is not so simple as that. The verdict of the electors is not just on results: it is to some extent an assent to this or that proposal for the future; but broadly speaking an election is an expression of approval or disapproval of what has happened. This is of course strictly in accordance with the "where the shoe pinches" theory. It does not imply any more than the theory does that the electorate are particularly intelligent: that their judgement as to what ought to be done is at all out of the ordinary. It does imply that, as the end of government is to promote the free life of all its citizens, all citizens must have their say as to how that free life is actually being hindered and how far the work of government is actually removing those hindrances.

But it will also be clear that this argument has its limitations. It does not meet anything like all the claims made for democratic government. It does not even support the claim that the general public can decide broad issues. It would not, for example, justify the democratic control of foreign policy. Foreign policy involves a judgement as to how the internal life of the country is to be preserved from danger from abroad. If we assume that the democratic voter is only concerned to be allowed to "live his own life," to be freed from hindrances to it, but that he has not the necessary knowledge to know what means should be taken to ensure that end, it follows that the ordinary man or woman has on the argument of "the shoe pinching" no particular competence to control foreign policy. Is he then to leave foreign policy entirely to "his betters"?

No democrat would assent. Let us see why.

What People Are Prepared To Do

Errors in foreign policy may mean that a country is faced with the threat of war which may involve, unless that threat is met in one way or another, the destruction of all in its life which its people hold dear. But there are only two conceivable ways in which a threat of war can be met, and both involve the severest sacrifices falling on the ordinary men and women in the country. One of the ways of course is to meet the threat of war by accepting its challenge and resisting it. The other has never been tried but it is advocated by Mr. Gandhi and extreme pacifists. It is to meet the threat of war by passive resistance. Let us first consider the second.

Passive resistance to invasion which would prevent the invader from destroying the soul of a country demands a heroism and goodness in the population of a kind which no people has ever yet shown. If a sincere pacifist statesman, say Mr. Gandhi in power in India, committed his country to this alternative by making the other alternative impossible, he might produce the most horrible disaster. If his people were not really prepared to act up to his principles, and he had incapacitated them from acting up to their own, the result would be disaster indeed. No statesman has a right to commit his country to action unless he has reason to believe that the people will respond to the challenge which that action involves.

The same point is obvious when we consider the conditions in which alone a democratic statesman can commit his country to war. If it be true that free men fight better than other men for what they hold dear, it is also true that they fight worse than others for what they do not hold dear. It is possible, as Nazi Germany has shown, for a government to get such control over the minds and wills of a people and to have imposed such discipline upon them, that they, the government, can make up their mind about what they intend the nation to do and then make their people ready to undergo almost any sacrifices in obedience to their will. But a democratic people is not disciplined in that way. Its government can never go much beyond what their people are prepared to do. It is therefore quite essential that its government should know what that is. No statesman can pursue a foreign policy of appeasement unless he knows how much his people will stand. No statesman can pursue a policy which may end in resistance to aggression unless he knows for what his people are prepared to fight. The weakness of British foreign policy in the period between the two wars was largely due to the fact that, because of the bad working of the democratic machinery or of faulty leadership or of a combination of both, British statesmen did not have this essential knowledge to guide them in their conduct of foreign policy. Britain found herself in a new position. The development of air power had made her vulnerable as she had never been before. The existence of the League of Nations meant the adoption of a new attitude to foreign policy. The spread of pacifism and semi-pacifism further confused the issue. Before the last war a foreign minister could say with confidence, that the British people would go a very long way to preserve peace but there were certain things which they would not stand, and he could have said what those things were. After the war that could no longer be said, and this had a disastrous effect on the conduct of foreign policy.

This need of knowledge of what people are prepared to do is not confined to foreign policy. In a democratic society at least, laws, if they are to be successful, must rest largely upon consent. The force behind government can do something, but not very much. If laws are to be effectively obeyed, their demands cannot go much beyond what people are prepared to do. Successful law-making therefore demands an understanding of the ways and the willingness of ordinary people. That understanding can, to some extent, be got without voting or the ordinary processes of democratic machinery. But in so far as democratic machinery produces the expert representative, it is probably as reliable a way as can be devised of ensuring that this necessary knowledge is in the hands of government and that the government pay attention to it.

It is important to notice that though "what people are prepared to do" is a matter of fact, it is fact of an odd kind. For any one who reflects on it knows that what people are prepared to do depends on the varying tone of their societies and that that tone depends on leadership, inspiration, and imponderables of that kind. What people are prepared to do is not a distinct fact, to be discovered in its distinct existence by scientific analysis. Indeed we may say in general about all the argument of these last few pages that we shall go wrong if we think of "the pinching of shoes" and "what people are prepared to do" as distinct facts, existing separately and there to be discovered. They are that to some extent but not altogether. In a small meeting the process of discovering what needs to be done and what people are prepared to do is also a process of getting people prepared to do something. Something of the same is true in the elaborate democratic processes which culminate in men and women recording their votes in the polling booths. They are, or at least ought to be, processes of discussion, discussion carried on in the most multifarious ways as it is in a healthy society, by means of the press, of clubs and societies of all kinds: in public-houses and in W.E.A. classes as well as, indeed more than, at political meetings. The process of discovering the sense of the meeting is also a process of making the sense of the meeting. So to some extent at least with a nation at large.

We shall come back to this point later. Meanwhile let us consider how far towards democracy these two arguments take us. They assert that government needs for its task knowledge which cannot be got by ordinary learning but is provided normally by the democratic machinery. That would not necessarily imply control. If the knowledge could be got in another way, presumably on this argument the democratic machinery would not be necessary. Mass observation may claim to be a scientific process of discovering accurately what is now a rather clumsy by-product of elections. There is no reason why Hitler or any other autocrat should not use such a process. It is part of any government's job to know these facts about its people even when its main purpose is to understand how to exploit them to serve its own evil ambitions.

These arguments only imply democracy when we remember that men in power need often to be compelled to serve the true purposes of government. Expert shoemakers, as we saw, do not always like to be told that their shoes are at fault. Men who have control over executive and administrative power easily forget that they are only servants and that their power has only value as an instrument. Hence all the democratic devices to ensure that government shall attend to the purposes for which it exists, shall be made to do something about the grievances and wishes of the ordinary people it is meant to serve. Hence the necessity for responsible government — for arrangements which make the government somehow responsible to the ordinary people as contrasted with the most elaborate arrangements for advising an irresponsible government, for seeing that government has the necessary information without compelling it to act on that information. If the theory of all this were properly put into practice it would mean that the government were given a free hand to deal with means. The purpose of the control exercised by the ordinary voters is to see that those means — the technical skill of the administrative are used to right ends.

THE WISDOM OF THE PLAIN MAN

This leads to a third argument for democracy where it is assumed that ordinary plain people have a certain wisdom which is denied to the expert, and that therefore they are the best judges of ends if not of means.

This argument can easily be so put as to be absurd. An expert is not necessarily a fool. It may be and often is true that experts are apt to give their minds an almost complete holiday outside their own special sphere. Who does not know the distinguished scientist who thinks that his scientific attainments in one sphere justify his making the most surprising generalizations in matters of which he has no knowledge? But knowledge even in a restricted sphere cannot be a greater handicap to sound judgement than ignorance in all spheres. Yet we are not wrong when we pray to be delivered from the clever ass and it is on the whole true that for a certain kind of practical wisdom — very important in politics — we do not natu-

rally go to the scientific expert. That does not mean that we go instead
to the most ignorant man we can find or to just any one. We go to some
one who has learnt wisdom from life.

It is an old story that wisdom in conduct is not learnt from books or
technical study, but from experience and character. We know what we
mean when we talk of men or women of "sound judgement" or of "common
sense." We distinguish them from the expert whom we rather distrust. We should defend this attitude by saying that the expert is a
specialist: that what is wanted for conduct is all-round experience of
people and things. "Sound judgement" or "common sense" are not the
products of ignorance. They are produced by experience of a certain kind,
by responsibility, by a varied acquaintance with men and things and by
an all-round experience. The expert or specialist on the other hand has
probably paid for his expert knowledge by having had to undergo a long
training which has removed him from the ordinary rough-and-tumble of
life. He has probably not had to check his judgements by practical experience. He has perhaps not had to pay for his mistakes. He has become
"academic" in the bad sense of that term.

If we think about the men and women whose judgement on practical
affairs and on conduct we respect, we should certainly agree that academic
education did not seem to be very important in their production. We
should say that some of them were learned and some not, some rich, some
poor. They have no special training or accomplishment. That is why we
contrast the one-sidedness of the expert with the good sense or common
sense of the *ordinary* man and why democrats think that the proposals of
the expert should be approved by the ordinary man.

There clearly is something in this, but we must be careful. "Common
sense" it is sometimes said, "is one of the rarest of qualities." The word
"common" is used in New England as a term of uncommon praise. It
means, I think, much what the word "plain" means in the north of England or Scotland. We were proud as children when some one described
our mother as "the plainest woman I have ever set eyes on," though we
used the ambiguity of the remark as a weapon to tease her. "Plain" meant,
as I think "common" means, that she had no pretensions and no pom-
posity; that she took people as she found them, and entirely disregarded
their external attributes, their rank or class or anything else. Such an
attitude of mind, receptive and humble, is essential to the true understanding of men and of life. It is found in all sorts of people who may have
no other particular accomplishments and are therefore regarded as ordinary. But in reality such people are neither common nor ordinary.

The democrat who stands up for the good sense and sound judgement of "the ordinary man" against the pronouncements and dicta of superior persons is really thinking of the good sense and sound judgement he has found — not by any manner of means in everybody — but in some humble, simple persons. This is really the secularized version of the Puritans' government by the elect. What is the difference, I once heard asked in a discussion, between government by the *élite* and government by the elect? The answer was: "The *élite* are people you choose; the elect are those whom God chooses." The untheological version of this would be to say that if you talk of *élite* you mean people characterized by some clearly marked and almost measurable quality — skill, training, birth, and so on; if you talk of the elect you mean men who have nothing of this about them but are nevertheless remarkable.

Practical wisdom, the democrat would say, shows itself in the most unexpected places. You must be prepared for it wherever it turns up, and you must not imagine you can, by any training or planning, produce it to order. The democratic leader turns up. He is recognized by his fellows and carries them with him. He has the power of calling out the best in ordinary people. Because he shares the life and experience of ordinary men and women he knows, almost unconsciously, "where the shoe pinches" and "what people are prepared to do," and because he shares the ordinary responsibilities of life, he has an all-round experience and is saved from the narrowness of the specialist. Knowledge of the common life and its possibilities; understanding of the things which produce in it bitterness and thwart men's activities are the wisdom most wanted for politics. The state will be wisely directed if the final control is in the hands of "ordinary" men — men not specialized in their vocation or training — who have "common sense" and "sound judgement." But those men are, in favourable circumstances, the men to whom others listen, and who furnish the real if informal leadership in a community. The great mass of really ordinary people will follow them, and to give power to everybody by means of universal suffrage is to give power to them.

This view still implies a judgement about the mass of ordinary men and women. It implies their power of recognizing "sound judgement" and "common sense" in their fellows; in being able to judge a man and ready to approve the natural leader and reject the charlatan. That they do not always do so is notorious. What is important to discover is whether we can say anything about the conditions favourable to the mass of men and women in society judging men well or ill.

DISCUSSION

The argument for democratic as contrasted with expert leadership is that political wisdom needs more than anything else an understanding of the common life; and that that wisdom is given not by expert knowledge but by a practical experience of life. If the defect of the expert is his onesidedness, the merit of the practical man of common-sense judgement will be his all-round experience. The simple agricultural societies where democracy flourishes and seems native to the soil produce naturally men of common sense and sound judgement, appraisers alike of men and horses. The men whom we readily think of as men of sound judgement though unlearned have often had that kind of training. The part played by the village cobbler or blacksmith in the democratic life of a village has often been noticed. The inhabitants of a natural democracy like the New England township described in Mr. Winston Churchill's *Coniston* are independent, accustomed to act on their own, and to make judgements within the scope of their experience.

Modern industrialism has taken away from the great mass of men in an industrialized community their independence. It has condemned very many of them to specialized and narrow lives. Their lives are far more specialized and far narrower than the lives of the experts whom our democratic argument has been putting in their place, and they are without the expert's skill or knowledge or his partial independence. Where under such conditions are the common-sense qualities and sound judgement of the ordinary man to be found? How can we keep a modern industrial society from becoming not a community but a mob, not a society of persons capable of judging for themselves, discussing and criticizing from their experience of life the proposals put before them, but a mass played upon by the clever people at the top? These, nowadays armed with new psychological techniques, claim to be able to manipulate those masses to their will, make them believe what the rulers want, hate what the rulers want, and even fight and die for what the rulers want.

For the real issue between the democrats and the anti-democrats is that democrats think of a society where men can and do act as responsible persons. The anti-democrats talk of the mob, or the herd, or the crowd. What these latter say of mobs or herds or crowds is as true as what the democrats say of the sound sense of the ordinary man who acts and thinks as an individual. No one can read a book like Ortega y Gasset's *The Revolt of the Masses* without recognizing the strength of the forces in modern society which go to the making of men into masses or crowds; or without seeing that, if they prevail, mass democracy must produce, as it has in so many countries produced, totalitarianism. . . .

But . . . modern industrialism has supplied an antidote in the working-class movement. If we consider what gives that movement its vitality, we see that it creates innumerable centres of discussion. Trade union branches, co-operative guild meetings, W.E.A. classes and discussion groups of all kinds provide conditions as far removed as possible from those that produce a mob. The key to democracy is the potency of discussion. A good discussion can draw out wisdom which is attainable in no other way. The success of anti-democratic totalitarian techniques has depended on the suppression of discussion. If the freedom of discussion is safeguarded and fostered, there is no necessity for the most urbanized of committees becoming a mob. Those of us who have seen anything of the spread of discussion in England during the war, in the Army, in A.R.P. posts, in shelters, in all kinds of places where people come together have seen something of how in discussion the "plain" man can come into his own.

THE PUBLIC PHILOSOPHY

by Walter Lippmann *

INTERNAL REVOLUTION IN THE DEMOCRACIES

A vigorous critic of democracy, Sir Henry Maine, writing in 1884 just as England was about to adopt general manhood suffrage, observed that "there could be no grosser mistake" than the impression that "Democracy differs from Monarchy in essence." For "the tests of success in the performance of the necessary and natural duties of a government are precisely the same in both cases." † These natural and necessary duties have to do with the defense and advancement abroad of the vital interests of the state and with its order, security, and solvency at home. Invariably

* Walter Lippmann, *The Public Philosophy* (Boston: 1955). Copyright 1955 by Walter Lippmann. Reprinted by permission of Atlantic — Little, Brown.
† Sir Henry Maine, *Popular Government* (1886), pp. 60–61.

these duties call for hard decisions. They are hard because the governors of the state must tax, conscript, command, prohibit; they must assert a public interest against private inclination and against what is easy and popular. If they are to do their duty, they must often swim against the tides of private feeling.

The hardness of governing was little realized in the early 1900's. For more than half a century, while democracy was making its historic advance, there had been a remarkable interlude during which the governments rarely had to make hard decisions. Since Waterloo there had been no world war, and after the American Civil War only a few short and localized wars. It was a time of expansion, development, liberation; there were new continents to be colonized and there was a new industrial system to be developed. It seemed as though mankind had outlived the tempests of history. The governments — which were increasingly democratic, liberal and humane — were spared the necessity of dealing with the hard issues of war and peace, of security and solvency, of constitutional order and revolution. They could be concerned with improvements, with the more and more and the better and better. Life was secure, liberty was assured, and the way was open to the pursuit of private happiness.

In this long peace, the liberals became habituated to the notion that in a free and progressive society it is a good thing that the government should be weak. For several generations the West had flourished under governments that did not have to prove their strength by making the hard decisions. It had been possible to dream, without being rudely awakened, that in the rivalry of the diverse interests all would somehow come out for the best. The government could normally be neutral and for the most part it could avoid making positive judgments of good and bad and of right and wrong. The public interest could be equated with that which was revealed in election returns, in sales reports, balance sheets, circulation figures, and statistics of expansion. As long as peace could be taken for granted, the public good could be thought of as being immanent in the aggregate of private transactions. There was no need for a governing power which transcended the particular interests and kept them in order by ruling over them.

All this was only, as we now know, a daydream during a brief spell of exceptionally fine weather. The dream ended with the outbreak of the First World War. Then we knew that the Age of Progress had not reformed the human condition of diversity and conflict; it had not mitigated the violence of the struggle for survival and domination. . . .

The strain of the war worked up a menacing popular pressure upon the weak governments. We can, I think, point to 1917 as the year when the pressure became so strong that the institutional framework of the established governments broke under it.

The strain became unbearable. 1917 was the year of the two Russian revolutions. It was the year of the American involvement which brought with it the declaration of the Wilsonian principles. For Italy it was the year of Caporetto. For Austria-Hungary it was the beginning of the end under the successor of Francis Joseph. For Germany it was the year of the July crisis and of the need of the Prussian monarchy to listen to the Reichstag and its demand for a negotiated peace. For France it was the year of the mutinies, and for Britain the year of mortal peril from the submarine. In eastern and central Europe tortured and infuriated masses brought down the historic states and the institutions of the old regime. In western Europe and in North America the breakthrough took the form — if I may use the term — of a deep and pervasive infiltration. Behind the façade, which was little changed, the old structure of executive government with the consent of a representative assembly was dismantled — not everywhere and not in all fields, but where it mattered the most — in the making of high policy for war and peace.

The existing governments had exhausted their imperium — their authority to bind and their power to command. With their traditional means they were no longer able to carry on the hyperbolic war; yet they were unable to negotiate peace. They had, therefore, to turn to the people. They had to ask still greater exertions and sacrifices. They obtained them by "democratizing" the conduct and the aims of the war: by pursuing total victory and by promising total peace.

In substance they ceded the executive power of decision over the strategical and the political conditions for concluding the war. In effect they lost control of the war. This revolution appeared to be a cession of power to the representative assemblies, and when it happened it was acclaimed as promising the end of the evils of secret diplomacy and the undemocratic conduct of unpopular wars. In fact, the powers which were ceded by the executive passed through the assemblies, which could not exercise them, to the mass of voters who, though unable also to exercise them, passed them on to the party bosses, the agents of pressure groups, and the magnates of the new media of mass communications.

The consequences were disastrous and revolutionary. The democracies became incapacitated to wage war for rational ends and to make a peace which would be observed or could be enforced.

THE PARALYSIS OF GOVERNMENTS

Perhaps, before going any further, I should say that I am a liberal democrat and have no wish to disenfranchise my fellow citizens. My hope is that both liberty and democracy can be preserved before the one destroys the other. Whether this can be done is the question of our time, what with more than half the world denying and despairing of it. Of one thing we may be sure. If it is to be done at all, we must be uninhibited in our examination of our condition. And since our condition is manifestly connected with grave errors in war and peace that have been committed by democratic governments, we must adopt the habit of thinking as plainly about the sovereign people as we do about the politicians they elect. It will not do to think poorly of the politicians and to talk with bated breath about the voters. No more than the kings before them should the people be hedged with divinity. Like all princes and rulers, like all sovereigns, they are ill-served by flattery and adulation. And they are betrayed by the servile hypocrisy which tells them that what is true and what is false, what is right and what is wrong, can be determined by their votes.

If I am right in what I have been saying, there has developed in this century a functional derangement of the relationship between the mass of the people and the government. The people have acquired power which they are incapable of exercising, and the governments they elect have lost powers which they must recover if they are to govern. What then are the true boundaries of the people's power? The answer cannot be simple. But for a rough beginning let us say that the people are able to give and to withhold their consent to being governed — their consent to what the government asks of them, proposes to them, and has done in the conduct of their affairs. They can elect the government. They can remove it. They can approve or disapprove its performance. But they cannot administer the government. They cannot themselves perform. They cannot normally initiate and propose the necessary legislation. A mass cannot govern. The people, as Jefferson said, are not "qualified to exercise themselves the Executive Department; but they are qualified to name the person who shall exercise it. . . . They are not qualified to legislate; with us therefore they only choose the legislators." *

Where mass opinion dominates the government, there is a morbid derangement of the true functions of power. The derangement brings about the enfeeblement, verging on paralysis, of the capacity to govern.

* *Works* (Ford ed. V, pp. 103–104, 1892–1898) cited in Yves R. Simon, *Philosophy of Democratic Government* (1951), p. 169.

This breakdown in the constitutional order is the cause of the precipitate and catastrophic decline of Western society. It may, if it cannot be arrested and reversed, bring about the fall of the West.

The propensity to this derangement and the vulnerability of our society to it have a long and complex history. Yet the more I have brooded upon the events which I have lived through myself, the more astounding and significant does it seem that the decline of the power and influence and self-confidence of the Western democracies has been so steep and so sudden. We have fallen far in a short span of time. However long the underlying erosion had been going on, we were still a great and powerful and flourishing community when the First World War began. What we have seen is not only decay — though much of the old structure was dissolving — but something which can be called an historic catastrophe. . . .

THE ENFEEBLED EXECUTIVE

In the effort to understand the malady of democratic government I have dwelt upon the underlying duality of functions: *governing*, that is, the administration of the laws and the initiative in legislating, and *representing* the living persons who are governed, who must pay, who must work, who must fight and, it may be, die for the acts of the government. I attribute the democratic disaster of the twentieth century to a derangement of these primary functions.

The power of the executive has become enfeebled, often to the verge of impotence, by the pressures of the representative assembly and of mass opinions. This derangement of the governing power has forced the democratic states to commit disastrous and, it could be, fatal mistakes. It has also transformed the assemblies in most, perhaps not in all, democratic states from the defenders of local and personal rights into boss-ridden oligarchies, threatening the security, the solvency, and the liberties of the state.

In the traditions of Western society, civilized government is founded on the assumption that the two powers exercising the two functions will be in balance — that they will check, restrain, compensate, complement, inform and vitalize each one the other.

In this century, the balance of the two powers has been seriously upset. Two great streams of evolution have converged upon the modern democracies to devitalize, to enfeeble, and to eviscerate the executive powers. One is the enormous expansion of public expenditure, chiefly for war and reconstruction; this has augmented the power of the assemblies which

vote the appropriations on which the executive depends. The other development which has acted to enfeeble the executive power is the growing
incapacity of the large majority of the democratic peoples to believe in
intangible realities. This has stripped the government of that imponderable authority which is derived from tradition, immemorial usage, conse-
cration, veneration, prescription, prestige, heredity, hierarchy.

At the beginning of our constitutional development the King, when
he had mastered the great barons, was the proprietor of the greatest wealth
in the realm. The crown was also the point from which radiated the imponderable powers to bind and to command. As the King needed money
and men for his wars, he summoned representatives of the counties and
the boroughs, who had the money and the men he needed. But the imponderable powers, together with very considerable power in land and in
men, were still in the King's own hands. Gradually, over the centuries, the
power of the Parliament over the supplies of the government grew larger.
They had to appropriate a larger proportion of a much greater total. At
the same time, in the white light of the enlightenment and the seculariza-
tion of men's minds, the imponderable powers of the crown diminished.

Under the stress and the strain of the great wars of the twentieth century, the executive power has become elaborately dependent upon the
assemblies for its enormous expenditures of men and of money. The executive has, at the same time, been deprived of very nearly all of his imponderable power: fearing the action of the representative assembly, he
is under great temptation to outwit it or bypass it, as did Franklin D.
Roosevelt in the period of the Second World War. It is significant, I
think, certainly it is at least suggestive, that while nearly all the Western
governments have been in deep trouble since the First World War, the
constitutional monarchies of Scandinavia, the Low Countries, and the
United Kingdom have shown greater capacity to endure, to preserve order
with freedom, than the republics of France, Germany, Spain and Italy. In
some measure that may be because in a republic the governing power,
being wholly secularized, loses much of its prestige; it is stripped, if one
prefers, of all the illusions of intrinsic majesty.

The evaporation of the imponderable powers, a total dependence upon
the assemblies and the mass electorates, has upset the balance of powers
between the two functions of the state. The executive has lost both its
material and its ethereal powers. The assemblies and the mass electorates
have acquired the monopoly of effective powers.

This is the internal revolution which has deranged the constitutional
system of the liberal democratic states.

The Totalitarian Counterrevolution

CERTAIN OF ITS LESSONS

We can learn something about the kind of incapacity which has brought on disaster for the modern democracies by the nature of the counterrevolutions that have undermined and overthrown so many of them. There are various types of counterrevolutions. The most notable are the Soviet Communist, Italian Fascist, German National Socialist, Spanish Falangist, Portuguese Corporatist, the Titoist, and Peronist. . . . Besides these organized counterrevolutionary movements, professing doctrines of an anti-liberal and undemocratic character, there is, in large areas of the world, a very strong tendency to nullify the democratic system behind the façade of democratic institutions. The countries where elections are free and genuine, where civil liberty is secure, are still powerful. But they embrace a shrinking minority of mankind.

Now in all these counterrevolutionary movements there are two common characteristics. One is the separation of the governing power from the large electorate. In the totalitarian states this is done by not holding free elections; in the great number of nontotalitarian but also nondemocratic states, it is done by controlling and rigging the elections.

The other common characteristic of the counterrevolutions is that political power, which is taken away from the electorate, the parties and the party bosses, is then passed to an elite corps marked off from the mass of the people by special training and by special vows. The totalitarian revolutions generally liquidate the elite of the old regime, and then recruit their own elite of specially trained and specially dedicated and highly disciplined men. Elsewhere, when the liberal democratic system fails, the new rulers are drawn from the older established elites — from the army officers, from the clergy, the higher bureaucracy and the diplomatic corps, from university professors.

It is significant that in the reaction against the practical failure of the democratic states, we find always that the electoral process is shut down to a minimum or shut off entirely, and that the executive function is taken over — more often than not with popular assent — by men with a special training and a special personal commitment to the business of ruling the state. In the enfeebled democracies the politicians have with rare exceptions been men without sure tenure of office. Many of the most important are novices, improvisers, and amateurs. After a counterrevolution has brought them down, their successors are almost certain to be either the elite of the new revolutionary party, or an elite drawn from predemocratic institutions like the army, the church, and the bureaucracy.

In their different ways — which ideologically may be at opposite ends of the world — the post-democratic rulers are men set apart from the masses of the people. They are not set apart only because they have the power to arrest others and to shoot them. They would not long hold on to that kind of power. They have also an aura of majesty, which causes them to be obeyed. That aura emanates from the popular belief that they have subjected themselves to a code and are under a discipline by which they are dedicated to ends that transcend their personal desires and their own private lives.

A PROGNOSIS

The nature of the counterrevolution reflects a radical deficiency in the modern liberal democratic state. This deficiency is, as I have been saying, the enfeeblement and virtual paralysis of the executive governing functions. The strong medicine of the counterrevolution is needed, on the one hand, to stop the electoral process from encroaching upon and invading the government, and, on the other hand, to invest the government not only with all material power but also with the imponderable force of majesty.

It is possible to govern a state without giving the masses of the people full representation. But it is not possible to go on for long without a government which can and does in fact govern. If, therefore, the people find that they must choose whether they will be represented in an assembly which is incompetent to govern, or whether they will be governed without being represented, there is no doubt at all as to how the issue will be decided. They will choose authority, which promises to be paternal, in preference to freedom which threatens to be fratricidal. For large communities cannot do without being governed. No ideal of freedom and of democracy will long be allowed to stand in the way of their being governed.

The plight of modern democracies is serious. They have suffered great disasters in this century and the consequences of these disasters are compounding themselves. The end is not yet clear. The world that is safe for democracy and is safely democratic is shrunken. It is still shrinking. For the disorder which has been incapacitating the democracies in this century is, if anything, becoming more virulent as time goes on.

A continuing practical failure to govern will lead — no one can say in what form and under what banners — to counterrevolutionary measures for the establishment of strong government. The alternative is to withstand and to reverse the descent towards counterrevolution. It is a much harder way. It demands popular assent to radical measures which will restore government strong enough to govern, strong enough to resist the encroachment of the assemblies and of mass opinions, and strong enough to guarantee private liberty against the pressure of the masses.

It would be foolish to attempt to predict whether the crisis of the democratic state will be resolved by such an internal restoration and revival or by counterrevolution. No doubt the danger of counterrevolution is greater in countries where the margins of life are thinner. No doubt the prospects of a restoration and revival are best in countries where the traditions of civility, as the public philosophy of Western society, have deep roots and a long history. . . .

THE ECLIPSE OF THE PUBLIC PHILOSOPHY

THE GREAT VACUUM

To speak of a public philosophy is, I am well aware, to raise dangerous questions, rather like opening Pandora's box.

Within the Western nations, as Father Murray has put it, there is "a plurality of incompatible faiths" *; there is also a multitude of secularized and agnostic people. Since there is so little prospect of agreement, and such certainty of dissension, on the content of the public philosophy, it seems expedient not to raise the issues by talking about them. It is easier to follow the rule that each person's beliefs are private and that only overt conduct is a public matter.

One might say that this prudent rule reflects and registers the terms of settlement of the religious wars and of the long struggle against exclusive authority in the realm of the spirit by "thrones or dominations, or principalities or powers."

Freedom of religion and of thought and of speech were achieved by denying both to the state and to the established church a sovereign monopoly in the field of religion, philosophy, morals, science, learning, opinion and conscience. The liberal constitutions, with their bills of rights, fixed the boundaries past which the sovereign — the King, the Parliament, the Congress, the voters — were forbidden to go.

Yet the men of the seventeenth and eighteenth centuries who established these great salutary rules would certainly have denied that a com-

* John Courtney Murray, S.J., "The Problem of Pluralism in America," in *Thought* (Fordham University, Summer, 1954).

munity could do without a general public philosophy. They were themselves the adherents of a public philosophy — of the doctrine of natural law, which held that there was law "above the ruler and the sovereign people . . . above the whole community of mortals." *

The traditions of civility spring from this principle, which was first worked out by the Stoics. As Ernest Barker says:

> The rational faculty of man was conceived as producing a common conception of law and order which possessed a universal validity. . . . This common conception included, as its three great notes, the three values of Liberty, Equality and the brotherhood or Fraternity of all mankind. This common conception, and its three great notes, have formed a European set of ideas for over two thousand years. It was a set of ideas which lived and moved in the Middle Ages; and St. Thomas Aquinas cherished the idea of a sovereign law of nature imprinted in the heart and nature of man, to which kings and legislators must everywhere bow. It was a set of ideas which lived and acted with an even greater animation from the days of the Reformation to those of the French Revolution . . . Spoken through the mouth of Locke, [they had justified] the English Revolution of 1688, and had recently served to inspire the American Revolution of 1776. . . . They were ideas of the proper conduct of states and governments in the area of internal affairs. They were ideas of the natural rights of man — of liberty, political and civic, with sovereignty residing essentially in the nation, and with free communication of thoughts and opinions; of equality before the law, and the equal repartition of public expenses among all the members of the public; of a general fraternity which tended in practice to be sadly restricted within the nation, but which could, on occasion, be extended by decree to protect all nations struggling for freedom.†

These traditions were expounded in the treatises of philosophers, were developed in the tracts of the publicists, were absorbed by the lawyers and applied in the courts. At times of great stress some of the endangered traditions were committed to writing, as in the Magna Carta and the Declaration of Independence. For the guidance of judges and lawyers, large portions were described — as in Lord Coke's examination of the common law. The public philosophy was in part expounded in the Bill of Rights of 1689. It was re-enacted in the first ten amendments of the Constitution of the United States. The largest part of the public philosophy was never

---

* Cf. Otto von Gierke, *Political Theories of the Middle Age*, translated with an introduction by Frederick William Maitland (London, Cambridge University Press, 1927), pp. 73–87; and more especially note #256. Also cf. Leo Strauss, *Natural Right and History* (1953).

† Sir Ernest Barker, *Traditions of Civility* (1948), pp. 10–12.

explicitly stated. Being the wisdom of a great society over the generations, it can never be stated in any single document. But the traditions of civility permeated the peoples of the West and provided a standard of public and private action which promoted, facilitated and protected the institutions of freedom and the growth of democracy.

The founders of our free institutions were themselves adherents of this public philosophy. When they insisted upon excluding the temporal power from the realm of the mind and the spirit, it was not that they had no public philosophy. It was because experience had taught them that as power corrupts, it corrupts the public philosophy. It was, therefore, a practical rule of politics that the government should not be given sovereignty and proprietorship over the public philosophy.

But as time went on, there fell out of fashion the public philosophy of the founders of Western institutions. The rule that the temporal power should be excluded from the realm of the mind and of the spirit was then subtly transformed. It became the rule that ideas and principles are private — with only subjective relevance and significance. Only when there is "a clear and present danger" to public order are the acts of speaking and publishing in the public domain. All the first and last things were removed from the public domain. All that has to do with what man is and should be, or how he should hold himself in the scheme of things, what are his rightful ends and the legitimate means, became private and subjective and publicly unaccountable. And so, the liberal democracies of the West became the first great society to treat as a private concern the formative beliefs that shape the character of its citizens.

This has brought about a radical change in the meaning of freedom. Originally it was founded on the postulate that there was a universal order on which all reasonable men were agreed: within that public agreement on the fundamentals and on the ultimates, it was safe to permit and it would be desirable to encourage, dissent and dispute. But with the disappearance of the public philosophy — and of a consensus on the first and last things — there was opened up a great vacuum in the public mind, yawning to be filled.

As long as it worked, there was an obvious practical advantage in treating the struggle for the ultimate allegiance of men as not within the sphere of the public interest. It was a way of not having to open the Pandora's box of theological, moral and ideological issues which divide the Western society. But in this century, when the hard decisions have had to be made, this rule of prudence has ceased to work. The expedient worked only as long as the general mass of the people were not seriously dissatisfied with things as they are. It was an expedient that looked towards reforms and improvement. But it assumed a society which was secure, progressive, expanding and unchallenged. That is why it was only in the fine Victorian weather, before the storm clouds of the great wars began to gather, that the liberal democratic policy of public agnosticism and practical neutrality in ultimate issues was possible.

THE NEGLECT OF THE PUBLIC PHILOSOPHY

We come, then, to a crucial question. If the discussion of public philosophy has been, so to speak, tabled in the liberal democracies, can we assume that, though it is not being discussed, there is a public philosophy? Is there a body of positive principles and precepts which a good citizen cannot deny or ignore? I am writing this book in the conviction that there is. It is a conviction which I have acquired gradually, not so much from a theoretical education, but rather from the practical experience of seeing how hard it is for our generation to make democracy work. I believe there is a public philosophy. Indeed there is such a thing as the public philosophy of civility. It does not have to be discovered or invented. It is known. But it does have to be revived and renewed.

The public philosophy is known as *natural law*, a name which, alas, causes great semantic confusion.* This philosophy is the premise of the institutions of the Western society, and they are, I believe, unworkable in communities that do not adhere to it. Except on the premises of this philosophy, it is impossible to reach intelligible and workable conceptions of popular election, majority rule, representative assemblies, free speech, loyalty, property, corporations and voluntary associations. The founders of these institutions, which the recently enfranchised democracies have inherited, were all of them adherents of some one of the various schools of natural law.

In our time the institutions built upon the foundations of the public philosophy still stand. But they are used by a public who are not being taught, and no longer adhere to, the philosophy. Increasingly, the people are alienated from the inner principles of their institutions. The question is whether and how this alienation can be overcome, and the rupture of the traditions of civility repaired.

Needless to say I am not about to argue that the rupture can be repaired by a neo-classical or neo-medieval restoration, or by some kind of romantic return to feudalism, folk-dancing and handicrafts. We cannot rub out

---

* Cf. Mortimer Adler, "The Doctrine of Natural Law in Philosophy," *University of Notre Dame Natural Law Institute Proceedings,* Vol. I, pp. 65–84.

the modern age, we cannot roll back the history that has made us what we are. We cannot start again as if there had been no advance of science, no spread of rationalism and secularism, no industrial revolution, no dissolution of the old habitual order of things, no sudden increase in the population. The poignant question is whether, and, if so, how modern men could make vital contact with the lost traditions of civility.

The appearance of things is quite obviously unpromising. There is radical novelty in our modern ways of life. The climate of feeling and the style of thought have changed radically. Modern men will first need to be convinced that the traditions of civility were not abandoned because they became antiquated. This is one of the roots of their unbelief and there is no denying its depth. Since the public philosophy preceded the advance of modern science and the industrial revolution, how can it be expected to provide a positive doctrine which is directly and practically relevant to the age we live in?

It does, one must admit, look like that, and quite evidently the original principles and precepts do not now provide the specific rules and patterns of a way of life in the circumstances of this age. A rereading of the political classics from Aristotle to Burke will not give the answers to the immediate and concrete questions: to the burning issues of diplomacy, military defense, trade, taxes, prices, and wages. Nor have the classical books anything to say about repairing automobiles, treating poliomyelitis, or proceeding with nuclear fission. As handbooks for the busy man, wanting to know how to do this or that, they are now lamentably out of date. The language is archaic, the idiom is strange, the images are unfamiliar, the practical precepts are addressed to forgotten issues.

But this irrelevance and remoteness might be the dust which has settled during the long time when philosophers and scholars and popular educators have relegated the public philosophy to the attic, when they have treated it as no longer usable by modern and progressive men. It is a neglected philosophy. For several generations it has been exceptional and indeed eccentric to use this philosophy in the practical discussion of public policies.

Neglect might well explain its dilapidated condition. If this were the explanation, it would encourage us to explore the question of a renascence. Could modern men again make vital contact with the traditions of civility? At least once before something of the sort did happen. The traditions were articulated in the Graeco-Roman world, and submerged in the West by the decline and the fall of the Western empire. Later on they were revived and renovated and remade in a great flowering of discovery and enterprise and creativity. The revival of learning did not provide maps for Columbus to use in discovering America. But it did produce much human wisdom which helped Columbus and his contemporaries to discover themselves and their possibilities.

The ancient world, we may remind ourselves, was not destroyed because the traditions were false. They were submerged, neglected, lost. For the men adhering to them had become a dwindling minority who were overthrown and displaced by men who were alien to the traditions, having never been initiated and adopted into them. May it not be that while the historical circumstances are obviously so different, something like that is happening again? . . .

The Defense of Civility

THE THESIS RESTATED

We have now made a reconnaissance in the public philosophy in order to test the chances of its revival. Our warrant for making this attempt rests on certain general findings about the condition of the Western world.

The first is that free institutions and democracy were conceived and established by men who adhered to a public philosophy. Though there have been many schools in this philosophy, there are fundamental principles common to all of them: that, in Cicero's words, "law is the bond of civil society," and that all men, governors and the governed, are always under, are never above, laws; that these laws can be developed and refined by rational discussion, and that the highest laws are those upon which all rational men of good will, when fully informed, will tend to agree.

The second finding from which we have proceeded, in our inquiry, is that the modern democracies have abandoned the main concepts, principles, precepts, and the general manner of thinking which I have been calling the public philosophy. I hold that liberal democracy is not an intelligible form of government and cannot be made to work except by men who possess the philosophy in which liberal democracy was conceived and founded. The prospects of liberal democracy in this time of mighty counterrevolutions are, therefore, bound up with the question whether the public philosophy is obsolete or whether it can be revived, reunited and renewed.

I believe that the public philosophy can be revived, and the reconnaissance which we have made has been a demonstration that when it is applied to such central concepts as popular sovereignty, property, freedom of speech, and education, the public philosophy clarifies the problems and opens the way towards rational and acceptable solutions. The revival of the public philosophy depends on whether its principles and precepts — which were articulated before the industrial revolution, before the era of rapid technological change, and before the rise of the mass democracies — depends on whether this old philosophy can be reworked for the modern age. If this cannot be done, then the free and democratic nations face the totalitarian challenge without a public philosophy which free men believe in and cherish, with no public faith beyond a mere official agnosticism, neutrality and indifference. There is not much doubt how the struggle is likely to end if it lies between those who, believing, care very much — and those who, lacking belief, cannot care very much.

THE COMMUNICATION OF THE PUBLIC PHILOSOPHY

We come now to the problem of communicating the public philosophy to the modern democracies. The problem has been, to be sure, only too obvious from the beginning. For, as we have seen, the public philosophy is in a deep contradiction with the Jacobin ideology, which is, in fact, the popular doctrine of the mass democracies. The public philosophy is addressed to the government of our appetites and passions by the reasons of a second, civilized, and, therefore, acquired nature. Therefore, the public philosophy cannot be popular. For it aims to resist and to regulate those very desires and opinions which are most popular. The warrant of the public philosophy is that while the regime it imposes is hard, the results of rational and disciplined government will be good. And so, while the right but hard decisions are not likely to be popular when they are taken, the wrong and soft decisions will, if they are frequent and big enough, bring on a disorder in which freedom and democracy are destroyed. . . .

THE MANDATE OF HEAVEN

. . . The public philosophy is in a large measure intellectually discredited among contemporary men. Because of that, what we may call the terms of discourse in public controversy are highly unfavorable to anyone who adheres to the public philosophy. The signs and seals of legitimacy, of rightness and of truth, have been taken over by men who reject, even when they are not the avowed adversaries of, the doctrine of constitutional democracy.

If the decline of the West under the misrule of the people is to be halted, it will be necessary to alter these terms of discourse. They are now set overwhelmingly against the credibility and against the rightness of the principles of the constitutional state; they are set in favor of the Jacobin conception of the emancipated and sovereign people.

I have been arguing, hopefully and wishfully, that it may be possible to alter the terms of discourse if a convincing demonstration can be made that the principles of the good society are not, in Sartre's phrase, invented and chosen — that the conditions which must be met if there is to be a good society are there, outside our wishes, where they can be discovered by rational inquiry, and developed and adapted and refined by rational discussion.

If eventually this were demonstrated successfully, it would, I believe, rearm all those who are concerned with the anomy of our society, with its progressive barbarization, and with its descent into violence and tyranny. Amidst the quagmire of moral impressionism they would stand again on hard intellectual ground where there are significant objects that are given and are not merely projected, that are compelling and are not merely wished. Their hope would be re-established that there is a public world, sovereign above the infinite number of contradictory and competing private worlds. Without this certainty, their struggle must be unavailing.

As the defenders of civility, they cannot do without the signs and seals of legitimacy, of rightness and of truth. For it is a practical rule, well known to experienced men, that the relation is very close between our capacity to act at all and our conviction that the action we are taking is right. This does not mean, of course, that the action *is* necessarily right. What is necessary to continuous action is that it shall be *believed* to be right. Without that belief, most men will not have the energy and will to persevere in the action. Thus satanism, which prefers evil as such, is present in some men and perhaps potential in many. Yet, except in a condition of the profoundest hysteria, as in a lynching, satanism cannot be preached to multitudes. Even Hitler, who was enormously satanic and delighted in monstrous evil, did nevertheless need, it would seem, to be reassured that he was not only a great man but, in a mysterious way, a righteous one.

William Jennings Bryan once said that to be clad in the armor of righteousness will make the humblest citizen of all the land stronger than all the hosts of error.* That is not quite true. But the reason the humblest citizen is not stronger than the hosts of error is that the latter also are clad in an armor which they at least believe is the armor of righteousness. Had they not been issued the armor of righteousness, they would not, as a matter of fact, be a host at all. For political

* Speech at Democratic National Convention (Chicago, 1896).

ideas acquire operative force in human affairs when, as we have seen, they acquire legitimacy, when they have the title of being right which binds men's consciences. Then they possess, as the Confucian doctrine has it, "the mandate of heaven."

In the crisis within the Western society, there is at issue now the mandate of heaven.

II. CAPITALISM

CAPITALISM is a distinctly modern word, hardly more than a century old. The essential conditions for capitalism developed slowly in the centuries after the fall of the Roman Empire, and slowly capitalistic theory emerged from the concepts of feudalism. During feudalism, life centered about the manor with its ordered hierarchy of relationships. In this rigidly structured society, functions and obligations were distributed in accordance with status and station. Church doctrine emphasized the primacy of a spiritual life guided by the clergy from the pope in Rome to the priest in the locality. Such material goods as were required for existence were provided by serfs, slaves and servants according to one's station and the customary obligations which had become traditional in the community. Ideologically, in a world devoted primarily to the goal of salvation, there was a disdain for worldly wealth. For the Bible counseled that it was easier for a camel to pass through the eye of a needle than for a rich man to enter the Kingdom of Heaven. Jesus had admonished man not to give thought to what one should eat, drink, or wear but to seek first the Kingdom of God. Indeed avarice, in Church doctrine, was considered a sin.

Of course, economic arrangements for producing and exchanging goods were required then as now; but these arrangements came within the purview of the prevailing ethic. Certain economic practices were either prohibited or markedly circumscribed. For example, to a very large extent modern capitalism is based on a credit economy, from which the creditors derive interest. We buy our homes and automobiles on time and pay interest for the privilege; likewise corporations and even governments borrow money in the form of bonds and pay the lender interest. But in the early medieval period interest was frowned upon and given the invidious appellation of usury. "Lend hoping for nothing again," St. Luke had written. And even earlier Aristotle had declared that the most odious form of wealth-getting was that achieved through usury. "For money was intended to be used in exchange, but not to increase at interest. And this term interest, which means the birth of money from money, is applied to the breeding of money because the offspring resembles the parent. Wherefore, of all modes of getting wealth this is the most unnatural." [1] Though the use of interest was one of the oldest economic practices it was also, until modern times, one of the most condemned. St. Thomas Aquinas, in his *Summa Theologica*, declared it a sin to take money for money lent. The Church so sought to stamp out the practice that between the twelfth and fourteenth centuries it not only refused to admit usurers to communion but declared that rulers who permitted usury were to be excommunicated. Yet usury survived and spread, and gradually the modern credit system developed and became ideologically acceptable.

Even as usury survived in spite of stringent prohibition so did other forms of economic activity which were forbidden. Forestalling, that is buying in advance, outside of the market; regrating, that is buying in bulk to sell back in the same market; and engrossing, that is "cornering" the market, were practices proscribed by craft and merchant guilds alike.

Perhaps the most characteristic economic doctrine of the medieval period was that known as the just price, for implicit in it were the ordered ethical, anti-profit-minded attitudes of the period. The price of an article, it was felt, involved far more than purely economic considerations, or to put the matter another way, economic and ethical considerations were so inextricably intertwined that elements of cost and need transcended the economic and entered the higher realm of social and religious values. Pricing, affecting as it did both buyers and sellers, was not just a transaction between individuals to be resolved by "higgling" in the market, but an interchange of goods and services which affected ultimately the entire community. It was therefore subject to community regulation by the guilds, the town and market authorities and ultimately of course by the Church. In the thirteenth century St. Thomas Aquinas wrote that "No man should sell a thing to another man for more than its worth." [2] While he granted that the just price of a thing could not be determined with "mathematical precision," nevertheless the *communis estimatio*, or common belief or estimate, could be a fair guide. Both buyer and seller were presumed to be protected by the just price, which town and guild authorities enforced in the market. In the fourteenth century Henry of Langenstein observed that "to leave the prices of goods at the discretion

[1] *Aristotle's Politics* (New York: The Modern Library, 1943), pp. 71–2.
[2] *The Political Ideas of St. Thomas Aquinas* (New York: Hafner Publishing Co., 1957), p. 144.

of the sellers is to give rein to the cupidity which goads almost all of them to seek excessive gain." [3]

The concept of the just price passed into Protestant thought as well. Supply and demand might be legitimate considerations in pricing but they were properly subject to the ethical restraints of the collective conscience of the community. As Martin Luther observed:

> A man should not say, "I will sell my wares as dear as I can or please," but "I will sell my wares as is right and proper." For thy selling should not be a work that is within thy own power or will, without all law and limit, as though thou wert a God, bounden to no one. But because thy selling is a work that thou performest to thy neighbor, it should be restrained within such law and conscience that thou mayest practice it without harm or injury to him. [4]

And in Puritan colonial Massachusetts, John Cotton attacked from the pulpit the practice of gouging, declaring it a false principle of trading, "that a man might sell as dear as he can, and buy as cheap as he can." [5] Indeed how much closer to medieval thought than to the present was the admonition of John Higginson in 1661, when he declared:

> My fathers and brethren, this is never to be forgotten that New England is originally a plantation of religion not a plantation of trade. Let merchants and such as are increasing cent per cent remember this, that worldly gain was not the end and design of the people of New England. [6]

It was only a century later, in the year of the signing of the Declaration of Independence, that Adam Smith published his *Wealth of Nations* and a new economic ideology was brought into the world. Of course a host of fundamental changes in the institutional structure of society had been taking place over the centuries, each affecting in some degree the economic processes. The art of printing had been discovered and with it came a new emphasis on learning. The compass was brought into general use and this led to increased trade, exploration, and colonization as discovery led to discovery. Political unification, nationalization, and expansion capitalized on the discovery and general use of gunpowder. Slowly but surely the old

[3] Quoted in R. H. Tawney, *Religion and the Rise of Capitalism* (New York: The New American Library, 1947), p. 43.

[4] Quoted in *ibid.*, p. 85.

[5] *Winthrop's Journal, History of New England* (1630–1649), edited by James K. Hosmer (New York: Charles Scribner's Sons, 1908), Vol. I, p. 317.

[6] Quoted in Thomas J. Wertenbaker, *The Puritan Oligarchy* (New York: Charles Scribner's Sons, 1946), p. 202.

ordered hierarchy of the medieval world, with its eyes focused on the heavens, crumbled in the wake of the revolutions in politics, science, religion, and commerce. In place of the intricate and static feudal arrangements in which the relationships of men were determined by station and tradition, a new class system arose which gave an increasingly prominent place to the entrepreneurs who became known as the bourgeoisie. These were the middle class townspeople — traders, merchants, and producers. A new fluidity in the social structure permitting horizontal, vertical, and geographical mobility was in part the response to an increasing emphasis on and acceptance of the role of worldly wealth in society. Along with the expansion of the political community came the expansion of the economic community. Trade routes and markets were protected by the political powers; and political rulers turned to merchants and moneylenders for their financial support. Indeed the possession of money — of gold and silver — became an increasingly important factor in politics, and it became accordingly an increasingly important mark of social prestige. The obscure and ostracized pawn-broker now paid interest for money held as well as took interest for money loaned, with the approval of the state. Modern banking came into being to facilitate the increasing production and exchange of goods. No longer were the money-lenders driven from the temple. Rather were they invited in. The fabulous fifteenth-century Medici family of Florence are an illustration in point. In fact their coat of arms of red balls on a gold field is supposedly the source of today's pawnbrokers' emblem of three gold balls. So vast was the banking power of the Medici that they maintained branch offices in all major cities of Europe. The family rose to such power that they not only ruled Florence for a time, but provided the Church with two popes and France with two queens. One might decry the new emphasis on wealth, but clearly the acquisitive urge, for goods and money, increasingly permeated all ranks in western society. The soldier-merchant-adventurer was an asset to a state, particularly if he brought back gold. The joint stock company came into being, one of the most notable of which was the English East India Company, chartered in 1600. Clearly the aggressive search for tangible, material wealth which overrode the medieval ethic with its numerous injunctions against acquisitive and pecuniary economics required a new ideology more in keeping with the modern worldly temper of events.

It was to fill this need that mercantilism, the first modern economic conception, came into being. As national states became more unified and royal authority more centralized under powerful monarchs with obedient bureaucracies, it became possible to give direction and control to economic activities and turn these to the advantage of the state. By restriction, sponsorship, taxation, and subsidy, governments assumed authority over economic life. As far as was possible they sought by these instruments of control to increase their power not only domestically, but in world politics as well. The national acquisition of gold and silver was encouraged, as was the effort to ensure an excess of exported goods over imported ones. Domestic industry and commerce were encouraged in the effort to achieve national self-sufficiency. And, of course, national defense was given the highest priority. Domestic monopoly was fostered at home as national monopoly was sought abroad. It was in all a frank recognition of the acutely political nature of economics in an age of expanding nationalism.

However, as nations failed to achieve an effective monopoly, even with their colonies in world trade, so did the monopoly system fail in the domestic market. The English Revolution of the seventeenth century, culminating in the supremacy of Parliament was the political counterpart of a social and economic revolution that would lead to the supremacy of the middle class. Royal restrictions, bounties and monopolies, if they favored some merchants, by the same token denied others. Increasingly, these restrictions were circumvented. And, with the American Revolution, it became apparent that mercantilism was inadequate to meet the larger needs of an empire. It was during this era in history that capitalism developed into the dominant economic theory of the West, and Adam Smith became its prophet.

Smith in *The Wealth of Nations* sought to answer the new questions of the times. If mercantilism was put aside, how could the wealth of a nation be fostered? How, if domestic economic regulations were reduced, could one ensure an adequate supply of the desired goods and services in the state? If the government did not regulate and direct economic activity, who would do so? And, finally and most consequentially, even if the economic needs of a nation were met under a new system, would such a system be ethically desirable? For even as no economic system is without its political implications so must every economic system have its ethical considerations. Whenever men meet to buy and sell, more than pecuniary matters of value are involved. Who performs what services, under what compulsions, and to what advantages are not matters that can be divorced from the larger issues of right and wrong in society. Thus, while the specific ethical judgements of the medieval period as they affected economic activity have been considerably modified to meet radically changed conditions, nevertheless ethical and inevitably political issues are involved in all modern economic ideologies. In the readings which follow it will be evident how important ethical argument is to political-economic issues, for none of the writers is content to rest his case on economic justification alone.

The selections below were first published as follows:

Adam Smith, *The Wealth of Nations* (1776)
John Maynard Keynes, *The General Theory of Employment Interest and Money* (1936)
Friedrich A. Hayek, *The Road to Serfdom* (1944)
David McCord Wright, *Democracy and Progress* (1948)

THE WEALTH OF NATIONS

by Adam Smith *

OF THE DIVISION OF LABOUR

The greatest improvement in the productive powers of labour, and the greater part of the skill, dexterity, and judgment with which it is anywhere directed, or applied, seem to have been the effects of the division of labour.

The effects of the division of labour, in the general business of society, will be more easily understood, by considering in what manner it operates in some particular manufactures. It is commonly supposed to be carried furthest in some very trifling ones; not perhaps that it really is carried further in them than in others of more importance: but in those trifling manufactures which are destined to supply the small wants of but a small number of people, the whole number of workmen must necessarily be small; and those employed in every different branch of the work can often be collected into the same workhouse, and placed at once under the view of the spectator. In those great manufactures, on the contrary, which are destined to supply the great wants of the great body of the people, every different branch of the work employs so great a number of workmen, that it is impossible to collect them all into the same workhouse. We can

---

* Adam Smith, *The Wealth of Nations* (New York: The Modern Library, 1937). By permission of Random House, Inc. Editor's footnotes omitted.

seldom see more, at one time, than those employed in one single branch. Though in such manufactures, therefore, the work may really be divided into a much greater number of parts, than in those of a more trifling nature, the division is not near so obvious, and has accordingly been much less observed.

To take an example, therefore, from a very trifling manufacture; but one in which the division of labour has been very often taken notice of, the trade of the pinmaker; a workman not educated to this business (which the division of labour has rendered a distinct trade), nor acquainted with the use of the machinery employed in it (to the invention of which the same division of labour has probably given occasion), could scarce, perhaps, with his utmost industry, make one pin in a day, and certainly could not make twenty. But in the way in which this business is now carried on, not only the whole work is a peculiar trade, but it is divided into a number of branches, of which the greater part are likewise peculiar trades. One man draws out the wire, another straights it, a third cuts it, a fourth points it, a fifth grinds it at the top for receiving the head; to make the head requires two or three distinct operations; to put it on is a peculiar business, to whiten the pins is another; it is even a trade by itself to put them into the paper; and the important business of making a pin is, in this manner, divided into about eighteen distinct operations, which, in some manufactories, are all performed by distinct hands, though in others the same man will sometimes perform two or three of them. I have seen a small manufactory of this kind where ten men only were employed, and where some of them consequently performed two or three distinct operations. But though they were very poor, and therefore but indifferently accommodated with the necessary machinery, they could, when they exerted themselves, make among them about twelve pounds of pins in a day. There are in a pound upwards of four thousand pins of a middling size. Those ten persons, therefore, could make among them upwards of forty-eight thousand pins in a day. Each person, therefore, making a tenth part of forty-eight thousand pins, might be considered as making four thousand eight hundred pins in a day. But if they had all wrought separately and independently, and without any of them having been educated to this peculiar business, they certainly could not each of them made twenty, perhaps not one pin in a day; that is, certainly, not the two hundred and fortieth, perhaps not the four thousand eight hundredth part of what they are at present capable of performing, in consequence of a proper division and combination of their different operations. . . .

This great increase of the quantity of work, which, in consequence of

the division of labour, the same number of people are capable of performing, is owing to three different circumstances; first, to the increase of
dexterity in every particular workman; secondly, to the saving of the time
which is commonly lost in passing from one species of work to another;
and lastly, to the invention of a great number of machines which facilitate
and abridge labour, and enable one man to do the work of many.

First, the improvement of the dexterity of the workman necessarily
increases the quantity of the work he can perform; and the division of
labour, by reducing every man's business to some one simple operation,
and by making this operation the sole employment of his life, necessarily
increases very much the dexterity of the workman. A common smith, who,
though accustomed to handle the hammer, has never been used to
make nails, if upon some particular occasion he is obliged to attempt
it, will scarce, I am assured, be able to make above two or three hundred
nails in a day, and those too very bad ones. A smith who has been accustomed to make nails, but whose sole or principal business has not been
that of a nailer, can seldom with his utmost diligence make more than
eight hundred or a thousand nails in a day. I have seen several boys under
twenty years of age who had never exercised any other trade but that of
making nails, and who, when they exerted themselves, could make, each
of them upwards of two thousand three hundred nails in a day. The
making of a nail, however, is by no means one of the simplest operations.
The same person blows the bellows, stirs or mends the fire as there is
occasion, heats the iron, and forges every part of the nail: in forging the
head too he is obliged to change his tools. The different operations into
which the making of a pin, or of a metal button, is subdivided, are all of
them much more simple, and the dexterity of the person, of whose life
it has been the sole business to perform them, is usually much greater. The
rapidity with which some of the operations of those manufacturers are
performed, exceeds what the human hand could, by those who had never
seen them, be supposed capable of acquiring.

Secondly, the advantage which is gained by saving the time commonly
lost in passing from one sort of work to another, is much greater than we
should at first view be apt to imagine it. It is impossible to pass very
quickly from one kind of work to another, that is carried on in a different
place, and with quite different tools. A country weaver, who cultivates a
small farm, must lose a good deal of time in passing from his loom to the
field, and from the field to his loom. When the two trades can be carried
on in the same workhouse, the loss of time is no doubt much less. It is
even in this case, however, very considerable. A man commonly saunters

a little in turning his hand from one sort of employment to another. When he first begins the new work he is seldom very keen and hearty; his mind, as they say, does not go to it, and for some time he rather trifles than applies to good purpose. The habit of sauntering and of indolent careless application, which is naturally, or rather necessarily acquired by every country workman who is obliged to change his work and his tools every half hour, and to apply his hand in twenty different ways almost every day of his life, renders him almost always slothful and lazy, and incapable of any vigorous application even on the most pressing occasions. Independent, therefore, of his deficiency in point of dexterity, this cause alone must always reduce considerably the quantity of work which he is capable of performing.

Thirdly, and lastly, everybody must be sensible how much labour is facilitated and abridged by the application of proper machinery. It is unnecessary to give any example. I shall only observe, therefore, that the invention of all those machines by which labour is so much facilitated and abridged, seems to have been originally owing to the division of labour. Men are much more likely to discover easier and readier methods of attaining any object, when the whole attention of their minds is directed towards that single object, than when it is dissipated among a great variety of things. But in consequence of the division of labour, the whole of every man's attention comes naturally to be directed towards some one very simple object. It is naturally to be expected, therefore, that some one or other of those who are employed in each particular branch of labour should soon find out easier and readier methods of performing their own particular work, wherever the nature of it admits of such improvement. A great part of the machines made use of in those manufactures in which labour is most subdivided, were originally the inventions of common workmen, who, being each of them employed in some very simple operation, naturally turned their thoughts towards finding out easier and readier methods of performing it. Whoever has been much accustomed to visit such manufacturers must frequently have been shewn very pretty machines, which were the inventions of such workmen in order to facilitate and quicken their own particular part of the work. In the first fire-engines, a boy was constantly employed to open and shut alternately the communication between the boiler and the cylinder, according as the piston either ascended or descended. One of those boys, who loved to play with his companions, observed that, by tying a string from the handle of the valve which opened this communication to another part of the machine, the valve would open and shut without his assistance, and leave him at

liberty to divert himself with his play-fellows. One of the greatest improvements that has been made upon this machine, since it was first invented,
was in this manner the discovery of a boy who wanted to save his own
labour.

All the improvements in machinery, however, have by no means been
the inventions of those who had occasion to use the machines. Many improvements have been made by the ingenuity of the makers of the
machines, when to make them became the business of a peculiar trade;
and some by that of those who are called philosophers or men of speculation, whose trade it is not to do anything, but to observe everything; and
who, upon that account, are often capable of combining together the
powers of the most distant and dissimilar objects. In the progress of
society, philosophy or speculation becomes, like every other employment,
the principal or sole trade and occupation of a particular class of citizens.
Like every other employment too, it is subdivided into a great number of
different branches, each of which affords occupation to a peculiar tribe or
class of philosophers; and this subdivision of employment in philosophy,
as well as in every other business, improves dexterity, and saves time. Each
individual becomes more expert in his own peculiar branch, more work is
done upon the whole, and the quantity of science is considerably increased
by it.

It is the great multiplication of the productions of all the different arts,
in consequence of the division of labour, which occasions, in a well-
governed society, that universal opulence which extends itself to the lowest
ranks of the people. Every workman has a great quantity of his own work
to dispose of beyond what he himself has occasion for; and every other
workman being exactly in the same situation, he is enabled to exchange
a great quantity of his own goods for a great quantity, or, what comes to
the same thing, for the price of a great quantity of theirs. He supplies them
abundantly with what they have occasion for, and they accommodate him
as amply with what he has occasion for, and a general plenty diffuses itself
through all the different ranks of the society.

OF THE PRINCIPLE WHICH GIVES OCCASION TO THE DIVISION OF LABOUR

This division of labour, from which so many advantages are derived, is
not originally the effect of any human wisdom, which foresees and intends
that general opulence to which it gives occasion. It is the necessary, though
very slow and gradual consequence of a certain propensity in human

nature which has in view no such extensive utility; the propensity to truck, barter, and exchange one thing for another.

Whether this propensity be one of those original principles in human nature, of which no further account can be given; or whether, as seems more probable, it be the necessary consequence of the faculties of reason and speech, it belongs not to our present subject to inquire. It is common to all men, and to be found in no other race of animals, which seem to know neither this nor any other species of contracts. Two greyhounds, in running down the same hare, have sometimes the appearance of acting in some sort of concert. Each turns her towards his companion, or endeavors to intercept her when his companion turns her towards himself. This, however, is not the effect of any contract, but of the accidental concurrence of their passions in the same object at that particular time. Nobody ever saw a dog make a fair and deliberate exchange of one bone for another with another dog. Nobody ever saw one animal by its gestures and natural cries signify to another, this is mine, that yours; I am willing to give this for that. When an animal wants to obtain something either of a man or of another animal, it has no other means of persuasion but to gain the favour of those whose service it requires. A puppy fawns upon its dam, and a spaniel endeavours by a thousand attractions to engage the attention of its master who is at dinner, when it wants to be fed by him. Man sometimes uses the same arts with his brethren, and when he has no other means of engaging them to act according to his inclinations, endeavours by every servile and fawning attention to obtain their good will. He has not time, however, to do this upon every occasion. In civilized society he stands at all times in need of the co-operation and assistance of great multitudes, while his whole life is scarce sufficient to gain the friendship of a few persons. In almost every other race of animals each individual, when it is grown up to maturity, is entirely independent, and in its natural state has occasion for the assistance of no other living creature. But man has almost constant occasion for the help of his brethren, and it is in vain for him to expect it from their benevolence only. He will be more likely to prevail if he can interest their self-love in his favour, and shew them that it is for their own advantage to do for him what he requires of them. Whoever offers to another a bargain of any kind, proposes to do this. Give me that which I want, and you shall have this which you want, is the meaning of every such offer; and it is in this manner that we obtain from one another the far greater part of those good offices which we stand in need of. It is not from the benevolence of the butcher, the brewer, or the baker, that we expect our dinner, but from their regard to their own interest. We address ourselves, not to their humanity but to their self-love, and never talk to them of our own necessities but of their advantages. Nobody but a beggar chooses to depend chiefly upon the benevolence of his fellow-citizens. Even a beggar does not depend upon it entirely. The charity of well-disposed people, indeed, supplies him with the whole fund of his subsistence. But though this principle ultimately provides him with all the necessaries of life which he has occasion for, it neither does nor can provide him with them as he has occasion for them. The greater part of his occasional wants are supplied in the same manner as those of other people, by treaty, by barter, and by purchase. With the money which one man gives him he purchases food. The old cloaths which another bestows upon him he exchanges for other old cloaths which suit him better, or for lodging, or for food, or for money, with which he can buy either food, cloaths, or lodging, as he has occasion.

As it is by treaty, by barter, and by purchase, that we obtain from one another the greater part of those mutual good offices which we stand in need of, so it is this same trucking disposition which originally gives occasion to the division of labour. In a tribe of hunters or shepherds, a particular person makes bows and arrows, for example, with more readiness and dexterity than any other. He frequently exchanges them for cattle or for venison with his companions; and he finds at last that he can in this manner get more cattle and venison, than if he himself went to the field to catch them. From a regard to his own interest, therefore, the making of bows and arrows grows to be his chief business, and he becomes a sort of armourer. Another excels in making the frames and covers of their little huts or movable houses. He is accustomed to be of use in this way to his neighbours, who reward him in the same manner with cattle and with venison, till at last he finds it his interest to dedicate himself entirely to this employment, and to become a sort of house-carpenter. In the same manner a third becomes a smith or a brazier; a fourth a tanner or dresser of hides or skins, the principal part of the clothing of savages. And thus the certainty of being able to exchange all that surplus part of the produce of his own labour, which is over and above his own consumption, for such parts of the produce of other men's labour as he may have occasion for, encourages every man to apply himself to a particular occupation, and to cultivate and bring to perfection whatever talent or genius he may possess for that particular species of business.

The difference of natural talents in different men is, in reality, much less than we are aware of; and the very different genius which appears to distinguish men of different professions, when grown up to maturity, is not upon many occasions so much the cause, as the effect of the division of labour. The difference between the most dissimilar characters, between a philosopher and a common street porter, for example, seems to arise not so much from nature as from habit, custom, and education. When they came into the world, and for the first six or eight years of their existence, they were, perhaps, very much alike, and neither their parents nor play-fellows could perceive any remarkable difference. About that age, or soon after, they come to be employed in very different occupations. The difference of talents comes then to be taken notice of, and widens by degrees, till at last the vanity of the philosopher is willing to acknowledge scarce any resemblance. But without the disposition to truck, barter, and exchange, every man must have procured to himself every necessary and conveniency of life which he wanted. All must have had the same duties to perform, and the same work to do, and there could have been no such difference of employment as could alone give occasion to any great difference of talents.

As it is this disposition which forms that difference of talents, so remarkable among men of different professions, so it is this same disposition which renders that difference useful. Many tribes of animals acknowledged to be all of the same species, derive from nature a much more remarkable distinction of genius, than what, antecedent to custom and education, appears to take place among men. By nature a philosopher is not in genius and disposition half so different from a street porter, as a mastiff is from a greyhound, or a greyhound from a spaniel, or this last from a shepherd's dog. Those different tribes of animals, however, though all of the same species, are of scarce any use to one another. The strength of the mastiff is not in the least supported either by the swiftness of the greyhound, or by the sagacity of the spaniel, or by the docility of the shepherd's dog. The effects of those different geniuses and talents, for want of the power or disposition to barter and exchange, cannot be brought into a common stock, and do not in the least contribute to the better accommodation and conveniency of the species. Each animal is still obliged to support and defend itself, separately and independently, and derives no sort of advantage from that variety of talents with which nature has distinguished its fellows. Among men, on the contrary, the most dissimilar geniuses are of use to one another; the different produces of their respective talents, by the general disposition to truck, barter, and exchange, being brought, as it were, into a common stock, where every man may purchase whatever part of the produce of other men's talents he has occasion for. . . .

OF THE REAL AND NOMINAL PRICE OF COMMODITIES, OR THEIR PRICE
IN LABOUR, AND THEIR PRICE IN MONEY

Every man is rich or poor according to the degree in which he can afford
to enjoy the necessaries, conveniences, and amusements of human life.
But after the division of labour has once thoroughly taken place, it is but
a very small part of these with which a man's own labour can supply him.
The far greater part of them he must derive from the labour of other
people, and he must be rich or poor according to the quantity of that
labour which he can command, or which he can afford to purchase. The
value of any commodity, therefore, to the person who possesses it, and
who means not to use or consume it himself, but to exchange it for other
commodities, is equal to the quantity of labour which it enables him to
purchase or command. Labour, therefore, is the real measure of the exchangeable value of all commodities.

The real price of everything, what everything really costs to the man
who wants to acquire it, is the toil and trouble of acquiring it. What everything is really worth to the man who has acquired it, and who wants to
dispose of it or exchange it for something else, is the toil and trouble which
it can save to himself, and which it can impose upon other people. What
is bought with money or with goods is purchased by labour, as much as
what we acquire by the toil of our own body. That money or those goods
indeed save us this toil. They contain the value of a certain quantity of
labour which we exchange for what is supposed at the time to contain the
value of an equal quantity. Labour was the first price, the original
purchase-money that was paid for all things. It was not by gold or by
silver, but by labour, that all the wealth of the world was originally
purchased; and its value, to those who possess it, and who want to exchange it for some new productions, is precisely equal to the quantity of
labour which it can enable them to purchase or command. . . .

But though labour be the real measure of the exchangeable value of
all commodities, it is not that by which their value is commonly estimated.
It is often difficult to ascertain the proportion between two different
quantities of labour. The time spent in two different sorts of work will
not always alone determine this proportion. The different degrees of hardship endured, and of ingenuity exercised, must likewise be taken into account. There may be more labour in an hour's hard work than in two
hours easy business; or in an hour's application to a trade which it cost
ten years labour to learn, than in a month's industry at an ordinary and

obvious employment. But it is not easy to find any accurate measure either of hardship or ingenuity. In exchanging indeed the different productions of different sorts of labour for one another, some allowance is commonly made for both. It is adjusted, however, not by any accurate measure, but by the higgling and bargaining of the market, according to that sort of rough equality which, though not exact, is sufficient for carrying on the business of common life.

Every commodity besides, is more frequently exchanged for, and thereby compared with, other commodities than with labour. It is more natural therefore, to estimate its exchangeable value by the quantity of some other commodity than by that of the labour which it can purchase. The greater part of people too understand better what is meant by a quantity of a particular commodity than by a quantity of labour. The one is a plain palpable object; the other an abstract notion, which, though it can be made sufficiently intelligible, is not altogether so natural and obvious.

But when barter ceases, and money has become the common instrument of commerce, every particular commodity is more frequently exchanged for money than for any other commodity. The butcher seldom carries his beef or his mutton to the baker, or the brewer, in order to exchange them for bread or for beer; but he carries them to the market, where he exchanges them for money, and afterwards exchanges that money for bread and for beer. The quantity of money which he gets for them regulates too the quantity of bread and beer which he can afterwards purchase. It is more natural and obvious to him, therefore, to estimate their value by the quantity of money, the commodity for which he immediately exchanges them, than by that of bread and beer, the commodities for which he can exchange them only by the intervention of another commodity; and rather to say that his butcher's meat is worth threepence or fourpence a pound, than that it is worth three or four pounds of bread, or three or four quarts of small beer. Hence it comes to pass that the exchangeable value of every commodity is more frequently estimated by the quantity of money, than by the quantity either of labour or of any other commodity which can be had in exchange for it.

Gold and silver, however, like every other commodity, vary in their value, are sometimes cheaper and sometimes dearer, sometimes of easier and sometimes of more difficult purchase. The quantity of labour which any particular quantity of them can purchase or command, or the quantity of other goods which it will exchange for, depends always upon the fertility or barrenness of the mines which happen to be known about the time when such exchanges are made. The discovery of the abundant mines of America reduced, in the sixteenth century, the value of gold and silver in Europe to about a third of what it had been before. As it costs less labour to bring those metals from the mine to the market, so when they were brought thither they could purchase or command less labour; and this revolution in their value, though perhaps the greatest, is by no means the only one of which history gives some account. But as a measure of quantity, such as the natural foot, fathom, or handful, which is continually varying in its own quantity, can never be an accurate measure of the quantity of other things; so a commodity which is itself continually varying in its own value, can never be an accurate measure of the value of other commodities. Equal quantities of labour, at all times and places, may be said to be of equal value to the labourer. In his ordinary state of health, strength and spirits; in the ordinary degree of his skill and dexterity, he must always lay down the same portion of his ease, his liberty, and his happiness. The price which he pays must always be the same, whatever may be the quantity of goods which he receives in return for it. Of these, indeed, it may sometimes purchase a greater and sometimes a smaller quantity; but it is their value which varies, not that of the labour which purchases them. At all times and places that is dear which it is difficult to come at, or which it costs much labour to acquire; and that cheap which is to be had easily, or with very little labour. Labour alone, therefore, never varying in its own value, is alone the ultimate and real standard by which the value of all commodities can at all times and places be estimated and compared. It is their real price; money is their nominal price only. . . .

Of the Natural and Market Price of Commodities

There is in every society or neighbourhood an ordinary or average rate both of wages and profit in every different employment of labour and stock. This rate is naturally regulated, as I shall show hereafter, partly by the general circumstances of the society, their riches or poverty, their advancing, stationary, or declining condition; and partly by the particular nature of each employment.

There is likewise in every society or neighbourhood an ordinary or average rate of rent, which is regulated too, as I shall show hereafter, partly by the general circumstances of the society or neighbourhood in which the land is situated, and partly by the natural or improved fertility of the land.

These ordinary or average rates may be called the natural rates of wages, profit, and rent, at the time and place in which they commonly prevail.

When the price of any commodity is neither more nor less than what is sufficient to pay the rent of the land, the wages of the labour, and the profits of the stock employed in raising, preparing, and bringing it to market, according to their natural rates, the commodity is then sold for what may be called its natural price.

The commodity is then sold precisely for what it is worth, or for what it really costs the person who brings it to market; for though in common language what is called the prime cost of any commodity does not comprehend the profit of the person who is to sell it again, yet if he sells it at a price which does not allow him the ordinary rate of profit in his neighbourhood, he is evidently a loser by the trade; since by employing his stock in some other way he might have made that profit. His profit, besides, is his revenue, the proper fund of his subsistence. As, while he is preparing and bringing the goods to market, he advances to his workmen their wages, or their subsistence; so he advances to himself, in the same manner, his own subsistence, which is generally suitable to the profit which he may reasonably expect from the sale of his goods. Unless they yield him this profit, therefore, they do not repay him what they may very properly be said to have really cost him.

Though the price, therefore, which leaves him this profit, is not always the lowest at which a dealer may sometimes sell his goods, it is the lowest at which he is likely to sell them for any considerable time; at least where there is perfect liberty, or where he may change his trade as often as he pleases.

The actual price at which any commodity is commonly sold is called its market price. It may either be above, or below, or exactly the same with its natural price.

The market price of every particular commodity is regulated by the proportion between the quantity which is actually brought to market, and the demand of those who are willing to pay the natural price of the commodity, or the whole value of the rent, labour, and profit, which must be paid in order to bring it thither. Such people may be called the effectual demanders, and their demand the effectual demand; since it may be sufficient to effectuate the bringing of the commodity to market. It is different from the absolute demand. A very poor man may be said in some sense to have a demand for a coach and six; he might like to have it; but his demand is not an effectual demand, as the commodity can never be brought to market in order to satisfy it.

When the quantity of any commodity which is brought to market falls short of the effectual demand, all those who are willing to pay the whole value of the rent, wages, and profit, which must be paid in order to bring it thither, cannot be supplied with the quantity which they want. Rather than want it altogether, some of them will be willing to give more. A competition will immediately begin among them, and the market price will rise more or less above the natural price, according as either the greatness of the deficiency, or the wealth and wanton luxury of the competitors, happen to animate more or less the eagerness of the competition. Among competitors of equal wealth and luxury the same deficiency will generally occasion a more or less eager competition, according as the acquisition of the commodity happens to be of more or less importance to them. Hence the exorbitant price of the necessaries of life during the blockade of a town or in a famine.

When the quantity brought to market exceeds the effectual demand, it cannot be all sold to those who are willing to pay the whole value of the rent, wages, and profit, which must be paid in order to bring it thither. Some part must be sold to those who are willing to pay less, and the low price which they give for it must reduce the price of the whole. The market price will sink more or less below the natural price, according as the greatness of the excess increases more or less the competition of the sellers, or according as it happens to be more or less important to them to get immediately rid of the commodity. The same excess in the importation of perishable, will occasion a much greater competition than in that of durable commodities; in the importation of oranges, for example, than in that of old iron.

When the quantity brought to market is just sufficient to supply the effectual demand and no more, the market price naturally comes to be either exactly, or as nearly as can be judged of, the same with the natural price. The whole quantity upon hand can be disposed of for this price, and cannot be disposed of for more. The competition of the different dealers obliges them all to accept of this price, but does not oblige them to accept of less.

The quantity of every commodity brought to market naturally suits itself to the effectual demand. It is the interest of all those who employ their land, labour, or stock, in bringing any commodity to market, that the quantity never should exceed the effectual demand; and it is the interest of all other people that it never should fall short of that demand.

If at any time it exceeds the effectual demand, some of the component parts of its price must be paid below their natural rate. If it is rent, the interest of the landlords will immediately prompt them to withdraw a part of their land; and if it is wages or profit, the interest of the labourers in the one case, and of their employers in the other, will prompt them to withdraw a part of their labour or stock from this employment. The quantity brought to market will soon be no more than sufficient to supply the effectual demand. All the different parts of its price will rise to their natural rate, and the whole price to its natural price.

If, on the contrary, the quantity brought to market should at any time fall short of the effectual demand, some of the component parts of its price must rise above their natural rate. If it is rent, the interest of all other landlords will naturally prompt them to prepare more land for the raising of this commodity; if it is wages or profit, the interest of all other labourers and dealers will soon prompt them to employ more labour and stock in preparing and bringing it to market. The quantity brought thither will soon be sufficient to supply the effectual demand. All the different parts of its price will soon sink to their natural rate, and the whole price to its natural price.

The natural price, therefore, is, as it were, the central price, to which the prices of all commodities are continually gravitating. Different accidents may sometimes keep them suspended a good deal above it, and sometimes force them down even somewhat below it. But whatever may be the obstacles which hinder them from settling in this center of repose and continuance, they are constantly tending towards it.

The whole quantity of industry annually employed in order to bring any commodity to market, naturally suits itself in this manner to the effectual demand. It naturally aims at bringing always that precise quantity thither which may be sufficient to supply, and no more than supply, that demand. . . .

Of Restraints upon the Importation from Foreign Countries of such Goods as can be produced at Home

The general industry of the society never can exceed what the capital of the society can employ. As the number of workmen that can be kept in employment by any particular person must bear a certain proportion to his capital, so the number of those that can be continually employed by all the members of a great society, must bear a certain proportion to the whole capital of that society, and never can exceed that proportion. No regulation of commerce can increase the quantity of industry in any society beyond what its capital can maintain. It can only divert a part of it into a direction into which it might not otherwise have gone; and it is by no means certain that this artificial direction is likely to be more advantageous to the society than that into which it would have gone of its own accord.

Every individual is continually exerting himself to find out the most advantageous employment for whatever capital he can command. It is his own advantage, indeed, and not that of the society, which he has in view. But the study of his own advantage naturally, or rather necessarily, leads him to prefer that employment which is most advantageous to the society.

First, every individual endeavours to employ his capital as near home as he can, and consequently as much as he can in the support of domestic industry; provided always that he can thereby obtain the ordinary, or not a great deal less than the ordinary profits of stock. . . .

Secondly, every individual who employs his capital in the support of domestic industry, necessarily endeavours so to direct that industry that its produce may be of the greatest possible value.

The produce of industry is what it adds to the subject or materials upon which it is employed. In proportion as the value of this produce is great or small, so will likewise be the profits of the employer. But it is only for the sake of profit that any man employs a capital in the support of industry; and he will always, therefore, endeavour to employ it in the support of that industry of which the produce is likely to be of the greatest value, or to exchange for the greatest quantity either of money or of other goods.

But the annual revenue of every society is always precisely equal to the exchangeable value of the whole annual produce of its industry, or rather is precisely the same thing with that exchangeable value. As every individual, therefore, endeavours as much as he can both to employ his capital in the support of domestic industry, and so to direct that industry that its produce may be of the greatest value; every individual necessarily labours to render the annual revenue of the society as great as he can. He generally, indeed, neither intends to promote the public interest, nor knows how much he is promoting it. By preferring the support of domestic to that of foreign industry, he intends only his own security; and by directing that industry in such a manner as its produce may be of the greatest value, he intends only his own gain, and he is in this, as in many other cases, led by an invisible hand to promote an end which was no part of his intention. Nor is it always the worse for the society that it was no part of it. By pursuing his own interest he frequently promotes that of the society more effectually than when he really intends to promote it. I have never known much good done by those who affected to trade for the public good. It is an affectation, indeed, not very common among merchants, and very few words need be employed in dissuading them from it.

What is the species of domestic industry which his capital can employ, and of which the produce is likely to be of the greatest value, every individual, it is evident, can, in his local situation, judge much better than any statesman or lawgiver can do for him. The statesman, who should attempt to direct private people in what manner they ought to employ their capitals, would not only load himself with a most unnecessary attention, but assume an authority which could safely be trusted, not only to no single person, but to no council or senate whatever, and which would nowhere be so dangerous as in the hands of a man who had folly and presumption enough to fancy himself fit to exercise it. . . .

THE GENERAL THEORY OF EMPLOYMENT, INTEREST, AND MONEY

by John Maynard Keynes *

CONCLUDING NOTES ON THE SOCIAL PHILOSOPHY TOWARDS WHICH THE GENERAL THEORY MIGHT LEAD

I

THE outstanding faults of the economic society in which we live are its failure to provide for full employment and its arbitrary and inequitable distribution of wealth and incomes. The bearing of the foregoing theory on the first of these is obvious. But there are also two important respects in which it is relevant to the second.

Since the end of the nineteenth century significant progress towards the removal of very great disparities of wealth and income has been achieved through the instrument of direct taxation—income tax and surtax and death duties—especially in Great Britain. Many people would wish

* John Maynard Keynes, The General Theory of Employment, Interest, and Money (New York: 1936). Reprinted by permission of Harcourt, Brace and Co., Inc.

to see this process carried much further, but they are deterred by two considerations; partly by the fear of making skilful evasions too much worth while and also of diminishing unduly the motive towards risk-taking, but mainly, I think, by the belief that the growth of capital depends upon the strength of the motive towards individual saving and that for a large proportion of this growth we are dependent on the savings of the rich out of their superfluity. Our argument does not affect the first of these considerations. But it may considerably modify our attitude towards the second. For we have seen that, up to the point where full employment prevails, the growth of capital depends not at all on a low propensity to consume but is, on the contrary, held back by it; and only in conditions of full employment is a low propensity to consume conducive to the growth of capital. Moreover, experience suggests that in existing conditions saving by institutions and through sinking funds is more than adequate, and that measures for the redistribution of incomes in a way likely to raise the propensity to consume may prove positively favourable to the growth of capital.

The existing confusion of the public mind on the matter is well illustrated by the very common belief that the death duties are responsible for a reduction in the capital wealth of the country. Assuming that the State applies the proceeds of these duties to its ordinary outgoings so that taxes on incomes and consumption are correspondingly reduced or avoided, it is, of course, true that a fiscal policy of heavy death duties has the effect of increasing the community's propensity to consume. But inasmuch as an increase in the habitual propensity to consume will in general (*i.e.* except in conditions of full employment) serve to increase at the same time the inducement to invest, the inference commonly drawn is the exact opposite of the truth.

Thus our argument leads towards the conclusion that in contemporary conditions the growth of wealth, so far from being dependent on the abstinence of the rich, as is commonly supposed, is more likely to be impeded by it. One of the chief social justifications of great inequality of wealth is, therefore, removed. I am not saying that there are no other reasons, unaffected by our theory, capable of justifying some measure of inequality in some circumstances. But it does dispose of the most important of the reasons why hitherto we have thought it prudent to move carefully. This particularly affects our attitude towards death duties: for there are certain justifications for inequality of incomes which do not apply equally to inequality of inheritances.

For my own part, I believe that there is social and psychological justification for significant inequalities of incomes and wealth, but not for such large disparities as exist to-day. There are valuable human activities which require the motive of money-making and the environment of private wealth-ownership for their full fruition. Moreover, dangerous human proclivities can be canalised into comparatively harmless channels by the existence of opportunities for money-making and private wealth, which, if they cannot be satisfied in this way, may find their outlet in cruelty, the reckless pursuit of personal power and authority, and other forms of self-aggrandisement. It is better that a man should tyrannise over his bank balance than over his fellow-citizens; and whilst the former is sometimes denounced as being but a means to the latter, sometimes at least it is an alternative. But it is not necessary for the stimulation of these activities and the satisfaction of these proclivities that the game should be played for such high stakes as at present. Much lower stakes will serve the purpose equally well, as soon as the players are accustomed to them. The task of transmuting human nature must not be confused with the task of managing it. Though in the ideal commonwealth men may have been taught or inspired or bred to take no interest in the stakes, it may still be wise and prudent statesmanship to allow the game to be played, subject to rules and limitations, so long as the average man, or even a significant section of the community, is in fact strongly addicted to the money-making passion.

II

There is, however, a second, much more fundamental inference from our argument which has a bearing on the future of inequalities of wealth; namely, our theory of the rate of interest. The justification for a moderately high rate of interest has been found hitherto in the necessity of providing a sufficient inducement to save. But we have shown that the extent of effective saving is necessarily determined by the scale of investment and that the scale of investment is promoted by a *low* rate of interest, provided that we do not attempt to stimulate it in this way beyond the point which corresponds to full employment. Thus it is to our best advantage to reduce the rate of interest to that point relatively to the schedule of the marginal efficiency of capital at which there is full employment.

There can be no doubt that this criterion will lead to a much lower rate of interest than has ruled hitherto; and, so far as one can guess at the schedules of the marginal efficiency of capital corresponding to increasing amounts of capital, the rate of interest is likely to fall steadily, if it should be practicable to maintain conditions of more or less continuous full employment—unless, indeed, there is an excessive change in the aggregate propensity to consume (including the State).

I feel sure that the demand for capital is strictly limited in the sense that it would not be difficult to increase the stock of capital up to a point where its marginal efficiency had fallen to a very low figure. This would not mean that the use of capital instruments would cost almost nothing, but only that the return from them would have to cover little more than their exhaustion by wastage and obsolescence together with some margin to cover risk and the exercise of skill and judgment. In short, the aggregate return from durable goods in the course of their life would, as in the case of short-lived goods, just cover their labour-costs of production *plus* an allowance for risk and the costs of skill and supervision.

Now, though this state of affairs would be quite compatible with some measure of individualism, yet it would mean the euthanasia of the rentier, and, consequently, the euthanasia of the cumulative oppressive power of the capitalist to exploit the scarcity-value of capital. Interest to-day rewards no genuine sacrifice, any more than does the rent of land. The owner of capital can obtain interest because capital is scarce, just as the owner of land can obtain rent because land is scarce. But whilst there may be intrinsic reasons for the scarcity of land, there are no intrinsic reasons for the scarcity of capital. An intrinsic reason for such scarcity, in the sense of a genuine sacrifice which could only be called forth by the offer of a reward in the shape of interest, would not exist, in the long run, except in the event of the individual propensity to consume proving to be of such a character that net saving in conditions of full employment comes to an end before capital has become sufficiently abundant. But even so, it will still be possible for communal saving through the agency of the State to be maintained at a level which will allow the growth of capital up to the point where it ceases to be scarce.

I see, therefore, the rentier aspect of capitalism as a transitional phase which will disappear when it has done its work. And with the disappearance of its rentier aspect much else in it besides will suffer a sea-change. It will be, moreover, a great advantage of the order of events which I am advocating, that the euthanasia of the rentier, of the functionless investor, will be nothing sudden, merely a gradual but prolonged continuance of what we have seen recently in Great Britain, and will need no revolution.

Thus we might aim in practice (there being nothing in this which is unattainable) at an increase in the volume of capital until it ceases to be scarce, so that the functionless investor will no longer receive a bonus;

and at a scheme of direct taxation which allows the intelligence and de- termination and executive skill of the financier, the entrepreneur *et hoc genus omne* (who are certainly so fond of their craft that their labour could be obtained much cheaper than at present), to be harnessed to the service of the community on reasonable terms of reward.

At the same time we must recognise that only experience can show how far the common will, embodied in the policy of the State, ought to be directed to increasing and supplementing the inducement to invest; and how far it is safe to stimulate the average propensity to consume, without forgoing our aim of depriving capital of its scarcity-value within one or two generations. It may turn out that the propensity to consume will be so easily strengthened by the effects of a falling rate of interest, that full employment can be reached with a rate of accumulation little greater than at present. In this event a scheme for the higher taxation of large incomes and inheritances might be open to the objection that it would lead to full employment with a rate of accumulation which was reduced considerably below the current level. I must not be supposed to deny the possibility, or even the probability, of this outcome. For in such matters it is rash to predict how the average man will react to a changed environ- ment. If, however, it should prove easy to secure an approximation to full employment with a rate of accumulation not much greater than at present, an outstanding problem will at least have been solved. And it would re- main for separate decision on what scale and by what means it is right and reasonable to call on the living generation to restrict their consump- tion, so as to establish, in course of time, a state of full investment for their successors.

III

In some other respects the foregoing theory is moderately conservative in its implications. For whilst it indicates the vital importance of establish- ing certain central controls in matters which are now left in the main to individual initiative, there are wide fields of activity which are un- affected. The State will have to exercise a guiding influence on the pro- pensity to consume partly through its scheme of taxation, partly by fixing the rate of interest, and partly, perhaps, in other ways. Furthermore, it seems unlikely that the influence of banking policy on the rate of interest will be sufficient by itself to determine an optimum rate of investment. I conceive, therefore, that a somewhat comprehensive socialisation of in- vestment will prove the only means of securing an approximation to full employment; though this need not exclude all manner of compromises and of devices by which public authority will co-operate with private initiative. But beyond this no obvious case is made out for a system of State Socialism which would embrace most of the economic life of the community. It is not the ownership of the instruments of production which it is important for the State to assume. If the State is able to determine the aggregate amount of resources devoted to augmenting the instruments and the basic rate of reward to those who own them, it will have accomplished all that is necessary. Moreover, the necessary measures of socialisation can be introduced gradually and without a break in the general traditions of society.

Our criticism of the accepted classical theory of economics has consisted not so much in finding logical flaws in its analysis as in pointing out that its tacit assumptions are seldom or never satisfied, with the result that it cannot solve the economic problems of the actual world. But if our central controls succeed in establishing an aggregate volume of output corresponding to full employment as nearly as is practicable, the classical theory comes into its own again from this point onwards. If we suppose the volume of output to be given, i.e. to be determined by forces outside the classical scheme of thought, then there is no objection to be raised against the classical analysis of the manner in which private self-interest will determine what in particular is produced, in what proportions the factors of production will be combined to produce it, and how the value of the final product will be distributed between them. Again, if we have dealt otherwise with the problem of thrift, there is no objection to be raised against the modern classical theory as to the degree of consilience between private and public advantage in conditions of perfect and imperfect competition respectively. Thus, apart from the necessity of central controls to bring about an adjustment between the propensity to consume and the inducement to invest, there is no more reason to socialise economic life than there was before.

To put the point concretely, I see no reason to suppose that the existing system seriously misemploys the factors of production which are in use. There are, of course, errors of foresight; but these would not be avoided by centralising decisions. When 9,000,000 men are employed out of 10,000,000 willing and able to work, there is no evidence that the labour of these 9,000,000 men is misdirected. The complaint against the present system is not that these 9,000,000 men ought to be employed on different tasks, but that tasks should be available for the remaining 1,000,000 men. It is in determining the volume, not the direction, of actual employment that the existing system has broken down.

Thus I agree with Gesell that the result of filling in the gaps in the classical theory is not to dispose of the "Manchester System," but to indicate the nature of the environment which the free play of economic forces requires if it is to realise the full potentialities of production. The central controls necessary to ensure full employment will, of course, involve a large extension of the traditional functions of government. Furthermore, the modern classical theory has itself called attention to various conditions in which the free play of economic forces may need to be curbed or guided. But there will still remain a wide field for the exercise of private initiative and responsibility. Within this field the traditional advantages of individualism will still hold good.

Let us stop for a moment to remind ourselves what these advantages are. They are partly advantages of efficiency—the advantages of decentralisation and of the play of self-interest. The advantage to efficiency of the decentralisation of decisions and of individual responsibility is even greater, perhaps, than the nineteenth century supposed; and the reaction against the appeal to self-interest may have gone too far. But, above all, individualism, if it can be purged of its defects and its abuses, is the best safeguard of personal liberty in the sense that, compared with any other system, it greatly widens the field for the exercise of personal choice. It is also the best safeguard of the variety of life, which emerges precisely from this extended field of personal choice, and the loss of which is the greatest of all the losses of the homogeneous or totalitarian state. For this variety preserves the traditions which embody the most secure and successful choices of former generations; it colours the present with the diversification of its fancy; and, being the handmaid of experiment as well as of tradition and of fancy, it is the most powerful instrument to better the future.

Whilst, therefore, the enlargement of the functions of government, involved in the task of adjusting to one another the propensity to consume and the inducement to invest, would seem to a nineteenth-century publicist or to a contemporary American financier to be a terrific encroachment on individualism, I defend it, on the contrary, both as the only practicable means of avoiding the destruction of existing economic forms in their entirety and as the condition of the successful functioning of individual initiative.

For if effective demand is deficient, not only is the public scandal of wasted resources intolerable, but the individual enterpriser who seeks to bring these resources into action is operating with the odds loaded against him. The game of hazard which he plays is furnished with many zeros, so that the players *as a whole* will lose if they have the energy and hope to deal all the cards. Hitherto the increment of the world's wealth has fallen short of the aggregate of positive individual savings; and the difference has been made up by the losses of those whose courage and initiative have not been supplemented by exceptional skill or unusual good fortune. But if effective demand is adequate, average skill and average good fortune will be enough.

The authoritarian state systems of to-day seem to solve the problem of unemployment at the expense of efficiency and of freedom. It is certain that the world will not much longer tolerate the unemployment which, apart from brief intervals of excitement, is associated—and, in my opinion, inevitably associated—with present-day capitalistic individualism. But it may be possible by a right analysis of the problem to cure the disease whilst preserving efficiency and freedom.

IV

I have mentioned in passing that the new system might be more favourable to peace than the old has been. It is worth while to repeat and emphasise that aspect.

War has several causes. Dictators and others such, to whom war offers, in expectation at least, a pleasurable excitement, find it easy to work on the natural bellicosity of their peoples. But, over and above this, facilitating their task of fanning the popular flame, are the economic causes of war, namely, the pressure of population and the competitive struggle for markets. It is the second factor, which probably played a predominant part in the nineteenth century, and might again, that is germane to this discussion.

I have pointed out in the preceding chapter that, under the system of domestic *laissez-faire* and an international gold standard such as was orthodox in the latter half of the nineteenth century, there was no means open to a government whereby to mitigate economic distress at home except through the competitive struggle for markets. For all measures helpful to a state of chronic or intermittent under-employment were ruled out, except measures to improve the balance of trade on income account.

Thus, whilst economists were accustomed to applaud the prevailing international system as furnishing the fruits of the international division of labour and harmonising at the same time the interests of different nations, there lay concealed a less benign influence; and those statesmen were moved by common sense and a correct apprehension of the true course of events, who believed that if a rich, old country were to neglect the struggle for markets its prosperity would droop and fail. But if nations can learn to provide themselves with full employment by their domestic policy (and, we must add, if they can also attain equilibrium in the trend of their population), there need be no important economic forces calculated to set the interest of one country against that of its neighbours. There would still be room for the international division of labour and for international lending in appropriate conditions. But there would no longer be a pressing motive why one country need force its wares on another or repulse the offerings of its neighbour, not because this was necessary to enable it to pay for what it wished to purchase, but with the express object of upsetting the equilibrium of payments so as to develop a balance of trade in its own favour. International trade would cease to be what it is, namely, a desperate expedient to maintain employment at home by forcing sales on foreign markets and restricting purchases, which, if successful, will merely shift the problem of unemployment to the neighbour which is worsted in the struggle, but a willing and unimpeded exchange of goods and services in conditions of mutual advantage.

V

Is the fulfilment of these ideas a visionary hope? Have they insufficient roots in the motives which govern the evolution of political society? Are the interests which they will thwart stronger and more obvious than those which they will serve?

I do not attempt an answer in this place. It would need a volume of a different character from this one to indicate even in outline the practical measures in which they might be gradually clothed. But if the ideas are correct—an hypothesis on which the author himself must necessarily base what he writes—it would be a mistake, I predict, to dispute their potency over a period of time. At the present moment people are unusually expectant of a more fundamental diagnosis; more particularly ready to receive it; eager to try it out, if it should be even plausible. But apart from this contemporary mood, the ideas of economists and political philosophers, both when they are right and when they are wrong, are more powerful than is commonly understood. Indeed the world is ruled by little else. Practical men, who believe themselves to be quite exempt from any intellectual influences, are usually the slaves of some defunct economist. Madmen in authority, who hear voices in the air, are distilling their frenzy from some academic scribbler of a few years back. I am sure that the power of vested interests is vastly exaggerated compared with the gradual encroachment of ideas. Not, indeed, immediately, but after a certain interval; for in the field of economic and political philosophy there are not many who are influenced by new theories after they are twenty-five or thirty years of age, so that the ideas which civil servants and politicians and even agitators apply to current events are not likely to be the newest. But, soon or late, it is ideas, not vested interests, which are dangerous for good or evil.

THE ROAD TO SERFDOM

by Friedrich A. Hayek *

PLANNING AND DEMOCRACY

The common features of all collectivist systems may be described, in a phrase ever dear to socialists of all schools, as the deliberate organization of the labors of society for a definite social goal. That our present society lacks such "conscious" direction toward a single aim, that its activities are guided by the whims and fancies of irresponsible individuals, has always been one of the main complaints of its socialist critics.

In many ways this puts the basic issue very clearly. And it directs us at once to the point where the conflict arises between individual freedom and collectivism. The various kinds of collectivism, communism, fascism, etc., differ among themselves in the nature of the goal toward which they want to direct the efforts of society. But they all differ from liberalism and individualism in wanting to organize the whole of society and all its resources for this unitary end and in refusing to recognize autonomous spheres in which the ends of the individuals are supreme. In short, they are totalitarian in the true sense of this new word which we have adopted to describe the unexpected but nevertheless inseparable manifestations of what in theory we call collectivism.

The "social goal," or "common purpose," for which society is to be organized is usually vaguely described as the "common good," the "general welfare," or the "general interest." It does not need much reflection to

* Friedrich A. Hayek, *The Road to Serfdom* (Chicago: 1944). By permission of the University of Chicago Press.

see that these terms have no sufficiently definite meaning to determine
a particular course of action. The welfare and the happiness of millions
cannot be measured on a single scale of less and more. The welfare of a
people, like the happiness of a man, depends on a great many things that
can be provided in an infinite variety of combinations. It cannot be adequately expressed as a single end, but only as a hierarchy of ends, a
comprehensive scale of values in which every need of every person is
given its place. To direct all our activities according to a single plan presupposes that every one of our needs is given its rank in an order of
values which must be complete enough to make it possible to decide
among all the different courses which the planner has to choose. It presupposes, in short, the existence of a complete ethical code in which all
the different human values are allotted their due place.

The conception of a complete ethical code is unfamiliar, and it requires some effort of imagination to see what it involves. We are not in
the habit of thinking of moral codes as more or less complete. The fact
that we are constantly choosing between different values without a social
code prescribing how we ought to choose does not surprise us and does
not suggest to us that our moral code is incomplete. In our society there
is neither occasion nor reason why people should develop common views
about what should be done in such situations. But where all the means
to be used are the property of society and are to be used in the name of
society according to a unitary plan, a "social" view about what ought to
be done must guide all decisions. In such a world we should soon find
that our moral code is full of gaps.

We are not concerned here with the question whether it would be
desirable to have such a complete ethical code. It may merely be pointed
out that up to the present the growth of civilization has been accompanied by a steady diminution of the sphere in which individual actions
are bound by fixed rules. The rules of which our common moral code
consists have progressively become fewer and more general in character.
From the primitive man, who was bound by an elaborate ritual in almost
every one of his daily activities, who was limited by innumerable taboos,
and who could scarcely conceive of doing things in a way different from
his fellows, morals have more and more tended to become merely limits
circumscribing the sphere within which the individual could behave as
he liked. The adoption of a common ethical code comprehensive enough
to determine a unitary economic plan would mean a complete reversal
of this tendency.

The essential point for us is that no such complete ethical code exists.

The attempt to direct all economic activity according to a single plan would raise innumerable questions to which the answer could be provided only by a moral rule, but to which existing morals have no answer and where there exists no agreed view on what ought to be done. People will have either no definite views or conflicting views on such questions, because in the free society in which we have lived there has been no occasion to think about them and still less to form common opinions about them.

Not only do we not possess such an all-inclusive scale of values: it would be impossible for any mind to comprehend the infinite variety of different needs of different people which compete for the available resources and to attach a definite weight to each. For our problem it is of minor importance whether the ends for which any person cares comprehend only his own individual needs, or whether they include the needs of his closer or even those of his more distant fellows — that is, whether he is egoistic or altruistic in the ordinary senses of these words. The point which is so important is the basic fact that it is impossible for any man to survey more than a limited field, to be aware of the urgency of more than a limited number of needs. Whether his interests center round his own physical needs, or whether he takes a warm interest in the welfare of every human being he knows, the ends about which he can be concerned will always be only an infinitesimal fraction of the needs of all men.

This is the fundamental fact on which the whole philosophy of individualism is based. It does not assume, as is often asserted, that man is egoistic or selfish or ought to be. It merely starts from the indisputable fact that the limits of our powers of imagination make it impossible to include in our scale of values more than a sector of the needs of the whole society, and that, since, strictly speaking, scales of value can exist only in individual minds, nothing but partial scales of values exist — scales which are inevitably different and often inconsistent with each other. From this the individualist concludes that the individuals should be allowed, within defined limits, to follow their own values and preferences rather than somebody else's; that within these spheres the individual's system of ends should be supreme and not subject to any dictation by others. It is this recognition of the individual as the ultimate judge of his ends, the belief that as far as possible his own views ought to govern his actions, that forms the essence of the individualist position.

This view does not, of course, exclude the recognition of social ends, or rather of a coincidence of individual ends which makes it advisable for men to combine for their pursuit. But it limits such common action to the instances where individual views coincide; what are called "social ends" are for it merely identical ends of many individuals — or ends to the achievement of which individuals are willing to contribute in return for the assistance they receive in the satisfaction of their own desires. Common action is thus limited to the fields where people agree on common ends. Very frequently these common ends will not be ultimate ends to the individuals but means which different persons can use for different purposes. In fact, people are most likely to agree on common action where the common end is not an ultimate end to them but a means capable of serving a great variety of purposes.

When individuals combine in a joint effort to realize ends they have in common, the organizations, like the state, that they form for this purpose are given their own system of ends and their own means. But any organization thus formed remains one "person" among others, in the case of the state much more powerful than any of the others, it is true, yet still with its separate and limited sphere in which alone its ends are supreme. The limits of this sphere are determined by the extent to which the individuals agree on particular ends; and the probability that they will agree on a particular course of action necessarily decreases as the scope of such action extends. There are certain functions of the state on the exercise of which there will be practical unanimity among its citizens; there will be others on which there will be agreement of a substantial majority; and so on, until we come to fields where, although each individual might wish the state to act in some way, there will be almost as many views about what the government should do as there are different people.

We can rely on voluntary agreement to guide the action of the state only so long as it is confined to spheres where agreement exists. But not only when the state undertakes direct control in fields where there is no such agreement is it bound to suppress individual freedom. We can unfortunately not indefinitely extend the sphere of common action and still leave the individual free in his own sphere. Once the communal sector, in which the state controls all the means, exceeds a certain proportion of the whole, the effects of its actions dominate the whole system. Although the state controls directly the use of only a large part of the available resources, the effects of its decisions on the remaining part of the economic system become so great that indirectly it controls almost everything. Where, as was, for example, true in Germany as early as 1928, the central and local authorities directly control the use of more than half the national income (according to an official German estimate then, 53 per cent), they control indirectly almost the whole economic life of the nation. There is, then, scarcely an individual end which is not dependent for its achievement on the action of the state, and the "social scale of values" which guides the state's action must embrace practically all individual ends.

It is not difficult to see what must be the consequences when democracy embarks upon a course of planning which in its execution requires more agreement than in fact exists. The people may have agreed on adopting a system of directed economy because they have been convinced that it will produce great prosperity. In the discussions leading to the decision, the goal of planning will have been described by some such term as "common welfare," which only conceals the absence of real agreement on the ends of planning. Agreement will in fact exist only on the mechanism to be used. But it is a mechanism which can be used only for a common end; and the question of the precise goal toward which all activity is to be directed will arise as soon as the executive power has to translate the demand for a single plan into a particular plan. Then it will appear that the agreement on the desirability of planning is not supported by agreement on the ends the plan is to serve. The effect of the people's agreeing that there must be central planning, without agreeing on the ends, will be rather as if a group of people were to commit themselves to take a journey together without agreeing where they want to go: with the result that they may all have to make a journey which most of them do not want at all. That planning creates a situation in which it is necessary for us to agree on a much larger number of topics than we have been used to, and that in a planned system we cannot confine collective action to the tasks on which we can agree but are forced to produce agreement on everything in order that any action can be taken at all, is one of the features which contributes more than most to determining the character of a planned system.

It may be the unanimously expressed will of the people that its parliament should prepare a comprehensive economic plan, yet neither the people nor its representatives need therefore be able to agree on any particular plan. The inability of democratic assemblies to carry out what seems to be a clear mandate of the people will inevitably cause dissatisfaction with democratic institutions. Parliaments come to be regarded as ineffective "talking shops," unable or incompetent to carry out the tasks for which they have been chosen. The conviction grows that if efficient planning is to be done, the direction must be "taken out of politics" and placed in the hands of experts — permanent officials or independent autonomous bodies.

The difficulty is well known to socialists. It will soon be half a century since the Webbs began to complain of "the increased incapacity of the House of Commons to cope with its work." * More recently, Professor Laski has elaborated the argument:

> It is common ground that the present parliamentary machine is quite unsuited to pass rapidly a great body of complicated legislation. The National Government, indeed, has in substance admitted this by implementing its economy and tariff measures not by detailed debate in the House of Commons but by a wholesale system of delegated legislation. A Labour Government would, I presume, build upon the amplitude of this precedent. It would confine the House of Commons to the two functions it can properly perform: the ventilation of grievances and the discussion of general principles of its measures. Its Bills would take the form of general formulae conferring wide powers on the appropriate government departments; and those powers would be exercised by Order in Council which could, if desired, be attacked in the House by means of a vote of no confidence. The necessity and value of delegated legislation has recently been strongly reaffirmed by the Donoughmore Committee; and its extension is inevitable if the process of socialisation is not to be wrecked by the normal methods of obstruction which existing parliamentary procedure sanctions.

And to make it quite clear that a socialist government must not allow itself to be too much fettered by democratic procedure, Professor Laski at the end of the same article raised the question "whether in a period of transition to Socialism, a Labour Government can risk the overthrow of its measures as a result of the next general election" — and left it significantly unanswered.†

* Sidney and Beatrice Webb, *Industrial Democracy* (1897), p. 800n.

† H. J. Laski, "Labour and the Constitution," *New Statesman and Nation*, No. 81 (new ser.), September 10, 1932, p. 277. In a book (*Democracy in Crisis* [1933], particularly p. 87) in which Professor Laski later elaborated these ideas, his determination that parliamentary democracy must not be allowed to form an obstacle to the realization of socialism is even more plainly expressed: not only would a socialist government "take vast powers and legislate under them by ordinance and decree" and "suspend the classic formulae of normal opposition" but the "continuance of parliamentary government would depend on its [i.e., the Labour government's] possession of guarantees from the Conservative Party that its work of transformation would not be disrupted by repeal in the event of its defeat at the polls"!

As Professor Laski invokes the authority of the Donoughmore Committee, it may be worth recalling that Professor Laski was a member of that committee and presumably one of the authors of its report.

It is important clearly to see the causes of this admitted ineffectiveness of parliaments when it comes to a detailed administration of the economic affairs of a nation. The fault is neither with the individual representatives nor with parliamentary institutions as such but with the contradictions inherent in the task with which they are charged. They are not asked to act where they can agree, but to produce agreement on everything — the whole direction of the resources of the nation. For such a task the system of majority decision is, however, not suited. Majorities will be found where it is a choice between limited alternatives; but it is a superstition to believe that there must be a majority view on everything. There is no reason why there should be a majority in favor of any one of the different possible courses of positive action if their number is legion. Every member of the legislative assembly might prefer some particular plan for the direction of economic activity to no plan, yet no one plan may appear preferable to a majority to no plan at all.

Nor can a coherent plan be achieved by breaking it up into parts and voting on particular issues. A democratic assembly voting and amending a comprehensive economic plan clause by clause, as it deliberates on an ordinary bill, makes nonsense. An economic plan, to deserve the name, must have a unitary conception. Even if a parliament could, proceeding step by step, agree on some scheme, it would certainly in the end satisfy nobody. A complex whole in which all the parts must be most carefully adjusted to each other cannot be achieved through a compromise between conflicting views. To draw up an economic plan in this fashion is even less possible than, for example, successfully to plan a military campaign by democratic procedure. As in strategy it would become inevitable to delegate the task to the experts.

Yet the difference is that, while the general who is put in charge of a campaign is given a single end to which, for the duration of the campaign, all the means under his control have to be exclusively devoted, there can be no such single goal given to the economic planner, and no similar limitation of the means imposed upon him. The general has not got to balance different independent aims against each other; there is for him only one supreme goal. But the ends of an economic plan, or of any part of it, cannot be defined apart from the particular plan. It is the essence of the economic problem that the making of an economic plan involves the choice between conflicting or competing ends — different needs of different people. But which ends do so conflict, which will have to be sacrificed if we want to achieve certain others, in short, which are the alternatives between which we must choose, can only be known to those who know all the facts; and only they, the experts, are in a position to decide which of the different ends are to be given preference. It is inevitable that they should impose their scale of preferences on the community for which they plan. . . .

It is the price of democracy that the possibilities of conscious control are restricted to the fields where true agreement exists and that in some fields things must be left to chance. But in a society which for its functioning depends on central planning this control cannot be made dependent on a majority's being able to agree; it will often be necessary that the will of a small minority be imposed upon the people, because this minority will be the largest group able to agree among themselves on the question at issue. Democratic government has worked successfully where, and so long as, the functions of government were, by a widely accepted creed, restricted to fields where agreement among a majority could be achieved by free discussion; and it is the great merit of the liberal creed that it reduced the range of subjects on which agreement was necessary to one on which it was likely to exist in a society of free men. It is now often said that democracy will not tolerate "capitalism." If "capitalism" means here a competitive system based on free disposal over private property, it is far more important to realize that only within this system is democracy possible. When it becomes dominated by a collectivist creed, democracy will inevitably destroy itself.

We have no intention, however, of making a fetish of democracy. It may well be true that our generation talks and thinks too much of democracy and too little of the values which it serves. It cannot be said of democracy, as Lord Acton truly said of liberty, that it "is not a means to a higher political end. It is itself the highest political end. It is not for the sake of a good public administration that it is required, but for the security in the pursuit of the highest objects of civil society, and of private life." Democracy is essentially a means, a utilitarian device for safeguarding internal peace and individual freedom. As such it is by no means infallible or certain. Nor must we forget that there has often been much more cultural and spiritual freedom under an autocratic rule than under some democracies — and it is at least conceivable that under the government of a very homogeneous and doctrinaire majority democratic government might be as oppressive as the worst dictatorship. Our point, however, is not that dictatorship must inevitably extirpate freedom but rather that planning leads to dictatorship because dictatorship is the most effective instrument of coercion and the enforcement of ideals and, as such, essential if central planning on a large scale is to be possible. The clash between planning and democracy arises simply from the fact that the latter is an obstacle to the suppression of freedom which the direction of economic activity requires. But in so far as democracy ceases to be a guaranty of individual freedom, it may well persist in some form under a totalitarian regime. A true "dictatorship of the proletariat," even if democratic in form, if it undertook centrally to direct the economic system, would probably destroy personal freedom as completely as any autocracy has ever done.

The fashionable concentration on democracy as the main value threatened is not without danger. It is largely responsible for the misleading and unfounded belief that, so long as the ultimate source of power is the will of the majority, the power cannot be arbitrary. The false assurance which many people derive from this belief is an important cause of the general unawareness of the dangers which we face. There is no justification for the belief that, so long as power is conferred by democratic procedure, it cannot be arbitrary; the contrast suggested by this statement is altogether false: it is not the source but the limitation of power which prevents it from being arbitrary. Democratic control *may* prevent power from becoming arbitrary, but it does not do so by its mere existence. If democracy resolves on a task which necessarily involves the use of power which cannot be guided by fixed rules, it must become arbitrary power. . . .

ECONOMIC CONTROL AND TOTALITARIANISM . . .

Our freedom of choice in a competitive society rests on the fact that, if one person refuses to satisfy our wishes, we can turn to another. But if we face a monopolist we are at his mercy. And an authority directing the whole economic system would be the most powerful monopolist conceivable. While we need probably not be afraid that such an authority would exploit this power in the manner in which a private monopolist would do so, while its purpose would presumably not be the extortion of maximum financial gain, it would have complete power to decide what we are to be given and on what terms. It would not only decide what commodities and services were to be available and in what quantities; it would be able to direct their distribution between districts and groups and could, if it wished, discriminate between persons to any degree it liked. If we remember why planning is advocated by most people, can there be much doubt that this power would be used for the ends of which the authority approves and to prevent the pursuits of ends which it disapproves?

The power conferred by the control of production and prices is almost unlimited. In a competitive society the prices we have to pay for a thing, the rate at which we can get one thing for another, depend on the quantities of other things of which by taking one, we deprive the other members of society. This price is not determined by the conscious will of anybody. And if one way of achieving our ends proves too expensive for us, we are free to try other ways. The obstacles in our path are not due to someone's disapproving of our ends but to the fact that the same means are also wanted elsewhere. In a directed economy, where the authority watches over the ends pursued, it is certain that it would use its powers to assist some ends and to prevent the realization of others. Not our own view, but somebody else's, of what we ought to like or dislike would determine what we should get. And since the authority would have the power to thwart any efforts to elude its guidance, it would control what we consume almost as effectively as if it directly told us how to spend our income. . . .

Who, Whom? . . .

We have already seen that the close interdependence of all economic phenomena makes it difficult to stop planning just where we wish and that, once the free working of the market is impeded beyond a certain degree, the planner will be forced to extend his controls until they become all-comprehensive. These economic considerations, which explain why it is impossible to stop deliberate control just where we should wish, are strongly reinforced by certain social or political tendencies whose strength makes itself increasingly felt as planning extends.

Once it becomes increasingly true, and is generally recognized, that the position of the individual is determined not by impersonal forces, not as a result of the competitive effort of many, but by the deliberate decision of authority, the attitude of the people toward their position in the social order necessarily changes. There will always exist inequalities which will appear unjust to those who suffer from them, disappointments which will appear unmerited, and strokes of misfortune which those hit have not deserved. But when these things occur in a society which is consciously directed, the way in which people will react will be very different from what it is when they are nobody's conscious choice.

Inequality is undoubtedly more readily borne, and affects the dignity of the person much less, if it is determined by impersonal forces than when it is due to design. In a competitive society it is no slight to a person, no offense to his dignity, to be told by any particular firm that it has no need for his services or that it cannot offer him a better job. It is true that in periods of prolonged mass unemployment the effect on many may be very similar. But there are other and better methods to prevent that scourge than central direction. But the unemployment or the loss of income which will always affect some in any society is certainly less degrading if it is the result of misfortune and not deliberately imposed by authority. However bitter the experience, it would be very much worse in a planned society. There individuals will have to decide not whether a person is needed for a particular job but whether he is of use for anything, and how useful he is. His position in life must be assigned to him by somebody else.

While people will submit to suffering which may hit anyone, they will not so easily submit to suffering which is the result of the decision of authority. It may be bad to be just a cog in an impersonal machine; but it is infinitely worse if we can no longer leave it, if we are tied to our place and to the superiors who have been chosen for us. Dissatisfaction of everybody with his lot will inevitably grow with the consciousness that it is the result of deliberate human decision.

Once government has embarked upon planning for the sake of justice, it cannot refuse responsibility for anybody's fate or position. In a planned society we shall all know that we are better or worse off than others, not because of circumstances which nobody controls, and which it is impossible to foresee with certainty, but because some authority wills it. And all our efforts directed toward improving our position will have to aim, not at foreseeing and preparing as well as we can for the circumstances over which we have no control, but at influencing in our favor the authority which has all the power. The nightmare of English nineteenth-century political thinkers, the state in which "no avenue to wealth and honor would exist save through the government," * would be realized in a completeness which they never imagined — though familiar enough in some countries which have since passed to totalitarianism.

As soon as the state takes upon itself the task of planning the whole economic life, the problem of the due station of the different individuals and groups must indeed inevitably become the central political problem. As the coercive power of the state will alone decide who is to have what, the only power worth having will be a share in the exercise of this direct-

---

* The actual words are those of the young Disraeli.

ing power. There will be no economic or social questions that would not be political questions in the sense that their solution will depend exclusively on who wields the coercive power, on whose are the views that will prevail on all occasions.

I believe it was Lenin himself who introduced to Russia the famous phrase "who, whom?" — during the early years of Soviet rule the byword in which the people summed up the universal problem of a socialist society.* Who plans whom, who directs and dominates whom, who assigns to other people their station in life, and who is to have his due allotted by others? These become necessarily the central issues to be decided solely by the supreme power.

More recently an American student of politics has enlarged upon Lenin's phrase and asserted that the problem of all government is "who gets what, when, and how." In a way this is not untrue. That all government affects the relative position of different people and that there is under any system scarcely an aspect of our lives which may not be affected by government action is certainly true. In so far as government does anything at all, its action will always have some effect on "who gets what, when, and how."

There are, however, two fundamental distinctions to be made. First, particular measures may be taken without the possibility of knowing how they will affect particular individuals and therefore without aiming at such particular effects. This point we have already discussed. Second, it is the extent of the activities of the government which decides whether everything that any person gets any time depends on the government, or whether its influence is confined to whether some people will get some things in some way at some time. Here lies the whole difference between a free and a totalitarian system.

The contrast between a liberal and a totally planned system is characteristically illustrated by the common complaints of Nazis and socialists of the "artificial separations of economics and politics" and by their equally common demand for the dominance of politics over economics. These phrases presumably mean not only that economic forces are now allowed to work for ends which are not part of the policy of the government but also that economic power can be used independently of government direction and for ends of which the government may not approve. But the alternative is not merely that there should be only one

* Cf. M. Muggeridge, *Winter in Moscow* (1934); Arthur Feiler, *The Experiment of Bolshevism* (1930).

power but that this single power, the ruling group, should have control over all human ends and particularly that it should have complete power over the position of each individual in society.

DEMOCRACY AND PROGRESS

by David McCord Wright *

POLITICAL DEMOCRACY AND THE ALTERNATIVES TO COMPETITION

Modern social thought is overwhelmingly characterized by an intense will to believe that we may change the economic organization of society without adverse effect on the quality of its political existence. Thus the first alternative usually proposed to hitherto accepted theories of dual action by competition and election is virtual abandonment of business competition, and extension of the elective method to economic affairs. Many economists write as if the holding of elections with universal suffrage were sufficient to protect the individual — no matter what our economic organization. For example, it may be said that as long as we elect the planners, or those who select them, we can control them; or that, if only the worker has a vote in the union (or in the management itself), he will be sufficiently protected.

Such extremely literal applications of political democracy to economic life make it necessary to remember the idea with which this book began — namely, that democracy is not a single simple standard but a complex of standards; and it is important to stress as background for our discussion a fact so evident that it is nearly always forgotten, that the competitive market in and of itself is already an application of the elective method to economic life. Viewed in the large, and with allowance for innumerable shortcomings, the competitive pricing system may be thought of as a perpetual election to decide what shall be produced. Money outlay forms the votes, advertising is the campaign literature, and the election returns — determining what goods shall be made and what not — are profit and

* David McCord Wright, *Democracy and Progress* (New York: 1948). By permission of The Macmillan Co.

loss. By this method we achieve such "democracy of choice" or of "preference" as we have secured. For it determines that virtually nothing gets produced long which the consumer is unwilling to buy.

Left-wing writers tend to protest analogies of this sort and to dwell upon the many defects of the process. But these defects are in themselves a valuable commentary upon the critics' own proposal — general reliance upon political election alone. Thus it may be said that advertising (the campaign literature of the economic election) is frequently silly, vicious, or untrue. But is absolute veracity or nobility an outstanding and characteristic quality of political campaign speeches? Or it may be said that the buyer (the economic "voter") does not really buy what he wants, since his personal expenditure is generally too small to compel products specially suited to his needs. His choice, therefore, is limited to the alternatives presented to him, and he may be said to have the "referendum" and the "recall" but not the "initiative." But how often in political life (even in the initiative) does a single voter pick his own candidate or proposal? Does he not also usually have to choose among alternatives put before him? As for the "impurity" or "imperfection" of the economic election — the "rigging of the market" — what of the purity of many political campaigns? Finally, some will object that in the economic election there are great discrepancies in "voting" power, because the man with a large income has many more "votes" (more money to spend) than the man with a small one. . . . Nevertheless, granted that power in the economic election is unequally distributed, does the possession of an equal personal vote really give each voter equal political power?

The assumption that an equal vote gives equal power and hence equal protection underlies nearly all the writings of those who feel that business competition is no longer necessary or desirable. Of the advocates of such views one may ask: How much effective control of U.M.W. policy does a vote in the union election give to the individual miner in John L. Lewis's union? How much power did the possession of a vote give the individual voter in Mayor Hague's Jersey City? Anyone with political experience will recognize that past the town meeting, or other small assembly where the individual may have a direct hearing, and indeed often even then, what counts is not simply a vote but control of the organization or influence with its members. In the bad old days a city boss could say, "I care not who casts the votes of my city as long as I can count them." The more flagrant abuses have passed. But still the organization with an integrated program, and a well drilled vote which can be "gotten out" when needed, holds major control. There are more ways of killing a cat than choking it!

Here, however, lies the dilemma of those who wish to rely upon the election method alone. One may grant that in cases of enormous abuse of power the citizens may combine and "throw the rascals out." They have thus a residual veto. But the effectiveness of this veto, and the degree of abuse needed to call forth its exercise, largely rest upon the economic independence of the voter. The power of the organization to perpetuate itself largely depends upon its degree of control over his economic life. Anyone who has had anything to do with reform movements in politics knows that the fear of economic reprisal is one of the most important factors keeping people from independent political action. Men are notoriously reluctant to vote against their bread and butter. Yet if the alternative to support is great financial loss or even starvation — and a man's vote or sympathies do get around despite the most improved election machinery — it is increasingly difficult to have effective opposition. The really crucial point is that in a large electorate the other side must organize in order to be effective. And if you are in a position to pick off and neutralize the leaders of the opposition before they have completed organization, the chances for effective democratic political action against you become almost nil.

The most obvious way to neutralize the opposition is by terror and persecution. But the beauty of the comprehensively planned state for the "ins" is that it makes possible a far more suave but almost equally effective method. Even in states like Beveridge's or Dr. Mordecai Ezekiel's, in which the shell of both private property rights and political democracy is permitted to survive, we are already in sight of self-perpetuating oligarchy. For investment is "planned" in advance, or fitted into a national investment "budget," and this implies large-scale control over the flow of resources, over unions, and over management. The individual who will not "cooperate" in setting a "proper" price, or in ruling out a "bad" invention, the man who talks too specifically about the abuses of power which he has encountered, can find it mysteriously difficult to get materials; or strange legal obstacles will develop for him. Who that has worked in Washington can deny this possibility? And how difficult to establish undoubted proof of favoritism. So far as the entrepreneur goes, how hard to show that the sudden interest of the Bureau of Internal Revenue in his income tax or of the antitrust division in his trade contacts is not all pure routine altruism! Could any better method of picking off able incipient organizers be devised? . . .

Let us run over again the problem of personal economic freedom in modern society. It is not hard to see how a self-sufficient farmer can be free — as long as he only wants to be a self-sufficient farmer. Provided merely that his property rights are respected, he can close his front gate and watch the "rest of the world go by." A man can also be independent in modern society by having an independent income — as long as he doesn't want to spend more than he gets — and he, too, need not fear economic oppression while his property rights are respected, and if he (or his trustee) has sense enough not to lose his money. But what about the great number of people who work for others? How can they be protected from oppression and bullying — especially when, in physical terms, they scarcely ever have more than a few hours' supply of food or even of water, and often very little more than that in terms of money?

The modern social thinker is inclined to believe that the prime hope for such people is in the trade union. Often this is the case. But we can no more depend upon unions alone for protection than we can depend upon elections alone. The essential guarantee — without which unions will rapidly degenerate — is alternative employment opportunities: a *bona fide* chance to get another job.

Left-wing writers make much of the differences in economic power which leave the individual worker unable to bargain effectively with a large concern. They seldom say anything about the differences in power which leave him unable to bargain effectively with a large union. But the energetic and ambitious young man who finds himself barred from the work he wishes by exorbitant fees and prolonged apprenticeships can tell a different story — as also can the worker, inside the union, who incurs the hostility of the leadership. Suppose a man works in a closed union in a closed-shop industry, with the check-off system. How can he protect himself from exploitation by the union? To impute to him any great power to protect himself is to be guilty of the cynical fallacy which led some of the popular writers on economics of the nineteenth century to say there could be no injustice because of "freedom of contract." To a union possessed of great funds for which there need be no accounting, with little effective control by the law, and with all the weapons of intimidation, fraud, and corruption at hand, the opportunity is wide for a tyranny from which there is no escape for the member save in a transfer to another industry.

The truth of the matter seems to be that unless the individual voter, in a union election just as in a political election, already possesses adequate independence, the election will almost inevitably become a farce. And in the last analysis this independence can be secured only through alternative employment opportunities of the kind which, though admittedly not perfect, the competitive system attempts to offer.

Yet it is precisely the transfer to other lines of employment which is increasingly limited by the trend of modern development. Let us suppose that the government embarks, as it has already partially done, upon a policy designed to give a more genuine democratic freedom to the worker. Let us assume a program of unemployment allowances, public employment agencies, dissemination of information regarding jobs, and schools for vocational reeducation. Are not these inadequate unless the worker is free to enter other fields without such things as exorbitant fees, fraudulent examinations, and unreasonable apprenticeships? There is no need to gild the lily. The right to "transfer" is a poor protection if there is not reasonably full employment . . . But it is also a poor protection if "democracy of management" is used in such a way as to create a number of rival closed groups between which movement is almost impossible; or if "full employment" is obtained by giving the central directorate such far-reaching power over economic life, and hiring and firing units, that no man can escape their grasp.

As one reflects upon matters like these it becomes apparent once more how political and personal freedom as well as technological creativeness is bound up with the institutions which give rise to "democracy of opportunity or aspiration" — the chance to rise on independent terms. Through the competitive market we get at once the diffusion of authority and the alternative opportunities which are needed. And though the force of public opinion and even state action may exclude certain methods of reaching wealth and power, this influence cannot be carried so far — if democracy is to survive — as to leave most men dependent upon the personal whim of dominant individuals or groups. The problem has been summed up by saying that we do not want a society in which promotion comes through "pull" rather than "push." "Push," to be sure, may be an unsympathetic word; but substitute "superior energy and foresight," and the point is equally well made.

Yet on the basis of what we have seen regarding the fear of economic reprisal and its effect on political election — and also the weakness of the single voter, acting alone, in a large electorate — it is questionable how long effective democracy can survive removal of the restraint upon state action which substantial reliance upon the competitive market implies. Further it is hard to see how personal freedom may be protected in our modern machine civilization without the alternative job opportunities of the competitive system. Some critics of course will say that, however sound our argument may be, it is too late: competition cannot be ensured any more, and even if it were it would not work. I believe them to be wrong. While the "free" competitive system could not be simply left alone we could get reasonable competition and stability if we wanted to, without too much state action. We shall consider this further. But suppose the critics are right. Let them then ask themselves: Do these arguments mean merely the end of competitive capitalism — or do they not mean the end of democracy too?

Democracy of opportunity, we must emphasize again, is one of the fundamental guarantees of political freedom. But if men are inherently unequal in capacity, and if they are allowed to go as far as their ability can take them, the results are bound to be an unequal distribution of wealth or of power — whether as unequal as the present distribution may be debated, but certainly much more unequal than most left-wing writers are willing to admit. . . .

THE FUTURE OF DEMOCRATIC PROGRESS . . .

Our argument has been that the competitive economic market furnished the best framework within which democratic progress could take place. We did not say that, in itself it was a guarantee of democratic progress, but we nevertheless maintained that without it democratic progress under modern conditions, would be virtually impossible. In other words, the competitive economic market, though not a sufficient condition for democracy and progress, is an overwhelmingly necessary one.

The line of thought pursued has been as follows: The administration of a complicated interdependent technology requires a hierarchy of highly trained and responsible technical operatives, even if the political state has nominally "withered away." Also, simply to maintain this technology, leaving aside all question of improving it, we must cultivate in the population some desire — even when stated in the most altruistic terms — to do a good job by holding responsible office. Yet at the very least skilled technological control cannot be left to just anyone, so that some form of selection is unavoidable; and, granted the joint necessity of some desire to hold position plus the need for selection among candidates, the inevitability of a degree of rivalry and disappointment immediately follows. The potentiality of rivalry and disappointment inheres in any form of integrated social life — if not, in fact, in all life. The relevant psychological approach for an interdependent society must run in terms of reconciliation to "legitimate" disappointment rather than preventing dissappointment. Economic peace is a generally accepted code of emulation and selection. What is needed is both the discovery of a selective code and the general acceptance of it — which, while recognizing and regularizing the constructive conflicts inherent in creative activity, will restrict to a minimum those forms of rivalry and conflict which are merely predatory and sterile.

In popular discussion our modern equalitarian bias has largely obscured this whole problem of selective method. Either the question is shunted to one side, or there is a foggy suggestion that the entire matter can be handled by "elections." Nevertheless, behind much modern left-wing propaganda lies a confused, subconscious feeling that conflict would be reduced to a minimum, and society run more efficiently, if a regime of "comprehensive" planning were adopted. By this is meant a system in which much the greater part of economic activity, especially new investment, is licensed or planned in advance by some organized and integrated central group.

In the long run, however, such an organization would prove incompatible both with political democracy and with technological progress. The technical operatives would come to form a self-perpetuating group, for under modern conditions, having control of production and economic life and hence of the actual existence of the population, they would also be in a position — directly or indirectly, roughly or suavely — to control the elections if the political state survived, or the population directly if it did not. Democracy, therefore, as Mr. Herbert of the International Ladies Garment Workers Union says, means pluralism. The life of the individual, economic, social, and political, must be divided among many organizations — all to some extent in competition with one another. This in the modern world means a relatively competitive society, and competition implies technical change. . . .

There is another aspect of the modern problem which must be faced. We have said that democratic political freedom is closely tied up with the decentralization, alternative work opportunities, and limited control of the competitive economic market. But how much competition would there be left if interproduct rivalry were abolished? The quasi-immortal corporation is an inevitable and valuable incident of large-scale enterprise (not necessarily, be it remembered, the same thing as monopoly), but it makes possible a perpetuation of strategic position probably stronger than the Victorian personal firm. Without interproduct competition, political as well as economic ossification of society would be likely. Thus not only our technical progress but our political freedom becomes associated with continual independent technical change. What hope is there for the future, what ideal of progress shall we set up?

Our distribution of wealth — the competitive market method of selection, and of control of those selected — has been attacked for many reasons. It has been attacked because it is unequal, because it creates self-perpetuating privilege, because it is wasteful, or, alternatively, because it causes both unemployment and the business cycle. Most of these criticisms are mistaken, or based largely on a false premise. Some form of inequality is inevitable; some privileges are bound to be inheritable while the family survives. The left wing is scarcely consistent in attacking the well-to-do both because they spend too much money and because they save too much. "Long-range" unemployment is the result not of "over-saving" but of the frustration of investment by pressure groups. The business cycle is not the result of the distribution of wealth. One version of the charge alone can be granted: The high savings and creative invention of our society, taken together, do make for rapid growth, and the *rapid growth* makes for instability. Assuming therefore that the process of growth can be stabilized, or counterbalanced, within reasonable bounds — a question already discussed — the usefulness of our social system comes to depend upon the usefulness of the growth and change which it makes possible.

Now of growth and change, as of competition, it may be said that they are nearly always necessary but not sufficient conditions for genuine progress. Mere change and mere expansion are not inevitably good. Indeed, the arguments earlier in this book concerning the "boundlessness" or "insatiability" of desires could easily be converted into saying that growth and change are futile. But our philosophy has rejected such a criterion. We have spoken, instead, of "better" wants and "better," or more satisfying, forms of action. In other words, democratic progress must be judged by a qualitative standard. Can the quantitative rise in "output per head" be justified in terms of a qualitative improvement in the nature of men's lives? That is the real question.

Behind the idea that human wants are insatiable, and therefore progress is futile, lies a basic fallacy. Wants as a whole, or the activity of wanting, as such, may be taken as insatiable, or alternatively as "constant." But this does not prove that particular wants will not be substantially satisfied. Thus, as output per head increases, the *quality* of the new wants and activities substituted by growth may rise. Also we may remedy many of the evils which now distress us without stopping the whole process of growth.

A good example is democracy of opportunity. We have seen that, if society is to give a satisfactory approach to "equality" of opportunity (the equality can never be absolute), the state must intervene by large-scale outlays on health and education so that the less privileged will not be unduly handicapped. But we also pointed out that, because the pursuit of relative economic inequality was a prime incentive of competitive growth and economic service, there was always a conflict between the extent to which equality of income and inheritance could be forced and the extent to which we could have continued growth. Also we said that economic inequality was both a useful and a relatively harmless form of distinction in a world in which some form of inequality (for example, power) was inevitable. All these apparently conflicting ideals may be substantially reconciled within the framework of democratic progress. For neither the amount needed to give men good health, nor that needed to give them good education, increases with infinite speed. To put it differently, the basic requirements for a "fair" start (an equal start being always impossible) do not necessarily rise as fast as the national income. Absolute outlay on "equalizing" expenditures for health and education may be constantly rising even when proportional sacrifice is unchanged. And since the absolute requirements for a fair start are not "boundless," democracy of opportunity may become constantly greater without imposing so high a progressive sacrifice as to cut off, or seriously retard, continued growth. Thus the mere quantitative rise in output per head can, in this instance, work to give greater satisfaction of the qualitative standard of democracy of opportunity.

One of the principal psychological advantages of socialism is that it is very easy for the individual worker to justify his position. However mistaken in fact he may be, he can always say that he is working for the public good because he is working for the state. The businessman, on the other hand, always finds it difficult to justify himself, and feels that in order to do so he must refute the charge that he is working solely for his own selfish interest. Therefore it is natural that when he is bitterly attacked, as he is today, he should instinctively turn for comfort to Adam Smith's doctrine of the "invisible hand." The famous misquotation from Adam Smith, "Every man working for his own selfish interest is nevertheless led by an invisible hand to promote the public good," furnishes an immediate means of justification to the businessman and an answer to his critics.

Of course, if the myth is literally accepted, it is hard to see why intervention by the state should ever be needed. Unfortunately, however, the pure doctrine of laissez faire has never been literally true. Even Smith himself did not state it so dogmatically; he actually said "in many instances," which is a very different thing from the "always" which the misquotation implies. If the capitalist clings to the dogma of laissez-faire economics, however, and tries to justify his system by saying supply and demand automatically always insure adequate social stability, he can never be really convincing. One of the principal obstacles which the believer in capitalism encounters in discussion is that he is nearly always assumed to say that the system will automatically adjust itself. Because this ability always to adjust within tolerable limits is demonstrably untrue, the defender of capitalism on such a ground is defeated before he has ever begun.

Yet, probably because of the psychological appeal of laissez faire already discussed, intelligent conservatism, recognizing the problems of effective demand, frequently does not attract business elements in the United States today. Rather we find an economic fundamentalism which seeks to overcome our problems by denying their existence. The trouble with the "modern" analysis is not that it is necessarily radical but that it is uncomfortable. The capitalist, as we have seen, does not want, indeed may not be able, to face the fact that competition and "supply and demand" will not always and automatically ensure either justice or stability. But since hardly anyone (certainly not the writer) would be willing to return to a regime of laissez faire, and since such a regime will inevitably be discredited by recurrent crises, inability or unwillingness of the capitalist world to adapt itself may well destroy the system. If conservatives prove unable to accept the valid elements of modern criticism, they cannot hope to refute the mistaken policies strangling the system. In such a case we may never get the relatively stable, free, democratic capitalism which lies within our grasp but rather some socialist or fascist hybrid. At the present time American capitalism bids fair to destroy itself through its own ignorance and, more important, lack of desire to learn.

We must be on our guard also for a different reason. The breakaway from blind adherence to laissez faire may bring another, and perhaps even greater, danger. For many businessmen who discard automatic adjustment consider that they are thereby free to discard the whole body of established capitalist thought. The results of this were particularly marked between world wars in Great Britain where a program of planned monopoly attracted the adherence of the most divergent groups. Large-scale labor and large-scale industry combined to throttle the new man and the new idea. If the philosophy of this book be accepted, such a program was neither more nor less than incipient economic fascism, and it was sometimes referred to as the conservative "corporative" state. Yet our business groups now play with the same idea.

We hear a great deal today of what business must "plan" — what it must do to give jobs. Over and over again we learn that business must have a "new attitude" in its work. But the individual firm is in no position by itself to do much toward full employment. Unless a business is to be run at a loss and the pay roll loaded down with useless employees, the businessman as a businessman has very little room for policy in this connection.

When a group of businessmen are gathered into an association, there is a little more leeway — but then the action taken is frequently harmful. It is easy to seek to prevent depression by tracking down "unfair" or "cutthroat" competition — too easy. Unfortunately, ideas of this sort do not furnish a sound analysis of the cause and cure of the business cycle. The root cause of cutthroat competition is usually the jerky expansion which is an inevitable concomitant of rapid change. Trying to prevent it will not solve the distortion of the structure of industry and the consequent shortage of demand which underlies the depression. All too often, instead the "prevention" is merely the cloak for comprehensive monopolization. It is rather by acting as an intelligent citizen that the businessman makes his most valuable contribution.

One of the paradoxes of modern radical criticism is that it often makes a businessman feel better as a monopolist than if he were conducting his business on more individualistic lines. There is unfortunately no necessary connection between the actual value of a man's work and the nobility of his avowed aims; a man may frequently be a better citizen if he sticks to trying to make money in the usual way than if he attempts to plan and "trade for the public good." But in the present state of public opinion, by assisting in essentially monopolistic restriction, he often obtains a public approval that is denied him if he takes what is in fact the more useful line of behavior. The easy coalition of the right-wing idea of unfair competition and left-wing ideas of planning or "cooperation" into a near-fascist regime of controlled monopoly is one of the chief dangers of our time.

There would appear, then, to be four main types of policy advocated in the modern world: (1) blind adherence to laissez faire at home and to economic isolationism abroad — which can only lead to eventual collapse; (2) planned monopolistic combination and log-rolled stagnation by business, labor, and government — a margin of otherwise unemployed must usually be occupied in armaments; (3) full-fledged socialism or fascism, which may be obtained either by direct seizure or by the more subtle hamstringing of the capitalist economy, public investment being used indefinitely "to fill the gap"; (4) removing barriers to investment and production so as to give the utmost freedom to the capitalist machinery, while standing ready to forestall disastrous deflation by the injection of purchasing power. Surely there can be little doubt as to which of these any believer in democracy and science should prefer.

There is, however, another aspect of the capitalist myth and the competitive market method which requires particular comment and justifies careful thought before interfering in economic affairs. It is characteristic of the competitive mechanism that it can never be standardized and reduced to routine without losing a large part of the energy and variety which are its most valuable attributes. Profits must be at the least proportional to risk, and risk is subjective rather than objective. Furthermore, the off chance, the one-in-a-hundred possibility, of supernormal profit is among the great impelling forces of investment. History shows that the extraordinary returns on investment rarely survive longer than a generation, and that labor's average real wages have persistently risen with the rise of the national income. The share of "capital," in the long run, has been remarkably constant. But if the attempt is made to limit the maximum expectation of the businessman, in advance, to "normal profits" — if, for example, he knows that as soon as he manages to increase profits his union will immediately strike — what reason is there to exert himself?

Competition in hope of supernormal profits is the force which gives both growth and realized normal profits. By limiting the hope to normal profits we cut off not merely the "excess" profits but the growth. The "purely competitive" ideal of the economic theorist is static and makes little or no allowance for dynamic investment. Yet the tendency of the human race is to demand absolute gospels and simple slogans. Selective codes such as hereditary right, seniority, or nose counting, employ objective standards easily appealed to. The competitive doctrine can never have comparable simplicity. Therefore it will always be less satisfying to those who believe in it and more vulnerable to adverse criticism.

Yet, come what may, there must be leaders under any system, and such leaders must be allowed to do their work and be protected from the jealousy of those not in power. So a new myth must be evolved. All wealth, it will be said, belongs to "us." The new privileged aristocracy are "our" servants, and we pay them well in money or titles or power, because of their great services to "us." For most people, differences in salary are always easier to rationalize than differences in profits or interest. But will this new myth be more literally accurate than the old? Will it make for more personal freedom, or less?

After all, "social myth" is but a euphemism for social lie. Adam Smith intended his myth merely as a convenient rough approximation. It is as pointless to object that it is not literally true as to object to the literal verity of Plato's myth of iron, brass, and golden men or the modern communists' myth of the labor theory of value. Is not much of our criticism of capitalism, when stripped of its verbiage, nearly as obvious as that there isn't any Santa Claus? Capitalism is not to be judged by mathematical "pure" competition but by alternatives in fact available. Rightly we do not trust Smith's doctrine as far as once we did. But will the new myth prove much more reliable? Can personal and economic freedom survive the end of change and business competition? That is a question which our children or grandchildren may well see answered. . . .

III. SOCIALISM

On the eve of the nineteenth century, in the course of the French Revolution in which he himself was a victim, the Marquis de Condorcet wrote a book of historical importance. It was entitled *Sketch For a Historical Picture of the Progress of the Human Mind*. It was a glowing prophecy, a statement of optimistic faith in the ability of the human race to attain eventually nothing less than the perfection of man. It was an appropriate expression of man's faith in science and his fellow man so characteristic of the "age of reason." "Our hopes," Condorcet wrote, "for the future condition of the human race can be subsumed under three important heads: the abolition of inequality between nations, the progress of equality within each nation, and the true perfection of mankind." [1] In his vision Condorcet foresaw the end of slavery, of race prejudice, of unequal treatment of the sexes, of discrimination based on nationality, indeed the end of war itself. Science would find cures for contagious diseases; longevity would increase, and man's morals would match the improvements in the other fields of learning.

For all of the excesses of the French Revolution it might well appear to the philosophical observer that the age of inevitable progress was at hand. The execution of the French king and many of the nobility symbolically, if barbarously, marked the death of the divine right theory of political authority. Political authority, henceforth, it might have appeared, would have to be justified by reason rather than sanctified by religion. Was not the age at hand that would give meaning to the Revolution's slogan of "liberty, equality, and fraternity"; and would not this new age realize in fact the immutable "Rights of Man"?

As democracy and capitalism swept forward in the nineteenth century the last vestiges of feudalism came under attack, and the old privileged

---

[1] Antoine-Nicholas de Condorcet, *Sketch For A Historical Picture of the Progress of the Human Mind*, translated by June Barraclough (New York: The Noonday Press, 1955) p. 174.

classes of the nobility and clergy gave way before the increasing power of the rising bourgeoisie. Against the traditional claims to power and privilege of the landed aristocracy the middle class called for liberty, equality, and self-government, while the lower class of laborers echoed the refrain. Throughout the nineteenth century, suffrage restrictions were swept aside in England, the United States, and Western Europe in recognition of the new-found power of democracy, against the claims of the landed classes. And, particularly in England, the special benefits accruing to the favored few under mercantilism were challenged, modified, and generally abolished in the face of the demands of the bourgeoisie to compete in a wider market without governmental sponsorship or restriction. This combined political and economic assault of the middle class upon the old order was known in England as liberalism. From England, liberalism spread to the Continent and to the United States. But this liberalism in turn came to be challenged by socialism.

To the socialist, the claims of early nineteenth-century liberalism to liberty in politics and economics failed to come to grips with the basic problems of conflict in society. In liberal theory liberty was interpreted as the absence of coercive governmental regulation; thus freedom was thought to be maximized where legislation was minimized. The ideology of liberalism thus posed a problem: the worker was extended political freedom by granting to him the franchise, but under the terms of economic and legal theory he was not to vote for economic reforms, for, it was argued, such reforms would increase governmental regulation and thereby diminish the area of economic freedom. The apparent conflict between wage-worker and capitalist in economic theory was however inevitably translated into a political one, as was evident with the rise of trade unionism and the increasing demand for ameliorative legislation.

Later in the nineteenth century liberalism underwent a modification in which conflict was rationalized as a recognized and accepted part of liberal ideology. The English philosopher Herbert Spencer in *Social Statics* (1851), and *The Man Versus the State* (1884), developed and popularized the thesis that the progress of civilization was dependent upon competition, or conflict, whereby through a law of nature the superior members of the race would succeed and prosper while the inferior members would fall by the wayside. It was thought by many that Darwin's studies supported this thesis and the term "social Darwinism" was often applied to it. Competition in a non-regulated (by government) economy was thought to be not only sound economics and sound jurisprudence but sound eugenics and ethics as well. For government, through ameliorative legislation, to tamper with this process not only would disturb the economic system but would violate a law of nature and of God. Spencer even went so far as to oppose governmental relief to the poor, and charged philanthropists with fuzzy thinking.

> Blind to the fact, that under the natural order of things society is constantly excreting its unhealthy, imbecile, slow, vacillating, faithless members, these unthinking, though well-meaning, men advocate an interference which not only stops the purifying process, but even increases the vitiation — absolutely encourages the multiplication of the reckless and incompetent by offering them an unfailing provision, and discourages the multiplication of the competent and provident by heightening the prospective difficulty of maintaining a family.[2]

This line of thinking was further expounded and popularized in the United States by William Graham Sumner, who was probably America's most respected sociologist of that century. In an essay entitled "The Challenge of Facts" Sumner noted:

> Every law or institution which protects persons at the expense of capital makes it easier for persons to live and to increase the number of consumers of capital while lowering all the motives to prudence and frugality by which capital is created. Hence every such law or institution tends to produce a large population, sunk in misery. All poor laws and all eleemosynary institutions and expenditures have this tendency. On the contrary, all laws and institutions which give security to capital against the interests of other persons than its owners, restrict numbers while preserving the means of subsistence. Hence every such law or institution tends to produce a small society on a high stage of comfort and well being. It follows that the antithesis commonly thought to exist between the protection of persons and the protection of property is in reality only an antithesis between numbers and quality. . . .
> Let it be understood that we cannot go outside of this alternative: liberty, inequality, survival of the fittest; non-liberty, equality, survival of the unfittest. The former carries society forward and favors all its best members; the latter carries society downwards and favors all its worst members.[3]

It was against this background of liberal ideology and economic institutions that socialism arose and gained political significance. For liberalism

---

[2] Herbert Spencer, *Social Statics* (New York: D. Appleton and Company, 1865), p. 355.
[3] William Graham Sumner, *The Challenge of Facts*, (New Haven: Yale University Press, 1914), pp. 27, 25.

appeared to offer no prospect of prosperity to the laboring classes other than that they individually remove themselves from the ranks of labor. To the social reformer it appeared that such an ideology departed from traditional humanitarian teachings of charity, co-operation and brotherly love. What had happened, it was asked, to the goals of liberty, equality, and fraternity? Capitalism, which in vanquishing feudalism had so spurred the growth of democracy, now found itself under attack by democrats who saw in the new economic system a new form of tyranny. As the masses attained political power they demanded as well some measure of control over the economic system. A host of reformers arose to lead them, offering myriad blueprints for the new society. In the course of the century there were anarchists, like Bakunin and Kropotkin, land taxers like Henry George, and socialists from Robert Owen to Karl Marx among countless others. But whatever the nature of the various schemes of social reform all had in common an indictment of the existing arrangements, particularly as these concerned the property system, and a plan intended to achieve a greater measure of equality in man's relationship with man.

It is important to note that socialism in all its various forms was not intended to be merely an economic system but an entire way of life. Both in the nineteenth century and today, socialism, in its non-communist form, has emphasized the role of economics in political and social affairs; the positive role of the government as the proper instrument for achieving social and economic amelioration; co-operation rather than competition; and the universal equality of men: but all these have been means to the end that men might achieve a fuller and more harmonious scheme for living together.

It is also significant to remember that socialism developed before the writings of Karl Marx. In the nineteenth century alone such reformers as Robert Owen, Saint-Simon and Charles Fourier were considered socialists as they sought to establish a more benevolent social and economic order. In other words, the social goals of socialism anteceded the economic theory. Marx dubbed these reformers "Utopian Socialists," for in his view they lacked a scientific understanding of human behavior and they were reaching for unrealistic, visionary schemes of perfection. Marx thought that with his class analysis of society and his dialectical materialism as an explanation of history his prophecy of the classless society was scientifically arrived at (see Chapter 4). While it is probably true that all forms of contemporary socialism are dependent in some fashion on Marx, all are also a departure from him.

The selections below were first published as follows:

Sidney and Beatrice Webb, *The Decay of Capitalist Civilization*
    (1923)
G. D. H. Cole, *World Socialism Restated* (1956)
Carlo Schmid, "Man and Technology" (1956)
Jawaharlal Nehru, "The Tragic Paradox of Our Age" (1958)
Mordecai Nesayahu, *The Road of Mapai* (1957)

THE DECAY OF CAPITALIST CIVILIZATION

by Sidney and Beatrice Webb *

INTRODUCTION

It is one of the illusions of each generation that the social institutions in which it lives are, in some peculiar sense, "natural," unchangeable and permanent. Yet for countless thousands of years social institutions have been successively arising, developing, decaying and becoming gradually superseded by others better adapted to contemporary needs. This book shows how we, the nations claiming to be the most advanced in civilization, are no less subject than our predecessors to this process of perpetual change. Just as the Sumerian, the Egyptian, the Greek, the Roman and the Christian medieval civilizations have passed away, our present capitalist civilization, as mortal as its predecessors, is dissolving before our eyes, not only in that "septic dissolution" diagnosed by the Dean of St. Paul's, brought upon us by war, and curable by genuine peace, but in that slower changing of the epochs which war may hasten, but which neither we nor anything else can hinder. The question, then, is not whether our present civilization will be transformed, but how it will be transformed. It may, by considerate adaptation, be made to pass gradually and peacefully into a new form. Or, if there is angry resistance instead of adaptation, it may crash, leaving mankind painfully to build up a new civilization from the lower level of a stage of social chaos and disorder in which not only the abuses but also the material, intellectual and moral gains of the previous order will have been lost.

Unfortunately many who assent to this general proposition of inevitable change, fail to realize what the social institutions are to which this law of change applies. To them the basis of all possible civilization is private property in a sense in which it is so bound up with human nature, that whilst men remain men, it is no more capable of decay or supersession than the rotation of the earth on its axis. But they misunderstand the position. It is not the sanction and security of personal possessions that forms the foundation of our capitalist system, but the institution of private ownership of the means by which the community lives.

At the risk of pedantry we define our meaning. By the term capitalism, or the capitalist system, or as we prefer, the capitalist civilization, we mean the particular stage in the development of industry and legal institutions in which the bulk of the workers find themselves divorced from the owner-ship of the instruments of production, in such a way as to pass into the position of wage earners, whose subsistence, security, and personal free-dom seem dependent on the will of a relatively small proportion of the nation; namely, those who own, and through their legal ownership control, the organization of the land, the machinery and the labor-force of the community, and do so with the object of making for themselves individual and private gains.

That the land and the other instruments of wealth production should be the private property of a relatively small class of individuals, with hardly more public responsibility attached to it than to the possession of a watch or walking-stick; that this private ownership should constitute the basis of the arrangement on which the rest of the community obtain their livelihood; and that it should carry with it the control and organization of the production and distribution of the commodities and services that are the very life of the nation — and this is what is meant by capitalism — this amazing arrangement, far from being eternal and ubiquitous through-out human history, has become the characteristic feature of the civiliza-tion of the United States only within three or four generations; and of Europe only within the last few centuries, through the unregulated squat-tings of commercial adventure on the derelict sites left by the gradual failure of the feudal system of land tenure and agriculture in the country, and of a relatively less important gild organization of manufacture and trading in the towns. We know that, in Europe, before the feudal system and the craft gilds existed, civilizations were based on different forms of slavery or serfdom, the family or the caste. These in their times seemed as rooted in human nature and as unchangeable as capitalism does. What is more, they lasted many centuries, and were thought out and organized in States and Churches as divine orders of society in which every man, from Emperor and Pope to serf and slave, was responsible to God for the use he made of his opportunities. The commercial squatting which, though it began in England under Henry VII., did not come into power until George III. was king, has never been authorized and organized politically and religiously in the old enduring fashion. The sages who thought it out as political economists declared that it had no concern with the Churches, and that the lawgivers must not meddle with it: its operations were to be godless and they were to be lawless. On these frankly buccaneering terms it undertook to secure the livelihood of the people, not as its aim, but as an incident of its devotion on principle to the art of getting rich quickly. Its sole claim to toleration was its success in fulfilling that cardinal condition.

It is the thesis of this book that though it never fulfilled the condition completely, and in many places violated it with every circumstance of outrage, yet there was a moment, roughly placeable at the middle of the nineteenth century, when it could claim that, in a hundred years, it had produced, on balance, a surprising advance in material civilization for greatly increased populations. But we must add that from that moment to the present it has been receding from defeat to defeat, beaten ever more and more hopelessly by the social problems created by the very civilization it has built up and the very fecundity it has encouraged. In short, that it began to decay before it reached maturity, and that history will regard capitalism, not as an epoch but as an episode, and in the main a tragic episode, or Dark Age, between two epochs. And, seeing that no individual owner recognizes himself as a dictator, let it be at once added that, as will presently be explained, the dictatorship is a class dictatorship, and each separate capitalist is as helpless in the face of the institution of ownership for private profit as are the wage-earners themselves. His control of the forces of competitive capitalism is, at bottom, no greater than a sailor's control of the wind. But as the institution makes each owner a member of a privileged class, and could be superseded by more advantageous arrangements if the class would give up its privileges, it is not altogether unfair to hold each and every member of the class responsible for the results of these privileges.

The labor and socialist movement of the world is essentially a revolt against the capitalist system of society.

We believe that the most advanced races are to-day, in knowledge, character and intelligence ripe for dispensing with this relation; for the supersession of industrial oligarchy by industrial democracy, and of the motive of pecuniary self-interest by that of public service. We realize that there have been, and over the greater part of the globe still are, other dictatorships more vicious in their motives and more disastrous in their results than the dictatorship of the owners of the instruments of production over the wage-earners. Such are the coercion of slaves by their proprietors, of vanquished races by their conquerors, of whole peoples by autocrats or oligarchies, basing themselves on a monopoly of political power by an individual or by a restricted aristocracy or other minority of race, class or creed. Running in and out of all these systems of oppression, sometimes waning, sometimes waxing, are the domestic tyrannies of the man over the woman, and of the parent over the child. Each of these separate and distinct forms of coercion of one human being by another has been embodied in peculiar economic, political or social laws and conventions: each has provoked, among virile races, its complementary movement of revolt and reform. Socialists, so long as they are true to the democracy in which socialism is rooted, are in sympathy with all these movements and are desirous of promoting them. They realize that, in the normal development of society, the abolition of chattel slavery, the establishment of political democracy, and the emancipation of women, must precede any general adoption of democracy in industry. The existence of one or other of these more obvious despotisms masks the despotism of the owners of the instruments of production over those who are dependent for their livelihood on being permitted to use them, and necessarily diverts attention from the specific evils of capitalism. But the primary purpose of the socialist is to focus attention on the peculiar kind of tyranny now exercised even in the most advanced political democracies, by a relatively small class of rich men over a mass of poor men.

The socialist indictment of the capitalist system of industry, and the society based upon it, has four main counts. History proves that, whilst national poverty may have other causes, whenever and wherever the greater part of the population are divorced from the ownership of the instruments of production, even where the aggregate production is relatively enormous, the bulk of the people live in penury, and large numbers of them are perpetually threatened by starvation. In the second place, this penury and its accompanying insecurity are rendered more hideous and humiliating by the relative comfort and luxury of the proprietary class, and by the shameless idleness of some of its members. The worst circumstance of capitalism is, however, neither the poverty of the wage-earner nor the luxury of the property owner, but, thirdly, the glaring inequality in personal freedom between the propertyless man and the member of the class that "lives by owning." Hour by hour, day by day, year in and year out, the two-thirds of the nation who depend for their daily or weekly housekeeping on gaining access to the instruments of production find themselves working under the orders of the relatively restricted class of those who own these instruments. The sanction for the orders is not legal punishment, but, ultimately, a starvation which is supposed to be optional. That is what is meant by the wage-earners when they complain of "wage slavery." Fourthly, the socialist believes that the very basis of the capitalist system is scientifically unsound, as a means of organizing the production and distribution of commodities and services, and fundamentally inconsistent with the spiritual advancement of the race. . . .

WORLD SOCIALISM RESTATED

by G. D. H. Cole *

REFLECTIONS ON HAVING BEEN A SOCIALIST FOR FIFTY YEARS

I have been a Socialist now for fifty years, ever since I was converted as a schoolboy by reading *News from Nowhere*: and nearly forty-eight years have gone by since, in my first term as an undergraduate at Oxford, I started and edited a Socialist journal. The time seems opportune for looking back, as well as forward, and for trying to see what has happened to the Socialist movement since I joined it half a century ago. First, I have to ask myself why, in those far-off days, I became a Socialist, and what has kept me constant to Socialism ever since — so firmly constant that I have never even for a moment entertained the thought of being anything else. I can still feel the glow of that conversion; and I find no difficulty in giving an account of it. I became a Socialist because, as soon as the case for a society of equals, set free from the twin evils of riches and poverty, mastership and subjection, was put to me, I knew that to be the only kind of society that could be consistent with human decency and fellowship and that in no other society could I have the right to be content. The society

* G. D. H. Cole, *World Socialism Restated* (London: 1957). By permission of *New Statesman and Nation*.

William Morris imagined seemed to me to embody the right sort of human relations, and to be altogether beautiful and admirable; and I decided to work for something as nearly resembling it as appeared possible, without at that stage of my conversion inquiring at all deeply into the ways and means.

That is to say, my initial conversion was essentially idealistic; and my Socialist convictions have always kept this foundation of idealism. I have always seen Socialism, not as historically necessary or determined, but as the embodiment of a social order which all decent men and women ought to want, and have envisaged it as the victory not of a class but of an idea. For this reason, though there is much in Marx's writings that I admire, I have never been a Marxist. I accept the class-struggle as a fact — though a more complex fact than Marx considered it to be. But I take no pleasure in it, save as a means to the classless society that I want to see established. I am, in terms of Engels's famous distinction an "utopian" rather than a "scientific" Socialist; and that makes me scrupulous about means as well as ends, for I do not like hurting people except for very cogent reasons, and I abominate cruelty, even when it is used to support causes I believe to be good.

PEACEABLY IF WE MAY

After all has been said, the case for Socialism is that it stands for a social order designed to maximise happiness and well-being, and to minimise pain and ill-fare; and such an order can exist only if men can learn to treat one another fairly and kindly and not to take pleasure in inflicting pain. They are unlikely to learn such behavior if, in their efforts to rebuild society on a better basis, they allow themselves to take pleasure in hurting those who stand in their way. A community of friends and lovers cannot be built on hatred, or by relying on force and violence as the principal means of bringing it about. In saying this, I am not denying that force and violence may need to be used; but I am saying that they should be used as little as possible, and always with a keen realisation of the harm they do to those who employ them and to whatever is accomplished by their means. The good society cannot be one in which men have become habituated to violence as the normal way of achieving their ends. Where Socialism is established by violence, it will carry the marks of its origin upon it, and will stand in need of great purgation before it can free itself of so evil an inheritance.

I do not believe that there was anything exceptional in the kind of conversion that made me a Socialist fifty years ago. I feel sure that many of my contemporaries who underwent a like conversion were moved by feelings closely akin to mine — at any rate in Great Britain and in other countries in which, broadly speaking, Socialism, as a movement, emerged out of bourgeois Radicalism and there was at least some tradition of free speech and personal liberty. It was probably different in countries which had no such tradition, so that Socialism could develop only as a revolt against the whole established order, and Socialists had to be revolutionaries because oppression left no other way of action open to them. Living in Great Britain, I was never in any doubt that there were elements in the existing society which, far from wishing to destroy, I must wish to carry over intact into the new society and to develop further rather than to replace. I cannot, however, reasonably expect that a citizen of Tsarist Russia or of Hohenzollern Prussia should have had similar feelings — or, more recently, an inhabitant of Germany under the Nazis or of Spain under Franco's rule. For, though there were elements even in these societies — cultural elements — that were worth keeping, they were so overlaid by evil political and economic institutions as to count for little in determining political attitudes among those who cherished ideals of human decency of conduct. I can see why Lenin felt as he did about Tsarist Russia; but I cannot, and never could, feel the same way about Great Britain, much though I revolted against many aspects of the British way of life as I saw it in my early Socialist days.

MORE THAN THE "WELFARE STATE"

And yet, being an idealist, with a vision of a possible society very different from that in which I was brought up, I regarded — and still regard — myself as more a revolutionary than a reformist. For Socialism means to me much more than a "Welfare State" from which the extremes of riches and poverty have been banished, and in which the great majority — or even everyone — is able to enjoy a tolerable standard of material living. To my mind, Socialism connotes equality, not necessarily in the sense of absolute equality of incomes, but in that of a cessation of class-distinctions that hold men apart and prevent them from mixing on equal terms. Accordingly, I want to make an end of the entire system of capitalism, which involves exploitation and class-division and is inconsistent with equal relations between man and man. I am in this sense a "revolutionary" Socialist; but it does not follow that I believe that Socialism can be established only by violent means. That, I think, depends on the situation that exists in each particular country or region, and it is foolish to be dogmatic about it *a priori*, as the Comintern was, at any rate in its early days. But it is equally foolish to proclaim dogmatically that Socialism can only come by the road of parliamentary democracy, as the protagonists of the revived Second International did in their reaction against proletarian dictatorship; for the democratic road may be barred by feudal or capitalist autocracy, so as to leave no way open that does not require resort to violent means. Moreover, even where the parliamentary road is open, it is all too easy for those who follow it to abandon the quest for Socialism and to rest content with such advances towards the Welfare State as can be made without attacking the fundamental inequalities of capitalist society; just as it is all too easy for those who set out to establish Socialism by violent means to sacrifice freedom and equality to the claims of authoritarianism and to mistake their own absolute rule for a higher form of democracy.

I do not pretend that in my early days as a Socialist I was nearly so alive to either of these dangers as I am today. I was, indeed, much more alive to the limitations of reformism than to the possible abuses of revolutionary power. I came into the Socialist movement as a left-winger; and on the left wing I have steadily remained. But I was never under any temptation to become a Communist, as I might have been had I been a Russian, or even a German. It always seemed to me plain commonsense to make the fullest use of parliamentary, and of other non-revolutionary, methods for achieving social reforms, even though such reforms could not, even in the long run, result in the establishment of Socialism; but I wanted the Socialist parties and the trade unions, while following this course, also to attack the fundamental institutions of capitalist society, and not to flinch if they found their attacks countered by violence on the part of their opponents. I was keenly critical of the Labour Party, in its behavior up to 1945, for failing to make any fundamental onslaught on capitalism and for showing far too little willingness to make common cause with the Socialists of other countries in a world crusade for Socialism. But I regarded the methods of Communism as entirely inappropriate to British conditions and to those of other countries in which the parliamentary road was open and freedom of speech and organisation were largely present.

THE LIMITED VISION OF SOCIAL DEMOCRACY

I confess that, in those early days, my vision was in the main limited to the more advanced countries, in which active Social Democratic and Labour movements existed and had considerable freedom of action. It must be borne in mind that when I became a Socialist the Russian Revolution was still in the future and there had been almost no awakening of either Socialism or even popular nationalism in the less developed countries. One envisaged the prospect of violent revolution in Russia, but hardly anywhere else — or, at all events, revolution outside Russia seemed altogether unlikely to take a Socialist form. Apart from Russia, one still thought of Socialism as essentially a movement of reaction against western capitalism and of Socialist policies in terms appropriate to the industrial societies of the West. Since then, mainly as a consequence of events in Russia, there has been a great social awakening in Asia and Africa and to some extent in Latin America; and in this awakening there has been a mingling of nationalist and Socialist elements which has made it imperative both to re-make Socialist thought in far more comprehensive world-wide terms and to revise earlier ideas about nationalism in its relation to Socialism. It is now necessary to envisage the movement towards Socialism as applying not only to highly industrialised societies accustomed to parliamentary government but also to many and highly diverse societies which possess neither developed industries nor any tradition of parliamentary practice; and this makes the older conception of Social Democracy clearly inadequate and even seriously misleading in relation to a great many countries now of importance in world affairs. It may not greatly alter the internal policies of Socialism in the industrialised western countries; but it is bound to affect fundamentally their international policies and the character of Socialism as a world movement.

EQUALITY FOR ALL THE PEOPLES

For one thing, this change has quite altered the character of the long-standing Socialist attack on imperialism and colonial exploitation. As long as there were, in effect, no Socialist or popular nationalist movements in the colonies of the Western powers or in other countries subject to imperialist penetration, Socialists could only protest against the exploitation of the colonial and quasi-colonial peoples and demand fairer treatment of them by their exploiters. Socialist colonial policy was inevitably reformist, and nothing more. But today it has become the plain duty of Socialists in all countries to take their stand energetically on the side of popular nationalism in the colonial and semi-colonial countries and to give full support to the claims of the exploited peoples to self-determination and to the control of their own development, in sharp opposition to all attempts to maintain imperialist rule or to insist on the preferential claims of white settlers or capitalist investors. This involves recognising to the full the human equality of all peoples, to the exclusion of every form of racial discrimination; and, over and above this, it involves allowing high priority to their claim to be helped by the more advanced peoples in the task of raising their standards of life.

The urgency of this claim I, like many other Socialists, have come to appreciate only gradually, as I have watched the rise of the new conscious-ness among the peoples of Asia and Africa. But there are, I fear, many Socialists who have not realised it even now, but continue to think of Socialism mainly in terms of what they hope to achieve by it in their own, relatively advanced, countries, and are even inclined to condone im-perialist policies that appear to work to their own countrymen's advan-tage. Such an attitude appears to me to be both morally false to Socialist principles and disastrous practically, because it leads to colonial wars in which the imperialists are bound to be worsted in the long run and be-cause it forfeits the chance to unite Socialists throughout the world in pursuit of a common ideal of human brotherhood and equality.

In this respect, then, my conception of Socialism has become deeper and broader than it was when I became a Socialist well before the First World War. What I feel about these matters now was, I think, implicit in the attitude I had then; but it was not explicit, or translated into terms of practical policy, as it needs to be now. Among other things, it greatly affects my attitude to Communism as a world movement; and before going further I must do my best to explain what this attitude is. That will be the theme of the next section.

ATTITUDE TO COMMUNISM

What attitude should left-wing Socialists who set a high value on per-sonal freedom and democracy take up towards Communism and the Com-munist parties whose advent has split the working-class movement into contending factions throughout the world? Many Socialists think it enough to assert and practise a thorough-going hostility to Communism and all its works, saying that Communism is a destroyer of democracy and of personal liberty, that it has imprisoned and maltreated millions of its citizens in "slave labour camps," and that it has revealed its true character in the innumerable purges and liquidations of its own leaders for political crimes of which no reasonable person believes many of them to have been guilty. This is indeed a formidable indictment, from which it is impos-sible to escape by attributing all the evil that has been done to discredited individuals, such as Stalin or Beria; for it is evident that the entire Com-munist leadership has been involved, and that many essential features of

Communist rule remain unchanged even now that it has become fashionable to denounce Stalin, as well as Trotsky, and to admit that serious "mistakes" have been made.

THE CASE AGAINST COMMUNISM AND WHAT IT LEAVES OUT

It is a plain fact of history that Communists, wherever they have held power, have been ruthless in suppressing opposition and in maintaining one-party dictatorial rule; that they have been callous about the infliction of suffering on anyone they have regarded as a political enemy or potential counter-revolutionary; that they have engaged in wholesale misrepresentation and often in plain lying about their opponents and have kept from their peoples the means of correcting their false statements by preventing them from acquiring true information; and that they have without scruple betrayed non-Communist Socialists who have attempted to work with them in the cause of working-class unity but have not been prepared to accept complete subjection to Communist Party control. It is no less a matter of history that after the First World War the Comintern, in pursuance of its campaign for world revolution, deliberately split the working-class movement in every country to which it could extend its influence, and thus opened the door wide to the various forms of Fascism that destroyed the movement in many countries — notably in Italy, Germany, and the Balkan States.

Nevertheless, though the indictment is heavy and unanswerable, it is not enough; for it ignores a number of vital facts. The first of these is that the Communists, whatever their vices, did carry through the Revolution in Russia and maintain it against all the efforts of world capitalism to encircle and destroy it, and that the Revolution in Russia did overthrow landlordism and capitalism and socialise the means of production, thus ensuring that the vast increase in productive power which was achieved after the desperate struggles of the early years should accrue in the long run to the benefit of the workers and peasants and should lift Russia from primitive barbarism to a leading position among the world's peoples. The second fact is that the Russian Revolution, though it did not usher in the world revolution for which the Bolsheviks hoped, did largely help to set on foot the great movements for emancipation among the peoples of Asia and Africa which are rapidly transforming the world into a much more equal community and are helping to destroy imperialism and racial discrimination and to attack at its roots the exploitation of the under-developed countries by the more advanced. The third fact is that, despite all the abuses of dictatorship in the Communist countries, it is unquestionable that the life of workers and peasants in Soviet Russia is immensely preferable to what they endured under Tsarism and that their status and opportunities for culture and good living — politics apart — have been immensely advanced.

In the light of these facts, deeply though I disapprove and hate many aspects of Communist rule and philosophy, I cannot regard Communism simply as an enemy to be fought. It is unrealistic to imagine that revolution could have been successfully carried through in Russia or in other parts of Eastern Europe and Asia by the methods of a "liberal" democracy of which no tradition, and for which no basis, existed in these societies, or that on the morrow of the Revolution they could have settled down under liberal-democratic regimes of the western type. Such regimes imply the existence of a readiness to accept the accomplished fact, and to accommodate oneself to it, that simply did not exist in Russia or China or in the other countries which have been conquered by Communism. To say that Russia or China ought not to have "gone Communist" is, in effect, to say that the Russian and Chinese revolutions ought not to have occurred at all; and, far from being willing to say this, I regard these two revolutions as the greatest achievements of the modern world. I do not mean that all the bad things that have been done in these countries since the revolutions have to be accepted as inevitable concomitants of the revolution. I think many of them need not, and ought not, to have happened. But I am not prepared to denounce the revolutions because of the abuses that took place under them: to do so would be sheer treason to the cause of world Socialism. I shall continue to denounce the abuses and to reject the Communist doctrines which are adduced to justify or extenuate them; but at the same time I am firmly on the side of these revolutions against their enemies, whether these enemies are feudal reactionaries, capitalists, or persons who proclaim themselves to be Socialists. . . .

THE ROAD TO SOCIALISM IN GREAT BRITAIN

The British Labour Government, between 1945 and 1950, not only placed on the statute book a number of important measures of social reform but also nationalised a substantial sector of the British economy — coal mines, inland transport, civil aviation, electricity and gas supply, and the Bank of England. In relation to other industries it took over considerable powers of control inherited from the war period; and it made some attempts to introduce a planned economy and to guide economic development into socially useful channels. It continued the high war taxes on large incomes, as well as on certain kinds of consumption; but it made no attack on the rights of property except by progressive taxes on incomes: so that the rich retained their capital wealth, even if it yielded them less income to spend. Nor did it do anything either to attack the rights of inheritance or to prevent the accumulation of new capital in private hands out of business profits placed to reserve — which had become the principal method of accumulating capital. It did not need to take special measures to maintain full employment; for in view of post-war demands labour was scarce in relation to the calls upon it — a situation which put the trade unions in a very strong bargaining position.

In the nationalised industries the Labour Government entrusted the management to state-appointed Boards or Commissions, instructed to pay their way, taking one year with another; and it introduced forms of joint consultation between these bodies and the workers employed, represented by their trade unions. It also set up Consumers' Councils, but gave them only insignificant powers. In practice, though a number of former trade union officials were given seats on the Boards and Commissions, the new managements were not very different from the old ones, except that they represented public monoplies and were obliged to consult their employees in matters of labour policy. There was certainly no fundamental change either in the position of the workers in these industries or in pricing and production policies as a result of nationalisation. Moreover, only one manufacturing industry — steel — was nationalised; and before anything could be done to reorganise it, Labour fell from office and the Conservatives sold it back to private ownership.

WHAT THE LABOUR GOVERNMENT ACHIEVED

Thus, what remained as the legacy of the years of Labour government was a capitalist economic system with a considerable nationalised sector inside it, and also a far-reaching structure of social insurance and other social services, including an extensive National Health Service and a substantial extension of public housing owned by local authorities — in short, not Socialism, but a Welfare State with a sector of public ownership.

I do not undervalue these achievements, which were real and substantial. But when so much had been done, the question was what to do next. Not much room was left for financing additional welfare legislation merely by further taxation of big *incomes*, though some was; and public control over privately owned industries became less and less viable when war controls were allowed to lapse as acute shortages were overcome, so that public planning became less and less effective. Profits were indeed high; but even if the Government had been in a position to take them over instead of allowing them to remain in private hands, most of the money would have been needed for investment in bringing industry up to date and would not have been available for increasing consumers' incomes. It was therefore necessary either to mark time or to make a frontal attack on the roots of economic inequality, so as to deprive the capitalist classes of their property rights.

It had to be admitted that there was little enthusiasm even among the workers for large-scale measures of further nationalisation of the kind already enacted, and that an election campaign fought mainly on this issue was unlikely to succeed, not so much because of the opposition it would arouse as because of the lukewarm reception it was likely to get from most of the voters. Yet only by taking over the more prosperous industries — the chief sources of capital accumulation — could the State gain the effective power to plan economic development or to control the distribution of the wealth produced. The only workable, non-revolutionary alternative to proceeding to nationalise the main industries with compensation to their owners was that of taxing private capital out of existence by some form of capital levy or by the abolition, or drastic limitation, of the right of inheritance — say, by restricting to a small amount what a person could leave to his heirs, and confiscating the rest for the public benefit. Neither a really big capital levy, however, nor a drastic inheritance tax was practicable unless the State took over the actual physical property affected, for clearly private persons would not be in a position to buy it. Thus, by choosing either of these courses, the State would have had to become the owner of a share in practically every business undertaking of any size, and would have had to carry on these undertakings as the partner of the capitalist owners of the shares still in private hands.

THE CASE FOR PUBLIC OWNERSHIP

Many Socialists feel a strong objection to such a policy of state partnership with capitalism, even if it would end up, in the not so long run, with the State as entire owner as more and more shares passed into its hands. But is there, within the limits of non-revolutionary action, any real alternative? Somehow, if Socialism is to come, the means of production must be transferred to public ownership, and the claims of private persons to live on returns from capital ownership must be swept away. And somehow, while the transition is going on, the instruments of production must be kept at work and regularly renewed. If this is done by nationalising one industry after another, with compensation, the problem remains of socialising the new property claims this compensation involves. Surely the right course is to combine the two methods and, while continuing to nationalise further industries, at the same time to take over property rights by levies on capital and on capital gains and especially by drastic taxes on inheritance?

VARIED FORMS OF SOCIALISATION

At any rate, that is my view. But, in order to give this policy a prospect of electoral success, it must be made clear that the purpose is not to create a further series of giant bureaucracies modelled on the existing Public Corporations, but to diffuse power and responsibility over a wide field and to make room for a wide diversity of forms of social ownership and control. There is nothing essentially Socialist in putting an industry under the management of a state-appointed Board with instructions to pay its way, including interest charges on the capital it employs. The great con-sumers' Co-operative Movement, which supplies its members on a non-profit basis, is just as much a form of social ownership as nationalisation, and in some fields is greatly to be preferred. Municipal public ownership, again, is better than state ownership in many branches of industry and service; and producers' co-operation is yet another acceptable alternative form, already in being on a small scale in a number of trades. There may well be other acceptable forms of social ownership and control which can be set going besides these variants. Nor is there any reason why all under-takings should be organised as monopolies, either local or national. There are many industries, made up of firms of widely varying size, that it would be absurd to unify under centralised management, instead of leaving them to compete under forms of public regulation that would prevent them from either exploiting their workers or overcharging the consumers. The capital of such firms could be publicly owned without subjecting them to centralised state management; and many of them could be converted into co-operative or semico-operative undertakings.

The essence of Socialism is not state management or bureaucratic control, which is deservedly unpopular, but the elimination of the claim of capital-owners to levy toll on producers and consumers, so as to constitute an exploiting class. In order to prevent this, it is necessary both to socialise capital and to control the salaries and expense allowances which the "high-ups" in industry are allowed to receive, and, of course, to ensure the payment of the best wages and the granting of the best working conditions society can afford. It is not necessary to enforce a uniform pattern on every sort of enterprise, or to reproduce in nationalised industry an income structure based on that which prevails in capitalist business. This, however, is what a Labour Government has tended so far to do. . . .

THE NEED FOR HIGH PRODUCTION

These, then, are the lines along which I believe the next British Labour Government should proceed. Under it, every worker will need to be asked to give his full co-operation in increasing productivity; for British standards of life cannot be maintained — much less, improved — unless British productivity keeps pace with that of other advanced countries, whatever their economic systems may be. Great Britain needs not only to be able to pay its way, by exporting enough to meet its requirements for imported food and materials, but also to have enough surplus to contribute largely — and, where necessary without payment — to the urgent demand of the underdeveloped countries for capital to speed up their economic growth and enable them to meet their pressing problems of rising population. A Socialist government no more than any other can afford to be slack about productivity: indeed it can do so least of all because its essential purpose is to improve living conditions both for its own people and for the impoverished peoples of the less advanced areas of the world. The workers, however, cannot be expected to rally with enthusiasm to the drive for higher output until they can be assured that the benefits will go to those who need them and not to the enrichment of the employing class or of a new managerial aristocracy that replaces it. For this reason, it is indispensable for a constitutional Socialist Party to make clear its determination to deal drastically with the possessing classes, who not only waste an appreciable part of the national product but, what is much more serious, stand in the way of national and international planning of production in the common service of mankind. . . .

SOCIALISM AND EQUALITY

In the preceding section, in discussing the next steps towards Socialism in Great Britain, I put great stress on the need to give a rapid advance towards social and economic equality a very high place among immediate objectives. I wanted to emphasise the point that, after all the achievements of the "Welfare State" policies adopted after 1945, Great Britain remains a society divided hardly less than before into social and economic classes. This remains true, even if the position of the classes near the bottom has considerably improved and the spendable incomes of many of the rich have been substantially reduced. We have still our so-called "public" schools at which the children of a limited class receive a "superior" education qualifying them for better paid and more prestigeful jobs; and these schools are overfull. Even if wages and earnings have risen faster than living costs, the claims to income of wage-workers and of persons who belong to the upper or professional classes are still judged by entirely different standards: so that no one ever enquires whether a highly skilled manual worker ought to be paid as much as, say, a business manager or a qualified professional engineer. I am not saying that he ought to be: only that the question is never asked. It is not asked, because class-divisions, even if they are blurred at some points, are still taken for granted and hardly questioned even by most workers themselves.

GETTING RID OF CLASS-DIVISION

I am, however, saying that, the more the costs of higher education are met out of public funds, the less case there is for paying large incomes to those who have received it, as if they or their parents had met the cost, and that I believe high incomes of every sort will have to come down. It is sometimes argued that those who stand for a big decrease in economic inequality are illogical if at the same time they defend the payment of higher wages to skilled than to less skilled workers. I do not see the force of this; for I am not arguing for absolute equality of incomes. As long as we continue to need to make use of economic incentives for getting more or better work done, some inequalities of payment will necessarily remain; and I doubt if anyone really believes that we can entirely dispense with such incentives at present. Socialists, however, must I feel wish to reduce over-all differences to the fullest possible extent and to come much nearer to judging all workers by a common standard, excluding all differentiation resting on a basis of social class.

It may be that in the very long run it will become possible to dispense with all monetary incentives and to adopt, if we so wish, a system of distribution "to each according to his needs." But we are clearly still a long way off any situation that would allow this to be done; nor would it, as matters are now, be even in accordance with the sentiment of the main body of rank-and-file workers. Let anyone who doubts this try to persuade a group of skilled workers that the labourers they work with ought to get the same wages as they do. Differences of payment, provided they are not of such magnitude as to set up class barriers and provided they have some real relation to differences of skill or responsibility, do correspond to most men's sentiment of what is fair and just; and it is even desirable that this should be so as long as money incentives continue to be needed. What Socialists require to insist on is not absolute equality of income for all but the combination of a really tolerable minimum standard with the smallest amount of occupational differentiation that is compatible with getting the more exacting jobs adequately manned and performed. What we must beware is lest, in accepting *some* inequality as needful, we throw away the argument for doing away with *class*-differences and allow ourselves to be induced to accept a continuance of differential treatment for persons who are regarded as having different class claims — for example, doctors or accountants as against compositors or engine-drivers or farm-workers or clerks.

THE MANAGERIAL SOCIETY

For evidently a society does not become Socialist merely by turning men and women into public employees, if they continue to be paid and graded much as they would be under a capitalist system. Such a society would be not Socialist, but only State Capitalist — a very different thing. This is the danger that lurks behind the notion of arriving at Socialism by way of piecemeal nationalisation, while adopting for the nationalised industries a social and economic hierarchy modelled on that of the capitalist enterprises that are left in being. How much difference is there, in social structure, between the personnel of the nationalised coal industry or transport service and that of Unilever or I. C. I.? Not, I think, a great deal; for these great private businesses too have passed under the managerial control of men who are much less capitalist owners than highly salaried administrators — men whose social status is not much further removed from that of the main body of their employees than the status of an ordinary coal-miner or railway engine-driver is from that of a member of the National Coal Board or the Transport Commission.

Of course, however great modern industries are organised and whatever the social system of which they form part, there will have to be at their head men entrusted with large powers of leadership and control. But it in no wise follows that these men should be rich, even if they should get rather bigger incomes than those who work under their supervision. If they are rich, as a result either of very big salaries or of excessive expense allowances that enable them to live much more luxuriously than other men, nothing can prevent them from constituting a privileged class and siding for the most part with any other specially privileged groups that are allowed to remain in being.

Socialists, then, can by no means afford to give up being *levellers* — to use a good old word that has gone too much into disuse. One key point at which it is necessary to keep on hitting hard is that of educational privilege. The "superior" classes must simply not be allowed to go on buying for their children a kind of class-education that is designed to encourage snobbery and the anti-social belief that those who have received it are entitled, as of right, to monopolise the more eligible jobs. It is no doubt impossible entirely to prevent children coming from impoverished and under-educated households, especially those with large families, from being to some extent handicapped in their chances of taking advantage of the openings for higher education, even if these are nominally made open to all. But it is possible to do a great deal to raise minimum educational standards and to provide broader highways to further education, as well as to make better provision for the children in big families, so as to give them a less unequal chance.

TOWARDS AN EQUAL SOCIETY

A Socialist society, as I see it, must be one in which there is a fairly close approximation to economic equality, so that no family can be living at a standard either so much above or so much below the common average as to prevent meeting and mixing, economically, on fairly equal terms. Of course, even in such a society there would remain differences of tastes and interests that would prevent universal mixing; but that is quite different from equal intercourse being prevented by economic barriers. However we go to work, it will take a long time to do away with the effects of the old class-barriers and to establish common norms of culture and social behaviour applicable irrespective of class-origins and traditions. The obstacles are bound to be formidable, most of all in the societies in which there is still an almost impassable gulf between illiterate, poverty-stricken peasants and small, educated classes which retain in many cases much of the feudal tradition, but also in the more advanced countries, in which it is easier for individuals to climb over the barriers into a superior class or group. We are all aware that Socialism cannot be made in a day, or made only by a change in the location of economic and political power — though it certainly cannot be made without such a change. An essential part of the building of Socialism is the establishment of a common culture and way of life open to the whole people, and resting on foundations of educational as well as of social and political and economic levelling. Nay more, it is essential that this levelling shall be achieved, not merely within each Socialist society, but over all the world. Socialism cannot be fully achieved in one country irrespective of what is happening elsewhere. It requires a concerted effort to put an end to primary poverty in every country, to open to all peoples the means of taking advantage of the full range of economic and social opportunity offered by the advance of knowledge and of what we are coming to call "scientific know-how." It involves a world war of mankind against want and ignorance, against squalor and disease, waged with all the constructive weapons men possess or can devise to serve the purposes of this great crusade. Finally, because it involves these things, it involves a great appeal to human idealism; for though a large part of the struggle must be against exploitation and the tyranny of men over men and for the achievement of higher material standards of living for the poor and oppressed of all countries, the final purpose is to raise not only the material standard but also the *quality* of human life and to enable mankind to live more nobly and in fuller fellowship as well as better in a material sense.

Every real Socialist knows and feels this. Indeed, we are often so ready to take it for granted as to be almost ashamed to mention it for fear of uttering empty platitudes; and some Socialists react so strongly against high-sounding idealistic phrases as to suspect insincerity whenever they are uttered. Nevertheless, it is impossible to express the spirit of world Socialism without appealing to ethical ideals; for Socialism — international Socialism — is in its essence the expression of a profoundly ethical attitude. Why do we want to establish a world-wide Socialist society? Simply because we believe that no other kind of society is compatible with universal fellowship and the fundamental equality inherent in the Rights of Man as man. . . .

Socialism and Personality

The familiar contrast between Socialism and Individualism has often been taken to mean that Socialism stands for the claims of society against those of the individual. This, however, is a most misleading view. The Individualism to which Socialists are opposed is not that which upholds the rights of the individual human being as such, but that which acclaims the right of a few individuals to ride roughshod over the rest — for example, of the charismatic Führer to impose his leadership regardless of other men's claims, or of the "captain" of industry or finance to pursue his quest of money or power at the expense of his competitors. Such forms of Individualism Socialists do roundly denounce in the name of democratic rights. They are against every claim that involves exalting the "rights" of the few above those of the many, whether the few be represented by a privileged class or caste or by a dominant individual with a lust for personal power and success.

This is an utterly different thing from being against the claims of the individual to seek happiness and well-being in his own way, provided he does not seek them at the expense of his fellow-men. Those who have most blatantly denied this claim have been, not Socialists, but military conquerors, absolute rulers, and also, in these latter days, the heads of great financial concerns, business combines, and predatory imperialist corporations; or they have been groups of men — great landowners, palace politicians, aristocratic castes — who have claimed a presumptive right to have their interests set apart from and preferred to those of ordinary men and women. It is in the cause of the individual as such, and not against him, that Socialists have waged war against all these claimants to a "divine" right to use common men as mere means to their ends.

In the world of today the common man is helpless if he attempts to act alone. In order to assert his claims, he has to make common cause with others who are similarly placed and suffer under an exploitation or imputation of inferiority like his own. Workers in modern industry can make no headway in protecting themselves unless they join together in trade unions for collective bargaining; peasants are helpless unless they form co-operative associations for making purchases in common, for access to the market on fair terms, and for the provision of credit. Nor is it only in the economic field that such common action is needed. Common men need also to join hands in political associations for pressing their claims upon governments, and in due course for bringing government under their own control. They have had to fight, and in some places are still fighting, hard battles for the right to form such combinations. Trade unions have won recognition in most countries only after prolonged persecution by the law, controlled by narrow ruling classes set on preventing the workers from asserting their rights. Even co-operative societies have often been obstructed and repressed by ruling classes determined to keep their peasants in thorough subjection; and, in the political field, the lower classes were until quite recently excluded in most countries from the right to vote, and their political associations violently broken up and their leaders again and again imprisoned, or even executed. These things were done by individualists or on behalf of privileged classes which, far from caring at all for the rights of the individual as such, contemned the common people and treated society as the playground of a superior minority, to which alone any human value was allowed.

EVERY INDIVIDUAL COUNTS

All this is so familiar a story that I need not dwell upon it. The Socialists have been, in one country after another, the protagonists in the struggle to establish the claim of every individual to count in his own right, and not to be treated simply as a means to other men's ends. They have fought, by collective means, for the individual, not against him; and they have stressed the need for solidarity in action only as a means to the recognition of the individual's rights. For example, not Socialists but their strongest opponents have advanced the notion that "Society" — with a big S — is something in itself superior to the individual man, who should find his highest satisfaction in serving it, not as a collection of individual human beings each with his personal and family life to live, but as an embodiment of collective power finding its highest expression in predatory war against other societies. Such ideas have been spread abroad, in our own day, not by Socialists, but by such men as Mussolini and Hitler, who rightly saw Socialism as their greatest enemy and set out ruthlessly to destroy it.

There is, nevertheless, a danger that Socialists, where they become engaged in battle with such evil forces as Fascism and class-autocracy of the Tsarist-Hohenzollern type, may be driven by the pressure of the struggle to adopt doctrines which endanger the rights of common people. Such dangers lurk in all theories that, exalting the class as the agent of social revolution, insist on the need for highly centralised, monolithic discipline as the means of ensuring fully unified action by the class as a whole. It would be quite wrong to accuse the Russians of ever forgetting that the purpose of the new society they have been struggling to build was to raise the quality of living for the great masses of Russian people who had been so bitterly repressed under Tsarism. The vast development of higher education and the immense stress laid on cultural development in the Soviet Union are a sufficient answer to any such accusation. It is, however, undoubtedly true that, in their hard struggle to achieve these advances, the leaders of Soviet society have been led on, or driven, to a denial of the value of free political and economic discussion and to a totalitarian imposition of certain opinions and ways of behavior that are inconsistent with the very freedom they profess to be seeking, and are accompanied by a ruthless dealing with dissidents irreconcilable with decent human relations. This evil tendency found its culminating expression in the so-called "personality cult" of Stalin as the supreme embodiment of the "value" of Soviet society; but it goes deeper than this, and is not to be cured by the substitution of group for personal leadership, if the group simply reproduces the same characteristics of monolithic conformity imposed from above.

WHAT IS A "FREE SOCIETY"?

A free society must be a society within which individuals and groups are free to differ, to give expression to their differences, and to organise for the collective furtherance of their opinions. I admit that a society engaged in civil war cannot be a free society, and that, while a civil war is in progress, the parties to it are forced to resort to ways of acting that forcibly suppress such freedoms. But the civil war in the Soviet Union ended a third of a century ago; and there has surely been ample time for the hard discipline which it required to be done away with. It will be answered that the Soviet Union, for the whole of its existence, has been continuously engaged in a struggle for survival against persistent enemies that have been seeking its destruction, and that this has justified it in maintaining its monolithic society as a necessary instrument of self-defence. I do not agree. I believe the Soviet Union would have been made stronger and not weaker by allowing opinion and policy within it to be formed by free, democratic discussion, both within the Communist Party and beyond it. Monolithic centralisation and suppression of dissident ideas cannot be pursued continuously for nearly forty years without disastrous effects on the minds of those who practise them, or without driving those who are persecuted under them into moods of irrational hatred such as are found among many Russian refugees abroad and, I do not doubt, in Russia too.

Hard lying is an exceedingly bad habit; and Communists have made so much a practice of it as to make it difficult to believe them even when they are uttering plain home truths — as they quite often do. If so many of their own leaders are, as they have told the world, abominable traitors and counter-revolutionary plotters, how is one to trust the rest? All too many of those who have been Communists and have then reacted against Communism appear to have suffered some lasting distortion of mental attitude, from which they cannot escape. "Double talk" and "double think" unhappily go close together.

Anti-Communism engenders similar distortions, even among those who have never been Communist. Some of them smell Communists everywhere, even in the most unlikely places, and are all too ready to brand as a "crypto" — or fellow-traveller — anyone with whom they happen to disagree. I have been so branded myself because, though I have been consistently critical of Communism on the grounds I have stated here, I have always refused to take· sides against either the Russian or Chinese Revolution or to accept as final a breach that divides the world working-class movement right down the middle. Doubtless, I *may* have been lying like a trooper all my life in the secret service of a doctrine I profess to detest; but at any rate *some* evidence is surely needed to back up such an imputation. The extreme anti-Communist, however, seems to need no evidence; and such irrational anti-Communism is especially prevalent in America, including the American trade unions, which have done their best to turn the I.C.F.T.U. into an agency for anti-Communist (and therewith anti-left-wing) propaganda.

SOCIALISM AND FRATERNITY

It is no more true that most left-wing Socialists are crypto-Communists than that most right-wingers are traitors, plotting with the bourgeoisie to compass the defeat of the working class. These mutual charges have the most damaging effects, apart from their sheer untruth. They create an atmosphere of mutual suspicion and hatred out of which a decent human society could not possibly be born, even as the outcome of a Socialist victory. A good society must be one in which, on the whole, men are prepared to trust one another's honesty and to look for ways of working together rather than for matters to quarrel about. A society built in the spirit of hatred and suspicion is bound to bear the marks of its origin, and to be perverted by the means it has made use of. I confess that I dislike and mistrust some of my fellow-Socialists — of the right wing and also of the left; but I do not glory in these sentiments: on the contrary, I try to keep them in check — though they will break out at times. To exalt and make a habit of them is to be false to the spirit of Socialism as a gospel of human fraternity and to poison Socialism at its roots. There are bad men, among Socialists as well as elsewhere; but I believe them to be few. Most of those who do evil in the Socialist movement are not bad men, but decent men perverted by false doctrine.

Of all false doctrines the most perverting is the belief that the knowledge of current policies is the exclusive possession either of a single generalissimo or Führer, or of an *elite* which has the mission of imposing it from above on the common run of the "faithful" and on the mass of the people. Leaders are of course needed to interpret and express plain men's desires better than such men can manage for themselves; and exceptional individuals can be vitally important sources of new ideas, which plain men can take up and adapt to their own ends. But unless discussion is free, leaders cannot interpret plain men's wishes because they cannot know plain men's thoughts; and plain men cannot take up great new ideas because they are kept from knowing about them. The establishment of a Socialist framework of social ownership and the ending of class-exploitation are not the making of a Socialist society, but only the foundations for it. Its making depends on the free play of the human spirit within the new framework; and if authoritarian centralism becomes the cornerstone of the new order the spirit cannot be free. The proper aim of Socialism is to set the human personality free, not to shut it up in a new collective prison.

MAN AND TECHNOLOGY

by Carlo Schmid *

Organic Development or Revolution? . . .

It may often be hard to tell whether one lives in a revolution or in a continuous development. Revolutions may approach on cat's paws and the new reality may not show itself everywhere with equal momentum and clearness. Some revolutions are protracted processes, and in some drastic instances, it was wellnigh impossible to tell the future from the initial steps.

Many phenomena may be explained by reference to the present while, in reality, they mark the first act of an upheaval. A sure sign that we today live in a revolutionary phase is the fact that the equations suited for yesterday do no more resolve themselves without a remainder. Often the awareness of this fact comes too late for man to master his new situation. Unfortunately, people then tend to substitute ideologies and reactionary attitudes for insight and constructive spirit and thus disaster runs its course.

* Carlo Schmid, *The Second Industrial Revolution* (Bonn: 1956). By permission of the Social Democratic Party of Germany.

Is it true that our era has created not just new but really revolutionary forms of production? I believe it is. The release of untold energies from nuclear fission and fusion, automation of many productive processes and electronic computers — these are features totally alien to our previous forms of production.

Work is not just faster and more efficient, we have no evolution but — to use a term from biology — what occurs are mutations. Production methods do not simply undergo modification, but spontaneous off-shoots of traditional methods emerge, techniques designed to reshape existing production processes, techniques which will therefore fundamentally change our social and political order, and perhaps even the very forms of human living.

What was the meaning of the first industrial revolution? It began when coal was first discovered as a source of energy, an event which occurred in England in the middle of the 18th century and in Germany about 130 years ago. It progressed further when James Watt's tea pot developed into a steam engine replacing the muscle power of man and beast as well as the power of water and wind. Suddenly, fewer workers produced more goods. The handicrafts as a form of production were replaced by mass production with its division of labour, permitting the use of unskilled workers and destroying the patriarchal society of craftsmen. New classes of employers and proletarians sprang up, facing each other willy-nilly in bitter class struggle.

The new transport media permitted an unprecedented exchange of goods the world over, and this in turn created the basis for an increase in world population beyond anything Malthus had foreseen. This increase affected particularly those countries which were beneficiaries of this first industrial revolution. The consequences for world politics are not unknown.

No one has better described the characteristics of the first industrial revolution than Marx and Engels in their Communist Manifesto.

But besides, Marx discovered other things. He discovered that this industrial revolution meant more than a turning upside down of current production methods; for him it involved the danger of man's self-alienation to a point where the idea of man and his reality fell apart. The great masses affected by this first industrial revolution would pay for the new splendour not merely by a transitional period of poverty but by a permanent impairment of their human dignity.

Only a change-over from a capitalist economy to a socialist one could create the material bases such that idea and reality of man might tally once more. It was not the deification of matter that prompted Marx and the Labour Movement to ponder over a change in living conditions in this world. Rather was it the sorrow over the degradation of man through merciless interaction of political, economic and social processes. It was the bitterness over the materialism of so-called anti-materialists that made them urge workers to take their liberation into their own hands. In this first industrial revolution, coal and iron replaced water and timber, and it happened that industrial progress and potential became largely tied to certain areas. The coal countries saw a concentration of industry and population. The absence of greater spread led to an increase of productivity in times of good business but also to increased susceptibility to crises, crises which meant mass unemployment and the creation of that human reservoir that would permit employers to keep wages down to minimum sufficient for labour to reproduce.

Politically, this fixed location of progress meant that only coal countries, they are all on the northern hemisphere, had a chance of taking a hand in world politics and of preserving their internal and external independence: in the last one hundred years, only countries along the coal belt have become or remained countries of historical significance. The others continued in their state of industrial underdevelopment even if they had once been the cradle of our civilization.

Certainly, a century later, electricity and the internal combustion engine permitted a greater regional spread of industry and the mechanization of small and medium-sized firms. A new middle class, a new category of qualified manual workers appeared. The national product rose faster than the population. But all this remained within the coordinates from which that epoch took its bearings.

Thus, many of Marx's findings and predictions kept their truth value also for this phase, though not all, since changes in production methods unknown to him and political constellations, while destroying the old middle class, produced a new middle class with small and medium-sized undertakings.

For the same reasons, agriculture remained largely stable. In social and political life, organized labour embarked on a struggle against impoverishment and after great efforts emerged as winners. Gradually, many decades later, the ill-effects of the industrial revolution wrought during its initial decades were mended. This was no automatic process but the result of labour's determination not to surrender but to fight and, through modifying and conditioning the decisive factors of our time, to change this world for the better.

The Labour Movement Faces New Tasks

Now the Labour Movement faces new tasks since it stands at the threshold of the second industrial revolution.

The release of nuclear power permits of much higher energies than the burning of oil and coal or the use of water power will ever yield. But where the mechanical energy available to man increases with the momentum of an explosion, it is not enough to produce more and to produce faster — what is needed are different methods of production. These "different" methods have a revolutionizing impact on man and on politics.

For one thing, through atomic energy also heavy industry is freed from the location of coal deposits. The economist Edgar Salin in Basle has shown that while it took 35,000 tons of coal to produce 100,000,000 kilowatts of electrical energy, and 3,500 freight cars to move the coal needed, in future 35 kilogrammes of enriched uranium is all that is needed to produce that energy, a weight you could stow away in a small suitcase and carry with you on a plane. This is not simply a change in the forms of production, it is an upheaval which will change the face of the earth.

Not tied to a particular habitat, this new source of energy permits in a great way the industrialization of those countries which got left behind in the first industrial revolution. There is no need for huge power lines, no coal mines need be dug, no costly railways built. A few plane loads will suffice to set up the key power stations. And also these new industrial areas will manage with a comparatively small number of technicians, i.e., no huge investments need be made for the training of a great skilled labour force, an incumbency which constitutes a major obstacle for the underdeveloped countries today. Moreover, the new production methods will fit fairly easily into the customary social pattern of those countries. This view can be substantiated.

While the production methods of the first industrial revolution were concentrated in Europe and North America and spread from there to the non-capitalist periphery, those of the second industrial revolution may make this periphery their main habitat. Thus, from this eccentric centre — if this paradox is permissible — a spontaneous transformation of society into a socialist order may take its start. In those countries, only the nation as a whole and not individual capitalists will be in a position to raise the requisite funds, except where foreign capital is invited. This latter case is unlikely in view of the passionate, though peaceful, national consciousness which swerves these so-called underdeveloped countries. Nationalism is merely the concrete form which their social emancipation takes.

Many years ago, the Swiss scholar Adrian Turel hinted at the consequences which would arise if technology were to move away from its original American and European domain to the colonial periphery. Industrialization in the 19th century — to quote Hans Freyer — was due essentially to the "unique phenomenon of European coal production, the white man's labour force, and the technical genius which had arisen in Western man. . . ."

Today, however, it is apparent that "non-white" countries are able not only to use but also to develop industrial technology although they had no part in the origins and the early phases of progress. The industrial development is becoming universal. Industrial development is the magic formula which may over night transform whole continents into modern world powers with a role to play in world history.

Accordingly, Europe and North America are faced with significant dialectical situations and changes. Some may think this to be the beginning "Decline of the West," but the present historic juncture may in my opinion also hold optimistic perspectives for us. At present, the old world is split in two hostile camps. It seems impossible that these two camps should reach a comprehensive settlement. It is possible, however, and in my opinion not utopian, to think that the present underdeveloped countries, through the untold potentialities afforded to them by technology, will more and more assume the role of mediators between the power blocs which so far determined world events. In decisive political issues this group of nations will throw their weight into the balance and affect the course of history. This is how the Asian leaders, largely Socialists, understood their role at the Bandung Conference last year.

This statement brings in a dilemma. These countries will, at least for some time, be dependent on states that will supply them with the new means of production and are ready to be their teachers. Who will this be, the West or the East? It will not be enough for the West to offer material assistance. It will be the loser in the competition with the East unless it is ready to recognize the one social order suitable for these countries, viz. Socialism. Burma, India, China, Indonesia and some others will never again resign themselves to a capitalist system. For them, capitalism would not mean civic freedom and progress but a revival of feudalism with its maharajahs and pashas. They will have too much self-esteem for that.

Socialism is no more restricted to the capitalist core of the world. In Marx' lifetime about a tenth of the world's population lived in industrialized countries. Since then, things have changed. In his day, people believed that our form of capitalism would spread over the whole world. This was a fallacy. The non-capitalist states exhibit an amazing resistance against the formative influence of old and new world capitalism.

A portion of the world's population far outnumbering that of the old industrial key areas has come into proximity of Socialism. These peoples have a world view different from ours. They may be able to infuse Socialist doctrine with conceptions and ideas hitherto alien to it, ideas other than those from English, French and German philosophy, sociology and economic theory.

The second industrial revolution has brushed aside the inescapable sequence of feudalism, capitalism and Socialism as a law of world-wide application. The change-over to Socialism at the periphery of the present capitalist world may occur before the victory of Socialism in the old industrial countries. We should keep an eye on this development, it really concerns us.

A SOCIALIST STATE NEEDED TO SUPPORT PROGRESS . . .

In the atomic age, monopolistic control of markets and of public opinion by uncontrolled and uncontrollable group interests can, under the cover of economic freedom, be practised more and more successfully. This mortal danger to us all can be checked only by subordinating the relevant plant to democratic authority and control and by planning and controlling the business trends of related industries.

Certainly the party of freedom-loving Socialism cannot aim at an abolition of economic freedom; all it wants is to see the inalienable rights of man assured which are greatly endangered in this new age by the travesty of economic freedom afforded by capitalism.

We are faced with a process which compels man to assume his destiny, making himself its master and not its object. Man will succeed only if, like the citizen in the political sphere, he will determine the development of the new processes by planning and consciously choosing his pattern of life. . . .

But, the release of nuclear energy for industrial purposes is not the only factor conducive to a change in our production methods. Perhaps so-called automation will precipitate even greater changes. It will develop faster than atomic energy: almost unnoticed, automation has begun to creep in.

AUTOMATION WILL CHANGE OUR LIVES . . .

The salient point is that in future there will not be factories with automatic machines in them but whole factories will be turned into automatons. In contrast to the first, the second industrial revolution will not only substitute machines for human muscular power but will also replace the human brain by mechanisms. Automatic mechanical devices will direct and control operations and reject defective products without man's help. This continuous qualitative and quantitative self-check is the decisive difference of present-day automation against the former use of automatic machines. . . .

The consequences for the workers will be tremendous; workshops will tend to be small and empty. Demands of a completely different order will be made on a person's qualification and abilities. Industrial production will be entirely different from that of today. It will revolutionize the structure of our society. There is no one who will remain unaffected. Accordingly, employers tend to belittle the significance and speedy advent of automation in the eyes of the public, as the American trade unions have noted. We are witnesses of a soft-pedalling campaign, a device not unknown in employers' circles. Therefore, Walter Reuther, one of the great leaders of the American trade union movement, raised his voice years ago and proclaimed it clearly as one of the most essential aims of the American trade unions to cushion the possible ill-effects of automation by timely measures.

Naturally automation will first make its appearance in big factories for mass-produced goods. But even medium-sized firms are changing over to automation. More and more electronic devices built by the big American firms are installed in medium-sized undertakings. Automation will spread rapidly in offices but also in many production processes of medium-sized plants; in fact, its scope is virtually unlimited. . . .

What will be the consequences?

(1) Automation will cut down on production costs. In anticipation of such savings, management will introduce these new devices. They will in fact be compelled to introduce them more quickly then we today imagine in order to stay in the race.

(2) Production will accelerate, involving a faster turnover of capital.

(3) Automation will economize on labour, or, to put it more bluntly, workers will be dismissed.

(4) There will occur economic readjustments at the factory level; rela-

tions between workers and technicians will change in favour of the latter. It may be that there will be two operatives for each technician.

(5) "Machines are more easily controlled than men" to hint at the words of an American businessman implying controls other than those of a technical nature. . . .

ALL MUST SHARE IN THE ADVANCES . . .

Naturally, every age has its pet utopias. Those of the first industrial revolution were altogether optimistic: machines were to discover man's happiness and make him free. The utopias of our time, on the other hand, are decidedly glum: the new age will degrade man and make him a robot, man will be at the mercy of technocrats while the last remnants of human freedom are sacrificed to the perfection of technology. In his terrifying utopia "1984," George Orwell has drawn a chart of such a world.

But even where no such books stir the minds there exists a general anxiety in the face of all those blessings which technology may have in store for us. The pessimistic outlook on our civilization, the characteristic disease of our age, does not originate with the fear of the H-bomb. One of its causes is rather the dwindling trust in the constructive social forces of industrial development. People fear that the new machines will not liberate them but still further enslave them, turning them into machines themselves — in short, they fear that this self-alienation which prompted Marx to develop his ideas, will worsen.

People fear that technological society may plunge into a new infantile stage and further impoverish their personalities. They fear that they might become the cave dwellers of the age of atomic power and automation; they fear that but for the mathematical and technical capacities of a chosen elite, their creative powers will die out.

In 1954, in his lecture before the Free University of Berlin, F. L. Neumann has made comments on this anxiety which no one will forget who heard or read them. Anxiety could be a warning signal but also a destructive predicament in that it keeps people from getting on their feet again. Finally, anxiety could have a cathartic effect and strengthen the self-confidence of man. Once it becomes clear that he has power to master the sources of danger he would be the better able to decide freely than if he had never passed through trial.

This last statement by Neumann seems to me a good description of the essential problem the second industrial revolution holds for us. In fact the problem is that of how to master the new power so that it will not be turned loose by the sorcerer's apprentice never to be tamed again. Our first task is to visualize some of the effects of automation which are bound to come. There will occur a variety of changes. A number of traditional occupations will have to go, new ones emerge.

A large group of qualified labour, so to speak the aristocracy of the existing working community, will lose its significance. Probably they will come down in station and be constrained to take on jobs way below their former level.

Workers in many industries will be "set free" or in other words dismissed. Some may believe that they can be reabsorbed by the very industries whose products made them redundant. But why should an economy cut down on expense items by creating new ones? If not all-out employment a kind of creeping unemployment will threaten us. Even now the number of workers bears an inverse relation to the rise in production.

Precisely in factories producing electronic apparatus, production per employee has more than doubled within a decade, *i.e.* merely half the employees are needed to maintain the production. The problem of purchasing power will assume new aspects: automation forces on us an economic structure with a fixed level of employment and stable purchasing power on the part of those employed — stability of income will be the motto. There will be comprehensive social rearrangements. Within the working community, salaried employers will increase considerably over manual labour. This involves not only social and sociological problems but — last not least — political ones. We know from decades of sad experiences how difficult it is to organize white-collar workers and to win their support for a party that has sprung from the Labour Movement.

Managerdom will be on the increase. We all are in danger to be victims of a technocracy which is capable to dominate everything and which might make its decisions not for man's sake but with a view to smooth operation of its automatons at the expense of man. These technocrats will have a stronger hold on public opinion than have the managers of today.

This leads us to examine the efficacy of present-day democratic methods. For, where it is only a matter of satisfying needs, a technocratic dictatorship is bound to be superior to democracy with its ethical tenets and its tendency towards compromise. Therefore, the main objective will be to revitalize the spiritual values of democracy, to strengthen the belief in their irreplaceable function, and to make men immune against the absolutist claims of technology. . . .

SPARE TIME — A CULTURAL AND SOCIAL PROBLEM

The main problem will be the fixing of working hours.

The only way to halt the dispossession of human labour by technology is to provide for a steady increase in the amount of spare time. Greater efficiency of human labour permits the introduction of shorter working hours and higher wage rates. . . .

So far, spare time has had three functions. First, it serves to balance tensions and make up for the loss of energy suffered in the industrial production process. Spare time serves the "reproduction of human labour-power" as Marx called it.

Spare time furthermore has meant recreation from the strains of a profession in which a person may be completely absorbed. Naturally, this aspect applies only to a small group of intellectual occupations and positions.

Finally, spare time has served to deaden a feeling of dissatisfaction caused by living conditions. The anaesthetics used are known to us all.

These traditional functions of spare time must needs lose their significance once spare time surpasses the number of hours spent on work in the production process. And accordingly, the problem of spare time takes a central position among the social issues raised by the second industrial revolution. The change in the ratio of working hours to spare time in favour of the latter could mean a change in man's life and being. How so? Hitherto man has been formed and determined by work in plant or workshop. In a society with its division of labour, form and content of dependent work rarely amounted to an "affirmation of his essence," or, to what Marx calls an "act of self-creation or self-objectification." Such work, as Marx shows, alienates man from nature and from himself, from humankind generally, to use Marx' words. In future, man will be formed and determined by freedom and the way he uses his freedom.

In modern society, the process of alienation has seized man because under the division of labour, work took up the major portion of the day. But if working hours come to be less than the amount of spare time, enabling man to make something of himself and to consider his work in the factory as merely complementary, his alienation might disappear. In fact this would lead to a state which Marx describes when he says, man is free when "he intuits himself in a world created by him."

Of course, this hypothesis holds only for the ideal case. There may be factors working in an opposite direction. The actualization of this hypothesis might fail through man's incapacity to use his freedom, or through shortcomings or breakdowns of social forces of integration such as family, church, trade unions, parties, schools etc. In my opinion, dangers in this field can only be overcome and turned to good account through structural changes in our economy along socialist lines. Perhaps we ought to start with such structural changes in order to be able to meet the new reality and channel its tide. I believe we should not wait till the new monster with its merciless demons has forced its law on us. The actualization of the hypothesis outlined might fail because man simply replaces the estranging compulsion to work by another kind of compulsion, viz. a subservience to prefabricated pastimes. Increased spare time will be a boon only if man has enough spiritual and emotional culture to know how to set himself activities without compulsory work to discipline him. Otherwise spare time will be a curse, a curse called boredom: an intellectual and emotional barrenness to which also highly specialized engineers are susceptible. It will not be enough to give people training, we will have to give them an education in the broad sense of the word. It seems highly doubtful that this can be achieved through our present school system. Even now, we must start with reform, for in twenty years' time, present-day teenagers will be exposed to the danger of spare time boredom. We must develop education in such a way that by the age of 30, 40 or 50, future man will know how to use his leisure.

So far leisure was a privilege of the upper classes; in future there could be leisure for all — a state of affairs which would at last invalidate Aristotle's saying that the upper classes fight, govern and philosophize while the common people should be confined to work.

These changes in our educational system should begin with primary schools and be carried through high schools, extension and extramural courses up to the universities. None of these institutions at present fulfil the requirements if we are to master the new era.

Education the way we advocate it cannot be simply intellectual or aesthetic. It must also be moral. It must provide man with fixed standards to determine his relationship to himself and his environment, such that he can be free and yet be an active member of a greater whole.

This broaches the problem of political education. There exists an undeniable affinity between technical intelligence and the mind of a totalitarian ruler, a significant fact of our age. However democracy should be the opposite of mechanical thought.

Education merits the name only if it makes man appreciate freedom not as an idol but as the highest life force, something which alone makes life worth living and which must not be subordinated to any other good, not even to technical progress. Rather does progress find its only justification in that it enables man to free himself from external compulsion.

. . . We cannot surrender the idea of man which is rooted in the notions of freedom, the good and the beautiful. And we cannot but do our utmost to make reality coincide with the idea of man — for if we renounce this aim we cease to be Socialists.

THE TRAGIC PARADOX OF OUR AGE

by Jawaharlal Nehru *

We have many grave internal problems to face. But even a consideration of these internal problems inevitably leads to a wider range of thought. Unless we have some clarity of vision or, at any rate, are clear as to the questions posed to us, we shall not get out of the confusion that afflicts the world today.

I do not pretend to have that clarity of thinking or to have any answers to our major questions. All I can say, in all humility, is that I am constantly thinking about these questions. In a sense, I might say that I rather envy those who have got fixed ideas and therefore need not take the trouble to look deeper into the problems of today.

Whether it is from the point of view of some religion, or ideology, they are not troubled with the mental conflicts which are always the accompaniment of great ages of transition. And yet, even though it may be more comfortable to have fixed ideas and be complacent, surely that is not to be commended, and that can only lead to stagnation and decay. The basic fact of today is the tremendous pace of change in human life. In my own life I have seen amazing changes, and I am sure that, in the course of the life of the next generation, these changes will be even greater, if humanity is not overwhelmed and annihilated by an atomic war.

* Jawaharlal Nehru, "Nehru on 'The Tragic Paradox of Our Age,' " *The New York Times Magazine* (September 7, 1958). Reprinted by permission of *The New York Times* and the *All India Congress Committee Economic Review* (August 15, 1958).

Nothing is so remarkable as the progressive conquest or understanding of the physical world by the mind of man today, and this process is continuing at a terrific pace. Man need no longer be a victim of external circumstances, at any rate to a very large extent. While there has been this conquest of external conditions, there is at the same time the strange spectacle of a lack of moral fiber and of self-control in man as a whole.

Conquering the physical world, he fails to conquer himself.

That is the tragic paradox of this atomic and sputnik age. The fact that nuclear tests continue, even though it is well recognized that they are very harmful in the present and in the future; the fact that all kinds of weapons of mass destruction are being produced and piled up, even though it is universally recognized that their use may well exterminate the human race, brings out this paradox with startling clarity.

Science is advancing far beyond the comprehension of a very great part of the human race, and posing problems which most of us are incapable of understanding, much less of solving. Hence the inner conflict and tumult of our times. On the one side there is this great and overpowering progress in science and technology and of their manifold consequences; on the other a certain exhaustion of civilization itself.

Religion comes into conflict with rationalism. The disciplines of religion and social usage fade away without giving place to other disciplines, moral or spiritual. Religion, as practiced, either deals with matters rather unrelated to our normal lives, and thus adopts an ivory-tower attitude, or is allied to certain social usages which do not fit in with the present age. Rationalism, on the other hand, with all its virtues, somehow appears to deal with the surface of things, without uncovering the inner core. Science itself has arrived at a stage where vast new possibilities and mysteries loom ahead. Matter and energy and spirit seem to overlap.

In ancient days life was simpler and more in contact with nature. Now it becomes more and more complex and more and more hurried, without time for reflection or even for questioning. Scientific developments have produced an enormous surplus of power and energy which are often used for the wrong purposes.

The old question still faces us as it has faced humanity for ages past: What is the meaning of life? The old days of faith do not appear to be adequate in a changing world; living should be a continuous adjustment to these changes and happenings. It is the lack of this adjustment that creates conflicts.

The old civilizations, with the many virtues that they possess, have obviously proved inadequate. The new Western civilization, with all its triumphs and achievements, and also with its atomic bombs, also appears inadequate and, therefore, the feeling grows that there is something wrong with our civilization. Indeed, essentially our problems are those of civilization itself.

Religion gave a certain moral and spiritual discipline; it also tried to perpetuate superstition and social usages. Indeed, those superstitions and social usages enmeshed and overwhelmed the real spirit of religion. Disillusionment followed.

Communism comes in the wake of this disillusionment and offers some kind of faith and some kind of discipline. To some extent it fills a vacuum. It succeeds, in some measure, by giving a content to man's life. But, in spite of its apparent success, it fails, partly because of its rigidity, but even more so because it ignores certain essential needs of human nature.

There is much talk in communism of the contradictions of capitalist society, and there is truth in that analysis. But we see the growing contradictions within the rigid framework of communism itself. Its suppression of individual freedom brings about powerful reactions. Its contempt for what might be called the moral and spiritual side of life not only ignores something that is basic in man but also deprives human behavior of standards and values. Its unfortunate association with violence encourages a certain evil tendency in human beings.

I have the greatest admiration for many of the achievements of the Soviet Union. Among these great achievements is the value attached to the child and the common man. Their systems of education and health are probably the best in the world. But it is said, and rightly, that there is suppression of individual freedom there. And yet the spread of education in all its forms is itself a tremendous liberating force which ultimately will not tolerate that suppression of freedom. This again is another contradiction. Unfortunately, communism became too closely associated with the necessity for violence and thus the idea which it placed before the world became a tainted one. Means distorted ends. We see here the powerful influence of wrong means and methods.

Communism charges the capitalist structure of society with being based on violence and class conflict. I think this is essentially correct, though that capitalist structure itself has undergone, and is continually undergoing, a change because of democratic, and other, struggles and inequality.

The question is how to get rid of this and have a classless society with equal opportunities for all. Can this be achieved through methods of violence, or can it be possible to bring about those changes through peaceful methods?

Communism has definitely allied itself to the approach of violence, even if it does not indulge normally in physical violence. Its language is of violence, its thought is violent and it does not seek to change by persuasion or peaceful, democratic pressures, but by coercion and, indeed, by destruction and extermination. Fascism has all these evil aspects of violence and extermination in their grossest forms and, at the same time, has no acceptable ideal.

This is completely opposed to the peaceful approach which Gandhi taught us. Communists, as well as anti-Communists, both seem to imagine that a principle can be stoutly defended only by the language of violence, and by condemning those who do not accept it. For both of them there are no shades; there is only black and white. That is the old approach of the bigoted aspects of some religions.

It is not the approach of tolerance, of feeling that perhaps others might have some share of the truths also. Speaking for myself, I find this approach wholly unscientific, unreasonable and uncivilized, whether it is applied in the realm of religion or economic theory or anything else. I prefer the old pagan approach of tolerance, apart from its religious aspects. But whatever we may think about it, we have arrived at a stage in the modern world where an attempt at forcible imposition of ideas on any large section of people is bound ultimately to fail. In present circumstances, this will lead to war and tremendous destruction. There will be no victory, only defeat for everyone. Even this we have seen in the last year or two — that it is not easy for even great powers to reintroduce colonial control over territories which have recently become independent.

This was exemplified by the Suez incident in 1956. Also, what happened in Hungary demonstrated that the desire for national freedom is stronger even than any ideology and cannot ultimately be suppressed. What happened in Hungary was not essentially a conflict between communism and anti-communism. It represented nationalism striving for freedom from foreign control.

This violence cannot possibly lead today to a solution of any major problem because violence has become much too terrible and destructive. The moral approach to this question has now been powerfully reinforced by the practical aspect.

If the society we aim at cannot be brought about by big-scale violence, will small-scale violence help? Surely not, partly because it produces an atmosphere of conflict and of disruption. It is absurd to imagine that out of conflict the social progressive forces are bound to win. In Germany, both the Communist party and the Social Democratic party were swept away by Hitler. This may well happen in other countries too. In India, any appeal to violence is particularly dangerous because of its inherent disruptive character. We have too many fissiparous tendencies for us to take risks. But all these are relatively minor considerations. The basic thing, I believe, is that wrong means will not lead to right results, and that is no longer merely an ethical doctrine but a practical proposition.

Some of us have been discussing this general background and, more especially, conditions in India. It is often said that there is a sense of frustration and depression in India, and that the old buoyance of spirit is not to be found at a time when enthusiasm and hard work are most needed. This is in evidence not merely in our country. It is, in a sense, a world phenomenon. An old and valued colleague said that this is due to our not having a philosophy of life and, indeed, the world also is suffering from this lack of a philosophical approach.

[The old colleague referred to is Dr. Sampurnanand, Chief Minister of the state of Uttar Pradesh.]

In our efforts to ensure material prosperity we have not paid any attention to the spiritual element in human nature. Therefore, in order to give the individual and the nation a sense of purpose, of something to live for and, if necessary, die for, we have to revive some philosophy of life and give, in the wider sense of the word, a spiritual background to our thinking.

We talk of the welfare state and of democracy and socialism. They are good concepts but they hardly convey a clear and unambiguous meaning. This was the argument, and then the question arose as to what our ultimate objective should be. Democracy and socialism are means to an end, not the end itself. We talk of the good of society. Is this something apart from, and transcending, the good of the individuals composing it? If the individual is ignored and sacrificed for what is considered the good of the society, is that the right objective to have?

It was agreed that the individual should not be so sacrificed and, indeed, that real social progress will come only when an opportunity is given to the individual to develop, provided the individual is not a selected group but comprises the whole community. The touchstone, therefore, should be how far any political or social theory enables the individual to rise above his petty self and thus think in terms of the good of all.

The law of life should not be the competition of acquisitiveness but cooperation, the good of each contributing to the good of all. In such a society, the emphasis will be on duties, not on rights; the rights will follow the performance of the duties. We have to give a new direction to education and evolve a new type of humanity.

This argument led to the old pedantic conception that everything, whether sentient or insentient, finds a place in the organic whole, that everything has a spark of what might be called the divine impulse, or the basic energy of the life force which pervades the universe. This leads to metaphysical regions which tend to take us away from the problems of life which face us.

I suppose that any line of thought sufficiently pursued leads us in some measure to metaphysics. Even science today is almost on the verge of all manner of imponderables. I do not propose to discuss these metaphysical aspects, but every argument indicates how the mind searches for something basic and underlying the physical world. If we really believed in this all-pervading concept of the principle of life, it might help us to get rid of some of our narrowness of race, caste or class and make us more tolerant and understanding in our approaches to life's problems. But obviously it does not solve any of these problems, and in a sense we remain where we were.

In India we talk of the welfare state and socialism. In a sense, every country, Socialist or Communist, accepts the ideal of the welfare state. Capitalism, in a few countries at least, has achieved this common welfare to a very large extent, though it has far from solved its own problems and there is a basic lack of something vital. Democracy allied to capitalism has undoubtedly toned down many of its evils and, in fact, it is different now from what it was a generation or two ago.

In industrially advanced countries there has been a continuous and steady upward trend of economic development. Even the terrible losses of world wars have not prevented this trend in so far as these highly developed countries are concerned. Further, this economic development has spread, though in varying degrees, to all classes. This does not apply to countries which are not industrially developed. Indeed, in those countries, the struggle for development is very difficult and sometimes, in spite of efforts, economic inequalities not only remain but tend to become worse.

Normally speaking, it may be said that the forces of a capitalist society, if left unchecked, tend to make the rich richer and the poor poorer, and thus increase the gap between them. This applies to countries as well as groups or regions or classes within the countries. Various democratic processes interfere with these normal trends. Capitalism itself has, therefore, developed some socialistic features even though its major aspects remain. Socialism, of course, deliberately wants to interfere with the normal processes, and this not only adds to the productive forces but lessens inequalities. But what is socialism? It is difficult to give a precise answer, and there are innumerable definitions of it. Some people probably think of socialism vaguely just as something which does good and which aims at equality. That does not take us very far.

Socialism is basically a different approach from that of capitalism, though I think it is true that the wide gap between them tends to lessen because many of the ideas of socialism are gradually incorporated even in the capitalist structure. Socialism is, after all, not only a way of life but a certain scientific approach to social and economic problems. If socialism is introduced in a backward and underdeveloped country, it does not suddenly make it any less backward. In fact, we have a backward and poverty-stricken socialism. Unfortunately, many of the political aspects of communism have tended to distort our vision of socialism. Also the technique of struggle evolved by communism has given violence a predominant part.

Socialism should, therefore, be considered apart from these political elements or the inevitability of violence. It tells us that the general character of social, political and intellectual life in a society is governed by its productive resources. As those productive resources change and develop so the life and thinking of the community changes.

Imperialism, or colonialism, suppressed, and suppresses, the progressive social forces. Inevitably, it aligns itself with certain privileged groups or classes because it is interested in preserving the social and economic *status quo*. Even after a country has become independent, it may continue to be economically dependent on other countries. This kind of thing is euphemistically called having close cultural and economic ties.

We discuss sometimes the self-sufficiency of the village. This should not be mixed up with the idea of decentralization, though it may be a part of it. While decentralization is, I think, desirable to the largest possible extent, if it leads to old and rather primitive methods of production, then it simply means that we do not utilize modern methods which have brought great material advance to some countries of the West. That is, we remain poor and, what is more, tend to become poorer because of the pressure of an increasing population.

I do not see any way out of our vicious circle of poverty except by utilizing the new sources of power which science has placed at our disposal. Being poor, we have no surplus to invest; we sink lower and lower.

We have to break through this barrier by profiting by new sources of power and modern techniques. But, in doing so, we should not forget the basic human element and the fact that our objective is individual improvement and lessening of inequalities; and we must not forget the ethical and spiritual aspects of life which are ultimately the basis of culture and civilization and which have given some meaning to life.

It has to be remembered that it is not by some magic adoption of the Socialist or capitalist method that poverty suddenly leads to riches. The only way is through hard work and increasing the productivity of the nation, and organizing an equitable distribution of its products. It is a lengthy and difficult process. In a poorly developed country, the capitalist method offers no chance. It is only through a planned approach on Socialist lines that steady progress can be attained, though even that will take time. As this process continues, the texture of our life and thinking gradually changes.

Planning is essential for this because, otherwise, we waste our resources, which are very limited. Planning does not mean a mere collection of projects or schemes but a thought-out approach of how to strengthen the base and pace of progress so that the community advances on all fronts. In India we have a terrible problem of extreme poverty in certain large regions, apart from the general poverty of the country. We have always a difficult choice before us: whether to concentrate on production by itself in selected and favorable areas, thus for the moment rather ignoring poor areas, or try to develop the backward areas at the same time, so as to lessen the inequalities between regions. A balance has to be struck and an integrated national plan evolved.

That national plan need not — and, indeed, should not — have rigidity. It need not be based on any dogma; but should rather take the existing facts into consideration. It may — and, I think, in present-day India it should — encourage private enterprise in many fields, though even that private enterprise must necessarily fit in with the national plan and have such controls as are considered necessary.

Land reforms have a peculiar significance because without them, more especially in a highly congested country like India, there can be no radical improvement in productivity in agriculture. But the main object of land reforms is a deeper one. They are meant to break up the old class structure of a society that is stagnant.

We want social security, but we have to recognize that social security comes only when a certain stage of development has been reached. Otherwise, we shall have neither social security nor any development.

It is clear that, in the final analysis, it is the quality of the human beings that counts. It is man that builds up the wealth of a nation, as well as its cultural progress. Hence, education and health are of high importance so as to produce that quality in human beings. We have to suffer here, also, from lack of resources, but still we have always to remember that it is right education and good health that will give the foundation for economic as well as cultural and spiritual progress.

A national plan has this as both a short-term objective and a long-term one. The long-term objective gives a true perspective. Without it, short-term planning is of little avail and will lead us into blind alleys. Planning will thus always be perspective planning, and hard, in view of the physical achievements for which we strive. In other words, it has to be physical planning, though it is obviously limited and conditioned by financial resources and economic conditions.

The problems that India faces are, to some extent, common to other countries, but much more so; there are new problems for which we have not got parallels or historical precedents elsewhere. What has happened in the past in the industrially advanced countries has little bearing on us today. As a matter of fact, the countries that are advanced today were economically better off than India today, in terms of per capita income, before their industrialization began.

Western economics, therefore, though helpful, has little bearing on our present-day problems. So also has Marxist economics, which is in many ways out of date, even though it throws considerable light on economic processes. We have thus to do our own thinking, profiting by the example of others, but essentially trying to find a path for ourselves suited to our own conditions.

In considering these economic aspects of our problems, we have always to remember the basic approach of peaceful means; and perhaps we might also keep in view the old pedantic ideal of the life force which is the inner base of everything that exists.

THE ROAD OF MAPAI

by Mordecai Nesayahu *

How does one differentiate between political parties? How does one evaluate political parties? Logic dictates that we do so on the basis of three major criteria:

A. The goals that the parties aim to achieve.

B. The means whereby they aim to achieve these goals . . .

C. And, finally, the extent and the manner in which these avowed goals are achieved when the party attains power.

We shall attempt to evaluate the road taken by Mapai — differentiating between it and other parties — in the light of these three questions. . . .

* Mordecai Nesayahu, *The Road of Mapai*, booklet distributed by the Mapai Information Department, Tel Aviv, Israel, translated especially for this volume by Erwin A. Tomaschoff. Notes regarding the political complexion of certain other Israeli political parties are included in the text; however, some brief comments on Mapai may prove to be of assistance to the student. Mapai, or the Israel Labor Party (Mifleget Poalei Eretz Israel) is described as "A Zionist Socialist party aiming at the ingathering of the Jewish People from the Diaspora, the upbuilding of the State of Israel, and a socialist regime founded on spiritual and political freedom." Its present leaders were foremost among those instrumental in creating the new state of Israel, and Mapai has been dominant in the national legislature of Israel, the Knesset. Of the 120 members of this Assembly, Mapai has, under a system of proportional representation, furnished from 40 to 47 members. It governs, therefore, through a coalition with certain other parties, as is indicated in the text. Of the sixteen or so cabinet portfolios within the coalition government of 1955, Mapai held nine, Mapam held two, and three other parties shared the remaining five. See *Facts and Figures*, Israel Office of Information, 1955, pp. 20ff.

PART A: THE GOALS

Although Mapai's national and social goals are closely interwoven, thus nurturing one another, we shall attempt, for the purposes of our analysis to define them separately.

The purpose of our many national goals is to provide a basis for and to nourish the general framework of national activity, and these goals are identical, in their broadest outlines for most of Israel's political parties, with the exception of the Communists on the one hand and Herut [an extremist party of the right] on the other, much as the latter two parties differ from each other. In contrast, the purpose of Mapai's social goals is to mold the character of the overall national framework, that is, of the developing state — in the light of a social goal that is unique to Mapai. . . .

WHAT ARE MAPAI'S UNIQUE SOCIAL GOALS?

A. PLACING THE NATIONAL ECONOMY AT THE DISPOSAL OF PUBLIC OWNERSHIP:

Public ownership does not necessarily mean nationalization. It includes nationalization, but does not necessarily call for it in each and every case; it embraces different forms (as appropriate for differing types of property) of ownership frameworks that are subjected either to public ownership or to public control, in both cases to either a greater or a lesser extent. State ownership should apply in the case of natural resources, power sources, key industries and essential public services. Ownership could take the form of [co-operative] ownership by the plant's workers in the case of branches of the economy where the industry's economic-technical character makes this possible. And it could and should take the form of more widespread ownership (i.e., not limited just to the plant's workers), but not too widespread (such as in the case of state ownership) — on a geographic or functional basis — in the case of enterprises where the cooperative form is not possible and state ownership not necessary. Only a varied combination such as this of the forms and extent of public ownership can avoid the pitfalls involved on the one hand in complete centralization (in the case of general state ownership), and on the other hand in the domination by the cooperatives (in the case where ownership resides exclusively in the plant's workers). Whether at the center of the national economy's circle stands the nationalized segment of the economy and whether at its circumference stands the cooperative segment, the main thing is that inside of the circle public ownership must be included in its differing forms — this is required for economic and technical development, and it is indicated by the unique experience of the Israel workers' movement. The above approach does not, however, preclude the continued existence of various forms of private ownership subject to government legislation and supervision in many branches of the economy.

Mapai sees as its special duty the development of the public sector of the economy. However, in its responsibility for the entire national economy, it welcomes and encourages any initiative on the part of private capital in the development of the national economy.

B. FROM THE PUBLIC NATURE OF OWNERSHIP OF THE ECONOMY SPRINGS THE DESIRABLE CHARACTER OF ITS MANAGEMENT:

Not the possession of capital, but rather the possession of skill, education and training should be the criteria in the choice of management. The interests of the public lie in the economic success of the nation's undertakings, which is also the key to social welfare. But there can be no economic success without effective management, just as there cannot be effective management in a modern economy without education and training — reinforced, of course, by suitable personal traits, talents, experience, and pioneering initiative.

C. PUBLIC OWNERSHIP CALLS FOR PUBLIC SUPERVISION OF MANAGEMENT NO LESS THAN IT CALLS FOR PROFESSIONAL-SCIENTIFIC MANAGEMENT:

Not only in the ownership of capital or land, but also in the possession of talent and knowledge there lurks the danger of the crystalization of [socio-economic] classes, of their isolation, and of the barring of control and [personnel] replacement. In a stratified society, a situation such as this is justified. But under public ownership this is a danger that must be fended off by constant public control. And while it is not ideal that party channels have the decisive voice in the appointment of management, they are, nevertheless, the only means of ensuring freedom of expression, organization, and the selection and control of the public councils that have supervision over management.

The degree of wage and salary differentials, and the criteria for their determination, are not matters that can be rigidly determined. They change with changing needs and changing opportunities. The duty of public supervision is to see that the power of decision in these matters is in the hands of public representatives, and not in the hands of the mana-

gers with regard to themselves. And the other function of public supervision — within the framework of public ownership of the economy — is
to ensure equal opportunities to all young people and to all talented
workers who are willing to devote themselves to studies that will give
them the education and practical training needed to enable them to ascend
the managerial ladder.

A publicly owned economy which combines in its structure the element
of public socialistic ownership, not present in a capitalist economy, with
that of democratic public control, not present in a Communist economy,
has from a national-social standpoint, an advantage not only over a
private economy but also over a state owned economy. In contrast to the
private economy, the profits of the public economy do not flow into the
private hands of the capitalists. Instead they are invested, for the major
part, in the development of the economy, while a minor portion is allocated to the satisfaction of various social needs, in accordance with the
decisions of the public's representatives. Of course, the owner of the
private enterprise may also reinvest the major portion of his profits in
the development of the economy, thereby contributing to the public
welfare. But not only is it true that most private capitalists, at least in
Israel, do not do this in practice, but, also, the structure of the private
economy is such that it permits owners to prefer their own interests over
the general-national or general-social interests. On the other hand, the
structure of the public economy, to the extent that it is true to itself, prefers the interests of developing the economy and of public service over
private interests, whatever they may be.

The advantage of a system of public ownership over one of state ownership — even when the latter is not absolute (an absolute system of state
ownership is not consistent with a democratic regime) — is that it is not
dependent, as under a system of public ownership, upon the government
budget.

A relative lack of dependence of the economy — and especially a public
economy — on the state, on the one hand, and upon the workers, on the
other hand, is essential to its economic development. Even where the
economy is state owned, in the one case, or cooperatively owned, in the
other, it is possible and necessary to ensure a certain measure of independence of this type. However, it is in the publicly owned economy in
its various forms (geographic area ownership, ownership by the entire
movement, ownership by all the workers of a specific section of the
economy, etc.) — where ownership is neither too limited, as in the co-
operative economy, and also not too wide, as wider state ownership — that

both the capacity for economic development and the efficacy of public control will tend to be the highest. The Israel Labor movement, more than any other labor movement in the world, has proved the essential and central role of the public economy in the upbuilding of a socialist-democratic regime.

NEITHER THE RIGHTIST NOR THE LEFTIST PARTIES SHARE WITH
MAPAI IN THIS CONCEPT OF THE STRUCTURE OF
A WORKERS SOCIETY:

The parties on the right . . . stand for private ownership. They also — to a lesser or greater extent — represent the interests of private capital in Israel. Mapai, on the other hand, not only stands for public ownership, but also sees capitalism as a means of denying society, both in theory and in practice, the opportunity to determine, as far as possible, its own destiny — especially in so vital an area as economics. . . .

The leftist parties . . . as long as they continue to identify themselves with the ideas of Marxism and Leninism also stand for public ownership of the economy, but they identify it with "the dictatorship of the proletariat," which is nothing but a dictatorship by one party — the so-called "Proletariat Party" — over the proletariat; a dictatorship that is the very antithesis of public ownership and control. Mapai not only stands for democracy, but also decries Communism as a dictatorial regime that deprives society, in practice and basically also in theory, of the opportunity to determine, as far as possible, its destiny in both the political and economic arenas. If it is true that the state is the means for social domination of the economy, and if the state itself is not subject to social control, then there is anyway a lack of [public] control of the economy — an even smaller measure of social control than exists today under a capitalistic regime.

The events of the past years in the U.S.S.R. have created ideological chaos . . . in the Communist camp, and among its admirers throughout the world. Stalin's most dastardly crimes were justified and explained away at the time by his followers. . . . Only the denunciation of these crimes by Stalin's heirs and the destruction of the Stalin myth by them could have brought about the confusion that we witness today. But all the latest events — including the violently anti-Israel and anti-Jewish line taken by Stalin's heirs — have not yet had the impact of eliciting from Ahdut Haavodah and Mapam [two political parties to the left of Mapai in Israel] more than reservations with regard to various disclosures of the Communist regime. These two parties have not yet shown in their ranks the degree of spiritual freedom and public courage needed to make a thorough and far-reaching ideological soul searching. . . .

Mapam continues to espouse "revolutionary socialism," in contrast to democratic socialism. It sees, as in earlier days, the Soviet regime as a basically socialist one. But Mapam's new platform completely ignores, and thereby implicitly answers in a "revolutionary Soviet" manner, one decisive question in the debate between democratic socialism and "revolutionary socialism" (as Mapam calls Communism today). The question is: should there be exclusive domination by one party and one party alone, or should there be political and spiritual freedom including freedom of party organization? The exclusive domination of the U.S.S.R. by the Communist Party is both a root and an expression of the tyranical regime of a monopolistic class which holds all the positions of power in Soviet society to an extent that is unparalleled by any other ruling class either at the present time or in the past. Most of the special privileges of this class are protected by the Communist Party's position of exclusive domination, and they will disappear with the collapse of the party dictatorship.

All the talk about "democratization" by the Soviet regime in Russia today — which is echoed in Mapam's platform — is without basis and is nothing but an insult to plain good-sense in the absence of democratic party politics in one of the forms existing in the Western world. But even in its new platform, Mapam's theory of Socialism has not yet reached this conclusion, despite the fact that in Israel Mapam in practice naturally supports all the forms of Western democracy. . . .

Both capitalism and communism — which presented itself as a social alternative to capitalism, but actually turned out to be only an economic alternative with reference to the implementation of the industrial revolution — are undergoing processes of basic internal change. There is a trend toward centralization in the decentralized capitalist economy, and a trend toward decentralization in the centralized Communist economy. There is a trend toward greater attention to demand — alongside the stress on production — under both forms of economy. And there is a trend toward stressing the scientific-professional element, which is struggling to free itself from the custody of capital under the capitalist regime and from the custody of political party bureaucracy under the Communist regime. Democratic socialism — even if it is, from the viewpoint of organizational strength, only a marginal factor in the world's regimes — constitutes not only the desired social alternative, but also the realistic substantive-internal alternative (on the backdrop of the processes of internal change) to the two world powers — to the extent that their leaderships steer them not toward atomic war, but rather toward atomic peace

Figuratively speaking, we may say that Mapai accepts neither Communism, which stands for paradise in heaven and hell on earth, nor capitalism, which means acceptance of the rocky terrain as it now essentially is — but, rather, democratic socialism, which calls for a slowly blossoming garden, cultivated, despite hardship and problems, successes and failures, on a terrain that is covered with many rocks.

It is no accident that the special task that faced the Zionist movement — the creation of a national society from its very foundations — was fulfilled mainly not by Jewish capitalism and certainly not by Jewish Communism, but rather by socialistic Zionism. Capitalism, unguided, anarchic, and intent only upon profit, was not suitable for laying the well thought out and planned foundations of basic sectors in agriculture, industry and services. It followed the lead of the public economy. And Communism was not consistent with a national movement based, first and foremost, upon voluntary effort, not only because of Communism's hostility toward Zionism, but also because of its very centralized nature, based upon coercion and lacking freedom. The national-public capital and the enterprising and organized labor that joined in creating a public economy — the fruit of socialistic Zionism's vision and initiative — were the pioneers in building up the new national society in the Land of Israel. From this viewpoint, Mapai's road is not a typical social-democratic one. In addition to being social-democratic with reference to the private economy in Israel, Mapai is the party of economic and public service development, the party of constructive socialism, and it serves as an example to its sister parties — the social-democratic parties of the world, and first and foremost of Asia and Europe. . . .

IV. COMMUNISM

"EVERYTHING happened differently in the U.S.S.R. and other Communist countries from what the leaders — even such prominent ones as Lenin, Stalin, Trotsky, and Bukharin — anticipated. They expected that the state would rapidly wither away, that democracy would be strengthened. The reverse happened. . . ." [1]

This *Marxist* indictment of Soviet Communism was penned by the former Communist Vice-President of Yugoslavia under the Tito regime. Its author, Milovan Djilas, has been considered a leading Yugoslavian Marxist theoretician and was, until quite recently, one of the heroes of world Communism. His increasingly bitter denunciation of both the Soviet and the Yugoslavian Communist regimes, and his approval of the heroic Hungarian revolution of 1956, may be considered as marking yet another in the series of grave crises with which the Communist movement has been recently faced. What is the background of these crises?

Following its costly but ultimately successful defense against the Nazi invasion, the Stalin regime succeeded in consolidating its power within the Soviet Union and achieved marked success in extending its sway over formerly independent peoples and territories. A galaxy of satellites were brought into the Soviet orbit, essentially through a combination of military and economic pressures, while the provision of personnel, funds, and other assistance furthered the cause of Communist parties in lands not contiguous to the "Socialist Fatherland." These gains were halted, at least temporarily, by the successful United States–United Nations defense of South Korea which was followed shortly by the death of Stalin in 1953. Stalin's unmourned death gave rise to the expected scramble for power on the part of his former subordinates, with the subsequent five year period having been marked by brutal infighting at the highest level of the party

[1] Milovan Djilas, *The New Class* (New York: Frederick H. Praeger, Inc., 1957), p. 37. For an abridgment of the central chapter of his book see the last selection in Part IV.

hierarchy,[2] not only within the Soviet Union, but also in the Communist parties throughout the world. A further deterrent to expansion of the Soviet sphere have been the abortive, but nonetheless significant, uprisings in parts of East Germany and Poland, with the Hungarian revolution of November, 1956 having assumed national proportions. There is considerable evidence that the ferment of discontent continues to be a factor of enormous importance, both within the U.S.S.R. and its satellites and in their relationship with the non-Communist world.

As Stalin's iron grip of the Soviet state and party was broken by death, there was also pierced the aura of menacing inscrutability with which he had veiled Russia during the decades of the 1930's and 1940's. As more sustained contact has been achieved, there has developed a soundly based realization of some of the internal difficulties faced by Soviet society, and recent years have seen a stream of valuable and authoritative writings on various aspects of life in the Soviet Union. We have now, for example, considerable evidence on the shortcomings of the Soviet collective farms; we know of the perennial difficulties encountered in achieving balanced production of basic commodities; the position and condition of labor in the U.S.S.R. These and many other internal problems and contradictions in that society are now much better understood.

The overall effect — especially of the most recent events and revelations — has been that of finally shattering the illusion of Communist monolithic singleness of purpose. Revealed now to the view and consideration of outsiders are some of the continuing crises of Communism. What is their nature, their extent, their precise significance? On the answer to these questions may very well turn the foreseeable future of Western civilization and the fate of a substantial portion of the world's people. A sobering reflection, to be sure, and rather astonishing when one recalls that it has been but little over a century since Karl Marx and Friedrich Engels warned that "A spectre is haunting Europe — the spectre of Communism." [3] At the time of this bold pronouncement in 1848 the frail apparition of Communism was easily suppressed by a small body of gendarmes, and it failed to realize any significant political successes during the remainder of the nineteenth century. Though defeated in its revolutionary moves and divided by countless schisms, the specter of Com-

---

[2] For some of the details of the intra-party struggle see the next-to-last selection in Part IV, *Crimes of the Stalin Era*, especially the concluding footnote.

[3] The *Manifesto* was, in fact, written by Marx and Engels as the platform of the "Communist League," a workingmen's association, the Central Board of which was hunted out by the Prussian Government shortly after publication of this document. The members of the Central Board were arrested, tried, and a number of them received prison sentences following the famous "Cologne Communist trial" in 1852.

munism continued to haunt Europe, attracting an assorted host of adherents. Its infusion in the Bolshevik formulation into the Russian polity,
and the subsequent development of that country, has certainly been of
utmost importance in drawing new adherents to Communism. But the
continued successes of the movement cannot be explained simply in terms
of the rebirth of Russian technological and military strength. The significance and challenge of Communism has long since transcended the Soviet
state. Marx's specter now permeates the world atmosphere, a development
dramatically symbolized by the orbiting Sputniks. Throughout Asia, in the
Middle East, along the fringes of Africa, in strife-torn republics of Central and South America, even within formerly remote islands of the Pacific,
Communism exerts a growing influence in countless ways. The responsible
statesman and citizen, the serious student, cannot ignore its relentless demands as it has become a factor in virtually every basic consideration of
foreign policy, as it has infiltrated and confused domestic political movements and has staked out its claim as the true analysis of politics, economics, and sociology.

While the theory and practice of Communism do not lend themselves
to rigid separation, the theoretical components of the movement play a
role of special importance in those areas outside of the Soviet orbit. The
conversion of two professors at Peking University [4] and the study of
Marxism by a young library assistant named Mao Tse-tung were to decisively affect the history of China. The acceptance of Marxism by Ho
Chi-minh was to shape the future of a substantial portion of Vietnam.
The Marxist *weltanschaung* of the Italian Togliatti, the Frenchman
Doriot, the German Koestler, were to play a role of great importance in
shaping the politics of Western Europe in the twentieth century; politics
which cannot be properly comprehended unless one understands at least
the basic elements of Communist theory. Nor can we properly grasp
the perspective of the successive leaders of the Soviet Union without a
comprehension of the fundamentals of Marxist thought, though there
may well have been important modifications and even major departures
from orthodox doctrine as it has been applied within the Soviet state. Such
changes and development in the doctrine represent, after all, modifications
from *Marxist* doctrine, and cannot be understood without reference to
the theories which were modified.

It is doubly necessary to stress the importance of Marxist theory in

---

[4] Ch'en Tu-hsiu and Li Ta-chao, a professor of literature and a historian respectively,
are considered to have been the founders of the Chinese Communist movement. See the
authoritative volume by Schwartz, *Chinese Communism and the Rise of Mao*. For something of Mao's views, see the selection in Part IV of this volume, *Let a Hundred Flowers
Bloom*.

view of the notable proclivity among many non-Communist people to dismiss political and social theory as being of little significance. No greater — or more dangerous — error could be made with regard to Communism, for the most basic element in its continuing appeal is precisely Marxist theory. A noted social scientist who has considered the relationship of Marxist theory and Soviet practice concludes:

> . . . it is the role of ideology as the medium for relating individuals to each other and to their environment which is probably its most important residual function in the Soviet Union. The function of Marxism and Communist ideology as a means of perception is, in itself, complex. In the first place, this ideology governs the way men look at the world and interpret it. The Soviet leaders were trained in a Marxist vocabulary; they talk and think, especially about the world abroad, in terms of economic interests, class groups, and class struggles. It is very doubtful, because it is wholly outside their direct personal training and experience, that they understand the ethical, and even religious, foundations of Western societies . . ." [5]

Nor is the importance of Marxist theory confined within the limits of the Soviet Union. Its appeal has been world wide, especially for young intellectuals and idealists during periods of crisis. In their view, Marxism appears to furnish techniques and goals for the rebuilding of society; it provides orientation amidst political chaos. Illustrative of the appeal of Marxist theory to the young intellectuals of Europe in the 1920's and 1930's is the account given by Arthur Koestler of his conversion to Communism through his initial study of Marxism.

> . . . Every page of Marx, and even more of Engels, brought a new revelation, and an intellectual delight which I had only experienced once before, at my first contact with Freud. . . . [*The Communist Manifesto*] as part of a closed system . . . made social philosophy fall into a lucid and comprehensive pattern, the demonstration of the historical relativity of institutions and ideals — of family, class, patriotism, bourgeois morality, sexual taboos — had the intoxicating effect of a sudden liberation from the rusty chains with which a pre-1914 middle-class childhood had cluttered one's mind. . . .
>
> I was ripe to be converted, as a result of my personal case-history; thousands of other members of the intelligentsia and the middle classes of my generation were ripe for it . . . [6]

[5] W. W. Rostow, *The Dynamics of Soviet Society* (New York: The New American Library and W. W. Norton and Co., Inc., 1952), p. 94.

[6] Richard Crossman, ed., *The God That Failed* (New York: Harper and Brothers, 1949), p. 20. Cf. the other selections by André Gide, Richard Wright, Arthur Koestler, Stephen Spender, Ignazio Silone and Louis Fischer on this same question.

Koestler continues:

> . . . I began for the first time to read Marx, Engels and Lenin in
> earnest. By the time I had finished with *Feuerbach* and *State and
> Revolution*, something had clicked in my brain which shook me like
> a mental explosion. To say that one had "seen the light" is a poor de-
> scription of the mental rapture which only the convert knows. . . .
> The new light seems to pour from all directions across the skull; the
> whole universe falls into pattern like the stray pieces of a jigsaw
> puzzle assembled by magic at one stroke. There is now an answer to
> every question, doubts and conflicts are a matter of the tortured past
> — a past already remote, when one had lived in dismal ignorance in
> the tasteless, colorless world of those who *don't know.* . . .[7]

For Koestler the new revelation was gradually destroyed by his experience within the Communist party, and by his observation of Communism in practice throughout Western Europe and the Soviet Union
during the decade of the 1930's. Other leaders of his generation, including
those who came to direct the destiny of nations, retained their allegiance,
and based their political policies to a greater or lesser extent on Marxist
theory as they understand it. For an initial understanding, therefore, of
the outlook and strategy of the Communist-led nations in particular, and
more generally for an understanding of the appeal of Communism to large
numbers within non-Communist countries, we must turn directly to a
consideration of these doctrines themselves. The selections which follow
represent a careful abridgment of a number of the most important Marxist
writings of the twentieth century; writings which, when supplemented
by *The Communist Manifesto* and excerpts from other writings of Marx
and Engels, should provide considerable background on the overall development of the theory.[8] Lenin's presentation of *The Teachings of Karl
Marx* is especially helpful in providing something of a sketch of the
Hegelian and Feuerbachian background of Marxist philosophy, and in
presenting the basic elements of its economic doctrine, the labor theory
of value, economic determinism, class struggle, and related concepts. Emphasis, however, has been placed on Marxist writings of the past half
century in view of the fact that the present crises of Communism to
which allusion has been made stem most directly from the views and actions of the twentieth century leaders of the Soviet Union. Especially

---

[7] *Ibid.*, p. 23. Emphasis in the original.

[8] There is available in English an excellent edition of the *Selected Works of Karl Marx
and Frederick Engels* published in two volumes by the Foreign Languages Publishing
House (Moscow: 1951). It is distributed by Lawrence and Wishart Ltd., London, and
contains virtually all of the basic selections necessary for the purposes of the ordinary
student.

important in revealing the Communist analysis of the contemporary world and their tactics for dealing with it are two of Lenin's famous works: *State and Revolution* and *Imperialism*. Lenin's successor, Joseph Stalin, purported to continue and to apply Leninism during his own period of ascendency, and the student will note in his *Foundations of Leninism* an immediate connection with the doctrines of *Imperialism*.

Finally, the student can understand more precisely the spirit in which Lenin and his successors have applied Marxist theory and conducted their Communist regimes through a consideration of Lenin's directive on *The Tasks of the Youth League*, in Mao Tse-tung's enigmatic suggestions *On the Correct Handling of Contradictions Among the People*, and in Khrushchev's report on *The Crimes of the Stalin Era*. The discussion of "National Communism" from *The New Class*, by Milovan Djilas, illustrates one of the most important current developments stemming from the continuing crisis in Communism.

The initial dates of publication for the readings in this section are as follows:

Karl Marx and Friedrich Engels, *Manifesto of the Communist Party* (1848)

V. I. Lenin, *The Teachings of Karl Marx* (1914)

Friederich Engels, *The Part Played by Labor in the Transition from Ape to Man* (1876)

Karl Marx and Friedrich Engels, *The German Ideology* (1845–46)

Karl Marx, *Introduction to the Critique of Political Economy* (1859)

V. I. Lenin, *State and Revolution* (1917)

V. I. Lenin, *Imperialism: The Highest Stage of Capitalism* (1917)

V. I. Lenin, *The Young Generation* (1920)

Joseph Stalin, *Foundations of Leninism* (1924)

Mao Tse-tung, *Let a Hundred Flowers Bloom* (1957)

Nikita Khrushchev, *Crimes of the Stalin Era* (1956)

Milovan Djilas, *The New Class: An Analysis of the Communist System* (1957)

MANIFESTO OF THE COMMUNIST PARTY

by Karl Marx and Friedrich Engels *

A spectre is haunting Europe — the spectre of Communism. All the powers of old Europe have entered into a holy alliance to exorcise this spectre: Pope and Czar, Metternich and Guizot, French Radicals and German police-spies.

Where is the party in opposition that has not been decried as communistic by its opponents in power? Where the Opposition that has not hurled back the branding reproach of Communism, against the more advanced opposition parties, as well as against its reactionary adversaries?

Two things result from this fact:

1. Communism is already acknowledged by all European powers to be itself a power.

2. It is high time that Communists should openly, in the face of the whole world, publish their views, their aims, their tendencies, and meet this nursery tale of the spectre of Communism with a manifesto of the party itself.

To this end, Communists of various nationalities have assembled in London, and sketched the following manifesto, to be published in the English, French, German, Italian, Flemish and Danish languages.

I. Bourgeois and Proletarians

The history of all hitherto existing society is the history of class struggles.

Freeman and slave, patrician and plebeian, lord and serf, guild-master and journeyman, in a word, oppressor and oppressed, stood in constant opposition to one another, carried on an uninterrupted, now hidden, now open fight, a fight that each time ended, either in a revolutionary recon-

* Karl Marx and Friedrich Engels, *Manifesto of the Communist Party* (New York: 1948). By permission of International Publishers.

stitution of society at large, or in the common ruin of the contending classes.

In the earlier epochs of history, we find almost everywhere a complicated arrangement of society into various orders, a manifold gradation of social rank. In ancient Rome we have patricians, knights, plebeians, slaves; in the Middle Ages, feudal lords, vassals, guild-masters, journeymen, apprentices, serfs; in almost all of these classes, again, subordinate gradations.

The modern bourgeois society that has sprouted from the ruins of feudal society, has not done away with class antagonisms. It has but established new classes, new conditions of oppression, new forms of struggle in place of the old ones.

Our epoch, the epoch of the bourgeoisie, possesses, however, this distinctive feature: It has simplified the class antagonisms. Society as a whole is more and more splitting up into two great hostile camps, into two great classes directly facing each other — bourgeoisie and proletariat.

From the serfs of the Middle Ages sprang the chartered burghers of the earliest towns. From these burgesses the first elements of the bourgeoisie were developed.

The discovery of America, the rounding of the Cape, opened up fresh ground for the rising bourgeoisie. The East-Indian and Chinese markets, the colonisation of America, trade with the colonies, the increase in the means of exchange and in commodities generally, gave to commerce, to navigation, to industry, an impulse never before known, and thereby, to the revolutionary element in the tottering feudal society, a rapid development.

The feudal system of industry, in which industrial production was monopolised by closed guilds, now no longer sufficed for the growing wants of the new markets. The manufacturing system took its place. The guild-masters were pushed aside by the manufacturing middle class; division of labour between the different corporate guilds vanished in the face of division of labour in each single workshop.

Meantime the markets kept ever growing, the demand ever rising. Even manufacture no longer sufficed. Thereupon, steam and machinery revolutionised industrial production. The place of manufacture was taken by the giant, modern industry, the place of the industrial middle class, by industrial millionaires — the leaders of whole industrial armies, the modern bourgeois.

Modern industry has established the world market, for which the discovery of America paved the way. This market has given an immense development to commerce, to navigation, to communication by land. This development has, in its turn, reacted on the extension of industry; and in proportion as industry, commerce, navigation, railways extended, in the same proportion the bourgeoisie developed, increased its capital, and pushed into the background every class handed down from the Middle Ages.

We see, therefore, how the modern bourgeoisie is itself the product of a long course of development, of a series of revolutions in the modes of production and of exchange.

Each step in the development of the bourgeoisie was accompanied by a corresponding political advance of that class. An oppressed class under the sway of the feudal nobility, it became an armed and self-governing association in the mediaeval commune; here independent urban republic (as in Italy and Germany), there taxable "third estate" of the monarchy (as in France); afterwards, in the period of manufacture proper, serving either the semi-feudal or the absolute monarchy as a counterpoise against the nobility, and, in fact, corner-stone of the great monarchies in general — the bourgeoisie has at last, since the establishment of modern industry and of the world market, conquered for itself, in the modern representative state, exclusive political sway. The executive of the modern state is but a committee for managing the common affairs of the whole bourgeoisie.

The bourgeoisie has played a most revolutionary role in history.

The bourgeoisie, wherever it has got the upper hand, has put an end to all feudal, patriarchal, idyllic relations. It has pitilessly torn asunder the motley feudal ties that bound man to his "natural superiors," and has left no other bond between man and man than naked self-interest, than callous "cash payment." It has drowned the most heavenly ecstasies of religious fervour, of chivalrous enthusiasm, of philistine sentimentalism, in the icy water of egotistical calculation. It has resolved personal worth into exchange value, and in place of the numberless indefeasible chartered freedoms, has set up that single, unconscionable freedom — Free Trade. In one word, for exploitation, veiled by religious and political illusions, it has substituted naked, shameless, direct, brutal exploitation.

The bourgeoisie has stripped of its halo every occupation hitherto honoured and looked up to with reverent awe. It has converted the physician, the lawyer, the priest, the poet, the man of science, into its paid wage-labourers.

The bourgeoisie has torn away from the family its sentimental veil, and has reduced the family relation to a mere money relation.

The bourgeoisie has disclosed how it came to pass that the brutal display of vigour in the Middle Ages, which reactionaries so much admire, found its fitting complement in the most slothful indolence. It has been the first to show what man's activity can bring about. It has accomplished wonders far surpassing Egyptian pyramids, Roman aqueducts, and Gothic cathedrals; it has conducted expeditions that put in the shade all former migrations of nations and crusades.

The bourgeoisie cannot exist without constantly revolutionising the instruments of production, and thereby the relations of production, and with them the whole relations of society. Conservation of the old modes of production in unaltered form, was, on the contrary, the first condition of existence for all earlier industrial classes. Constant revolutionising of production, uninterrupted disturbance of all social conditions, everlasting uncertainty and agitation distinguish the bourgeois epoch from all earlier ones. All fixed, fast-frozen relations, with their train of ancient and venerable prejudices and opinions, are swept away, all new-formed ones become antiquated before they can ossify. All that is solid melts into air, all that is holy is profaned, and man is at last compelled to face with sober senses his real conditions of life and his relations with his kind.

The need of a constantly expanding market for its products chases the bourgeoisie over the whole surface of the globe. It must nestle everywhere, settle everywhere, establish connections everywhere.

The bourgeoisie has through its exploitation of the world market given a cosmopolitan character to production and consumption in every country. To the great chagrin of reactionaries, it has drawn from under the feet of industry the national ground on which it stood. All old-established national industries have been destroyed or are daily being destroyed. They are dislodged by new industries, whose introduction becomes a life and death question for all civilised nations, by industries that no longer work up indigenous raw material, but raw material drawn from the remotest zones; industries whose products are consumed, not only at home, but in every quarter of the globe. In place of the old wants, satisfied by the production of the country, we find new wants, requiring for their satisfaction the products of distant lands and climes. In place of the old local and national seclusion and self-sufficiency, we have intercourse in every direction, universal inter-dependence of nations. And as in material, so also in intellectual production. The intellectual creations of individual nations become common property. National one-sidedness and narrow-mindedness become more and more impossible, and from the numerous national and local literatures there arises a world literature.

The bourgeoisie, by the rapid improvement of all instruments of production, by the immensely facilitated means of communication, draws all nations, even the most barbarian, into civilisation. The cheap prices of its commodities are the heavy artillery with which it batters down all Chinese walls, with which it forces the barbarians' intensely obstinate hatred of foreigners to capitulate. It compels all nations, on pain of extinction, to adopt the bourgeois mode of production; it compels them to introduce what it calls civilisation into their midst, *i.e.*, to become bourgeois themselves. In a word, it creates a world after its own image.

The bourgeoisie has subjected the country to the rule of the towns. It has created enormous cities, has greatly increased the urban population as compared with the rural, and has thus rescued a considerable part of the population from the idiocy of rural life. Just as it has made the country dependent on the towns, so it has made barbarian and semi-barbarian countries dependent on the civilised ones, nations of peasants on nations of bourgeois, the East on the West.

More and more the bourgeoisie keeps doing away with the scattered state of the population, of the means of production, and of property. It has agglomerated population, centralised means of production, and has concentrated property in a few hands. The necessary consequence of this was political centralisation. Independent, or but loosely connected provinces, with separate interests, laws, governments and systems of taxation, became lumped together into one nation, with one government, one code of laws, one national class interest, one frontier and one customs tariff.

The bourgeoisie, during its rule of scarce one hundred years, has created more massive and more colossal productive forces than have all preceding generations together. Subjection of nature's forces to man, machinery, application of chemistry to industry and agriculture, steam-navigation, railways, electric telegraphs, clearing of whole continents for cultivation, canalisation of rivers, whole populations conjured out of the ground — what earlier century had even a presentiment that such productive forces slumbered in the lap of social labour?

We see then that the means of production and of exchange, which served as the foundation for the growth of the bourgeoisie, were generated in feudal society. At a certain stage in the development of these means of production and of exchange, the conditions under which feudal society produced and exchanged, the feudal organisation of agriculture and manufacturing industry, in a word, the feudal relations of property became no longer compatible with the already developed productive forces; they became so many fetters. They had to be burst asunder; they were burst asunder.

Into their place stepped free competition, accompanied by a social and political constitution adapted to it, and by the economic and political sway of the bourgeois class.

A similar movement is going on before our own eyes. Modern bourgeois society with its relations of production, of exchange and of property, a society that has conjured up such gigantic means of production and of exchange, is like the sorcerer who is no longer able to control the powers of the nether world whom he has called up by his spells. For many a decade past the history of industry and commerce is but the history of the revolt of modern productive forces against modern conditions of production, against the property relations that are the conditions for the existence of the bourgeoisie and of its rule. It is enough to mention the commercial crises that by their periodical return put the existence of the entire bourgeois society on trial, each time more threateningly. In these crises a great part not only of the existing products, but also of the previously created productive forces, are periodically destroyed. In these crises there breaks out an epidemic that, in all earlier epochs, would have seemed an absurdity — the epidemic of over-production. Society suddenly finds itself put back into a state of momentary barbarism; it appears as if a famine, a universal war of devastation had cut off the supply of every means of subsistence; industry and commerce seem to be destroyed. And why? Because there is too much civilisation, too much means of subsistence, too much industry, too much commerce. The productive forces at the disposal of society no longer tend to further the development of the conditions of bourgeois property; on the contrary, they have become too powerful for these conditions, by which they are fettered, and no sooner do they overcome these fetters than they bring disorder into the whole of bourgeois society, endanger the existence of bourgeois property. The conditions of bourgeois society are too narrow to comprise the wealth created by them. And how does the bourgeoisie get over these crises? On the one hand by enforced destruction of a mass of productive forces; on the other, by the conquest of new markets, and by the more thorough exploitation of the old ones. That is to say, by paving the way for more extensive and more destructive crises, and by diminishing the means whereby crises are prevented.

The weapons with which the bourgeoisie felled feudalism to the ground are now turned against the bourgeoisie itself.

But not only has the bourgeoisie forged the weapons that bring death to itself; it has also called into existence the men who are to wield those weapons — the modern working class — the proletarians.

In proportion as the bourgeoisie, *i.e.*, capital, is developed, in the same proportion is the proletariat, the modern working class, developed — a class of labourers, who live only so long as they find work, and who find work only so long as their labour increases capital. These labourers, who must sell themselves piecemeal, are a commodity, like every other article of commerce, and are consequently exposed to all the vicissitudes of competition, to all the fluctuations of the market.

Owing to the extensive use of machinery and to division of labour, the work of the proletarians has lost all individual character, and, consequently, all charm for the workman. He becomes an appendage of the machine, and it is only the most simple, most monotonous, and most easily acquired knack, that is required of him. Hence, the cost of production of a workman is restricted, almost entirely, to the means of subsistence that he requires for his maintenance, and for the propagation of his race. But the price of a commodity, and therefore also of labour, is equal to its cost of production. In proportion, therefore, as the repulsiveness of the work increases, the wage decreases. Nay more, in proportion as the use of machinery and division of labour increases, in the same proportion the burden of toil also increases, whether by prolongation of the working hours, by increase of the work exacted in a given time, or by increased speed of the machinery, etc.

Modern industry has converted the little workshop of the patriarchal master into the great factory of the industrial capitalist. Masses of labourers, crowded into the factory, are organised like soldiers. As privates of the industrial army they are placed under the command of a perfect hierarchy of officers and sergeants. Not only are they slaves of the bourgeois class, and of the bourgeois state; they are daily and hourly enslaved by the machine, by the over-looker, and, above all, by the individual bourgeois manufacturer himself. The more openly this despotism proclaims gain to be its end and aim, the more petty, the more hateful and the more embittering it is.

The less the skill and exertion of strength implied in manual labour, in other words, the more modern industry develops, the more is the labour of men superseded by that of women. Differences of age and sex have no longer any distinctive social validity for the working class. All are instruments of labour, more or less expensive to use, according to their age and sex.

No sooner has the labourer received his wages in cash, for the moment escaping exploitation by the manufacturer, than he is set upon by the other portions of the bourgeoisie, the landlord, the shopkeeper, the pawn-broker, etc.

The lower strata of the middle class — the small tradespeople, shop-keepers, and retired tradesmen generally, the handicraftsmen and peas-ants — all these sink gradually into the proletariat, partly because their diminutive capital does not suffice for the scale on which modern industry is carried on, and is swamped in the competition with the large capital-ists, partly because their specialised skill is rendered worthless by new methods of production. Thus the proletariat is recruited from all classes of the population.

The proletariat goes through various stages of development. With its birth begins its struggle with the bourgeoisie. At first the contest is car-ried on by individual labourers, then by the work people of a factory, then by the operatives of one trade, in one locality, against the individual bour-geois who directly exploits them. They direct their attacks not against the bourgeois conditions of production, but against the instruments of production themselves; they destroy imported wares that compete with their labour, they smash machinery to pieces, they set factories ablaze, they seek to restore by force the vanished status of the workman of the Middle Ages.

At this stage the labourers still form an incoherent mass scattered over the whole country, and broken up by their mutual competition. If any-where they unite to form more compact bodies, this is not yet the con-sequence of their own active union, but of the union of the bourgeoisie, which class, in order to attain its own political ends, is compelled to set the whole proletariat in motion, and is moreover still able to do so for a time. At this stage, therefore, the proletarians do not fight their enemies, but the enemies of their enemies, the remnants of absolute monarchy, the landowners, the non-industrial bourgeois, the petty bourgeoisie. Thus the whole historical movement is concentrated in the hands of the bour-geoisie; every victory so obtained is a victory for the bourgeoisie.

But with the development of industry the proletariat not only increases in number; it becomes concentrated in greater masses, its strength grows, and it feels that strength more. The various interests and conditions of life within the ranks of the proletariat are more and more equalised, in proportion as machinery obliterates all distinctions of labour and nearly everywhere reduces wages to the same low level. The growing competition among the bourgeois, and the resulting commercial crises, make the wages of the workers ever more fluctuating. The unceasing improvement of machinery, ever more rapidly developing, makes their livelihood more and more precarious; the collisions between individual workmen and individual bourgeois take more and more the character of collisions between two classes. Thereupon the workers begin to form combinations (trade unions) against the bourgeoisie; they club together in order to keep up the rate of wages; they found permanent associations in order to make provision beforehand for these occasional revolts. Here and there the contest breaks out into riots.

Now and then the workers are victorious, but only for a time. The real fruit of their battles lies, not in the immediate result, but in the ever expanding union of the workers. This union is furthered by the improved means of communication which are created by modern industy, and which place the workers of different localities in contact with one another. It was just this contact that was needed to centralise the numerous local struggles, all of the same character, into one national struggle between classes. But every class struggle is a political struggle. And that union, to attain which the burghers of the Middle Ages, with their miserable highways, required centuries, the modern proletarians, thanks to railways, achieve in a few years.

This organisation of the proletarians into a class, and consequently into a political party, is continually being upset again by the competition between the workers themselves. But it ever rises up again, stronger, firmer, mightier. It compels legislative recognition of particular interests of the workers, by taking advantage of the divisions among the bourgeoisie itself. Thus the ten-hour bill in England was carried.

Altogether, collisions between the classes of the old society further the course of development of the proletariat in many ways. The bourgeoisie finds itself involved in a constant battle. At first with the aristocracy; later on, with those portions of the bourgeoisie itself whose interests have become antagonistic to the progress of industry at all times with the bourgeoisie of foreign countries. In all these battles it sees itself compelled to appeal to the proletariat, to ask for its help, and thus, to drag it into the political arena. The bourgeoisie itself, therefore, supplies the proletariat with its own elements of political and general education, in other words, it furnishes the proletariat with weapons for fighting the bourgeoisie.

Further, as we have already seen, entire sections of the ruling classes are, by the advance of industry, precipitated into the proletariat, or are at least threatened in their conditions of existence. These also supply the proletariat with fresh elements of enlightenment and progress.

Finally, in times when the class struggle nears the decisive hour, the process of dissolution going on within the ruling class, in fact within the whole range of old society, assumes such a violent, glaring character, that a small section of the ruling class cuts itself adrift, and joins the revolutionary class, the class that holds the future in its hands. Just as, therefore, at an earlier period, a section of the nobility went over to the bourgeoisie, so now a portion of the bourgeoisie goes over to the proletariat, and in particular, a portion of the bourgeois ideologists, who have raised themselves to the level of comprehending theoretically the historical movement as a whole.

Of all the classes that stand face to face with the bourgeoisie today, the proletariat alone is a really revolutionary class. The other classes decay and finally disappear in the face of modern industry; the proletariat is its special and essential product.

The lower middle class, the small manufacturer, the shopkeeper, the artisan, the peasant, all these fight against the bourgeoisie, to save from extinction their existence as fractions of the middle class. They are therefore not revolutionary, but conservative. Nay more, they are reactionary, for they try to roll back the wheel of history. If by chance they are revolutionary, they are so only in view of their impending transfer into the proletariat; they thus defend not their present, but their future interests; they desert their own standpoint to adopt that of the proletariat.

The "dangerous class," the social scum (*Lumpenproletariat*), that passively rotting mass thrown off by the lowest layers of old society, may, here and there, be swept into the movement by a proletarian revolution; its conditions of life, however, prepare it far more for the part of a bribed tool of reactionary intrigue.

The social conditions of the old society no longer exist for the proletariat. The proletarian is without property; his relation to his wife and children has no longer anything in common with bourgeois family relations; modern industrial labour, modern subjection to capital, the same in England as in France, in America as in Germany, has stripped him of every trace of national character. Law, morality, religion, are to him so many bourgeois prejudices, behind which lurk in ambush just as many bourgeois interests.

All the preceding classes that got the upper hand, sought to fortify their already acquired status by subjecting society at large to their conditions of appropriation. The proletarians cannot become masters of the productive forces of society, except by abolishing their own previous mode of appropriation, and thereby also every other previous mode of appropriation. They have nothing of their own to secure and to fortify; their mission is to destroy all previous securities for, and insurances of, individual property.

All previous historical movements were movements of minorities, or in the interest of minorities. The proletarian movement is the self-conscious, independent movement of the immense majority, in the interest of the immense majority. The proletariat, the lowest stratum of our present society, cannot stir, cannot raise itself up, without the whole super-incumbent strata of official society being sprung into the air.

Though not in substance, yet in form, the struggle of the proletariat with the bourgeoisie is at first a national struggle. The proletariat of each country must, of course, first of all settle matters with its own bourgeoisie.

In depicting the most general phases of the development of the proletariat, we traced the more or less veiled civil war, raging within existing society, up to the point where that war breaks out into open revolution, and where the violent overthrow of the bourgeoisie lays the foundation for the sway of the proletariat.

Hitherto, every form of society has been based, as we have already seen, on the antagonism of oppressing and oppressed classes. But in order to oppress a class, certain conditions must be assured to it under which it can, at least, continue its slavish existence. The serf, in the period of serfdom, raised himself to membership in the commune, just as the petty bourgeois, under the yoke of feudal absolutism, managed to develop into a bourgeois. The modern labourer, on the contrary, instead of rising with the progress of industry, sinks deeper and deeper below the conditions of existence of his own class. He becomes a pauper, and pauperism develops more rapidly than population and wealth. And here it becomes evident, that the bourgeoisie is unfit any longer to be the ruling class in society, and to impose its conditions of existence upon society as an over-riding law. It is unfit to rule because it is incompetent to assure an existence to its slave within his slavery, because it cannot help letting him sink into such a state, that it has to feed him, instead of being fed by him. Society can no longer live under this bourgeoisie, in other words, its existence is no longer compatible with society.

The essential condition for the existence and sway of the bourgeois class, is the formation and augmentation of capital; the condition for capital is wage-labour. Wage-labour rests exclusively on competition between the labourers. The advance of industry, whose involuntary promoter is the bourgeoisie, replaces the isolation of the labourers, due to competition, by their revolutionary combination, due to association. The development of modern industry, therefore, cuts from under its feet the very foundation on which the bourgeoisie produces and appropriates products. What the bourgeoisie therefore produces, above all, are its own grave-diggers. Its fall and the victory of the proletariat are equally inevitable.

II. PROLETARIANS AND COMMUNISTS

In what relation do the Communists stand to the proletarians as a whole?

The Communists do not form a separate party opposed to other working class parties.

They have no interests separate and apart from those of the proletariat as a whole.

They do not set up any sectarian principles of their own, by which to shape and mould the proletarian movement.

The Communists are distinguished from the other working class parties by this only: 1. In the national struggles of the proletarians of the different countries, they point out and bring to the front the common interests of the entire proletariat, independently of all nationality. 2. In the various stages of development which the struggle of the working class against the bourgeoisie has to pass through, they always and everywhere represent the interests of the movement as a whole.

The Communists, therefore, are on the one hand, practically, the most advanced and resolute section of the working class parties of every country, that section which pushes forward all others; on the other hand, theoretically, they have over the great mass of the proletariat the advantage of clearly understanding the line of march, the conditions, and the ultimate general results of the proletarian movement.

The immediate aim of the Communists is the same as that of all the other proletarian parties: Formation of the proletariat into a class, overthrow of bourgeois supremacy, conquest of political power by the proletariat.

The theoretical conclusions of the Communists are in no way based on ideas or principles that have been invented, or discovered, by this or that would-be universal reformer.

They merely express, in general terms, actual relations springing from an existing class struggle, from a historical movement going on under our very eyes. The abolition of existing property relations is not at all a distinctive feature of Communism.

All property relations in the past have continually been subject to historical change consequent upon the change in historical conditions.

The French Revolution, for example, abolished feudal property in favour of bourgeois property.

The distinguishing feature of Communism is not the abolition of property generally, but the abolition of bourgeois property. But modern bourgeois private property is the final and most complete expression of the system of producing and appropriating products that is based on class antagonisms, on the exploitation of the many by the few.

In this sense, the theory of the Communists may be summed up in the single sentence: Abolition of private property.

We Communists have been reproached with the desire of abolishing the right of personally acquiring property as the fruit of a man's own labour, which property is alleged to be the groundwork of all personal freedom, activity and independence. Hard-won, self-acquired, self-earned property! Do you mean the property of the petty artisan and of the small peasant, a form of property that preceded the bourgeois form? There is no need to abolish that; the development of industry has to a great extent already destroyed it, and is still destroying it daily.

Or do you mean modern bourgeois private property?

But does wage-labour create any property for the labourer? Not a bit. It creates capital, *i.e.*, that kind of property which exploits wage-labour, and which cannot increase except upon condition of begetting a new supply of wage-labour for fresh exploitation. Property, in its present form, is based on the antagonism of capital and wage-labour. Let us examine both sides of this antagonism.

To be a capitalist, is to have not only a purely personal, but a social *status* in production. Capital is a collective product, and only by the united action of many members, nay, in the last resort, only by the united action of all members of society, can it be set in motion.

Capital is therefore not a personal, it is a social, power.

When, therefore, capital is converted into common property, into the property of all members of society, personal property is not thereby transformed into social property. It is only the social character of the property that is changed. It loses its class character.

Let us now take wage-labour.

The average price of wage-labour is the minimum wage, *i.e.*, that quantum of the means of subsistence which is absolutely requisite to keep the labourer in bare existence as a labourer. What, therefore, the wage-labourer appropriates by means of his labour, merely suffices to prolong and reproduce a bare existence. We by no means intend to abolish this personal appropriation of the products of labour, an appropriation that is

made for the maintenance and reproduction of human life, and that leaves
no surplus wherewith to command the labour of others. All that we want
to do away with is the miserable character of this appropriation, under
which the labourer lives merely to increase capital, and is allowed to live
only insofar as the interest of the ruling class requires it.

In bourgeois society, living labour is but a means to increase accumulated labour. In Communist society, accumulated labour is but a means to
widen, to enrich, to promote the existence of the labourer.

In bourgeois society, therefore, the past dominates the present; in Communist society, the present dominates the past. In bourgeois society capital
is independent and has individuality, while the living person is dependent
and has no individuality.

And the abolition of this state of things is called by the bourgeois,
abolition of individuality and freedom! And rightly so. The abolition of
bourgeois individuality, bourgeois independence, and bourgeois freedom
is undoubtedly aimed at.

By freedom is meant, under the present bourgeois conditions of production, free trade, free selling and buying.

But if selling and buying disappears, free selling and buying disappears
also. This talk about free selling and buying, and all the other "brave
words" of our bourgeoisie about freedom in general, have a meaning, if
any, only in contrast with restricted selling and buying, with the fettered
traders of the Middle Ages, but have no meaning when opposed to the
Communist abolition of buying and selling, of the bourgeois conditions of
production, and of the bourgeoisie itself.

You are horrified at our intending to do away with private property.
But in your existing society, private property is already done away with
for nine-tenths of the population; its existence for the few is solely due to
its non-existence in the hands of those nine-tenths. You reproach us,
therefore, with intending to do away with a form of property, the necessary condition for whose existence is the non-existence of any property
for the immense majority of society.

In a word, you reproach us with intending to do away with your
property. Precisely so; that is just what we intend.

From the moment when labour can no longer be converted into capital,
money, or rent, into a social power capable of being monopolised, *i.e.*,
from the moment when individual property can no longer be transformed
into bourgeois property, into capital, from that moment, you say, individuality vanishes.

You must, therefore, confess that by "individual" you mean no other person than the bourgeois, than the middle class owner of property. This person must, indeed, be swept out of the way, and made impossible.

Communism deprives no man of the power to appropriate the products of society; all that it does is to deprive him of the power to subjugate the labour of others by means of such appropriation.

It has been objected, that upon the abolition of private property all work will cease, and universal laziness will overtake us.

According to this, bourgeois society ought long ago to have gone to the dogs through sheer idleness; for those of its members who work, acquire nothing, and those who acquire anything, do not work. The whole of this objection is but another expression of the tautology: There can no longer be any wage-labour when there is no longer any capital.

All objections urged against the Communist mode of producing and appropriating material products, have, in the same way, been urged against the Communist modes of producing and appropriating intellectual products. Just as, to the bourgeois, the disappearance of class property is the disapearance of production itself, so the disappearance of class culture is to him identical with the disappearance of all culture.

That culture, the loss of which he laments, is, for the enormous majority, a mere training to act as a machine.

But don't wrangle with us so long as you apply, to our intended abolition of bourgeois property, the standard of your bourgeois notions of freedom, culture, law, etc. Your very ideas are but the outgrowth of the conditions of your bourgeois production and bourgeois property, just as your jurisprudence is but the will of your class made into a law for all, a will whose essential character and direction are determined by the economic conditions of existence of your class.

The selfish misconception that induces you to transform into eternal laws of nature and of reason, the social forms springing from your present mode of production and form of property — historical relations that rise and disappear in the progress of production — this misconception you share with every ruling class that has preceded you. What you see clearly in the case of ancient property, what you admit in the case of feudal property, you are of course forbidden to admit in the case of your own bourgeois form of property.

Abolition of the family! Even the most radical flare up at this infamous proposal of the Communists.

On what foundation is the present family, the bourgeois family, based?

On capital, on private gain. In its completely developed form this family exists only among the bourgeoisie. But this state of things finds its complement in the practical absence of the family among the proletarians, and in public prostitution.

The bourgeois family will vanish as a matter of course when its complement vanishes, and both will vanish with the vanishing of capital.

Do you charge us with wanting to stop the exploitation of children by their parents? To this crime we plead guilty.

But, you will say, we destroy the most hallowed of relations, when we replace home education by social.

And your education! Is not that also social, and determined by the social conditions under which you educate, by the intervention of society, direct or indirect, by means of schools, etc.? The Communists have not invented the intervention of society in education; they do but seek to alter the character of that intervention, and to rescue education from the influence of the ruling class.

The bourgeois claptrap about the family and education, about the hallowed co-relation of parent and child, becomes all the more disgusting, the more, by the action of modern industry, all family ties among the proletarians are torn asunder, and their children transformed into simple articles of commerce and instruments of labour.

But you Communists would introduce community of women, screams the whole bourgeoisie in chorus.

The bourgeois sees in his wife a mere instrument of production. He hears that the instruments of production are to be exploited in common, and, naturally, can come to no other conclusion than that the lot of being common to all will likewise fall to the women.

He has not even a suspicion that the real point aimed at is to do away with the status of women as mere instruments of production.

For the rest, nothing is more ridiculous than the virtuous indignation of our bourgeois at the community of women which, they pretend, is to be openly and officially established by the Communists. The Communists have no need to introduce community of women; it has existed almost from time immemorial.

Our bourgeois, not content with having the wives and daughters of their proletarians at their disposal, not to speak of common prostitutes, take the greatest pleasure in seducing each other's wives.

Bourgeois marriage is in reality a system of wives in common and thus, at the most, what the Communists might possibly be reproached with is that they desire to introduce, in substitution for a hypocritically concealed, an openly legalised community of women. For the rest, it is self-evident, that the abolition of the present system of production must bring with it the abolition of the community of women springing from that system, *i.e.*, of prostitution both public and private.

The Communists are further reproached with desiring to abolish countries and nationality.

The workingmen have no country. We cannot take from them what they have not got. Since the proletariat must first of all acquire political supremacy, must rise to be the leading class of the nation, must constitute itself *the* nation, it is, so far, itself national, though not in the bourgeois sense of the word.

National differences and antagonisms between peoples are vanishing gradually from day to day, owing to the development of the bourgeoisie, to freedom of commerce, to the world market, to uniformity in the mode of production and in the conditions of life corresponding thereto.

The supremacy of the proletariat will cause them to vanish still faster. United action, of the leading civilised countries at least, is one of the first conditions for the emancipation of the proletariat.

In proportion as the exploitation of one individual by another is put an end to, the exploitation of one nation by another will also be put an end to. In proportion as the antagonism between classes within the nation vanishes, the hostility of one nation to another will come to an end.

The charges against Communism made from a religious, a philosophical, and, generally, from an ideological standpoint, are not deserving of serious examination.

Does it require deep intuition to comprehend that man's ideas, views, and conceptions, in one word, man's consciousness, changes with every change in the conditions of his material existence, in his social relations and in his social life?

What else does the history of ideas prove, than that intellectual production changes its character in proportion as material production is changed? The ruling ideas of each age have ever been the ideas of its ruling class.

When people speak of ideas that revolutionise society, they do but express the fact that within the old society the elements of a new one have been created, and that the dissolution of the old ideas keeps even pace with the dissolution of the old conditions of existence.

When the ancient world was in its last throes, the ancient religions were overcome by Christianity. When Christian ideas succumbed in the 18th century to rationalist ideas, feudal society fought its death-battle with the then revolutionary bourgeoisie. The ideas of religious liberty and freedom of conscience, merely gave expression to the sway of free competition within the domain of knowledge.

"Undoubtedly," it will be said, "religion, moral, philosophical and juridical ideas have been modified in the course of historical development. But religion, morality, philosophy, political science, and law, constantly survived this change."

"There are, besides, eternal truths, such as Freedom, Justice, etc., that are common to all states of society. But Communism abolishes eternal truths, it abolishes all religion, and all morality, instead of constituting them on a new basis; it therefore acts in contradiction to all past historical experience."

What does this accusation reduce itself to? The history of all past society has consisted in the development of class antagonisms, antagonisms that assumed different forms at different epochs.

But whatever form they may have taken, one fact is common to all past ages, *viz.*, the exploitation of one part of society by the other. No wonder, then, that the social consciousness of past ages, despite all the multiplicity and variety it displays, moves within certain common forms, or general ideas, which cannot completely vanish except with the total disappearance of class antagonisms.

The Communist revolution is the most radical rupture with traditional property relations; no wonder that its development involves the most radical rupture with traditional ideas.

But let us have done with the bourgeois objections to Communism.

We have seen above, that the first step in the revolution by the working class, is to raise the proletariat to the position of ruling class, to establish democracy.

The proletariat will use its political supremacy to wrest, by degrees, all capital from the bourgeoisie, to centralise all instruments of production in the hands of the state, *i.e.*, of the proletariat organised as the ruling class; and to increase the total of productive forces as rapidly as possible.

Of course, in the beginning, this cannot be effected except by means of despotic inroads on the rights of property, and on the conditions of bourgeois production; by means of measures, therefore, which appear economically insufficient and untenable, but which, in the course of the movement, outstrip themselves, necessitate further inroads upon the old social order, and are unavoidable as a means of entirely revolutionising the mode of production.

These measures will of course be different in different countries.

Nevertheless in the most advanced countries, the following will be pretty generally applicable.

1. Abolition of property in land and application of all rents of land to public purposes.

2. A heavy progressive or graduated income tax.

3. Abolition of all right of inheritance.

4. Confiscation of the property of all emigrants and rebels.

5. Centralisation of credit in the hands of the state, by means of a national bank with state capital and an exclusive monopoly.

6. Centralisation of the means of communication and transport in the hands of the state.

7. Extension of factories and instruments of production owned by the state; the bringing into cultivation of waste lands, and the improvement of the soil generally in accordance with a common plan.

8. Equal obligation of all to work. Establishment of industrial armies, especially for agriculture.

9. Combination of agriculture with manufacturing industries; gradual abolition of the distinction between town and country, by a more equable distribution of the population over the country.

10. Free education for all children in public schools. Abolition of child factory labour in its present form. Combination of education with industrial production, etc.

When, in the course of development, class distinctions have disappeared, and all production has been concentrated in the hands of a vast association of the whole nation, the public power will lose its political character. Political power, properly so called, is merely the organised power of one class for oppressing another. If the proletariat during its contest with the bourgeoisie is compelled, by the force of circumstances, to organise itself as a class; if, by means of a revolution, it makes itself the ruling class, and, as such sweeps away by force the old conditions of production, then it will, along with these conditions, have swept away the conditions for the existence of class antagonisms, and of classes generally, and will thereby have abolished its own supremacy as a class.

In place of the old bourgeois society, with its classes and class antagonisms, we shall have an association, in which the free development of each is the condition for the free development of all. . . .

IV. Position of the Communists in Relation to the Various
Existing Opposition Parties

Section II has made clear the relations of the Communists to the existing working class parties, such as the Chartists in England and the
Agrarian Reformers in America.

The Communists fight for the attainment of the immediate aims, for
the enforcement of the momentary interests of the working class; but in
the movement of the present, they also represent and take care of the
future of that movement. In France the Communists ally themselves with
the Social-Democrats, against the conservative and radical bourgeoisie,
reserving, however, the right to take up a critical position in regard to
phrases and illusions traditionally handed down from the great Revolution.

In Switzerland they support the Radicals, without losing sight of the
fact that this party consists of antagonistic elements, partly of Democratic
Socialists, in the French sense, partly of radical bourgeois.

In Poland they support the party that insists on an agrarian revolution
as the prime condition for national emancipation, that party which fo-
mented the insurrection of Cracow in 1846.

In Germany they fight with the bourgeoisie whenever it acts in a revolutionary way, against the absolute monarchy, the feudal squirearchy, and
the petty bourgeoisie.

But they never cease, for a single instant, to instil into the working class
the clearest possible recognition of the hostile antagonism between bourgeoisie and proletariat, in order that the German workers may straightway
use, as so many weapons against the bourgeoisie, the social and political
conditions that the bourgeoisie must necessarily introduce along with its
supremacy, and in order that, after the fall of the reactionary classes in
Germany, the fight against the bourgeoisie itself may immediately begin.

The Communists turn their attention chiefly to Germany, because that
country is on the eve of a bourgeois revolution that is bound to be carried
out under more advanced conditions of European civilisation and with a
much more developed proletariat than what existed in England in the
17th and in France in the 18th century, and because the bourgeois revolution in Germany will be but the prelude to an immediately following
proletarian revolution.

In short, the Communists everywhere support every revolutionary movement against the existing social and political order of things.

In all these movements they bring to the front, as the leading question in each case, the property question, no matter what its degree of development at the time.

Finally, they labour everywhere for the union and agreement of the democratic parties of all countries.

The Communists disdain to conceal their views and aims. They openly declare that their ends can be attained only by the forcible overthrow of all existing social conditions. Let the ruling classes tremble at a Communist revolution. The proletarians have nothing to lose but their chains. They have a world to win.

Workingmen of all countries, unite!

THE TEACHINGS OF KARL MARX

by V. I. Lenin *

KARL MARX

Karl Marx was born May 5, 1818, in the city of Trier, in the Rhine province of Prussia. His father was a lawyer — a Jew, who in 1824 adopted Protestantism. The family was well-to-do, cultured, but not revolutionary. After graduating from the *Gymnasium* in Trier, Marx entered first the University at Bonn, later Berlin University, where he studied jurisprudence, but devoted most of his time to history and philosophy. At the conclusion of his university course in 1841, he submitted his doctoral dissertation on Epicure's philosophy. Marx at that time was still an adherent of Hegel's idealism. In Berlin he belonged to the circle of "Left Hegelians" . . . who sought to draw atheistic and revolutionary conclusions from Hegel's philosophy.

After graduating from the University, Marx moved to Bonn in the expectation of becoming a professor. However, the reactionary policy of the government, . . . forced Marx to abandon the idea of pursuing an academic career. The development of the ideas of Left Hegelianism in Germany was very rapid at that time. Ludwig Feuerbach in particular, after

* V. I. Lenin, *The Teachings of Karl Marx* (New York: 1930). By permission of International Publishers.

1836, began to criticise theology and to turn to materialism, which by 1841 had gained the upper hand in his conceptions . . . *The Essence of Christianity* . . . : in 1843 his . . . *Principles of the Philosophy of the Future* appeared. Of these works of Feuerbach, Engels subsequently wrote: "One must himself have experienced the liberating effect of these books." "We" (the Left Hegelians, including Marx) "at once became Feuerbachists." At that time the radical bourgeois of the Rhine province, who had certain points of contact with the Left Hegelians, founded in Cologne, an opposition paper, the *Rheinische Zeitung* [*Rhenish Gazette*], which began to appear on January 1, 1842. Marx and Bruno Bauer were invited to be the chief contributors, and in October, 1842, Marx became the paper's editor-in-chief and moved from Bonn to Cologne. . . . Marx's newspaper work revealed to him that he was not sufficiently acquainted with political economy, and he set out to study it diligently. . . .

In September, 1844, Friedrich Engels, who from then on was Marx's closest friend, came in for a few days to Paris. Both of them took a very active part in the seething life of the revolutionary groups of Paris (where Proudhon's doctrine was then of particular importance; later Marx decisively parted ways with that doctrine in his *Poverty of Philosophy*, 1847). Waging a sharp struggle against the various doctrines of petty-bourgeois Socialism, they worked out the theory and tactics of revolutionary *proletarian Socialism*, otherwise known as Communism (Marxism). For this phase of Marx's activities, see Marx's works of 1844–1848. In 1845, at the insistence of the Prussian government, Marx was banished from Paris as a dangerous revolutionist. From Paris he moved to Brussels. In the spring of 1847 Marx and Engels joined a secret propaganda society bearing the name *Bund der Kommunisten* [*Communist League*], at whose second congress they took a prominent part (London, November, 1847), and at whose behest they composed the famous *Manifesto of the Communist Party* which appeared in February, 1848. With the clarity and brilliance of genius, this work outlines a new conception of the world; it represents consistent materialism extended also to the realm of social life; it proclaims dialectics as the most comprehensive and profound doctrine of development; it advances the theory of the class struggle and of the world-historic revolutionary role of the proletariat as the creator of a new Communist society.

When the February, 1848, Revolution broke out, Marx was banished from Belgium. He returned to Paris and from there, after the March Revolution, to Cologne, in Germany. From June 1, 1848, to May 19, 1849, the *Neue Rheinische Zeitung* [*New Rhenish Gazette*] was published in

Cologne with Marx as editor-in-chief. The new doctrine found excellent corroboration in the course of the revolutionary events of 1848–1849, as it has subsequently been corroborated by all the proletarian and democratic movements of all the countries of the world. Victorious counter-revolution in Germany first instigated court proceedings against Marx (he was acquitted February 9, 1849), then banished him from Germany (May 16, 1849). He first went to Paris, from where he was also banished after the demonstration of June 13, 1849. He then went to London, where he lived to the end of his days. . . .

MARX'S TEACHING

Marxism is the system of the views and teachings of Marx. Marx was the genius who continued and completed the three chief ideological currents of the nineteenth century, represented respectively by the three most advanced countries of humanity: classical German philosophy, classical English political economy, and French Socialism combined with French revolutionary doctrines. . . .

PHILOSOPHIC MATERIALISM

Beginning with the years 1844–1845, when his views were definitely formed, Marx was a materialist, and especially a follower of Feuerbach; even in later times, he saw Feuerbach's weak side only in this, that his materialism was not sufficiently consistent and comprehensive. For Marx, Feuerbach's world-historic and "epoch-making" significance consisted in his having decisively broken away from the idealism of Hegel, and in his proclamation of materialism, which even in the eighteenth century, especially in France, had become "a struggle not only against the existing political institutions, and against . . . religion and theology, but also . . . against every form of metaphysics" (as "intoxicated speculation" in contradistinction to "sober philosophy") . . .

> For Hegel . . . the thought process (which he actually transforms into an independent subject, giving to it the name of "idea") is the demiurge [creator] of the real. . . . In my view, on the other hand, the ideal is nothing other than the material when it has been transposed and translated inside the human head. [*Capital*, Vol. I.]

In full conformity with Marx's materialist philosophy, and expounding it, Engels wrote in *Anti-Dühring* . . . :

The unity of the world does not consist in its existence. . . . The real unity of the world consists in its materiality, and this is proved . . . by the long and laborious development of philosophy and natural science. . . . Motion is the form of existence of matter. Never and nowhere has there been or can there be matter without motion. . . . Matter without motion is just as unthinkable as motion without matter. . . . If we enquire . . . what thought and consciousness are, whence they come we find that they are products of the human brain, and that man himself is a product of nature, developing in and along with his environment. Obviously, therefore, the products of the human brain, being in the last analysis likewise products of nature, do not contradict the rest of nature, but correspond to it.

Again: "Hegel was an idealist; that is to say, for him the thoughts in his head were not more or less abstract reflections . . . of real things and processes; but, on the contrary, things and their evolution were, for Hegel, only reflections in reality of the Idea that existed somewhere even prior to the world."

In his *Ludwig Feuerbach* . . . Engels writes:

The great basic question of all, and especially of recent, philosophy, is the question of the relationship between thought and existence, between spirit and nature. . . . Which is prior to the other: spirit or nature? Philosophers are divided into two great camps, according to the way in which they have answered this question. Those who declare that spirit existed before nature, and who, in the last analysis, therefore, assume in one way or another that the world was created . . . have formed the idealist camp. The others, who regard nature as primary, belong to the various schools of materialism.

Any other use (in a philosophic sense) of the terms idealism and materialism is only confusing. Marx decidedly rejected not only idealism, always connected in one way or another with religion, but also the views of Hume and Kant, that are especially widespread in our day, as well as agnosticism, criticism, positivism in various forms; he considered such philosophy as a "reactionary" concession to idealism, at best as a "shamefaced manner of admitting materialism through the back door while denying it before the world." . . . It is especially important that we should note Marx's opinion concerning the relation between freedom and necessity: "Freedom is the recognition of necessity. Necessity is blind only in so far as it is not understood" (Engels, *Anti-Dühring*). This means acknowledgment of the objective reign of law in nature and of the dialectical transformation of necessity into freedom (at the same time, an acknowledgment of the transformation of the unknown but knowable "thing-in-itself" into the "thing-for-us," of the "essence of things" into "phenomena"). Marx and Engels pointed out the following major shortcomings of the "old" materialism . . . : (1) it was "predominantly mechanical," not taking into account the latest developments of chemistry and biology (in our day it would be necessary to add the electric theory of matter); (2) it was non-historical, non-dialectical (was metaphysical, in the sense of being anti-dialectical), and did not apply the standpoint of evolution consistently and all-sidedly; (3) it regarded "human nature" abstractly, and not as a "synthesis" of (definite, concrete-historical) "social relationships" — and thus only "interpreted" the world, whereas it was a question of "changing" it, that is, it did not grasp the significance of "practical revolutionary activity."

DIALECTICS

Marx and Engels regarded Hegelian dialectics, the theory of evolution most comprehensive, rich in content and profound, as the greatest achievement of classical German philosophy. All other formulations of the principle of development, of evolution, they considered to be one-sided, poor in content, distorting and mutilating the actual course of development of nature and society (a course often consummated in leaps and bounds, catastrophes, revolutions).

> Marx and I were almost the only persons who rescued conscious dialectics . . . [from the swamp of idealism, including Hegelianism] by transforming it into the materialist conception of nature. . . . Nature is the test of dialectics, and we must say that science has supplied a vast and daily increasing mass of material for this test, thereby proving that, in the last analysis, nature proceeds dialectically and not metaphysically. [This was written before the discovery of radium, electrons, the transmutation of elements, etc.]

Again, Engels writes:

> The great basic idea that the world is not to be viewed as a complex of fully fashioned objects, but as a complex of processes, in which apparently stable objects, no less than the images of them inside our heads (our concepts), are undergoing incessant changes, arising here and disappearing there, and which with all apparent accident and in spite of all momentary retrogression, ultimately constitutes a progressive development — this great basic idea has, particularly since the time of Hegel, so deeply penetrated the general consciousness that hardly any one will now venture to dispute it in its general form. But it is one thing to accept it in words, quite an-

other thing to put it in practice on every occasion and in every field of investigation.

In the eyes of dialectic philosophy, nothing is established for all time, nothing is absolute or sacred. On everything and in everything it sees the stamp of inevitable decline; nothing can resist it save the unceasing process of formation and destruction, the unending ascent from the lower to the higher — a process of which that philosophy itself is only a simple reflection within the thinking brain.

Thus dialectics, according to Marx, is "the science of the general laws of motion both of the external world and of human thinking."

This revolutionary side of Hegel's philosophy was adopted and developed by Marx. Dialectical materialism "does not need any philosophy towering above the other sciences." Of former philosophies there remain "the science of thinking and its laws — formal logic and dialectics." Dialectics, as the term is used by Marx in conformity with Hegel, includes what is now called the theory of cognition, or epistemology, or gnoseology, a science that must contemplate its subject matter in the same way — historically, studying and generalising the origin and development of cognition, the transition from *non*-consciousness to consciousness. In our times, the idea of development, of evolution, has almost fully penetrated social consciousness, but it has done so in other ways, not through Hegel's philosophy. Still, the same idea, as formulated by Marx and Engels on the basis of Hegel's philosophy, is much more comprehensive, much more abundant in content than the current theory of evolution. A development that repeats, as it were, the stages already passed, but repeats them in a different way, on a higher plane ("negation of negation"); a development, so to speak, in spirals, not in a straight line; a development in leaps and bounds, catastrophes, revolutions; "intervals of gradualness"; transformation of quantity into quality; inner impulses for development, imparted by the contradiction, the conflict of different forces and tendencies reacting on a given body or inside a given phenomenon or within a given society; interdependence, and the closest, indissoluble connection between *all* sides of every phenomenon (history disclosing ever new sides), a connection that provides the one world-process of motion proceeding according to law — such are some of the features of dialectics as a doctrine of evolution more full of meaning than the current one. . . .

MATERIALIST CONCEPTION OF HISTORY

Realising the inconsistency, the incompleteness, and the one-sidedness of the old materialism, Marx became convinced that it was necessary "to harmonise the science of society with the materialist basis, and to reconstruct it in accordance with this basis." If, speaking generally, materialism explains consciousness as the outcome of existence, and not conversely, then, applied to the social life of mankind, materialism must explain *social* consciousness as the outcome of *social* existence. "Technology," writes Marx in the first volume of *Capital*, "reveals man's dealings with nature, discloses the direct productive activities of his life, thus throwing light upon social relations and the resultant mental conceptions." In the preface to A *Contribution to the Critique of Political Economy* Marx gives an integral formulation of the fundamental principles of materialism as applied to human society and its history, in the following words:

> In the social production of the means of life, human beings enter into definite and necessary relations which are independent of their will — production relations which correspond to a definite stage of the development of their productive forces. The totality of these production relations constitutes the economic structure of society, the real basis upon which a legal and political superstructure arises and to which definite forms of social consciousness correspond. The mode of production of the material means of life determines, in general, the social, political, and intellectual processes of life. It is not the consciousness of human beings that determines their existence, but, conversely, it is their social existence that determines their consciousness. At a certain stage of their development, the material productive forces of society come into conflict with the existing production relationships, or, what is but a legal expression for the same thing, with the property relationships within which they have hitherto moved. From forms of development of the productive forces, these relationships turn into their fetters. A period of social revolution then begins. With the change in the economic foundation, the whole gigantic superstructure is more or less rapidly transformed. In considering such transformations we must always distinguish between the material changes in the economic conditions of production, changes which can be determined with the precision of natural science, and the legal, political, religious, aesthetic, or philosophic, in short, ideological forms, in which human beings become conscious of this conflict and fight it out to an issue.
>
> Just as little as we judge an individual by what he thinks of himself, just so little can we appraise such a revolutionary epoch in accordance with its own consciousness of itself. On the contrary, we have to explain this consciousness as the outcome of the contradictions of material life, of the conflict existing between social productive forces and production relationships. . . . In broad outline we can designate the Asiatic, the classical, the feudal, and the modern bourgeois forms of production as progressive epochs in the economic formation of society. . . .

The discovery of the materialist conception of history, or, more correctly, the consistent extension of materialism to the domain of social phenomena, obviated the two chief defects in earlier historical theories. For, in the first place, those theories, at best, examined only the ideological motives of the historical activity of human beings without investigating the origin of these ideological motives, or grasping the objective conformity to law in the development of the system of social relationships, or discerning the roots of these social relationships in the degree of development of material production. In the second place, the earlier historical theories ignored the activities of the *masses*, whereas historical materialism first made it possible to study with scientific accuracy the social conditions of the life of the masses and the changes in these conditions. At best, pre-Marxist "sociology" and historiography gave an accumulation of raw facts collected at random, and a description of separate sides of the historic process. Examining the *totality* of all the opposing tendencies, reducing them to precisely definable conditions in the mode of life and the method of production of the various *classes* of society, discarding subjectivism and free will in the choice of various "leading" ideas or in their interpretation, showing how all the ideas and all the various tendencies, without exception, have their roots in the condition of the material forces of production, Marxism pointed the way to a comprehensive, an all-embracing study of the rise, development, and decay of socio-economic structures. People make their own history; but what determines their motives, that is, the motives of people in the mass; what gives rise to the clash of conflicting ideas and endeavours; what is the sum total of all these clashes among the whole mass of human societies; what are the objective conditions for the production of the material means of life that form the basis of all the historical activity of man; what is the law of the development of these conditions — to all these matters Marx directed attention, pointing out the way to a scientific study of history as a unified and true-to-law process despite its being extremely variegated and contradictory.

CLASS STRUGGLE

That in any given society the strivings of some of the members conflict with the strivings of others; that social life is full of contradictions; that history discloses to us a struggle among peoples and societies, and also within each nation and each society, manifesting in addition an alternation between periods of revolution and reaction, peace and war, stagnation and rapid progress or decline — these facts are generally known. Marxism provides a clue which enables us to discover the reign of law in this seeming labyrinth and chaos: the theory of the class struggle. Nothing but the study of the totality of the strivings of all the members of a given society, or group of societies, can lead to the scientific definition of the result of these strivings. Now, the conflict of strivings arises from differences in the situation and modes of life of the *classes* into which society is divided.

> The history of all human society, past and present [wrote Marx in 1848, in the *Communist Manifesto*; except the history of the primitive community, Engels added], has been the history of class struggles. Freeman and slave, patrician and plebeian, baron and serf, guild-burgess and journeyman — in a word, oppressor and oppressed — stood in sharp opposition each to the other. They carried on perpetual warfare, sometimes masked, sometimes open and acknowledged; a warfare that invariably ended either in a revolutionary change in the whole structure of society or else in the common ruin of the contending classes. . . . Modern bourgeois society, rising out of the ruins of feudal society, did not make an end of class antagonisms. It merely set up new classes in place of the old; new conditions of oppression; new embodiments of struggle. Our own age, the bourgeois age, is distinguished by this — that it has simplified class antagonisms. More and more, society is splitting up into two great hostile camps, into two great and directly contraposed classes: bourgeoisie and proletariat.

Since the time of the great French Revolution, the class struggle as the actual motive force of events has been most clearly manifest in all European history. During the Restoration period in France, there were already a number of historians (Thierry, Guizot, Mignet, Thiers) who, generalising events, could not but recognise in the class struggle the key to the understanding of all the history of France. In the modern age — the epoch of the complete victory of the bourgeoisie, of representative institutions, of extended (if not universal) suffrage, of cheap daily newspapers widely circulated among the masses, etc., of powerful and ever-expanding organisations of workers and employers, etc. — the class struggle (though sometimes in a highly one-sided, "peaceful," "constitutional" form), has shown itself still more obviously to be the mainspring of events. The following passage from Marx's *Communist Manifesto* will show us what Marx demanded of social sciences as regards an objective analysis of the situation of every class in modern society as well as an analysis of the conditions of development of every class.

> Among all the classes that confront the bourgeoisie to-day, the proletariat alone is really revolutionary. Other classes decay and

perish with the rise of large-scale industry, but the proletariat is the most characteristic product of that industry. The lower middle class — small manufacturers, small traders, handicraftsmen, peasant proprietors — one and all fight the bourgeoisie in the hope of safe-guarding their existence as sections of the middle class. They are, therefore, not revolutionary, but conservative. Nay, more, they are reactionary, for they are trying to make the wheels of history turn backwards. If they ever become revolutionary, it is only because they are afraid of slipping down into the ranks of the proletariat; they are not defending their present interests, but their future interests; they are forsaking their own standpoint, in order to adopt that of the proletariat.

In a number of historical works . . . Marx gave brilliant and profound examples of materialist historiography, an analysis of the position of *each* separate class, and sometimes of that of various groups or strata within a class, showing plainly why and how "every class struggle is a political struggle." The above quoted passage is an illustration of what a complex network of social relations and *transitional stages* between one class and another, between the past and the future, Marx analyses in order to arrive at the resultant of the whole historical development.

Marx's economic doctrine is the most profound, the most many-sided, and the most detailed confirmation and application of his teaching.

Marx's Economic Doctrine

"It is the ultimate aim of this work to reveal the economic law of mo-tion of modern society" (that is to say, capitalist, bourgeois society), writes Marx in the preface to the first volume of *Capital*. The study of the pro-duction relationships in a given, historically determinate society, in their genesis, their development, and their decay — such is the content of Marx's economic teaching. In capitalist society the dominant feature is the production of *commodities*, and Marx's analysis therefore begins with an analysis of a commodity.

Value

A commodity is, firstly, something that satisfies a human need; and, secondly, it is something that is exchanged for something else. The utility of a thing gives it *use-value*. Exchange-value (or simply, value) presents itself first of all as the proportion, the ratio, in which a certain number of use-values of one kind are exchanged for a certain number of use-values of another kind. Daily experience shows us that by millions upon millions of such exchanges, all and sundry use-values in themselves very different and not comparable one with another, are equated to one another. Now, what is common in these various things which are constantly weighed one against another in a definite system of social relationships? That which is common to them is that they are *products of labour*. In exchanging products, people equate to one another most diverse kinds of labour. The production of commodities is a system of social relationships in which different producers produce various products (the social division of labour), and in which all these products are equated to one another in exchange. Consequently, the element common to all commodities is not concrete labour in a definite branch of production, not labour of one particular kind, but *abstract* human labour — human labour in general. All the labour power of a given society, represented in the sum total of values of all commodities, is one and the same human labour power. Millions upon millions of acts of exchange prove this. Consequently, each particular commodity represents only a certain part of *socially necessary* labour time. The magnitude of the value is determined by the amount of socially necessary labour, or by the labour time that is socially requisite for the production of the given commodity of the given use-value. ". . . Exchanging labour products of different kinds one for another, they equate the values of the exchanged products; and in doing so they equate the different kinds of labour expended in production, treating them as homogeneous human labour. They do not know that they are doing this, but they do it." As one of the earlier economists said, value is a relationship between two persons, only he should have added that it is a relationship hidden beneath a material wrapping. We can only understand what value is when we consider it from the point of view of a system of social production relationships in one particular historical type of society; and, moreover, of relationships which present themselves in a mass form, the phenomenon of exchange repeating itself millions upon millions of times. "As values, all commodities are only definite quantities of congealed labour time." Having made a detailed analysis of the twofold character of the labour incorporated in commodities, Marx goes on to analyse the *form of value and of money*. His main task, then, is to study the *origin* of the money form of value, to study the *historical process* of the development of exchange, beginning with isolated and casual acts of exchange ("simple, isolated, or casual value form," in which a given quantity of one commodity is exchanged for a given quantity of another), passing on to the universal form of value, in which a number of different commodities are exchanged for one and the same particular commodity, and ending with the money form of value, when gold becomes this particular commodity, the universal equivalent. Being the highest product of the development of exchange and of commodity production, money masks the social character of individual labor, and hides the social tie between the various producers who come together in the market. Marx analyses in great detail the various functions of many; and it is essential to note that here (as generally in the opening chapters of *Capital*) what appears to be an abstract and at times purely deductive mode of exposition in reality reproduces a gigantic collection of facts concerning the history of the development of exchange and commodity production.

> Money . . . presupposes a definite level of commodity exchange. The various forms of money (simple commodity equivalent or means of circulation, or means of payment, treasure, or international money) indicate, according to the different extent to which this or that function is put into application, and according to the comparative predominance of one or other of them, very different grades of the social process of production. [*Capital*, Vol. I.]

SURPLUS VALUE

At a particular stage in the development of commodity production, money becomes transformed into capital. The formula of commodity circulation was C-M-C (commodity — money — commodity); the sale of one commodity for the purpose of buying another. But the general formula of capital, on the contrary, is M-C-M (money — commodity — money); purchase for the purpose of selling — at a profit. The designation "surplus value" is given by Marx to the increase over the original value of money that is put into circulation. The fact of this "growth" of money in capitalist society is well known. Indeed, it is this "growth" which transforms money into *capital*, as a special, historically defined, social relationship of production. Surplus value cannot arise out of the circulation of commodities, for this represents nothing more than the exchange of equivalents; it cannot arise out of an advance in prices, for the mutual losses and gains of buyers and sellers would equalise one another; and we are concerned here, not with what happens to individuals, but with a mass or average or social phenomenon. In order that he may be able to receive surplus value, "Moneybags must . . . find in the market a commodity whose use-value has the peculiar quality of being a source of value" — a commodity, the actual process of whose use is at the same time the process of the creation of value. Such a commodity exists. It is human labour power. Its use is labour, and labour creates value. The owner of money buys labour power at its value, which is determined, like the value of every other commodity, by the socially necessary labour time requisite for its production (that is to say, the cost of maintaining the worker and his family). Having bought labour power, the owner of money is entitled to use it, that is to set it to work for the whole day — twelve hours, let us suppose. Meanwhile, in the course of six hours ("necessary" labour time) the labourer produces sufficient to pay back the cost of his own maintenance; and in the course of the next six hours ("surplus" labour time), he produces a "surplus" product for which the capitalist does not pay him — surplus product or surplus value. In capital, therefore, from the viewpoint of the process of production, we have to distinguish between two parts: first, constant capital, expended for the means of production (machinery, tools, raw materials, etc.), the value of this being (all at once or part by part) transferred, unchanged, to the finished product; and, secondly, variable capital, expended for labour power. The value of this latter capital is not constant, but grows in the labour process, creating surplus value. To express the degree of exploitation of labour power by capital, we must therefore compare the surplus value, not with the whole capital, but only with the variable capital. Thus, in the example just given, the rate of surplus value, as Marx calls this relationship, will be 6:6, *i.e.*, 100%.

There are two historical prerequisites to the genesis of capital: first, accumulation of a considerable sum of money in the hands of individuals living under conditions in which there is a comparatively high development of commodity production. Second, the existence of workers who are "free" in a double sense of the term: free from any constraint or restriction as regards the sale of their labour power; free from any bondage to the soil or to the means of production in general — *i.e.*, of propertyless workers, of "proletarians" who cannot maintain their existence except by the sale of their labour power.

There are two fundamental ways in which surplus value can be increased: by an increase in the working day ("absolute surplus value"); and by a reduction in the necessary working day ("relative surplus value"). Analysing the former method, Marx gives an impressive picture of the struggle of the working class for shorter hours and of government interference, first (from the fourteenth century to the seventeenth) in order to lengthen the working day, and subsequently (factory legislation of the nineteenth century) to shorten it. Since the appearance of *Capital*, the history of the working-class movement in all lands provides a wealth of new facts to amplify this picture. . . .

The accumulation of capital, accelerating the replacement of workers by machinery, creating wealth at the one pole and poverty at the other, gives birth to the so-called "reserve army of labour," to a "relative over-abundance" of workers or to "capitalist over-population." This assumes the most diversified forms, and gives capital the possibility of expanding production at an exceptionally rapid rate. This possibility, in conjunction with enhanced facilities for credit and with the accumulation of capital in the means of production, furnishes, among other things the key to the understanding of the *crises* of overproduction that occur periodically in capitalist countries — first about every ten years, on an average, but sub-sequently in a more continuous form and with a less definite periodicity. From accumulation of capital upon a capitalist foundation we must dis-tinguish the so-called "primitive accumulation": the forcible severance of the worker from the means of production, the driving of the peasants off the land, the stealing of the communal lands, the system of colonies and national debts, of protective tariffs, and the like. "Primitive accumu-lation" creates, at one pole, the "free" proletarian: at the other, the owner of money, the capitalist. . . .

In agriculture, as in industry, capitalism improves the production process only at the price of the "martyrdom of the producers."

> The dispersion of the rural workers over large areas breaks down their powers of resistance at the very time when concentration is increasing the powers of the urban operatives in this respect. In modern agriculture, as in urban industry, the increased productivity and the greater mobility of labour are purchased at the cost of dev-astating labour power and making it a prey to disease. Moreover, every advance in capitalist agriculture is an advance in the art, not only of robbing the worker, but also of robbing the soil. . . . Capi-talist production, therefore, is only able to develop the technique and the combination of the social process of production by simul-taneously undermining the foundations of all wealth — the land and the workers. [*Capital*, Vol. I.]

SOCIALISM

From the foregoing it is manifest that Marx deduces the inevitability of the transformation of capitalist society into Socialist society wholly and exclusively from the economic law of the movement of contemporary society. The chief material foundation of the inevitability of the coming of Socialism is the socialisation of labour in its myriad forms, advancing ever more rapidly, and conspicuously so, throughout the half century that has elapsed since the death of Marx — being especially plain in the growth of large-scale production, of capitalist cartels, syndicates, and trusts; but also in the gigantic increase in the dimensions and the power of finance capital. The intellectual and moral driving force of this transformation is the proletariat, the physical carrier trained by capitalism itself. The contest of the proletariat with the bourgeoisie, assuming various forms which grow continually richer in content, inevitably becomes a political struggle aiming at the conquest of political power by the proletariat ("the dictatorship of the proletariat"). The socialisation of production cannot fail to lead to the transfer of the means of production into the possession of society, to the "expropriation of the expropriators." An immense increase in the productivity of labour; a reduction in working hours; replacement of the remnants, the ruins of petty, primitive, individual production by collective and perfected labour — such will be the direct consequences of this transformation. Capitalism breaks all ties between agriculture and industry; but at the same time, in the course of its highest development, it prepares new elements for the establishment of a connection between the two, uniting industry and agriculture upon the basis of the conscious use of science and the combination of collective labour, the redistribution of population (putting an end at one and the same time to rural seclusion and unsociability and savagery, and to the unnatural concentration of enormous masses of population in huge cities). A new kind of family life, changes in the position of women and in the upbringing of the younger generation, are being prepared by the highest forms of modern capitalism; the labour of women and children, the break-up of the patriarchal family by capitalism, necessarily assume in contemporary society the most terrible, disastrous, and repulsive forms. . . .

> . . . It is plain, moreover, that the composition of the combined labour personnel out of individuals of both sexes and various ages — although in its spontaneously developed and brutal capitalist form (wherein the worker exists for the process of production instead of the process of production existing for the worker) it is a pestilential source of corruption and slavery — under suitable conditions cannot fail to be transformed into a source of human progress. [*Capital*, Vol. I.]

In the factory system are to be found "the germs of the education of the future. . . . This will be an education which, in the case of every child over a certain age, will combine productive labour with instruction and physical culture, not only as a means for increasing social production, but as the only way of producing fully developed human beings" (*ibid.*, p. 522). Upon the same historical foundation, not with the sole idea of throwing light on the past, but with the idea of boldly foreseeing the future and boldly working to bring about its realisation, the Socialism of Marx propounds the problems of nationality and the state. The nation is a necessary product, an inevitable form, in the bourgeois epoch of social development. The working class cannot grow strong, cannot mature, cannot consolidate its forces, except by "establishing itself as the nation," except by being "national" ("though by no means in the bourgeois sense of the term"). But the development of capitalism tends more and more to break down the partitions that separate the nations one from another, does away with national isolation, substitutes class antagonisms for national antagonisms. In the more developed capitalist countries, therefore, it is perfectly true that "the workers have no fatherland," and that "united action" of the workers, in the civilised countries at least, "is one of the first conditions requisite for the emancipation of the workers" (*Communist Manifesto*). . . .

THE PART PLAYED BY LABOR

by Frederick Engels and Karl Marx

THE PART PLAYED BY LABOR IN THE TRANSITION FROM APE TO MAN *

Labor is the source of all wealth, the political economists assert. It is this, next to nature, which supplies it with the material that it converts into wealth. But it is even infinitely more than this. It is the prime basic condition for all human existence, and this to such an extent that, in a sense, we have to say that labor created man himself. . . .

. . . the development of labor necessarily helped to bring the members

* Frederick Engels, *The Part Played by Labor in the Transition from Ape to Man* (New York: 1950). By permission of International Publishers.

of society closer together by multiplying cases of mutual support, joint activity, and by making clear the advantage of this joint activity to each individual. In short, men in the making arrived at the point where *they had something to say* to one another. The urge created its organ; the undeveloped larynx of the ape was slowly but surely transformed by means of modulation in order to produce constantly more developed modulation, and the organs of the mouth gradually learned to pronounce one articulate letter after another.

Comparison with animals proves that this explanation of the origin of language from and in the process of labor is the only correct one. The little that even the most highly developed animals need to communicate with one another can be communicated without the aid of articulate speech. In a state of nature, no animal feels handicapped by its inability to speak or to understand human speech. It is quite different when it has been tamed by man. The dog and the horse, by association with man, have developed such a good ear for articulate speech that they easily learn to understand any language within the range of their circle of ideas. Moreover they have acquired the capacity for feelings such as affection for man, gratitude, etc., which were previously foreign to them. Anyone who has had much to do with such animals will hardly be able to escape the conviction that there are plenty of cases where they *now* feel their inability to speak is a defect, although, unfortunately, it can no longer be remedied owing to their vocal organs being too specialized in a definite direction. However, where the organ exists, within certain limits even this inability disappears. . . .

First labor, after it and then with it speech — these were the two most essential stimuli under the influence of which the brain of the ape gradually changed into that of man, which for all its similarity is far larger and more perfect. Hand in hand with the development of the brain went the development of its most immediate instruments — the sense organs. . . .

The reaction on labor and speech of the development of the brain and its attendant senses, of the increasing clarity of consciousness, power of abstraction and of judgment, gave both labor and speech an ever-renewed impulse to further development, a development which, far from reaching its conclusion when man finally became distinct from the monkey, continued on the whole to make powerful progress, varying in degree and direction among different peoples and at different times, and here and there even interrupted by local or temporary regression. This further development has been strongly urged forward, on the one hand, and guided along more definite directions, on the other hand, by a new element which came into play with the appearance of fully fledged man, namely, *society*.

. . . This "predatory economy" of animals plays an important part in the gradual transformation of species by forcing them to adapt themselves to other than the usual food, thanks to which their blood acquires a different chemical composition and the whole physical constitution gradually alters, while species that were once established die out. There is no doubt that this predatory economy has powerfully contributed to the transition of our ancestors from ape to man. In a race of apes that far surpassed all others in intelligence and adaptability, this predatory economy could not help leading to a continual increase in the number of plants used for food and to the devouring of more and more edible parts of alimentary plants. In short, it led to the food becoming more and more varied, hence also the substances entering the body, the chemical premises for the transition to man. But all that was not yet labor in the proper sense of the word. Labor begins with the making of tools. And what are the most ancient tools that we find — the most ancient judging by the heirlooms of prehistoric man that have been discovered, and by the mode of life of the earliest historical peoples and of the rawest of contemporary savages? They are hunting and fishing implements, the former at the same time serving as weapons. But hunting and fishing presuppose the transition from an exclusively vegetable diet to the concomitant use of meat, and this is another important step in the process of transition from ape to man. . . .

By the co-operation of hands, organs of speech and brain, not only in each individual but also in society, human beings became capable of executing more and more complicated operations, and of setting themselves, and achieving, higher and higher aims. With each generation labor itself became different, more perfect, more diversified. Agriculture was added to hunting and cattle raising; then spinning, weaving, metalworking, pottery, and navigation. Along with trade and industry there appeared finally art and science. From tribes there developed nations and states. Law and politics arose, and with them the fantastic mirror image of human things in the human mind: religion. In the face of all these creations, which appeared in the first place as products of the mind and which seemed to dominate human societies, the more modest productions of the working hand retreated into the background, the more so since the mind that planned the labor already at a very early stage of development of society (for example, already in the primitive family), was able to have the labor that had been planned carried out by other hands than its own. All merit for the swift advance of civilization was ascribed to the mind, to the development and activity of the brain. Men became accustomed to explain their actions from their thoughts instead of from their needs (which in any case are reflected and come to consciousness in the mind); and so there arose in the course of time that idealistic outlook on the world which, especially since the end of the ancient world, has dominated men's minds. It still rules them to such a degree that even the most materialistic natural scientists of the Darwinian school are still unable to form any clear idea of the origin of man, because under this ideological influence they do not recognize the part that has been played therein by labor.

. . . But if animals exert a lasting effect on their environment it happens unintentionally and, as far as the animals themselves are concerned, it is an accident. The further removed men are from animals, however, the more their effect on nature assumes the character of premeditated, planned action directed towards definite ends known in advance. . . .

THE ECONOMIC INTERPRETATION OF HISTORY *

The themes developed by Engels in his speculations on the transition from ape to man are found in a more fully developed form in Marx's *Critique of Political Economy*, where one discovers a broad application of his fundamental thesis of the economic interpretation of history. Marx begins his analysis of history in this selection at approximately the point at which Engels ends his conjectures on the transformation of the primeval ape into the human beings with whose history Marx is here concerned.

In the social production which men carry on they enter into definite relations that are indispensable and independent of their will; these relations of production correspond to a definite stage of development of their material powers of production. The sum total of these relations of production constitutes the economic structure of society — the real founda-

* Karl Marx, From the *Introduction to the Critique of Political Economy* (Berlin: 1859). This excerpt is from *Capital and Other Writings by Karl Marx*, edited by Max Eastman, pp. 10–11 (New York: 1932). Copyright 1932 by The Modern Library. Reprinted by permission of Random House, Inc.

tion, on which rise legal and political superstructures and to which correspond definite forms of social consciousness. The mode of production in material life determines the general character of the social, political and spiritual processes of life. It is not the consciousness of men that determines their existence, but, on the contrary, their social existence determines their consciousness. At a certain stage of their development, the material forces of production in society come in conflict with the existing relations of production, or — what is but a legal expression for the same thing — with the property relations within which they had been at work before. From forms of development of the forces of production these relations turn into their fetters. Then comes the period of social revolution. With the change of the economic foundation the entire immense superstructure is more or less rapidly transformed. In considering such transformations the distinction should always be made between the material transformation of the economic conditions of production which can be determined with the precision of natural science, and the legal, political, religious, aesthetic or philosophic — in short ideological forms in which men become conscious of this conflict and fight it out. Just as our opinion of an individual is not based on what he thinks of himself, so can we not judge of such a period of transformation by its own consciousness; on the contrary, this consciousness must rather be explained from the contradictions of material life, from the existing conflict between the social forces of production and the relations of production. No social order ever disappears before all the productive forces, for which there is room in it, have been developed; and new higher relations of production never appear before the material conditions of their existence have matured in the womb of the old society. Therefore, mankind always takes up only such problems as it can solve; since, looking at the matter more closely, we will always find that the problem itself arises only when the material conditions necessary for its solution already exist or are at least in the process of formation. In broad outlines we can designate the Asiatic, the ancient, the feudal, and the modern bourgeois methods of production as so many epochs in the progress of the economic formation of society. The bourgeois relations of production are the last antagonistic form of the social process of production — antagonistic not in the sense of individual antagonism, but of one arising from conditions surrounding the life of individuals in society; at the same time the productive forces developing in the womb of bourgeois society create the material conditions for the solution of that antagonism. This social formation constitutes, therefore, the closing chapter of the prehistoric stage of human society.

OUTLINES OF A FUTURE SOCIETY *

With the "closing chapter of the prehistoric stage of human society"— the stage in which natural-grown societies necessarily generate class antagonisms — mankind will be free to enter the classless society of the future. This ultimate goal to which Marxism points is of absolutely crucial importance in its overall theory, but it has been dealt with only sketchily by Marxists and inadequately discussed. In *The German Ideology* Marx suggested something of the nature of the future society.

The division of labor presents just the first example of the fact that so long as men find themselves in a natural-grown society, so long therefore as the split exists between the individual and the common interest, so long as activities are not divided voluntarily but by a process of natural growth, man's own act becomes to him an alien power standing over against him, dominating him, instead of being ruled by him. That is to say that according as labor begins to be divided, everyone has a definite, circumscribed sphere of activity which is put upon him and from which he cannot escape. He is hunter, fisherman or shepherd or "critical critic," and must remain so if he does not want to lose the means of subsistence — whereas in the Communist society, where each one does not have a circumscribed sphere of activity but can train himself in any branch he chooses, society by regulating the common production makes it possible for me to do this today and that tomorrow, to hunt in the morning, to fish in the afternoon, to carry on cattle-breeding in the evening, also to criticize the food — just as I please — without becoming either hunter, fisherman, shepherd or critic. This setting-fast of social activity, this consolidation of our own product into an objective power over us, which outgrows our control, thwarts our expectations, brings our calculations to nothing, is one of the principal distinguishing points in historic evolution up to this day. . . .

In all history up to now it is certainly an empiric fact that single individuals, with the expansion of their activity to a world historic scale, have become more and more enslaved to an alien power . . . a power which has become steadily more massive . . . But it is just as empirically grounded that through the overthrow of the existing social order, through

---

* Karl Marx and Friedrich Engels, *The German Ideology.* This work was written in 1845–46, but only one section was published as an article in 1847. The work was first published in full in 1932. *Ibid.,* pp. 1–2.

the Communist revolution . . . and what is the same thing, the abolition of private property, this power . . . will be dissolved, and then the
emancipation of every single individual will be achieved to the same extent
that history transforms itself completely into world history. That the
genuine spiritual riches of the individual depend entirely upon the richness
of the actual relations in which he stands, is clear from the above. Single
individuals will in this way only be freed from the various national and
local limitations, put into practical relation to the productive activity
(including spiritual production) of the whole world, and placed in a position to acquire the capacity to enjoy this all-sided production of the whole
earth. — That *all-sided* dependence, that natural-grown form of the
world historical cooperation of individuals, will be transformed by the
Communist revolution into a control and conscious domination of those
powers that are born of the mutual reactions of men, and which have
heretofore imposed upon them and ruled over them as powers completely
alien.

STATE AND REVOLUTION

by V. I. Lenin *

POSTSCRIPT TO THE FIRST EDITION

This pamphlet was written in August and September, 1917. . . . However, the second part of the pamphlet (devoted to the "Experience of
the Russian Revolutions of 1905 and 1917,") will probably have to be
put off for a long time. It is more pleasant and useful to go through the
"experience of the revolution" than to write about it. . . .

THE STATE AS THE PRODUCT OF THE IRRECONCILABILITY
OF CLASS ANTAGONISMS

What is now happening to Marx's doctrine has, in the course of history,
often happened to the doctrines of other revolutionary thinkers and leaders

* V. I. Lenin, *State and Revolution* (New York: 1932). By permission of International
Publishers.

of oppressed classes struggling for emancipation. During the lifetime of great revolutionaries, the oppressing classes have visited relentless persecution on them and received their teaching with the most savage hostility, the most furious hatred, the most ruthless campaign of lies and slanders. After their death, attempts are made to turn them into harmless icons, canonise them, and surround their *names* with a certain halo for the "consolation" of the oppressed classes and with the object of duping them, while at the same time emasculating and vulgarising the *real essence* of their revolutionary theories and blunting their revolutionary edge. At the present time, the bourgeoisie and the opportunists within the labour movement are co-operating in this work of adulterating Marxism. They omit, obliterate, and distort the revolutionary side of its teaching, its revolutionary soul. They push to the foreground and extol what is, or seems, acceptable to the bourgeoisie. . . .

In such circumstances, the distortion of Marxism being so widespread, it is our first task to *resuscitate* the real teachings of Marx on the state. For this purpose it will be necessary to quote at length from the works of Marx and Engels themselves. . . .

Let us begin with the most popular of Engels' works, *The Origin of the Family, Private Property, and the State.* . . .

Summarising his historical analysis Engels says:

> The state is therefore by no means a power imposed on society from the outside; just as little is it "the reality of the moral idea," "the image and reality of reason," as Hegel asserted. Rather, it is a product of society at a certain stage of development; it is the admission that this society has become entangled in an insoluble contradiction with itself, that it is cleft into irreconcilable antagonisms which it is powerless to dispel. But in order that these antagonisms, classes with conflicting economic interests, may not consume themselves and society in sterile struggle, a power apparently standing above society becomes necessary, whose purpose is to moderate the conflict and keep it within the bounds of "order"; and this power arising out of society, but placing itself above it, and increasingly separating itself from it, is the state.

Here we have, expressed in all its clearness, the basic idea of Marxism on the question of the historical role and meaning of the state. The state is the product and the manifestation of the *irreconcilability* of class antagonisms. The state arises when, where, and to the extent that the class antagonisms *cannot* be objectively reconciled. And, conversely, the existence of the state proves that the class antagonisms *are* irreconcilable.

It is precisely on this most important and fundamental point that distortions of Marxism arise along two main lines.

On the one hand, the bourgeois, and particularly the petty-bourgeois, ideologists, compelled under the pressure of indisputable historical facts to admit that the state only exists where there are class antagonisms and the class struggle, "correct" Marx in such a way as to make it appear that the state is an organ for *reconciling* the classes. According to Marx, the state could neither arise nor maintain itself if a reconciliation of classes were possible. But with the petty-bourgeois and philistine professors and publicists, the state — and this frequently on the strength of benevolent references to Marx! — becomes a conciliator of the classes. According to Marx, the state is an organ of class *domination,* an organ of *oppression* of one class by another; its aim is the creation of "order" which legalises and perpetuates this oppression by moderating the collisions between the classes. . . .

. . . if the state is the product of the irreconcilable character of class antagonisms, if it is a force standing *above* society and "increasingly separating itself from it," then it is clear that the liberation of the oppressed class is impossible not only without a violent revolution, *but also without the destruction* of the apparatus of state power, which was created by the ruling class and in which this "separation" is embodied. . . .

SPECIAL BODIES OF ARMED MEN, PRISONS, ETC. . . .

Engels develops the conception of that "power" which is termed the state — a power arising from society, but placing itself above it and becoming more and more separated from it. What does this power mainly consist of? It consists of special bodies of armed men who have at their disposal prisons, etc.

We are justified in speaking of special bodies of armed men, because the public power peculiar to every state is not "absolutely identical" with the armed population, with its "self-acting armed organisation."

Like all the great revolutionary thinkers, Engels tries to draw the attention of the class-conscious workers to that very fact which to prevailing philistinism appears least of all worthy of attention, most common and sanctified by solid, indeed, one might say, petrified prejudices. A standing army and police are the chief instruments of state power. But can this be otherwise? . . .

Here the question regarding the privileged position of the officials as organs of state power is clearly stated. The main point is indicated as follows: what is it that places them *above* society? . . .

> As the state arose out of the need to hold class antagonisms in check; but as it, at the same time, arose in the midst of the conflict of these classes, it is, as a rule, the state of the most powerful, economically dominant class, which by virtue thereof becomes also the dominant class politically, and thus acquires new means of holding down and exploiting the oppressed class. . . .

Not only the ancient and feudal states were organs of exploitation of the slaves and serfs, but

> the modern representative state is the instrument of the exploitation of wage-labour by capital. By way of exception, however, there are periods when the warring classes so nearly attain equilibrium that the state power, ostensibly appearing as a mediator, assumes for the moment a certain independence in relation to both. . . .

In a democratic republic, Engels continues, "wealth wields its power indirectly, but all the more effectively," first, by means of "direct corruption of the officials" (America); second, by means of "the alliance of the government with the stock exchange" (France and America).

At the present time, imperialism and the domination of the banks have "developed" to an unusually fine art both these methods of defending and asserting the omnipotence of wealth in democratic republics of all descriptions. . . .

We must also note that Engels quite definitely regards universal suffrage as a means of bourgeois domination. Universal suffrage, he says, obviously summing up the long experience of German Social-Democracy, is "an index of the maturity of the working class; it cannot, and never will, be anything else but that in the modern state." . . .

A general summary of his views is given by Engels in the most popular of his works in the following words:

> The state, therefore, has not existed from all eternity. There have been societies which managed without it, which had no conception of the state and state power. At a certain stage of economic development, which was necessarily bound up with the cleavage of society into classes, the state became a necessity owing to this cleavage. We are now rapidly approaching a stage in the development of production at which the existence of these classes has not only ceased to be a necessity, but is becoming a positive hindrance to production. They will disappear as inevitably as they arose at an earlier stage. Along with them, the state will inevitably disappear. The society that

organises production anew on the basis of a free and equal association
of the producers will put the whole state machine where it will then
belong: in the museum of antiquities, side by side with the spinning
wheel and the bronze axe. . . .

THE "WITHERING AWAY" OF THE STATE AND VIOLENT REVOLUTION

Engels' words regarding the "withering away" of the state enjoy such
popularity, they are so often quoted, and they show so clearly the essence
of the usual adulteration by means of which Marxism is made to look like
opportunism, that we must dwell on them in detail. Let us quote the
whole passage from which they are taken.

> The proletariat seizes state power, and then transforms the means
> of production into state property. But in doing this, it puts an end
> to itself as the proletariat, it puts an end to all class differences and
> class antagonisms, it puts an end also to the state as the state. Former
> society, moving in class antagonisms, had need of the state, that
> is, an organisation of the exploiting class at each period for the
> maintenance of its external conditions of production; therefore,
> in particular, for the forcible holding down of the exploited class
> in the conditions of oppression (slavery, bondage or serfdom, wage-
> labour) determined by the existing mode of production. The state
> was the official representative of society as a whole, its embodiment
> in a visible corporate body; but it was this only in so far as it was the
> state of that class which itself, in its epoch, represented society as a
> whole: in ancient times, the state of the slave-owning citizens; in the
> Middle Ages, of the feudal nobility; in our epoch, of the bourgeoisie.
> When ultimately it becomes really representative of society as a
> whole, it makes itself superfluous. As soon as there is no longer any
> class of society to be held in subjection; as soon as, along with class
> domination and the struggle for individual existence based on the
> former anarchy of production, the collisions and excesses arising from
> these have also been abolished, there is nothing more to be repressed,
> and a special repressive force, a state, is no longer necessary. The first
> act in which the state really comes forward as the representative of
> society as a whole — the seizure of the means of production in the
> name of society — is at the same time its last independent act as a
> state. The interference of a state power in social relations becomes
> superfluous in one sphere after another, and then becomes dormant
> of itself. Government over persons is replaced by the administration
> of things and the direction of the processes of production. The state
> is not "abolished," *it withers away*. It is from this standpoint that we
> must appraise . . . the demand of the so-called Anarchists that the
> state should be abolished overnight. . . . [*Anti-Dühring*]*

* Friedrich Engels, *Anti-Dühring* (1877), London and New York, 1933. — Ed.

. . . Engels at the very outset of his argument says that, in assuming state power, the proletariat by that very act "puts an end to the state as the state." . . . Engels speaks here of the destruction of the bourgeois state by the proletarian revolution, while the words about its withering away refer to the remains of *proletarian* statehood *after* the Socialist revolution. The bourgeois state does not "wither away," according to Engels, but is "put an end to" by the proletariat in the course of the revolution. What withers away after the revolution is the proletarian state or semi-state.

Secondly, the state is a "special repressive force." This splendid and extremely profound definition of Engels' is given by him here with complete lucidity. It follows from this that the "special repressive force" of the bourgeoisie for the suppression of the proletariat, of the millions of workers by a handful of the rich, must be replaced by a "special repressive force" of the proletariat for the suppression of the bourgeoisie (the dictatorship of the proletariat). It is just this that constitutes the destruction of "the state as the state." It is just this that constitutes the "act" of "the seizure of the means of production in the name of society." And it is obvious that such a substitution of one (proletarian) "special repressive force" for another (bourgeois) "special repressive force" can in no way take place in the form of a "withering away."

Thirdly, as to the "withering away" or, more expressively and colourfully, as to the state "becoming dormant," Engels refers quite clearly and definitely to the period *after* "the seizure of the means of production [by the state] in the name of society," that is, *after* the Socialist revolution. We all know that the political form of the "state" at that time is complete democracy. But it never enters the head of any of the opportunists who shamelessly distort Marx that when Engels speaks here of the state "withering away," or "becoming dormant," he speaks of *democracy*. At first sight this seems very strange. But it is "unintelligible" only to one who has not reflected on the fact that democracy is *also* a state and that, consequently, democracy will *also* dissappear when the state disappears. The bourgeois state can only be "put an end to" by a revolution. The state in general, *i.e.*, most complete democracy, can only "wither away."

Fourthly, having formulated his famous proposition that "the state withers away," Engels at once explains concretely that this proposition is directed equally against the opportunists and the Anarchists. . . .

Fifthly, in the same work of Engels, from which every one remembers his argument on the "withering away" of the state, there is also a disquisition on the significance of a violent revolution. The historical analysis of its role becomes, with Engels, a veritable panegyric on violent revolution. This, of course, "no one remembers"; to talk or even to think of the im-

portance of this idea is not considered good form by contemporary
Socialist parties, and in the daily propaganda and agitation among the
masses it plays no part whatever. Yet it is indissolubly bound up with the
"withering away" of the state in one harmonious whole.

Here is Engels' argument:

> . . . That force, however, plays another role (other than that of a
> diabolical power) in history, a revolutionary role; that, in the words
> of Marx, it is the midwife of every old society which is pregnant with
> the new; that it is the instrument with whose aid social movement
> forces its way through and shatters the dead, fossilised political
> forms — of this there is not a word in Herr Dühring. It is only with
> sighs and groans that he admits the possibility that force will perhaps
> be necessary for the overthrow of the economic system of exploitation
> — unfortunately! because all use of force, forsooth, demoralises the
> person who uses it. And this in spite of the immense moral and
> spiritual impetus which has resulted from every victorious revolu-
> tion! . . .

How can this panegyric on violent revolution . . . be combined with the
theory of the "withering away" of the state to form one doctrine? . . .

We have already said above and shall show more fully later that the
teaching of Marx and Engels regarding the inevitability of a violent revolution refers to the bourgeois state. It *cannot* be replaced by the proletarian
state (the dictatorship of the proletariat) through "withering away," but,
as a general rule, only through a violent revolution. . . . The necessity of
systematically fostering among the masses *this* and just this point of view
about violent revolution lies at the root of the *whole* of Marx's and Engels'
teaching. . . .

The replacement of the bourgeois by the proletarian state is impossible
without a violent revolution. The abolition of the proletarian state, *i.e.*,
of all states, is only possible through "withering away." . . .

It is instructive to compare with this general statement of the idea of
the state disappearing after classes have disappeared, the statement contained in the *Communist Manifesto*, written by Marx and Engels . . .

> In depicting the most general phases of the development of the
> proletariat, we traced the more or less veiled civil war, raging within
> existing society, up to the point where that war breaks out into open
> revolution, and where the violent overthrow of the bourgeoisie lays
> the foundation for the sway of the proletariat. . . .
>
> The proletariat will use its political supremacy to wrest by degrees
> all capital from the bourgeoisie, to centralise all instruments of
> production in the hands of the state, *i.e.*, of the proletariat organised
> as the ruling class; and to increase the total of productive forces as
> rapidly as possible.

Here we have a formulation of one of the most remarkable and most important ideas of Marxism on the subject of the state, namely, the idea of the "dictatorship of the proletariat" . . . "*the proletariat organised as the ruling class.*" . . .

The doctrine of the class struggle, as applied by Marx to the question of the state and of the Socialist revolution, leads inevitably to the recognition of the *political rule* of the proletariat, of its dictatorship, *i.e.*, of a power shared with none and relying directly upon the armed force of the masses. The overthrow of the bourgeoisie is realisable only by the transformation of the proletariat into the *ruling class*, able to crush the inevitable and desperate resistance of the bourgeoisie, and to organise, for the new economic order, *all* the toiling and exploited masses.

The proletariat needs state power, the centralised organisation of force, the organisation of violence, both for the purpose of crushing the resistance of the exploiters and for the purpose of *guiding* the great mass of the population — the peasantry, the petty-bourgeoisie, the semi-proletarians — in the work of organising Socialist economy.

By educating a workers' party, Marxism educates the vanguard of the proletariat, capable of assuming power and of *leading the whole people* to Socialism, of directing and organising the new order, of being the teacher, guide and leader of all the toiling and exploited in the task of building up their social life without the bourgeoisie and against the bourgeoisie. . . .

But, if the proletariat needs the state, as a *special* form of organisation of violence *against* the capitalist class, the following question arises almost automatically: is it thinkable that such an organisation can be created without a preliminary break-up and destruction of the state machinery created for *its own* use by the bourgeoisie? The *Communist Manifesto* leads straight to this conclusion. . . .

The problem of the state is put concretely: how did the bourgeois state, the state machinery necessary for the rule of the bourgeoisie, come into being? What were its changes, what its evolution in the course of the bourgeois revolutions and in the face of the independent actions of the oppressed classes? What are the tasks of the proletariat relative to this state machinery?

The centralised state power peculiar to bourgeois society came into being in the period of the fall of absolutism. Two institutions are especially characteristic of this state machinery: bureaucracy and the standing army. . . .

The development, perfecting and strengthening of the bureaucratic and military apparatus has been going on through all the bourgeois revolutions of which Europe has seen so many since the fall of feudalism. It is

particularly the petty-bourgeoisie that is attracted to the side of the big
bourgeoisie and to its allegiance, largely by means of this apparatus, which
provides the upper strata of the peasantry, small artisans and tradesmen
with a number of comparatively comfortable, quiet and respectable berths
raising their holders *above* the people. . . .

But the longer the process of "re-apportioning" the bureaucratic apparatus among the various bourgeois and petty-bourgeois parties (among
the Cadets, S.-R.'s and Mensheviks, if we take the case of Russia) goes
on, the more clearly the oppressed classes, with the proletariat at their
head, realise that they are irreconcilably hostile to the *whole* of bourgeois
society. Hence the necessity for all bourgeois parties, even for the most
democratic and "revolutionary-democratic" among them, to increase their
repressive measures against the revolutionary proletariat, to strengthen the
apparatus of repression, *i.e.*, the same state machinery. Such a course of
events compels the revolution *"to concentrate all its forces of destruction"*
against the state power, and to regard the problem as one, not of perfecting
the machinery of the state, but of *breaking up and annihilating it.* . . .

At the present time, world history is undoubtedly leading, on an incomparably larger scale than in 1852, to the "concentration of all the
forces" of the proletarian revolution for the purpose of "destroying" the
state machinery. . . .

In 1907 Mehring published . . . extracts from a letter by Marx to
Weydemeyer dated March 5, 1852. In this letter, among other things, is
the following noteworthy observation:

> As far as I am concerned, the honour does not belong to me for
> having discovered the existence either of classes in modern society
> or of the struggle between the classes. Bourgeois historians a long
> time before me expounded the historical development of this class
> struggle, and bourgeois economists, the economic anatomy of classes.
> What was new on my part, was to prove the following: (1) that the
> existence of classes is connected only with certain historical struggles
> which arise out of the development of production [*historische
> Entwicklungskämpfe der Produktion*]; (2) that class struggle neces-
> sarily leads to the dictatorship of the proletariat; (3) that this dic-
> tatorship is itself only a transition to the abolition of all classes and
> to a classless society. . . .

. . . The theory of the class struggle was *not* created by Marx, but by the
bourgeoisie *before* Marx and is, generally speaking, *acceptable* to the
bourgeoisie. He who recognises *only* the class struggle is not yet a Marxist;
he may be found not to have gone beyond the boundaries of bourgeois
reasoning and politics. To limit Marxism to the teaching of the class

struggle means to curtail Marxism — to distort it, to reduce it to something which is acceptable to the bourgeoisie. A Marxist is one who *extends* the acceptance of class struggle to the acceptance of the *dictatorship of the proletariat*. . . .

. . . the state during this period inevitably must be a state that is democratic *in a new way* (for the proletariat and the poor in general) and dictatorial *in a new way* (against the bourgeoisie).

Further, the substance of the teachings of Marx about the state is assimilated only by one who understands that the dictatorship of a *single* class is necessary not only for any class society generally, not only for the *proletariat* which has overthrown the bourgeoisie, but for the entire *historic period* which separates capitalism from "classless society," from Communism. The forms of bourgeois states are exceedingly variegated, but their essence is the same: in one way or another, all these states are in the last analysis inevitably a *dictatorship of the bourgeoisie*. The transition from capitalism to Communism will certainly bring a great variety and abundance of political forms, but the essence will inevitably be only one: *the dictatorship of the proletariat*. . . .

WHAT IS TO REPLACE THE SHATTERED STATE MACHINERY?

. . . To replace this machinery by "the proletariat organised as the ruling class," by "establishing democracy" — such was the answer of the *Communist Manifesto*.

Without resorting to Utopias, Marx waited for the *experience* of a mass movement to produce the answer to the problem as to the exact forms which this organisation of the proletariat as the ruling class will assume and as to the exact manner in which this organisation will be combined with the most complete, most consistent "establishment of democracy."

The experiment of the Commune, meagre as it was, was subjected by Marx to the most careful analysis in his *The Civil War in France*. . . .

> The Commune was formed of municipal councillors, chosen by universal suffrage in various wards of the town, responsible and revocable at short terms. The majority of its members were naturally working men, or acknowledged representatives of the working class.
> . . . Instead of continuing to be the agent of the Central Government, the police was at once stripped of its political attributes, and turned into the responsible and at all times revocable agent of the Commune. So were the officials of all other branches of the administration. From the members of the Commune downwards, the public service had to be done at *workmen's wages*. . . .

Thus the Commune would appear to have replaced the shattered state machinery "only" by fuller democracy: abolition of the standing army: all officials to be fully elective and subject to recall. . . . as a matter of fact this "only" signifies a gigantic replacement of one type of institution by others of a fundamentally different order. Here we observe a case of "transformation of quantity into quality" . . .

In this connection the Commune's measure emphasised by Marx, particularly worthy of note, is: the abolition of all representation allowances, and of all money privileges in the case of officials, the reduction of the remuneration of *all* servants of the state to *"workingmen's wages."* Here is shown, more clearly than anywhere else, the *break* from a bourgeois democracy to a proletarian democracy, from the democracy of the oppressors to the democracy of the oppressed classes, from the state as a "special force for suppression" of a given class to the suppression of the oppressors by the *whole force* of the majority of the people — the workers and the peasants. . . .

The reduction of the remuneration of the highest state officials seems "simply" a demand of naive, primitive democracy. . . . the transition from capitalism to Socialism is *impossible* without "return," in a measure, to "primitive" democracy (how can one otherwise pass on to the discharge of all the state functions by the majority of the population and by every individual of the population?); . . . Capitalist culture has *created* large-scale production, factories, railways, the postal service, telephones, etc., and *on this basis* the great majority of functions of the old "state power" have become so simplified and can be reduced to such simple operations of registration, filing and checking that they will be quite within the reach of every literate person, and it will be possible to perform them for "workingmen's wages," which circumstance can (and must) strip those functions of every shadow of privilege, of every appearance of "official grandeur." . . .

The Destruction of Parliamentarism

The Commune — says Marx — was to be a working, not a parliamentary body, executive and legislative at the same time. . . .

To decide once every few years which member of the ruling class is to repress and oppress the people through parliament — this is the real essence of bourgeois parliamentarism, not only in parliamentary-constitutional monarchies, but also in the most democratic republics. . . .

The venal and rotten parliamentarism of bourgeois society is replaced in the Commune by institutions in which freedom of opinion and discussion does not degenerate into deception, for the parliamentarians must themselves work, must themselves execute their own laws, must themselves verify their results in actual life, must themselves be directly responsible to their electorate. Representative institutions remain, but parliamentarism as a special system, as a division of labour between the legislative and the executive functions, as a privileged position for the deputies, *no longer exists.* Without representative institutions we cannot imagine democracy, not even proletarian democracy; but we can and *must* think of democracy without parliamentarism . . .

We are not Utopians, we do not indulge in "dreams" of how best to do away *immediately* with all administration, with all subordination; these Anarchist dreams, based upon a lack of understanding of the task of proletarian dictatorship, are basically foreign to Marxism, and, as a matter of fact, they serve but to put off the Socialist revolution until human nature is different. No, we want the Socialist revolution with human nature as it is now, with human nature that cannot do without subordination, control, and "managers."

But if there be subordination, it must be to the armed vanguard of all the exploited and the labouring — to the proletariat. The specific "commanding" methods of the state officials can and must begin to be replaced — immediately, within twenty-four hours — by the simple functions of "managers" and bookkeepers, functions which are now already within the capacity of the average city dweller and can well be performed for "workingmen's wages."

. . . Such a beginning, on the basis of large-scale production, of itself leads to the gradual "withering away" of all bureaucracy, to the gradual creation of a new order . . . an order which has nothing to do with wage slavery, an order in which the more and more simplified functions of control and accounting will be performed by each in turn, will then become a habit, and will finally die out as *special* functions of a special stratum of the population. . . .

To organise the *whole* national economy like the postal system, in such a way that the technicians, managers, bookkeepers as well as *all* officials, should receive no higher wages than "workingmen's wages," all under the control and leadership of the armed proletariat — this is our immediate aim. This is the kind of state and economic basis we need. This is what will produce the destruction of parliamentarism, while retaining representative institutions. This is what will free the labouring classes from the prostitution of these institutions by the bourgeoisie. . . .

> If anything is certain, it is that our party and the working class can
> only come to power under the form of the democratic republic. This
> is, indeed, the specific form for the dictatorship of the proletariat, as
> has already been shown by the great French Revolution. . . .

Engels repeats here in a particularly emphatic form the fundamental
idea which runs like a red thread throughout all Marx's work, namely,
that the democratic republic is the nearest approach to the dictatorship of
the proletariat. For such a republic — without in the least setting aside
the domination of capital, and, therefore, the oppression of the masses and
the class struggle — inevitably leads to such an extension, development,
unfolding and sharpening of that struggle that, as soon as the possibility
arises for satisfying the fundamental interests of the oppressed masses, this
possibility is realised inevitably and solely in the dictatorship of the
proletariat, in the guidance of these masses by the proletariat. . . .

From the point of view of the proletariat and the proletarian revolution,
Engels, like Marx, insists on democratic centralism, on one indivisible
republic. The federal republic he considers either as an exception and a
hindrance to development, or as a transitional form from a monarchy to
a centralised republic, as a "step forward" under certain special conditions. . . .

. . . when Engels says that in a democratic republic, "no less" than in a
monarchy, the state remains a "machine for the oppression of one class
by another," this by no means signifies that the *form* of oppression is a
matter of indifference to the proletariat, as some Anarchists "teach." A
wider, freer and more open *form* of the class struggle and of class oppression enormously assists the proletariat in its struggle for the abolition of
all classes.

. . . why only a new generation will be able completely to throw out all
the state rubbish — this question is bound up with the question of overcoming democracy, to which we now turn.

ENGELS ON THE OVERCOMING OF DEMOCRACY . . .

In the current arguments about the state, the mistake is constantly
made against which Engels cautions here, and which we have indiciated
above, namely, it is constantly forgotten that the destruction of the state
means also the destruction of democracy; that the withering away of the
state also means the withering away of democracy.

At first sight such a statement seems exceedingly strange and incomprehensible; indeed, some one may even begin to fear lest we be ex-

pecting the advent of such an order of society in which the principle of the subordination of the minority to the majority will not be respected — for is not a democracy just the recognition of this principle?

No, democracy is *not* identical with the subordination of the minority to the majority. Democracy is a *state* recognising the subordination of the minority to the majority, *i.e.*, an organisation for the systematic use of *violence* by one class against the other, by one part of the population against another.

We set ourselves the ultimate aim of destroying the state, *i.e.*, every organised and systematic violence, every use of violence against man in general. We do not expect the advent of an order of society in which the principle of subordination of minority to majority will not be observed. But, striving for Socialism, we are convinced that it will develop into Communism; that, side by side with this, there will vanish all need for force, for the *subjection* of one man to another, and of one part of the population to another, since people will *grow accustomed* to observing the elementary conditions of social existence *without force and without subjection.*

In order to emphasise this element of habit, Engels speaks of a *new generation,* "reared under new and free social conditions," which "will be able to throw on the scrap heap all this state rubbish" — every kind of state, including even the democratic-republican state. . . .

On the basis of what *data* can the future evolution of future Communism be considered?

On the basis of the fact that *it has its origin* in capitalism, that it develops historically from capitalism, that it is the result of the action of a social force to which capitalism *has given birth.* There is no shadow of an attempt on Marx's part to conjure up a Utopia, to make idle guesses about that which cannot be known. Marx treats the question of Communism in the same way as a naturalist would treat the question of the evolution of, say, a new biological species, if he knew that such and such was its origin, and such and such the direction in which it changed.

. . . historically, there must undoubtedly be a special stage or epoch of *transition* from capitalism to Communism. . . .

Between capitalist and Communist society — Marx continues — lies the period of the revolutionary transformation of the former into the latter. To this also corresponds a political transition period, in which the state can be no other than *the revolutionary dictatorship of the proletariat.*

This conclusion Marx bases on an analysis of the role played by the proletariat in modern capitalist society, on the data concerning the evolution of this society, and on the irreconcilability of the opposing interests of the proletariat and the bourgeoisie.

Earlier the question was put thus: to attain its emancipation, the proletariat must overthrow the bourgeoisie, conquer political power and establish its own revolutionary dictatorship.

Now the question is put somewhat differently: the transition from capitalist society, developing towards Communism, towards a Communist society, is impossible without a "political transition period," and the state in this period can only be the revolutionary dictatorship of the proletariat.

What, then, is the relation of this dictatorship to democracy?

. . . On the basis of all that has been said above, one can define more exactly how democracy changes in the transition from capitalism to Communism.

In capitalist society, under the conditions most favourable to its development, we have more or less complete democracy in the democratic republic. But this democracy is always bound by the narrow framework of capitalist exploitation, and consequently always remains, in reality, a democracy for the minority, only for the possessing classes, only for the rich. Freedom in capitalist society always remains just about the same as it was in the ancient Greek republics: freedom for the slave-owners. The modern wage-slaves, owing to the conditions of capitalist exploitation, are so much crushed by want and poverty that "democracy is nothing to them," "politics is nothing to them"; that, in the ordinary peaceful course of events, the majority of the population is debarred from participating in social and political life. . . .

But from this capitalist democracy — inevitably narrow, subtly rejecting the poor, and therefore hypocritical and false to the core — progress does not march onward, simply, smoothly and directly, to "greater and greater democracy," as the liberal professors and petty-bourgeois opportunists would have us believe. No, progress marches onward, *i.e.*, towards Communism, through the dictatorship of the proletariat; it cannot do otherwise, for there is no one else and no other way to *break the resistance* of the capitalist exploiters. . . .

Democracy for the vast majority of the people, and suppression by force, *i.e.*, exclusion from democracy, of the exploiters and oppressors of the people — this is the modification of democracy during the *transition* from capitalism to Communism.

Only in Communist society, when the resistance of the capitalists has been completely broken, when the capitalists have disappeared, when there are no classes (*i.e.*, there is no difference between the members of society in their relation to the social means of production), *only then* "the state ceases to exist," and "*it becomes possible to speak of freedom.*" Only then a really full democracy, a democracy without any exceptions, will be possible and will be realised. And only then will democracy itself begin to *wither away* due to the simple fact that, freed from capitalist slavery, from the untold horrors, savagery, absurdities and infamies of capitalist exploitation, people will gradually *become accustomed* to the observance of the elementary rules of social life that have been known for centuries and repeated for thousands of years in all school books; they will become accustomed to observing them without force, without compulsion, without subordination, without the *special apparatus* for compulsion which is called the state.

The expression "the state *withers away*," is very well chosen, for it indicates both the gradual and the elemental nature of the process. Only habit can, and undoubtedly will, have such an effect; for we see around us millions of times how readily people get accustomed to observe the necessary rules of life in common, if there is no exploitation, if there is nothing that causes indignation, that calls forth protest and revolt and has to be *suppressed*.

Thus, in capitalist society, we have a democracy that is curtailed, poor, false; a democracy only for the rich, for the minority. The dictatorship of the proletariat, the period of transition to Communism, will, for the first time, produce democracy for the people, for the majority, side by side with the necessary suppression of the minority — the exploiters. Communism alone is capable of giving a really complete democracy, and the more complete it is the more quickly will it become unnecessary and wither away of itself.

In other words: under capitalism we have a state in the proper sense of the word, that is, special machinery for the suppression of one class by another, and of the majority by the minority at that. Naturally, for the successful discharge of such a task as the systematic suppression by the exploiting minority of the exploited majority, the greatest ferocity and savagery of suppression are required, seas of blood are required, through which mankind is marching in slavery, serfdom, and wage-labour. . . .

Finally, only Communism renders the state absolutely unnecessary, for there is *no one* to be suppressed — "no one" in the sense of a *class*, in the sense of a systematic struggle with a definite section of the population. We are not Utopians, and we do not in the least deny the possibility and inevitability of excesses on the part of *individual persons*, nor the need to suppress *such* excesses. But, in the first place, no special machinery, no special apparatus of repression is needed for this; this will be done by the armed people itself, as simply and as readily as any crowd of civilised people, even in modern society, parts a pair of combatants or does not allow a woman to be outraged. And, secondly, we know that the fundamental social cause of excesses which consist in violating the rules of social life is the exploitation of the masses, their want and their poverty. With the removal of this chief cause, excesses will inevitably begin to *"wither away."* We do not know how quickly and in what succession, but we know that they will wither away. With their withering away, the state will also *wither away.*

Without going into Utopias, Marx defined more fully what can *now* be defined regarding this future, namely, the difference between the lower and higher phases (degrees, stages) of Communist society.

First Phase of Communist Society . . .

> What we are dealing with here [analysing the program of the party] is not a Communist society which has *developed* on its own foundations, but, on the contrary, one which is just *emerging* from capitalist society, and which therefore in all respects — economic, moral and intellectual — still bears the birthmarks of the old society from whose womb it sprung.

And it is this Communist society — a society which has just come into the world out of the womb of capitalism, and which, in all respects, bears the stamp of the old society — that Marx terms the "first," or lower, phase of Communist society. . . .

The first phase of Communism, therefore, still cannot produce justice and equality; differences, and unjust differences, in wealth will still exist, but the *exploitation* of man by man will have become impossible, because it will be impossible to seize as private property the *means of production*, the factories, machines, land, and so on. . . .

Marx not only takes into account with the greatest accuracy the inevitable inequality of men; he also takes into account the fact that the mere conversion of the means of production into the common property of the whole of society ("Socialism" in the generally accepted sense of the word) *does not remove* the defects of distribution and the inequality of "bourgeois right" which *continue to rule* as long as the products are divided "according to work performed."

> But these defects — Marx continues — are unavoidable in the first phase of Communist society, when, after long travail, it first emerges from capitalist society. Justice can never rise superior to the economic conditions of society and the cultural development conditioned by them.

And so, in the first phase of Communist society (generally called Socialism) "bourgeois right" is *not* abolished in its entirety. . . .

. . . "He who does not work, shall not eat" — this Socialist principle is *already* realised; "for an equal quantity of labour, an equal quantity of products" — this Socialist principle is also *already* realised. However, this is not yet Communism, and this does not abolish "bourgeois right," which gives to unequal individuals, in return for an unequal (in reality unequal) amount of work, an equal quantity of products.

This is a "defect," says Marx, but it is unavoidable during the first phase of Communism; for, if we are not to fall into Utopianism, we cannot imagine that, having overthrown capitalism, people will at once learn to work for society *without any standards of right*; indeed, the abolition of capitalism *does not immediately lay* the economic foundations for *such* a change. . . .

HIGHER PHASE OF COMMUNIST SOCIETY

Marx continues:

> In a higher phase of Communist society, when the enslaving subordination of individuals in the division of labour has disappeared, and with it also the antagonism between mental and physical labour; when labour has become not only a means of living, but itself the first necessity of life; when, along with the all-round development of individuals, the productive forces too have grown, and all the springs of social wealth are flowing more freely — it is only at that stage that it will be possible to pass completely beyond the narrow horizon of bourgeois rights, and for society to inscribe on its banners: from each according to his ability; to each according to his needs! . . .

The economic basis for the complete withering away of the state is that high stage of development of Communism when the antagonism between mental and physical labour disappears, that is to say, when one of the principal sources of modern *social* inequality disappears — a source, moreover, which it is impossible to remove immediately by the mere conversion of the means of production into public property, by the mere expropriation of the capitalists.

This expropriation will make a gigantic development of the productive forces *possible*. . . . we have a right to say, with the fullest confidence, that the expropriation of the capitalists will inevitably result in a gigantic development of the productive forces of human society. But how rapidly this development will go forward, how soon it will reach the point of breaking away from the division of labour, of removing the antagonism between mental and physical labour, of transforming work into the "first necessity of life" — this we do not and *cannot* know.

Consequently, we have a right to speak solely of the inevitable withering away of the state, emphasising the protracted nature of this process and its dependence upon the rapidity of development of the *higher phase* of Communism; leaving quite open the question of lengths of time, or the concrete forms of withering away, since material for the solution of such questions is *not available*.

The state will be able to wither away completely when society has realised the rule: "From each according to his ability; to each according to his needs," *i.e.*, when people have become accustomed to observe the fundamental rules of social life, and their labour is so productive, that they voluntarily work *according to their ability*. . . .

From the bourgeois point of view, it is easy to declare such a social order "a pure Utopia," and to sneer at the Socialists . . .

Ignorance — for it has never entered the head of any Socialist to "promise" that the highest phase of Communism will arrive; while the great Socialists, in *foreseeing* its arrival, presupposed both a productivity of labour unlike the present and a person not like the present man in the street, capable of spoiling, without reflection . . . the stores of social wealth, and of demanding the impossible.

Until the "higher" phase of Communism arrives, the Socialists demand the *strictest* control, *by society and by the state*, of the quantity of labour and the quantity of consumption; only this control must *start* with the expropriation of the capitalists, with the control of the workers over the capitalists, and must be carried out, not by a state of bureaucrats, but by a state of *armed workers*. . . .

Consequently, for a certain time not only bourgeois rights, but even the bourgeois state remains under Communism, without the bourgeoisie!

This may look like a paradox, or simply a dialectical puzzle for which Marxism is often blamed by people who would not make the least effort to study its extraordinarily profound content.

But, as a matter of fact, the old surviving in the new confronts us in life at every step, in nature as well as in society. Marx did not smuggle a scrap of "bourgeois" rights into Communism of his own accord; he indicated what is economically and politically inevitable in a society issuing *from the womb* of capitalism.

Democracy is of great importance for the working class in its struggle for freedom against the capitalists. But democracy is by no means a limit one may not overstep; it is only one of the stages in the course of development from feudalism to capitalism, and from capitalism to Communism.

Democracy means equality. The great significance of the struggle of the proletariat for equality, and the significance of equality as a slogan, are apparent, if we correctly interpret it as meaning the abolition of *classes.* But democracy means only *formal* equality. Immediately after the attainment of equality for all members of society *in respect of* the ownership of the means of production, that is, of equality of labour and equality of wages, there will inevitably arise before humanity the question of going further from formal equality to real equality, *i.e.,* to realising the rule, "From each according to his ability; to each according to his needs." By what stages, by means of what practical measures humanity will proceed to this higher aim — this we do not and cannot know. . . .

Democracy is a form of the state — one of its varieties. Consequently, like every state, it consists in organised, systematic application of force against human beings. This on the one hand. On the other hand, however, it signifies the formal recognition of the equality of all citizens, the equal right of all to determine the structure and administration of the state. This, in turn, is connected with the fact that, at a certain stage in the development of democracy, it first rallies the proletariat as a revolutionary class against capitalism, and gives it an opportunity to crush, to smash to bits, to wipe off the face of the earth the bourgeois state machinery — even its republican variety: the standing army, the police, and bureaucracy; then it substitutes for all this a *more* democratic, but still a state machinery in the shape of armed masses of workers, which becomes transformed into universal participation of the people in the militia.

Here "quantity turns into quality": *such* a degree of democracy is bound up with the abandonment of the framework of bourgeois society, and the beginning of its Socialist reconstruction. If *every one* really takes part in the administration of the state, capitalism cannot retain its hold. In its turn, capitalism, as it develops, itself creates *prerequisites* for "every one" *to be able* really to take part in the administration of the state. Among such prerequisites are: universal literacy, already realised in most of the advanced capitalist countries, then the "training and disciplining" of millions of workers by the huge, complex, and socialised apparatus of the post-office, the railways, the big factories, large-scale commerce, banking, etc., etc.

With such *economic* prerequisites it is perfectly possible, immediately, within twenty-four hours after the overthrow of the capitalists and bureaucrats, to replace them, in the control of production and distribution, in the business of *control* of labour and products, by the armed workers, by the whole people in arms. (The question of control and accounting must not be confused with the question of the scientifically educated staff of engineers, agronomists and so on. These gentlemen work today, obeying the capitalists; they will work even better tomorrow, obeying the armed workers.) . . .

The whole of society will have become one office and one factory, with equal work and equal pay.

But this "factory" discipline, which the proletariat will extend to the whole of society after the defeat of the capitalists and the overthrow of the exploiters, is by no means our ideal, or our final aim. It is but a *foothold* necessary for the radical cleansing of society of all the hideousness and foulness of capitalist exploitation, *in order to advance further.*

. . . Socialism will shorten the working day, raise the *masses* to a new life, create such conditions for the *majority* of the population as to enable *everybody*, without exception, to perform "state functions," and this will lead to a *complete withering away* of every state in general. . . .

. . . the whole of the class-conscious proletariat will be with us — not for a "shifting of the relation of forces," but for the *overthrow of the bourgeoisie*, the *destruction* of bourgeois parliamentarianism, for a democratic republic after the type of the Commune, or a republic of Soviets of Workers' and Soldiers' Deputies, the revolutionary dictatorship of the proletariat.

IMPERIALISM

by V. I. Lenin *

THE HIGHEST STAGE OF CAPITALISM

. . . the main purpose of the book was and remains: to present, on the basis of the summarised returns of irrefutable bourgeois statistics, and the admissions of bourgeois scholars of all countries, a *general picture* of the world capitalist system in its international relationships at the beginning of the twentieth century — on the eve of the first world imperialist war.

To a certain extent it will be useful for many Communists in advanced capitalist countries to convince themselves by the example of this pamphlet, *legal, from the standpoint of the tsarist censor,* of the possibility — and necessity — of making use of even the slight remnants of legality which still remain at the disposal of the Communists, say, in contemporary America or France, after the recent wholesale arrests of Communists, in order to explain the utter falsity of social-pacifist views and hopes for "world democracy." The most essential of what should be added to this censored pamphlet I shall try to present in this preface.

In the pamphlet I proved that the war of 1914–18 was imperialistic (that is, an annexationist, predatory, plunderous war) on the part of both sides; it was a war for the division of the world, for the partition and repartition of colonies, "spheres of influence" of finance capital, etc.

Proof of what was the true social, or rather, the true class character of the war is naturally to be found, not in the diplomatic history of the war, but in an analysis of the *objective* position of the ruling *classes in all* belligerent countries. In order to depict this objective position one must not take examples or isolated data (in view of the extreme complexity of social life it is always quite easy to select any number of examples or separate data to prove any point one desires), but the *whole* of the data concerning the *basis* of economic life in *all* the belligerent countries and the *whole* world.

* V. I. Lenin, *Imperialism: The Highest Stage of Capitalism* (New York: 1939). By permission of International Publishers.

It is precisely irrefutable summarised data of this kind that I quoted in describing the *partition of the world* in the period of 1876 to 1914 . . . and the distribution of the *railways* all over the world in the period of 1890 to 1913. . . . Railways combine within themselves the basic capitalist industries: coal, iron and steel; and they are the most striking index of the development of international trade and bourgeois-democratic civilisation. . . . I showed how the railways are linked up with large-scale industry, with monopolies, syndicates, cartels, trusts, banks and the financial oligarchy. The uneven distribution of the railways, their uneven development — sums up, as it were, modern world monopolist capitalism. And this summing up proves that imperialist wars are absolutely inevitable under *such* an economic system, *as long as* private property in the means of production exists. . . .

What is the economic basis of this historically important world phenomenon? Precisely the parasitism and decay of capitalism which are the characteristic features of its highest historical stage of development, *i.e.,* imperialism. As has been shown in this pamphlet, capitalism has now brought to the front a *handful* (less than one-tenth of the inhabitants of the globe; less than one-fifth, if the most "generous" and liberal calculations were made) of very rich and very powerful states which plunder the whole world simply by "clipping coupons." Capital exports produce an income of eight to ten billion francs per annum, according to pre-war prices and pre-war bourgeois statistics. Now, of course, they produce much more than that.

Obviously, out of such enormous *super-profits* (since they are obtained over and above the profits which capitalists squeeze out of the workers of their "home" country) it is quite *possible to bribe* the labour leaders and the upper stratum of the labour aristocracy. And the capitalists of the "advanced" countries are bribing them; they bribe them in a thousand different ways, direct and indirect, overt and covert.

This stratum of bourgeoisified workers, or the "labour aristocracy," who are quite philistine in their mode of life, in the size of their earnings and in their outlook, serves as the principal prop of the Second International, and, in our days, the principal *social* (not military) *prop of the bourgeoisie.* They are the real *agents of the bourgeoisie in the labour movement,* the labour lieutenants of the capitalist class, real channels of reformism and chauvinism. In the civil war between the proletariat and the bourgeoisie they inevitably, and in no small numbers, stand side by side with the bourgeoisie, with the "Versaillese" against the "Communards."

Not the slightest progress can be made toward the solution of the practical problems of the Communist movement and of the impending social revolution unless the economic roots of this phenomenon are understood and unless its political and sociological significance is appreciated.

Imperialism is the eve of the proletarian social revolution. This has been confirmed since 1917 on a world-wide scale. . . .

During the last fifteen or twenty years, especially since the Spanish-American War (1898), and the Anglo-Boer War (1899–1902), the economic and also the political literature of the two hemispheres has more and more often adopted the term "imperialism" in order to define the present era. . . .

CONCENTRATION OF PRODUCTION AND MONOPOLIES

The enormous growth of industry and the remarkably rapid process of concentration of production in ever-larger enterprises represent one of the most characteristic features of capitalism. Modern censuses of production give very complete and exact data on this process. . . .

. . . This transformation of competition into monopoly is one of the most important — if not the most important — phenomena of modern capitalist economy, and we must deal with it in greater detail. But first we must clear up one possible misunderstanding.

American statistics say: 3,000 giant enterprises in 250 branches of industry, as if there were only a dozen large-scale enterprises for each branch of industry. But this is not the case. Not in every branch of industry are there large-scale enterprises; and, moreover, a very important feature of capitalism in its highest stage of development is so-called "combined production," that is to say, the grouping in a single enterprise of different branches of industry, which either represent the consecutive stages in the working up of raw materials (for example, the smelting of iron ore into pig iron, the conversion of pig iron into steel, and then, perhaps, the manufacture of steel goods) — or are auxiliary to one another (for example, the utilisation of waste or of by-products, the manufacture of packing materials, etc.). . . .

Fifty years ago, when Marx was writing *Capital*, free competition appeared to most economists to be a "natural law." Official science tried, by a conspiracy of silence, to kill the works of Marx, which by a theoretical and historical analysis of capitalism showed that free competition gives rise to the concentration of production, which, in turn, at a certain stage of development, leads to monopoly. Today, monopoly has become a fact. The economists are writing mountains of books in which they describe the diverse manifestations of monopoly, and continue to declare in chorus that "Marxism is refuted." But facts are stubborn things, as the English proverb says, and they have to be reckoned with, whether we like it or not. The facts show that differences between capitalist countries, *e.g.*, in the matter of protection or free trade, only give rise to insignificant variations in the form of monopolies or in the moment of their appearance; and that the rise of monopolies, as the result of the concentration of production, is a general and fundamental law of the present stage of development of capitalism.

For Europe, the time when the new capitalism *definitely* superseded the old can be established with fair precision: it was the beginning of the twentieth century. . . .

Thus, the principal stages in the history of monopolies are the following: 1) 1860–70, the highest stage, the apex of development of free competition; monopoly is in the barely discernible, embryonic stage. 2) After the crisis of 1873, a wide zone of development of cartels; but they are still the exception. They are not yet durable. They are still a transitory phenomenon. 3) The boom at the end of the nineteenth century and the crisis of 1900–03. Cartels become one of the foundations of the whole of economic life. Capitalism has been transformed into imperialism. . . .

. . . Capitalism in its imperialist stage arrives at the threshold of the most complete socialisation of production. In spite of themselves, the capitalists are dragged, as it were, into a new social order, a transitional social order from complete free competition to complete socialisation.

Production becomes social, but appropriation remains private. The social means of production remain the private property of a few. The general framework of formally recognised free competition remains, but the yoke of a few monopolists on the rest of the population becomes a hundred times heavier, more burdensome and intolerable. . . .

Translated into ordinary human language this means that the development of capitalism has arrived at a stage when, although commodity production still "reigns" and continues to be regarded as the basis of economic life, it has in reality been undermined and the big profits go to the "geniuses" of financial manipulation. At the basis of these swindles and manipulations lies socialised production; but the immense progress of humanity, which achieved this socialisation, goes to benefit the speculators. . . .

Monopoly! This is the last word in the "latest phase of capitalist development." But we shall only have a very insufficient, incomplete, and poor notion of the real power and the significance of modern monopolies if we do not take into consideration the part played by the banks.

THE BANKS AND THEIR NEW ROLE

The principal and primary function of banks is to serve as an intermediary in the making of payments. In doing so they transform inactive money capital into active capital, that is, into capital producing a profit; they collect all kinds of money revenues and place them at the disposal of the capitalist class.

As banking develops and becomes concentrated in a small number of establishments the banks become transformed, and instead of being modest intermediaries they become powerful monopolies having at their command almost the whole of the money capital of all the capitalists and small business men and also a large part of the means of production and of the sources of raw materials of the given country and in a number of countries. The transformation of numerous modest intermediaries into a handful of monopolists represents one of the fundamental processes in the transformation of capitalism into capitalist imperialism. For this reason we must first of all deal with the concentration of banking. . . .

SIX BIG BERLIN BANKS

Year	Branches in Germany	Deposit Banks and Exchange Offices	Constant Holdings in German Joint Stock Banks	Total Establishments
1895	16	14	1	42
1900	21	40	8	80
1911	104	276	63	450

These simple figures show perhaps better than long explanations how the concentration of capital and the growth of their turnover is radically changing the significance of the banks. Scattered capitalists are transformed into a single collective capitalist. When carrying the current accounts of a few capitalists, the banks, as it were, transact a purely technical and exclusively auxiliary operation. When, however, these operations grow to enormous dimensions we find that a handful of monopolists control all the operations, both commercial and industrial, of the whole of capitalist society. They can, by means of their banking connections, by running current accounts and transacting other financial operations, first *ascertain exactly* the position of the various capitalists, then *control* them, influence them by restricting or enlarging, facilitating or hindering their credits, and finally they can *entirely determine* their fate, determine their income, deprive them of capital, or, on the other hand, permit them to increase their capital rapidly and to enormous dimensions, etc. . . .

. . . Germany is *governed* by not more than three hundred magnates of capital, and the number of these is constantly diminishing. At all events, banks in all capitalist countries, no matter what the law in regard to them may be, greatly intensify and accelerate the process of concentration of capital and the formation of monopolies. The banking system, Marx wrote half a century ago in *Capital*, "presents indeed the form of common book-keeping and distribution of means of production on a social scale, but only the form." . . . It is "common distribution of means of production" that, from the formal point of view, grows out of the development of modern banks, the most important of which, numbering from three to six in France, and from six to eight in Germany, control billions and billions. In point of fact, however, the distribution of means of production is by no means "common," but private, *i.e.*, it conforms to the interests of big capital, and primarily, of very big monopoly capital, which operates in conditions in which the masses of the population live in want, in which the whole development of agriculture hopelessly lags behind the development of industry and within industry itself the "heavy industries" exact tribute from all other branches of industry. . . .

The building, so to speak, of the great capitalist monopolies is therefore going on full steam ahead in all "natural" and "supernatural" ways. A sort of division of labour amongst some hundreds of kings of finance who reign over modern capitalist society is being systematically developed. . . .

Thus, the beginning of the twentieth century marks the turning point from the old capitalism to the new, from the domination of capital in general to the domination of finance capital.

FINANCE CAPITAL AND FINANCIAL OLIGARCHY . . .

The concentration of production; the monopoly arising therefrom; the merging or coalescence of banking with industry — this is the history of the rise of finance capital and what gives the term "finance capital" its content. . . .

Finance capital, concentrated in a few hands and exercising a virtual monopoly, exacts enormous and ever-increasing profits from the floating of companies, issue of stock, state loans, etc., tightens the grip of financial oligarchies and levies tribute upon the whole of society for the benefit of monopolists. Here is an example, taken from a multitude of others, of the methods of "business" of the American trusts, quoted by Hilferding: in 1887, Havemeyer founded the Sugar Trust by amalgamating fifteen small firms, whose total capital amounted to $6,500,000. Suitably "watered," as the Americans say, the capital of the trust was increased to $50,000,000. This "over-capitalisation" anticipated the monopoly profits, in the same way as the United States Steel Corporation anticipated its profits by buying up as many iron fields as possible. In fact, the Sugar Trust set up monopoly prices on the market, which secured it such profits that it could pay 10 per cent dividend on capital "watered" *sevenfold, or about 70 per cent on the capital actually invested at the time of the creation of the trust!* In 1909, the capital of the Sugar Trust was increased to $90,000,000. In twenty-two years, it had increased its capital more than tenfold. . . .

It is characteristic of capitalism in general that the ownership of capital is separated from the application of capital to production, that money capital is separated from industrial or productive capital, and that the rentier, who lives entirely on income obtained from money capital, is separated from the entrepreneur and from all who are directly concerned in the management of capital. Imperialism, or the domination of finance capital, is that highest stage of capitalism in which this separation reaches vast proportions. The supremacy of finance capital over all other forms of capital means the predominance of the rentier and of the financial oligarchy; it means the crystallisation of a small number of financially "powerful" states from among all the rest. The extent to which this process is going on may be judged from the statistics on emissions, *i.e.*, the issue of all kinds of securities. . . .

Neymarck estimates the total amount of issued securities current in the world in 1910 at about 815,000,000,000 francs. Deducting from this amounts which might have been duplicated, he reduces the total to 575–600,000,000,000, which is distributed among the various countries as follows (we will take 600,000,000,000):

FINANCIAL SECURITIES CURRENT IN 1910
(*In billions of francs*)

Great Britain	142 ⎫	Japan	12
United States	132 ⎪ 479	Holland	12.5
France	110 ⎬	Belgium	7.5
Germany	95 ⎭	Spain	7.5
Russia	31	Switzerland	6.25
Austria-Hungary	24	Denmark	3.75
Italy	14	Sweden, Norway, Rumania, etc.	2.5
		TOTAL	600.00

From these figures we at once see standing out in sharp relief four of the richest capitalist countries, each of which controls securities to amounts ranging from 100 to 150 billion francs. Two of these countries, England and France, are the oldest capitalist countries, and, as we shall see, possess the most colonies; the other two, the United States and Germany, are in the front rank as regards rapidity of development and the degree of extension of capitalist monopolies in industry. Together, these four countries own 479,000,000,000 francs, that is, nearly 80 per cent of the world's finance capital. Thus, in one way or another, nearly the whole world is more or less the debtor to and tributary of these four international banker countries, the four "pillars" of world finance capital.

It is particularly important to examine the part which export of capital plays in creating the international network of dependence and ties of finance capital.

THE EXPORT OF CAPITAL

Under the old capitalism, when free competition prevailed, the export of *goods* was the most typical feature. Under modern capitalism, when monopolies prevail, the export of *capital* has become the typical feature.

Capitalism is commodity production at the highest stage of development, when labour power itself becomes a commodity. The growth of internal exchange, and particularly of international exchange, is the characteristic distinguishing feature of capitalism. The uneven and spasmodic character of the development of individual enterprises, of individual branches of industry and individual countries, is inevitable under the capitalist system. England became a capitalist country before any other, and in the middle of the nineteenth century, having adopted free trade, claimed to be the "workshop of the world," the great purveyor of manufactured goods to all countries, which in exchange were to keep her supplied with raw materials. But in the last quarter of the nineteenth century, *this* monopoly was already undermined. Other countries, protecting themselves by tariff walls, had developed into independent capitalist states. On the threshold of the twentieth century, we see a new type of monopoly coming into existence. Firstly, there are monopolist capitalist combines in all advanced capitalist countries; secondly, a few rich countries, in which the accumulation of capital reaches gigantic proportions, occupy a monopolist position. An enormous "superabundance of capital" has accumulated in the advanced countries. . . .

. . . The necessity for exporting capital arises from the fact that in a few countries capitalism has become "over-ripe" and (owing to the backward state of agriculture and the impoverished state of the masses) capital cannot find "profitable" investment.

Here are approximate figures showing the amount of capital invested abroad by the three principal countries:

CAPITAL INVESTED ABROAD
(*In billions of francs*)

Year	Great Britain	France	Germany
1862	3.6	—	—
1872	15.0	10 (1869)	—
1882	22.0	15 (1880)	?
1893	42.0	20 (1890)	?
1902	62.0	27–37	12.5
1914	75–100	60	44.0

This table shows that the export of capital reached formidable dimensions only in the beginning of the twentieth century. . . .

The capital exporting countries have divided the world among themselves in the figurative sense of the term. But finance capital has also led to the *actual* division of the world.

THE DIVISION OF THE WORLD AMONG CAPITALIST COMBINES

Monopolist capitalist combines — cartels, syndicates, trusts — divide among themselves, first of all, the whole internal market of a country, and impose their control, more or less completely, upon the industry of that country. But under capitalism the home market is inevitably bound up with the foreign market. Capitalism long ago created a world market. As the export of capital increased, and as the foreign and colonial relations and the "spheres of influence" of the big monopolist combines expanded, things "naturally" gravitated towards an international agreement among these combines, and towards the formation of international cartels.

This is a new stage of world concentration of capital and production, incomparably higher than the preceding stages. . . .

. . . International cartels show to what point capitalist monopolies have developed, and they *reveal the object* of the struggle between the various capitalist groups. This last circumstance is the most important; it alone shows us the historico-economic significance of events; for the *forms* of the struggle may and do constantly change in accordance with varying, relatively particular, and temporary causes, but the *essence* of the struggle, its class *content, cannot* change while classes exist. . . . The capitalists divide the world, not out of any particular malice, but because the degree of concentration which has been reached forces them to adopt this method in order to get profits. And they divide it in proportion to "capital," in proportion to "strength," because there cannot be any other system of division under commodity production and capitalism. But strength varies with the degree of economic and political development. . . .

The epoch of modern capitalism shows us that certain relations are established between capitalist alliances, *based* on the economic division of the world; while parallel with this fact and in connection with it, certain relations are established between political alliances, between states, on the basis of the territorial division of the world, of the struggle for colonies, of the "struggle for economic territory."

THE DIVISION OF THE WORLD AMONG THE GREAT POWERS . . .

Hence, we are passing through a peculiar period of world colonial policy, which is closely associated with the "latest stage in the development of capitalism," with finance capital. . . .

For Great Britain, the period of the enormous expansion of colonial conquests is that between 1860 and 1880, and it was also very considerable in the last twenty years of the nineteenth century. For France and Germany this period falls precisely in these last twenty years. We saw above that the apex of pre-monopoly capitalist development, of capitalism in which free competition was predominant, was reached in the 'sixties and 'seventies of the last century. We now see that it is *precisely after that period* that the "boom" in colonial annexations begins, and that the struggle for the territorial division of the world becomes extraordinarily keen. It is beyond doubt, therefore, that capitalism's transition to the stage of monopoly capitalism, to finance capital, is *bound up* with the intensification of the struggle for the partition of the world. . . .

. . . at the end of the nineteenth century the heroes of the hour in England were Cecil Rhodes and Joseph Chamberlain, open advocates of imperialism, who applied the imperialist policy in the most cynical manner.

It is not without interest to observe that even at that time these leading British bourgeois politicians fully appreciated the connection between what might be called the purely economic and the politico-social roots of modern imperialism. Chamberlain advocated imperialism by calling it a "true, wise and economical policy," and he pointed particularly to the German, American and Belgian competition which Great Britain was encountering in the world market. Salvation lies in monopolies, said the capitalists as they formed cartels, syndicates and trusts. Salvation lies in monopolies, echoed the political leaders of the bourgeoisie, hastening to appropriate the parts of the world not yet shared out. . . .

. . . We ask, is there *under capitalism* any means of removing the disparity between the development of productive forces and the accumulation of capital on the one side, and the division of colonies and "spheres of influence" for finance capital on the other side — other than by resorting to war? . . .

THE CRITIQUE OF IMPERIALISM

The enormous dimensions of finance capital concentrated in a few hands and creating an extremely extensive and close network of ties and relationships which subordinate not only the small and medium, but also even the very small capitalists and small masters, on the one hand, and the intense struggle waged against other national state groups of financiers for the division of the world and domination over other countries, on the other hand, cause the wholesale transition of the possessing classes to the side of imperialism. The signs of the times are a "general" enthusiasm regarding its prospects, a passionate defence of imperialism, and every possible embellishment of its real nature. The imperialist ideology also penetrates the working class. There is no Chinese Wall between it and the other classes. The leaders of the so-called "Social-Democratic" Party of Germany are today justly called "social-imperialists," that is, socialists in words and imperialists in deeds; but as early as 1902, Hobson noted the existence of "Fabian imperialists" who belonged to the opportunist Fabian Society in England.

Bourgeois scholars and publicists usually come out in defence of imperialism in a somewhat veiled form, and obscure its complete domination and its profound roots; they strive to concentrate attention on partial and secondary details and do their very best to distract attention from the main issue by means of ridiculous schemes for "reform," such as police supervision of the trusts and banks, etc. Less frequently cynical and frank imperialists speak out and are bold enough to admit the absurdity of the idea of reforming the fundamental features of imperialism. . . .

In the United States, the imperialist war waged against Spain in 1898 stirred up the opposition of the "anti-imperialists," the last of the Mohicans of bourgeois democracy. They declared this war to be "criminal"; they denounced the annexation of foreign territories as being a violation of the Constitution, and denounced the "Jingo treachery" by means of which Aguinaldo, leader of the native Filipinos, was deceived (the Americans promised him the independence of his country, but later they landed troops and annexed it). They quoted the words of Lincoln:

> When the white man governs himself, that is self-government; but when he governs himself and also governs another man, that is more then self-government — that is despotism.

But while all this criticism shrank from recognizing the indissoluble bond between imperialism and the trusts, and, therefore, between imperialism and the very foundations of capitalism; while it shrank from joining up with the forces engendered by large-scale capitalism and its development — it remained a "pious wish." . . .

Therefore, in the realities of the capitalist system, and not in the banal philistine fantasies of English parsons, or of the German "Marxist," Kautsky, "inter-imperialist" or "ultra-imperialist" alliances, no matter what form they may assume, whether of one imperialist coalition against another, or of a general alliance embracing *all* the imperialist powers, are *inevitably* nothing more than a "truce" in periods between wars. Peaceful alliances prepare the ground for wars, and in their turn grow out of wars; the one is the condition for the other, giving rise to alternating forms of peaceful and non-peaceful struggle out of *one and the same* basis of imperialist connections and the relations between world economics and world politics. . . .

THE PLACE OF IMPERIALISM IN HISTORY

We have seen that the economic quintessence of imperialism is monopoly capitalism. This very fact determines its place in history, for monopoly that grew up on the basis of free competition, and precisely out of free competition, is the transition from the capitalist system to a higher social-economic order. We must take special note of the four principal forms of monopoly, or the four principal manifestations of monopoly capitalism, which are characteristic of the epoch under review.

Firstly, monopoly arose out of the concentration of production at a very advanced stage of development. This refers to the monopolist capitalist combines, cartels, syndicates and trusts. We have seen the important part that these play in modern economic life. At the beginning of the twentieth century, monopolies acquired complete supremacy in the advanced countries. And although the first steps towards the formation of the cartels were first taken by countries enjoying the protection of high tariffs (Germany, America), Great Britain, with her system of free trade, was not far behind in revealing the same basic phenomenon, namely, the birth of monopoly out of the concentration of production.

Secondly, monopolies have accelerated the capture of the most important sources of raw materials, especially for the coal and iron industries, which are the basic and most highly cartelised industries in capitalist society. The monopoly of the most important sources of raw materials has enormously increased the power of big capital, and has sharpened the antagonism between cartelised and non-cartelised industry.

Thirdly, monopoly has sprung from the banks. The banks have developed from modest intermediary enterprises into the monopolists of finance capital. Some three or five of the biggest banks in each of the foremost capitalist countries have achieved the "personal union" of industrial and bank capital, and have concentrated in their hands the disposal of thousands upon thousands of millions which form the greater part of the capital and income of entire countries. A financial oligarchy, which throws a close net of relations of dependence over all the economic and political institutions of contemporary bourgeois society without exception — such is the most striking manifestation of this monopoly.

Fourthly, monopoly has grown out of colonial policy. To the numerous "old" motives of colonial policy, finance capital has added the struggle for the sources of raw materials, for the export of capital, for "spheres of influence," *i.e.*, for spheres for profitable deals, concessions, monopolist profits and so on; in fine, for economic territory in general. . . .

The extent to which monopolist capital has intensified all the contradictions of capitalism is generally known. It is sufficient to mention the high cost of living and the oppression of the cartels. This intensification of contradictions constitutes the most powerful driving force of the transitional period of history, which began from the time of the definite victory of world finance capital.

Monopolies, oligarchy, the striving for domination instead of the striving for liberty, the exploitation of an increasing number of small or weak nations by an extremely small group of the richest or most powerful nations — all these have given birth to those distinctive characteristics of imperialism which compel us to define it as parasitic or decaying capitalism. More and more prominently there emerges, as one of the tendencies of imperialism, the creation of the "bondholding" (rentier) state, the usurer state, in which the bourgeoisie lives on the proceeds of capital exports and by "clipping coupons." It would be a mistake to believe that this tendency to decay precludes the possibility of the rapid growth of capitalism. It does not. In the epoch of imperialism, certain branches of industry, certain strata of the bourgeoisie and certain countries betray, to a more or less degree, one or other of these tendencies. On the whole, capitalism is growing far more rapidly than before. But this growth is not only becoming more and more uneven in general; its unevenness also manifests itself, in particular, in the decay of the countries which are richest in capital (such as England). . . .

From all that has been said in this book on the economic nature of imperialism, it follows that we must define it as capitalism in transition, or, more precisely, as moribund capitalism. It is very instructive in this respect to note that the bourgeois economists, in describing modern capitalism, frequently employ terms like "interlocking," "absence of isolation," etc.; "in conformity with their functions and course of development," banks are "not purely private business enterprises; they are more and more outgrowing the sphere of purely private business regulation." . . . Riesser, who uttered the words just quoted, declares with all seriousness that the "prophecy" of the Marxists concerning "socialisation" has "not come true."

What then does this word "interlocking" express? It merely expresses the most striking feature of the process going on before our eyes. It shows that the observer counts the separate trees, but cannot see the wood. It slavishly copies the superficial, the fortuitous, the chaotic. It reveals the observer as one who is overwhelmed by the mass of raw material and is utterly incapable of appreciating its meaning and importance. Ownership of shares and relations between owners of private property "interlock in a haphazard way." But the underlying factor of this interlocking, its very base, is the changing social relations of production. When a big enterprise assumes gigantic proportions, and, on the basis of exact computation of mass data, organises according to plan the supply of primary raw materials to the extent of two-thirds, or three-fourths of all that is necessary for tens of millions of people; when the raw materials are transported to the most suitable place of production, sometimes hundreds or thousands of miles away, in a systematic and organised manner; when a single centre directs all the successive stages of work right up to the manufacture of numerous varieties of finished articles; when these products are distributed according to a single plan among tens and hundreds of millions of consumers (as in the case of the distribution of oil in America and Germany by the American "oil trust") — then it becomes evident that we have socialisation of production, and not mere "interlocking"; that private economic relations and private property relations constitute a shell which is no longer suitable for its contents, a shell which must inevitably begin to decay if its destruction be delayed by artificial means; a shell which may continue in a state of decay for a fairly long period (particularly if the cure of the opportunist abscess is protracted), but which will inevitably be removed. . . .

THE TASKS OF THE YOUTH LEAGUE

by V. I. Lenin *

You must train yourselves to become Communists. The task of the Young Communist League is to organise its practical activities in such a way that, in learning, organising, uniting and fighting, it shall train its members and all those who look upon it as their leader, train them to become Communists. The whole object of the training, education and tuition of the youth of today should be to imbue them with Communist ethics.

But is there such a thing as Communist ethics? Is there such a thing as Communist morality? Of course there is. Often it is made to appear that we have no ethics of our own; and very often the bourgeoisie accuse us Communists of repudiating all ethics. This is a method of shuffling concepts, of throwing dust in the eyes of the workers and peasants.

In what sense do we repudiate ethics and morality?

In the sense that they were preached by the bourgeoisie, who declared that ethics were God's commandments. We, of course, say that we do not believe in God, and that we know perfectly well that the clergy, the landlords and the bourgeoisie spoke in the name of God in order to pursue their own exploiters' interests. Or, instead of deducing these ethics from the commandments of morality, from the commandments of God, they deduced them from idealistic or semi-idealistic phrases, which were always very similar to God's commandments.

We repudiate all morality that is taken outside of human, class concepts.

* V. I. Lenin, *The Young Generation* (New York: 1920). By permission of International Publishers.

We say that this is deception, a fraud, which clogs the brains of the workers and peasants in the interests of the landlords and capitalists.

We say that our morality is entirely subordinated to the interests of the class struggle of the proletariat. Our morality is deduced from the class struggle of the proletariat.

The old society was based on the oppression of all the workers and peasants by the landlords and capitalists. We had to destroy this, we had to overthrow this; but for this we had to create unity. God will not create such unity.

This unity could be created only by the factories and workers, only by the proletariat, trained, and roused from its age-long slumber; only when that class was formed did the mass movement begin which led to what we see now — the victory of the proletariat revolution in one of the weakest countries in the world, a country which for three years has repelled the attacks of the bourgeoisie of the whole world. And we see that the proletarian revolution is growing all over the world. We now say, on the basis of experience, that the proletariat alone could create the compact force that could take the lead of the disunited and scattered peasantry, that could withstand all the attacks of the exploiters. This class alone can help the toiling masses to unite, to rally and completely withstand all attacks upon, completely consolidate and completely build up, Communist society.

That is why we say that for us there is no such thing as morality taken outside of human society; such a morality is a fraud. For us, morality is subordinated to the interests of the class struggle of the proletariat.

FOUNDATIONS OF LENINISM

by Joseph Stalin *

Lenin combines all these conclusions into one general conclusion that *"imperialism is the eve of the socialist revolution."* . . .

The very approach to the question of the proletarian revolution, of the

* Joseph Stalin, *Foundations of Leninism* (New York: 1939). By permission of International Publishers.

character of the revolution, of its scope, of its depth, the scheme of the revolution in general, changes accordingly.

Formerly, the analysis of the conditions for the proletarian revolution was usually approached from the point of view of the economic state of individual countries. Now, this approach is no longer adequate. Now the matter must be approached from the point of view of the economic state of all or the majority of countries, from the point of view of the state of world economy; for individual countries and individual national economies have ceased to be self-sufficient units, have become links in a single chain called world economy; for the old "cultured" capitalism has evolved into imperialism, and imperialism is a world system of financial enslavement and colonial oppression of the vast majority of the population of the earth by a handful of "advanced" countries.

Formerly, it was the accepted thing to speak of the existence or absence of objective conditions for the proletarian revolution in individual countries, or, to be more precise, in one or another developed country. Now this point of view is no longer adequate. Now we must speak of the existence of objective conditions for the revolution in the entire system of world imperialist economy as an integral unit; the existence within this system of some countries that are not sufficiently developed industrially cannot serve as an insurmountable obstacle to the revolution, *if* the system as a whole, or, more correctly, *because* the system as a whole is already ripe for revolution. . . .

. . . Now the proletarian revolution must be regarded primarily as the result of the development of the contradictions within the world system of imperialism, as the result of the snapping of the chain of the imperialist world front in one country or another.

Where will the revolution begin? Where, in what country, can the front of capital be pierced first?

Where industry is more developed, where the proletariat constitutes the majority, where there is more culture, where there is more democracy — that was the reply usually given formerly.

No, objects the Leninist theory of revolution; *not necessarily where industry is more developed,* and so forth. The front of capital will be pierced where the chain of imperialism is weakest, for the proletarian revolution is the result of the breaking of the chain of the world imperialist front at its weakest link; and it may turn out that the country which has started the revolution, which has made a breach in the front of capital, is less developed in a capitalist sense than other, more developed, countries, which have, however, remained within the framework of capitalism.

In 1917 the chain of the imperialist world front proved to be weaker in Russia than in the other countries. It was there that the chain gave way and provided an outlet for the proletarian revolution. Why? Because in Russia a great popular revolution was unfolding, and at its head marched the revolutionary proletariat, which had such an important ally as the vast mass of the peasantry who were oppressed and exploited by the land-lords. Because the revolution there was opposed by such a hideous repre-sentative of imperialism as tsarism, which lacked all moral prestige and was deservedly hated by the whole population. The chain proved to be weaker in Russia, although that country was less developed in a capitalist sense than, say, France or Germany, England or America.

Where will the chain break in the near future? Again, where it is weak-est. It is not precluded that the chain may break, say, in India. Why? Because that country has a young, militant, revolutionary proletariat, which has such an ally as the national liberation movement — an undoubtedly powerful and undoubtedly important ally. Because there the revolution is opposed by such a well-known foe as foreign imperialism, which lacks all moral credit and is deservedly hated by the oppressed and exploited masses of India. . . .

. . . the heroes of the Second International asserted . . . that between the bourgeois-democratic revolution and the proletarian revolution there is a chasm, or at any rate a Chinese Wall, separating one from the other by a more or less protracted interval of time, during which the bourgeoisie, having come into power develops capitalism, while the proletariat accumu-lates strength and prepares for the "decisive struggle" against capitalism. This interval is usually calculated to extend over many decades, if not longer. It need hardly be proved that this Chinese Wall "theory" is totally devoid of scientific meaning under the conditions of imperialism, that it is and can be only a means of concealing and camouflaging the counter-revolutionary aspirations of the bourgeoisie. It need hardly be proved that under the conditions of imperialism, which is pregnant with collisions and wars; under the conditions of the "eve of the socialist revolution," when "flourishing" capitalism is becoming "moribund" capitalism and the revo-lutionary movement is growing in all countries of the world; when imperi-alism is allying itself with all reactionary forces without exception, down to and including tsarism and serfdom, thus making imperative the coalition of all revolutionary forces, from the proletarian movement of the West to the national liberation movement of the East; when the overthrow of the survivals of the regime of feudal serfdom becomes impossible without a revolutionary struggle against imperialism — it need hardly be proved that the bourgeois-democratic revolution, in a more or less developed country, must under such circumstances verge upon the proletarian revolution, that the former must pass into the latter. The history of the revolution in Russia has provided palpable proof that this thesis is correct and incontrovertible. It was not without reason that Lenin, as far back as 1905, on the eve of the first Russian revolution, in his pamphlet *Two Tactics*, depicted the bourgeois-democratic revolution and the socialist revolution as two links in the same chain, as a single and integral picture of the sweep of the Russian revolution: . . .

Further, I might refer to Lenin's well-known articles *On the Provisional Government* (1905), where, depicting the prospects of the unfolding Russian revolution, he assigns to the Party the task of "striving to make the Russian revolution not a movement of a few months, but a movement of many years, so that it may lead, not merely to slight concessions on the part of the powers that be, but to the complete overthrow of those powers"; where, enlarging further on these prospects and linking them with the revolution in Europe, he goes on to say:

> And if we succeed in doing that, then . . . the revolutionary conflagration will spread all over Europe; the European worker, languishing under bourgeois reaction, will rise in his turn and will show us "how it is done"; then the revolutionary wave in Europe will sweep back again into Russia and will convert an epoch of a few revolutionary years into an epoch of several revolutionary decades. . . . (*Selected Works*, Vol. III, p. 31.)

This, then, is the position in regard to Lenin's idea of the bourgeois-democratic revolution passing into the proletarian revolution, of utilising the bourgeois revolution . . . To proceed. Formerly, the victory of the revolution in one country was considered impossible, on the assumption that it would require the combined action of the proletarians of all or at least of a majority of the advanced countries to achieve victory over the bourgeoisie. Now this point of view no longer accords with the facts. Now we must proceed from the possibility of such a victory, for the uneven and spasmodic character of the development of the various capitalist countries under the conditions of imperialism, the development, within imperialism, of catastrophic contradictions leading to inevitable wars, the growth of the revolutionary movement in all countries of the world — all this leads, not only to the possibility, but also to the necessity of the victory of the proletariat in individual countries. The history of the Russian revolution is direct proof of this. At the same time, however, it must be borne in mind that the overthrow of the bourgeoisie can be successfully accomplished only when certain absolutely necessary conditions exist, in the absence of which there can be even no question of the proletariat taking power.

Here is what Lenin says about these conditions in his pamphlet "*Left-Wing" Communism, an Infantile Disorder:*

> The fundamental law of revolution, which has been confirmed by all revolutions, and particularly by all three Russian revolutions in the twentieth century, consists in the following: it is not enough for revolution that the exploited and oppressed masses should understand the impossibility of living in the old way and demand changes; for revolution it is necessary that the exploiters should not be able to live and rule in the old way. Only when the "lower classes" *do not want* the old way, and when the "upper classes" *cannot carry on in the old way* — only then can revolution triumph. This truth may be expressed in other words: *Revolution is impossible without a nation-wide crisis (affecting both the exploited and the exploiters).** It follows that for revolution it is essential, first, that a majority of the workers (or at least a majority of the class conscious, thinking, politically active workers) should fully understand the necessity for revolution and be ready to sacrifice their lives for it; secondly, that the ruling classes should be passing through a governmental crisis which would draw even the most backward masses into politics . . . weaken the government and make it possible for the revolutionaries to overthrow it rapidly. (*Selected Works,* Vol. X, p. 127.)

But the overthrow of the power of the bourgeoisie and establishment of the power of the proletariat in one country still does not mean that the complete victory of socialism has been ensured. After consolidating its power and taking the peasantry in tow, the proletariat of the victorious country can and must build up a socialist society. But does this mean that it will thereby achieve the complete and final victory of socialism, *i.e.,* does it mean that with the forces of only one country it can finally consolidate socialism and fully guarantee that country against intervention and, consequently, also against restoration? No, it does not. For this the victory of the revolution in at least several countries is needed. Therefore, the development and support of revolution in other countries is an essential task of the victorious revolution. Therefore, the revolution in the victorious country must regard itself not as a self-sufficient entity but as an aid, as a means of hastening the victory of the proletariat in other countries.

Lenin expressed this thought in a nutshell when he said that the task of the victorious revolution is to do "the utmost possible in one country *for* the development, support and awakening of the revolution *in all countries.*" (*Selected Works,* Vol. VII, p. 182.)

* My italics. — Joseph Stalin.

These, in general, are the characteristic features of Lenin's theory of proletarian revolution.

LET A HUNDRED FLOWERS BLOOM

by Mao Tse-tung *

Our general subject is the correct handling of contradictions among the people. For convenience's sake, let us discuss it under twelve sub-headings. Although reference will be made to contradictions between ourselves and our enemies, this discussion will center mainly on contradictions among the people.

Two Different Types of Contradictions

Never has our country been as united as it is today. The victories of the bourgeois-democratic revolution and the socialist revolution, coupled with our achievements in socialist construction, have rapidly changed the face of old China. Now we see before us an even brighter future. The days of national disunity and turmoil which the people detested have gone forever. Led by the working class and the Communist party, and united as one, our 600 million people are engaged in the great work of building socialism. Unification of the country, unity of the people, and unity among our various nationalities — these are the basic guarantees for the sure triumph of our cause. However, this does not mean that there are no longer any contradictions in our society. It would be naive to imagine that there are no more contradictions. To do so would be to fly in the face of objective reality. We are confronted by two types of social contradictions — contradictions between ourselves and the enemy and contradictions among the people. These two types of contradictions are totally different in nature. . . .

* Mao Tse-tung, Chairman, Communist Party of China, *Let a Hundred Flowers Bloom*, the complete text of "On the Correct Handling of Contradictions Among the People," speech to the Supreme State Conference, Peking, February 27, 1957. The translation is taken from the special supplement to *The New Leader*, with notes and an introduction by G. F. Hudson. By permission of *The New Leader*.

In the conditions existing in China today, what we call contradictions among the people include the following:

Contradictions within the working class, contradictions within the peasantry, contradictions within the intelligentsia, contradictions between the working class and the peasantry, contradictions between the working class and the peasantry on the one hand and the intelligentsia on the other, contradictions between the working class and other sections of the working people on the one hand and the national bourgeoisie on the other, contradictions within the national bourgeoisie, and so forth. Our People's Government is a government that truly represents the interests of the people and serves the people, yet certain contradictions do exist between the Government and the masses. These include contradictions between the interests of the state, collective interests and individual interests; between democracy and centralism; between those in positions of leadership and the led, and contradictions arising from the bureaucratic practices of certain state functionaries in their relations with the masses. All these are contradictions among the people; generally speaking, underlying the contradictions among the people is the basic identity of the interests of the people. . . .

Ours is a people's democratic dictatorship, led by the working class and based on the worker-peasant alliance. What is this dictatorship for? Its first function is to suppress the reactionary classes and elements and those exploiters in the country who range themselves against the socialist revolution, to suppress all those who try to wreck our socialist construction; that is to say, to solve the contradictions between ourselves and the enemy within the country — for instance, to arrest, try and sentence certain counter-revolutionaries, and for a specified period of time deprive landlords and bureaucrat-capitalists of their right to vote and freedom of speech — all this comes within the scope of our dictatorship. To maintain law and order and safeguard the interests of the people, it is likewise necessary to exercise dictatorship over robbers, swindlers, murderers, arsonists, hooligans and other scoundrels who seriously disrupt social order.

The second function of this dictatorship is to protect our country from subversive activities and possible aggression by the external enemy. Should that happen, it is the task of this dictatorship to solve the external contradiction between ourselves and the enemy. The aim of this dictatorship is to protect all our people so that they can work in peace and build China into a socialist country with a modern industry, agriculture, science and culture.

Who is to exercise this dictatorship? Naturally, it must be the working class and the entire people led by it. Dictatorship does not apply in the ranks of the people. The people cannot possibly exercise dictatorship over themselves; nor should one section of them oppress another section. Law-breaking elements among the people will be dealt with according to law, but this is different in principle from using the dictatorship to suppress enemies of the people. What applies among the people is democratic centralism. Our constitution lays it down that citizens of the People's Republic of China enjoy freedom of speech, of the press, of assembly, of association, of procession, of demonstration, of religious belief and so on. Our constitution also provides that state organs must practice democratic centralism and must rely on the masses, that the personnel of state organs must serve the people. Our socialist democracy is democracy in the widest sense, such as is not to be found in any capitalist country. Our dictatorship is known as the people's democratic dictatorship, led by the working class and based on the worker-peasant alliance. That is to say, democracy operates within the ranks of the people, while the working class, uniting with all those enjoying civil rights, the peasantry in the first place, enforces dictatorship over the reactionary classes and elements and all those who resist socialist transformation and oppose socialist construction. By civil rights, we mean political freedom and democratic rights.

But this freedom is freedom with leadership, and this democracy is democracy under centralized guidance, not anarchy. Anarchy does not conform to the interests or wishes of the people.

Certain people in our country were delighted when the Hungarian events took place. They hoped that something similar would happen in China, that thousands upon thousands of people would demonstrate in the streets against the People's Government. Such hopes ran counter to the interests of the masses and therefore could not possibly get their support. In Hungary, a section of the people deceived by domestic and foreign counter-revolutionaries made the mistake of resorting to acts of violence against the People's Government, with the result that both the state and the people suffered for it. The damage done to the country's economy in a few weeks of rioting will take a long time to repair.

There were other people in our country who took a wavering attitude toward the Hungarian events because they were ignorant about the actual world situation. They felt that there was too little freedom under our people's democracy and that there was more freedom under Western parliamentary democracy. They ask for the adoption of the two-party system of the West, where one party is in office and the other out of office. But this so-called two-party system is nothing but a means of maintaining the dictatorship of the bourgeoisie; under no circumstances can it safeguard the freedom of the working people. As a matter of fact, freedom and democracy cannot exist in the abstract; they only exist in the concrete.

In a society where there is class struggle, the exploiting classes are free to exploit the working people while the working people have no freedom from being exploited; where there is democracy for the bourgeoisie, there can be no democracy for the proletariat and other working people. In some capitalist countries, the Communist parties are allowed to exist legally, but only to the extent that they do not endanger the fundamental interests of the bourgeoisie; beyond that, they are not permitted legal existence.

Those who demand freedom and democracy in the abstract regard democracy as an end and not a means. Democracy sometimes seems to be an end, but it is in fact only a means. Marxism teaches us that democracy is part of the superstructure and belongs to the category of politics. That is to say, in the last analysis it serves the economic base. The same is true of freedom. Both democracy and freedom are relative, not absolute, and they come into being and develop under specific historical circumstances. . . .

This is how things stand today: The turbulent class struggles waged by the masses on a large scale characteristic of the revolutionary periods have, in the main, concluded, but class struggle is not entirely over. While the broad masses of the people welcome the new system, they are not yet quite accustomed to it. Government workers are not sufficiently experienced and should continue to examine and explore ways of dealing with questions relating to specific policies.

In other words, time is needed for our socialist system to grow and consolidate itself, for the masses to get accustomed to the new system, and for Government workers to study and acquire experience. It is imperative that at this juncture we raise the question of distinguishing contradictions among the people from contradictions between ourselves and the enemy, as well as the question of the proper handling of contradictions among the people, so as to rally the people of all nationalities in our country to wage a new battle — the battle against nature — to develop our economy and culture, enable all our people to go through this transition period in a fairly smooth way, make our new system secure, and build up our new state.

THE SUPPRESSION OF COUNTER-REVOLUTION . . .

After liberation, we rooted out a number of counter-revolutionaries. Some were sentenced to death because they had committed serious crimes.

This was absolutely necessary; it was the demand of the people. It was done to free the masses from long years of oppression by counter-revolutionaries and all kinds of local tyrants — in other words, to set free the productive forces. If we had not done so, the masses would not have been able to lift their heads.

Since 1956, however, there has been a radical change in the situation. Taking the country as a whole, the main force of counter-revolution has been rooted out. Our basic task is no longer to set free the productive forces but to protect and expand them in the context of the new relations of production. Some people do not understand that our present policy fits the present situation and our past policy fitted the past situation; they want to make use of the present policy to reverse decisions on past cases and to deny the great success we achieved in suppressing counter-revolution. This is quite wrong, and the people will not permit it.

As regards the suppression of counter-revolution, the main thing is that we have achieved successes, but mistakes have also been made. There were excesses in some cases, and in other cases counter-revolutionaries were overlooked. . . .

AGRICULTURAL COOPERATION

We have a farm population of over 500 million, so the situation of our peasants has a very important bearing on the development of our economy and the consolidation of our state power. In my view, the situation is basically sound. The organization of agricultural cooperatives has been successfully completed, and this has solved a major contradiction in our country — that between socialist industrialization and individual farm economy. The organization of cooperatives was completed swiftly, and so some people were worried that something untoward might occur. Some things did go wrong, but, fortunately, they were not so serious.

The movement on the whole is healthy. The peasants are working with a will, and last year, despite the worst floods, droughts and typhoons in years, they were still able to increase the output of food crops. Yet, some people have stirred up a miniature typhoon; they are grousing that cooperative farming won't do, that it has no superior qualities. . . .

THE QUESTION OF INDUSTRIALISTS AND BUSINESSMEN

The year 1956 saw the transformation of privately owned industrial and commercial enterprises into joint state-private enterprises as well as the organization of cooperatives in agriculture and handicrafts as part of the transformation of our social system. The speed and smoothness with which this was carried out are closely related to the fact that we treated the contradiction between the working class and the national bourgeoisie as a contradiction among the people. Has this class contradiction been resolved completely? No, not yet. A considerable period of time is still required to do so. However, some people say that the capitalists have been so remolded that they are now not much different from the workers and that further remolding is unnecessary. Others go so far as to say that the capitalists are even a bit better than the workers. Still others ask, if remolding is necessary, why does not the working class undergo remolding? Are these opinions correct? Of course not. . . .

THE QUESTION OF INTELLECTUALS

Contradictions within the ranks of the people in our country also find expression among our intellectuals. Several million intellectuals who worked for the old society have come to serve the new society. The question that now arises is how they can best meet the needs of the new society and how we can help them do so. This is also a contradiction among the people.

Most of our intellectuals have made marked progress during the past seven years. They express themselves in favor of the socialist system. Many of them are diligently studying Marxism and some have become Communists. Their number, though small, is growing steadily. There are, of course, still some intellectuals who are skeptical of socialism or who do not approve of it, but they are in a minority.

China needs as many intellectuals as she can get to carry through the colossal task of socialist construction. We should trust intellectuals who are really willing to serve the cause of socialism, radically improve our relations with them and help them solve whatever problems have to be solved, so that they can give full play to their talents. Many of our comrades are not good at getting along with intellectuals. They are stiff with them, lack respect for their work, and interfere in scientific and cultural matters in a way that is uncalled for. We must do away with all such shortcomings.

Our intellectuals have made some progress, but they should not be complacent. They must continue to remold themselves, gradually shed their bourgeois world outlook and acquire a proletarian, Communist world outlook, so that they can fully meet the needs of the new society and closely unite with the workers and peasants. This change in world outlook is a fundamental one, and up to now it cannot yet be said that most of our intellectuals have accomplished it. We hope that they will continue making progress and, in the course of work and study, gradually acquire a Communist world outlook, get a better grasp of Marxism-Leninism, and identify themselves with the workers and peasants. We hope they will not stop halfway or, what is worse, slip back, for if they do they will find themselves in a blind alley. . . .

. . . Not to have a correct political point of view is like having no soul. Ideological remolding in the past was necessary and has yielded positive results. But it was carried on in a somewhat rough and ready way, and the feelings of some people were hurt — this was not good. We must avoid such shortcomings in the future. All departments and organizations concerned should take up their responsibilities with regard to ideological and political work. This applies to the Communist party, the Youth League, Government departments responsible for this work, and especially heads of educational institutions and teachers. Our educational policy must enable everyone who gets an education to develop morally, intellectually and physically and become a cultured, socialist-minded worker. We must spread the idea of building our country through hard work and thrift. We must see to it that all our young people understand that ours is still a very poor country, that we cannot change this situation radically in a short time, and that only through the united efforts of our younger generation and all our people working with their own hands can our country be made strong and prosperous within a period of several decades. It is true that the establishment of our socialist system has opened the road leading to the ideal state of the future, but we must work hard, very hard indeed, if we are to make that ideal a reality. Some of our young people think that everything ought to be perfect once a socialist society is established and that they should be able to enjoy a happy life, ready-made, without working for it. This is unrealistic. . . .

ON "LETTING A HUNDRED FLOWERS BLOSSOM" AND "LETTING A
HUNDRED SCHOOLS OF THOUGHT CONTEND" AND "LONG-TERM
COEXISTENCE AND MUTUAL SUPERVISION"

"Let a hundred flowers blossom" and "let a hundred schools of thought contend," "long-term coexistence and mutual supervision" — how did these slogans come to be put forward?

They were put forward in the light of the specific conditions existing in China, on the basis of the recognition that various kinds of contradictions still exist in a socialist society, and in response to the country's urgent need to speed up its economic and cultural development.

The policy of letting a hundred flowers blossom and a hundred schools of thought contend is designed to promote the flourishing of the arts and the progress of science; it is designed to enable a socialist culture to thrive in our land. Different forms and styles in art can develop freely, and different schools in science can contend freely. We think that it is harmful to the growth of art and science if administrative measures are used to impose one particular style of art or school of thought and to ban another. Questions of right and wrong in the arts and sciences should be settled through free discussions in artistic and scientific circles and in the course of practical work in the arts and sciences. They should not be settled in summary fashion. A period of trial is often needed to determine whether something is right or wrong. In the past, new and correct things often failed at the outset to win recognition from the majority of people and had to develop by twists and turns in struggle. Correct and good things have often at first been looked upon not as fragrant flowers but as poisonous weeds; Copernicus's theory of the solar system and Darwin's theory of evolution were once dismissed as erroneous and had to win through over bitter opposition. Chinese history offers many similar examples. In socialist society, conditions for the growth of new things are radically different from and far superior to those in the old society. Nevertheless, it still often happens that new, rising forces are held back and reasonable suggestions smothered.

The growth of new things can also be hindered, not because of deliberate suppression but because of lack of discernment. That is why we should take a cautious attitude in regard to questions of right and wrong in the arts and sciences, encourage free discussion, and avoid hasty conclusions. We believe that this attitude will facilitate the growth of the arts and sciences.

Marxism has also developed through struggle. At the beginning, Marxism was subjected to all kinds of attack and regarded as a poisonous weed. It is still being attacked and regarded as a poisonous weed in many parts of the world. However, it enjoys a different position in the socialist countries. But, even in these countries, there are non-Marxist as well as anti-Marxist ideologies. It is true that in China socialist transformation, insofar as a change in the system of ownership is concerned, has in the main been completed, and the turbulent, large-scale, mass class struggles characteristic of the revolutionary periods have in the main concluded. But remnants of the overthrown landlord and comprador classes still exist, the bourgeoisie still exists, and the petty bourgeoisie has only just begun to remold itself. Class struggle is not yet over. The class struggle between the proletariat and the bourgeoisie, the class struggle between various political forces, and the class struggle in the ideological field between the proletariat and the bourgeoisie will still be long and devious and at times may even become very acute. The proletariat seeks to transform the world according to its own world outlook; so does the bourgeoisie. In this respect, the question of whether socialism or capitalism will win is still not really settled. Marxists are still a minority of the entire population as well as of the intellectuals. Marxism therefore must still develop through struggle. Marxism can only develop through struggle — this is true not only in the past and present, it is necessarily true in the future also. What is correct always develops in the course of struggle with what is wrong. The true, the good and the beautiful always exist in comparison with the false, the evil and the ugly, and grow in struggle with the latter. As mankind in general rejects an untruth and accepts a truth, a new truth will begin struggling with new erroneous ideas. Such struggles will never end. This is the law of development of truth, and it is certainly also the law of development of Marxism. . . .

People may ask: Since Marxism is accepted by the majority of the people in our country as the guiding ideology, can it be criticized? Certainly it can. As a scientific truth, Marxism fears no criticism. If it did and could be defeated in argument, it would be worthless. In fact, are not the idealists criticizing Marxism every day and in all sorts of ways? As for those who harbor bourgeois and petty-bourgeois ideas and do not wish to change, are not they also criticizing Marxism in all sorts of ways? Marxists should not be afraid of criticism from any quarter. Quite the contrary, they need to steel and improve themselves and win new positions in the teeth of criticism and the storm and stress of struggle. Fighting against wrong ideas is like being vaccinated — a man develops greater immunity from disease after the vaccine takes effect. Plants raised in hot-houses are not likely to be robust. Carrying out the policy of letting a hundred flowers blossom and a hundred schools of thought contend will not weaken but strengthen the leading position of Marxism in the ideological field.

What should our policy be toward non-Marxist ideas? As far as unmistakable counter-revolutionaries and wreckers of the socialist cause are concerned, the matter is easy; we simply deprive them of their freedom of speech. But it is quite a different matter when we are faced with incorrect ideas among the people. Will it do to ban such ideas and give them no opportunity to express themselves? Certainly not. It is not only futile but very harmful to use crude and summary methods to deal with ideological questions among the people, with questions relating to the spiritual life of man. You may ban the expression of wrong ideas, but the ideas will still be there. On the other hand, correct ideas, if pampered in hot-houses without being exposed to the elements or immunized against disease, will not win out against wrong ones. That is why it is only by employing methods of discussion, criticism and reasoning that we can really foster correct ideas, overcome wrong ideas and really settle issues. . . .

On the surface, these two slogans — let a hundred flowers blossom and a hundred schools of thought contend — have no class character; the proletariat can turn them to account, and so can the bourgeoisie and other people. But different classes, strata and social groups each have their own views on what are fragrant flowers and what are poisonous weeds. So what, from the point of view of the broad masses of the people, should be a criterion today for distinguishing between fragrant flowers and poisonous weeds?

In the political life of our country, how are our people to determine what is right and what is wrong in our words and actions? Basing ourselves on the principles of our constitution, the will of the overwhelming majority of our people and the political programs jointly proclaimed on various occasions by our political parties and groups, we believe that, broadly speaking, words and actions can be judged right if they:

1. Help to unite the people of our various nationalities, and do not divide them.

2. Are beneficial, not harmful, to socialist transformation and socialist construction.

3. Help to consolidate, not undermine or weaken, the people's democratic dictatorship.

4. Help to consolidate, not undermine or weaken, democratic centralism.

5. Tend to strengthen, not to cast off or weaken, the leadership of the Communist party.

6. Are beneficial, not harmful, to international socialist solidarity and the solidarity of the peace-loving peoples of the world.

Of these six criteria, the most important are the socialist path and the leadership of the Party. These criteria are put forward in order to foster, and not hinder, the free discussion of various questions among the people. Those who do not approve of these criteria can still put forward their own views and argue their cases. When the majority of the people have clear-cut criteria to go by, criticism and self-criticism can be conducted along proper lines, and these criteria can be applied to people's words and actions to determine whether they are fragrant flowers or poisonous weeds. These are political criteria. Naturally, in judging the truthfulness of scientific theories or assessing the esthetic value of works of art, other pertinent criteria are needed, but these six political criteria are also applicable to all activities in the arts or sciences. In a socialist country like ours, can there possibly be any useful scientific or artistic activity which runs counter to these political criteria? . . .

We all know that supervision over the Communist party is mainly exercised by the working people and Party membership. But we will benefit even more if the other democratic parties do this as well. Of course, advice and criticism exchanged between the Communist party and the other democratic parties will play a positive role in mutual supervision only when they conform to the six political criteria given above. That is why we hope that the other democratic parties will all pay attention to ideological remolding and strive for long-term coexistence and mutual supervision with the Communist party so as to meet the needs of the new society.

CONCERNING DISTURBANCES CREATED BY SMALL NUMBERS OF PEOPLE

In 1956, small numbers of workers and students in certain places went on strike. The immediate cause of these disturbances was the failure to satisfy certain of their demands for material benefits, of which some should and could be met, while others were out of place or excessive and therefore could not be met for the time being. But a more important cause was bureaucracy on the part of those in positions of leadership. In some cases, responsibility for such bureaucratic mistakes should be placed on the higher authorities and those at lower levels should not be made to bear all the blame. Another cause for these disturbances was that the ideological and political educational work done among the workers and students was inadequate. In the same year, members of a small number of agricultural cooperatives also created disturbances, and the main causes were also bureaucracy on the part of the leadership and lack of educational work among the masses. . . .

CAN BAD THINGS BE TURNED INTO GOOD THINGS?

As I have said, in our society it is bad when groups of people make disturbances, and we do not approve of it. But when disturbances do occur, they force us to learn lessons from them, to overcome bureaucracy and educate the cadres and the people. In this sense, bad things can be turned into good things. Disturbances thus have a dual character. All kinds of disturbances can be looked at in this way.

It is clear to everybody that the Hungarian events were not a good thing. But they, too, had a dual character. Because our Hungarian comrades took proper action in the course of these events, what was a bad thing turned ultimately into a good thing. The Hungarian state is now more firmly established than ever, and all other countries in the socialist camp have also learned a lesson. . . .

The First World War was followed by the birth of the Soviet Union with a population of 200 million. The Second World War was followed by the emergence of the socialist camp with a combined population of 900 million. If the imperialists should insist on launching a third world war, it is certain that several hundred million more will turn to socialism; then there will not be much room left in the world for the imperialists, while it is quite likely that the whole structure of imperialism will utterly collapse.

Given specific conditions, the two aspects of a contradiction invariably turn into their respective opposites as a result of the struggle between them. Here, the conditions are important. Without specific conditions, neither of the two contradictory aspects can transform itself into its opposite. Of all the classes in the world, the proletariat is the most eager to change its position; next comes the semi-proletariat. The former possesses nothing at all, while the latter is not much better off. The present situation in which the United States controls a majority in the United Nations and dominates many parts of the world is a transient one, which will eventually be changed. China's situation as a poor country denied her rights in international affairs will also be changed. A poor country will be changed into a rich country, a country denied her rights into a country enjoying her rights — a transformation of things into their opposites. Here, the decisive conditions are the socialist system and the concerted efforts of a united people.

THE PRACTICE OF ECONOMY

. . . A dangerous tendency has shown itself of late among many of our personnel — an unwillingness to share the joys and hardships of the masses, a concern for personal position and gain. This is very bad. One way of overcoming this dangerous tendency is, in our campaign, to increase production and practice economy, to streamline our organizations and transfer cadres to lower levels so that a considerable number of them will return to productive work. We must see to it that all cadres and all our people constantly bear in mind that, while ours is a big socialist country, it is an economically backward and poor country, and that this is a very great consideration. If we want to see China rich and strong, we must be prepared for several decades of intensive effort which will include, among other things, carrying out a policy of building our country through hard work and thrift — of practicing strict economy and combating waste.

CHINA'S PATH TO INDUSTRIALIZATION

In discussing our path to industrialization, I am here concerned principally with the relationship between the growth of heavy industry, light industry and agriculture. Heavy industry is the core of China's economic construction. This must be affirmed. But, at the same time, full attention must be paid to the development of agriculture and light industry. . . .

In order to make our country into an industrial power, we must learn conscientiously from the advanced experience of the Soviet Union. The Soviet Union has been building socialism for forty years, and we treasure its experience.

Let us consider who designed and equipped so many important factories for us. Was it the United States? Or Britain? No, neither of them. Only the Soviet Union was willing to do so, because it is a socialist country and our ally. In addition to the Soviet Union, some brother countries of Eastern Europe also gave us assistance. It is perfectly sure that we should learn from the good experience of all countries, socialist or capitalist, but the main thing is still to learn from the Soviet Union.

Now here are two different attitudes in learning from others. One is a doctrinaire attitude: transplanting everything, whether suited or not to the conditions of our country. This is not a good attitude. Another attitude is to use our heads and learn those things which suit conditions in our country, that is, to absorb whatever experience is useful to us. This is the attitude we should adopt.

To strengthen our solidarity with the Soviet Union, to strengthen our solidarity with all socialist countries — this is our fundamental policy, herein lies our basic interest. Then there are the Asian and African countries, and all the peace-loving countries and peoples — we must strengthen and develop our solidarity with them. United with these two forces, we will not stand alone. As for the imperialist countries, we should also unite with their peoples and strive to coexist in peace with those countries, do business with them and prevent any possible war, but under no circumstances should we harbor any unrealistic notions about those countries.

CRIMES OF THE STALIN ERA

by Nikita S. Khrushchev *

Comrades! . . .

After Stalin's death the Central Committee of the party began to implement a policy of explaining concisely and consistently that it is impermissible and foreign to the spirit of Marxism-Leninism to elevate one person, to transform him into a superman possessing supernatural characteristics, akin to those of a god. Such a man supposedly knows everything, sees everything, thinks for everyone, can do anything, is infallible in his behavior.

Such a belief about a man, and specifically about Stalin, was cultivated among us for many years.

The objective of the present report is not a thorough evaluation of Stalin's life and activity. Concerning Stalin's merits, an entirely sufficient number of books, pamphlets and studies had already been written in his lifetime. The role of Stalin in the preparation and execution of the Socialist Revolution, in the Civil War, and in the fight for the construction of socialism in our country, is universally known. Everyone knows this well.

At present, we are concerned with a question which has immense importance for the party now and for the future — with how the cult of the person of Stalin has been gradually growing, the cult which became at a

* Nikita S. Khrushchev, First Secretary, Communist Party of the Soviet Union, *Crimes of the Stalin Era: Special Report to the 20th Congress of the Communist Party of the Soviet Union*, Closed Session, February 24–25, 1956. The translation, and two of the footnotes, are taken from the special supplement to *The New Leader*, as annotated by Boris I. Nicolaevsky, and with an introduction by Anatole Shub. By permission of *The New Leader*.

certain specific stage the source of a whole series of exceedingly serious and grave perversions of party principles, of party democracy, of revolutionary legality.

Because of the fact that not all as yet realize fully the practical consequences resulting from the cult of the individual, the great harm caused by the violation of the principle of collective direction of the party and because of the accumulation of immense and limitless power in the hands of one person, the Central Committee of the party considers it absolutely necessary to make the material pertaining to this matter available to the 20th Congress of the Communist Party of the Soviet Union. . . .

In December 1922, in a letter to the Party Congress, Vladimir Ilyich [Lenin] wrote: "After taking over the position of Secretary General, Comrade Stalin accumulated in his hands immeasurable power and I am not certain whether he will be always able to use this power with the required care."

This letter — a political document of tremendous importance, known in the party history as Lenin's "testament" — was distributed among the delegates to the 20th Party Congress. You have read it and will undoubtedly read it again more than once. You might reflect on Lenin's plain words, in which expression is given to Vladimir Ilyich's anxiety concerning the party, the people, the state, and the future direction of party policy.

Vladimir Ilyich said: "Stalin is excessively rude, and this defect, which can be freely tolerated in our midst and in contacts among us Communists, becomes a defect which cannot be tolerated in one holding the position of the Secretary General. Because of this, I propose that the comrades consider the method by which Stalin would be removed from this position and by which another man would be selected for it, a man who, above all, would differ from Stalin in only one quality, namely, greater tolerance, greater loyalty, greater kindness and more considerate attitude toward the comrades, a less capricious temper, etc." . . .

When we analyze the practice of Stalin in regard to the direction of the party and of the country, when we pause to consider everything which Stalin perpetrated, we must be convinced that Lenin's fears were justified. The negative characteristics of Stalin, which, in Lenin's time, were only incipient, transformed themselves during the last years into a grave abuse of power by Stalin, which caused untold harm to our party.

We have to consider seriously and analyze correctly this matter in order that we may preclude any possibility of a repetition in any form whatever of what took place during the life of Stalin, who absolutely did not tolerate collegiality in leadership and in work, and who practiced brutal violence, not only toward everything which opposed him, but also toward that which seemed, to his capricious and despotic character, contrary to his concepts.

Stalin acted not through persuasion, explanation and patient cooperation with people, but by imposing his concepts and demanding absolute submission to his opinion. Whoever opposed this concept or tried to prove his viewpoint and the correctness of his position was doomed to removal from the leading collective and to subsequent moral and physical annihilation. This was especially true during the period following the 17th Party Congress, when many prominent party leaders and rank-and-file party workers, honest and dedicated to the cause of Communism, fell victim to Stalin's despotism. . . .

Worth noting is the fact that, even during the progress of the furious ideological fight against the Trotskyites, the Zinovievites, the Bukharinites and others, extreme repressive measures were not used against them. The fight was on ideological grounds. But some years later, when socialism in our country was fundamentally constructed, when the exploiting classes were generally liquidated, when the Soviet social structure had radically changed, when the social basis for political movements and groups hostile to the party had violently contracted, when the ideological opponents of the party were long since defeated politically — then the repression directed against them began.

It was precisely during this period (1935–1937–1938) that the practice of mass repression through the Government apparatus was born, first against the enemies of Leninism — Trotskyites, Zinovievites, Bukharinites, long since politically defeated by the party — and subsequently also against many honest Communists, against those party cadres who had borne the heavy load of the Civil War and the first and most difficult years of industrialization and collectivization, who actively fought against the Trotskyites and the rightists for the Leninist party line.

Stalin originated the concept "enemy of the people." This term automatically rendered it unnecessary that the ideological errors of a man or men engaged in a controversy be proven; this term made possible the usage of the most cruel repression, violating all norms of revolutionary legality, against anyone who in any way disagreed with Stalin, against those who were only suspected of hostile intent, against those who had bad reputations. This concept "enemy of the people" actually eliminated the possibility of any kind of ideological fight or the making of one's views known on this or that issue, even those of a practical character. In the main, and in actuality, the only proof of guilt used, against all norms of current legal science, was the "confession" of the accused himself; and, as subsequent probing proved, "confessions" were acquired through physical pressures against the accused. This led to glaring violations of revolutionary legality and to the fact that many entirely innocent persons, who in the past had defended the party line, became victims.

We must assert that, in regard to those persons who in their time had opposed the party line, there were often no sufficiently serious reasons for their physical annihilation. The formula "enemy of the people" was specifically introduced for the purpose of physically annihilating such individuals. . . .

Lenin's wisdom in dealing with people was evident in his work with cadres.

An entirely different relationship with people characterized Stalin. Lenin's traits — patient work with people, stubborn and painstaking education of them, the ability to induce people to follow him without using compulsion, but rather through the ideological influence on them of the whole collective — were entirely foreign to Stalin. He discarded the Leninist method of convincing and educating, he abandoned the method of ideological struggle for that of administrative violence, mass repressions and terror. He acted on an increasingly larger scale and more stubbornly through punitive organs, at the same time often violating all existing norms of morality and of Soviet laws.

Arbitrary behavior by one person encouraged and permitted arbitrariness in others. Mass arrests and deportations of many thousands of people, execution without trial and without normal investigation created conditions of insecurity, fear and even desperation.

This, of course, did not contribute toward unity of the party ranks and of all strata of working people, but, on the contrary, brought about annihilation and the expulsion from the party of workers who were loyal but inconvenient to Stalin.

Our party fought for the implementation of Lenin's plans for the construction of socialism. This was an ideological fight. Had Leninist principles been observed during the course of this fight, had the party's devotion to principles been skillfully combined with a keen and solicitous concern for people, had they not been repelled and wasted but rather drawn to our side, we certainly would not have had such a brutal violation of revolutionary legality and many thousands of people would not have fallen victim to the method of terror. Extraordinary methods would then have been resorted to only against those people who had in fact committed criminal acts against the Soviet system. . . .

Stalin, on the other hand, used extreme methods and mass repressions at a time when the Revolution was already victorious, when the Soviet state was strengthened, when the exploiting classes were already liquidated and socialist relations were rooted solidly in all phases of national economy, when our party was politically consolidated and had strengthened itself both numerically and ideologically. It is clear that here Stalin showed in a whole series of cases his intolerance, his brutality and his abuse of power. Instead of proving his political correctness and mobilizing the masses, he often chose the path of repression and physical annihilation, not only against actual enemies, but also against individuals who had not committed any crimes against the party and the Soviet Government. Here we see no wisdom but only a demonstration of the brutal force which had once so alarmed V. I. Lenin.

Lately, especially after the unmasking of the Beria gang, the Central Committee looked into a series of matters fabricated by this gang. This revealed a very ugly picture of brutal willfulness connected with the incorrect behavior of Stalin. As facts prove, Stalin, using his unlimited power, allowed himself many abuses, acting in the name of the Central Committee, not asking for the opinion of the Committee members nor even of the members of the Central Committee's Political Bureau; often he did not inform them about his personal decisions concerning very important party and government matters. . . .

The commission has become acquainted with a large quantity of materials in the NKVD archives and with other documents and has established many facts pertaining to the fabrication of cases against Communists, to false accusations, to glaring abuses of socialist legality, which resulted in the death of innocent people. It became apparent that many party, Soviet and economic activists, who were branded in 1937–1938 as "enemies," were actually never enemies, spies, wreckers, etc., but were always honest Communists; they were only so stigmatized and, often, no longer able to bear barbaric tortures, they charged themselves (at the order of the investigative judges — falsifiers) with all kinds of grave and unlikely crimes. . . .

It was determined that of the 139 members and candidates of the party's Central Committee who were elected at the 17th Congress, 98 persons, *i.e.*, 70 per cent, were arrested and shot (mostly in 1937–1938). . . .

The same fate met not only the Central Committee members but also the majority of the delegates to the 17th Party Congress. Of 1,966 delegates with either voting or advisory rights, 1,108 persons were arrested on charges of anti-revolutionary crimes, *i.e.*, decidedly more than a majority. . . .

We should recall that the 17th Party Congress is historically known as the Congress of Victors. Delegates to the Congress were active participants in the building of our socialist state; many of them suffered and fought for party interests during the pre-Revolutionary years in the conspiracy and at the civil-war fronts; they fought their enemies valiantly and often nervelessly looked into the face of death. . . .

Now, when the cases of some of these so-called "spies" and "saboteurs" were examined, it was found that all their cases were fabricated. Confessions of guilt of many arrested and charged with enemy activity were gained with the help of cruel and inhuman tortures.

At the same time, Stalin, as we have been informed by members of the Political Bureau of that time, did not show them the statements of many accused political activists when they retracted their confessions before the military tribunal and asked for an objective examination of their cases. There were many such declarations, and Stalin doubtless knew of them. . . .

Many thousands of honest and innocent Communists have died as a result of this monstrous falsification of such "cases," as a result of the fact that all kinds of slanderous "confessions" were accepted, and as a result of the practice of forcing accusations against oneself and others. In the same manner were fabricated the "cases" against eminent party and state workers — Kossior, Chubar, Postyshev, Kosarev and others.

In those years repressions on a mass scale were applied which were based on nothing tangible and which resulted in heavy cadre losses to the party.

The vicious practice was condoned of having the NKVD prepare lists of persons whose cases were under the jurisdiction of the Military Collegium and whose sentences were prepared in advance. Yezhov would send these lists to Stalin personally for his approval of the proposed punishment. In 1937-1938, 383 such lists containing the names of many thousands of party, Soviet, Komsomol, Army and economic workers were sent to Stalin. He approved these lists.

A large part of these cases are being reviewed now and a great part of them are being voided because they were baseless and falsified. Suffice it to say that from 1954 to the present time the Military Collegium of the Supreme Court has rehabilitated 7,679 persons, many of whom were rehabilitated posthumously.

Mass arrests of party, Soviet, economic and military workers caused tremendous harm to our country and to the cause of socialist advancement.

Mass repressions had a negative influence on the moral-political condition of the party, created a situation of uncertainty, contributed to the spreading of unhealthy suspicion, and sowed distrust among Communists. All sorts of slanderers and careerists were active. . . .

Only because our party has at its disposal such great moral-political strength was it possible for it to survive the difficult events in 1937–1938 and to educate new cadres. There is, however, no doubt that our march forward toward socialism and toward the preparation of the country's defense would have been much more successful were it not for the tremendous loss in the cadres suffered as a result of the baseless and false mass repressions in 1937–1938. . . .

In such a situation, there is no need for any sanction, for what sort of a sanction could there be when Stalin decided everything? He was the chief prosecutor in these cases. Stalin not only agreed to, but on his own initiative issued, arrest orders. We must say this so that the delegates to the Congress can clearly undertake and themselves assess this and draw the proper conclusions.

Facts prove that many abuses were made on Stalin's orders without reckoning with any norms of party and Soviet legality. Stalin was a very distrustful man, sickly suspicious; we know this from our work with him. He could look at a man and say: "Why are your eyes so shifty today?" or "Why are you turning so much today and avoiding to look me directly in the eyes?" The sickly suspicion created in him a general distrust even toward eminent party workers whom he had known for years. Everywhere and in everything he saw "enemies," "two-facers" and "spies." Possessing unlimited power, he indulged in great willfulness and choked a person morally and physically. A situation was created where one could not express one's own will.

When Stalin said that one or another should be arrested, it was necessary to accept on faith that he was an "enemy of the people." Meanwhile, Beria's gang, which ran the organs of state security, outdid itself in proving the guilt of the arrested and the truth of materials which it falsified. And what proofs were offered? The confessions of the arrested, and the investigative judges accepted these "confessions." And how is it possible that a person confesses to crimes which he has not committed? Only in one way — because of application of physical methods of pressuring him, tortures, bringing him to a state of unconsciousness, deprivation of his judgment, taking away of his human dignity. In this manner were "confessions" acquired. . . .

The power accumulated in the hands of one person, Stalin, led to serious consequences during the Great Patriotic War. . . .

Before the war, our press and all our political-educational work was characterized by its bragging tone: When an enemy violates the holy Soviet soil, then for every blow of the enemy we will answer with three blows, and we will battle the enemy on his soil and we will win without much harm to ourselves. But these positive statements were not based in all areas on concrete facts, which would actually guarantee the immunity of our borders. . . .

Documents which have now been published show that by April 3, 1941 Churchill, through his Ambassador to the USSR, Cripps, personally warned Stalin that the Germans had begun regrouping their armed units with the intent of attacking the Soviet Union. . . .

Despite these particularly grave warnings, the necessary steps were not taken to prepare the country properly for defense and to prevent it from being caught unawares.

Did we have time and the capabilities for such preparations? Yes, we had the time and capabilities. Our industry was already so developed that it was capable of supplying fully the Soviet Army with everything that it needed. This is proven by the fact that, although during the war we lost almost half of our industry and important industrial and food-production areas as the result of enemy occupation of the Ukraine, Northern Caucasus and other western parts of the country, the Soviet nation was still able to organize the production of military equipment in the eastern parts of the country, install there equipment taken from the western industrial areas, and to supply our armed forces with everything which was necessary to destroy the enemy.

Had our industry been mobilized properly and in time to supply the Army with the necessary matériel, our wartime losses would have been decidedly smaller. Such mobilization had not been, however, started in time. And already in the first days of the war it became evident that our Army was badly armed, that we did not have enough artillery, tanks and planes to throw the enemy back.

Soviet science and technology produced excellent models of tanks and artillery pieces before the war. But mass production of all this was not organized, and, as a matter of fact, we started to modernize our military equipment only on the eve of the war. As a result, at the time of the enemy's invasion of the Soviet land we did not have sufficient quantities

either of old machinery which was no longer used for armament production or of new machinery which we had planned to introduce into armament production.

The situation with anti-aircraft artillery was especially bad; we did not
organize the production of anti-tank ammunition. Many fortified regions
had proven to be indefensible as soon as they were attacked, because the
old arms had been withdrawn and new ones were not yet available there.

This pertained, alas, not only to tanks, artillery and planes. At the outbreak of the war we did not even have sufficient numbers of rifles to arm
the mobilized manpower. . . .

And what were the results of this carefree attitude, this disregard of
clear facts? The result was that already in the first hours and days the
enemy had destroyed in our border regions a large part of our Air Force,
artillery and other military equipment; he annihilated large numbers of
our military cadres and disorganized our military leadership; consequently
we could not prevent the enemy from marching deep into the country.

Very grievous consequences, especially in reference to the beginning of
the war, followed Stalin's annihilation of many military commanders and
political workers during 1937–1941 because of his suspiciousness and through
slanderous accusations.* During these years repressions were instituted
against certain parts of military cadres beginning literally at the company
and battalion commander level and extending to the higher military centers; during this time the cadre of leaders who had gained military experience in Spain and in the Far East was almost completely liquidated. . . .

The question arises: And where are the military, on whose shoulders
rested the burden of the war? . . .

Not Stalin, but the party as a whole, the Soviet Government, our heroic
Army, its talented leaders and brave soldiers, the whole Soviet nation —
these are the ones who assured the victory in the Great Patriotic War. . . .

The magnificent and heroic deeds of hundreds of millions of people of
the East and of the West during the fight against the threat of fascist
subjugation which loomed before us will live centuries and millennia in
the memory of thankful humanity. . . .

The main role and the main credit for the victorious ending of the war

---

* Nicolaevsky notes that "We now know from revelations by former members of the
German secret police that Stalin wiped out a vast part of the command personnel of
the Red Army on the basis of false documents which Stalin's personal secretariat had
received from Nazi agents. The false documents on the basis of which Marshal Tukhachev-
sky and his closest colleagues were executed were turned over by Nazi agents to L. Z.
Mekhlis, a trusted member of Stalin's personnel secretariat, who flew to Berlin for that
purpose in May 1937."

belongs to our Communist party, to the armed forces of the Soviet Union, and to the tens of millions of Soviet people raised by the party. . . .

Comrades, let us reach for some other facts. The Soviet Union is justly considered as a model of a multinational state because we have in practice assured the equality and friendship of all nations which live in our great Fatherland.

All the more monstrous are the acts whose initiator was Stalin and which are rude violations of the basic Leninist principles of the nationality policy of the Soviet state. We refer to the mass deportations from their native places of whole nations, together with all Communists and Komsomols without any exception; this deportation action was not dictated by any military considerations.

Thus, already at the end of 1943, when there occurred a permanent breakthrough at the fronts of the Great Patriotic War benefiting the Soviet Union, a decision was taken and executed concerning the deportation of all the Karachai from the lands on which they lived.

In the same period, at the end of December 1943, the same lot befell the whole population of the Autonomous Kalmyk Republic. In March 1944, all the Chechen and Ingush peoples were deported and the Chechen-Ingush Autonomous Republic was liquidated. In April 1944, all Balkars were deported to faraway places from the territory of the Kabardino-Balkar Autonomous Republic and the Republic itself was renamed the Autonomous Kabardian Republic.

The Ukrainians avoided meeting this fate only because there were too many of them and there was no place to which to deport them. Otherwise, he would have deported them also. . . .

Not only a Marxist-Leninist but also no man of common sense can grasp how it is possible to make whole nations responsible for inimical activity, including women, children, old people, Communists and Komsomols, to use mass repression against them, and to expose them to misery and suffering for the hostile acts of individual persons or groups of persons.

After the conclusion of the Patriotic War, the Soviet nation stressed with pride the magnificent victories gained through great sacrifices and tremendous efforts. The country experienced a period of political enthusiasm. The party came out of the war even more united; in the fire of the war, party cadres were tempered and hardened. Under such conditions nobody could have even thought of the possibility of some plot in the party.

And it was precisely at this time that the so-called "Leningrad affair" was born. As we have now proven, this case was fabricated. Those who innocently lost their lives included Comrades Voznesensky, Kuznetsov, Rodionov, Popkov, and others. . . .

How did it happen that these persons were branded as enemies of the people and liquidated? . . .

We must state that, after the war, the situation became even more complicated. Stalin became even more capricious, irritable and brutal; in particular his suspicion grew. His persecution mania reached unbelievable dimensions. Many workers were becoming enemies before his very eyes. After the war, Stalin separated himself from the collective even more. Everything was decided by him alone without any consideration for anyone or anything.

This unbelievable suspicion was cleverly taken advantage of by the abject *provocateur* and vile enemy, Beria, who had murdered thousands of Communists and loyal Soviet people. The elevation of Voznesensky and Kuznetsov alarmed Beria. As we have now proven, it had been precisely Beria who had "suggested" to Stalin the fabrication by him and by his confidants of materials in the form of declarations and anonymous letters, and in the form of various rumors and talks. . . .

We know that there have been at times manifestations of local bourgeois nationalism in Georgia as in several other republics. The question arises: Could it be possible that, in the period during which the resolutions referred to above were made, nationalist tendencies grew so much that there was a danger of Georgia's leaving the Soviet Union and joining Turkey? . . .

As it developed, there was no nationalistic organization in Georgia. Thousands of innocent people fell victim to willfulness and lawlessness. All of this happened under the "genial" leadership of Stalin, "the great son of the Georgian nation," as Georgians like to refer to Stalin. . . .

The willfulness of Stalin showed itself not only in decisions concerning the internal life of the country but also in the international relations of the Soviet Union. . . .

I recall the first days when the conflict between the Soviet Union and Yugoslavia began artificially to be blown up. Once, when I came from Kiev to Moscow, I was invited to visit Stalin, who, pointing to the copy of a letter lately sent to Tito, asked me, "Have you read this?"

Not waiting for my reply, he answered, "I will shake my little finger — and there will be no more Tito. He will fall."

We have dearly paid for this "shaking of the little finger." This statement reflected Stalin's mania for greatness, but he acted just that way: "I will shake my little finger — and there will be no Kossior"; "I will shake

my little finger once more and Postyshev and Chubar will be no more";
"I will shake my little finger again — and Voznesensky, Kuznetsov and
many others will disappear."

But this did not happen to Tito. No matter how much or how little
Stalin shook, not only his little finger but everything else that he could
shake, Tito did not fall. Why? The reason was that, in this case of disagreement with the Yugoslav comrades, Tito had behind him a state and
a people who had gone through a severe school of fighting for liberty and
independence, a people which gave support to its leaders.

You see to what Stalin's mania for greatness led. He had completely
lost consciousness of reality; he demonstrated his suspicion and haughti-
ness not only in relation to individuals in the USSR, but in relation to
whole parties and nations. . . .

Let us also recall the "affair of the doctor-plotters." . . . Actually there
was no "affair" outside of the declaration of the woman doctor Timashuk,
who was probably influenced or ordered by someone (after all, she was
an unofficial collaborator of the organs of state security) to write Stalin
a letter in which she declared that doctors were applying supposedly improper methods of medical treatment.

Such a letter was sufficient for Stalin to reach an immediate conclusion
that there are doctor-plotters in the Soviet Union. He issued orders to
arrest a group of eminent Soviet medical specialists. He personally issued
advice on the conduct of the investigation and the method of interroga-
tion of the arrested persons. He said that the academician Vinogradov
should be put in chains, another one should be beaten. Present at this
Congress as a delegate is the former Minister of State Security, Comrade
Ignatiev. Stalin told him curtly, "If you do not obtain confessions from
the doctors we will shorten you by a head." . . .

Stalin personally called the investigative judge, gave him instructions,
advised him on which investigative methods should be used; these methods
were simple — beat, beat and, once again, beat.

Shortly after the doctors were arrested, we members of the Political
Bureau received protocols with the doctors' confessions of guilt. After
distributing these protocols, Stalin told us, "You are blind like young kit-
tens; what will happen without me? The country will perish because you
do not know how to recognize enemies."

The case was so presented that no one could verify the facts on which
the investigation was based. There was no possibility of trying to verify
facts by contacting those who had made the confessions of guilt.

We felt, however, that the case of the arrested doctors was questionable. We knew some of these people personally because they had once treated us. When we examined this "case" after Stalin's death, we found it to be fabricated from beginning to end. . . .

Stalin's reluctance to consider life's realities and the fact that he was not aware of the real state of affairs in the provinces can be illustrated by his direction of agriculture.

All those who interested themselves even a little in the national situation saw the difficult situation in agriculture, but Stalin never even noted it. Did we tell Stalin about this? Yes, we told him, but he did not support us. Why? Because Stalin never traveled anywhere, did not meet city and *kolkhoz* workers; he did not know the actual situation in the provinces.

He knew the country and agriculture only from films. And these films had dressed up and beautified the existing situation in agriculture. Many films so pictured *kolkhoz* life that the tables were bending from the weight of turkeys and geese. Evidently, Stalin thought that it was actually so.

Vladimir Ilyich Lenin looked at life differently; he was always close to the people; he used to receive peasant delegates and often spoke at factory gatherings; he used to visit villages and talk with the peasants.

Stalin separated himself from the people and never went anywhere. This lasted ten years. The last time he visited a village was in January 1928, when he visited Siberia in connection with grain deliveries. How then could he have known the situation in the provinces? . . .

We are currently beginning slowly to work our way out of a difficult agricultural situation. . . .

Comrades! If we sharply criticize today the cult of the individual which was so widespread during Stalin's life and if we speak about the many negative phenomena generated by this cult which is so alien to the spirit of Marxism-Leninism, various persons may ask: How could it be? Stalin headed the party and the country for 30 years and many victories were gained during his lifetime. Can we deny this? In my opinion, the question can be asked in this manner only by those who are blinded and hopelessly hypnotized by the cult of the individual, only by those who do not understand the essence of the revolution and of the Soviet state, only by those who do not understand, in a Leninist manner, the role of the party and of the nation in the development of the Soviet society. . . .

Some comrades may ask us: Where were the members of the Political Bureau of the Central Committee? Why did they not assert themselves against the cult of the individual in time? And why is this being done only now?

First of all, we have to consider the fact that the members of the Political Bureau viewed these matters in a different way at different times. Initially, many of them backed Stalin actively because Stalin was one of the strongest Marxists and his logic, his strength and his will greatly influenced the cadres and party work. . . .

Later, however, Stalin, abusing his power more and more, began to fight eminent party and Government leaders and to use terroristic methods against honest Soviet people. As we have already shown, Stalin thus handled such eminent party and Government leaders as Kossior, Rudzutak, Eikhe, Postyshev and many others. . . .

In the situation which then prevailed I have talked often with Nikolai Alexandrovich Bulganin; once when we two were traveling in a car, he said, "It has happened sometimes that a man goes to Stalin on his invitation as a friend. And, when he sits with Stalin, he does not know where he will be sent next — home or to jail." *

It is clear that such conditions put every member of the Political Bureau in a very difficult situation. And, when we also consider the fact that in the last years the Central Committee plenary sessions were not convened and that the sessions of the Political Bureau occurred only occasionally, from time to time, then we will understand how difficult it was for any member of the Political Bureau to take a stand against one or another unjust or improper procedure, against serious errors and shortcomings in the practices of leadership. . . .

Let us consider the first Central Committee plenum after the 19th Party Congress when Stalin, in his talk at the plenum, characterized Vyacheslav Mikhailovich Molotov and Anastas Ivanovich Mikoyan and suggested that these old workers of our party were guilty of some baseless charges. It is not excluded that had Stalin remained at the helm for another several months, Comrades Molotov and Mikoyan would probably have not delivered any speeches at this Congress.†

* It is pertinent to note that these traveling companions of long-standing have apparently made their last trip together for the foreseeable future. As "good-will ambassadors" Bulganin and Khrushchev journeyed many tens of thousands of miles together, but it is believed that Bulganin backed the anti-Khrushchev faction which was allegedly led by Molotov in mid-1957. On March 27, 1958, Khrushchev personally succeeded Marshal Bulganin as Premier of the USSR, thus openly acquiring control of both the party and the Soviet state. Through his action he has finally and openly abandoned the principles of collective leadership set forth in this tract.

† It may be predicted with no less certainty that "Comrades Molotov and . . ." many others who were considered key figures in the "collective leadership" which was in power at the time of the 20th Party Congress will not be delivering any speeches at the next Congress. At this time it is not possible to ascertain with certainty the present situation of many of the members of the "collective leadership," but it is clear that Khrushchev's consolidation of power has moved far within a two-year period. Marshal Zhukov has been replaced as Defense Minister, and on February 2, 1958, Radio Moscow noted that

Stalin evidently had plans to finish off the old members of the Political Bureau. He often stated that Political Bureau members should be replaced by new ones.

His proposal, after the 19th Congress, concerning the election of 25 persons to the Central Committee Presidium, was aimed at the removal of the old Political Bureau members and the bringing in of less experienced persons so that these would extol him in all sorts of ways.

We can assume that this was also a design for the future annihilation of the old Political Bureau members and, in this way, a cover for all shameful acts of Stalin, acts which we are now considering. . . .

We should, in all seriousness, consider the question of the cult of the individual. We cannot let this matter get out of the party, especially not to the press. It is for this reason that we are considering it here at a closed Congress session. We should know the limits; we should not give ammunition to the enemy; we should not wash our dirty linen before their eyes. I think that the delegates to the Congress will understand and assess properly all these proposals. . . .

Comrades! We must abolish the cult of the individual decisively, once and for all; we must draw the proper conclusions concerning both ideological-theoretical and practical work. It is necessary for this purpose:

First, in a Bolshevik manner to condemn and to eradicate the cult of the individual as alien to Marxism-Leninism and not consonant with the principles of party leadership and the norms of party life, and to fight inexorably all attempts at bringing back this practice in one form or another.

To return to and actually practice in all our ideological work the most important theses of Marxist-Leninist science about the people as the

---

ex-Foreign Minister Dmitri T. Shepilov had been assigned to serve as head of a scientific institute in the Kirghiz S.S.R. At the same time it was revealed that ex-Deputy Prime Minister Lazar M. Kaganovich was serving as a building materials executive somewhere in the Urals. Molotov, too, had been assigned to "diplomatic service" in far away places. Whether removal of these former leaders, some of whom had a strong popular following, to remote regions will prove to be a first step in their ultimate liquidation remains to be seen. It may be noted that ominous rumblings have been forthcoming from *Pravda* which do not augur well for them, and the uncertainty of their situation is emphasized with each new report. On May 12, 1958, *Time* reported *Pravda* as having published "two front-page editorials warning that the party 'cannot forget' the opposition of 'Malenkov, Kaganovich, Molotov and Shepilov.' At a Lenin birthday celebration in Khrushchev's presence, Party Secretary Petr Pospelov attacked the fallen 'antiparty group' by name for their 'fierce resistance.' Finally, Khrushchev himself joined vigorously and enthusiastically in the denunciations, and, in a speech on agriculture at Kiev, singled out Georgy Malenkov as 'one of the main culprits' responsible as Stalin's right hand and successor 'for all shortcomings.' " In view of the serious character of these "shortcomings," as detailed in the preceding denunciation, the implications of such an accusation would appear to be grave.

creator of history and as the creator of all material and spiritual good of humanity, about the decisive role of the Marxist party in the revolutionary fight for the transformation of society, about the victory of communism. . . .

We are absolutely certain that our party, armed with the historical resolutions of the 20th Congress, will lead the Soviet people along the Leninist path to new successes, to new victories. . . .

Long live the victorious banner of our party — Leninism!

NATIONAL COMMUNISM

by Milovan Djilas *

1.

In essence, Communism is only one thing, but it is realized in different degrees and manners in every country. Therefore it is possible to speak of various Communist systems, i.e., of various forms of the same manifestation.

The differences which exist between Communist states — differences that Stalin attempted futilely to remove by force — are the result, above all, of diverse historical backgrounds. Even the most cursory observation reveals how, for example, contemporary Soviet bureaucracy is not without a connecting link with the Czarist system in which the officials were, as Engels noted, "a distinct class." Somewhat the same thing can also be said of the manner of government in Yugoslavia. When ascending to power, the Communists face in the various countries different cultural and technical levels and varying social relationships, and are faced with different national intellectual characters. These differences develop even farther, in a special way. Because the general causes which brought them to power are identical, and because they have to wage a struggle against common internal and foreign opponents, the Communists in separate countries are immediately compelled to fight jointly and on the basis of a

* Milovan Djilas, *The New Class: An Analysis of the Communist System* (New York: 1957). By permission of Frederick A. Praeger, Inc.

similar ideology. International Communism, which was at one time the task of revolutionaries, eventually transformed itself, as did everything else in Communism, and became the common ground of Communist bureaucracies, fighting one another on nationalistic considerations. Of the former international proletariat, only words and empty dogmas remained. Behind them stood the naked national and international interests, aspirations, and plans of the various Communist oligarchies, comfortably entrenched.

The nature of authority and property, a similar international outlook, and an identical ideology inevitably identify Communist states with one another. Nevertheless, it is wrong to ignore and underestimate the significance of the inevitable differences in degree and manner between Communist states. The degree, manner, and form in which Communism will be realized, or its purpose, is just as much of a given condition for each of them as is the essence of Communism itself. No single form of Communism, no matter how similar it is to other forms, exists in any way other than as national Communism. In order to maintain itself, it must become national. . . .

The differences between Communist countries will, as a rule, be as great as the extent to which the Communists were independent in coming to power. Concretely speaking, only the Communists of three countries — the Soviet Union, China, and Yugoslavia — independently carried out revolutions or, in their own way and at their own speed, attained power and began "the building of socialism." These three countries remained independent as Communist states even in the period when Yugoslavia was — as China is today — under the most extreme influence of the Soviet Union; that is, in "brotherly love" and in "eternal friendship" with it. In a report at a closed session of the Twentieth Congress, Khrushchev revealed that a clash between Stalin and the Chinese government had barely been averted. The case of the clash with Yugoslavia was not an isolated case, but only the most drastic and the first to occur. In the other Communist countries the Soviet government enforced Communism by "armed missionaries" — its army. The diversity of manner and degree of the development in these countries has still not attained the stage reached in Yugoslavia and China. However, to the extent that ruling bureaucracies gather strength as independent bodies in these countries, and to the extent that they recognize that obedience to and copying of the Soviet Union weaken themselves, they endeavor to "pattern" themselves on Yugoslavia; that is, to develop independently. The Communist East European countries did not become satellites of the U.S.S.R. because they benefited from it, but because they were too weak to prevent it. As soon as they become stronger, or as soon as favorable conditions are created, a yearning for independence and for protection of "their own people" from Soviet hegemony will rise among them.

With the victory of a Communist revolution in a country a new class comes into power and into control. It is unwilling to surrender its own hard-gained *privileges*, even though it subordinates its *interests* to a similar class in another country, solely in the cause of ideological solidarity.

Where a Communist revolution has won victory independently, a separate, distinct path of development is inevitable. Friction with other Communist countries, especially with the Soviet Union as the most important and most imperialistic state, follows. The ruling national bureaucracy in the country where the victorious revolution took place has already become independent in the course of the armed struggle and has tasted the blessings of authority and of "nationalization" of property. Philosophically speaking, it has also grasped and become conscious of its own essence, "its own state," its authority, on the basis of which it claims equality.

This does not mean that this involves only a clash — when it comes to that — between two bureaucracies. A clash also involves the revolutionary elements of a subordinated country, because they do not usually tolerate domination and they consider that relationships between Communist states must be as ideally perfect as predicted in dogma. The masses of the nation, who spontaneously thirst for independence, cannot remain unperturbed in such a clash. In every case the nation benefits from this: it does not have to pay tribute to a foreign government; and the pressure on the domestic government, which no longer desires, and is not permitted, to copy foreign methods, is also diminished. Such a clash also brings in external forces, other states and movements. However, the nature of the clash and the basic forces in it remain. Neither Soviet nor Yugoslav Communists stopped being what they are — not before, nor during, nor after their mutual bickerings. Indeed, the diverse types of degree and manner with which they insured their monopoly led them mutually to deny the existence of socialism in the opposite camp. After they settled their differences, they again acknowledged the existence of socialism elsewhere, becoming conscious that they must respect mutual differences if they wanted to preserve that which was identical in essence and most important to them.

The subordinate Communist governments in East Europe can, in fact must, declare their independence from the Soviet government. No one can say how far this aspiration for independence will go and what disagreements will result. The result depends on numerous unforeseen internal and external circumstances. However, there is no doubt that a national Communist bureaucracy aspires to more complete authority for itself. This is demonstrated by the anti-Tito processes in Stalin's time in the East European countries; it is shown also by the current unconcealed emphasis on "one's own path to socialism," which has recently come to light sharply in Poland and Hungary. The central Soviet government has found itself in difficulty because of the nationalism existing even in those governments which it installed in the Soviet republics (Ukraine, Caucasia), and still more so with regard to those governments installed in the East European countries. Playing an important role in all of this is the fact that the Soviet Union was unable, and will not be able in the future, to assimilate the economies of the East European countries.

The aspirations toward national independence must of course have greater impetus. These aspirations can be retarded and even made dormant by external pressure or by fear on the part of the Communists of "imperialism" and the "bourgeoisie," but they cannot be removed. On the contrary, their strength will grow.

It is impossible to foresee all of the forms that relations between Communist states will assume. Even if cooperation between Communist states of different countries should in a short time result in mergers and federations, so can clashes between Communist states result in war. An open, armed clash between the U.S.S.R. and Yugoslavia was averted not because of the "socialism" in one or the other country, but because it was not in Stalin's interest to risk a clash of unforeseeable proportions. Whatever will happen between Communist states will depend on all those factors which ordinarily affect political events. The interests of the respective Communist bureaucracies, expressed variously as "national" or as "united," along with the unchecked tendency toward ever increasing independence on a national basis, will, for the time being, play an important role in the relationships among the Communist countries.

2.

The concept of national Communism had no meaning until the end of World War II, when Soviet imperialism was manifested not only with regard to the capitalist but the Communist states as well. This concept developed above all from the Yugoslav-U.S.S.R. clash. The renunciation of Stalin's methods by the "collective leadership" of Khrushchev-Bulganin may perhaps modify relations between the U.S.S.R. and other Communist countries, but it cannot resolve them. In the U.S.S.R. operations are not concerned solely with Communism but are simultaneously concerned with the imperialism of the Great Russian — Soviet — state. This imperialism can change in form and method, but it can no more disappear than can the aspirations of Communists of other countries for independence.

A similar development awaits the other Communist states. According to strength and conditions, they too will attempt to become imperialistic in one way or another. . . .

The basic cause of an imperialistic policy is completely hidden in the exploitative and despotic nature of the new class. In order that that class might manifest itself as imperialistic, it was necessary for it to attain a prescribed strength and to appear in appropriate circumstances. It already had this strength when World War II began. The war itself abounded in possibilities for imperialistic combinations. The small Baltic states were not necessary for the security of so large a state as the U.S.S.R., particularly in modern war. These states were non-aggressive and even allies; however, they were an attractive morsel for the insatiable appetite of the great Russian Communist bureaucracy. . . .

. . . Soviet imperialism, by political, police and military methods, had to compensate for its own economic and other weaknesses. Imperialism in the military form, which was only an advanced stage of the old Czarist military-feudal imperialism, also corresponded to the internal structure of the Soviet Union in which the police and administrative apparatus, centralized in one personality, played a major role. Stalinism was a mixture of a personal Communist dictatorship and militaristic imperialism.

These forms of imperialism developed: joint stock companies, absorption of the exports of the East European countries by means of political pressure at prices below the world market, artificial formation of a "socialist world market," control of every political act of subordinate parties and states, transformation of the traditional love of Communists toward the "socialist fatherland" into deification of the Soviet state, Stalin, and Soviet practices. . . .

Now the Soviet Union entered into the predominantly economic and political phase of its imperialistic policy. Or so it appears, judging from current facts.

Today national Communism is a general phenomenon in Communism. To varying degrees all Communist movements — except that of the U.S.S.R. against which it is directed — are gripped by national Communism. In its time, in the period of Stalin's ascendancy, Soviet Communism also was national Communism. At that time Russian Communism abandoned internationalism, except as an instrument of its foreign policy. Today Soviet Communism is compelled, even if indefinitely, to acknowledge a new reality in Communism.

Changing internally, Soviet imperialism was also compelled to alter its views toward the external world. From predominantly administrative controls, it advanced toward gradual economic integration with the East European countries. This is being accomplished by means of mutual planning in important branches of economy, in which the local Communist governments today mainly voluntarily concur, still sensing themselves weaker externally and internally.

Such a situation cannot remain for long, because it conceals a fundamental contradiction. On the one hand national forms of Communism become stronger, but on the other, Soviet imperialism does not diminish.

Recognition of national forms of Communism, which the Soviet government did with clenched teeth, has immense significance and conceals within itself very considerable dangers for Soviet imperialism.

It involves freedom of discussion to a certain extent; this means ideological independence too. Now the fate of certain heresies in Communism will depend not only on the tolerance of Moscow, but on their national potentialities. Deviation from Moscow that strives to maintain its influence in the Communist world on a "voluntary" and "ideologic" basis cannot possibly be checked. . . .

National modifications in Communism jeopardize Soviet imperialism, particularly in the imperialism of the Stalin epoch, but not Communism either as a whole or in essence. On the contrary, where Communism is in control these changes are able to influence its direction and even to strengthen it and make it acceptable externally. National Communism is in harmony with non-dogmaticism, that is, with the anti-Stalinist phase in the development of Communism. In fact, it is a basic form of this phase.

3.

National Communism is unable to alter the nature of current international relationships between states or within workers' movements. But its role in these relationships may be of great significance.

Thus, for example, Yugoslav Communism, as a form of national Communism, played an extremely important role in the weakening of Soviet imperialism and in the downgrading of Stalinism inside the Communist movement. The motives for changes which are occurring in the Soviet

Union and in the East European countries are to be found, above all, in the countries themselves. They appeared first in Yugoslavia — in the Yugoslav way. And there, too, they were first completed. . . .

4.

National Communism similar to that in Yugoslavia could be of immense international significance in Communist parties of non-Communist states. It could be of even greater significance there than in Communist parties which are actually in power. This is relevant above all to the Communist parties in France and Italy, which encompass a significant majority of the working class and which are, along with several parties in Asia the only ones of major significance in the non-Communist world.

Until now, the manifestations of national Communism in these parties have been without major significance and impetus. However, they have been inevitable. They could, in the final analysis, lead to profound and essential changes in these parties.

These parties have to contend with the Social Democrats — who are able to channel the dissatisfied masses toward themselves by means of their own socialist slogans and activity. This is not the only reason for the eventual deviation of these parties from Moscow. Lesser reasons may be seen in the periodic and unanticipated reversals of Moscow and of the other ruling Communist parties. Such reversals lead these and other non-ruling Communist parties into a "crisis of conscience" — to spit on what until yesterday they extolled, then suddenly to change their line. Neither oppositionist propaganda nor administrative pressure will play a fundamental role in the transformation of these parties.

The basic causes for deviation of these parties from Moscow may be found in the nature of the social system of the countries in which they operate. If it becomes evident — and it appears likely — that the working class of these countries is able through parliamentary forms to arrive at some improvement in its position, and also to change the social system itself, the working class will abandon the Communists regardless of its revolutionary and other traditions. Only small groups of Communist dogmaticists can look dispassionately at the disassociation of the workers; serious political leaders in a given nation will endeavor to avoid it even at the cost of weakening ties with Moscow.

Parliamentary elections which give a huge number of votes to Communists in these countries do not accurately express the actual strength of Communist parties. To a significant degree they are an expression of dissatisfaction and delusion. Stubbornly following the Communist leaders, the masses will just as easily abandon them the moment it becomes obvious to them that the leaders are sacrificing national institutions, or the concrete prospects of the working class, to their bureaucratic nature, or to the "dictatorship of the proletariat" and ties with Moscow.

Of course, all of this is hypothesis. But even today these parties are finding themselves in a difficult situation. If they really wish to be adherents of parliamentarianism, their leaders will have to renounce their anti-parliamentary nature, or change over to their own national Communism which would, since they are not in control, lead to disintegration of their parties.

The leaders of Communist parties in these countries are driven to experiment with the idea of national Communism and national forms by all of these factors: by the strengthening of the possibility that the transformation of society and the improvement of position of the workers will be attained by democratic means; by Moscow's reversals, which by the downgrading of the cult of Stalin ultimately resulted in destruction of the ideologic center; by concurrence of the Social Democrats; by tendencies toward unification of the West on a profound and enduring social basis as well as a military one; by military strengthening of the Western bloc which offers increasingly fewer prospects for "brotherly aid" for the Soviet army; and by the impossibility of new Communist revolutions without a world war. At the same time fear of the inevitable result of a transition to parliamentarianism, and of a breaking off with Moscow, prevents these leaders from doing anything of real significance. Increasingly deeper social differences between the East and the West work with relentless force. The clever Togliatti is confused, and the robust Thorez is wavering. External and internal party life is beginning to bypass them.

Emphasizing that today a parliament can serve as a "form of transition to socialism," Khrushchev intended at the Twentieth Congress to facilitate manipulation of the Communist parties in "capitalist countries," and to stimulate the cooperation of Communists and Social Democrats and the formation of "People's Fronts." Something like this appeared realistic to him, according to his words, because of the changes which had resulted in the strengthening of Communism and because of peace in the world. With that he tacitly acknowledged to everyone the obvious impossibility of Communist revolutions in the developed countries, as well as the impossibility of further expansion of Communism under current conditions without the danger of a new world war. The policy of the Soviet state has been reduced to a status quo, while Communism has descended to gradual acquisition of new positions in a new way.

A crisis has actually begun in the Communist parties of the non-Communist states. If they change over to national Communism, they risk forsaking their very nature; and if they do not change over, they face the loss of followers. Their leaders, those who represent the spirit of Communism in these parties, will be forced into the most cunning manipulations and unscrupulous measures if they are to extricate themselves from this contradiction. It is improbable that they will be able to check disorientation and disintegration. They have reached a state of conflict with the real tendencies of development in the world and in their countries that obviously lead toward new relationships.

National Communism outside of the Communist states inevitably leads toward renunciation of Communism itself, or toward the disintegration of the Communist parties. Its possibilities are greater today in the non-Communist states, but obviously, only along the lines of separation from Communism itself. Therefore, national Communism in these parties will emerge victorious only with difficulty and slowly, in successive outbursts.

In the Communist parties that are not in power it is evident that national Communism — despite its intent to stimulate Communism and strengthen its nature — is simultaneously the heresy that nibbles at Communism as such. National Communism per se is contradictory. Its nature is the same as that of Soviet Communism, but it aspires to detach itself into something of its own, nationally. In reality, national Communism is Communism in decline.

V . ELITISM

a . Racial Elitism

THE MYTH of racial superiority is the fullest expression of the belief in the inequality of men. For, the myth asserts, not only are men unequal when considered individually, but the masses of mankind may be graded on a scale of superiority and inferiority when they are classified by the mystical and elusive category of race. It is no coincidence that most racists are also advocates of elitism in politics; or that elitists tend to advocate the ideology of racism. For the one belief system tends to complement the other. If men are not created equal, as Locke and the authors of the Declaration of Independence maintained, then they are created unequal. What is the source of this inequality? The racists attribute this to some factor in the blood, the genes or some natural force that is beyond the control of man or his environment. The age-old argument between heredity and environment as the dominant conditioning force upon men is thus resolved in favor of heredity.

Generally speaking, racism is a modern ideology. It is largely a by-product of the expansion of the European culture into other parts of the world and the efforts of the colonizers and their descendants to maintain their political supremacy. For all the eighteenth-century avowals of the equality of men, the colonization of the Americas, India, Africa, and Australia brought European settlers into contact and conflict with the natives of these conquered areas where inequality was the practice if not the overt principle. Though the Declaration of Independence proclaimed the equality of men, the American Indians were driven westward and the system of Negro slavery expanded. The conquered Indians and the chattel slaves were hardly thought of as equals by the early settlers, and it was easy to relate the differences in culture with the differences in physical characteristics to give rise to the belief in racial inequality.

It was not, however, until the arguments over abolition arose that racism received systematized expression in this country. Then in the pre-Civil War debates the champions of white supremacy came forward to defend slavery, which was of course an extreme form of institutionalized racial inequality. "He who is by nature not his own but another's man, is by nature a slave," Aristotle had maintained in his *Politics*. "From the hour of their birth, some are marked out for subjection, others for rule." In the pre-Civil War debates Aristotle, the Bible, and historical precedent were all refurbished to justify the institution of slavery. Endless claims were made that the Negro was a naturally inferior race suitable only to slavery. One of the most extreme statements concerning the inequality of men was made by Governor J. H. Hammond of South Carolina when he advocated the "mud-sill" theory of society.

> In all social systems there must be a class to do the menial duties, to perform the drudgery of life. That is, a class requiring but a low order of intellect and but little skill. Its requisites are vigor, docility, fidelity. Such a class you must have or you would not have that other class which leads progress, civilization, and refinement. It constitutes the very mud-sill of society and of political government; and you might as well attempt to build a house in the air, as to build either the one or the other, except on this mud-sill. Fortunately for the South, she found a race adapted to that purpose to her hand. . . . We use them for our purpose and call them slaves.[1]

Slavery was thus viewed not as a symptom of social retrogression but rather as a source of civilization. John C. Calhoun, denouncing the belief in the equality of men, argued that it is the "inequality of conditions between the front and rear ranks, in the march of progress, which gives so strong an impulse to the former to maintain their position and to the latter to press forward into their files. This gives to progress its greatest impulse." [2]

While the Civil War settled the issue of slavery in the United States, it did not by any means resolve the issue of racism. From the Ku Klux Klan to the White Citizens' Councils, from segregated housing in Chicago to segregated schools in Columbia, South Carolina, the Negro has been stymied in his efforts to realize the basic principles enunciated in the Declaration of Independence. Racism, in one form or another, has been

---

[1] Speech in Senate, March 4, 1858, *Congressional Globe*, 35th Congress, 1st session, appendix, p. 71.
[2] "A Disquisition on Government" in *The Works of John C. Calhoun*, edited by Richard K. Crallé (New York: D. Appleton and Co., 1854), Vol. I, p. 57.

used as a political instrument in the United States as well as elsewhere to serve the interests of the dominant racial and religious groups.

While the slavery issue accentuated racism and racist ideology in the United States, the nineteenth century saw this ideology develop on the continent and in England as well. Yet beyond the strategies of political advantage which led to the acceptance of racist ideology in the nineteenth and twentieth centuries, who were the major propounders of this doctrine? In a sense, there were many. Early efforts in ethnology and philology had led to descriptive classifications of the peoples of the world in terms of size of heads, stature, pigmentation, hair texture and various linguistic attributes. While none of these early descriptive efforts to classify mankind ever achieved the status of scientific evidence or definitive truth, a new race consciousness, one might say, took hold of historians, anthropologists and politicians. Imposing terms, such as brachycephalic (broad-skulled) and dolichocephalic (long-skulled) were introduced into the discussion of races in 1842 by the Swedish scientist, Anders Retzius. But undoubtedly it was the French litterateur and diplomat Arthur de Gobineau, who was the most ideologically influential figure in the course of modern racism.

Count de Gobineau (1816–1882) was of that small and disenchanted French aristocracy which resented the rise of popular democracy in the world and ridiculed the idea of progress. Like the French monarchists of the early nineteenth century, Count de Maistre and the Marquis de Bonald, Count de Gobineau sought to check the spread of liberalism, with its easy optimism and trust in majority rule. Like other racists before and after him, Gobineau coupled to his belief in racial superiority a belief in minority rule. Human character he believed to be directly the result of racial inheritance. The races of mankind had, he believed, separate character and propensities, as well as different colors, sizes, and shapes. It was, he felt, as impossible to change a person's character by education as it was to change the color of his skin by the same process. All was determined by race: all art, all politics, all civilizations. Indeed, the rise and fall of civilizations were the direct result of racial combinations.

Gobineau believed that there had been a primitive white race called Aryas, who came out of Central Asia. As these Aryas invaded Egypt, India, and Assyria they brought about the great civilizations which flourished there in ancient days. When they entered Greece and Rome and Western Europe they brought civilization with them. However, in every instance they crossed their blood with the subject peoples and thus in time each civilization floundered and fell. Miscegenation thus is the cause of decadence. Witty, even in his pessimism, Gobineau despaired for the future of his own civilization with its democratic disregard of what he conceived to be the facts of racial inequality. "We do not come from the ape," he once wrote, "but we are rapidly getting there." [3]

Gobineau's influence upon European thought is quite beyond estimate, for it is evident he influenced many who had never read his four-volume *Essay on The Inequality of Races* (1855). His essay was read and admired by Nietzsche, Schopenhauer, and Richard Wagner. Indeed Wagner, who was a thoroughgoing Nordic racist, and Gobineau were personal friends. While Wagner turned racism to the advantage of German nationalism, Gobineau always thought of racism in terms of an international Aryan elite. He believed that there was no longer a pure race, Aryan or other. Only within the Aryan race, he felt, there was still a remnant of pure stock which existed on the aristocratic class level. Yet this point was usually overlooked by the German racists who used Gobineau's ideas for national purposes.

It is one of the ironies of modern history that German racism took much of its ideology from the Frenchman, Gobineau, and the renegade Englishman, Houston Stewart Chamberlain. Unlike the urbane Gobineau, Chamberlain blatantly turned racism into a German national ideology. In place of Aryan, Chamberlain used the word Teuton. The Teutons throughout history were the race that possessed all virtue, all culture, those who had controlled the destinies of civilizations. On the other hand the Jews were a menacing and destructive influence on Teutonic culture. It is obviously an easy step from the tirades of Chamberlain to the tirades of Hitler. Both equated "German" with "Teuton" and "Aryan." The defeat of Germany in 1918 seemed to both to spell the decline of the human race. A few years after World War I, Chamberlain and Hitler met, and one can guess exchanged ideas on racial inequality. In 1923 Chamberlain wrote to Hitler his reactions to their visit. "At one blow," he wrote, "you have transformed the state my soul was in. Germany's vitality is proved if in this hour of its deepest need it can produce a Hitler." [4] And Hitler, in discussing in *Mein Kampf* the causes of the collapse of Germany, lamented that only a few recognized "the planlessness and thoughtlessness of the policy of the Reich, and were, accordingly, very well aware of its inner weakness and hollowness, but they were only the outsiders of political life; the official authorities of the government passed by the observa-

---

[3] Quoted in Jacques Barzun, *Race, A Study in Modern Superstition* (London: Methuen & Co., 1938), p. 72.

[4] Adolf Hitler, *Mein Kampf* (New York: Reynal & Hitchcock, 1941), p. 395, fn.

tions of a Houston Stewart Chamberlain just as indifferently as this is still the case with us today." [5] Chamberlain's racist ideology served as German propaganda in two world wars. His ideology was rephrased by Hitler, but little that was new or more consistent was added. However, Hitler unlike Chamberlain, was able to put the ideology into practice.

Racism continued in the United States even as we combatted racism abroad. While Americans deplored the use of concentration camps in Hitler's Germany, they nevertheless, early in World War II, removed a hundred thousand Americans of Japanese descent from their homes on the West Coast to relocation centers further inland. Clearly this move was inspired by reasoning along lines of racial distrust. In the United States xenophobia has often come into evidence along racial lines. As German racists have extolled the Teuton, American racist ideology has usually proclaimed the Anglo-Saxon as the superior race. Late in the nineteenth century Josiah Strong (1847–1916) wrote a little book called *Our Country* (1885). It attacked Romanism, Mormonism, Immigration, Socialism, Urbanization, and Intemperance as the great evils facing America. And it extolled the virtues of the Anglo-Saxon, who was credited with being representative of two great ideas in history: civil liberty and spiritual Christianity. Not only were 130,000 copies of the first edition sold but most of the chapters were reprinted in newspapers as well. *Our Country* was, apparently, an immediate commercial success because it was stating a point of view that thousands of Americans concurred in. In 1891 the book went into a new edition, in which form it was available for America's late nineteenth-century imperialism. *Our Country* expressed, in milder form, the thoughts of Senator A. J. Beveridge, who wrote during the Spanish-American War that it was "the most holy war ever waged by one nation against another — a war for civilization, a war for a permanent peace, a war which, under God, although we knew it not, swung open to the republic the portals of commerce of the world. . . . Fellow Americans, we are God's chosen people." [6]

In America opponents of mass immigration argued that the influx of Orientals and eastern Europeans would eventually mongrelize the native American stock and so bring about the decline of the United States. Madison Grant (1865–1937) was one of the most influential spokesmen of this line of thought. In *The Passing of the Great Race* (1916) Grant, like Houston Stewart Chamberlain, advanced an explanation of the course of

---

[5] *Ibid.*, p. 369.
[6] "The March of the Flag," *Modern Eloquence* (Philadelphia: John D. Morris and Company, 1903), XI, 226, 242.

European history in terms of race. As the historian Henry Fairfield Osborn observed in his preface to Grant's book, "race has played a far larger part than either language or nationality in moulding the destinies of men; race implies heredity and heredity implies all the moral, social and intellectual characteristics and traits which are the springs of politics and government."

By 1921 Grant's book had gone into four editions and was translated into German and French. Grant declared that *The Passing of the Great Race* was written to "rouse his fellow-Americans to the overwhelming importance of race and to the folly of the 'Melting Pot' theory. . . ." Indeed Grant credits the book and the discussions about it with influencing Congress "to adopt discriminating and restrictive measures against the immigration of undesirable races and peoples." He was referring, of course, to the Immigration Act of 1921 which established the national origins system for controlling the entry of persons into the United States. Today, under the national origins plan, the total annual immigration has been set at 154,657. However, each country has a quota which is made up of one-sixth of one percent of the number of people in the United States in 1920 who came from that country. In effect, this allows about 72% of the total possible immigration to those from Britain, Ireland and Germany. Fifty-six countries have quotas of only 100 persons. This is true, for instance, of all Asiatic countries with the exception of Japan which has a quota of 185. Madison Grant's theory is thus clearly incorporated into the law of the land.

The politics of race have special significance today at opposite ends of the world: the Union of South Africa and the United States. In parts of both countries the traditional political, social and economic rule of white over black is at issue. In South Africa, the post-war governments have sought to achieve an increasing measure of separation between the races through the "apartheid" policy. In the United States the "separate but equal" doctrine was overthrown by the Supreme Court in 1954, thereby making integration, not segregation, the law of the land. However, as the tragic experience of Little Rock, Arkansas, has demonstrated, racial elitism continues to be one of the basic issues of our times.

The selections below were first published as follows:

Josiah Strong, *Our Country* (1885)
Houston Stewart Chamberlain, *Foundations of the Nineteenth Century* (1910)
Adolf Hitler, *Mein Kampf* (1925)
N. J. J. Olivier, "Apartheid — A Slogan or a Solution" (1953)
Herbert R. Sass, "Mixed Schools and Mixed Blood" (1956)

THE ANGLO-SAXON AND THE WORLD'S FUTURE

by Josiah Strong *

Every race which has deeply impressed itself on the human family has been the representative of some great idea — one or more — which has given direction to the nation's life and form to its civilization. Among the Egyptians this seminal idea was life, among the Persians it was light, among the Hebrews it was purity, among the Greeks it was beauty, among the Romans it was law. The Anglo-Saxon is the representative of two great ideas, which are closely related. One of them is that of civil liberty. Nearly all of the civil liberty of the world is enjoyed by Anglo-Saxons: the English, the British colonists, and the people of the United States. To some, like the Swiss, it is permitted by the sufferance of their neighbors; others, like the French, have experimented with it; but, in modern times, the peoples whose love of liberty has won it, and whose genius for self-government has preserved it, have been Anglo-Saxons. The noblest races have always been lovers of liberty. The love ran strong in early German blood, and has profoundly influenced the institutions of all the branches of the great German family; but it was left for the Anglo-Saxon branch fully to recognize the right of the individual to himself, and formally to declare it the foundation stone of government.

The other great idea of which the Anglo-Saxon is the exponent is that of a pure *spiritual* Christianity. It was no accident that the great reformation of the sixteenth century originated among a Teutonic, rather than a Latin people. It was the fire of liberty burning in the Saxon heart that flamed up against the absolutism of the Pope. Speaking roughly, the peoples of Europe which are Celtic are Roman Catholic, and those which are Teutonic are Protestant; and where the Teutonic race was purest, there Protestantism spread with the greatest rapidity. But, with beautiful exceptions, Protestantism on the continent has degenerated into mere

* Josiah Strong, *Our Country* (New York: The Baker and Taylor Co., 1891).

formalism. . . . Evidently it is chiefly to the English and American peoples that we must look for the evangelization of the world.

It is not necessary to argue to those for whom I write that the two great needs of mankind, that all men may be lifted up into the light of the highest Christian civilization, are, first, a pure, spiritual Christianity, and second, civil liberty. Without controversy, these are the forces which, in the past, have contributed most to the elevation of the human race, and they must continue to be, in the future, the most efficient ministers to its progress. It follows, then, that the Anglo-Saxon, as the great representative of these two ideas, the depositary of these two greatest blessings, sustains peculiar relations to the world's future, is divinely commissioned to be, in a peculiar sense, his brother's keeper. Add to this the fact of his rapidly increasing strength in modern times, and we have well-nigh a demonstration of his destiny. In 1700 this race numbered less than 6,000,000 souls. In 1800, Anglo-Saxons (I use the term somewhat broadly to include all English-speaking peoples) had increased to about 20,500,000, and now, in 1890, they number more than 120,000,000 having multiplied almost six-fold in ninety years. At the end of the reign of Charles II the English colonists in America numbered 200,000. During these two hundred years, our population has increased two hundred and fifty-fold. And the expansion of this race has been no less remarkable than its multiplication. In one century the United States has increased its territory ten-fold, while the enormous acquisition of foreign territory by Great Britain — and chiefly within the last hundred years — is wholly unparalleled in history. This mighty Anglo-Saxon race, though comprising only one-thirteenth part of mankind now rules more than one-third of the earth's surface, and more than one-fourth of its people. And if this race, while growing from 6,000,000 to 120,000,000, thus gained possession of a third portion of the earth, is it to be supposed that when it numbers 1,000,000,000, it will lose the disposition, or lack the power to extend its sway?

This race is multiplying not only more rapidly than any other European race, but more rapidly than *all* the races of continental Europe taken together. There is no exact knowledge of the population of Europe early in the century. We know, however, that the increase on the continent during the ten years from 1870 to 1880 was 6.89 per cent. If this rate of increase is sustained for a century, the population on the continent in 1980 will be 534,000,000; while the one Anglo-Saxon race, if it should multiply for a hundred years as fast as from 1870 to 1880, would in 1980 number 1,111,000,000 souls, an incredible increase, of course.

What then will be the probable numbers of this race a hundred years hence? It is hazardous to venture a prophecy, but we may weigh probabilities. In studying this subject several things must be borne in mind. Heretofore, the great causes which have operated to check the growth of population in the world have been war, famine, and pestilence; but, among civilized peoples, these causes are becoming constantly less operative. Paradoxical as it seems, the invention of more destructive weapons of war renders war less destructive; commerce and wealth have removed the fear of famine, and pestilence is being brought more and more under control by medical skill and sanitary science. Moreover, Anglo-Saxons, with the exception of the people of Great Britain, who now compose less than one-third of this race, are much less exposed to these checks upon growth than the races of Europe. Again, Europe is crowded, and is constantly becoming more so, which will tend to reduce continually the ratio of increase; while over two-thirds of the Anglo-Saxons occupy lands which invite almost unlimited expansion — the United States, Canada, Australia, and South Africa. Again, emigration from Europe, which will probably increase, is very largely into Anglo-Saxon countries; and, though these foreign elements exert a modifying influence on the Anglo-Saxon stock, their descendants are certain to be Anglo-Saxonized. From 1870 to 1880, Germany lost 987,000 inhabitants by emigration, most of whom came to the United States. In one generation, their children will be counted Anglo-Saxons. This race has been undergoing an unparalleled expansion during the eighteenth and nineteenth centuries, and the conditions for its continued growth are singularly favorable.

We are now prepared to ask what light statistics cast on the future. In Great Britain, from 1840 to 1850, the ratio of increase of the population was 2.49 per cent; during the next ten years it was 5.44 per cent; the next ten years, it was 8.60; from 1870 to 1880, it was 10.57; and from 1880 to 1889 it was 10.08 per cent. That is, for fifty years the ratio of increase has been rapidly rising.

It is not unlikely to continue rising for some time to come; but, remembering that the population is dense, in making our estimate for the next hundred years, we will suppose the ratio of increase to be only one-half as large as that from 1870 to 1880, which would make the population in 1980, 57,000,000. All the great colonies of Britain, except Canada, which has a great future, show a very high ratio of increase in population; that of Australia, from 1870 to 1880, was 56.50 per cent; that of South Africa was 73.28. It is quite reasonable to suppose that the colonies, taken together, will double their population once in twenty-five years for the next century. In the United States, population has, on the average, doubled once in twenty-five years since 1685. Adopting this ratio, then, for the English colonies, their 11,000,000 in 1880 will be 176,000,000 in 1980 and about 234,000,000 in 1990. Turning now to our own country, we find in the following table the ratio of increase of population for each decade of years since 1800:

From 1800 to 1810	36.38 per cent.		
" 1810 " 1820	34.80	"	"
" 1820 " 1830	33.11	"	"
" 1830 " 1840	32.66	"	"
" 1840 " 1850	35.87	"	"
" 1850 " 1860	35.58	"	"
" 1860 " 1870	22.59	"	"
" 1870 " 1880	30.06	"	"
" 1880 " 1890	24.57	"	"

Here we see a falling ratio of increase of about one per cent every ten years from 1800 to 1840 — a period when immigration was inconsiderable. During the next twenty years the ratio was decidedly higher, because of a large immigration. It fell off during the war, and again arose from 1870 to 1880, while it seems to have fallen from 1880 to 1890.

If the rate of increase for the next century is as great with immigration as it was from 1800 to 1840 without immigration, we shall have a falling ratio of increase of about one per cent every ten years. Beginning, then, with an increase of twenty-four per cent from 1890 to 1900, our population in 1990 would be 373,000,000, making the total Anglo-Saxon population of the world, at that time, 667,000,000, as compared with 570,000,000 inhabitants of continental Europe. When we consider how much more favorable are the conditions for the increase of population in Anglo-Saxon countries than in continental Europe, and remember that we have reckoned the growth of European population at its rate of increase from 1870 to 1880, while we have reckoned Anglo-Saxon growth at much less than its rate of increase during the same ten years, we may be reasonably confident that a hundred years hence this one race will outnumber all the peoples of continental Europe. And it is possible that, by the close of the next century, the Anglo-Saxons will outnumber all the other civilized races of the world. Does it not look as if God were not only preparing in our Anglo-Saxon civilization the die with which to stamp the peoples of the earth, but as if he were also massing behind that die the mighty power with which to press it? My confidence that this race is eventually to give its civilization to mankind is not based on mere numbers — China forbid!

I look forward to what the world has never yet seen united in the same race; viz., the greatest numbers, *and* the highest civilization.

There can be no reasonable doubt that North America is to be the great home of the Anglo-Saxon, the principal seat of his power, the center of his life and influence. Not only does it constitute seven-elevenths of his possessions, but here his empire is unsevered, while the remaining four-elevenths are fragmentary and scattered over the earth. Australia will have a great population; but its disadvantages, as compared with North America, are too manifest to need mention. Our continent has room and resources and climate, it lies in the pathway of the nations, it belongs to the zone of power, and already, among Anglo-Saxons, do we lead in population and wealth. Of England, Franklin once wrote: "That pretty island which, compared to America, is but a stepping-stone in a brook, scarce enough of it above water to keep one's shoes dry." England can hardly hope to maintain her relative importance among Anglo-Saxon peoples when her "pretty island" is the home of only one-twentieth part of that race. With the wider distribution of wealth, and increasing facilities of intercourse, intelligence and influence are less centralized, and peoples become more homogeneous; and the more nearly homogeneous peoples are, the more do *numbers tell*.

America is to have the great preponderance of numbers and of wealth, and by the logic of events will follow the scepter of controlling influence. This will be but the consummation of a movement as old as civilization — a result to which men have looked forward for centuries. . . .

It may be easily shown, and is of no small significance, that the two great ideas of which the Anglo-Saxon is the exponent are having a fuller development in the United States than in Great Britain. There the union of Church and State tends strongly to paralyze some of the members of the body of Christ. Here there is no such influence to destroy spiritual life and power. Here, also, has been evolved the form of government consistent with the largest possible civil liberty. Furthermore, it is significant that the marked characteristics of this race are being here emphasized most. Among the most striking features of the Anglo-Saxon is his money-making power — a power of increasing importance in the widening commerce of the world's future. We have seen, in a preceding chapter, that, although England is by far the richest nation of Europe, we have already outstripped her in the race after wealth, and we have only begun the development of our vast resources.

Again, another marked characteristic of the Anglo-Saxon is what may be called an instinct or genius for colonizing. His unequaled energy, his indomitable perseverance, and his personal independence, made him a pioneer. He excels all others in pushing his way into new countries. It was those in whom this tendency was strongest that came to America, and this inherited tendency has been further developed by the westward sweep of successive generations across the continent. So noticeable has this characteristic become that English visitors remark it. Charles Dickens once said that the typical American would hesitate to enter heaven unless assured that he could go farther west.

Again, nothing more manifestly distinguishes the Anglo-Saxon than his intense and persistent energy, and he is developing in the United States an energy which, in eager activity and effectiveness, is peculiarly American. This is due partly to the fact that Americans are much better fed than Europeans, and partly to the undeveloped resources of a new country, but more largely to our climate, which acts as a constant stimulus. Ten years after the landing of the Pilgrims, the Rev. Francis Higginson, a good observer, wrote: "A sup of New England air is better than a whole flagon of English ale." Thus early had the stimulating effect of our climate been noted. Moreover, our social institutions are stimulating. In Europe the various ranks of society are, like the strata of the earth, fixed and fossilized. There can be no great change without a terrible upheaval, a social earthquake. Here society is like the waters of the sea, mobile; as General Garfield said, and so signally illustrated in his own experience, that which is at the bottom to-day may one day flash on the crest of the highest wave. Every one is free to become whatever he can make of himself; free to transform himself from a rail-splitter or a tanner or a canal-boy, into the nation's President. Our aristocracy, unlike that of Europe, is open to all comers. Wealth, position, influence, are prizes offered for energy; and every farmer's boy, every apprentice and clerk, every friendless and penniless immigrant, is free to enter the lists. Thus many causes co-operate to produce here the most forceful and tremendous energy in the world.

What is the significance of such facts? These tendencies infold the future; they are the mighty alphabet with which God writes his prophecies. May we not, by a careful laying together of the letters, spell out something of his meaning? It seems to me that God, with infinite wisdom and skill, is training the Anglo-Saxon race for an hour sure to come in the world's future. Heretofore there has always been in the history of the world a comparatively unoccupied land westward, into which the crowded countries of the East have poured their surplus populations. But the widening waves of migration, which millenniums ago rolled east and west from the valley of the Euphrates, meet to-day on our Pacific coast. There are no more new worlds. The unoccupied arable lands of the earth are limited, and will soon be taken. The time is coming when the pressure of population on the means of subsistence will be felt here as it is now felt in Europe and Asia. Then will the world enter upon a new stage of its history — *the final competition of races, for which the Anglo-Saxon is being schooled.* Long before the thousand millions are here, the mighty *centrifugal* tendency, inherent in this stock and strengthened in the United States, will assert itself. Then this race of unequaled energy, with all the majesty of numbers and the might of wealth behind it— the representative, let us hope, of the largest liberty, the purest Christianity, the highest civilization — having developed peculiarly aggressive traits calculated to impress its institutions upon mankind, will spread itself over the earth. If I read not amiss, this powerful race will move down upon Mexico, down upon Central and South America, out upon the islands of the sea, over upon Africa and beyond. And can any one doubt that the results of this competition of races will be the "survival of the fittest?" "Any people," says Dr. Bushnell, "that is physiologically advanced in culture, though it be only in a degree beyond another which is mingled with it on strictly equal terms, is sure to live down and finally live out its inferior. Nothing can save the inferior race but a ready and pliant assimilation. Whether the feebler and more abject races are going to be regenerated and raised up, is already very much of a question. What if it should be God's plan to people the world with better and finer material?

"Certain it is, whatever expectations we may indulge, that there is a tremendous overbearing surge of power in the Christian nations, which, if the others are not speedily raised to some vastly higher capacity, will inevitably submerge and bury them forever. These great populations of Christendom — what are they doing, but throwing out their colonies on every side, and populating themselves, if I may so speak, into the possession of all countries and climes?" * To this result no war of extermination is needful; the contest is not one of arms, but of vitality and of civilization. "At the present day," says Mr. Darwin, "civilized nations are everywhere supplanting barbarous nations, excepting where the climate opposes a deadly barrier; and they succeed mainly, though not exclusively through their arts, which are the products of the intellect." † Thus the Finns were supplanted by the Aryan races in Europe

* *Christian Nurture*, pp. 207, 213.
† *Descent of Man*, vol. I, p. 154.

and Asia, the Tartars by the Russians, and thus the aborigines of North America, Australia and New Zealand are now disappearing before the all-conquering Anglo-Saxons. It seems as if these inferior tribes were only precursors of a superior race, voices in the wilderness crying: "Prepare ye the way of the Lord!" The savage is a hunter; by the incoming of civilization, the game is driven away and disappears before the hunter becomes a herder or an agriculturist. The savage is ignorant of many diseases of civilization which, when he is exposed to them, attack him before he learns how to treat them. Civilization also has its vices, of which the uninitiated savage is innocent. He proves an apt learner of vice, but dull enough in the school of morals.

Every civilization has its destructive and preservative elements. The Anglo-Saxon race would speedily decay but for the salt of Christianity. Bring savages into contact with our civilization, and its destructive forces become operative at once, while years are necessary to render effective the saving influences of Christian instruction. Moreover, the pioneer wave of our civilization carries with it more scum than salt. Where there is one missionary, there are hundreds of miners or traders or adventurers ready to debauch the native.

Whether the extinction of inferior races before the advancing Anglo-Saxon seems to the reader sad or otherwise, it certainly appears probable. I know of nothing except climatic conditions to prevent this race from populating Africa as it has peopled North America. And those portions of Africa which are unfavorable to Anglo-Saxon life are less extensive than was once supposed. The Dutch Boers, after two centuries of life there, are as hardy as any race on earth. The Anglo-Saxon has established himself in climates totally diverse — Canada, South Africa, and India — and, through several generations, has preserved his essential race characteristics. He is not, of course, superior to climatic influences; but even in warm climates, he is likely to retain his aggressive vigor long enough to supplant races already enfeebled. Thus, in what Dr. Bushnell calls "the out-populating power of the Christian stock," may be found God's final and complete solution of the dark problem of heathenism among many inferior peoples. . . .

Is there room for reasonable doubt that this race, unless devitalized by alcohol and tobacco, is destined to dispossess many weaker races, assimilate others, and mold the remainder, until, in a very true and important sense, it has Anglo-Saxonized mankind? Already "the English language, saturated with Christian ideas, gathering up into itself the best thought of all the ages, is the great agent of Christian civilization throughout the world; at this moment affecting the destinies and molding the character of half the human race." * Jacob Grimm, the German philologist, said of this language: "It seems chosen, like its people, to rule in future times in a still greater degree in all the corners of the earth." He predicted, indeed, that the language of Shakespeare would eventually become the language of mankind. Is not Tennyson's noble prophecy to find its fulfillment in Anglo-Saxondom's extending its domination and influence —

> "Till the war-drum throbs no longer, and the battle-flags are furl'd
> In the Parliament of man, the Federation of the world." †

In my own mind there is no doubt that the Anglo-Saxon is to exercise the commanding influence in the world's future; but the exact nature of that influence is, as yet, undetermined. How far his civilization will be materialistic and atheistic, and how long it will take thoroughly to Christianize and sweeten it, how rapidly he will hasten the coming of the kingdom wherein dwelleth righteousness, or how many ages he may retard it, is still uncertain; *but is now being swiftly determined*. Let us weld together in a chain the various links of our logic which we have endeavored to forge. Is it manifest that the Anglo-Saxon holds in his hands the destinies of mankind for ages to come? Is it evident that the United States is to be the home of this race, the principal seat of his power, the great center of his influence? Is it true . . . that the great West is to dominate the nation's future? Has it been shown . . . that this generation is to determine the character, and hence the destiny of the West? Then may God open the eyes of this generation! When Napoleon drew up his troops before the Mamelukes, under the shadow of the Pyramids, pointing to the latter, he said to his soldiers: "Remember that from yonder heights forty centuries look down on you." Men of this generation, from the pyramid top of opportunity on which God has set us, *we look down on forty centuries!* We stretch our hand into the future with power to mold the destinies of unborn millions.

> "We are living, we are dwelling,
> In a grand and awful time,
> In an age on ages telling —
> To be living is sublime!"

Notwithstanding the great perils which threaten it, I cannot think our civilization will perish; but I believe it is fully in the hands of the

* Rev. N. G. Clark, D.D.
† "Locksley Hall."

Christians of the United States, during the next ten or fifteen years, to hasten or retard the coming of Christ's kingdom in the world by hundreds, and perhaps thousands, of years. We of this generation and nation occupy the Gibraltar of the ages which commands the world's future.

FOUNDATIONS OF THE NINETEENTH CENTURY

by Houston Stewart Chamberlain *

Let us attempt a glance into the depths of the soul. What are the specific intellectual and moral characteristics of this Germanic race? Certain anthropologists would fain teach us that all races are equally gifted; we point to history and answer: that is a lie! The races of mankind are markedly different in the nature and also in the extent of their gifts, and the Germanic races belong to the most highly gifted group, the group usually termed Aryan. Is this human family united and uniform by bonds of blood? Do these stems really all spring from the same root? I do not know and I do not much care; no affinity binds more closely than elective affinity, and in this sense the Indo-European Aryans certainly form a family. In his *Politics* Aristotle writes (i.5): "If there were men who in physical stature alone were so pre-eminent as the representatives of the Gods, then every one would admit that other men by right must be subject unto them. If this, however, is true in reference to the body, then there is still greater justification for distinguishing between pre-eminent and commonplace souls." Physically and mentally the Aryans are pre-eminent among all peoples; for that reason they are by right, as the Stagirite expresses it, the lords of the world. Aristotle puts the matter still more concisely when he says, "Some men are by nature free, others slaves"; this perfectly expresses the moral aspect. For freedom is by no means an abstract thing, to which every human being

* Houston Stewart Chamberlain, *Foundations of the Nineteenth Century* (New York: 1912). Reprinted by permission of Dodd, Mead & Company.

has fundamentally a claim; a right to freedom must evidently depend upon capacity for it, and this again presupposes physical and intellectual power. One may make the assertion, that even the mere conception of freedom is quite unknown to most men. Do we not see the *homo syriacus* develop just as well and as happily in the position of slave as of master? Do the Chinese not show us another example of the same nature? Do not all historians tell us that the Semites and half-Semites, in spite of their great intelligence, never succeeded in founding a State that lasted, and that because every one always endeavoured to grasp all power for himself, thus showing that their capabilities were limited to despotism and anarchy, the two opposites of freedom? And here we see at once what great gifts a man must have in order that one may say of him, he is "by nature free," for the first condition of this is the power of creating. Only a State-building race can be free; the gifts which make the individual an artist and philosopher are essentially the same as those which, spread through the whole mass as instinct, found States and give to the individual that which hitherto had remained unknown to all nature: the idea of freedom. As soon as we understand this, the near affinity of the Germanic peoples to the Greeks and Romans strikes us, and at the same time we recognise what separates them. In the case of the Greeks the individualistic creative character predominates, even in the forming of constitutions; in the case of the Romans it is communistic legislation and military authority that predominate; the Germanic races, on the other hand, have individually and collectively perhaps less creative power, but they possess a harmony of qualities, maintaining the balance between the instinct of individual freedom, which finds its highest expression in creative art, and the instinct of public freedom which creates the State; and in this way they prove themselves to be the equals of their great predecessors. Art more perfect in its creations, so far as form is concerned, there may have been, but no art has ever been more powerful in its creations than that which includes the whole range of things human between the winged pen of Shakespeare and the etching-tool of Albrecht Dürer, and which in its own special language — music — penetrates deeper into the heart than any previous attempt to create immortality out of that which is mortal — to transform matter into spirit. And in the meantime the European States, founded by Germanic peoples, in spite of their, so to speak, improvised, always provisional and changeable character — or rather perhaps thanks to this character — proved themselves to be the most enduring as well as the most powerful in the world. In spite of all storms of war, in spite of the deceptions of that ancestral enemy, the chaos of peoples, which carried its poison into the very heart of our nation, freedom and its correlative, the State, remained, through all the ages the creating and saving ideal, even though the balance between the two often seemed to be upset: we recognise that more clearly to-day than ever.

In order that this might be so, that fundamental and common "Aryan" capacity of free creative power had to be supplemented by another quality, the incomparable and altogether peculiar Germanic loyalty (*Treue*). If that intellectual and physical development which leads to the idea of freedom and which produces on the one hand art, philosophy, science, on the other constitutions (as well as all the phenomena of culture which this word implies), is common to the Hellenes and Romans as well as to the Germanic peoples, so also is the extravagant conception of loyalty a specific characteristic of the Teuton. . . . Julius Caesar at once recognised not only the military prowess but also the unexampled loyalty of the Teutons and hired from among them as many cavalrymen as he could possibly get. In the battle of Pharsalus, which was so decisive for the history of the world, they fought for him; the Romanised Gauls had abandoned their commander in the hour of need, the Germanic troops proved themselves as faithful as they were brave. This loyalty to a master chosen of their own free will is the most prominent feature in the Germanic character; from it we can tell whether pure Germanic blood flows in the veins or not. The German mercenary troops have often been made the object of ridicule, but it is in them that the genuine costly metal of this race reveals itself. The very first autocratic Emperor, Augustus, formed his personal bodyguard of Teutons; where else could he have found unconditional loyalty? During the whole time that the Roman Empire in the east and the west lasted, this same post of honour was filled by the same people, but they were always brought from farther and farther north, because with the so-called "Latin culture" the plague of disloyalty had crept more deeply into the country; finally, a thousand years after Augustus, we find Anglo-Saxons and Normans in this post, standing on guard around the throne of Byzantium. Hapless Germanic Lifeguardsman! Of the political principles, which forcibly held together the chaotic world in a semblance of order, he understood just as little as he did of the quarrels concerning the nature of the Trinity, which cost him many a drop of blood: but one thing he understood: to be loyal to the master he had himself chosen. When in the time of Nero the Frisian delegates left the back seats which had been assigned to them in the Circus and proudly sat down on the front benches of the senators among the richly adorned foreign delegates, what was it that gave these poor men, who came to Rome to beg for land to cultivate, such a bold spirit of independence? Of what alone could they boast? "That no one in the world surpassed the Teuton in loyalty." * Karl Lamprecht has written so beautifully about this great fundamental characteristic of loyalty in its historical significance that I should reproach myself if I did not quote him here. He has just spoken of the "retainers" who in the old German State pledge themselves to their chief to be true unto death and prove so, and then he adds: "In the formation of this body of retainers we see one of the most magnificent features of the specifically Germanic view of life, the feature of loyalty. Not understood by the Roman but indispensable to the Teuton, the need of loyalty existed even at that time, that ever-recurring German need of closest personal attachment, of complete devotion to each other, perfect community of hopes, efforts and destinies. Loyalty never was to our ancestors a special virtue, it was the breath of life of everything good and great; upon it rested the feudal State of the Early and the co-operative system of the Later Middle Ages, and who could conceive the military monarchy of the present day without loyalty? . . . Not only were songs sung about loyalty, men lived in it. The retinue of the King of the Franks, the courtiers of the great Karolingians, the civil and military ministers of our mediaeval Emperors, the officials of the centres of administration under our Princes since the fourteenth and the fifteenth centuries are merely new forms of the old Germanic conception. For the wonderful vitality of such institutions consisted in this, that they were not rooted in changing political or even moral conditions, but in the primary source of Germanicism itself, the need of loyalty." †

However true and beautiful every word that Lamprecht has here written, I do not think that he has made quite clear the "primary source." Loyalty, though distinguishing the Teutons from mongrel races, is not altogether a specific Germanic trait. One finds it in almost all purely bred races, nowhere more than among the negroes, for example, and — I would ask — what man could be more faithful than the noble dog? No, in order to reveal that "primary source of Germanicism," we must show what is the nature of this Germanic loyalty, and we can only succeed in doing so if we have grasped the fact that freedom is the intellectual basis of the whole Germanic nature. For the characteristic feature of this loyalty is its free self-determination. The human character resembles

---

* Tacitus: *Annals* xiii, 54.
† Lamprecht: *Deut. Gesch.*, 2nd ed. i, 136.

the nature of God as the theologians represent it: complex and yet in-
discernible, an inseparable unity. This loyalty and this freedom do not
grow the one out of the other, they are two manifestations of the same
character which reveals itself to us on one occasion more from the intellectual on another more from the moral side. The negro and the dog
serve their masters, whoever they may be: that is the morality of the
weak, or as Aristotle says, of the man who is born to be a slave; the
Teuton chooses his master, and his loyalty is therefore loyalty to himself: that is the morality of the man who is born free. But loyalty as
displayed by the Teuton was unexampled. The disloyalty of the extrav-
agantly gifted proclaimer of poetical and political freedom, *i.e.*, of the
Hellene, was proverbial from time immemorial; the Roman was loyal
only in the defence of his own, German loyalty remained, Lamprecht
says, "incomprehensible to him"; here, as everywhere in the sphere of
morals, we see an affinity with the Indo-Aryans; but these latter people
so markedly lacked the artistic sense which urges men on to adventure
and to the establishment of a free life, that their loyalty never reached
that creative importance in the world's history which the same quality
attained under the influence of the Germanic races. Here again, as before, in the consideration of the feeling of freedom, we find a higher
harmony of character in the Teuton; hence we may say that no one
in the world, not even the greatest, has surpassed him. One thing is certain: if we wish to sum up in a single word the historic greatness of the
Teuton — always a perilous undertaking, since everything living is of
Protean nature — we must name his loyalty. That is the central point
from which we can survey his whole character, or better, his personality.
But we must remember that this loyalty is not the primary source, as
Lamprecht thinks, not the root but the blossom—the fruit by which we
recognise the tree. Hence it is that this loyalty is the finest touchstone
for distinguishing between genuine and false Germanicism; for it is not
by the roots but by the fruit that we distinguish the species; we should
not forget that with unfavourable weather many a tree has no blossoms
or only poor ones, and this often happens in the case of hard-pressed
Teutons. The root of their particular character is beyond all doubt that
power of imagination which is common to all Aryans and peculiar to
them alone and which appeared in greatest luxuriance among the
Hellenes. I spoke of this in the beginning of the chapter on Hellenic art
and philosophy; from that root everything springs, art, philosophy, politics,
science; hence, too, comes the peculiar sap which tinges the flower of
loyalty. The stem then is formed by the positive strength — the physical

and the intellectual, which can never be separated; in the case of the
Romans, to whom we owe the firm bases of family and State, this stem
was powerfully developed. But the real blossoms of such a tree are those
which mind and sentiment bring to maturity. Freedom is an expansive
power which scatters men, Germanic loyalty is the bond which by its
inner power binds men more closely than the fear of the tyrant's sword:
freedom signifies thirst after direct self-discovered truth, loyalty the reverence for that which has appeared to our ancestors to be true; freedom
decides its own destiny and loyalty holds that decision unswervingly
and for ever. Loyalty to the loved one, to friend, parents, and fatherland
we find in many places; but here, in the case of the Teuton, something
is added, which makes the great instinct become a profoundly deep
spiritual power, a principle of life. Shakespeare represents the father
giving his son as the best advice for his path through life, as the one
admonition which includes all others, these words:

This above all: to thine own self be true!

The principle of Germanic loyalty is evidently not the necessity of attachment, as Lamprecht thinks, but on the contrary the necessity of constancy within a man's own autonomous circle; self-determination testifies
to it; in it freedom proves itself; by it the vassal, the member of the
guild, the official, the officer asserts his independence. For the free man,
to serve means to command himself. "It was the Germanic races who
first introduced into the world the idea of personal freedom," says
Goethe. What in the case of the Hindoos was metaphysics and in so
far necessarily negative, seclusive, has been here transferred to life as
an ideal of mind, it is the "breath of life of everything great and good,"
a star in the night, to the weary a spur, to the storm-tossed an anchor
of safety. In the construction of the Germanic character loyalty is the
necessary perfection of the personality, which without it falls to pieces.
Immanuel Kant has given a daring, genuinely Germanic definition of
personality: it is, he says, "freedom and independence of the mechanism
of all nature"; and what it achieves he has summed up as follows: "That
which elevates man above himself (as part of the world of sense), at-
taches him to an order of things which only the understanding can conceive, and which has the whole world of sense subject to it, is Personality."
But without loyalty this elevation would be fatal: thanks to it alone
the impulse of freedom can develop and bring blessing instead of a
curse. Loyalty in this Germanic sense cannot originate without freedom, but it is impossible to see how an unlimited, creative impulse to

freedom could exist without loyalty. Childish attachment to nature is a proof of loyalty; it enables man to raise himself above nature, without falling shattered to the ground, like the Hellenic Phaethon. Therefore it is that Goethe writes: "Loyalty preserves personality!" Germanic loyalty is the girdle that gives immortal beauty to the ephemeral individual, it is the sun without which no knowledge can ripen to wisdom, the charm which alone bestows upon the free individual's passionate action the blessing of permanent achievement. . . .

FORWARD GLANCE

I sometimes regret that, in a book like this, moralising would be so out of place as to be almost an offence against good taste. When we see those splendid "barbarians" glowing with youth, free, making their entry into history endowed with all those qualities which fit them for the very highest place; when next we realise how they, the conquerors, the true "Freeborn" of Aristotle, contaminate their pure blood by mixture with the impure races of the slave-born; how they accept their schooling from the unworthy descendants of noble progenitors, and force their way with untold toil out of the night of this Chaos towards a new dawn; — then we have to acknowledge the further fact that every day adds new enemies and new dangers to those which already exist — that these new enemies, like the former ones, are received by the Teutons with open arms, that the voice of warning is carelessly laughed at, and that while every enemy of our race, with full consciousness and the perfection of cunning, follows his own designs, we — still great, innocent barbarians — concentrate ourselves upon earthly and heavenly ideals, upon property, discoveries, inventions, brewing, art, metaphysics, love, and heaven knows what else! and with it all there is ever a tinge of the impossible, of that which cannot be brought to perfection, of the world beyond, otherwise we should remain lying idle on our bearskins! Who could help moralising when he sees how we, without weapons, without defence, unconscious of any danger, go on our way, constantly befooled, ever ready to set a high price on what is foreign and to set small store by what is our own — we, the most learned of all men, and yet ignorant beyond all others of the world around us, the greatest discoverers and yet stricken with chronic blindness! Who could help crying with Ulrich von Hutten: "Oh! unhappy Germany, unhappy by thine own choice! thou that with eyes to see seest not, and with clear understanding understandest not!" But I will not do it. I feel that this is not my business, and to tell the truth this haughty pococurantism is so characteristic a feature that I should regret its loss. The Teuton is no pessimist like the Hindoo, he is no good critic; he really thinks little in comparison with other Aryans; his gifts impel him to act and to feel. To call the Germans a "nation of thinkers" is bitter irony; a nation of soldiers and shopkeepers would certainly be more correct, or of scholars and artists — but of thinkers? — these are thinly sown. Hence it was that Luther went so far as to call the Germans "blind people"; the rest of the Germanic races are the same in scarcely less degree; for analytical thought belongs to seeing, and to that again capacity, time, practice. The Teuton is occupied with other things; he has not yet completed his "entrance into the history of the world"; he must first have taken possession of the whole earth, investigated nature on all sides, made the powers subject to him; he must first have developed the expression of art to a perfection yet unknown, and have collected an enormous store of historical knowledge — then perhaps he will have time to ask himself what is going on immediately around him. Till then he will continue to walk on the edge of the precipice with the same calmness as on a flowering meadow. That cannot be changed, for this pococurantism is, as I said above, characteristic of the Teuton. The Greeks and the Romans were not unlike this: the former continued to think and invent artistically, the latter to add conquest to conquest without ever becoming conscious of themselves like the Jews, without ever noticing in the least how the course of events was gradually wiping them from off the face of the earth; they did not fall dead like other nations; they descended slowly into Hades full of life to the last, vigorous to the last, in the proud consciousness of victory.

And I, a modest historian, who can neither influence the course of events nor possess the power of looking clearly into the future, must be satisfied if in fulfilling the purpose of this book I have succeeded in showing the distinction between the Germanic and the Non-Germanic. That the Teuton is one of the greatest, perhaps the very greatest power in the history of mankind, no one will wish to deny, but in order to arrive at a correct appreciation of the present time, it behoved us to settle once for all who could and who could not be regarded as Teuton. In the nineteenth century, as in all former centuries, but of course with widely different grouping and with constantly changing relative power, there stood side by side in Europe these "Heirs" — the chaos of half-breeds, relics of the former Roman Empire, the Germanising of which is falling off — the Jews — and the Germans, whose contamination by mixture with the half-breeds and the descendants of other Non-Aryan races is on the increase. No arguing about "humanity" can alter the fact that this means a struggle. Where the struggle is not waged with cannon-balls, it goes on silently in the heart of society by marriages, by the annihilation of distances which furthers intercourse, by the varying powers of resistance in the different types of mankind, by the shifting of wealth, by the birth of new influences and the disappearance of others, and by many other motive powers. But this struggle, silent though it be, is above all others a struggle for life and death.

NATION AND RACE

by Adolf Hitler *

Any crossing of two beings not at exactly the same level produces a medium between the level of the two parents. This means: the offspring will probably stand higher than the racially lower parent, but not as high as the higher one. Consequently, it will later succumb in the struggle against the higher level. Such mating is contrary to the will of Nature for a higher breeding of all life. The precondition for this does not lie in associating superior and inferior, but in the total victory of the former. The stronger must dominate and not blend with the weaker, thus sacrificing his own greatness. Only the born weakling can view this as cruel, but he after all is only a weak and limited man; for if this law did not prevail, any conceivable higher development of organic living beings would be unthinkable.

The consequence of this racial purity, universally valid in Nature, is not only the sharp outward delimitation of the various races, but their uniform character in themselves. The fox is always a fox, the goose a goose, the tiger a tiger, etc., and the difference can lie at most in the varying measure of force, strength, intelligence, dexterity, endurance, etc.,

* The selections from Adolf Hitler's Mein Kampf (translated by Ralph Manheim) 1943, are reprinted by permission of and arrangement with Houghton Mifflin Company, the authorized publishers.

of the individual specimens. But you will never find a fox who in his inner attitude might, for example, show humanitarian tendencies toward geese, as similarly there is no cat with a friendly inclination toward mice.

Therefore, here, too, the struggle among themselves arises less from inner aversion than from hunger and love. In both cases, Nature looks on calmly, with satisfaction, in fact. In the struggle for daily bread all those who are weak and sickly or less determined succumb, while the struggle of the males for the female grants the right or opportunity to propagate only to the healthiest. And struggle is always a means for improving a species' health and power of resistance and, therefore, a cause of its higher development.

If the process were different, all further and higher development would cease and the opposite would occur. For, since the inferior always predominates numerically over the best, if both had the same possibility of preserving life and propagating, the inferior would multiply so much more rapidly that in the end the best would inevitably be driven into the background, unless a correction of this state of affairs were undertaken. Nature does just this by subjecting the weaker part to such severe living conditions that by them alone the number is limited, and by not permitting the remainder to increase promiscuously, but making a new and ruthless choice according to strength and health.

No more than Nature desires the mating of weaker with stronger individuals, even less does she desire the blending of a higher with a lower race, since, if she did, her whole work of higher breeding, over perhaps hundreds of thousands of years, might be ruined with one blow.

Historical experience offers countless proofs of this. It shows with terrifying clarity that in every mingling of Aryan blood with that of lower peoples the result was the end of the cultured people. North America, whose population consists in by far the largest part of Germanic elements who mixed but little with the lower colored peoples, shows a different humanity and culture from Central and South America, where the predominantly Latin immigrants often mixed with the aborigines on a large scale. By this one example, we can clearly and distinctly recognize the effect of racial mixture. The Germanic inhabitant of the American continent, who has remained racially pure and unmixed, rose to be master of the continent; he will remain the master as long as he does not fall a victim to defilement of the blood.

The result of all racial crossing is therefore in brief always the following:

(a) Lowering of the level of the higher race,

(b) Physical and intellectual regression and hence the beginning of a slowly but surely progressing sickness.

To bring about such a development is, then, nothing else but to sin against the will of the eternal creator.

And as a sin this act is rewarded.

When man attempts to rebel against the iron logic of Nature, he comes into struggle with the principles to which he himself owes his existence as a man. And this attack must lead to his own doom. . . .

Everything we admire on this earth today — science and art, technology and inventions — is only the creative product of a few peoples and originally perhaps of *one* race. On them depends the existence of this whole culture. If they perish, the beauty of this earth will sink into the grave with them.

However much the soil, for example, can influence men, the result of the influence will always be different depending on the races in question. The low fertility of a living space may spur the one race to the highest achievements; in others it will only be the cause of bitterest poverty and final undernourishment with all its consequences. The inner nature of peoples is always determining for the manner in which outward influences will be effective. What leads the one to starvation trains the other to hard work.

All great cultures of the past perished only because the originally creative race died out from blood poisoning.

The ultimate cause of such a decline was their forgetting that all culture depends on men and not conversely; hence that to preserve a certain culture the man who creates it must be preserved. This preservation is bound up with the rigid law of necessity and the right to victory of the best and stronger in this world.

Those who want to live, let them fight, and those who do not want to fight in this world of eternal struggle do not deserve to live.

Even if this were hard — that is how it is! Assuredly, however, by far the harder fate is that which strikes the man who thinks he can overcome Nature, but in the last analysis only mocks her. Distress, misfortune, and diseases are her answer.

The man who misjudges and disregards the racial laws actually forfeits the happiness that seems destined to be his. He thwarts the triumphal march of the best race and hence also the precondition for all human progress, and remains, in consequence, burdened with all the sensibility of man, in the animal realm of helpless misery.

It is idle to argue which race or races were the original representative of human culture and hence the real founders of all that we sum up under the word "humanity." It is simpler to raise this question with regard to the present, and here an easy, clear answer results. All the human culture, all the results of art, science, and technology that we see before us today, are almost exclusively the creative product of the Aryan. This very fact admits of the not unfounded inference that he alone was the founder of all higher humanity, therefore representing the prototype of all that we understand by the word "man." He is the Prometheus of mankind from whose bright forehead the divine spark of genius has sprung at all times, forever kindling anew that fire of knowledge which illumined the night of silent mysteries and thus caused man to climb the path to mastery over the other beings of this earth. Exclude him — and perhaps after a few thousand years darkness will again descend on the earth, human culture will pass, and the world turn to a desert.

If we were to divide mankind into three groups, the founders of culture, the bearers of culture, the destroyers of culture, only the Aryan could be considered as the representative of the first group. From him originate the foundations and walls of all human creation, and only the outward form and color are determined by the changing traits of character of the various peoples. He provides the mightiest building stones and plans for all human progress and only the execution corresponds to the nature of the varying men and races. In a few decades, for example, the entire east of Asia will possess a culture whose ultimate foundation will be Hellenic spirit and Germanic technology, just as much as in Europe. Only the *outward* form — in part at least — will bear the features of Asiatic character. It is not true, as some people think, that Japan adds European technology to its culture; no, European science and technology are trimmed with Japanese characteristics. The foundation of actual life is no longer the special Japanese culture, although it determines the color of life — because outwardly, in consequence of its inner difference, it is more conspicuous to the European — but the gigantic scientific-technical achievements of Europe and America; that is, of Aryan peoples. Only on the basis of these achievements can the Orient follow general human progress. They furnish the basis of the struggle for daily bread, create weapons and implements for it, and only the outward form is gradually adapted to Japanese character.

If beginning today all further Aryan influence on **Japan** should stop, assuming that Europe and America should perish, Japan's present rise in science and technology might continue for a short time; but even in a few years the well would dry up, the Japanese special character would gain, but the present culture would freeze and sink back into the slumber from which it was awakened seven decades ago by the wave of Aryan culture. Therefore, just as the present Japanese development owes its life to Aryan origin, long ago in the gray past foreign influence and foreign spirit awakened the Japanese culture of that time. The best proof of this is furnished by the fact of its subsequent sclerosis and total petrifaction. This can occur in a people only when the original creative racial nucleus has been lost, or if the external influence which furnished the impetus and the material for the first development in the cultural field was later lacking. But if it is established that a people receives the most essential basic materials of its culture from foreign races, that it assimilates and adapts them, and that then, if further external influence is lacking, it rigidifies again and again, such a race may be designated as "culture-bearing," but never as "culture-creating." An examination of the various peoples from this standpoint points to the fact that practically none of them were originally culture-founding, but almost always culture-bearing.

Approximately the following picture of their development always results:

Aryan races — often absurdly small numerically — subject foreign peoples, and then, stimulated by the special living conditions of the new territory (fertility, climatic conditions, etc.) and assisted by the multitude of lower-type beings standing at their disposal as helpers, develop the intellectual and organizational capacities dormant within them. Often in a few millenniums or even centuries they create cultures which originally bear all the inner characteristics of their nature, adapted to the above-indicated special qualities of the soil and subjected beings. In the end, however, the conquerors transgress against the principle of blood purity, to which they had first adhered; they begin to mix with the subjugated inhabitants and thus end their own existence; for the fall of man in paradise has always been followed by his expulsion.

After a thousand years and more, the last visible trace of the former master people is often seen in the lighter skin color which its blood left behind in the subjugated race, and in a petrified culture which it had originally created. For, once the actual and spiritual conqueror lost himself in the blood of the subjected people, the fuel for the torch of human progress was lost! Just as, through the blood of the former masters, the color preserved a feeble gleam in their memory, likewise the night of cultural life is gently illumined by the remaining creations of the former light-bringers. They shine through all the returned barbarism and too often inspire the thoughtless observer of the moment with the opinion that he beholds the picture of the present people before him, whereas he is only gazing into the mirror of the past.

It is then possible that such a people will a second time, or even more often in the course of its history, come into contact with the race of those who once brought it culture, and the memory of former encounters will not necessarily be present. Unconsciously the remnant of the former master blood will turn toward the new arrival, and what was first possible only by compulsion can now succeed through the people's own will. A new cultural wave makes its entrance and continues until those who have brought it are again submerged in the blood of foreign peoples. . . .

The progress of humanity is like climbing an endless ladder; it is impossible to climb higher without first taking the lower steps. Thus, the Aryan had to take the road to which reality directed him and not the one that would appeal to the imagination of a modern pacifist. The road of reality is hard and difficult, but in the end it leads where our friend would like to bring humanity by dreaming, but unfortunately removes more than bringing it closer.

Hence it is no accident that the first cultures arose in places where the Aryan, in his encounters with lower peoples, subjugated them and bent them to his will. They then became the first technical instrument in the service of a developing culture.

Thus, the road which the Aryan had to take was clearly marked out. As a conquerer he subjected the lower beings and regulated their practical activity under his command, according to his will and for his aims. But in directing them to a useful, though arduous activity, he not only spared the life of those he subjected; perhaps he gave them a fate that was better than their previous so-called "freedom." As long as he ruthlessly upheld the master attitude, not only did he really remain master, but also the preserver and increaser of culture. For culture was based exclusively on his abilities and hence on his actual survival. As soon as the subjected people began to raise themselves up and probably approached the conqueror in language, the sharp dividing wall between master and servant fell. The Aryan gave up the purity of his blood and, therefore, lost his sojourn in the paradise which he had made for himself. He became submerged in the racial mixture, and gradually, more and more, lost his cultural capacity, until at last, not only mentally but also physically, he began to resemble the subjected aborigines more than his own ancestors. For a time he could live on the existing cultural benefits, but then petrifaction set in and he fell a prey to oblivion.

Thus cultures and empires collapsed to make place for new formations.

Blood mixture and the resultant drop in the racial level is the sole cause of the dying out of old cultures; for men do not perish as a result of lost wars, but by the loss of that force of resistance which is contained only in pure blood.

All who are not of good race in this world are chaff.

And all occurrences in world history are only the expression of the races' instinct of self-preservation, in the good or bad sense. . . .

The mightiest counterpart to the Aryan is represented by the Jew. In hardly any people in the world is the instinct of self-preservation developed more strongly than in the so-called "chosen." Of this, the mere fact of the survival of this race may be considered the best proof. Where is the people which in the last two thousand years has been exposed to so slight changes of inner disposition, character, etc., as the Jewish people? What people, finally, has gone through greater upheavals than this one — and nevertheless issued from the mightiest catastrophes of mankind unchanged? What an infinitely tough will to live and preserve the species speaks from these facts!

The mental qualities of the Jew have been schooled in the course of many centuries. Today he passes as "smart," and this in a certain sense he has been at all times. But his intelligence is not the result of his own development, but of visual instruction through foreigners. For the human mind cannot climb to the top without steps; for every step upward he needs the foundation of the past, and this in the comprehensive sense in which it can be revealed only in general culture. All thinking is based only in small part on man's own knowledge, and mostly on the experience of the time that has preceded. The general cultural level provides the individual man, without his noticing it as a rule, with such a profusion of preliminary knowledge that, thus armed, he can more easily take further steps of his own. The boy of today, for example, grows up among a truly vast number of technical acquisitions of the last centuries, so that he takes for granted and no longer pays attention to much that a hundred years ago was a riddle to even the greatest minds, although for following and understanding our progress in the field in question it is of decisive importance to him. If a very genius from the twenties of the past century should suddenly leave his grave today, it would be harder for him even intellectually to find his way in the present era than for an average boy of fifteen today. For he would lack all the infinite preliminary education which our present contemporary unconsciously, so to speak, assimilates while growing up amidst the manifestations of our present general civilization.

Since the Jew — for reasons which will at once become apparent — was never in possession of a culture of his own, the foundations of his intellectual work were always provided by others. His intellect at all times developed through the cultural world surrounding him.

The reverse process never took place.

For if the Jewish people's instinct of self-preservation is not smaller but larger than that of other peoples, if his intellectual faculties can easily arouse the impression that they are equal to the intellectual gifts of other races, he lacks completely the most essential requirement for a cultured people, the idealistic attitude.

In the Jewish people the will to self-sacrifice does not go beyond the individual's naked instinct of self-preservation. Their apparently great sense of solidarity is based on the very primitive herd instinct that is seen in many other living creatures in this world. It is a noteworthy fact that the herd instinct leads to mutual support only as long as a common danger makes this seem useful or inevitable. The same pack of wolves which has just fallen on its prey together disintegrates when hunger abates into its individual beasts. The same is true of horses which try to defend themselves against an assailant in a body, but scatter again as soon as the danger is past.

It is similar with the Jew. His sense of sacrifice is only apparent. It exists only as long as the existence of the individual makes it absolutely necessary. However, as soon as the common enemy is conquered, the danger threatening all averted and the booty hidden, the apparent harmony of the Jews among themselves ceases, again making way for their old causal tendencies. The Jew is only united when a common danger forces him to be or a common booty entices him; if these two grounds are lacking, the qualities of the crassest egoism come into their own, and in the twinkling of an eye the united people turns into a horde of rats, fighting bloodily among themselves.

If the Jews were alone in this world, they would stifle in filth and offal; they would try to get ahead of one another in hate-filled struggle and exterminate one another, in so far as the absolute absence of all sense of self-sacrifice, expressing itself in their cowardice, did not turn battle into comedy here too.

So it is absolutely wrong to infer any ideal sense of sacrifice in the Jews from the fact that they stand together in struggle, or, better expressed, in the plundering of their fellow men.

Here again the Jew is led by nothing but the naked egoism of the individual.

That is why the Jewish state — which should be the living organism for preserving and increasing a race — is completely unlimited as to territory. For a state formation to have a definite spatial setting always presupposes an idealistic attitude on the part of the state-race, and especially a correct interpretation of the concept of work. In the exact measure in which this attitude is lacking, any attempt at forming, even of preserving, a spatially delimited state fails. And thus the basis on which alone culture can arise is lacking.

Hence the Jewish people, despite all apparent intellectual qualities, is without any true culture, and especially without any culture of its own. For what sham culture the Jew today possesses is the property of other peoples, and for the most part it is ruined in his hands.

In judging the Jewish people's attitude on the question of human culture, the most essential characteristic we must always bear in mind is that there has never been a Jewish art and accordingly there is none today either; that above all the two queens of all the arts, architecture and music, owe nothing original to the Jews. What they do accomplish in the field of art is either patchwork or intellectual theft. Thus, the Jew lacks those qualities which distinguish the races that are creative and hence culturally blessed.

To what an extent the Jew takes over foreign culture, imitating or rather ruining it, can be seen from the fact that he is mostly found in the art which seems to require least original invention, the art of acting. But even here, in reality, he is only a "juggler," or rather an ape; for even here he lacks the last touch that is required for real greatness; even here he is not the creative genius, but a superficial imitator, and all the twists and tricks that he uses are powerless to conceal the inner lifelessness of his creative gift. Here the Jewish press most lovingly helps him along by raising such a roar of hosannahs about even the most mediocre bungler, just so long as he is a Jew, that the rest of the world actually ends up by thinking that they have an artist before them, while in truth it is only a pitiful comedian.

No, the Jew possesses no culture-creating force of any sort, since the idealism, without which there is no true higher development of man, is not present in him and never was present. Hence his intellect will never have a constructive effect, but will be destructive, and in very rare cases perhaps will at most be stimulating, but then as the prototype of the "force which always wants evil and nevertheless creates good." Not through him does any progress of mankind occur, but in spite of him.

Since the Jew never possessed a state with definite territorial limits and therefore never called a culture his own, the conception arose that this was a people which should be reckoned among the ranks of the *nomads*. This is a fallacy as great as it is dangerous. The nomad does possess a definitely limited living space, only he does not cultivate it like a sedentary peasant, but lives from the yield of his herds with which he wanders about in his territory. The outward reason for this is to be found in the small fertility of a soil which simply does not permit of settlement. The deeper cause, however, lies in the disparity between the technical culture of an age or people and the natural poverty of a living space. There are territories in which even the Aryan is enabled only by his technology, developed in the course of more than a thousand years, to live in regular settlements, to master broad stretches of soil and obtain from it the requirements of life. If he did not possess this technology, either he would have to avoid these territories or likewise have to struggle along as a nomad in perpetual wandering, provided that his thousand-year-old education and habit of settled residence did not make this seem simply unbearable to him. We must bear in mind that in the time when the American continent was being opened up, numerous Aryans fought for their livelihood as trappers, hunters, etc., and often in larger troops with wife and children, always on the move, so that their existence was completely like that of the nomads. But as soon as their increasing number and better implements permitted them to clear the wild soil and make a stand against the natives, more and more settlements sprang up in the land.

Probably the Aryan was also first a nomad, settling in the course of time, but for that very reason he was never a Jew! No, the Jew is no nomad; for the nomad had also a definite attitude toward the concept of work which could serve as a basis for his later development in so far as the necessary intellectual premises were present. In him the basic idealistic view is present, even if in infinite dilution, hence in his whole being he may seem strange to the Aryan peoples, but not unattractive. In the Jew, however, this attitude is not at all present; for that reason he was never a nomad, but only and always a *parasite* in the body of other peoples. That he sometimes left his previous living space has nothing to with his own purpose, but results from the fact that from time to time he was thrown out by the host nations he had misused. His spreading is a typical phenomenon for all parasites; he always seeks a new feeding ground for his race.

This, however, has nothing to do with nomadism, for the reason that a Jew never thinks of leaving a territory that he has occupied, but remains where he is, and he sits so fast that even by force it is very hard to drive him out. His extension to ever-new countries occurs only in the moment in which certain conditions for his existence are there present, without which

— unlike the nomad — he would not change his residence. He is and remains the typical parasite, a sponger who like a noxious bacillus keeps spreading as soon as a favorable medium invites him. And the effect of his existence is also like that of spongers: wherever he appears, the host people dies out after a shorter or longer period.

Thus, the Jew of all times has lived in the states of other peoples, and there formed his own state, which, to be sure, habitually sailed under the disguise of "religious community" as long as outward circumstances made a complete revelation of his nature seem inadvisable. But as soon as he felt strong enough to do without the protective cloak, he always dropped the veil and suddenly became what so many of the others previously did not want to believe and see: the Jew.

APARTHEID — A SLOGAN OR A SOLUTION?

by N. J. J. Olivier *

The South African policy of "apartheid" has caused world-wide comment and discussion. In the world outside South Africa such comments have usually ranged from bitter denunciation to mild and indifferent justification. Born and bred in South Africa, and belonging to the Afrikaans-speaking section of the European population, this writer has no doubts whatsover that such a policy, from a human, ethical, Christian, and scientific point of view, is one which, if carried into effect, would improve race relations in South Africa and would lead to human happiness and a spirit of good will between white and black; although convinced that such improvement, happiness, and good will could be achieved only by a sane and just implementation of a policy of separate development — a term preferable to that of "apartheid" — the writer realizes that it is well-nigh impossible to deal exhaustively with the subject in a single article, the more so since he has no illusions about the magnitude of the task facing

* N. J. J. Olivier, "Apartheid — A Slogan or a Solution?" *Journal of International Affairs*, Volume VII, Number 2 (New York: 1953), pp. 136–43. By permission of *Journal of International Affairs*.

anyone who attempts to justify the South African policy before a world forum which is almost completely ignorant of the South African background and realities of life.

The policy of apartheid, formerly also called segregation, is, in principle, the traditional policy followed by successive generations and governments in South Africa in relations between white and black — a policy of white South Africa to save itself and its way of life from total extinction by the numerically superior, illiterate, and relatively primitive black masses.

In the beginning of the seventeenth century the greatest portion of the southernmost part of the African continent was practically uninhabited. When the Dutch colonists settled at the Cape in 1652, the migratory Bantu tribes had scarcely crossed the northern borders of what is today the Union of South Africa. In the course of time the eastward and northward expansion of the white colony had to meet the southward-moving Bantu tribes; at the end of the eighteenth century they met and clashed in the eastern parts of the present Cape Province. It is therefore a complete fallacy to state that the Bantu in South Africa have a stronger aboriginal claim to the country than the Europeans: the Bantu were at that time as much foreigners as the whites were. Equally fallacious is the prevailing assumption that the Bantu had to part with their land under duress, and that the whites stole their land from them; in this connection the whites in South Africa have a record far superior to their brethren in North America!

In the wars following the contact between white and black, the Bantu were eventually vanquished and brought under the direct control of the Europeans and the European government, thereby putting an effective end to the devastating strife between the various Bantu tribes themselves. It would have been a comparatively easy task for the Europeans of that time to withdraw their protection, to allow the Bantu to annihilate themselves by internecine wars, and even to assist in this annihilation; they could, in other words, have followed the course adopted in North America and Australia. Instead, compelled by their religious convictions and humanitarian principles, they accepted the onerous duty of trusteeship over these barbarous and warlike peoples — the task of Christianizing, civilizing, educating them, leading them to a fuller and happier life. It cannot be denied that, in this connection, South Africa has a record of which she can rightly be proud.

It is a well-known fact that the Europeans in South Africa have a distinctive race or color consciousness. To anyone ignorant of the present-day facts of South African life and their historical background, this attitude toward race relations is often mystifying. To the scientific and open-minded observer, however, such an attitude is completely understandable and justifiable. The simple truth is that it was (and still is) a direct and inevitable result of the vast differences between the two groups, and was (and still is) fundamentally nothing other than a determined attempt by the whites to preserve their identity, their way of life, and their continued existence. Consider the following facts:

The Racial Differences. That racial differences do exist, nobody would deny; that the Bantu and the Europeans in South Africa belong to two distinct racial types, with distinct and unalterable biological characteristics is also a fact so evident that no one would attempt to deny it. It is only natural that the European colonists came to regard these distinctive characteristics as so many racial differences, and since they were wont to associate with people of their own racial type, they considered these differences, according to their taste and traditions, as æsthetically disagreeable.

The Differences in Civilization, Culture, and General Way of Life. The colonists came into contact with a people whose level of civilization was not only far lower, but clearly primitive. Their general culture, material and otherwise, and their way of life were characteristic of a primitive people, and of course vastly different from those of the European colonists. Their warlike nature, their social institutions, their legal and administrative system, their primitive subsistence economy, their language — all these accentuated the differences between white and black.

The Difference in Religion. The primitive level of civilization and culture was accompanied by a similarly primitive religious system; ancestor worship and witchcraft were two of the main facets of this system, pervading almost the whole political, social, and economic field. In contrast, the European colonists were deeply imbued with the Christian faith and the Protestant principles, and many had fled to South Africa for the sake of religious freedom. The Bible and their religion played a significant role in their everyday lives, and was a source of inestimable comfort and succor in the many and varied depredations they so patiently suffered. It is exactly because of this that they felt themselves duty-bound not to annihilate these heathen but to convert them to Christianity and to bring them to accept salvation in Jesus Christ.

The Difference in Numbers. From the outset the European colonists were greatly outnumbered; there is no doubt that if they had decided on a course of assimilation, they would have disappeared into the black heathendom of Africa as effectively as if they had been completely vanquished in war. Of necessity they had to arm and protect themselves against this ever-growing menace, and how could it better be done than by throwing an impenetrable armor around themselves — the armor of racial purity and self-preservation?

Thus it is evident that the origin of South African color consciousness is understandable and justifiable. The difference in color, as the most evident racial difference, became tantamount to a difference between one way of life and another, between barbarism and civilization, between heathenism and Christianity, between overwhelming numbers and practically insignificant numbers. Although some of the facets of the problem may have changed, this color consciousness remains as active as ever; it has become a tradition into which almost every white child is born, and an indivisible part of his mental make-up.

Let us consider, in the light of the four points mentioned above, the main aspects of European-Bantu relations as they exist today:

(1) The racial differences are as pronounced today as they were 300 years ago. The European population has in a remarkable way succeeded in preserving its identity as a group racially distinct from the Bantu.

(2) The differences in civilization and culture have become somewhat less because of European influence and activities, especially in the educational and missionary fields. A very small percentage of the Bantu population has completed the process of acculturation and has become completely Europeanized and civilized; among the rest (the overwhelming majority) western civilization and culture have been accepted in varying degrees, but in general by far the bigger section of the Bantu population is still in a relatively primitive stage of development, although not wholly untouched by western civilization. It is the educated minority group that the outside world generally sees; this group is the most vociferous and most clamorous, feeling the restrictions placed by European overlordship as unbearable and unjustifiable. That so small a number of Bantu has become completely Europeanized, in spite of the long contact with Europeans and their civilization and in spite of educational and missionary activities, is due mainly to their tenacious clinging to old customs and usages and to their preponderance in numbers. The urbanization of large numbers of Bantu as a result of industrial development and their integration into the economic life and activities in the European (non-native) area, must of course hasten the disintegration of the tribal system and their acceptance of European ideas and ways of life.

(3) What has been said above about the differences in civilization and culture also applies to the differences in religion. Only a minority of the Bantu has become Christian in the full sense.

(4) The numerical preponderance of the Bantu is still on the increase. This can be ascribed, *inter alia*, to the absence of internecine strife, the non-occurrence of famine, the provision of medical services — all due to European intervention or assistance — coupled with the absence of birth-control measures. At the moment there are about eight and one-half million Bantu in the Union of South Africa as against approximately two and one-half million Europeans; the Bantu population thus outnumbers the white population 3.4 to one. It has been estimated that in another 50 years the Bantu population will have increased to approximately 20-22 million, and the European population to about six million.* With this unique situation, it is understandable that white South Africa views with scepticism suggestions concerning their racial policies put forward by countries where the problem does not exist. The matter is made much worse in that the Bantu of the Union of South Africa are but a fringe of the vast Bantu population on the African continent.

From these facts it follows that no European community in South Africa would be willing to commit suicide by following a policy which would lead to its own political, economic, and social subservience with eventual extinction, either by force or assimilation.

The crux of South Africa's native problem could thus be succinctly stated as follows: the European population has the unalterable and indomitable determination first, to preserve its identity and continued existence as a separate, distinctive entity; and second, to retain and exercise its right of political self-determination at all costs. On the other hand, the Bantu population must be afforded the right of national self-expression, in politics, economics, and the like. In other words, it is impossible to follow indefinitely a policy by which the Bantu or at least the educated and civilized section of it, would be denied political rights and economic opportunities. Bearing in mind the facts and considerations stated above, the only possible solution of these two apparently irreconcilable principles lies in the acceptance and application of the policy of separate development.

Such a policy aims at the gradual and systematic disentanglement of the two groups, making it possible for each to exercise political rights and enjoy economic opportunities within its own territory. It means a large-

---

* These estimates do not take into consideration the almost 1,500,000 other non-Europeans in the Union.

scale development of the existing native areas within the Union of South Africa. Approximately thirteen per cent of the area of the Union has been put aside for exclusive native use; by far the greater portion of this area consists of fertile agricultural land, with an excellent rainfall. These territories have become denuded and eroded as a result of the primitive agricultural methods employed by the inhabitants, and they are in general under-developed and poor, mainly because industrial and urban development has been confined to the European areas. There is, however, not the least doubt that these territories could be developed on the basis of a diversified economy, to the extent that they could accommodate two to three times their present population, which numbers somewhat over three million. If the size of the present native areas makes such a policy unrealizeable in its full extent, then only one alternative remains: the extension of these areas either within the Union or in collaboration with other governments. Considering the agricultural methods employed by the natives in their areas at the present time, it would be nonsensical to consider a large-scale extension of these areas at present. As a matter of fact, the time may arrive when the European groups in the Union and elsewhere in Southern Africa would be compelled, in their own interests, no longer to think in terms of the reservation of land for the natives, but of the reservation of land for the Europeans, leaving the rest of the continent to the native.

It is quite clear that the European population, possibly with international assistance, will have to bear the brunt of the development and will have to assist for many years to come with capital, technical skill, and management, especially for the development of the basic services (transport, power, water) and primary and secondary industries. By following a policy of decentralization in the non-native area, it would be possible to create fairly large-scale industrial activities in the vicinity of the native areas, enabling the natives to obtain remunerative employment without any harmful effects on their social and family life. In general, the economies of the native and non-native areas will probably be integrated to form an economic whole.

Politically, the policy of separate development envisages the creation of a number of Bantu territorial units with an increasing measure of self-government. The basic principles to be applied in this connection are that Europeans living in the native areas will be citizens of the European state; natives living in the European area will be integrated into the political machinery of the various native areas. What the eventual form of collaboration between the European sector and the various native sectors will be is difficult to foretell, but it is quite possible that it may develop along federal lines, eventually resulting in a United States of Southern Africa or a Southern Africa Confederation. Only an arrangement of this sort can do justice to the political and economic aspirations of the native peoples, and still guarantee the Europeans' continued political existence. Such a policy aims at forestalling the race conflict that is inherent in the present situation by removing the root cause of the problem — the intermixture of the races. The same solution was put in force in the former British India by its partition into the two separate states of India and Pakistan. When it is considered that this division was brought about solely because of the religious differences between Hindus and Muslims, how much stronger is the claim for a territorial division in Southern Africa!

The main obstacles to the implementation of this policy are those of land and labor. The former has been dealt with briefly above; as regards the latter, it is worth remembering that the availability of relatively large numbers of unskilled native laborers has resulted in a general unwillingness to mechanize and rationalize. There is a scandalous waste of manpower and there probably will be for as long as the present policy continues. While recognizing the important role "cheap" native labor plays in the economic structure of the European area, one can hardly argue that this could not be changed in the course of two or three generations. The natural increase of the European population, immigration, mechanization and rationalization, more efficient use of available labor, coupled with the system of migratory native labor — these may all be factors that would assist in decreasing the number of natives at present living in the European area. The contention that a policy of separate development must of necessity lead to economic disruption and chaos is without substance.

As could be expected, opinions in South Africa are in no way unanimous as to the course that should be adopted. In the main, two opposing schools of thought may be distinguished: that of "integration" and that of separate development. The first school favors the increasing integration of the native population into the economic life of the European area, and the removal of all restrictions hampering the permanent settlement of natives in the European towns and cities. It is generally conceded that economic integration will eventually lead to political, economic, and social equality between white and black. Some of the people favoring integration, however, refuse to admit this obvious fact, believing that it would be possible to have complete integration and still "keep the native in his place."

Among integrationists one finds the following groups, listed in order of increasing number of followers: (1) Those in favor of the immediate granting of political equality between white and black, regardless of differences in civilization and culture. The Communists are practically the only ones subscribing to this view. (2) Those favoring the placing of the natives on a separate voters' roll, with limited representation in the legislative institutions. The majority favors a weighted franchise. (3) Those favoring a common voters' roll, with a weighted franchise in the case of natives, *i.e.*, only natives possessing certain qualifications (as regards the level of civilization reached) to be enrolled. (4) Those favoring a common roll for all, white and black, who possess certain defined qualifications. (5) Those in favor of the creation of the parallel legislative institutions, in essence amounting to the creation of a white parliament and of a black parliament. (6) Those favoring the retention of the present position and opposed to any material extension of the present political rights of natives, regardless of the extent of economic integration.

Very often the integrationists favoring the latter two policies are regarded, and regard themselves, as protagonists of the "apartheid" policy; although believing in the necessity and desirability of the economic integration of white and black, they are convinced that a policy of political and social discrimination can be maintained. Some even propagate the curtailment of the limited political rights at present enjoyed by the natives.

Those subscribing to a general "apartheid" policy can be classified as follows: (1) As in (6) above. (2) As in (5) above. (3) Those favoring curtailment of the political rights at present exercised by natives. (4) Those favoring a larger measure of territorial separation, with the retention of present native political rights in the European area and the gradual development of local governing institutions in the native areas. (5) Those in favor of eventually complete, or almost complete, territorial separation with the removal of the present political representation of natives in the Union Parliament and the development of legislative institutions in the native areas. There are minor differences as to the form and measure of self-government that is to develop in the natives' own areas.

All this must appear rather bewildering to an outsider. It would, however, simplify matters if it is remembered (a) that probably no less than 95 per cent of the whites in South Africa are strenuously opposed to any form of political equality in the European area, now or in the future; (b) that the majority still believes in economic integration. But an increasing section is beginning to see the inevitable difficulties ahead if (b) is continued and (a) is held as an unalterable conviction, as undoubtedly will be the case. It is this increasing section of the white population that sees in a constructive policy of separate development the only possible avenue of escape for white and black. . . .

MIXED SCHOOLS AND MIXED BLOOD

by Herbert Ravenel Sass *

1

What may well be the most important physical fact in the story of the United States is one which is seldom emphasized in our history books. It is the fact that throughout the three and a half centuries of our existence we have kept our several races biologically distinct and separate. Though we have encouraged the mixing of many different strains in what has been called the American "melting pot," we have confined this mixing to the white peoples of European ancestry, excluding from our "melting pot" all other races. The result is that the United States today is overwhelmingly a pure white nation, with a smaller but considerable Negro population in which there is some white blood, and a much smaller American Indian population.

The fact that the United States is overwhelmingly pure white is not only important; it is also the most distinctive fact about this country when considered in relation to the rest of the New World. Except Canada, Argentina, and Uruguay, none of the approximately twenty-five other countries of this hemisphere has kept its races pure. Instead (though each contains some pure-blooded individuals) all these countries are products of an amalgamation of races — American Indian and white or American Indian, Negro, and white. In general the pure-blooded white nations have outstripped the far more numerous American mixed-blood nations in most of the achievements which constitute progress as commonly defined.

These facts are well known. But now there lurks in ambush, as it were, another fact: we have suddenly begun to move toward abandonment of our 350-year-old system of keeping our races pure and are preparing to

* Copyright © 1956 by The Atlantic Monthly Company, Boston 16, Massachusetts.

adopt instead a method of racial amalgamation similar to that which has created the mixed-blood nations of this hemisphere; except that the amalgamation being prepared for this country is not Indian and white but Negro and white. It is the deep conviction of nearly all white Southerners in the states which have large Negro populations that the mingling or integration of white and Negro children in the South's primary schools would open the gates to miscegenation and widespread racial amalgamation.

This belief is at the heart of our race problem, and until it is realized that this is the South's basic and compelling motive, there can be no understanding of the South's attitude.

It must be realized too that the Negroes of the U.S.A. are today by far the most fortunate members of their race to be found anywhere on earth. Instead of being the hapless victim of unprecedented oppression, it is nearer the truth that the Negro in the United States is by and large the product of friendliness and helpfulness unequaled in any comparable instance in all history. Nowhere else in the world, at any time of which there is record, has a helpless, backward people of another color been so swiftly uplifted and so greatly benefited by a dominant race.

What America, including the South, has done for the Negro is the truth which should be trumpeted abroad in rebuttal of the Communist propaganda. In failing to utilize this truth we have deliberately put aside a powerful affirmative weapon of enormous potential value to the free world and have allowed ourselves to be thrown on the defensive and placed in an attitude of apologizing for our conduct in a matter where actually our record is one of which we can be very proud.

We have permitted the subject of race relations in the United States to be used not as it should be used, as a weapon for America, but as a weapon for the narrow designs of the new aggressive Negro leadership in the United States. It cannot be so used without damage to this country, and that damage is beyond computation. Instead of winning for America the plaudits and trust of the colored peoples of Asia and Africa in recognition of what we have done for our colored people, our pro-Negro propagandists have seen to it that the United States appears as an international Simon Legree — or rather a Dr. Jekyll and Mr. Hyde with the South in the villainous role.

2

The South has had a bad time with words. Nearly a century ago the word slavery, even more than the thing itself, did the South irreparable damage. In a strange but real way the misused word democracy has injured the South; its most distinctive — and surely its greatest — period has been called undemocratic, meaning illiberal and reactionary, because it resisted the onward sweep of a centralizing governmental trend alien to our federal republic and destructive of the very "cornerstone of liberty," local self-government. Today the word segregation and, perhaps even more harmful, the word prejudice blacken the South's character before the world and make doubly difficult our effort to preserve not merely our own way of life but certain basic principles upon which our country was founded.

Words are of such transcendent importance today that the South should long ago have protested against these two. They are now too firmly imbedded in the dialectic of our race problem to be got rid of. But that very fact renders all the more necessary a careful scrutiny of them. Let us first consider the word segregation.

Segregation is sometimes carelessly listed as a synonym of separation, but it is not a true synonym and the difference between the two words is important.

Segregation, from the Latin *segregatus* (set apart from the flock), implies isolation; separation carries no such implication. Segregation is what we have done to the American Indian — whose grievous wrongs few reformers and still fewer politicians ever bother their heads about. By use of force and against his will we have segregated him, isolated him, on certain small reservations which had and still have somewhat the character of concentration camps.

The South has not done that to the Negro. On the contrary, it has shared its countryside and its cities with him in amity and understanding, not perfect by any means, and careful of established folk custom, but far exceeding in human friendliness anything of the kind to be found in the North. Not segregation of the Negro race as the Indian is segregated on his reservations — and as the Negro is segregated in the urban Harlems of the North — but simply *separation* of the white and Negro races in certain phases of activity is what the South has always had and feels that it must somehow preserve even though the time-honored, successful, and completely moral "separate but equal" principle no longer has legal sanction.

Until the Supreme Court decision forbidding compulsory racial separation in the public schools, the South was moving steadily toward abandonment or relaxation of the compulsory separation rule in several important fields. This is no longer true. Progress in racial relations has been stopped short by the ill-advised insistence of the Northern-directed Negro leadership upon the one concession which above all the white South will not and cannot make — public school integration.

Another word which is doing grave damage to the South today is prejudice, meaning race prejudice — a causeless hostility often amounting to hatred which white Southerners are alleged to feel in regard to the Negro. Here again the South, forgetful of the lessons of its past, has failed to challenge effectively an inaccurate and injurious word. Not prejudice but preference is the word that truth requires.

Between prejudice and preference there is vast difference. Prejudice is a preconceived unfavorable judgment or feeling without sound basis. Preference is a natural reaction to facts and conditions observed or experienced, and through the action of heredity generation after generation it becomes instinctive. Like separateness, it exists throughout the animal kingdom. Though the difference between two races of an animal species may be so slight that only a specialist can differentiate between them, the individuals of one race prefer as a rule to associate with other individuals of that race.

One can cite numerous examples among birds and mammals. In the human species the history of our own country provides the most striking example of race preference. The white men and women, chiefly of British, German, Dutch, and Scandinavian stocks, who colonized and occupied what is now the United States were strongly imbued with race preference. They did not follow the example of the Spanish and Portuguese (in whom for historical reasons the instinct of race preference was much weaker) who in colonizing South and Central America amalgamated with the Indians found in possession of the land and in some cases with the Negroes brought over as slaves. Instead, the founders of the future United States maintained their practice of non-amalgamation rigorously, with only slight racial blendings along the fringes of each group.

Hence it is nonsense to say that racial discrimination, the necessary consequence of race preference, is "un-American." Actually it is perhaps the most distinctively American thing there is, the reason why the American people — meaning the people of the United States — are what they are. Today when racial discrimination of any kind or degree is instantly denounced as both sinful and stupid, few stop to reflect that this nation is built solidly upon it.

The truth is, of course, that there are many different kinds and degrees of racial discrimination. Some of them are bad — outdated relics of an earlier time when conditions were unlike those of today, and these should be, and were being, abolished until the unprecedented decree of the Supreme Court in the school cases halted all progress. But not all kinds of racial discrimination are evil — unless we are prepared to affirm that our forefathers blundered in "keeping the breed pure."

Thus it is clear that discrimination too is a misused word as commonly employed in the realm of racial relations. It does not necessarily imply either stupidity or sin. It is not a synonym for injustice, and it is very far from being, as many seem to think, a synonym for hatred. The Southern white man has always exercised discrimination in regard to the Negro but — except for a tiny and untypical minority of the white population — he has never hated the Negro. I have lived a fairly long life in a part of the South — the South Carolina Lowcountry — where there are many thousands of Negroes, and since early boyhood I have known many of them well, in some cases for years, in town and country. I know how I feel about them and how the white people of this old plantation region, the high and the low, the rich and the poor, the large landowner and the white mechanic, feel about them.

I am sure that among white Carolinians there is, as yet, almost no hatred of the Negro, nor is there anything that can accurately be called race prejudice. What does exist, strongly and ineradicably, is race preference. In other words, we white Southerners prefer our own race and wish to keep it as it is.

This preference should not and in fact cannot be eliminated. It is much bigger than we are, a far greater thing than our racial dilemma. It is — and here is another basic fact of great significance — an essential element in Nature's huge and complex mechanism. It is one of the reasons why evolution, ever diversifying, ever discriminating, ever separating race from race, species from species, has been able to operate in an ascending course so that what began aeons ago as something resembling an amoeba has now become Man. In preferring its own race and in striving to prevent the destruction of that race by amalgamation with another race, the white South is not flouting Nature but is in harmony with her.

3

If the Negro also prefers his own race and wishes to preserve its identity, then he is misrepresented by his new aggressive leadership which, whether or not this is its deliberate aim, is moving toward a totally different result. Let us see why that is so.

The crux of the race problem in the South, as I have said, is the nearly universal belief of the Southern white people that only by maintaining a certain degree of separateness of the races can the racial integrity of the white South be safeguarded. Unfortunately the opinion has prevailed outside the South that only a few Southerners hold this conviction — a handful of demagogic politicians and their most ignorant followers — and that "enlightened" white Southerners recognize the alleged danger of racial amalgamation as a trumped-up thing having no real substance.

Nothing could be farther from the truth. Because the aggressive Northern-Negro leadership continues to drive onward, the white South (except perhaps that part which is now more Western than Southern and in which Negroes are few) is today as united in its conviction that its racial integrity must be protected as it was when the same conviction drove its people — the slaveholder and the non-slaveholder, the high and the low, the educated and the ignorant — to defend the outworn institution of Negro slavery because there seemed to be no other way to preserve the social and political control needed to prevent the Africanization of the South by a combination of fanatical Northern reformers and millions of enfranchised Negroes. The South escaped that fate because after a decade of disastrous experiment the intelligent people of the victorious North realized that the racial program of their social crusaders was unsound, or at least impracticable, and gave up trying to enforce it.

Now in a surging revival of that "Reconstruction" crusade — a revival which is part dedicated idealism, part understandable racial ambition, part political expediency national and international — the same social program is again to be imposed upon the South. There are new conditions which help powerfully to promote it: the Hitlerite excesses in the name of race which have brought all race distinctions into popular disrepute; the notion that the white man, by divesting himself of race consciousness, may appease the peoples of Asia and Africa and wean them away from Communism.

In addition, a fantastic perversion of scientific authority has been publicized in support of the new crusade. Though everywhere else in Nature (as well as in all our plant breeding and animal breeding) race and heredity are recognized as of primary importance, we are told that in the human species race is of no importance and racial differences are due not to heredity but to environment. Science has proved, so we are told, that all races are equal and, in essentials, identical.

Science has most certainly not proved that all races are equal, much less identical; and, as the courageous geneticist, Dr. W. C. George of the University of North Carolina, has recently pointed out, there is overwhelming likelihood that the biological consequences of white and Negro integration in the South would be harmful. It would not be long before these biological consequences became visible. But there is good hope that we shall never see them, because any attempt to force a program of racial integration upon the South would be met with stubborn, determined, and universal opposition, probably taking the form of passive resistance of a hundred kinds. Though secession is not conceivable, persistance in an attempt to compel the South to mingle its white and Negro children in its public schools would split the United States in two as disastrously as in the sixties and perhaps with an even more lamentable aftermath of bitterness.

For the elementary public school is the most critical of those areas of activity where the South must and will at all costs maintain separateness of the races. The South must do this because, although it is a nearly universal instinct, race preference is not active in the very young. Race preference (which the propagandists miscall race prejudice or hate) is one of those instincts which develop gradually as the mind develops and which, if taken in hand early enough, can be prevented from developing at all.

Hence if the small children of the two races in approximately equal numbers — as would be the case in a great many of the South's schools — were brought together intimately and constantly and grew up in close association in integrated schools under teachers necessarily committed to the gospel of racial integration, there would be many in whom race preference would not develop. This would not be, as superficial thinkers might suppose, a good thing, the happy solution of the race problem in America. It might be a solution of a sort, but not one that the American people would desire. It would inevitably result, beginning with the least desirable elements of both races, in a great increase of racial amalgamation, the very process which throughout our history we have most sternly rejected. For although to most persons today the idea of mixed mating is disagreeable or even repugnant, this would not be true of the new generations brought up in mixed schools with the desirability of racial integration as a basic premise. Among those new generations mixed matings would become commonplace, and a greatly enlarged mixed-blood population would result.

That is the compelling reason, though by no means the only reason, why the South will resist, with all its resources of mind and body, the mixing of the races in its public schools. It is a reason which, when its validity is generally recognized, will quickly enlist millions of non-Southerners in support of the South's position. The people of the North and West do not favor the transformation of the United States into a nation

Boston

composed in considerable part of mixed bloods any more than the people of the South do. Northern support of school integration in the South is due to the failure to realize its inevitable biological effect in regions of large Negro population. If Northerners did realize this, their enthusiasm for mixed schools in the South would evaporate at once.

4

There are other cogent reasons for the white South's stand: the urgent necessity of restoring the Constitution and our federal form of government before they are permanently destroyed by the Court's usurpation of power; the equally urgent necessity of re-establishing law and precedent instead of sociological and psychological theory as the basis of the Court's decisions; the terrible damage which racial integration would do to the South's whole educational system, black as well as white. These and other aspects have been fully and effectively explored and need not be touched upon here.

But the underlying and compelling reason for the South's refusal to operate mixed schools — its belief that mixed schools will result in ulti-mate racial amalgamation — has been held virtually taboo and if men-tioned in the North is not examined at all but is summarily dismissed as not worthy of consideration. The amalgamation "bogey," it is said, is not really believed by intelligent Southerners but is a smoke screen used to hide the South's real motives, which are variously described, ranging from plain sadism to a shrewd determination to deprive the Negro of education so that he can never displace the Southern white man. Besides, it is confidently alleged, the Negro does not wish to destroy the identity of his race by merging it with the white race.

Both those statements are incorrect. As already pointed out, the fear that mixed schools in the South would open the way to racial amalgama-tion is not a bogey or a smoke screen or a pretense of any kind but the basic animating motive of the white South in resisting the drive of the N.A.A.C.P. and its supporters. The second statement is as erroneous as the first. The Negro leaders do want racial amalgamation; they not only want the right to amalgamate through legal intermarriage but they want that right to be exercised widely and frequently.

It is only natural and human that they should feel this way. The truth is that these ambitious, intelligent, often amalgamated, and often genu-inely dedicated Negro men and women feel about this matter exactly as white men and women would feel if they were similarly constituted and circumstanced — fusion of the two races would solve the Negro's problem at once. How much of the Negro rank and file consciously seeks amalgamation is a question; to· the Southern Negro in particular the thought of intermarriage is still new and strange. As for the Northern leaders of the movement, some of them make no bones about it, and when they do evade the question they do so only for reasons of strategy.

But actually it does not matter much whether or not intermarriage is the admitted aim of the N.A.A.C.P. strategists. To suppose that, proclaiming the virtual identity of the races, we can promote all other degrees of race mixing but stop short of interracial mating is — if I may use an overworked but vivid simile — like going over Niagara Falls in a barrel in the expectation of stopping three fourths of the way down. The South is now the great bulwark against intermarriage. A very few years of thoroughly integrated schools would produce large numbers of indoctrinated young Southerners free from all "prejudice" against mixed matings.

It is because there the adolescent and "unprejudiced" mind can be reached that the integrationists have chosen the Southern schools as their primary target; and it is precisely because the adolescent and therefore defenseless mind would there be exposed to brain-washing which it would not know how to refute that the white South will not operate integrated public schools. If the South fails to defend its young children who are not yet capable of defending themselves, if it permits their wholesale impregnation by a propaganda persuasive and by them unanswerable, the salutary instinct of race preference which keeps the races separate, as in Nature, will be destroyed before it develops and the barriers against racial amalgamation will go down.

This is the new and ominous fact which, as was said at the beginning of this article, lurks in ambush, concealed like a viper in the school integration crusade. Success of that crusade would mean that after three and a half centuries of magnificent achievement under a system of racial separateness and purity, we would tacitly abandon that system and instead would begin the creation of a mixed American race by the fusion of the two races which, as H. G. Wells expressed it, are at opposite extremes of the human species.

Many well-meaning persons have suddenly discovered that the tenets of the Christian religion and the professions of our democratic faith compel us to accept the risks of this hybridization. No one who will face up to the biological facts and really think the problem through can believe any such thing or see the partial suicide of the white race in America (and of the Negro race also) as anything other than a crime against both religion and civilization.

I have tried to show here the basic and compelling reason why the Southern people, who know the facts of life in the South better than any doctrinaire sociologist viewing the scene from his ivory tower, see no possible course save to stand firm in their resistance to school integration no matter what may be the consequences of their resistance. When a people believes that something even dearer than its life is threatened, there isn't much use in pointing out its duty to obey the law which threatens it, especially when it is almost unanimously of the opinion that the law is a perversion. And the South has ample precedent for resistance. In a much firmer sense the Prohibition Amendment was the law of the land, and the North even more than the South made a mockery of it. So too was the federal fugitive slave act the law of the land, yet many Northern states nullified and openly violated it.

Moreover, fortifying the South for its ordeal is the conviction that it is defending something far greater than itself: that integrity of race and that pride of race which all great peoples have — the Chinese, the Japanese, the Arabs, the Jews, for instance — and without which no people is worth its salt. There is good hope that before too long this will begin to be recognized outside the South. The current pseudoscientific buncombe about racial identity is at last being questioned openly. It will be exploded completely with the ending of the leftist-liberal taboo which has practically sealed the lips of geneticists able and willing to discuss racial realities, and our Lysenko-like excursion in the realm of race will come to an end. Then it will be seen that the South, in maintaining the actuality and the great significance of racial differences, has not been "racist" in any evil sense but has been the defender of something permanently important to the whole American people; and that the Supreme Court, in launching the Negro on an offensive which cannot and should not succeed, has dealt a terrible blow to his advancement and his happiness.

b. Political Elitism

ALEXIS DE TOCQUEVILLE, discussing the development of *Democracy in America* at mid-19th century, described the central political issue of his day as an epochal struggle between the rising tide of democracy and a receding aristocracy. Tocqueville believed he discerned overpowering historical forces behind the advancing democracy: a vast clergy which had "opened its ranks to all classes, to the poor and the rich" alike; the enormous increase throughout Europe of commerce and finance; vastly increased opportunities for common-born practitioners of law and statecraft; ever greater opportunities for careers in science, the requirement for which was talent, not high birth: "Henceforward every new discovery, every new want which it engendered, and every new desire which craved satisfaction, was a step toward the universal level." [1] Tocqueville's reading of European history convinced him that "we shall scarcely meet with a single great event, in the lapse of seven hundred years, which has not turned to the advantage of equality." [2]

His prescience proved to be remarkable, and the powerful trends toward equality which he discerned and described in classic fashion were soon to be powerfully reinforced by the organized political demands of a variety of socialist and communist parties. [3] Equality, complete equality, was the central demand of these parties, and remains so to this day, as is evidenced in the following statement by one of its best known, contemporary proponents:

> An essential part of the building of Socialism is the establishment of a common culture and way of life open to the whole people, and resting on foundations of educational as well as of social and political and economic levelling. Nay more, it is essential that this levelling

[1] Alexis de Tocqueville, *Democracy in America*, The World's Classics edition, edited by Henry Steele Commager, Oxford University Press (London: 1955), pp. 3-4.

[2] *Ibid.*

[3] Cf. *The Communist Manifesto*, Part IV, for some of the specific reforms designed to remove social and economic inequality, e.g., abolition of all right of inheritance; heavy, progressive income taxes; abolition of property in land; free public education for all, etc. Similar and related demands were made by the various socialist parties.

shall be achieved, not merely within each Socialist society, but over all the world . . .[4]

The forces behind this insistent demand for leveling were overpowering in Tocqueville's view; the outcome of the struggle between democracy and aristocracy being virtually inevitable, for

> The gradual development of the equality of conditions is . . . a providential fact, and it possesses all the characteristics of a Divine decree: it is universal, it is durable, it constantly eludes all human interference, and all events as well as all men contribute to its progress. . . .
> . . . If the men of our time were led by attentive observation and by sincere reflection to acknowledge that the gradual and progressive development of social equality is at once the past and future of their history, this solitary truth would confer the sacred character of a Divine decree upon the change. To attempt to check democracy would be in that case to resist the will of God; and the nations would then be constrained to make the best of the social lot awarded to them by Providence.[5]

Viewed from the perspective of the inevitable triumph of democracy, the most pressing political duty of even a responsible aristocrat would be that of helping to direct and educate the new democracy; "to purify its morals; to direct its energies, to substitute a knowledge of business for its inexperience, and an acquaintance with its true interests for its blind propensities." [6] "A new science of politics is indispensable to a new world"; for, should men of good will fail in this task, Tocqueville foresaw the development of a new kind of universal tyranny.

> I believe that it is easier to establish an absolute and despotic government among a people in which the conditions of society are equal, than among any other; and I think that if such a government were once established among such a people, it would not only oppress men, but would eventually strip each of them of several of the highest qualities of humanity. Despotism, therefore, appears to me peculiarly to be dreaded in democratic ages.[7]

Though acutely aware of the pitfalls in the path of the onrushing democratic movement, Tocqueville was impelled to view its progress with "a kind of religious dread . . ." [8] — quite in contrast to many of his influ-

---

[4] G. D. H. Cole, *World Socialism Restated*, p. 33. See Part III, under *Socialism*, for substantial excerpts from this tract.

[5] Tocqueville, *op. cit.*, pp. 5–6.

[6] *Ibid.*, pp. 6–7.

[7] *Ibid.*, pp. 583–4.

[8] *Ibid.*, p. 6.

ential contemporaries, some of whom foresaw a calamitous outcome to the democratic revolution and set themselves firmly in resistance to it.[9] Chief among the opponents of democracy, both in the scope and profundity of his attack and in the vitriolic fervor with which he pressed it, stands the figure of Friedrich Nietzsche. Against the encroaching demands for equality, leveling, socialism, and against Christianity, he loosed Olympian thunderbolts, lighting the intellectual heavens with the searing brilliance of his aphorisms and prose-poetry. Conceiving himself the prophet of a new — and higher — epoch, he donned the guise of Zarathustra, "coming down from the mountain" [10] to the market place to smash the democratic idols with the "hammer-strokes" of his new philosophy. The dominant ideals of modernity — democracy, socialism, Marxism — would produce, argued Nietzsche, not utopias, but degradation. They would lead mankind to the epoch which Huxley was later to characterize as "Brave New World," a world in which "the highest qualities of humanity" would indeed be lost; the world of "the last man." [11] In an extraordinary passage Nietzsche summarized this danger for man — for mankind — as follows:

> . . . There are few pains so grievous as to have seen, divined, or experienced how an exceptional man has missed his way and deteriorated; but he who has the rare eye for the universal danger of "man" himself *deteriorating*, he who like us has recognised the extraordinary fortuitousness which has hitherto played its game in respect to the future of mankind . . . suffers from an anguish with which no other is to be compared. He sees at a glance all that could still *be made out of man* through a favourable accumulation and augmentation of human powers and arrangements; he knows with all the knowledge of his conviction how unexhausted man still is for the greatest possibilities, and how often in the past the type man has stood in presence of mysterious decisions and new paths: he knows still better from his painfulest recollections on what wretched obstacles promising developments of the highest rank have hitherto usually gone to pieces, broken down, sunk, and become contemptible. The universal *degeneracy of mankind* to the level of the "man of the future" — as idealised by the socialistic fools and shallow-pates

[9] Cf. Bagehot on *The English Constitution*; Adams on *The Degradation of the Democratic Dogma*; the writings of Herbert Spencer and the "Social Darwinists"; Comte Arthur de Gobineau's *The Inequality of Human Races* and many others in the same vein.

[10] Cf. Matthew, 8:1: "When he was come down from the mountain, great multitudes followed him." Nietzsche's attack on Christianity is heightened by the Biblical imagery; his Zarathustra, like the Zarathustra of old, was the prophet of a new religion, a new philosophy, a new society. Cf. *Ecce Homo*, in which he reveals something of his intention in Zarathustra.

[11] See the first excerpt in this Part entitled *Excerpts from Nietzsche*.

— this degeneracy and dwarfing of man to an absolutely gregarious animal (or as they call it, to a man of "free society"), this brutalising of man into a pigmy with equal rights and claims, is undoubtedly *possible*. He who has thought out this possibility to its ultimate conclusion knows another loathing unknown to the rest of mankind — and perhaps also a new *mission!* [12]

It was to this "new mission" that Nietzsche devoted himself without restraint, creating — and destroying — with a desperate intensity. It was clearly part of his intention that his work should have political consequences of the greatest importance, and in this expectation he was not mistaken, although betrayed. Nietzsche called for the creation, the spontaneous creation, of a new nobility, a European aristocracy whose aspirations and achievements would transcend all earlier "political elites." Possessing the vigor and courage of Greek warriors, the subtlety and intelligence of renaissance gentlemen, and fortified, about all, by what Nietzsche termed the "master morality," this new aristocracy could first unite Europe, ending a disastrous epoch of petty, national politics. It would then bring the rest of the world under its sway, advancing mankind to heights hitherto undreamed of. . . .

It has been the destructive aspects of Nietzsche's work which have been more readily grasped and acted upon, for Zarathustra was a destroyer, as well as a creator; the smashing of old idols must precede the erection of the new. Nietzsche set himself the task of delivering the final blows to Christianity, to the Biblical morality and their associated human standards, so that a new morality might arise. The indirect consequences of his teaching can hardly be overestimated, for the twentieth century has indeed witnessed spectacles which Nietzsche's contemporaries would have thought no longer within the range of human potentialities. New political elites have, indeed, arisen, and — under their leadership — substantial portions of mankind have demonstrated the capacity to return to fathomless depths of barbarism. This new barbarism has emphatically rejected the fundamental standards of Western civilization, including its religious beliefs; but, while the old standards have been largely destroyed, there has not yet appeared a higher morality. Rather, the Western world has fallen victim to an enervating nihilism.

Nietzsche's role in these developments has been of fundamental importance, yet it would be eminently unfair to conclude that he would have been a proponent of the elitist political movements which, some

[12] Friedrich Nietzsche, *Beyond Good and Evil* (New York: Modern Library, Random House, 1954), pp. 496–97. Emphasis in the original.

decades after his death, tyrannized over mankind under the banners of Fascism and National Socialism. Indeed, his contempt for demagogic tyrants of the stamp of Mussolini and Hitler would have known no bounds. Literally engulfed would he have been by "a great nausea" had he lived to witness leaders of the "Black Shirt" and "Brown Shirt" elites mouthing his phrases and vulgarizing his arguments. Yet the comparison of certain of Nietzsche's writings with those of the theoreticians and leaders of the Italian and German totalitarian parties reveals their kinship, however crude and debased they may have become in their interpretation by Nazi and Fascist propagandists. It is true that they distorted Nietzsche's arguments, ignored his overall intention, and mutilated his principles in their attempts to apply them; yet it was with some partial grasp of his mission that they launched their movements. On this score it is instructive to compare "the leadership principle," and the doctrines of elitism, as applied by the Fascists and Nazis with Nietzsche's conception of "the new aristocracy"; their glorification of the state with Nietzsche's contempt for this "cold monster." One should contrast the Nazi racial doctrine [13] with Nietzsche's qualified and rather tentative suggestions on this subject.[14] The Nietzschean concept of "the will to power" was seized upon by Nazi and Fascist theorists, yet here, as in other areas, one might conclude that he anticipated the abuse to which it would be put by the twentieth century elitists: "It is the age of the masses: they lie on their belly before everything that is passive. And so also in *politics*. A statesman who rears up for them a new Tower of Babel, some monstrosity of empire and power, they call 'great' . . ."[15] The transformation of some of Nietzsche's views in their application by the Fascists and Nazis led, in some instances, to their virtual antithesis — for example, the revival of virulent Italian and German nationalism, in contrast to his plea for a European aristocracy.

Nietzsche's views were indeed transformed in their application by the political elitists, yet a crude correspondence remains which suggests the possibility of certain inadequacies in their original formulation and presentation. Specifically, the new elitist theories drew heavily upon Nietzsche's attack on the democratic, socialistic ideals of equality. In place of these

[13] Consider especially the selection from *Mein Kampf* in Section A of Part V. The doctrines of political elitism do not, necessarily, place stress on racial theories, and the selections which follow suggest many points of contrast between the National Socialist and Fascist doctrines. For example, in opposition to the Nazi view, Mussolini asserted: "Race; it is an emotion, not a reality; ninety-five per cent of it is emotion." See his essay on *The Doctrine of Fascism*, portions of which follow in this section.

[14] Cf. *Beyond Good and Evil*, pp. 562ff.

[15] *Ibid.*, p. 550. Emphasis in the original.

ideals of equality, which Nietzsche subjected to a deep and provocative analysis, they proposed their antithesis — *inequality*. And the tyrants of the twentieth century were to give expression to this standard in a variety of ways. But the entire blame for the misunderstanding and misapplication of Nietzsche's teaching cannot be placed entirely on the heads of the new political elitists, for there is oftentimes a lack of specificity in his writings, which, when augmented by his passionate recklessness of expression, makes his work inherently self-defeating.[16] It was virtually inevitable that in the realm of political action Nietzsche's thought would be taken less seriously by those to whom he intended to speak than by those, who, though unable to understand the higher reaches of his thought, nevertheless attempted to follow what they construed to be his political teaching.

A proper study of Nietzsche's writings then reveals the most comprehensive and thoughtful formulation of the outlook which helped to pave the way for the political elitism of the twentieth century. Included in this section are excerpts from *Thus Spoke Zarathustra*, which was first published in its entirety in 1892; *Beyond Good and Evil*, published in 1886; and *The Genealogy of Morals*, published in 1887. Before contrasting Nietzsche's teaching with the doctrines of Fascism and National Socialism which follow, the student is well advised to consider the warning of Dr. Carl Mayer that "it is only after they have formed and informed the spirit of a time that ideas become instrumental in the formation of a moral-intellectual background. It is not as pure thoughts but as intellectual movements that they become potent." [17] In any event, a few decades after Nietzsche's death, Europe was to be devastated by the total wars which he had feared and even forecast, and from the material and moral rubble of the Continent there arose a succession of political elitist movements. There developed in Italy the Fascist state under the leadership of Benito Mussolini, whose well-known statement of *The Doctrine of Fascism* is included almost in its entirety. It was first published in the *Enciclopedia Italiana* in 1932. Even more revealing of the nature of the Fascist attack on liberal democracy is the article by Corrado Gini, one of the movement's foremost theoreticians, who published his analysis of "The Scientific Basis of Fascism" in 1927. Gini's position in the move-

---

[16] In this respect, it would appear that Nietzsche did not heed his own teaching, for he wrote that ". . . a spirit who is sure of himself speaks softly; he seeks secrecy, he lets himself be awaited. A philosopher is recognized by the fact that he shuns three brilliant and noisy things — fame, princes, and women: which is not to say that they do not come to him. He shuns every glaring light: therefore he shuns his time and its 'daylight.' Therein he is as a shadow; the deeper sinks the sun, the greater grows the shadow."

[17] Carl Mayer, "The Origin of National Socialism," *Social Research*, Vol. 9, 1942, p. 241.

ment was such that he headed the state commission charged with the drafting of the Italian legislative reforms designed to introduce "the organic state" based upon corporations or syndicates.

Concluding this section are two selections which illustrate something of National Socialism, that manifestation of political elitism which arose in Germany and overcame for a time all opposition. The following selection from Hitler's *Mein Kampf,* which was published in 1925, indicates something of the theoretical basis on which he attacked parliamentarianism and asserted his principle of leadership. No analysis of these doctrines would be complete, however, without some consideration of their application. The concluding selection on "Nazi Conspiracy and Aggression," which was published in 1946, is designed to illustrate the most terrible aspects of the National Socialist movement as they manifested themselves during the horrors of the Second World War, when for a time the Nazis were free to give vent to their darkest aspirations. Evidence gathered during the Nuremberg trials reveals a spectacle of scarcely human tyranny, the full nature of which is beyond comprehension. For a brief period the world was subjected to the rule of a twentieth-century "blond beast," who, *in the words of Nietzsche,* if not in his spirit, reverted "to the innocence of the beast-of-prey conscience," and came "from a ghostly bout of murder, arson, rape, and torture, with bravado and a moral equanimity, as though merely some wild student's prank had been played, perfectly convinced that the poets have now an ample theme to sing and celebrate." [18]

The readings in this Part were first published as follows:

Friedrich Nietzsche: *Thus Spoke Zarathustra* (1892)
       Beyond Good and Evil (1886)
       The Genealogy of Morals (1887)
Benito Mussolini, *The Doctrine of Fascism* (1932)
Corrado Gini, *The Scientific Basis of Fascism* (1927)
Adolf Hitler, *Mein Kampf* (1925)
United States Government, *Nazi Conspiracy and Aggression* (1946)

[18] Friedrich Nietzsche, *The Genealogy of Morals,* from *The Philosophy of Nietzsche* (New York: The Modern Library, 1954), pp. 651–2.

EXCERPTS FROM NIETZSCHE

by Friedrich Nietzsche *

THUS SPOKE ZARATHUSTRA

THE LAST MAN

"They have something of which they are proud. What do they call that which makes them proud? Education they call it; it distinguishes them from goatherds. That is why they do not like to hear the word 'contempt' applied to them. Let me then address their pride. Let me speak to them of what is most contemptible: but that is the *last man*."

And thus spoke Zarathustra to the people: "The time has come for man to set himself a goal. The time has come for man to plant the seed of his highest hope. His soil is still rich enough. But one day this soil will be poor and domesticated, and no tall tree will be able to grow in it. Alas, the time is coming when man will no longer shoot the arrow of his longing beyond man, and the string of his bow will have forgotten how to whir!

"I say unto you: one must still have chaos in oneself to be able to give birth to a dancing star. I say unto you: you still have chaos in yourselves.

"Alas, the time is coming when man will no longer give birth to a star. Alas, the time of the most despicable man is coming, he that is no longer able to despise himself. Behold, I show you the *last man*.

" 'What is love? What is creation? What is longing? What is a star?' thus asks the last man, and he blinks.

"The earth has become small, and on it hops the last man, who makes everything small. His race is as ineradicable as the flea-beetle; the last man lives longest.

" 'We have invented happiness,' say the last men, and they blink. They have left the regions where it was hard to live, for one needs warmth. One still loves one's neighbor and rubs against him, for one needs warmth.

---

* Friedrich Nietzsche, *Thus Spoke Zarathustra* in *The Portable Nietzsche* (New York: 1954), edited and translated by Walter Kaufmann. Copyright 1954 by The Viking Press and reprinted with their permission.

"Becoming sick and harboring suspicion are sinful to them: one proceeds carefully. A fool, whoever still stumbles over stones or human beings! A little poison now and then: that makes for agreeable dreams. And much poison in the end, for an agreeable death.

"One still works, for work is a form of entertainment. But one is careful lest the entertainment be too harrowing. One no longer becomes poor or rich: both require too much exertion. Who still wants to rule? Who obey? Both require too much exertion.

"No shepherd and one herd! Everybody wants the same, everybody is the same: whoever feels different goes voluntarily into a madhouse.

" 'Formerly, all the world was mad,' say the most refined, and they blink.

"One is clever and knows everything that has ever happened: so there is no end of derision. One still quarrels, but one is soon reconciled — else it might spoil the digestion.

"One has one's little pleasure for the day and one's little pleasure for the night: but one has a regard for health.

" 'We have invented happiness,' say the last men, and they blink."

Beyond Good and Evil *

THE FREE SPIRIT

Will they be new friends of "truth," these coming philosophers? Very probably, for all philosophers hitherto have loved their truths. But assuredly they will not be dogmatists. It must be contrary to their pride, and also contrary to their taste, that their truth should still be truth for every one — that which has hitherto been the secret wish and ultimate purpose of all dogmatic efforts. "My opinion is *my* opinion: another person has not easily a right to it" — such a philosopher of the future will say, perhaps. One must renounce the bad taste of wishing to agree with many people. "Good" is no longer good when one's neighbour takes it into his mouth. And how could there be a "common good"! The expression contradicts itself; that which can be common is always of small value. In the end things must be as they are and have always been — the great things remain for the great, the abysses for the profound, the delicacies and thrills for the refined, and, to sum up shortly, everything rare for the rare.

Need I say expressly after all this that they will be free, *very* free spirits, these philosophers of the future — as certainly also they will not be merely free spirits, but something more, higher, greater, and fundamentally differ-

* Friedrich Nietzsche, *The Philosophy of Nietzsche* (New York: 1954). By permission of The Modern Library and George Allen and Unwin, London.

ent, which does not wish to be misunderstood and mistaken? But while I say this, I feel under *obligation* almost as much to them as to ourselves (we free spirits who are their heralds and forerunners), to sweep away from ourselves altogether a stupid old prejudice and misunderstanding, which, like a fog, has too long made the conception of "free spirit" obscure. In every country of Europe, and the same in America, there is at present something which makes an abuse of this name: a very narrow, prepossessed, enchained class of spirits, who desire almost the opposite of what our intentions and instincts prompt — not to mention that in respect to the *new* philosophers who are appearing, they must still more be closed windows and bolted doors. Briefly and regrettably, they belong to the *levellers*, these wrongly named "free spirits" — as glib-tongued and scribe-fingered slaves of the democratic taste and its "modern ideas": all of them men without solitude, without personal solitude, blunt, honest fellows to whom neither courage nor honourable conduct ought to be denied; only, they are not free, and are ludicrously superficial, especially in their innate partiality for seeing the cause of almost *all* human misery and failure in the old forms in which society has hitherto existed — a notion which happily inverts the truth entirely! What they would fain attain with all their strength, is the universal, green-meadow happiness of the herd, together with security, safety, comfort, and alleviation of life for every one; their two most frequently chanted songs and doctrines are called "Equality of Rights" and "Sympathy with all Sufferers" — and suffering itself is looked upon by them as something which must be *done away with*. We opposite ones, however, who have opened our eye and conscience to the question how and where the plant "man" has hitherto grown most vigorously, believe that this has always taken place under the opposite conditions, that for this end the dangerousness of his situation had to be increased enormously, his inventive faculty and dissembling power (his "spirit") had to develop into subtlety and daring under long oppression and compulsion, and his Will to Life had to be increased to the unconditioned Will to Power: — we believe that severity, violence, slavery, danger in the street and in the heart, secrecy, stoicism, tempter's art and devilry of every kind, — that everything wicked, terrible, tyrannical, predatory, and serpentine in man, serves as well for the elevation of the human species as its opposite: — we do not even say enough when we only say *this much*; and in any case we find ourselves here, both with our speech and our science, at the *other* extreme of all modern ideology and gregarious desirability, as their antipodes perhaps? What wonder that we "free spirits" are not exactly the most communicative spirits? that we do not wish to betray in every respect *what* a spirit can free itself from, and *where* perhaps it will then be driven? . . .

"THE NATURAL HISTORY OF MORALS"

Inasmuch as in all ages, as long as mankind has existed, there have also been human herds (family alliances, communities, tribes, peoples, states, churches), and always a great number who obey in proportion to the small number who command — in view, therefore, of the fact that obedience has been most practised and fostered among mankind hitherto, one may reasonably suppose that, generally speaking, the need thereof is now innate in every one, as a kind of *formal conscience* which gives the command: "Thou shalt unconditionally do something, unconditionally refrain from something"; in short, "Thou shalt." This need tries to satisfy itself and to fill its form with a content; according to its strength, impatience, and eagerness, it at once seizes as an omnivorous appetite with little selection, and accepts whatever is shouted into its ear by all sorts of commanders — parents, teachers, laws, class prejudices, or public opinion. The extraordinary limitation of human development, the hesitation, protractedness, frequent retrogression, and turning thereof, is attributable to the fact that the herd-instinct of obedience is transmitted best, and at the cost of the art of command. If one imagine this instinct increasing to its greatest extent, commanders and independent individuals will finally be lacking altogether; or they will suffer inwardly from a bad conscience, and will have to impose a deception on themselves in the first place in order to be able to command: just as if they also were only obeying. This condition of things actually exists in Europe at present — I call it the moral hypocrisy of the commanding class. They know no other way of protecting themselves from their bad conscience than by playing the role of executors of older and higher orders (of predecessors, of the constitution, of justice, of the law, or of God himself), or they even justify themselves by maxims from the current opinions of the herd, as "first servants of their people," or "instruments of the public weal." On the other hand, the gregarious European man nowadays assumes an air as if he were the only kind of man that is allowable; he glorifies his qualities, such as public spirit, kindness, deference, industry, temperance, modesty, indulgence, sympathy, by virtue of which he is gentle, endurable, and useful to the herd, as the peculiarly human virtues. In cases, however, where it is believed that the leader and bellwether cannot be dispensed with, attempt after attempt is made nowadays to replace commanders by the summing together of clever gregarious men: all representative constitutions, for example, are of this origin. In spite of all, what a blessing, what a deliverance from a weight becoming unendurable, is the appearance of an absolute ruler for these gregarious Europeans — of this fact the effect of the appearance of Napoleon was the last great proof: the history of the influence of Napoleon is almost the history of the higher happiness to which the entire century has attained in its worthiest individuals and periods.

The man of an age of dissolution which mixes the races with one another, who has the inheritance of a diversified descent in his body — that is to say, contrary, and often not only contrary, instincts and standards of value, which struggle with one another and are seldom at peace — such a man of late culture and broken lights, will, on an average, be a weak man. His fundamental desire is that the war which is *in him* should come to an end; happiness appears to him in the character of a soothing medicine and mode of thought (for instance, Epicurean or Christian); it is above all things the happiness of repose, of undisturbedness, of repletion, of final unity — it is the "Sabbath of Sabbaths," to use the expression of the holy rhetorician, St. Augustine, who was himself such a man. . . .

As long as the utility which determines moral estimates is only gregarious utility, as long as the preservation of the community is only kept in view, and the immoral is sought precisely and exclusively in what seems dangerous to the maintenance of the community, there can be no "morality of love to one's neighbour." Granted even that there is already a little constant exercise of consideration, sympathy, fairness, gentleness, and mutual assistance, granted that even in this condition of society all those instincts are already active which are latterly distinguished by honourable names as "virtues," and eventually almost coincide with the conception "morality": in that period they do not as yet belong to the domain of moral valuations — they are still *ultra-moral*. A sympathetic action, for instance, is neither called good nor bad, moral nor immoral, in the best period of the Romans; and should it be praised, a sort of resentful disdain is compatible with this praise, even at the best, directly the sympathetic action is compared with one which contributes to the welfare of the whole, to the *res publica*. After all, "love to our neighbour" is always a secondary matter, partly conventional and arbitrarily manifested in relation to our *fear of our neighbour*. After the fabric of society seems on the whole established and secured against external dangers, it is this fear of our neighbour which again creates new perspectives of moral valuation. Certain strong and dangerous instincts, such as the love of enterprise, foolhardiness, revengefulness, astuteness, rapacity, and love of power, which up till then had not only to be honoured from the point of view of general utility — under other names, of course, than those here given — but had to be fostered and cultivated (because they were perpetually required in the common danger against the common enemies), are now felt in their dangerousness to be doubly strong — when the outlets for them are lacking — and are gradually branded as immoral and given over to calumny. The contrary instincts and inclinations now attain to moral honour; the gregarious instinct gradually draws its conclusions. How much or how little dangerousness to the community or to equality is contained in an opinion, a condition, an emotion, a disposition, or an endowment — that is now the moral perspective; here again fear is the mother of morals. It is by the loftiest and strongest instincts, when they break out passionately and carry the individual far above and beyond the average, and the low level of the gregarious conscience, that the self-reliance of the community is destroyed; its belief in itself, its backbone, as it were, breaks; consequently these very instincts will be most branded and defamed. The lofty independent spirituality, the will to stand alone, and even the cogent reason, are felt to be dangers; everything that elevates the individual above the herd, and is a source of fear to the neighbour, is henceforth called *evil*; the tolerant, unassuming, self-adapting, self-equalising disposition, the *mediocrity* of desires, attains to moral distinction and honour. Finally, under very peaceful circumstances, there is always less opportunity and necessity for training the feelings to severity and rigour; and now every form of severity, even in justice, begins to disturb the conscience; a lofty and rigourous nobleness and self-responsibility almost offends, and awakens distrust, "the lamb," and still more "the sheep," wins respect. There is a point of diseased mellowness and effeminacy in the history of society, at which society itself takes the part of him who injures it, the part of the *criminal*, and does so, in fact, seriously and honestly. To punish, appears to it to be somehow unfair — it is certain that the idea of "punishment" and "the obligation to punish" are then painful and alarming to people. "Is it not sufficient if the criminal be rendered *harmless*? Why should we still punish? Punishment itself is terrible!" — with these questions gregarious morality, the morality of fear, draws its ultimate conclusion. If one could at all do away with danger, the cause of fear, one would have done away with this morality at the same time, it would no longer be necessary, it *would not consider itself* any longer necessary! — Whoever examines the conscience of the present-day European, will always elicit the same imperative from its thousand moral folds and hidden recesses, the imperative of the timidity of the herd: "we wish that some time or other there may be *nothing more to fear!*" Some time or other — the will and the way *thereto* is nowadays called "progress" all over Europe.

The Genealogy of Morals *

GOOD AND EVIL

The revolt of the slaves in morals begins in the very principle of *resentment* becoming creative and giving birth to values — a resentment experienced by creatures who, deprived as they are of the proper outlet of action, are forced to find their compensation in an imaginary revenge. While every aristocratic morality springs from a triumphant affirmation of its own demands, the slave morality says "no" from the very outset to what is "outside itself," "different from itself," and "not itself": and this "no" is its creative deed. This volte-face of the valuing standpoint — this *inevitable* gravitation to the objective instead of back to the subjective — is typical of "resentment": the slave-morality requires as the condition of its existence an external and objective world, to employ physiological terminology, it requires objective stimuli to be capable of action at all — its action is fundamentally a reaction. The contrary is the case when we come to the aristocrat's system of values: it acts and grows spontaneously, it merely seeks its antithesis in order to pronounce a more grateful and exultant "yes" to its own self; — its negative conception, "low," "vulgar," "bad," is merely a pale late-born foil in comparison with its positive and fundamental conception (saturated as it is with life and passion), of "we aristocrats, we good ones, we beautiful ones, we happy ones."

When the aristocratic morality goes astray and commits sacrilege on reality, this is limited to that particular sphere with which it is *not* sufficiently acquainted — a sphere, in fact, from the real knowledge of which it disdainfully defends itself. It misjudges, in some cases, the sphere which it despises, the sphere of the common vulgar man and the low people: on the other hand, due weight should be given to the consideration that in any case the mood of contempt, of disdain, of superciliousness, even on the supposition that it *falsely* portrays the object of its contempt, will always be far removed from that degree of falsity which will always characterise the attacks — in effigy, of course — of the vindictive hatred and revengefulness of the weak in onslaughts on their enemies. In point of fact, there is in contempt too strong an admixture of nonchalance, of casualness, of boredom, of impatience, even of personal exultation, for it to be capable of distorting its victim into a real caricature or a real monstrosity. Attention again should be paid to the almost benevolent *nuances*

* Friedrich Nietzsche, *The Philosophy of Nietzsche* (New York: 1954). By permission of The Modern Library and George Allen and Unwin, London.

which, for instance, the Greek nobility imports into all the words by which it distinguishes the common people from itself; note how continuously a kind of pity, care, and consideration imparts its honeyed *flavour*, until at last almost all the words which are applied to the vulgar man survive finally as expressions for "unhappy," "worthy of pity" . . . The "well-born" simply *felt* themselves the "happy"; they did not have to manufacture their happiness artificially through looking at their enemies, or in cases to talk and lie themselves into happiness (as is the custom with all resentful men); and similarly, complete men as they were, exuberant with strength, and consequently *necessarily* energetic, they were too wise to dissociate happiness from action — activity becomes in their minds necessarily counted as happiness . . . all in sharp contrast to the "happiness" of the weak and the oppressed, with their festering venom and malignity, among whom happiness appears essentially as a narcotic, a deadening, a quietude, a peace, a "Sabbath," an enervation of the mind and relaxation of the limbs, — in short, a purely *passive* phenomenon. While the aristocratic man lived in confidence and openness with himself . . . the resentful man, on the other hand, is neither sincere nor naïf, nor honest and candid with himself. His soul *squints*; his mind loves hidden crannies, tortuous paths and backdoors, everything secret appeals to him as *his* word, *his* safety, *his* balm; he is past master in silence, in not forgetting, in waiting, in provisional self-depreciation and self-abasement. A race of such *resentful* men will of necessity eventually prove more *prudent* than any aristocratic race, it will honour prudence on quite a distinct scale, as, in fact, a paramount condition of existence, while prudence among aristocratic men is apt to be tinged with a delicate flavour of luxury and refinement; so among them it plays nothing like so integral a part as that complete certainty of function of the governing *unconscious* instincts, or as indeed a certain lack of prudence, such as a vehement and valiant charge, whether against danger or the enemy, or as those ecstatic bursts of rage, love, reverence, gratitude, by which at all times noble souls have recognised each other. When the resentment of the aristocratic man manifests itself, it fulfils and exhausts itself in an immediate reaction, and consequently instills no *venom*: on the other hand, it never manifests itself at all in countless instances, when in the case of the feeble and weak it would be inevitable. An inability to take seriously for any length of time their enemies, their disasters, their *misdeeds* — that is the sign of the full strong natures who possess a superfluity of moulding plastic force, that heals completely and produces forgetfulness: a good example of this in the modern world is Mirabeau, who had no memory for any insults and meannesses which were practised on him, and who was only incapable of forgiving because he forgot. Such a man indeed shakes off with a shrug many a worm which would have buried itself in another; it is only in characters like these that we see the possibility (supposing, of course, that there is such a possibility in the world) of the real "*love* of one's enemies." What respect for his enemies is found, forsooth, in an aristocratic man — and such a reverence is already a bridge to love! He insists on having his enemy to himself as his distinction. He tolerates no other enemy but a man in whose character there is nothing to despise and *much* to honour! On the other hand, imagine the "enemy" as the resentful man conceives him — and it is here exactly that we see his work, his creativeness; he has conceived "the evil enemy," the "evil one," and indeed that is the root idea from which he now evolves as a contrasting and corresponding figure a "good one," himself — his very self!

The method of this man is quite contrary to that of the aristocratic man, who conceives the root idea "good" spontaneously and straight away, that is to say, out of himself, and from that material then creates for himself a concept of "bad"! This "bad" of aristocratic origin and that "evil" out of the cauldron of unsatisfied hatred — the former an imitation, an "extra," an additional nuance; the latter, on the other hand, the original, the beginning, the essential act in the conception of a slave-morality — these two words "bad" and "evil," how great a difference do they mark, in spite of the fact that they have an identical contrary in the idea "good." But the idea "good" is *not* the same: much rather let the question be asked: "Who is really evil according to the meaning of the morality of resentment?" In all sternness let it be answered thus: — *just* the good man of the other morality, just the aristocrat, the powerful one, the one who rules, but who is distorted by the venomous eye of resentfulness, into a new colour, a new signification, a new appearance. This particular point we would be the last to deny: the man who learned to know those "good" ones only as enemies, learned at the same time not to know them only as "*evil enemies*," and the same men who *inter pares* were kept so rigorously in bounds through convention, respect, custom, and gratitude, though much more through mutual vigilance and jealousy *inter pares*, these men who in their relations with each other find so many new ways of manifesting consideration, self-control, delicacy, loyalty, pride, and friendship, these men are in reference to what is outside their circle (where the foreign element, a *foreign* country, begins), not much better than beasts of prey, which have been let loose. They enjoy there freedom from all social control, they feel that in the wilderness they can give vent with impunity to that tension which is produced by enclosure and imprisonment in the peace of society, they *revert* to the innocence of the beast-of-prey conscience, like jubilant monsters, who perhaps come from a ghostly bout of murder, arson, rape, and torture, with bravado and a moral equanimity, as though merely some wild student's prank had been played, perfectly convinced that the poets have now an ample theme to sing and celebrate. It is impossible not to recognize at the core of all these aristocratic races the beast of prey; the magnificent *blond brute,* avidly rampant for spoil and victory; this hidden core needed an outlet from time to time, the beast must get loose again, must return into the wilderness — the Roman, Arabic, German, and Japanese nobility, the Homeric heroes, the Scandinavian Vikings, are all alike in this need. It is the aristocratic races who have left the idea "Barbarian" on all the tracks in which they have marched; nay, a consciousness of this very barbarianism, and even a pride in it, manifests itself even in their highest civilisation (for example, when Pericles says to his Athenians in that celebrated funeral oration, "Our audacity has forced a way over every land and sea, rearing everywhere imperishable memorials of itself for *good* and for *evil*"). This audacity of aristocratic races, mad, absurd, and spasmodic as may be its expression; the incalculable and fantastic nature of their enterprises, — Pericles sets in special relief and glory, the [lightheartedness] of the Athenians, their nonchalance and contempt for safety, body, life, and comfort, their awful joy and intense delight in all destruction, in all the ecstasies of victory and cruelty, — all these features become crystallised, for those who suffered thereby in the picture of the "barbarian," of the "evil enemy," perhaps of the "Goth" and of the "Vandal." The profound, icy mistrust which the German provokes, as soon as he arrives at power, — even at the present time, — is always still an aftermath of that inextinguishable horror with which for whole centuries Europe has regarded the wrath of the blond Teuton beast (although between the old Germans and ourselves there exists scarcely a psychological, let alone a physical, relationship). I have once called attention to the embarrassment of Hesiod, when he conceived the series of social ages, and endeavoured to express them in gold, silver, and bronze. He could only dispose of the contradiction, with which he was confronted, by the Homeric world, an age magnificent indeed, but at the same time so awful and so violent, by making two ages out of one, which he henceforth placed one behind the other — first, the age of the heroes and demigods, as that world had remained in the memories of the aristocratic families, who found therein their own ancestors; secondly, the bronze age, as that corresponding age appeared to the descendants of the oppressed, spoiled, ill-treated, exiled, enslaved; namely, as an age of bronze, as I have said, hard, cold, terrible, without feelings and without conscience, crushing everything, and be-spattering everything with blood. Granted the truth of the theory now believed to be true, that the very *essence of all civilisation* is to *train* out of man, the beast of prey, a tame and civilised animal, a domesticated animal, it follows indubitably that we must regard as the real *tools of civilisation* all those instincts of reaction and resentment, by the help of which the aristocratic races, together with their ideals, were finally de-graded and overpowered; though that has not yet come to be synonymous with saying that the bearers of those tools also *represented* the civilisation. It is rather the contrary that is not only probable — nay, it is *palpable* today; these bearers of vindictive instincts that have to be bottled up, these descendants of all European and non-European slavery, especially of the pre-Aryan population — these people, I say, represent the *decline* of humanity! These "tools of civilisation" are a disgrace to humanity, and constitute in reality more of an argument against civilisation, more of a reason why civilisation should be suspected. One may be perfectly justified in being always afraid of the blonde beast that lies at the core of all aristocratic races, and in being on one's guard: but who would not a hundred times prefer to be afraid, when one at the same time admires, than to be immune from fear, at the cost of being perpetually obsessed with the loathsome spectacle of the distorted, the dwarfed, the stunted, the envenomed? And is that not our fate? What produces today our re-pulsion towards "man"? — for we *suffer* from "man," there is no doubt about it. It is not fear; it is rather that we have nothing more to fear from men; it is that the worm "man" is in the foreground and pullulates; it is that the "tame man," the wretched mediocre and unedifying creature, has learned to consider himself a goal and a pinnacle, an inner meaning, an historic principle, a "higher man"; yes, it is that he has a certain right so to consider himself, in so far as he feels that in contrast to that excess of deformity, disease, exhaustion, and effeteness whose odour is beginning to pollute present-day Europe, he at any rate has achieved a relative suc-cess, he at any rate still says "yes" to life.

I cannot refrain at this juncture from uttering a sigh and one last hope. What is it precisely which I find intolerable? That which I alone cannot get rid of, which makes me choke and faint? Bad air! Bad air! That some-thing misbegotten comes near me; that I must inhale the odour of the entrails of a misbegotten soul! — That excepted, what can one not endure in the way of need, privation, bad weather, sickness, toil, solitude? In point of fact, one manages to get over everything, born as one is to a burrowing and battling existence; one always returns once again to the light, one always lives again one's golden hour of victory — and then one stands as one was born, unbreakable, tense, ready for something more difficult, for something more distant, like a bow stretched but the tauter by every strain. But from time to time do ye grant me — assuming that "beyond good and evil" there are goddesses who can grant — one glimpse, grant me but one glimpse only, of something perfect, fully realised, happy, mighty, triumphant, of something that still gives cause for fear! A glimpse of a man that justifies the existence of man, a glimpse of an incarnate human happiness that realises and redeems, for the sake of which one may hold fast to *the belief in man!* For the position is this: in the dwarfing and levelling of the European man lurks *our* greatest peril, for it is this outlook which fatigues — we see today nothing which wishes to be greater, we surmise that the process is always still backwards, still backwards towards something more attenuated, more inoffensive, more cunning, more comfortable, more mediocre, more indifferent, more Chinese, more Christian — man, there is no doubt about it, grows always "better" — the destiny of Europe lies even in this — that in losing the fear of man, we have also lost the hope in man, yea, the will to be man. The sight of man now fatigues. — What is present-day Nihilism if it is not *that?* — We are tired of *man*.

It is primarily involved in this hypothesis of the origin of the bad conscience, that that alteration was no gradual and no voluntary alteration, and that it did not manifest itself as an organic adaptation to new conditions, but as a break, a jump, a necessity, an inevitable fate, against which there was no resistance and never a spark of resentment. And secondarily, that the fitting of a hitherto unchecked and amorphous population into a fixed form, starting as it had done in an act of violence, could only be accomplished by acts of violence and nothing else — that the oldest "State" appeared consequently as a ghastly tyranny, a grinding ruthless piece of machinery, which went on working, till this raw material of a semi-animal populace was not only thoroughly kneaded and elastic, but also *moulded.* I used the word "State"; my meaning is self-evident, namely, a herd of blonde beasts of prey, a race of conquerors and masters, which with all its war-like organisation and all its organising power pounces with its terrible claws on a population, in numbers possibly tremendously superior, but as yet formless, as yet nomad. Such is the origin of the "State." That fantastic theory that makes it begin with a contract is, I think, disposed of. He who can command, he who is a master by "nature," he who comes on the scene forceful in deed and gesture — what has he to do with contracts? Such beings defy calculation, they come like fate, without cause, reason, notice, excuse, they are there as the lightning is there, too terrible, too sudden, too convincing, too "different," to be personally even hated. Their work is an instinctive creating and impressing of forms, they are the most involuntary, unconscious artists that there are: — their appearance produces instantaneously a scheme of sovereignty which is *live*, in which the functions are partitioned and apportioned, in which above all no part is received or finds a place, until pregnant with a "meaning" in regard to the whole. They are ignorant of the meaning of guilt, responsibility, consideration, are these born organisers; in them predominates that terrible artist-egoism, that gleams like brass, and that knows itself justified to all eternity, in its work, even as a mother in her child. It is not in *them* that there grew the bad conscience, that is elementary — but it would not have grown *without them*, repulsive growth as it was, it would be missing, had not a tremendous quantity of freedom been expelled from the world by the stress of their hammer-strokes, their artist violence, or been at any rate made invisible and, as it were, *latent*. This *instinct of freedom* forced into being latent — it is already clear — this instinct of freedom forced back, trodden back, imprisoned within itself, and finally only able to find vent and relief in itself; this, only this, is the beginning of the "bad conscience."

The more normal is this sickliness in man — and we cannot dispute this normality — the higher honour should be paid to the rare cases of psychical and physical powerfulness, the *windfalls* of humanity, and the more strictly should the sound be guarded from that worst of air, the air of the sick-room. Is that done? The sick are the greatest danger for the healthy; it is not from the strongest that harm comes to the strong, but from the weakest. Is that known? Broadly considered, it is not for a minute the fear of man, whose diminution should be wished for; for this fear forces the strong to be strong, to be at times terrible — it preserves in its integrity the sound type of man. What is to be feared, what does work with a fatality found in no other fate, is not the great fear of, but the great *nausea* with, man; and equally so the great pity for man. Supposing that both these things were one day to espouse each other, then inevitably the maximum of monstrousness would immediately come into the world — the "last will" of man, his will for nothingness, Nihilism. And, in sooth, the way is well paved thereto. He who not only has his nose to smell with, but also has eyes and ears, he sniffs almost wherever he goes today an air something like that of a mad-house, the air of a hospital — I am speaking, as stands to reason, of the cultured areas of mankind, of every kind of "Europe" that there is in fact in the world. The *sick* are the great danger of man, *not* the evil, *not* the "beasts of prey." . . .

. . . Away with this "perverse world"! Away with this shameful sodden-ness of sentiment! Preventing the sick making the healthy sick — for that is what such a soddenness comes to — this ought to be our supreme object in the world — but for this it is above all essential that the healthy should remain *separated* from the sick, that they should even guard them-selves from the look of the sick, that they should not even associate with the sick. Or may it, perchance, be their mission to be nurses or doctors? But they could not mistake and disown *their* mission more grossly — the higher *must* not degrade itself to be the tool of the lower, the pathos of distance must to all eternity keep their missions also separate. The right of the happy to existence, the right of bells with a full tone over the discordant cracked bells, is verily a thousand times greater: they alone are the *sureties* of the future, they alone are *bound* to man's future. What they can, what they must do, that can the sick never do, should never do! but if *they are* to be enabled to do what *only* they must do, how can they possibly be free to play the doctor, the comforter, the "Saviour" of the sick? . . . And therefore good air! good air! and away, at any rate, from the neighbourhood of all the madhouses and hospitals of civilisation! And therefore good company, *our own* company, or solitude, if it must be so! but away, at any rate, from the evil fumes of internal corruption and the secret worm-eaten state of the sick! that, forsooth, my friends, we may defend ourselves, at any rate for still a time, against the two worst plagues that could have been reserved for us — against the *great nausea with man!* against the *great pity for man!*

THE DOCTRINE OF FASCISM

by Benito Mussolini *

(i) FUNDAMENTAL IDEAS

1. Like every sound political conception, Fascism is both practice and thought; action in which a doctrine is immanent, and a doctrine which, arising out of a given system of historical forces, remains embedded in them and works there from within. Hence it has a form correlative to the contingencies of place and time, but it has also a content of thought which raises it to a formula of truth in the higher level of the history of thought. In the world one does not act spiritually as a human will dominating other wills without a conception of the transient and particular reality under which it is necessary to act, and of the permanent and universal reality in which the first has its being and its life. In order to know men it is necessary to know man; and in order to know man it is necessary to know reality and its laws. There is no concept of the State which is not fundamentally a concept of life: philosophy or intuition, a system of ideas which develops logically or is gathered up into a vision or into a faith, but which is always, at least virtually, an organic conception of the world.

2. Thus Fascism could not be understood in many of its practical manifestations as a party organization, as a system of education, as a discipline, if it were not always looked at in the light of its whole way of conceiving life, a spiritualized way. The world seen through Fascism is not this material world which appears on the surface, in which man is an individual separated from all others and standing by himself, and in which he is governed by a natural law that makes him instinctively live a life of selfish and momentary pleasure. The man of Fascism is an individual who is nation and fatherland, which is a moral law, binding

---

* Benito Mussolini, *The Doctrine of Fascism*. This statement appeared initially in the *Enciclopedia Italiana* in 1932. Translation by Michael Oakeshott in *The Social and Political Doctrines of Contemporary Europe* (New York: 1942). By permission of Cambridge University Press.

together individuals and the generations into a tradition and a mission, suppressing the instinct for a life enclosed within the brief round of pleasure in order to restore within duty a higher life free from the limits of time and space: a life in which the individual, through the denial of himself, through the sacrifice of his own private interests, through death itself, realizes that completely spiritual existence in which his value as a man lies.

3. Therefore it is a spiritualized conception, itself the result of the general reaction of modern times against the flabby materialistic positivism of the nineteenth century. Anti-positivistic, but positive: not sceptical, nor agnostic, nor pessimistic, nor passively optimistic, as are, in general, the doctrines (all negative) that put the centre of life outside man, who with his free will can and must create his own world. Fascism desires an active man, one engaged in activity with all his energies: it desires a man virilely conscious of the difficulties that exist in action and ready to face them. It conceives of life as a struggle, considering that it behoves man to conquer for himself that life truly worthy of him, creating first of all in himself the instrument (physical, moral, intellectual) in order to construct it. Thus for the single individual, thus for the nation, thus for humanity. Hence the high value of culture in all its forms (art, religion, science), and the enormous importance of education. Hence also the essential value of work, with which man conquers nature and creates the human world (economic, political, moral, intellectual).

4. This positive conception of life is clearly an ethical conception. It covers the whole of reality, not merely the human activity which controls it. No action can be divorced from moral judgment; there is nothing in the world which can be deprived of the value which belongs to everything in its relation to moral ends. Life, therefore, as conceived by the Fascist, is serious, austere, religious: the whole of it is poised in a world supported by the moral and responsible forces of the spirit. The Fascist disdains the "comfortable" life.

5. Fascism is a religious conception in which man is seen in his immanent relationship with a superior law and with an objective Will that transcends the particular individual and raises him to conscious membership of a spiritual society. Whoever has seen in the religious politics of the Fascist regime nothing but mere opportunism has not understood that Fascism besides being a system of government is also, and above all, a system of thought.

6. Fascism is an historical conception, in which man is what he is only in so far as he works with the spiritual process in which he finds himself,

in the family or social group, in the nation and in the history in which all nations collaborate. From this follows the great value of tradition, in memories, in language, in customs, in the standards of social life. Outside history man is nothing. Consequently Fascism is opposed to all the individualistic abstractions of a materialistic nature like those of the eighteenth century; and it is opposed to all Jacobin utopias and innovations. It does not consider that "happiness" is possible upon earth, as it appeared to be in the desire of the economic literature of the eighteenth century, and hence it rejects all teleological theories according to which mankind would reach a definitive stabilized condition at a certain period in history. This implies putting oneself outside history and life, which is a continual change and coming to be. Politically, Fascism wishes to be a realistic doctrine; practically, it aspires to solve only the problems which arise historically of themselves and that of themselves find or suggest their own solution. To act among men, as to act in the natural world, it is necessary to enter into the process of reality and to master the already operating forces.

7. Against individualism, the Fascist conception is for the State; and it is for the individual in so far as he coincides with the State, which is the conscience and universal will of man in his historical existence. It is opposed to classical Liberalism, which arose from the necessity of reacting against absolutism, and which brought its historical purpose to an end when the State was transformed into the conscience and will of the people. Liberalism denied the State in the interests of the particular individual; Fascism reaffirms the State as the true reality of the individual. And if liberty is to be the attribute of the real man, and not of that abstract puppet envisaged by individualistic Liberalism, Fascism is for liberty. And for the only liberty which can be a real thing, the liberty of the State and of the individual within the State. Therefore, for the Fascist, everything is in the State, and nothing human or spiritual exists, much less has value, outside the State. In this sense Fascism is totalitarian, and the Fascist State, the synthesis and unity of all values, interprets, develops and gives strength to the whole life of the people.

8. Outside the State there can be neither individuals nor groups (political parties, associations, syndicates, classes). Therefore Fascism is opposed to Socialism, which confines the movement of history within the class struggle and ignores the unity of classes established in one economic and moral reality in the State; and analogously it is opposed to class syndicalism. Fascism recognizes the real exigencies for which the socialist and syndicalist movement arose, but while recognizing them wishes to

bring them under the control of the State and give them a purpose within the corporative system of interests reconciled within the unity of the State.

9. Individuals form classes according to the similarity of their interests, they form syndicates according to differentiated economic activities within these interests; but they form first, and above all, the State, which is not to be thought of numerically as the sum-total of individuals forming the majority of a nation. And consequently Fascism is opposed to Democracy, which equates the nation to the majority, lowering it to the level of that majority; nevertheless it is the purest form of democracy if the nation is conceived, as it should be, qualitatively and not quantitatively, as the most powerful idea (most powerful because most moral, most coherent, most true) which acts within the nation as the conscience and the will of a few, even of One, which ideal tends to become active within the conscience and the will of all — that is to say, of all those who rightly constitute a nation by reason of nature, history or race, and have set out upon the same line of development and spiritual formation as one conscience and one sole will. Not a race, nor a geographically determined region, but as a community historically perpetuating itself, a multitude unified by a single idea, which is the will to existence and to power: consciousness of itself, personality.

10. This higher personality is truly the nation in so far as it is the State. It is not the nation that generates the State, as according to the old naturalistic concept which served as the basis of the political theories of the national States of the nineteenth century. Rather the nation is created by the State, which gives to the people, conscious of its own moral unity, a will and therefore an effective existence. The right of a nation to independence derives not from a literary and ideal consciousness of its own being, still less from a more or less unconscious and inert acceptance of a *de facto* situation, but from an active consciousness, from a political will in action and ready to demonstrate its own rights: that is to say, from a state already coming into being. The State, in fact, as the universal ethical will, is the creator of right.

11. The nation as the State is an ethical reality which exists and lives in so far as it develops. To arrest its development is to kill it. Therefore the State is not only the authority which governs and gives the form of laws and the value of spiritual life to the wills of individuals, but it is also a power that makes its will felt abroad, making it known and respected, in other words, demonstrating the fact of its universality in all the necessary directions of its development. It is consequently organization and expansion, at least virtually. Thus it can be likened to the human will which

knows no limits to its development and realizes itself in testing its own limitlessness.

12. The Fascist State, the highest and most powerful form of personality, is a force, but a spiritual force, which takes over all the forms of the moral and intellectual life of man. It cannot therefore confine itself simply to the functions of order and supervision as Liberalism desired. It is not simply a mechanism which limits the sphere of the supposed liberties of the individual. It is the form, the inner standard and the discipline of the whole person; it saturates the will as well as the intelligence. Its principle, the central inspiration of the human personality living in the civil community, pierces into the depths and makes its home in the heart of the man of action as well as of the thinker, of the artist as well as of the scientist: it is the soul of the soul.

13. Fascism, in short, is not only the giver of laws and the founder of institutions, but the educator and promoter of spiritual life. It wants to remake, not the forms of human life, but its content, man, character, faith. And to this end it requires discipline and authority that can enter into the spirits of men and there govern unopposed. Its sign, therefore, is the Lictors' rods, the symbol of unity, of strength and justice.

(ii) Political and Social Doctrine

1. When in the now distant March of 1919 I summoned to Milan, through the columns of the *Popolo d' Italia,* my surviving supporters who had followed me since the constitution of the Fasces of Revolutionary Action, founded in January 1915, there was no specific doctrinal plan in my mind. I had known and lived through only one doctrine, that of the Socialism of 1903–4 up to the winter of 1914, almost ten years. My experience in this had been that of a follower and of a leader, but not that of a theoretician. My doctrine, even in that period, had been a doctrine of action. An unequivocal Socialism, universally accepted, did not exist after 1905, when the Revisionist Movement began in Germany under Bernstein and there was formed in opposition to that, in the see-saw of tendencies, an extreme revolutionary movement, which in Italy never emerged from the condition of mere words, whilst in Russian Socialism it was the prelude to Bolshevism. Reform, Revolution, Centralization — even the echoes of the terminology are now spent; whilst in the great river of Fascism are to be found the streams which had their source in Sorel, Peguy, in the Lagardelle of the *Mouvement Socialiste* and the groups of Italian Syndicalists, who between 1904 and 1914 brought a note of novelty

into Italian Socialism, which by that time had been devitalized and drugged by fornication with Giolitti, in *Pagine Libere* of Olivetti, *La Lupa* of Orano and *Divenire Sociale* of Enrico Leone.

In 1919, at the end of the War, Socialism as a doctrine was already dead: it existed only as hatred, it had still only one possibility, especially in Italy, that of revenge against those who had wished for the War and who should be made to expiate it. The *Popolo d' Italia* expressed it in its sub-title — "The Newspaper of Combatants and Producers." The word "producers" was already the expression of a tendency. Fascism was not given out to the wet nurse of a doctrine elaborated beforehand round a table: it was born of the need for action; it was not a party, but in its first two years it was a movement against all parties. The name which I gave to the organization defined its characteristics. Nevertheless, whoever rereads, in the now crumpled pages of the time, the account of the constituent assembly of the *Fasci italiani di Combattimento* will not find a doctrine, but a series of suggestions, of anticipations, of admonitions, which when freed from the inevitable vein of contingency, were destined later, after a few years, to develop into a series of doctrinal attitudes which made of Fascism a self-sufficient political doctrine able to face all others, both past and present. "If the bourgeoisie," I said at that time, "thinks to find in us a lightning-conductor, it is mistaken. We must go forward in opposition to Labour. . . . We want to accustom the working classes to being under a leader, to convince them also that it is not easy to direct an industry or a commercial undertaking successfully. . . . We shall fight against technical and spiritual retrogression. . . . The successors of the present regime still being undecided, we must not be unwilling to fight for it. We must hasten; when the present regime is superseded, we must be the ones to take its place. The right of succession belongs to us because we pushed the country into the War and we lead it to victory. The present method of political representation cannot be sufficient for us, we wish for a direct representation of individual interests. . . . It might be said against this programme that it is a return to the corporations. It doesn't matter! . . . I should like, nevertheless, the Assembly to accept the claims of national syndicalism from the point of view of economics. . . ."

It is not surprising that from the first day in the Piazza San Sepolero there should resound the word "Corporation" which was destined in the course of the revolution to signify one of the legislative and social creations at the base of the regime?

2. The years preceding the March on Rome were years during which the necessity of action did not tolerate enquiries or complete elaborations

of doctrine. Battles were being fought in the cities and villages. There
were discussions, but — and this is more sacred and important — there
were deaths. People knew how to die. The doctrine — beautiful, well-
formed, divided into chapters and paragraphs and surrounded by a commentary — might be missing; but there was present something more
decisive to supplant it — Faith. Nevertheless, he who recalls the past with
the aid of books, articles, votes in Parliament, the major and the minor
speeches, he who knows how to investigate and weigh evidence, will find
that the foundations of the doctrine were laid while the battle was raging.
It was precisely in these years that Fascist thought armed itself, refined
itself, moving towards one organization of its own. The problems of the
individual and the State; the problems of authority and liberty; political
and social problems and those more specifically national; the struggle
against liberal, democratic, socialist, Masonic, demagogic doctrines was
carried on at the same time as the "punitive expeditions." But since the
"system" was lacking, adversaries ingenuously denied that Fascism had any
power to make a doctrine of its own, while the doctrine rose up, even
though tumultuously, at first under the aspect of a violent and dogmatic
negation, as happens to all ideas that break new ground, then under the
positive aspect of a constructive policy which, during the years 1926, 1927,
1928, was realized in the laws and institutions of the regime.

Fascism is to-day clearly defined not only as a regime but as a doctrine.
And I mean by this that Fascism to-day, self-critical as well as critical of
other movements, has an unequivocal point of view of its own, a criterion,
and hence an aim, in face of all the material and intellectual problems
which oppress the people of the world.

3. Above all, Fascism, in so far as it considers and observes the future
and the development of humanity quite apart from the political considerations of the moment, believes neither in the possibility nor in the utility
of perpetual peace. It thus repudiates the doctrine of Pacifism — born of
a renunciation of the struggle and an act of cowardice in the face of
sacrifice. War alone brings up to their highest tension all human energies
and puts the stamp of nobility upon the peoples who have the courage
to meet it. All other trials are substitutes, which never really put a man
in front of himself in the alternative of life and death. A doctrine, therefore, which begins with a prejudice in favour of peace is foreign to
Fascism; as are foreign to the spirit of Fascism, even though acceptable by
reason of the utility which they might have in given political situations,
all internationalistic and socialistic systems which, as history proves, can
be blown to the winds when emotional, idealistic and practical movements

storm the hearts of peoples. Fascism carries over this anti-pacifist spirit even into the lives of individuals. The proud motto of the *Squadrista*, "Me ne frego," written on the bandages of a wound is an act of philosophy which is not only stoical, it is the epitome of a doctrine that is not only political: it is education for combat, the acceptance of the risks which it brings; it is a new way of life for Italy. Thus the Fascist accepts and loves life, he knows nothing of suicide and despises it; he looks on life as duty, ascent, conquest: life which must be noble and full: lived for oneself, but above all for those others near and far away, present and future.

4. The "demographic" policy of the regime follows from these premises. Even the Fascist does in fact love his neighbour, but this "neighbour" is not for him a vague and ill-defined concept; love for one's neighbour does not exclude necessary educational severities, and still less differentiations and distances. Fascism rejects universal concord, and, since it lives in the community of civilized peoples, it keeps them vigilantly and suspiciously before its eyes, it follows their states of mind and the changes in their interests and it does not let itself be deceived by temporary and fallacious appearances.

5. Such a conception of life makes Fascism the precise negation of that doctrine which formed the basis of the so-called Scientific or Marxian Socialism: the doctrine of historical Materialism, according to which the history of human civilizations can be explained only as the struggle of interest between the different social groups and as arising out of change in the means and instruments of production. That economic improvements — discoveries of raw materials, new methods of work, scientific inventions — should have an importance of their own, no one denies, but that they should suffice to explain human history to the exclusion of all other factors is absurd: Fascism believes, now and always, in holiness and in heroism, that is in acts in which no economic motive — remote or immediate — plays a part. With this negation of historical materialism, according to which men would be only by-products of history, who appear and disappear on the surface of the waves while in the depths the real directive forces are at work, there is also denied the immutable and irreparable "class struggle" which is the natural product of this economic conception of history, and above all it is denied that the class struggle can be the primary agent of social changes. Socialism, being thus wounded in these two primary tenets of its doctrine, nothing of it is left save the sentimental aspiration — old as humanity — towards a social order in which the sufferings and the pains of the humblest folk could be alleviated. But here Fascism rejects the concept of an economic "happiness" which

would be realized socialistically and almost automatically at a given moment of economic evolution by assuring to all a maximum prosperity. Fascism denies the possibility of the materialistic conception of "happiness" and leaves it to the economists of the first half of the eighteenth century; it denies, that is, the equation of prosperity with happiness, which would transform men into animals with one sole preoccupation: that of being well-fed and fat, degraded in consequence to a merely physical existence.

6. After Socialism, Fascism attacks the whole complex of democratic ideologies and rejects them both in their theoretical premises and in their applications or practical manifestations. Fascism denies that the majority, through the mere fact of being a majority, can rule human societies; it denies that this majority can govern by means of a periodical consultation; it affirms the irremediable, fruitful and beneficent inequality of men, who cannot be levelled by such a mechanical and extrinsic fact as universal suffrage. By democratic regimes we mean those in which from time to time the people is given the illusion of being sovereign, while true effective sovereignty lies in other, perhaps irresponsible and secret, forces. Democracy is a regime without a king, but with very many kings, perhaps more exclusive, tyrannical and violent than one king even though a tyrant. This explains why Fascism, although before 1922 for reasons of expediency it made a gesture of republicanism, renounced it before the March on Rome, convinced that the question of the political forms of a State is not pre-eminent to-day, and that studying past and present monarchies, past and present Republics it becomes clear that monarchy and republic are not to be judged *sub specie aeternitatis*, but represent forms in which the political evolution, the history, the tradition, the psychology of a given country are manifested. Now Fascism overcomes the antithesis between monarchy and republic which retarded the movements of democracy, burdening the former with every defect and defending the latter as the regime of perfection. Now it has been seen that there are inherently reactionary and absolutistic republics, and monarchies that welcome the most daring political and social innovations.

7. "Reason, Science," said Renan (who was inspired before Fascism existed) in one of his philosophical Meditations, "are products of humanity, but to expect reason directly from the people and through the people is a chimera. It is not necessary for the existence of reason that everybody should know it. In any case, if such an initiation should be made, it would not be made by means of base democracy, which apparently must lead to the extinction of every difficult culture, and every

higher discipline. The principle that society exists only for the prosperity and the liberty of the individuals who compose it does not seem to conform with the plans of nature, plans in which the species alone is taken into consideration and the individual seems to be sacrificed. It is strongly to be feared lest the last word of democracy thus understood (I hasten to say that it can also be understood in other ways) would be a social state in which a degenerate mass would have no other care than to enjoy the ignoble pleasures of vulgar men."

Thus far Renan. Fascism rejects in democracy the absurd conventional lie of political equalitarianism clothed in the dress of collective irresponsibility and the myth of happiness and indefinite progress. But if democracy can be understood in other ways, that is, if democracy means not to relegate the people to the periphery of the State, then Fascism could be defined as an "organized, centralized, authoritarian democracy."

8. In face of Liberal doctrines, Fascism takes up an attitude of absolute opposition both in the field of politics and in that of economics. It is not necessary to exaggerate — merely for the purpose of present controversies — the importance of Liberalism in the past century, and to make of that which was one of the numerous doctrines sketched in that century a religion of humanity for all times, present and future. Liberalism flourished for no more than some fifteen years. It was born in 1830, as a reaction against the Holy Alliance that wished to drag Europe back to what it had been before 1789, and it had its year of splendour in 1848 when even Pius IX was a Liberal. Immediately afterwards the decay set in. If 1848 was a year of light and of poetry, 1849 was a year of darkness and of tragedy. The Republic of Rome was destroyed by another Republic, that of France. In the same year Marx launched the gospel of the religion of Socialism with the famous *Communist Manifesto*. In 1851 Napoleon III carried out his unliberal *coup d'état* and ruled over France until 1870, when he was dethroned by a popular revolt, but as a consequence of a military defeat which ranks among the most resounding that history can relate. The victor was Bismarck, who never knew the home of the religion of liberty or who were its prophets. It is symptomatic that a people of high culture like the Germans should have been completely ignorant of the religion of liberty during the whole of the nineteenth century. It was, there, no more than a parenthesis, represented by what has been called the "ridiculous Parliament of Frankfort" which lasted only a season. Germany has achieved her national unity outside the doctrines of Liberalism, against Liberalism, a doctrine which seems foreign to the German soul, a soul essentially monarchical, whilst Liberalism is the historical and logical be-

ginning of anarchism. The stages of German unity are the three wars of 1864, 1866 and 1870, conducted by "Liberals" like Moltke and Bismarck. As for Italian unity, Liberalism has had in it a part absolutely inferior to the share of Mazzini and of Garibaldi, who were not Liberals. Without the intervention of the unliberal Napoleon we should not have gained Lombardy, and without the help of the unliberal Bismarck at Sadowa and Sedan, very probably we should not have gained Venice in 1866; and in 1870 we should not have entered Rome. From 1870–1915 there occurs the period in which the very priests of the new creed had to confess the twilight of their religion: defeated as it was by decadence in literature, by activism in practice. Activism: that is to say, Nationalism, Futurism, Fascism. The "Liberal" century, after having accumulated an infinity of Gordian knots, tried to untie them by the hecatomb of the World War. Never before has any religion imposed such a cruel sacrifice. Were the gods of Liberalism thirsty for blood? Now Liberalism is about to close the doors of its deserted temples because the peoples feel that its agnosticism in economics, its indifferentism in politics and in morals, would lead, as they have led, the States to certain ruin. In this way one can understand why all the political experiences of the contemporary world are anti-Liberal, and it is supremely ridiculous to wish on that account to class them outside of history; as if history were a hunting ground reserved to Liberalism and its professors, as if Liberalism were the definitive and no longer surpassable message of civilization.

9. But the Fascist repudiations of Socialism, Democracy, Liberalism must not make one think that Fascism wishes to make the world return to what it was before 1789, the year which has been indicated as the year of the beginning of the liberal-democratic age. One does not go backwards. The Fascist doctrine has not chosen De Maistre as its prophet. Monarchical absolutism is a thing of the past and so also is every theocracy. So also feudal privileges and division into impenetrable and isolated castes have had their day. The theory of Fascist authority has nothing to do with the police State. A party that governs a nation in a totalitarian way is a new fact in history. References and comparisons are not possible. Fascism takes over from the ruins of Liberal Socialistic democratic doctrines those elements which still have a living value. It preserves those that can be called the established facts of history, it rejects all the rest, that is to say the idea of a doctrine which holds good for all times and all peoples. If it is admitted that the nineteenth century has been the century of Socialism, Liberalism and Democracy, it does not follow that the twentieth must also be the century of Liberalism, Socialism and Democracy. Political

doctrines pass; peoples remain. It is to be expected that this century may be that of authority, a century of the "Right," a Fascist century. If the nineteenth was the century of the individual (Liberalism means individualism) it may be expected that this one may be the century of "collectivism" and therefore the century of the State. That a new doctrine should use the still vital elements of other doctrines is perfectly logical. No doctrine is born quite new, shining, never before seen. No doctrine can boast of an absolute "originality." It is bound, even if only historically, to other doctrines that have been, and to develop into other doctrines that will be. Thus the scientific socialism of Marx is bound to the Utopian Socialism of the Fouriers, the Owens and the Saint-Simons; thus the Liberalism of the nineteenth century is connected with the whole "Enlightenment" of the eighteenth century. Thus the doctrines of democracy are bound to the *Encyclopédie*. Every doctrine tends to direct the activity of men towards a determined objective; but the activity of man reacts upon the doctrine, transforms it, adapts it to new necessities or transcends it. The doctrine itself, therefore, must be, not words, but an act of life. Hence, the pragmatic veins in Fascism, its will to power, its will to be, its attitude in the face of the fact of "violence" and of its own courage.

10. The keystone of Fascist doctrine is the conception of the State, of its essence, of its tasks, of its ends. For Fascism the State is an absolute before which individuals and groups are relative. Individuals and groups are "thinkable" in so far as they are within the State. The Liberal State does not direct the interplay and the material and spiritual development of the groups, but limits itself to registering the results; the Fascist State has a consciousness of its own, a will of its own, on this account it is called an "ethical" State. In 1929, at the first quinquennial assembly of the regime, I said: "For Fascism, the State is not the night-watchman who is concerned only with the personal security of the citizens; nor is it an organization for purely material ends, such as that of guaranteeing a certain degree of prosperity and a relatively peaceful social order, to achieve which a council of administration would be sufficient, nor is it a creation of mere politics with no contact with the material and complex reality of the lives of individuals and the life of peoples. The State, as conceived by Fascism and as it acts, is a spiritual and moral fact because it makes concrete the political, juridical, economic organization of the nation and such an organization is, in its origin and in its development, a manifestation of the spirit. The State is the guarantor of internal and external security, but it is also the guardian and the transmitter of the spirit of the people as it has been elaborated through the centuries in language, custom, faith. The

State is not only present, it is also past, and above all future. It is the State which, transcending the brief limit of individual lives, represents the immanent conscience of the nation. The forms in which States express themselves change, but the necessity of the State remains. It is the State which educates citizens for civic virtue, makes them conscious of their mission, calls them to unity; harmonizes their interests in justice; hands on the achievements of thought in the sciences, the arts, in law, in human solidarity; it carries men from the elementary life of the tribe to the highest human expression of power which is Empire; it entrusts to the ages the names of those who died for its integrity or in obedience to its laws; it puts forward as an example and recommends to the generations that are to come the leaders who increased its territory and the men of genius who gave it glory. When the sense of the State declines and the disintegrating and centrifugal tendencies of individuals and groups prevail, national societies move to their decline."

11. From 1929 up to the present day these doctrinal positions have been strengthened by the whole economico-political evolution of the world. It is the State alone that grows in size, in power. It is the State alone that can solve the dramatic contradictions of capitalism. What is called the crisis cannot be overcome except by the State, within the State. Where are the shades of the Jules Simons who, at the dawn of liberalism, proclaimed that "the State must strive to render itself unnessary and to prepare for its demise"; of the MacCullochs who, in the second half of the last century, affirmed that the State must abstain from too much governing? And faced with the continual, necessary and inevitable interventions of the State in economic affairs what would the Englishman Bentham now say, according to whom industry should have asked of the State only to be left in peace? Or the German Humboldt, according to whom the "idle" State must be considered the best? It is true that the second generation of liberal economists was less extremist than the first, and already Smith himself opened, even though cautiously, the door to State intervention in economics. But when one says liberalism, one says the individual; when one says Fascism, one says the State. But the Fascist State is unique; it is an original creation. It is not reactionary, but revolutionary in that it anticipates the solutions of certain universal problems. These problems are no longer seen in the same light: in the sphere of politics they are removed from party rivalries, from the supreme power of parliament, from the irresponsibility of assemblies; in the sphere of economics they are removed from the sphere of the syndicates' activities — activities that were ever widening their scope and increasing their power both on the workers'

side and on the employers' — removed from their struggles and their designs; in the moral sphere they are divorced from ideas of the need for order, discipline and obedience, and lifted into the plane of the moral commandments of the fatherland. Fascism desires the State to be strong, organic and at the same time founded on a wide popular basis. The Fascist State has also claimed for itself the field of economics and, through the corporative, social and educational institutions which it has created, the meaning of the State reaches out to and includes the farthest off-shoots; and within the State, framed in their respective organizations, there revolve all the political, economic and spiritual forces of the nation. A State founded on millions of individuals who recognize it, feel it, are ready to serve it, is not the tyrannical State of the medieval lord. It has nothing in common with the absolutist States that existed either before or after 1789. In the Fascist State the individual is not suppressed, but rather multiplied, just as in a regiment a soldier is not weakened but multiplied by the number of his comrades. The Fascist State organizes the nation, but it leaves sufficient scope to individuals; it has limited useless or harmful liberties and has preserved those that are essential. It cannot be the individual who decides in this matter, but only the State.

12. The Fascist State does not remain indifferent to the fact of religion in general and to that particular positive religion which is Italian Catholicism. The State has no theology, but it has an ethic. In the Fascist State religion is looked upon as one of the deepest manifestations of the spirit; it is, therefore, not only respected, but defended and protected. The Fascist State does not create a "God" of its own, as Robespierre once, at the height of the Convention's foolishness, wished to do; nor does it vainly seek, like Bolshevism, to expel religion from the minds of men; Fascism respect the God of the ascetics, of the saints, of the heroes, and also God as seen and prayed to by the simple and primitive heart of the people.

13. The Fascist State is a will to power and to government. In it the tradition of Rome is an idea that has force. In the doctrine of Fascism Empire is not only a territorial, military or mercantile expression, but spiritual or moral. One can think of an empire, that is to say a nation that directly or indirectly leads other nations, without needing to conquer a single square kilometre of territory. For Fascism the tendency to Empire, that is to say, to the expansion of nations, is a manifestation of vitality; its opposite, staying at home, is a sign of decadence: peoples who rise or re-rise are imperialist, peoples who die are renunciatory. Fascism is the doctrine that is most fitted to represent the aims, the states of mind,

of a people, like the Italian people, rising again after many centuries of abandonment or slavery to foreigners. But Empire calls for discipline, co-ordination of forces, duty and sacrifice; this explains many aspects of the practical working of the regime and the direction of many of the forces of the State and the necessary severity shown to those who would wish to oppose this spontaneous and destined impulse of the Italy of the twentieth century, to oppose it in the name of the superseded ideologies of the nineteenth, repudiated wherever great experiments of political and social transformation have been courageously attempted: especially where, as now, peoples thirst for authority, for leadership, for order. If every age has its own doctrine, it is apparent from a thousand signs that the doctrine of the present age is Fascism. That it is a doctrine of life is shown by the fact that it has resuscitated a faith. That this faith has conquered minds is proved by the fact that Fascism has had its dead and its martyrs.

Fascism henceforward has in the world the universality of all of those doctrines which, by fulfilling themselves, have significance in the history of the human spirit.

THE SCIENTIFIC BASIS OF FASCISM

by Corrado Gini *

A few years ago, political scientists would hardly have ventured even to imagine the existence, among our civilized countries, of a government which would not hesitate to place limitations upon any of the liberties of the individual that had been regarded from the beginning of the last century as a sacred heritage of human individuality; a government which would concentrate the effective control of a great part of public power in the hands of few, or of a single person, so as to give almost the impression of a dictatorship; a government which would propose to reform the constitutional and administrative organization of the state, openly char-

* Corrado Gini, 'The Scientific Basis of Fascism," *Political Science Quarterly*, Volume 42 (New York: 1927), pp. 99–115. By permission of the Academy of Political Science.

acterizing its action in doing so as revolutionary; a government, moreover, which would not shrink from proclaiming itself as representative of the minority of the nation and which would announce its intention to win the consent of the majority by the exercise of force. If the Fascist party, resting on such principles, has attained to power, and thereafter has succeeded not only in maintaining itself, but in strengthening its position and in acquiring the support of large elements even outside of Italy, is not this fact a demonstration that the premises which the scientific world adopts as the basis of political theory and political practice are at least incomplete, if not inexact, in so far as they fail to meet the exigencies of certain situations which can occur in the lives of nations?

The first, perhaps, of these premises, and the one which appears the most obvious, is that the government should rest upon the consent of the majority of the citizens and interpret the will of that majority. To-day it would be difficult to deny that the Fascist government enjoys the support of the great majority of the Italian population; but there certainly have been periods, or at least one period, in which that administration did not possess the support of such a majority.

On the other hand, at times when many could have believed that there was no basis for doubt on the subject, the head of the administration, and of the Fascist party, did not hesitate to declare that he was accumulating the necessary force in entire confidence of acquiring the consent of the majority little by little in the future. His expression of his confidence in such terms revealed his assumption that he did not possess it at the time. Again, at times when there was more foundation for doubt concerning the extent of the support of the majority, important spokesmen of the Fascist party proclaimed, amid the applause of the Black Shirts, that the Fascists were disposed to fight and die rather than relinquish power. The impression of objective persons was that those favorable to the Fascist regime constituted, at a given moment, a genuine minority, but a minority ready to die for their chosen cause, while the majority, composed of elements more or less openly opposed to the Fascist regime, did not manifest any comparable interest in the contest.

In this last statement there is, I believe, a basis for criticism of the postulate indicated as the first of those ordinarily set up. That postulate takes for granted — if you examine it carefully — that the majority and the minority which take shape in connection with various questions manifest in the solution of those questions an interest, if not identical with their own magnitude, at least in the same order of magnitude; this, I suggest, is taken for granted not with respect to particular individuals, but with regard to the average of the majority or minority. If we accept the foregoing interpretation as correct, the postulate which we may call that of the right of the majority may be generalized and transformed into the postulate of the paramountcy of interests, according to which the government is to be administered by the part of the population which represents the prevailing interests.

In the ordinary political life of a people, the hypothesis of a corresponding order of magnitude of the interest which the majority and the minority, on the average, manifest in bringing particular questions to solutions seems acceptable; and this justifies the adoption of the postulate of the majority as the basis of the ordinary political life of the nation. . . .

The existence of a government in the hands of the minority is not, after all, when carefully analyzed, in antithesis to the liberal concept of political life, neither as a *means* in so far as the minority government represents the results of the free action of the citizenry, nor, on the other hand, as a *result*, in so far as the minority government satisfies the prevailing interests. But a more obvious gap existed between the liberal theory and the nationalistic theory which was gradually adopted by the Fascist party; and this irreconcilability was destined to show itself very early. The liberal theory assumes that society consists of an aggregate of individuals who must look after their own interests and it regards the state as an emanation of the individual wills intended to eliminate the conflicts between the interests of individuals. The nationalistic theory, on the contrary, views society as a true and distinct organism of a rank superior to that of the individuals who compose it, an organism endowed with a life of its own and with interests of its own. These interests result from the coordination of the desires for the time being of the current generation together with the interests of all the future generations which are to constitute the future life of the nation. Often enough these are in harmony one with the other, but occasionally the interests of future generations are opposed to those of the present generation, and in any case they may differ notably, if not in direction, at least in intensity. The agency destined to give effect to these higher interests of society is the state, sacrificing, wherever necessary, the interests of the individual and operating in opposition to the will of the present generation.

Hence the concept of the government as an agency to which is entrusted a mission of historical character, a mission which summarizes its very reason for existence. It is an agency, not for the changeable wishes of numerical majorities or of major interests, but rather for the effectuation of a program corresponding to the interests of the national organism.

In consequence, therefore, there is the tendency to free the administration from the constant control of parliamentary majorities. Once the program of the administration is approved, the administration henceforth derives its authority directly from the program itself and cannot permit others to interfere with it in giving effect to the program. The justification of measures of restraint upon individual liberties follows from this point of view, although these measures may be opposed to the desire of the majority or, theoretically, of even the entire body of citizens, when such measures of restraint are thought to be necessary in order to give effect to a program identified with the interests of a nation.

The concept which I have outlined briefly seems to be in harmony with that of the Conservative party and especially that of the Conservative branch of the Popular party in so far as the latter sees in certain institutions — such as those of private property, the family, and the Church — cohesive social forces which must be maintained regardless of the individual wishes of particular citizens. It is not surprising that the supporters of these principles who had been identified with the Liberal and Popular parties in the political struggles of recent years should have abandoned the last-named parties in order to remain favorable to Fascism.

This concept has also points of contact with the Socialist concept in that both assume the ideal of a collectivity superior to the interests of the individuals composing it. On the other hand, Fascism in no sense whatever withholds due recognition of the social importance and individual rights of the laboring classes. On the contrary, Fascism sees in them the living forces of the nation destined to renew the upper classes of society in the course of the ceaseless shift which goes on among the constituent elements of the national organism.

The essential difference between Fascism and the Socialistic current of thought, which has drifted off from the original programs of Communism and Collectivism, consists to-day in the concept of organic unity to which the interest of the individual must be subordinated. The Fascists perceive this unity in the nation, while the Socialists recognize it, at least theoretically — even at the cost of sacrificing their native land — in the larger human society.

This contrast explains why a fairly large part, if not, indeed, the very nucleus, of the Fascist movement has been built up of ex-Socialists who abandoned their party because of, or in consequence of, the war. This observation is particularly true of the younger element in the Socialistic party, including young men of a practical turn, often restless in temperament, who had rallied to the Socialist party not so much because of its positive economic program, as because of its negative program of protest against the aimless individualism of the Liberal regime, and who found in Fascism the means for effectuating their desire to take a part and to reconstruct. It was this element of Socialist origin — to which, as is well known, the head of the party himself belonged — which gave tone to the Fascist program and distinguished it from the position of the former Nationalist party, a position more theoretical than practical in character.

And in a sense this explains the attitude of the Fascist party towards international or supra-national organisms such as the League of Nations, the International Labour Office, and the like. It is an attitude of natural aversion from organisms tending to place limits upon the free action of the national organism, and, consequently, in a certain sense actually to weaken that organism. On this basis is to be explained the effort not to extend one iota beyond what is necessary the function of such international organisms or the participation of the national government in their proceedings.

The nationalist theories had as their fundamental basis the organic concept of society. Naturally, the acceptance of these theories was destined to bring about the discussion of organic representation which, both before and shortly after the war, had many supporters in Italy and abroad and which had recently been given some effect in the national economic councils of certain countries. This problem was one of the principal matters assigned by the Italian government to a commission of eighteen members, men engaged in public affairs and professors of law and social sciences. The commission was appointed with instructions to prepare for the government a draft of the legislative reforms to be introduced into the organic structure of the state. The majority of the commission favored the introduction into the Parliament of organic representation based upon professional corporations or syndicates. The authorities of the administration accepted the proposal in the form which the writer had the honor of suggesting, to the effect that the organic representation should be provided for in the Senate, which thus would be intended to become elective in part. Without entering upon a discussion of the details which this reform is to embody, it is perhaps worth while to emphasize the fundamental reason for introducing into the country's legislative machinery organic representation supplementary to individual representation, which to-day rests upon a geographic basis in most countries. I may be permitted at this point to quote the opening paragraphs of the report wherein I had the honor to submit to the government my proposals in this connection.

The principle that all citizens, so far as they possess legal capacity to do so, may participate with equal suffrage rights in the political life of the state — the principle which is at the very basis of universal suffrage — fits in with the concept of the state as a means of satisfying the individual aims of citizens. If, indeed, the action of the state possesses an *absolute* importance which varies with the individuals belonging to the several categories of the population, particularly in proportion to their respective wealth, it cannot, on the other hand, he said that the action of the state assumes a *relative* importance systematically different in the lives of those individuals. The poor man's vital necessity for positive action on the part of the state is no less than that of the rich man and in this sense the action of the state cannot be regarded as less important for the poor than for the rich.

But, on the other hand, when the state is regarded as an entity, that is, as an organism standing apart with its own objects and its own requirements, and when individuals are regarded as means to satisfy such objects and such requirements, it is natural that individuals be called upon to participate in the political life of the nation in no other proportion than that of the importance which they assume in the life of the state.

The two points of view have in fact always made themselves effective in the political organization of the state, offsetting each other to some extent. It is easy to understand, however, why the second point of view should come little by little to be emphasized more definitely according as the organization of the state is buttresesd in consequence of the extension of its functions, all the more since, in the exercise of the functions more recently assumed, it is easily possible that the object of the state should differ from the simple sum of the aims and objects of the individuals which compose it. This last hypothesis is borne out with particular frequency in the field of political economy, which in recent years has come to absorb so large a part of the activity of the state; hence it is readily comprehensible why emphasis has been more and more placed upon the necessity for organic representation of the economic functions of the different categories of citizens supplementary to their individual political representation.

In the last paragraph of the foregoing quotation I have drawn attention to the intensification and expansion of the functions of the state. This is one of the manifestations, or rather a consequence, of the progressive organization of society. If, indeed, we may to-day speak appropriately of society as a true and distinct organism — that is to say a totality of elements mutually bound one to the others, existing in a state of equilibrium and possessing the qualities necessary for self-preservation and eventually for the restoration of equilibrium — this is something that probably could not be said with quite as much exactitude for past ages. With the increasing density of populations, the multiplication of all the means of communication, the further subdivision of labor, the increasing refinement of the economic feeling of individuals, the sharpening of the faculty of foresight, it is hardly to be denied that the bonds among regions, among various classes and among individuals have been multiplied, the reactions are more effective and more rapid, equilibrium is, consequently, more nearly stable, and the restoration or readjustment is more rapid and more complete after some abnormal disturbance.

However much reason may exist for questioning whether the interests of the nation have always been properly interpreted and whether the intervention of public authority in economic life during and after the war has assumed exaggerated proportions, with perhaps prejudicial consequences, nevertheless it is undeniable that this intervention finds a partial justification in the increasingly strong tendency of modern society toward organization. . . .

There was no genuine and distinct reaction against the development of the Fascist Government on the part of the majority even though some measures of an unusual character produced at first an unfavorable impression in certain circles. The disorganization which had come to exist during the administrations which preceded Fascism made the great majority of the nation feel the necessity of a strong hand and a united will.

We have witnessed during these years in Italy one of those resumptions of power by a limited number of persons, which, historians tell us, occur from time to time in the life of nations; and it has been a resumption fortunately not requiring a civil war for its fulfilment. The exercise of sovereign and political authority, according to the observation of historians, appears to be concentrated at the outset in the hands of a single individual, and then, little by little, its privileges are expanded through a constantly larger group until it ends by being regarded as a right which theoretically belongs to all the individuals who constitute the nation. But after some time the democratic regime reveals symptoms of degeneration and a monarch, a tyrant or a dictator, or whatever name he may bear, steps in, and the cycle once more begins its course. . . .

The uncertain point in connection with the system of Fascism, now effectuated, is the lack of an objective standard whereby to interpret the interests of the nation. We must not conceal from ourselves the danger that a minority, which has come into power through the exercise of force or in consequence of unexpected developments, will go on maintaining itself by force and yet retain the intention of serving in good faith the true interests of the nation and purporting to carry out the program inspired by those interests, but not in reality corresponding to them. The fact that such an error of foresight may be committed in good faith does not make it any the less dangerous for the nation. On the other hand, it is an error much more easily committed when the number of persons actually endowed with power is very limited.

Nor is it to be denied that a state of affairs in which the prevailing interests are indeed the interests of the majority and fit in well with the higher interests of the nation is clearly to be preferred. But it is when agreement is lacking and not when it exists that the problem presents itself; and in such a case there can be no doubt as to the choice between the desires of the majority on the one hand, and on the other, the paramount interests of a minority which are in harmony with those higher interests of the nation. The objectivity and practical character of the standard suggested by the principle of the majority clearly cannot be a sufficient reason for maintaining that principle in circumstances wherein, as we have observed, its very basic premises do not exist.

It is perhaps in order to add that a government administered by a minority can be regarded in no other fashion than as a transitional solution. Either such a minority government succeeds — because of the excellence of its administration — in winning the consent of the majority, or it embitters the latter and arouses on its part a reaction which ends by making the interests of the majority prevail, and sooner or later it brings about the fall of the minority government. When the President of Council declared that he was accumulating force in anticipation of the consent of the majority, he clearly indicated that he was tending toward a government based upon consent as the position of national stability. It is the general impression that the Fascist Government has succeeded in this program and to-day possesses a great majority behind it in Italy.

In order that the danger to which I have alluded above may be less imminent and the winning of the consent of the majority easier, it is undoubtedly very desirable that the government should maintain the utmost contact with the people and take account of the impressions produced on them by governmental measures, not remaining deaf to suggestions emanating from the people. . . .

On the other hand, the success of a government in which the effective administration of authority is confined to one person or a few persons depends, in the last analysis, upon the quality of this person or of these few persons. The conviction is widely held in Italy that the Fascist regime could hardly have succeeded or persisted if it had not had at its head an individual of the exceptional qualities of Mussolini; and this explains the authority, almost unlimited in extent, which he possesses among the Fascists, and the respect which even those who are wholly opposed to his regime, or indifferent to it, have for him personally.

In conclusion, it seems to me that there can be no doubt that the Fascist experiment has had highly satisfactory results in Italy. Among those who have had an opportunity to compare the present situation of Italy with that which existed under the preceding administrations, there is no uncertainty whatever in this connection. The concentration of power in the hands of few men has permitted the revaluation of national ideals, the reestablishment abroad of the prestige of Italy, and the restoration of domestic order. This last achievement has greatly facilitated the economic recovery of the country, dating from the early part of 1922, and that has hastened the financial adjustment in progress. Moreover, the rapid solution of many pending problems has been made possible by the concentration of political authority and many reforms great and small have been effected, some long matters of deep study and others new — reforms which in the aggregate deserve favorable judgment.

But all this does not signify, as I see it, that the success of the Fascist government makes it desirable to attempt analogous experiments in other countries or in other conditions. It is an experiment which exceptional conditions have made necessary and the success of which was realized by an exceptional man, rather than a system of government suitable for all times and all countries. This does not mean that from the experiment itself there may not be learned lessons from which all countries may profit, with regard, for example, to the mutual relations and operation of legislative and executive agencies, with regard also to the organization of parties for purposes of organic representation, with regard finally to the use and abuse of individual liberties.

One other conclusion may be drawn by many from the foregoing considerations to the effect that, in the last analysis, force is what determines a political party's tenure of power. This conclusion, of course, is in no sense novel. It would not be correct if by "force" we understood merely the physical force derived from muscular strength. But if, on the other hand, we understand "force" in the larger sense to represent the power derived from the intellect no less than from the muscles, and, over and above that derived from the intellect, the force which is derived from the weight of interests and the intensity of feeling, the conclusion I have indicated is hardly to be doubted, I think. Originally electoral contests were assemblies of armed individuals generally aware of one another's equal power and consequently regarding themselves as equal, one to the other; they were willing, therefore, to refrain from struggling, and instead found it more practical to agree beforehand in allowing the victory to rest in the hands of the more numerous group, in the conviction that the latter would have won it in any event if the question were put to the decision of arms and not amicably settled. But where the reality of the situation has advanced far beyond the assumption of equal power, either because of diverse social qualities, for example, such as characterize the relations of white and colored races in the United States, or because of the difference in intensity of feeling and of interests such as characterizes the relations during recent years of the Nationalist and Social Democratic parties in Italy — in situations of this sort, there is no legal device or philosophical theory which can prevent the more powerful party from securing the upper hand and actually conquering the place of power, just as there is nothing except some external force which can prevent the body lighter than air from rising, and the body heavier than air from falling to the earth.

MEIN KAMPF

by Adolf Hitler *

I had always hated parliament, but not as an institution in itself. On the contrary, as a freedom-loving man I could not even conceive of any other possibility of government, for the idea of any sort of dictatorship would, in view of my attitude toward the House of Habsburg, have seemed to me a crime against freedom and all reason.

What contributed no little to this was that as a young man, in consequence of my extensive newspaper reading, I had, without myself realizing it, been inoculated with a certain admiration for the British Parliament, of which I was not easily able to rid myself. The dignity with which the

* The selections from Adolf Hitler's Mein Kampf (translated by Ralph Manheim), 1943, are reprinted by permission of and arrangement with Houghton Mifflin Company, the authorized publishers.

Lower House there fulfilled its tasks (as was so touchingly described in our press) impressed me immensely. Could a people have any more exalted form of self-government?

But for this very reason I was an enemy of the Austrian parliament. I considered its whole mode of conduct unworthy of the great example. To this the following was now added:

The fate of the Germans in the Austrian state was dependent on their position in the Reichsrat. Up to the introduction of universal and secret suffrage, the Germans had had a majority, though an insignificant one, in parliament. Even this condition was precarious, for the Social Democrats, with their unreliable attitude in national questions, always turned against German interests in critical matters affecting the Germans — in order not to alienate the members of the various foreign nationalities. Even in those days the Social Democracy could not be regarded as a German party. And with the introduction of universal suffrage the German superiority ceased even in a purely numerical sense. There was no longer any obstacle in the path of the further de-Germanization of the state.

For this reason my instinct of national self-preservation caused me even in those days to have little love for a representative body in which the Germans were always misrepresented rather than represented. Yet these were deficiencies which, like so many others, were attributable, not to the thing in itself, but to the Austrian state. I still believed that if a German majority were restored in the representative bodies, there would no longer be any reason for a principled opposition to them, that is, as long as the old state continued to exist at all.

These were my inner sentiments when for the first time I set foot in these halls as hallowed as they were disputed. For me, to be sure, they were hallowed only by the lofty beauty of the magnificent building. A Hellenic miracle on German soil!

How soon was I to grow indignant when I saw the lamentable comedy that unfolded beneath my eyes!

Present were a few hundred of these popular representatives who had to take a position on a question of most vital economic importance.

The very first day was enough to stimulate me to thought for weeks on end.

The intellectual content of what these men said was on a really depressing level, in so far as you could understand their babbling at all; for several of the gentlemen did not speak German, but their native Slavic languages or rather dialects. I now had occasion to hear with my own ears what previously I had known only from reading the newspapers. A wild gesticulating mass screaming all at once in every different key, presided over by a good-natured old uncle who was striving in the sweat of his brow to revive the dignity of the House by violently ringing his bell and alternating gentle reproofs with grave admonitions.

I couldn't help laughing.

A few weeks later I was in the House again. The picture was changed beyond recognition. The hall was absolutely empty. Down below everybody was asleep. A few deputies were in their places, yawning at one another; one was "speaking." A vice-president of the House was present, looking into the hall with obvious boredom.

The first misgivings arose in me. From now on, whenever time offered me the slightest opportunity, I went back and, with silence and attention, viewed whatever picture presented itself, listened to the speeches in so far as they were intelligible, studied the more or less intelligent faces of the elect of the peoples of this woe-begone state — and little by little formed my own ideas.

A year of this tranquil observation sufficed totally to change or eliminate my former view of the nature of this institution. My innermost position was no longer against the misshapen form which this idea assumed in Austria; no, by now I could no longer accept the parliament as such. Up till then I had seen the misfortune of the Austrian parliament in the absence of a German majority, now I saw that its ruination lay in the whole nature and essence of the institution as such.

A whole series of questions rose up in me.

I began to make myself familiar with the democratic principle of majority rule as the foundation of this whole institution, but devoted no less attention to the intellectual and moral values of these gentlemen, supposedly the elect of the nations, who were expected to serve this purpose.

Thus I came to know the institution and its representatives at once.

In the course of a few years, my knowledge and insight shaped a plastic model of that most dignified phenomenon of modern times: the parliamentarian. He began to impress himself upon me in a form which has never since been subjected to any essential change.

Here again the visual instruction of practical reality had prevented me from being stifled by a theory which at first sight seemed seductive to so many, but which none the less must be counted among the symptoms of human degeneration.

The Western democracy of today is the forerunner of Marxism which without it would not be thinkable. It provides this world plague with the culture in which its germs can spread. In its most extreme form, parliamentarianism created a "monstrosity of excrement and fire," * in which, however, sad to say, the "fire" seems to me at the moment to be burned out.

I must be more than thankful to Fate for laying this question before me while I was in Vienna, for I fear that in Germany at that time I would have found the answer too easily. For if I had first encountered this absurd institution known as "parliament" in Berlin, I might have fallen into the opposite fallacy, and not without seemingly good cause have sided with those who saw the salvation of the people and the Reich exclusively in furthering the power of the imperial idea, and who nevertheless were alien and blind at once to the times and the people involved.

In Austria this was impossible.

Here it was not so easy to go from one mistake to the other. If parliament was worthless, the Habsburgs were even more worthless — in no event, less so. To reject "parliamentarianism" was not enough, for the question still remained open: what then? The rejection and abolition of the Reichsrat would have left the House of Habsburg the sole governing force, a thought which, especially for me, was utterly intolerable.

The difficulty of this special case led me to a more thorough contemplation of the problem as such than would otherwise have been likely at such tender years.

What gave me most food for thought was the obvious absence of any responsibility in a single person.

The parliament arrives at some decision whose consequences may be ever so ruinous — nobody bears any responsibility for this, no one can be taken to account. For can it be called an acceptance of responsibility if, after an unparalleled catastrophe, the guilty government resigns? Or if the coalition changes, or even if parliament is itself dissolved?

Can a fluctuating majority of people ever be made responsible in any case?

Isn't the very idea of responsibility bound up with the individual?

But can an individual directing a government be made practically responsible for actions whose preparation and execution must be set exclusively to the account of the will and inclination of a multitude of men?

Or will not the task of a leading statesman be seen, not in the birth of a creative idea or plan as such, but rather in the art of making the brilliance of his projects intelligible to a herd of sheep and blockheads, and subsequently begging for their kind approval?

---

* "Spottgeburt aus Dreck und Feuer." Should be "von Dreck und Feuer." Goethe's Faust, Part 1, 5356: Faust to Mephistopheles.

Is it the criterion of the statesman that he should possess the art of persuasion in as high degree as that of political intelligence in formulating great policies or decisions? Is the incapacity of a leader shown by the fact that he does not succeed in winning for a certain idea the majority of a mob thrown together by more or less savory accidents?

Indeed, had this mob ever understood an idea before success proclaimed its greatness?

Isn't every deed of genius in this world a visible protest of genius against the inertia of the mass?

And what should the statesman do, who does not succeed in gaining the favor of this mob for his plans by flattery?

Should he buy it?

Or, in view of the stupidity of his fellow citizens, should he renounce the execution of the tasks which he has recognized to be vital necessities? Should he resign or should he remain at his post?

In such a case, doesn't a man of true character find himself in a hopeless conflict between knowledge and decency, or rather honest conviction?

Where is the dividing line between his duty toward the general public and his duty toward his personal honor?

Mustn't every true leader refuse to be thus degraded to the level of a political gangster?

And, conversely, mustn't every gangster feel that he is cut out for politics, since it is never he, but some intangible mob, which has to bear the ultimate responsibility?

Mustn't our principle of parliamentary majorities lead to the demolition of any idea of leadership?

Does anyone believe that the progress of this world springs from the mind of majorities and not from the brains of individuals?

Or does anyone expect that the future will be able to dispense with this premise of human culture?

Does it not, on the contrary, today seem more indispensable than ever?

By rejecting the authority of the individual and replacing it by the numbers of some momentary mob, the parliamentary principle of majority rule sins against the basic aristocratic principle of Nature, though it must be said that this view is not necessarily embodied in the present-day decadence of our upper ten thousand.

The devastation caused by this institution of modern parliamentary rule is hard for the reader of Jewish newspapers to imagine, unless he has learned to think and examine independently. It is, first and foremost, the cause of the incredible inundation of all political life with the most in-

ferior, and I mean the most inferior, characters of our time. Just as the
true leader will withdraw from all political activity which does not consist
primarily in creative achievement and work, but in bargaining and haggling for the favor of the majority, in the same measure this activity will
suit the small mind and consequently attract it.

The more dwarfish one of these present-day leather-merchants is in spirit
and ability, the more clearly his own insight makes him aware of the lamentable figure he actually cuts — that much more will he sing the praises
of a system which does not demand of him the power and genius of a
giant, but is satisfied with the craftiness of a village mayor, preferring in
fact this kind of wisdom to that of a Pericles. And this kind doesn't have
to torment himself with responsibility for his actions. He is entirely removed from such worry, for he well knows that, regardless what the result
of his "statesmanlike" bungling may be, his end has long been written in
the stars: one day he will have to cede his place to another equally great
mind, for it is one of the characteristics of this decadent system that the
number of great statesmen increases in proportion as the stature of the
individual decreases. With increasing dependence on parliamentary majorities it will inevitably continue to shrink, since on the one hand great
minds will refuse to be the stooges of idiotic incompetents and big-mouths,
and on the other, conversely, the representatives of the majority, hence of
stupidity, hate nothing more passionately than a superior mind.

For such an assembly of wise men of Gotham, it is always a consolation
to know that they are headed by a leader whose intelligence is at the level
of those present: this will give each one the pleasure of shining from time
to time — and, above all, if Tom can be master, what is to prevent Dick
and Harry from having their turn too?

This invention of democracy is most intimately related to a quality
which in recent times has grown to be a real disgrace, to wit, the cowardice
of a great part of our so-called "leadership." What luck to be able to hide
behind the skirts of a so-called majority in all decisions of any real importance!

Take a look at one of these political bandits. How anxiously he begs
the approval of the majority for every measure, to assure himself of the
necessary accomplices, so he can unload the responsibility at any time. And
this is one of the main reasons why this type of political activity is always
repulsive and hateful to any man who is decent at heart and hence courageous, while it attracts all low characters — and anyone who is unwilling
to take personal responsibility for his acts, but seeks a shield, is a cowardly
scoundrel. When the leaders of a nation consist of such vile creatures, the

results will soon be deplorable. Such a nation will be unable to muster the courage for any determined act; it will prefer to accept any dishonor, even the most shameful, rather than rise to a decision; for there is no one who is prepared of his own accord to pledge his person and his head for the execution of a dauntless resolve.

For there is one thing which we must never forget: in this, too, the majority can never replace the man. It is not only a representative of stupidity, but of cowardice as well. And no more than a hundred empty heads make one wise man will an heroic decision arise from a hundred cowards.

The less the responsibility of the individual leader, the more numerous will be those who, despite their most insignificant stature, feel called upon to put their immortal forces in the service of the nation. Indeed, they will be unable to await their turn; they stand in a long line, and with pain and regret count the number of those waiting ahead of them, calculating almost the precise hour at which, in all probability, their turn will come. Consequently, they long for any change in the office hovering before their eyes, and are thankful for any scandal which thins out the ranks ahead of them. And if some man is unwilling to move from the post he holds, this in their eyes is practically a breach of a holy pact of solidarity. They grow vindictive, and they do not rest until the impudent fellow is at last overthrown, thus turning his warm place back to the public. And, rest assured, he won't recover the position so easily. For as soon as one of these creatures is forced to give up a position, he will try at once to wedge his way into the "waiting-line" unless the hue and cry raised by the others prevents him. . . . The haggling and bargaining for the individual portfolios represented Western democracy of the first water. And the results corresponded to the principles applied. Particularly the change of individual personalities occurred in shorter and shorter terms, ultimately becoming a veritable chase. In the same measure, the stature of the "statesmen" steadily diminished until finally no one remained but that type of parliamentary gangster whose statesmanship could only be measured and recognized by their ability in pasting together the coalitions of the moment; in other words, concluding those pettiest of political bargains which alone demonstrate the fitness of these representatives of the people for practical work. . . .

But what attracted me no less was to compare the ability and knowledge of these representatives of the people and the tasks which awaited them. In this case, whether I liked it or not, I was impelled to examine more closely the intellectual horizon of these elect of the nations themselves, and in so doing, I could not avoid giving the necessary attention to the processes which lead to the discovery of these ornaments of our public life.

The way in which the real ability of these gentlemen was applied and placed in the service of the fatherland, in other words, the technical process of their activity — was also worthy of thorough study and investigation.

The more determined I was to penetrate these inner conditions, to study the personalities and material foundations with dauntless and penetrating objectivity, the more deplorable became my total picture of parliamentary life. Indeed, this is an advisable procedure in dealing with an institution which, in the person of its representatives, feels obliged to bring up "objectivity" in every second sentence as the only proper basis for every investigation and opinion. Investigate these gentlemen themselves and the laws of their sordid existence, and you will be amazed at the result.

There is no principle which, objectively considered, is as false as that of parliamentarianism.

Here we may totally disregard the manner in which our fine representatives of the people are chosen, how they arrive at their office and their new dignity. That only the tiniest fraction of them rise in fulfillment of a general desire, let alone a need, will at once be apparent to anyone who realizes that the political understanding of the broad masses is far from being highly enough developed to arrive at definite general political views of their own accord and seek out the suitable personalities.

The thing we designate by the word "public opinion" rests only in the smallest part on experience or knowledge which the individual has acquired by himself, but rather on an idea which is inspired by so-called "enlightenment," often of a highly persistent and obtrusive type.

Just as a man's denominational orientation is the result of upbringing, and only the religious need as such slumbers in his soul, the political opinion of the masses represents nothing but the final result of an incredibly tenacious and thorough manipulation of their mind and soul.

By far the greatest share in their political "education," which in this case is most aptly designated by the word "propaganda," falls to the account of the press. It is foremost in performing this "work of enlightenment" and thus represents a sort of school for grown-ups. This instruction, however, is not in the hands of the state, but in the claws of forces which are in part very inferior. In Vienna as a very young man I had the best opportunity to become acquainted with the owners and spiritual manufacturers of this machine for educating the masses. At first I could not help but be amazed at how short a time it took this great evil power within the state to create a certain opinion even where it meant totally falsifying profound desires and views which surely existed among the public. In a few days a ridiculous episode had become a significant state action, while, conversely, at the same time, vital problems fell a prey to public oblivion, or rather were simply filched from the memory and consciousness of the masses. . . .

These scum manufacture more than three quarters of the so-called "public opinion," from whose foam the parliamentarian Aphrodite arises. To give an accurate description of this process and depict it in all its false-hood and improbability, one would have to write volumes. But even if we disregard all this and examine only the given product along with its ac-tivity, this seems to me enough to make the objective lunacy of this institu-tion dawn on even the naïvest mind.

This human error, as senseless as it is dangerous, will most readily be understood as soon as we compare democratic parliamentarianism with a truly Germanic democracy.

The distinguishing feature of the former is that a body of, let us say five hundred men, or in recent times even women, is chosen and entrusted with making the ultimate decision in any and all matters. And so for practical purposes they alone are the government; for even if they do choose a cabinet which undertakes the external direction of the affairs of state, this is a mere sham. In reality this so-called government cannot take a step without first obtaining the approval of the general assembly. Conse-quently, it cannot be made responsible for anything, since the ultimate decision never lies with it, but with the majority of parliament. In every case it does nothing but carry out the momentary will of the majority. Its political ability can only be judged according to the skill with which it understands how either to adapt itself to the will of the majority or to pull the majority over to its side. Thereby it sinks from the heights of real government to the level of a beggar confronting the momentary majority. Indeed, its most urgent task becomes nothing more than either to secure the favor of the existing majority, as the need arises, or to form a majority with more friendly inclinations. If this succeeds, it may "govern" a little while longer; if it doesn't succeed, it can resign. The soundness of its pur-poses as such is beside the point.

For practical purposes, this excludes all responsibility.

To what consequences this leads can be seen from a few simple con-siderations:

The internal composition of the five hundred chosen representatives of the people, with regard to profession or even individual abilities, gives a picture as incoherent as it is usually deplorable. For no one can believe that these men elected by the nation are elect of spirit or even intelligence! It is to be hoped that no one will suppose that the ballots of an electorate which is anything else than brilliant will give rise to statesmen by the hundreds. Altogether we cannot be too sharp in condemning the absurd notion that geniuses can be born from general elections. In the first place, a nation only produces a real statesman once in a blue moon and not a hundred or more at once; and in the second place, the revulsion of the masses for every outstanding genius is positively instinctive. Sooner will a camel pass through a needle's eye than a great man be "discovered" by an election.

In world history the man who really rises above the norm of the broad average usually announces himself personally.

As it is, however, five hundred men, whose stature is to say the least modest, vote on the most important affairs of the nation, appoint governments which in every single case and in every special question have to get the approval of the exalted assembly, so that policy is really made by five hundred.

And that is just what it usually looks like.

But even leaving the genius of these representatives of the people aside, bear in mind how varied are the problems awaiting attention, in what widely removed fields solutions and decisions must be made, and you will realize how inadequate a governing institution must be which transfers the ultimate right of decision to a mass assembly of people, only a tiny fraction of which possess knowledge and experience of the matter to be treated. The most important economic measures are thus submitted to a forum, only a tenth of whose members have any economic education to show. This is nothing more nor less than placing the ultimate decision in a matter in the hands of men totally lacking in every prerequisite for the task.

The same is true of every other question. The decision is always made by a majority of ignoramuses and incompetents, since the composition of this institution remains unchanged while the problems under treatment extend to nearly every province of public life and would thereby presuppose a constant turn over in the deputies who are to judge and decide on them, since it is impossible to let the same persons decide matters of transportation as, let us say, a question of high foreign policy. Otherwise these men would all have to be universal geniuses such as we actually seldom encounter once in centuries. Unfortunately we are here confronted, for the most part, not with "thinkers," but with dilettantes as limited as they are conceited and inflated, intellectual *demi-monde* of the worst sort. And this is the source of the often incomprehensible frivolity with which these gentry speak and decide on things which would require careful meditation even in the greatest minds. Measures of the gravest significance for the future of a whole state, yes, of a nation, are passed as though a game of *schafkopf* or *tarock*,* which would certainly be better suited to their abilities, lay on the table before them and not the fate of a race. . . .

And thereby every practical responsibility can lie in the obligation of an individual and not in a parliamentary bull session.

Juxtaposed to this is the truly Germanic democracy characterized by the free election of a leader and his obligation fully to assume all responsibility for his actions and omissions. In it there is no majority vote on individual questions, but only the decision of an individual who must answer with his fortune and his life for his choice.

If it be objected that under such conditions scarcely anyone would be prepared to dedicate his person to so risky a task, there is but one possible answer:

Thank the Lord, Germanic democracy means just this: that any old climber or moral slacker cannot rise by devious paths to govern his national comrades,† but that, by the very greatness of the responsibility to be assumed, incompetents and weaklings are frightened off.

But if, nevertheless, one of these scoundrels should attempt to sneak in, we can find him more easily, and mercilessly challenge him: Out, cowardly scoundrel! Remove your foot, you are besmirching the steps; the front steps of the Pantheon of history are not for sneak-thieves, but for heroes!

PERSONALITY AND THE CONCEPTION OF THE FOLKISH STATE

The folkish National Socialist state sees its chief task in *educating and preserving the bearer of the state.* It is not sufficient to encourage the racial elements as such, to educate them and finally instruct them in the needs

---

* *Schafkopf* is a four-handed card-game widely played in Germany. *Tarock.* Three-handed card-game of Italian origin (*tarocco*), popular in Austria and southern Germany.

† "*Volksgenosse.*" Brockhaus defines: In contrast to the concept of citizen which is based on the idea of legal equality in the state, the designation for all members of the same national community (*Volksgemeinschaft*), especially those who form a working association in the service of the nation as a whole. As used by the National Socialists, it might be translated as "racial comrades." I have chosen the more neutral term "national comrades" because the National Socialists did not coin the term and it occurs frequently in the speeches of parliamentarians who were not even noted for their anti-Semitism.

of practical life; the state must also adjust its own organization to this task.

It would be lunacy to try to estimate the value of man according to his race, thus declaring war on the Marxist idea that men are equal, unless we are determined to draw the ultimate consequences. And the ultimate consequence of recognizing the importance of blood — that is, of the racial foundation in general — is the transference of this estimation to the individual person. In general, I must evaluate peoples differently on the basis of the race they belong to, and the same applies to the individual men within a national community. The realization that peoples are not equal transfers itself to the individual man within a national community, in the sense that men's minds cannot be equal, since here, too, the blood components, though equal in their broad outlines, are, in particular cases, subject to thousands of the finest differentiations.

The first consequence of this realization might at the same time be called the cruder one: an attempt to promote in the most exemplary way those elements within the national community that have been recognized as especially valuable from the racial viewpoint and to provide for their special increase.

This task is cruder because it can be recognized and solved almost mechanically. It is more difficult to recognize among the whole people the minds that are most valuable in the intellectual and ideal sense, and to gain for them that influence which not only is the due of these superior minds, but which above all is beneficial to the nation. This sifting according to capacity and ability cannot be undertaken mechanically; it is a task which the struggle of daily life unceasingly performs.

A philosophy of life which endeavors to reject the democratic mass idea and give this earth to the best people — that is, the highest humanity — must logically obey the same aristocratic principle within this people and make sure that the leadership and the highest influence in this people fall to the best minds. Thus, it builds, not upon the idea of the majority, but upon the idea of personality.

Anyone who believes today that a folkish National Socialist state must distinguish itself from other states only in a purely mechanical sense, by a superior construction of its economic life — that is, by a better balance between rich and poor, or giving broad sections of the population more right to influence the economic process, or by fairer wages by elimination of excessive wage differentials — has not gone beyond the most superficial aspect of the matter and has not the faintest idea of what we call a philosophy. All the things we have just mentioned offer not the slightest guaranty of continued existence, far less of any claim to greatness. A people which did not go beyond these really superficial reforms would not obtain the least guaranty of victory in the general struggle of nations. A movement which finds the content of its mission only in such a general leveling, assuredly just as it may be, will truly bring about no great and profound, hence real, reform of existing conditions, since its entire activity does not, in the last analysis, go beyond externals, and does not give the people that inner armament which enables it, with almost inevitable certainty I might say, to overcome in the end those weaknesses from which we suffer today.

To understand this more easily, it may be expedient to cast one more glance at the real origins and causes of human cultural development.

The first step which outwardly and visibly removed man from the animal was that of invention. Invention itself is originally based on the finding of stratagems and ruses, the use of which facilitates the life struggle with other beings, and is sometimes the actual prerequisite for its favorable course. These most primitive inventions do not yet cause the personality to appear with sufficient distinctness, because, of course, they enter the consciousness of the future, or rather the present, human observer, only as a mass phenomenon. Certain dodges and crafty measures which man, for example, can observe in the animal catch his eye only as a summary fact, and he is no longer in a position to establish or investigate their origin, but must simply content himself with designating such phenomena as "instinctive."

But in our case this last word means nothing at all. For anyone who believes in a higher development of living creatures must admit that every expression of their life urge and life struggle must have had a beginning; that *one* subject must have started it, and that subsequently such a phenomenon repeated itself more and more frequently and spread more and more, until at last it virtually entered the subconscious of all members of a given species, thus manifesting itself as an instinct.

This will be understood and believed more readily in the case of man. His first intelligent measures in the struggle with other beasts assuredly originate in the actions of individual, particularly able subjects. Here, too, the personality was once unquestionably the cause of decisions and acts which later were taken over by all humanity and regarded as perfectly self-evident. Just as any obvious military principle, which today has become, as it were, the basis of all strategy, originally owed its appearance to one absolutely distinct mind, and only in the course of many, perhaps even thousands of years, achieved universal validity and was taken entirely for granted.

Man complements this first invention by a second: he learns to place other objects and also living creatures in the service of his own struggle for self-preservation; and thus begins man's real inventive activity which today is generally visible. These material inventions, starting with the use of stone as a weapon and leading to the domestication of beasts, giving man artificial fire, and so on up to the manifold and amazing inventions of our day, show the individual creator the more clearly, the closer the various inventions lie to the present day, or the more significant and incisive they are. At all events, we know that all the material inventions we see about us are the result of the creative power and ability of the individual personality. And all these inventions in the last analysis help to raise man more and more above the level of the animal world and finally to remove him from it. Thus, fundamentally, they serve the continuous process of higher human development. But the very same thing which once, in the form of the simplest ruse, facilitated the struggle for existence of the man hunting in the primeval forest, again contributes, in the shape of the most brilliant scientific knowledge of the present era, to alleviate mankind's struggle for existence and to forge its weapons for the struggles of the future. All human thought and invention, in their ultimate effects, primarily serve man's struggle for existence on this planet, even when the so-called practical use of an invention or a discovery or a profound scientific insight into the essence of things is not visible at the moment. All these things together, by contributing to raise man above the living creatures surrounding him, strengthen him and secure his position, so that in every respect he develops into the dominant being on this earth.

Thus, all inventions are the result of an individual's work. All these individuals, whether intentionally or unintentionally, are more or less great benefactors of all men. Their work subsequently gives millions, nay, billions of human creatures, instruments with which to facilitate and carry out their life struggle.

If in the origin of our present material culture we always find individuals in the form of inventors, complementing one another and one building upon another, we find the same in the practice and execution of the things devised and discovered by the inventors. For all productive processes in turn must in their origin be considered equivalent to inventions, hence dependent on the individual. Even purely theoretical intellectual work, which in particular cases is not measurable, yet is the premise for all further material inventions, appears as the exclusive product of the individual person. It is not the mass that invents and not the majority that organizes or thinks, but in all things only and always the individual man, the person.

A human community appears well organized only if it facilitates the labors of these creative forces in the most helpful way and applies them in a manner beneficial to all. The most valuable thing about the invention itself, whether it lie in the material field or in the world of ideas, is primarily the inventor as a personality. Therefore, to employ him in a way benefiting the totality is the first and highest task in the organization of a national community. Indeed, the organization itself must be a realization of this principle. Thus, also, it is redeemed from the curse of mechanism and becomes a living thing. *It must itself be an embodiment of the endeavor to place thinking individuals above the masses, thus subordinating the latter to the former.*

Consequently, the organization must not only not prevent the emergence of thinking individuals from the mass; on the contrary it must in the highest degree make this possible and easy by the nature of its own being. In this it must proceed from the principle that the salvation of mankind has never lain in the masses, but in its creative minds, which must therefore really be regarded as benefactors of the human race. To assure them of the most decisive influence and facilitate their work is in the interest of the totality. Assuredly this interest is not satisfied, and is not served by the domination of the unintelligent or incompetent, in any case uninspired masses, but solely by the leadership of those to whom Nature has given special gifts for this purpose.

The selection of these minds, as said before, is primarily accomplished by the hard struggle for existence. Many break and perish, thus showing that they are not destined for the ultimate and in the end only a few appear to be chosen. In the fields of thought, artistic creation, even, in fact, of economic life, this selective process is still going on today, though, especially in the latter field, it faces a grave obstacle. The administration of the state and likewise the power embodied in the organized military might of the nation are also dominated by these ideas. Here, too, the idea of personality is everywhere dominant — its authority downward and its responsibility toward the higher personality above. Only political life has today completely turned away from this most natural principle. While all human culture is solely the result of the individual's creative activity, everywhere, and particularly in the highest *leadership* of the national community, the *principle of the value of the majority* appears decisive, and from that high place begins to gradually poison all life; that is, in reality to dissolve it. The destructive effect of the Jew's activity in other national bodies is basically attributable only to his eternal efforts to undermine the position of the personality in the host-peoples and to replace it by the mass. Thus, the organizing principle of Aryan humanity is replaced by the destructive principle of the Jew. He becomes "a ferment of decomposition" among peoples and races, and in the broader sense a dissolver of human culture.

Marxism presents itself as the perfection of the Jew's attempt to exclude the pre-eminence of personality in all fields of human life and replace it by the numbers of the mass. To this, in the political sphere, corresponds the parliamentary form of government, which, from the smallest germ cells of the municipality up to the supreme leadership of the Reich, we see in such disastrous operation, and in the economic sphere, the system of a trade-union movement which does not serve the real interests of the workers, but exclusively the destructive purposes of the international world Jew. In precisely the measure in which the economy is withdrawn from the influence of the personality principle and instead exposed to the influences and effects of the masses, it must lose its efficacy in serving all and benefiting all, and gradually succumb to a sure retrogression. All the shop organizations which, instead of taking into account the interests of their employees, strive to gain influence on production, serve the same purpose. They injure collective achievement, and thus in reality injure individual achievement. For the satisfaction of the members of a national body does not in the long run occur exclusively through mere theoretical phrases, but by the goods of daily life that fall to the individual and the ultimate resultant conviction that a national community in the sum of its achievement guards the interests of individuals.

It is of no importance whether Marxism, on the basis of its mass theory, seems capable of taking over and carrying on the economy existing at the moment. Criticism with regard to the soundness or unsoundness of this principle is not settled by the proof of its capacity to *administer* the existing order for the future, but exclusively by the proof that it can itself *create* a higher culture. Marxism might a thousand times take over the existing economy and make it continue to work under its leadership, but even success in this activity would prove nothing in the face of the fact that it would not be in a position, by applying its principle *itself*, to create the same thing which today it takes over in a finished state.

Of this Marxism has furnished practical proof. Not only that it has nowhere been able to found and create a culture by itself; actually it has not been able to continue the existing ones in accordance with its principles, but after a brief time has been forced to return to the ideas embodied in the personality principle, in the form of *concessions;* — even in its own organization it cannot dispense with these principles.

The folkish philosophy is basically distinguished from the Marxist philosophy by the fact that it not only recognizes the value of race, but with it the importance of the personality, which it therefore makes one of the pillars of its entire edifice. These are the factors which sustain its view of life.

If the National Socialist movement did not understand the fundamental importance of this basic realization, but instead were merely to perform superficial patchwork on the present-day state, or even adopt the mass standpoint as its own — then it would really constitute nothing but a party in competition with the Marxists; in that case, it would not possess the right to call itself a philosophy of life. If the social program of the movement consisted only in pushing aside the personality and replacing it by the masses, National Socialism itself would be corroded by the poison of Marxism, as is the case with our bourgeois parties.

The folkish state must care for the welfare of its citizens by recognizing in all and everything the importance of the value of personality, thus in all fields preparing the way for that highest measure of productive performance which grants to the individual the highest measure of participation.

And accordingly, the folkish state must free all leadership and especially the highest — that is, the political leadership — entirely from the parliamentary principle of majority rule — in other words, mass rule — and instead absolutely guarantee the right of the personality.

From this the following realization results:

The best state constitution and state form is that which, with the most unquestioned certainty, raises the best minds in the national community to leading position and leading influence.

But as, in economic life, the able men cannot be appointed from above, but must struggle through for themselves, and just as here the endless schooling, ranging from the smallest business to the largest enterprise, occurs spontaneously, with life alone giving the examinations, obviously political minds cannot be "discovered." Extraordinary geniuses permit of no consideration for normal mankind.

From the smallest community cell to the highest leadership of the entire Reich, the state must have the personality principle anchored in its organization.

There must be no majority decisions, but only responsible persons, and the word "council" must be restored to its original meaning. Surely every man will have advisers by his side, but *the decisions will be made by one man.*

The principle which made the Prussian army in its time into the most wonderful instrument of the German people must some day, in a transferred sense, become the principle of the construction of our whole state conception: *authority of every leader downward and responsibility upward.*

Even then it will not be possible to dispense with those corporations which today we designate as parliaments. But their councillors will then actually give counsel; responsibility, however, can and may be borne only by *one* man, and therefore only he alone may possess the authority and right to command.

Parliaments as such are necessary, because in them, above all, personalities to which special responsible tasks can later be entrusted have an opportunity gradually to rise up.

This gives the following picture:

The folkish state, from the township up to the Reich leadership, has no representative body which decides anything by the majority, but only *advisory bodies* which stand at the side of the elected leader, receiving their share of work from him, and in turn if necessary assuming unlimited responsibility in certain fields, just as on a larger scale the leader or chairman of the various corporations himself possesses.

As a matter of principle, the folkish state does not tolerate asking advice or opinions in special matters — say, of an economic nature — of men who, on the basis of their education and activity, can understand nothing of the subject. It, therefore, divides its representative bodies from the start into *political and professional chambers.*

In order to guarantee a profitable cooperation between the two, a special *senate* of the élite always stands over them.

In no chamber and in no senate does a vote ever take place. They are working institutions and not voting machines. The individual member has an advisory, but never a determining, voice. The latter is the exclusive privilege of the responsible chairman.

This principle — absolute responsibility unconditionally combined with absolute authority — will gradually breed an élite of leaders such as today, in this era of irresponsible parliamentarianism, is utterly inconceivable.

Thus, the political form of the nation will be brought into agreement with that law to which it owes its greatness in the cultural and economic field.

As regards the possibility of putting these ideas into practice I beg you not to forget that the parliamentary principle of democratic majority rule has by no means always dominated mankind, but on the contrary is to be found only in brief periods of history, which are always epochs of the decay of peoples and states.

But it should not be believed that such a transformation can be accomplished by purely theoretical measures from above, since logically it may not even stop at the state constitution, but must permeate all other legislation, and indeed all civil life. Such a fundamental change can and will only take place through a movement which is itself constructed in the spirit of these ideas and hence bears the future state within itself.

Hence the National Socialist movement should today adapt itself entirely to these ideas and carry them to practical fruition within its own organization, so that some day it may not only show the state these same guiding principles, but can also place the completed body of its own state at its disposal.

NAZI CONSPIRACY AND AGGRESSION *

JUDGMENT . . .

This indictment charges the defendants with crimes against peace by the planning, preparation, initiation, and waging of wars of aggression, which were also wars in violation of intentional treaties, agreements, and assurances; with war crimes; and with crimes against humanity. The defendants are also charged with participating in the formulation or execution of a common plan or conspiracy to commit all these crimes. . . .

THE COMMON PLAN OF CONSPIRACY AND AGGRESSIVE WAR

The Tribunal now turns to the consideration of the crimes against peace charged in the indictment. Count one of the indictment charges the de-

---

* Nazi Conspiracy and Aggression, Opinion and Judgment, Office of United States Chief of Counsel for Prosecution of Axis Criminality, United States Government Printing Office (Washington: 1947).

fendants with conspiring or having a common plan to commit crimes against peace. Count two of the indictment charges the defendants with committing specific crimes against peace by planning, preparing, initiating, and waging wars of aggression against a number of other States. It will be convenient to consider the question of the existence of a common plan and the question of aggressive war together, and to deal later in this judgment with the question of the individual responsibility of the defendants.

The charges in the indictment that the defendants planned and waged aggressive wars are charges of the utmost gravity. War is essentially an evil thing. Its consequences are not confined to the belligerent states alone, but affect the whole world.

To initiate a war of aggression, therefore, is not only an international crime; it is the supreme international crime differing only from other war crimes in that it contains within itself the accumulated evil of the whole.

The first acts of aggression referred to in the indictment are the seizure of Austria and Czechoslovakia; and the first war of aggression charged in the indictment is the war against Poland begun on the 1st September 1939.

Before examining that charge it is necessary to look more closely at some of the events which preceded these acts of aggression. The war against Poland did not come suddenly out of an otherwise clear sky; the evidence has made it plain that this war of aggression, as well as the seizure of Austria and Czechoslovakia, was premeditated and carefully prepared, and was not undertaken until the moment was thought opportune for it to be carried through as a definite part of the preordained scheme and plan.

For the aggressive designs of the Nazi Government were not accidents arising out of the immediate political situation in Europe and the world; they were a deliberate and essential part of Nazi foreign policy.

From the beginning, the National Socialist movement claimed that its object was to unite the German people in the consciousness of their mission and destiny, based on inherent qualities of race, and under the guidance of the Fuehrer.

For its achievement, two things were deemed to be essential: The disruption of the European order as it had existed since the Treaty of Versailles, and the creation of a Greater Germany beyond the frontiers of 1914. This necessarily involved the seizure of foreign territories.

War was seen to be inevitable, or at the very least, highly probable, if these purposes were to be accomplished. The German people, therefore, with all their resources, were to be organized as a great political-military army, schooled to obey without question any policy decreed by the State.

PREPARATION FOR AGGRESSION

In "Mein Kampf" Hitler had made this view quite plain. It must be remembered that "Mein Kampf" was no mere private diary in which the secret thoughts of Hitler were set down. Its contents were rather proclaimed from the house tops. It was used in the schools and universities and among the Hitler Youth, in the SS and the SA, and among the German people generally, even down to the presentation of an official copy to all newly married people. By the year 1945 over 6½ million copies had been circulated. The general contents are well known. Over and over again Hitler asserted his belief in the necessity of force as the means of solving international problems, as in the following quotation:

> "The soil on which we now live was not a gift bestowed by Heaven on our forefathers. They had to conquer it by risking their lives. So also in the future, our people will not obtain territory, and therewith the means of existence, as a favor from any other people, but will have to win it by the power of a triumphant sword."

"Mein Kampf" contains many such passages, and the extolling of force as an instrument of foreign policy is openly proclaimed.

The precise objectives of this policy of force are also set forth in detail. The very first page of the book asserts that "German-Austria must be restored to the great German Motherland," not on economic grounds, but because "people of the same blood should be in the same Reich."

The restoration of the German frontiers of 1914 is declared to be wholly insufficient, and if Germany is to exist at all, it must be as a world power with the necessary territorial magnitude.

"Mein Kampf" is quite explicit in stating where the increased territory is to be found:

> "Therefore we National Socialists have purposely drawn a line through the line of conduct followed by prewar Germany in foreign policy. We put an end to the perpetual Germanic march towards the south and west of Europe, and turn our eyes towards the lands of the east. We finally put a stop to the colonial and trade policy of the prewar times, and pass over to the territorial policy of the future.
>
> "But when we speak of new territory in Europe today, we must think principally of Russia and the border states subject to her."

"Mein Kampf" is not to be regarded as a mere literary exercise, nor as an inflexible policy or plan incapable of modification.

Its importance lies in the unmistakable attitude of aggression revealed throughout its pages.

WAR CRIMES AND CRIMES AGAINST HUMANITY

The evidence relating to war crimes has been overwhelming, in its volume and its detail. It is impossible for this judgment adequately to review it, or to record the mass of documentary and oral evidence that has been presented. The truth remains that war crimes were committed on a vast scale, never before seen in the history of war. They were perpetrated in all the countries occupied by Germany, and on the high seas, and were attended by every conceivable circumstance of cruelty and horror. There can be no doubt that the majority of them arose from the Nazi conception of "total war," with which the aggressive wars were waged. For in this conception of "total war" the moral ideas underlying the conventions which seek to make war more humane are no longer regarded as having force or validity. Everything is made subordinate to the overmastering dictates of war. Rules, regulations, assurances, and treaties, all alike, are of no moment; and so, freed from the restraining influence of international law, the aggressive war is conducted by the Nazi leaders in the most barbaric way. Accordingly, war crimes were committed when and wherever the Fuehrer and his close associates thought them to be advantageous. They were for the most part the result of cold and criminal calculation.

On some occasions war crimes were deliberately planned long in advance. In the case of the Soviet Union, the plunder of the territories to be occupied, and the ill-treatment of the civilian population, were settled in minute detail before the attack was begun. As early as the autumn of 1940, the invasion of the territories of the Soviet Union was being considered. From that date onwards, the methods to be employed in destroying all possible opposition were continuously under discussion.

Similarly, when planning to exploit the inhabitants of the occupied countries for slave labor on the very greatest scale, the German Government conceived it as an integral part of the war economy, and planned and organized this particular war crime down to the last elaborate detail.

Other war crimes, such as the murder of prisoners of war who had escaped and been recaptured, or the murder of commandos or captured airmen, or the destruction of the Soviet commissars, were the result of direct orders circulated through the highest official channels.

The Tribunal proposes, therefore, to deal quite generally with the question of war crimes, and to refer to them later when examining the responsibility of the individual defendants in relation to them. Prisoners of war were ill-treated and tortured and murdered, not only in defiance of the well-established rules of international law, but in complete disregard of the elementary dictates of humanity. Civilian populations in occupied territories suffered the same fate. Whole populations were deported to Germany for the purposes of slave labor upon defense works, armament production and similar tasks connected with the war effort. Hostages were taken in very large numbers from the civilian populations in all the occupied countries, and were shot as suited the German purposes. Public and private property was systematically plundered and pillaged in order to enlarge the resources of Germany at the expense of the rest of Europe. Cities and towns and villages were wantonly destroyed without military justification or necessity.

The territories occupied by Germany were administered in violation of the laws of war. The evidence is quite overwhelming of a systematic rule of violence, brutality, and terror. . . .

The practice of keeping hostages to prevent and to punish any form of civil disorder was resorted to by the Germans; an order issued by the defendant Keitel on the 16th September 1941, spoke in terms of fifty or a hundred lives from the occupied areas of the Soviet Union for one German life taken. The order stated that "it should be remembered that a human life in unsettled countries frequently counts for nothing, and a deterrent effect can be obtained only by unusual severity." The exact number of persons killed as a result of this policy is not known, but large numbers were killed in France and the other occupied territories in the west, while in the east the slaughter was on an even more extensive scale. In addition to the killing of hostages, entire towns were destroyed in some cases; such massacres as those of Oradour-sur-Glane in France and Lidice in Czechoslovakia, both of which were described to the Tribunal in detail, are examples of the organized use of terror by the occupying forces to beat down and destroy all opposition to their rule.

One of the most notorious means of terrorizing the people in occupied territories was the use of concentration camps. They were first established in Germany at the moment of the seizure of power by the Nazi Government. Their original purpose was to imprison without trial all those persons who were opposed to the Government, or who were in any way obnoxious to German authority. With the aid of a secret police force, this practice was widely extended, and in course of time concentration camps became places of organized and systematic murder, where millions of people were destroyed.

In the administration of the occupied territories the concentration camps were used to destroy all opposition groups. The persons arrested by the Gestapo were as a rule sent to concentration camps. They were conveyed to the camps in many cases without any care whatever being taken for them, and great numbers died on the way. Those who arrived at the camp were subject to systematic cruelty. They were given hard physical labor, inadequate food, clothes, and shelter, and were subject at all times to the rigors of a soulless regime, and the private whims of individual guards. In the report of the War Crimes Branch of the Judge Advocate's Section of the Third United States Army, under date 21st June 1945, the conditions at the Flossenburg concentration camp were investigated, and one passage may be quoted:

> "Flossenburg concentration camp can best be described as a factory dealing in death. Although this camp had in view the primary object of putting to work the mass slave labor, another of its primary objects was the elimination of human lives by the methods employed in handling the prisoners. Hunger and starvation rations, sadism, inadequate clothing, medical neglect, disease, beatings, hangings, freezing, forced suicides, shooting, etc., all played a major role in obtaining their object. Prisoners were murdered at random; spite killings against Jews were common; injections of poison and shooting in the neck were everyday occurrences; epidemics of typhus and spotted fever were permitted to run rampant as a means of eliminating prisoners; life in this camp meant nothing. Killing became a common thing — so common that a quick death was welcomed by the unfortunate ones."

A certain number of the concentration camps were equipped with gas chambers for the wholesale destruction of the inmates, and with furnaces for the burning of the bodies. Some of them were, in fact, used for the extermination of Jews as part of the "final solution" of the Jewish problem. Most of the non-Jewish inmates were used for labor, although the conditions under which they worked made labor and death almost synonymous terms. Those inmates who became ill and were unable to work were either destroyed in the gas chambers or sent to special infirmaries, where they were given entirely inadequate medical treatment, worse food, if possible, than the working inmates, and left to die.

The murder and ill-treatment of civilian populations reached its height in the treatment of the citizens of the Soviet Union and Poland. . . .

The Tribunal has before it an affidavit of one Hermann Graebe, dated 10 November 1945, describing the immense mass murders which he witnessed. He was the manager and engineer in charge of the branch of the

Solingen firm of Josef Jung in Spolbunow, Ukraine, from September 1941 to January 1944. He first of all described the attack upon the Jewish ghetto at Rowno:

> ". . . Then the electric floodlights which had been erected all round the ghetto were switched on. SS and militia details of four to six members entered or at least tried to enter the houses. Where the doors and windows were closed, and the inhabitants did not open upon the knocking, the SS men and militia broke the windows, forced the doors with beams and crowbars, and entered the dwelling. The owners were driven on to the street just as they were, regardless of whether they were dressed or whether they had been in bed . . . Car after car was filled. Over it hung the screaming of women and children, the cracking of whips and rifle shots."

Graebe then described how a mass execution at Dubno, which he witnessed on the 5th October 1942, was carried out:

> ". . . Now we heard shots in quick succession from behind one of the earth mounds. The people who had got off the trucks, men, women, and children of all ages, had to undress upon the orders of an SS man, who carried a riding or dog whip . . . Without screaming or crying, these people undressed, stood around by families, kissed each other, said farewells, and waited for the command of another SS man, who stood near the excavation, also with a whip in his hand . . . At that moment the SS man at the excavation called something to his comrade. The latter counted off about 20 persons, and instructed them to walk behind the earth mound . . . I walked around the mound and stood in front of a tremendous grave; closely pressed together, the people were lying on top of each other so that only their heads were visible. The excavation was already two-thirds full; I estimated that it contained about a thousand people . . . Now already the next group approached, descended into the excavation, lined themselves up against the previous victims and were shot."

The foregoing crimes against the civilian population are sufficiently appalling, and yet the evidence shows that at any rate in the east, the mass murders and cruelties were not committed solely for the purpose of stamping out opposition or resistance to the German occupying forces. In Poland and the Soviet Union these crimes were part of a plan to get rid of whole native populations by expulsion and annihilation, in order that their territory could be used for colonization by Germans. Hitler had written in "Mein Kampf" on these lines, and the plan was clearly stated by Himmler in July 1942, when he wrote:

> "It is not our task to Germanize the east in the old sense, that is to teach the people there the German language and the German law, but to see to it that only people of purely Germanic blood live in the east."

In August 1942, the policy for the eastern territories as laid down by Bormann was summarized by a subordinate of Rosenberg as follows:

> "The Slavs are to work for us. Insofar as we do not need them, they may die. Therefore, compulsory vaccination and Germanic health services are superfluous. The fertility of the Slavs is undesirable."

It was Himmler again who stated in October 1943:

> "What happens to a Russian, a Czech, does not interest me in the slightest. What the nations can offer in the way of good blood of our type, we will take. If necessary, by kidnapping their children and raising them here with us. Whether nations live in prosperity or starve to death interests me only insofar as we need them as slaves for our Kultur, otherwise it is of no interest to me."

In Poland the intelligentsia had been marked down for extermination as early as September 1939, and in May 1940 the defendant Frank wrote in his diary of "taking advantage of the focussing of world interest on the western front, by wholesale liquidation of thousands of Poles, first leading representatives of the Polish intelligentsia." Earlier, Frank had been directed to reduce the "entire Polish economy to an absolute minimum necessary for bare existence. The Poles shall be the slaves of the Greater German World Empire." In January 1940 he recorded in his diary that "cheap labor must be removed from the general government by hundreds of thousands. This will hamper the native biological propagation." So successfully did the Germans carry out this policy in Poland that by the end of the war one-third of the population had been killed, and the whole of the country devastated.

It was the same story in the occupied area of the Soviet Union. At the time of the launching of the German attack in June 1941, Rosenberg told his collaborators:

> "The object of feeding the German people stands this year without a doubt at the top of the list of Germany's claims on the east, and there the southern territories and the northern Caucasus will have to serve as a balance for the feeding of the German people . . . A very extensive evacuation will be necessary, without any doubt, and it is sure that the future will hold very hard years in store for the Russians."

PERSECUTION OF THE JEWS

The persecution of the Jews at the hands of the Nazi Government has been proved in the greatest detail before the Tribunal. It is a record of consistent and systematic inhumanity on the greatest scale. Ohlendorf, chief of Amt. III in the RSHA from 1939 to 1943, and who was in command of one of the Einsatz groups in the campaign against the Soviet Union testified as to the methods employed in the extermination of the Jews. He said that he employed firing squads to shoot the victims in order to lessen the sense of individual guilt on the part of his men; and the 90,000 men, women, and children who were murdered in 1 year by his particular group were mostly Jews.

When the witness Bach-Zelewski was asked how Ohlendorf could admit the murder of 90,000 people, he replied:

> "I am of the opinion that when, for years, for decades, the doctrine is preached that the Slav race is an inferior race, and Jews not even human, then such an outcome is inevitable."

But the defendant Frank spoke the final words of this chapter of Nazi history when he testified in this court:

> "We have fought against Jewry; we have fought against it for years; and we have allowed ourselves to make utterances and my own diary has become a witness against me in this connection — utterances which are terrible * * *. A thousand years will pass and this guilt of Germany will still not be erased."

The anti-Jewish policy was formulated in point 4 of the party program which declared, "Only a member of the race can be a citizen. A member of the race can only be one who is of German blood, without consideration of creed. Consequently, no Jew can be a member of the race." Other points of the program declared that Jews should be treated as foreigners, that they should not be permitted to hold public office, that they should be expelled from the Reich if it were impossible to nourish the entire population of the State, that they should be denied any further immigration into Germany, and that they should be prohibited from publishing German newspapers. The Nazi Party preached these doctrines throughout its history. "Der Stuermer" and other publications were allowed to disseminate hatred of the Jews and in the speeches and public declarations of the Nazi leaders, the Jews were held up to public ridicule and contempt.

With the seizure of power, the persecution of the Jews was intensified.

A series of discriminatory laws was passed, which limited the offices and professions permitted to Jews; and restrictions were placed on their family life and their rights of citizenship. By the autumn of 1938, the Nazi policy towards the Jews had reached the stage where it was directed towards the complete exclusion of Jews from German life. Pogroms were organized, which included the burning and demolishing of synagogues, the looting of Jewish businesses, and the arrest of prominent Jewish businessmen. A collective fine of 1 billion marks was imposed on the Jews, the seizure of Jewish assets was authorized, and the movement of Jews was restricted by regulations to certain specified districts and hours. The creation of ghettoes was carried out on an extensive scale, and by an order of the security police Jews were compelled to wear a yellow star to be worn on the breast and back. . . .

The Nazi persecution of Jews in Germany before the war, severe and repressive as it was, cannot compare, however, with the policy pursued during the war in the occupied territories. Originally the policy was similar to that which had been in force inside Germany. Jews were required to register, were forced to live in ghettoes, to wear the yellow star, and were used as slave laborers. In the summer of 1941, however, plans were made for the "final solution" of the Jewish question in Europe. This "final solution" meant the extermination of the Jews, which early in 1939 Hitler had threatened would be one of the consequences of an outbreak of war, and a special section in the Gestapo under Adolf Eichmann, as head of section B-4, of the Gestapo, was formed to carry out the policy.

The plan for exterminating the Jews was developed shortly after the attack on the Soviet Union. Einsatzgruppen of the security police and SD, formed for the purpose of breaking the resistance of the population of the areas lying behind the German armies in the east, were given the duty of exterminating the Jews in those areas. The effectiveness of the work of the Einsatzgruppen is shown by the fact that in February 1942, Heydrich was able to report that Esthonia had already been cleared of Jews and that in Riga the number of Jews had been reduced from 29,500 to 2,500. Altogether the Einsatzgruppen operating in the occupied Baltic States killed over 135,000 Jews in 3 months. . . .

These atrocities were all part and parcel of the policy inaugurated in 1941, and it is not surprising that there should be evidence that one or two German officials entered vain protests against the brutal manner in which the killings were carried out. But the methods employed never conformed to a single pattern. The massacres of Rowno and Dubno, of which the German engineer Graebe spoke, were examples of one method, the systematic extermination of Jews in concentration camps, was another. Part of the "final solution" was the gathering of Jews from all German occupied Europe in concentration camps. Their physical condition was the test of life or death. All who were fit to work were used as slave laborers in the concentration camps; all who were not fit to work were destroyed in gas chambers and their bodies burnt. Certain concentration camps such as Treblinka and Auschwitz were set aside for this main purpose. With regard to Auschwitz, the Tribunal heard the evidence of Hoess, the commandant of the camp from May 1, 1940 to December 1, 1943. He estimated that in the camp of Auschwitz alone in that time 2,500,000 persons were exterminated, and that a further 500,000 died from disease and starvation. Hoess described the screening for extermination by stating in evidence —

> "We had two SS doctors on duty at Auschwitz to examine the incoming transports of prisoners. The prisoners would be marched by one of the doctors who would make spot decisions as they walked by. Those who were fit for work were sent into the camp. Others were sent immediately to the extermination plants. Children of tender years were invariably exterminated since by reason of their youth they were unable to work. Still another improvement we made over Treblinka was that at Treblinka the victims almost always knew that they were to be exterminated and at Auschwitz we endeavored to fool the victims into thinking that they were to go through a delousing process. Of course, frequently they realized our true intentions and we sometimes had riots and difficulties due to that fact. Very frequently women would hide their children under their clothes, but of course when we found them we would send the children in to be exterminated."

He described the actual killing by stating:

> "It took from 3 to 15 minutes to kill the people in the death chamber, depending upon climatic conditions. We knew when the people were dead because their screaming stopped. We usually waited about one-half hour before we opened the doors and removed the bodies. After the bodies were removed our special commandos took off the rings and extracted the gold from the teeth of the corpses."

Beating, starvation, torture, and killing were general. The inmates were subjected to cruel experiments at Dachau in August 1942; victims were immersed in cold water until their body temperature was reduced to 28° C., when they died immediately. Other experiments included high altitude experiments in pressure chambers, experiments to determine how long human beings could survive in freezing water, experiments with poison bullets, experiments with contagious diseases, and experiments dealing with sterilization of men and women by X-rays and other methods.

Evidence was given of the treatment of the inmates before and after their extermination. There was testimony that the hair of women victims was cut off before they were killed, and shipped to Germany, there to be used in the manufacture of mattresses. The clothes, money, and valuables of the inmates were also salvaged and sent to the appropriate agencies for disposition. After the extermination the gold teeth and fillings were taken from the heads of the corpses and sent to the Reichsbank. After cremation the ashes were used for fertilizer, and in some instances attempts were made to utilize the fat from the bodies of the victims in the commercial manufacture of soap. Special groups traveled through Europe to find Jews and subject them to the "final solution." German missions were sent to such satellite countries as Hungary and Bulgaria, to arrange for the shipment of Jews to extermination camps and it is known that by the end of 1944, 400,000 Jews from Hungary had been murdered at Auschwitz. Evidence has also been given of the evacuation of 110,000 Jews from part of Rumania for "liquidation." Adolf Eichmann, who had been put in charge of this program by Hitler, has estimated that the policy pursued resulted in the killing of 6,000,000 Jews, of which 4,000,000 were killed in the extermination institutions.

VI. NATIONALISM

IT IS appropriate that the concluding section of this volume should include a broad variety of selections illustrative of the phenomenon of nationalism; for of the ideologies which have been dealt with nationalism is perhaps the most ubiquitous, its tenets have persistently invaded and modified each of the other dominant ideologies of the present day. It is for this reason, among others, that nationalism is particularly difficult to define and describe, since its elements are oftentimes infused into movements which term themselves primarily "democratic," "socialist," "liberal-capitalist," "fascist," etc. Since, with the notable exception of Mussolini's Fascism and Hitler's violent nationalism, the basic orientation of these other movements is non-nationalistic, and in the case of Communism, even *anti*-nationalistic, it is all the more necessary to search for the roots of nationalism and to discover, if possible, its essential characteristics, however they may be modified in any particular political movement.

Though nationalism as a specific and politically powerful doctrine is hardly more than a few centuries old, its roots in Western political life may be traced back to that time when human associations were first extended beyond their initial limits of the family and tribe. This development of the political association, as it is illustrated by Greek and Roman experience, is sketched with extraordinary clarity and beauty, though from a non-philosophic orientation, by Fustel de Coulanges in his classic work, *The Ancient City*.[1] What were the ties, the beliefs, he asks, which bound men into the ever larger associations of the family, the tribe, and finally the *polis*? [2] He answers that with respect to the Greeks and Romans:

[1] Fustel de Coulanges, *The Ancient City* (New York: Doubleday & Co., Inc., 1956). Published originally in 1864 as *La Cité Antique*, translated by Willard Small.

[2] Coulanges generally uses this word to designate such political associations as those of Athens, Sparta, Corinth, etc. The word *polis* will be used throughout this discussion, rather than such unsatisfactory and unnecessary substitutes as "city," "city-state," "state," etc.

When we sought the most ancient beliefs of these men, we found a religion which had their dead ancestors for its object, and for its principal symbol the sacred fire. It was this religion that founded the family and established the first laws. But this race has also had in all its branches another religion — the one whose principal figures were Zeus, Here, Athene, Juno, that of the Hellenic Olympus, and of the Roman Capitol.[3]

Men were united by sacred ties, by a religious worship restricted initially to the family, but subsequently extended, while there also gradually developed a parallel worship of the divinities of the *polis*. The sacred things of the family, the tribe, and the *polis* were all connected especially with the soil, the native soil, for the ancient religions forbade men to quit the land "where their divine ancestors reposed."[4] The intensity of this attachment to the "fatherland" is forcefully illustrated by the account given of the founding of Rome by Romulus:

The day for the foundation having arrived, he first offers a sacrifice. . . . Romulus dug a small trench, of a circular form, and threw into it a clod of earth, which he had brought from the city of Alba.[5] Then each of his companions, approaching by turns, following his example, threw in a little earth, which he had brought from the country from which he had come. This rite is remarkable, and reveals to us a notion of the ancients to which we must call attention. . . . A man could not quit his dwelling-place without taking with him his *soil and his ancestors*. This rite had to be accomplished, so that he might say, pointing out the new place which he had adopted, *This is still the land of my fathers, terra patrum, patria; here is my country, for here are the manes of my family*.[6]

Coulanges thus reveals to us as part of the ancient foundations of patriotism the attachment of men to these things which they held most sacred, especially their attachment to the *sacred soil*, which had been sanctified by their immortal ancestors, and with which there was associated a body of religious rites and customs by which they were distinguished from strangers. Summing up its meaning, Coulanges contends that

The word *country* among the ancients, signified the land of the fathers, *terra patria* — fatherland. The fatherland of every man was that part of the soil which his domestic or national religion had sanctified, the land where the remains of his ancestors were deposited, and which their souls occupied. His little fatherland was the family

[3] Coulanges, *op. cit.*, pp. 120–21.
[4] *Ibid.*, p. 136.
[5] His former home. See *ibid.*, p. 135.
[6] *Ibid.*, p. 136, emphasis supplied.

enclosure with its tomb and its hearths. The great fatherland was the city, with its prytaneus and its heroes, with its sacred enclosure, with its territory marked out by religion. "Sacred fatherland" the Greeks called it. Nor was it a vain word; this soil was, indeed, sacred to man, for his gods dwelt there. State, city, fatherland: these words were no abstraction, as they are among the moderns; they really represented a group of local divinities, with a daily worship and beliefs that had a powerful influence over the soul.[7]

The unending and internecine struggle between various factions within the ancient *polis* may be taken as but one indication that the standard of patriotism was not unequivocally understood or applied;[8] however, its ultimately problematic character does not diminish its immediate, political relevance. This was duly acknowledged in classical political philosophy, which contended that there would be a diminution in the quality and intensity of patriotism should the size of the *polis* be increased beyond a certain size in population or territory. This view was based, in part, on the presumption that men are capable of only a limited number of close ties of affection and of knowing well a rather limited body of fellow citizens. Confirmation of this view may be found in the consensus of contemporary historians that patriotism was, in fact, considerably diffused and diminished, following the general disappearance of the independent *polis* of antiquity with its incorporation into larger kingdoms and empires of various descriptions. One of the most eminent historians concerned with the subject of nationalism suggests that during this period it "would be more accurate to say that on top of natural local patriotism was superimposed a more artificial patriotism."[9] This "artificial patriotism," which Professor Hayes at times terms "nationalism," was, in his view, of little consequence politically.

During the thousand years which separate Luther and Machiavelli from Pope Gregory the Great and which we designate, for lack of a better term, the middle ages, there were few signs of nationalism anywhere in Europe. The Europeans during this long period had many loyalties — to Catholic Church, to bishop or abbot, to parish priest, to lay lord, to tribal chieftain, to duke or count or baron, to

[7] *Ibid.*, p. 198.

[8] See Aristotle's *Politics*, Book III; cf. his *Constitution of the Athenians*, especially his discussion of the political policy of Theramenes, who consistently defended the cause of his fatherland, both against external enemies and against those internal factions of oligarchs and democrats who placed partisan interests above those of the common good. A translation of this work by Livio Stecchini is available from The Free Press (Glencoe, Illinois: 1950).

[9] Carlton J. H. Hayes, *Essays on Nationalism* (New York: The Macmillan Co., 1937), pp. 24–25.

guild of merchants or of craftsmen, to manor or town, to realism or nominalism, to St. Francis or St. Dominic, to pope or emperor, to Christendom in arms against Islam. Nationalities surely persisted throughout the period and undoubtedly there was an acutely nascent consciousness of national differences toward the close of the middle ages, the result of the crusades, of the rise of vernacular literature, and of the ambitious efforts of monarchs in western Europe, but if there was an object of popular loyalty superior to all others it was not the nation but Christendom.[10]

It would follow from this analysis that nationalism in its present-day manifestations must have developed essentially in the period following the fragmentation of Christendom, in the centuries following the Reformation. There was, in fact, seen at this time the development of national churches and of national vernaculars for ecclesiastical and literary use. This period witnessed also the virtual end of many feudal institutions as there developed powerful monarchies which extended control and stabilized large areas; the locus, as it were, of a variety of centripetal forces. Among these forces were the new processes of manufacture, trade, and refined instruments of commerce which accelerated the development of foreign trade.

The impact of these developments was manifested in varying degrees throughout Europe. In England especially they appeared to accompany an increasing political and cultural unity, at least within the ruling classes. In France, the development was less clear cut, for loyalty to the province continued powerful. And the forces of centralization had hardly begun to manifest themselves in the area incorporated by twentieth-century Germany. Of this area it has been reiterated by historians that

> At the opening of the eighteenth century, conditions . . . had changed very little since the Thirty Years' War. One glance at the political map will show that Germany was a masterpiece of partition, entanglement and confusion. It comprised approximately eighteen hundred separate territories of various sizes and forms of government, over which an equal number of sovereigns ruled. Each of these territories was practically a distinct sovereignty. The theory uniting them rested not upon a feeling of German nationalism, but rather upon the idea of universality.[11]

The development of national unity which had, at the opening of the eighteenth century, made such uncertain progress had — a mere century

---

[10] Hays, op. cit., p. 28.
[11] Robert R. Ergang, Herder and the Foundations of German Nationalism (New York: Columbia University Press, 1931), Columbia University studies in history, economics and public law, p. 13.

and a half later — swept over Europe and made itself felt powerfully throughout most of the world. An especially virulent feeling of national consciousness manifested itself in Germany and Italy of the twentieth century, yet throughout the eighteenth century these areas were the most fragmented, and it seemed, the least likely to develop into unified nations.

How may the swiftness and magnitude of this change be explained? At least one thing is certain: the rise of nationalism in Europe in the eighteenth and nineteenth centuries paralleled the triumph of certain new developments in political philosophy. It may, then, prove helpful to explore certain relationships between them. By way of a beginning, the student may examine the suggestion of E. H. Carr that "the founder of modern nationalism as it began to take shape in the 19th century was Rousseau, who, rejecting the embodiment of the nation in the personal sovereign or the ruling class, boldly identified 'nation' and 'people'; . . ." [12] A related suggestion is made by another of the best known interpreters of nationalism, Hans Kohn, who finds that Rousseau "saw the necessity of establishing the collective personality of the nation as the new center and justification of society and social order." [13] It is certainly true that Rousseau emphasized the importance of patriotism; in one of his earliest writings there is an indication of the important role which it was to play in his work:

> It is certain that the greatest miracles of virtue have been produced by patriotism: this fine and lively feeling, which gives to the force of self-love all the beauty of virtue, lends it an energy which without disfiguring it, makes it the most heroic of all passions. This it is that produces so many immortal actions, the glory of which dazzles our feeble eyes; and so many great men, whose old-world virtues pass for fables now that patriotism is made mock of.[14]

Rousseau adds that "the love of one's country, which is a hundred times more lively and delightful than the love of a mistress, cannot be conceived except by experiencing it." [15] One of his last and greatest works, *Emile*, begins with illustrations of the "immortal actions" of these patriots of ancient Sparta and Rome, and similar references abound in all his major works. Patriotism is a central concern of Rousseau's certainly, but his emphasis on love of country presents an enigma to modernity. That the citizen of the ancient *polis* was moved by powerful emotions of patriotism

[12] Edward Hallett Carr, *Nationalism and After* (London: Macmillan & Co., 1945), p. 7.
[13] Hans Kohn, *Nationalism: Its Meaning and History* (New York: D. Van Nostrand Company, 1955), p. 21.
[14] Jean J. Rousseau, *The Social Contract and Discourses* (New York: Everyman's Library, E. P. Dutton and Co., Inc., 1950), pp. 301–2.
[15] *Ibid.*, p. 302.

is understandable in view of the myriad ties of religion which have been discussed. Nor was it difficult for classical political thought to understand patriotism in view of its concern with the *natural qualities of the political association*. Rousseau, however, by no means shared this perspective. As a social contract theorist he began rather from the understanding that prior to the creation of civil society men lived in a *state of nature*; that in this pre-social state of nature they possessed certain rights, and "that, to secure these rights, governments are instituted among men, deriving their just powers from the consent of the governed; that whenever any form of government becomes destructive of these ends, it is the right of the people to alter or to abolish it, and to institute a new government . . ." [16]

The question which then presents itself is whether the citizen of a social contract society, being aware of its *artificial and subordinate character*, can experience the emotion of patriotism which tied earlier men to the *polis*. The social contract theorists who preceded Rousseau implied not, and anticipated the development of essentially commercial societies which would be more stable and prosperous for their very *lack* of patriotism. This proposed solution to the political problem was seen by Rousseau as inadequate, and in attacking this position he argues:

> Let it be admitted that luxury is a certain indication of wealth; that it even serves, if you will, to increase such wealth; what conclusion is to be drawn from this paradox, so worthy of the times? And what will become of virtue if riches are to be acquired at any cost? The politicians of the ancient world were always talking of morals and virtue; ours speak of nothing but commerce and money.[17]

The social contract state constructed according to the formula of Hobbes and Locke might produce a comfortable bourgeoisie; it would never produce true *citizens*, the virtuous, patriotic citizens of an ancient Sparta or Rome. Such citizen-virtue had been the product of the sound laws and the comprehensive system of education by which every aspect of the human character was properly developed. But what had been the source of these institutions? Rousseau's answer to this question was, in some ways, very similar to the position held in classical political thought, *i.e.*, the foundations of the good society must be laid by a great law-giver or legislator, for example, by such men as Lycurgus, Moses, or Romulus,[18]

---

[16] *The Declaration of Independence*, July 4, 1776.

[17] Rousseau, *op. cit.*, p. 161.

[18] *Ibid.*, pp. 37–42, Book II, ch. vii. Following Machiavelli, Rousseau suggests that the real founder of Rome, its true legislator, was Numa Pompilius, who, "finding a very savage people, and wishing to reduce them to civil obedience by the arts of peace, had recourse to religion as the most necessary and assured support of any civil society. . . ." *Discourses*, I, xi.

who were the legislators, the virtual creators, of the Spartan, Jewish, and Roman nations respectively. That few legislators have been successful in their undertaking is not surprising, for "those who dare to undertake the institution of a people must feel themselves capable, as it were, of changing human nature, of transforming each individual, who by himself is a perfect and solitary whole, into a part of a much greater whole from which he in a manner receives his life and being . . ." [19] Yet some legislators have succeeded. For example, it was, says Rousseau, Moses who

> first conceived and executed a bold plan that involved building a nation out of a swarm of wretched fugitives who possessed no arts, no arms, no talents, no virtues, no courage, and who — with not a single square foot of territory that they might call their own — were in sober truth a troop of outcasts upon the face of the earth. It was Moses who dared to transform this gang of servile migrants into a political body — a free people. He bestowed upon it, at a time when it was wandering about in the wilderness, the stable institutions — proof against time, fortune, and conquest — that five thousand years have not sufficed to destroy or even change. Even in our time, when the nation itself no longer exists, those institutions endure — as strong now as they were in their early days.[20]

How was *Moses* able to accomplish this "true miracle"? It is in answering this question that Rousseau provides one of the basic conceptions of modern nationalism. The particular success of Moses is said to have stemmed from the fact that:

> Determined as he was that his people should never be absorbed by other peoples, he gave them customs and folkways that would not blend with those of other nations. He imposed rites upon them, and ceremonies to be performed within the bosom of their families. He devised a thousand goads to keep them always on their toes — and to make sure that they would always seem strangers when thrown with other men; and each fraternal bond he established among the individual members of his republic became yet another barrier that separated them from their neighbors and prevented their assimilation by them. That is why this strange nation — often dispersed, often apparently wiped out of existence, but always utterly faithful to its law — survives even today, scattered among other peoples but never absorbed by them. That is, again, why its mores, its laws, its rites maintain their vigor, and why they will perpetuate themselves as long as the world itself goes on — despite the hatred and persecution of the remainder of mankind.[21]

[19] *Op. cit.*, p. 38.

[20] J. Jacques Rousseau, *Considerations on the Government of Poland*. Translation by Willmore Kendall, Minnesota Bookstore (Minneapolis: 1947), p. 3.

[21] *Ibid*. In the same vein, Rousseau suggests to a future legislator for Poland that "if you will but make sure that no Pole shall be capable of becoming a Russian, Russia will —

Since such statesmen as Europe possessed in Rousseau's day were not following the wise policy of Moses, Rousseau struck out at "the Europe-wide tendency to imitate the tastes and mores of the French"; furthermore

> Say what you like, in our day there is no longer any such thing as a Frenchman, a German, a Spaniard; there is not even any such thing as an Englishman. Nowadays we have only Europeans, all with the same tastes, the same passions, the same mores — necessarily, since none of them has had a national character impressed upon him by national institutions. . . . all of them aspire to nothing save luxury; all of them are without passions, save only that for money . . . Wherever they find money to steal and women to corrupt, there they have their fatherland.[22]

Rousseau's analysis of the current situation of European man, along with his elaborately developed political and educational theories for the rebuilding of Europe along truly national lines after the anticipated revolution, had an impact beyond calculation. By way of a single illustration, it again may be noted that while among German speaking people there had been, as we have seen, a notable lack of national feeling, the influence of Rousseau's writings laid the foundations for a radical transformation. It has been said of Johann Herder, "the German Rousseau," [23] that "from Rousseau he borrowed the idea of the artificiality of the culture of his age, and thereafter endeavored to bring his generation back to a life founded on the laws of nature. Rousseau's nature gospel was, in a sense, to become the foundation of Herder's idea of nationality." [24] And this idea was to become a central theme in the work of "the father of German nationalism." In developing his philosophy of history, Herder "regarded each nationality as an organic unit and each branch of culture as an organic part of the larger unit." He frequently used the phrase, "the physiology of the whole national group." [25] This view was compatible with his notion that

> The family is a product of Nature. The most natural state is, therefore, a state composed of a single people with a single national character. A people can maintain its national character for thousands of

---

I promise you — never subjugate Poland." *Considerations on the Government of Poland,* p. 6.

[22] *Ibid.,* pp. 6–7.

[23] Ergang, *op. cit.,* p. 60.

[24] *Ibid.,* p. 60.

[25] *Ibid.,* p. 85. With an eye to later developments it is interesting to note that "Herder used various terms to express this unity of action in the national group; *Nationalgeist,* i, 263; iii, 30; viii, 392 . . . *Seele des Volks* . . . *Geist der Nation* . . . *Genius des Volks* . . . *Geist des Volks* . . ."

years and, if its prince, who shares this heritage, has a concern for it, it can be developed through education along the lines most natural to it. For a people is a natural growth like a family, only spread more widely. Nothing seems, therefore, more clearly opposed to the aims which all governments should have in view than the expansion of states beyond their natural limits, the indiscriminate mingling of various nations and human types under one sceptre. The sceptre of a human ruler has neither the strength nor the range which would enable it to weld together such heterogeneous materials into a unity. So rulers are reduced to sticking them together, as it were, in order to constitute what is described as the "machine" of government — a fragile and lifeless contrivance between the separate parts of which no mutual sympathy is possible. In an empire of this kind even the best of monarchs can with difficulty regard himself as the Father of his country. Such an empire is a reproduction, on the stage of history, of the apocalyptic vision of the Great Beast with the head of a lion, the tail of a dragon, the wings of an eagle and the feet of a bear.[26] But a political conglomeration of this kind is in no sense a fatherland. Such artificial constructions resemble the wooden horse of Troy. They cannot move by their own impulsion. Nevertheless, they form part of a system of equilibrium in which each part guarantees the permanence of the other. Yet individually each is lifeless because it lacks a national character and personality. They are drawn together by an external force, and it is only the curse of destiny which could condemn them to immortality: for the statecraft that produced them is an art which juggles with peoples and human beings as though they were lifeless bodies. But history shows plainly enough that these products of human pride are made of clay, and that, like all earthly clay, they are doomed to be broken or washed away.[27]

The true history of mankind, Herder contends, would be the work of genuine nationalities, and to such national groups he, like Rousseau, "ascribed growth, maturity and decay, the fundamental characteristics of everything organic . . ."[28] Just as every nationality is subject to an

[26] Cf. the *Revelation* of St. John the Divine, Chapter XIII, 2, "The Beasts from the Sea and from the Earth."

[27] J. G. von Herder, "The Nation as an Enlarged Family," from *Modern Political Doctrines*, edited by Sir Alfred Zimmern (Oxford: The Clarendon Press, 1939), pp. 165–6.

[28] Ergang, p. 85. Compare this aspect of Herder's teaching with those various suggestions by Rousseau in *The Social Contract* that there is some sort of natural history of peoples. "Most peoples, like most men, are docile only in youth; as they grow old they become incorrigible." Book II, viii. The recognition of this problem is of supreme importance to the potential legislator, in Rousseau's view, since "there is for nations, as for men, a period of youth, or, shall we say, maturity, before which they should not be made subject to laws . . . Russia will never be really civilized, because it was civilized too soon. Peter had a genius for imitation; but he lacked true genius, which is creative and makes all from nothing. . . ." II, viii.

invariable law of change, so it is with its distinctive language also. Every nation must then express itself in its period of growth through the development of its unique language, its particular literature, mores and art. The culmination of this view is finally the belief that language

> is not the invention of individual men who coined the words; it is the expression of the collective experience of the group. The poet does not sit down and laboriously manufacture poetry; he writes when the national soul moves him and he writes what it inspires. The individual prophets, writers, artists or poets are but the means employed by the national soul to give expression to a national religion, a national language, or a national literature.[29]

The further development of these views within German idealistic philosophy may be traced from Herder through Fichte and Hegel. The initial selection which follows, Fichte's considerations of "The Special Quality of German People," was published in 1808. It concerns itself with the character of national languages, continuing the development noted in Herder's formulation. This same theme, along with related problems, is taken up by Ernest Renan in his famous essay, "What Is a Nation?" which was published in 1882. As has been suggested, the breadth and complexity of the phenomenon of nationalism as it has developed in the modern world is so great that to understand it adequately the student will have to discover not only its philosophic roots, but will have also to identify its manifestations within the other dominant ideologies of our day. The remaining selections may facilitate his task. Mazzini's famous statement on *The Duties of Man* illustrates the prevalent, twentieth century notion embodied in the principle of "self-determination" that the political boundaries of the state should coincide with the limits of the ethnic group. *The Duties of Man* was written by Mazzini as a series of essays to be read especially by the Italian working class. They were published between 1844 and 1858.

The principle of self-determination was given powerful political expression by President Woodrow Wilson, who contended that no genuine peace could be achieved unless it was generally applied as the basis for settlement of the principal issues of the First World War. Some of his views on this issue are presented in his 1918 statement and pertinent articles of "The Fourteen Points."

The present importance of nationalism as one of the major factors underlying the turbulent mid-century developments in the Middle East is becoming ever more evident, and something of its nature and role in this

---

[29] Ergang, *op. cit.*, p. 87.

context is illustrated by the statements of Prime Minister Ben Gurion and President Nasser. The resurrection of Israel as a sovereign state and President Nasser's conception of a "United Arab Republic" highlight some of the problematic aspects of the application of the doctrine of nationalism. It is clear that the development of a Jewish nation and the attempt to bring together the diverse peoples and non-contiguous territories of the "Arab world" involve many trans-national considerations. Prime Minister Ben Gurion's statement was delivered in 1946, two years prior to the creation of the State of Israel, while President Nasser's articles were published in 1954, shortly before he assumed his present position. Something of the basic importance of the nationalistic appeal in winning independence for India can be seen in Prime Minister Nehru's autobiographical writing, *Toward Freedom*. Paradoxically enough, application of similar nationalistic arguments now appear to present a threat to the unity of India, as separatists seek virtually autonomous "lingual states." Will these demands culminate in political partition of the sort which carved from British India the bifurcated areas of Pakistan? Or can a viable solution be found within the context of the principles of federalism to effectively meet the demands of the Dravidians and other lingual groups who are currently pleading for separate states? The following excerpt from Phillips Talbot's commentary on the program of the Dravidian Progressive Federation effectively illustrates some of the additional stresses produced within the heterogeneous, continental-nation-state by application of the principles of nationalistic self-determination.

The selections in this Part were first published as follows:

J. G. Fichte, *The Special Quality of German People* (1808)
Ernest Renan, *What Is A Nation?* (1882)
Joseph Mazzini, *The Duties of Man* (1884)
Woodrow Wilson, *Self-Determination as the Basis for Peace* (1918)
                The Fourteen Points, Articles VI–XIII (1918)
David Ben Gurion, *Israel's National Aspirations* (1946)
Gamal Abdul Nasser, *The Philosophy of the Egyptian Revolution* (1954)
Jawaharlal Nehru, *Toward Freedom* (1936)
Phillips Talbot, *Notes from a Tamilnad Tour, A Letter from Phillips Talbot* (1957)

THE SPECIAL QUALITY OF GERMAN PEOPLE

by J. G. Fichte *

. . . in my opinion the cause of a complete contrast between the Germans and the other peoples of Teutonic descent, is . . . the change of language. Here, as I wish to point out distinctly at the very beginning, it is not a question of the special quality of the language retained by the one branch or adopted by the other; on the contrary, the importance lies solely in the fact that in the one case something native is retained, while in the other case something foreign is adopted. Nor is it a question of the previous ancestry of those who continue to speak an original language; on the contrary, the importance lies solely in the fact that this language continues to be spoken, for men are formed by language far more than language is formed by men.

A language that has become lifeless and thus essentially meaningless very easily lends itself to perversion and to misuse in glossing over every kind of human corruption, in a way that is not possible in a language which has never died. I take as my example the three notorious words Humanity, Popularity, and Liberality. When these words are used in speaking to a German who has learnt no language but his own they are to him nothing but a meaningless noise, which has no relationship of sound to remind him of anything he knows already and so takes him completely out of his circle of observation and beyond any observation possible to him. Now, if the unknown word nevertheless attracts his attention by its foreign, distinguished and euphonious tone, and if he thinks that what sounds so lofty must also have some lofty meaning, he must have this meaning explained to him from the very beginning and as something entirely new to him, and he can only blindly accept this explanation. So he becomes tacitly accustomed to acknowledge as really existing and valuable

* J. G. Fichte, "Addresses to the German Nation (1808)." *Modern Political Doctrines* (Oxford: 1939), edited by Sir Alfred Zimmern. By permission of The Clarendon Press, Oxford.

something which, if left to himself, he would perhaps never have found worth mentioning. Let no one believe that the case is much different with the neo-Latin peoples, who utter those words as if they were words of their mother-tongue. Without a scholarly study of antiquity and of its actual language they understand the roots of those words just as little as the German does. Now, if instead of the word Humanity [*Humanität*], we had said to a German the word *Menschlichkeit*, which is its literal translation, he would have understood us without further historical explanation, but he would have said: "Well, to be a man [*Mensch*] and not a wild beast is not very much after all." Now it may be that no Roman would ever have said that; but the German would say it, because in his language manhood [*Menschheit*] has remained an idea of the senses only and has never become a symbol of a supersensuous idea as it did among the Romans. Our ancestors had taken note of the separate human virtues and designated them symbolically in language perhaps long before it occurred to them to combine them in a single concept as contrasted with animal nature; and that is no discredit to our ancestors as compared with the Romans. Now anyone who, in spite of this, wished to introduce that foreign and Roman symbol artificially and, as it were, by a trick into the language of the Germans would obviously be lowering their ethical standard in passing on to them as distinguished and commendable something which may perhaps be so in the foreign language, but which the German, in accordance with the ineradicable nature of his national power of imagination, only regards as something already familiar that must be kept in its place. A closer examination might enable us to demonstrate that those Teutonic races which adopted the Latin language experienced, even in the beginning, similar degradations of their former ethical standard because of inappropriate foreign symbols; but on this circumstance we do not now wish to lay too great a stress.

Further, if in speaking to the German, instead of the words Popularity [*Popularität*] and Liberality [*Liberalität*], I should use the expressions, "striving for favour with the great mob," and "not having the mind of a slave," which is how they must be literally translated, he would, to begin with, not even obtain a clear and vivid sense-image such as was certainly obtained by a Roman of old. The latter saw every day with his own eyes the supple politeness of an ambitious candidate to all and sundry, and outbursts of the slave mind too; and those words vividly re-presented these things to him. Even from the Roman of a later period these sights were removed by the change in the form of government and the introduction of Christianity; and, besides, his own language was beginning to a great extent to die away in his own mouth. This was more especially due to Christianity, which was alien to him, and which he could neither ward off nor thoroughly assimilate. How was it possible for this language, already half dead in its own home, to be transmitted alive to a foreign people? How could it now be transmitted to us Germans? Moreover, as regards to the symbolic mental content of both those expressions, there is in the word Popularity, even from its very origin, something base, which was perverted in their mouths and became a virtue, owing to the corruption of the nation and of its constitution. The German never falls into this perversion, so long as it is put before him in his own language. But when Liberality is translated by saying that a man has not the soul of a slave, or, to give it a modern rendering, has not a lackey's way of thinking, he once more replies that to say this also means very little.

Moreover, into these verbal images, which even in their pure form among the Romans arose at a low stage of ethical culture or designated something positively base, there were stealthily introduced during the development of the neo-Latin languages the idea of lack of seriousness about social relations, the idea of self-abandonment, and the idea of heartless laxity. In order to bring these things into esteem among us, use was made of the respect we have for antiquity and foreign countries to introduce the same words into the German language. It was done so quietly that no one was fully aware of what was actually intended. The purpose and the result of all admixture has always been this: first of all to deprive the hearer of the immediate comprehensibility and definiteness which are the inherent qualities of every primitive language; then, when he has been prepared to accept such words in blind faith, to supply him with the explanation that he needs: and, finally, in this explanation to mix vice and virtue together in such a way that it is no easy matter to separate them again. Now, if the true meaning of those three foreign words, assuming them to have a meaning, had been expressed to the German in his own words and within his own circle of verbal images, in this way: *Menschen-freundlichkeit* (friendliness to man), *Leutseligkeit* (condescension or affability), and *Edelmut* (noblemindedness), he would have understood them; but the base associations we have mentioned could never have been slipped into those designations. Within the range of German speech such a wrapping-up in incomprehensibility and darkness arises either from clumsiness or evil design; it is to be avoided, and the means always ready to hand is to translate into right and true German. But in the neo-Latin languages this incomprehensibility is of their very nature and origin, and there is no means of avoiding it, for they do not possess any living language by which they might examine the dead one; indeed, when one looks at the matter closely, they are entirely without a mother-tongue.

With this our immediate task is performed, which was to find the characteristic that differentiates the German from the other peoples of Teutonic descent. The difference arose at the moment of the separation of the common stock and consists in this, that the German speaks a language which has been alive ever since it first issued from the force of nature, whereas the other Teutonic races speak a language which has movement on the surface only but is dead at the root. To this circumstance alone, to life on the one hand and death on the other, we assign the difference; but we are not in any way taking up the further question of the intrinsic value of the German language. Between life and death there is no comparison; the former has infinitely more value than the latter. To make a direct comparison between German and neo-Latin languages is therefore futile; it is to discuss things which are not worth discussing. If the intrinsic value of the German language is to be discussed, at the very least a language of equal rank, a language equally primitive, as, for example, Greek, must enter the lists; but such a comparison is far beyond our present purpose.

What an immeasurable influence on the whole human development of a people the character of its language may have — its language, which accompanies the individual into the most secret depths of his mind in thought and will and either hinders him or gives him wings, which unites within its domain the whole mass of men who speak it into one single and common understanding, which is the true point of meeting and mingling for the world of the senses and the world of spirits and fuses the ends of both in each other in such a fashion that it is impossible to tell to which of the two it belongs itself — how different the results of this influence may prove to be where the relation is as life to death, all this in general is easily perceived. In the first place, the German has a means of investigating his living language more thoroughly by comparing it with the closed Latin language, which differs very widely from his own in the development of verbal images; on the other hand, he has a means of understanding Latin more clearly in the same way. This is not possible to a member of the neo-Latin peoples, who fundamentally remains a captive in the sphere of one and the same language. Then the German, in learning the original Latin, at the same time acquires to a certain extent the derived languages also; and if he should learn the former more thoroughly than a foreigner does, which for the reason given the German will very likely be able to do, he at the same time learns to understand this foreigner's own language far more thoroughly and to possess it far more intimately than does the foreigner himself who speaks it. Hence the German, if only he makes use of all his advantages, can always be superior to the foreigner and understand him fully, even better than the foreigner understands himself, and can translate the foreigner to the fullest extent. On the other hand, the foreigner can never understand the true German without a thorough and extremely laborious study of the German language, and there is no doubt that he will leave what is genuinely German untranslated. The things in these languages which can only be learnt from the foreigner himself are mostly new fashions of speech due to boredom and caprice, and one is very modest when one consents to receive instruction of this kind. In most cases one would be able, instead, to show foreigners how they ought to speak according to the primitive language and its law of change, and to show that the new fashion is worthless and offends against ancient and traditional good usage.

In addition to the special consequence just mentioned, the whole wealth of consequences we spoke of comes about of itself.

It is, however, our intention to treat these consequences as a whole, fundamentally and comprehensively, from the point of view of the bond that unites them, in order to give in this way a thorough description of the German in contrast to the other Teutonic races. For the present I briefly indicate these consequences thus:

(1) Where the people has a living language, mental culture influences life; where the contrary is the case, mental culture and life go their way independently of each other.

(2) For the same reason, a people of the former kind is really and truly in earnest about all mental culture and wishes it to influence life; whereas a people of the latter kind looks upon mental culture rather as an ingenious game and has no wish to make it anything more. The latter have intelligence; the former have intelligence and depth of personality (Gemüth).

(3) From No. 2 it follows that the former has honest diligence and earnestness in all things, and takes pains, whereas the latter is easy-going and guided by its happy nature.

(4) From all this together it follows that in a nation of the former kind the mass of the people is capable of education, and the educators of such a nation test their discoveries on the people and wish to influence it; whereas in a nation of the latter kind the educated classes separate themselves from the people and regard it as nothing more than a blind instrument of their plans.

WHAT IS A NATION?

by Ernest Renan *

I propose to ask you to join with me in analysing an idea which, though it appears simple, yet lends itself to the most dangerous misunderstandings. Human society assumes the most varied forms, great masses of human beings, such as we see in China; in Egypt and in the older Babylonia; the tribe as exemplified by the Hebrews and Arabs; the city, as in Athens and Sparta; the unions of various countries, as in the Achaemenian, Roman and Carlovingian empires; communities having no mother country but held together by the bond of religion, as the Israelites and the Parsees; nations such as France, England and most modern European autonomous States; confederations, as in Switzerland and America; relationships, such as those set up by race, or rather by language, between the different branches of Germans or Slavs: all these various groupings exist, or have existed, and to ignore the differences between them is to create a serious confusion. At the time of the French Revolution it was believed that the institutions of small independent towns, such as Sparta and Rome, could be applied to our great nations comprising thirty or forty million inhabitants. Nowadays, we observe a graver error. The terms "race" and "nation" are confused, and we see attributed to ethnographic, or rather linguistic, groups a sovereignty analogous to that of actually existing peoples. Let us try to arrive at some degree of exactness with regard to these difficult questions in which the least confusion at the outset of the argument as to the meaning of words may lead in the end to the most fatal errors. Our task is a delicate one; it amounts almost to vivisection; and we are going to treat the living as usually we treat the dead. We shall proceed coldly and with the most complete impartiality.

* Ernest Renan, "What Is a Nation?" *Modern Political Doctrines*, edited by Sir Alfred Zimmern (Oxford: 1939). By permission of The Clarendon Press, Oxford.

I

Since the end of the Roman Empire, or rather since the dismemberment of the empire of Charlemagne, Western Europe appears to us as divided into nations, some of which have, at certain periods, tried to establish a hegemony over others, without ever achieving any permanent success. Where Charles V, Louis XIV and Napoleon I failed, no man in the future will probably ever succeed. To set up a new Roman Empire or a new empire such as that of Charlemagne has become an impossibility. Europe is so much divided that any attempt at universal domination would immediately produce a coalition that would compel the ambitious nation to retire within its natural limits. A kind of durable balance has been established. Centuries may pass, but France, England, Germany and Russia, in spite of all their adventures, will retain their distinct historical individuality, like pieces on a draughtboard, the squares of which are ever varying in size and importance, but never quite blend completely.

Nations, thus conceived, are a fairly recent phenomenon in history. Such nations were unknown in ancient times. Egypt, China and old Chaldaea were by no manner of means nations. They were flocks led by an offspring of the Sun or an offspring of Heaven. There were no Egyptian citizens, any more than there are Chinese citizens. The classical antique world had its republics and royal towns, its confederations of local republics and its empires, but it hardly had a nation in our sense of the word. Athens, Sparta, Sidon and Tyre are small centres of patriotism, however admirable; they are cities possessing relatively small territories. Gaul, Spain and Italy, before their absorption into the Roman Empire, were assemblies of tribes, often in league with one another, but without central institutions or dynasties. Nor could the empires of Assyria or Persia or that of Alexander point to any mother country. There were never any Assyrian patriots; nor was the empire of Persia anything but a vast feudal estate. There is not a nation that traces its origin back to Alexander's colossal enterprise, which was yet so fertile in its consequences for the general history of civilization.

The Roman Empire came much nearer to being a mother country. Roman rule, at first so hard to bear, very soon became loved in return for the immense benefit conferred by the suppression of war. It was a grand association, synonymous with order, peace and civilization. During its closing period, men of lofty mind, enlightened clerics and the educated classes had a real sense of "the Roman Peace," as opposed to the menacing chaos of barbarism. But an empire twelve times as great as France is to-day could not be termed a State in the modern sense of the word. The split between

East and West was inevitable. In the third century attempts at a Gallic empire failed; and it was the Germanic invasion that ushered into the world the principle which afterwards served as a basis for the existence of nationalities.

What in fact did the Germanic peoples accomplish from the time of their great invasions in the fifth century to the last Norman conquests in the tenth? They effected little change in the essential character of races, but they imposed dynasties and a military aristocracy on more or less important areas within the former empire of the West, and these areas assumed the names of their invaders. Hence we have a France, a Burgundy, a Lombardy, and — later on — a Normandy. The rapid superiority won by the Frankish Empire renewed, for a brief period, the unity of the West. But about the middle of the ninth century this empire was shattered beyond repair. The Treaty of Verdun laid down its dividing lines, immutable in principle, and from that time France, Germany, England, Italy and Spain march forward, by ways often tortuous and beset by countless hazards, to their full national existence such as we see spread out before us to-day.

What is, in fact, the distinguishing mark of these various States? It is the fusion of the populations that compose them. There is no analogy between the countries we have just mentioned and the state of affairs in Turkey, where Turk, Slav, Greek, Armenian, Arab, Syrian and Kurd are as distinct to-day as at the time of the conquest. Two essential circumstances contributed to this result. First, the fact that the Germanic peoples adopted Christianity as soon as they came into more or less permanent contact with the Greek and Latin peoples. When victor and vanquished have the same religion, or rather when the victor adopts the religion of the vanquished, there can be no question of the Turkish system of complete discrimination according to a man's religion. The second circumstance was that the victors forgot their own language. The grandsons of Clovis, Alaric, Gondebaud, Alboin and Rollo spoke the Roman tongue. This fact was itself the consequence of another important particular circumstance, viz., that the Franks, Burgundians, Goths, Lombards and Normans were accompanied by very few women of their own race. During several generations the chiefs married none but German wives. But their concubines and their children's nurses were Latins, and the whole tribe married Latin women, with the result that, from the time of the settlement of the Franks and Goths on Roman soil, the *lingua francica* and the *lingua gothica* had but a very short career. It was not so in England, since the Anglo-Saxon invaders doubtless brought wives with them. The

British population fled before them, and furthermore, Latin was no longer, or rather had never been, the dominant language in Britain. If, in the fifth century, Old French had been the general language in Gaul, Clovis and his men would not have deserted their Germanic tongue in favour of Old French.

Hence we get the following most important result, namely that, in spite of the brutality of the invaders, the pattern laid down by them became, in the course of time, the very pattern of the nation. Quite rightly, France became the name of a country containing but an imperceptible minority of Franks. In the tenth century, in the early songs of Charlemagne, which perfectly reflect the spirit of the age, all the inhabitants of France appear as Frenchmen. The idea of any difference of race in the population of France, which stands out so clearly in Gregory of Tours, does not occur at all in French writers or poets after the time of Hugh Capet. The difference between noble and serf is accentuated to the highest degree, but it is in no sort of way an ethnic difference. It is a difference in courage, custom and education, transmitted by birth. The idea that the origin of all this lies in conquest occurs to no one. Already in the thirteenth century we see established, with all the force of dogma, the spurious system according to which nobility owed its origin to a privilege conferred by the King in recognition of great services rendered to the nation, so that every noble is a man ennobled. The same thing happened after almost all the Norman conquests; after one or two generations the Norman invaders were no longer distinguishable from the rest of the population. Nevertheless, they had exercised a marked influence, having given to the conquered country a nobility, military habits and a feeling of patriotism — things which it had never known before.

To forget and — I will venture to say — to get one's history wrong, are essential factors in the making of a nation; and thus the advance of historical studies is often a danger to nationality. Historical research, in fact, casts fresh light upon those deeds of violence which have marked the origin of all political formations, even of those which have been followed by the most beneficial results. Unity is always realized by brute force. The union of North and South in France was the result of a reign of terror and extermination carried on for nearly a century. The French monarchy, which is generally regarded as typifying a steady process of crystallization and as having brought about the most perfect example of national unity known to history, when studied more closely loses its glamour. It was cursed by the nation that it was engaged in moulding, and to-day it is only those who can see the past in perspective who can appreciate the value of its achievement.

These great laws in the history of Western Europe become obvious by contrast. Many countries have failed in such an enterprise as that which the king of France, partly by his tyranny and partly by his justice, brought to so admirable a conclusion. Beneath the crown of St. Stephen, Magyars and Slavs have remained as distinct as they were eight hundred years ago. The House of Habsburg, far from blending the diverse elements in its dominions, has kept them apart and often in opposition to each other. In Bohemia the Czech and German elements are superposed like oil and water in a glass. The Turkish policy of separating nationalities according to religion has had very much graver consequences, since it has entailed the ruin of the East. Take a town like Salonica or Smyrna, and you will find five or six communities, each with its own memories and almost nothing in common. Now it is of the essence of a nation that all individuals should have much in common, and further that they should all have forgotten much. No French citizen knows whether he is a Burgundian, an Alan, a Taifal or a Visigoth, while every French citizen must have forgotten the massacre of St. Bartholomew's and the massacres in the South in the thirteenth century. Not ten families in France can prove their Frankish descent, and even if they could, such a proof would be inherently unsound, owing to the innumerable unknown alliances capable of upsetting all genealogical systems.

The modern nation is, therefore, the historic consequence of a series of facts converging towards the same point. Sometimes unity has been brought about by a dynasty, as in the case of France; at other times it has been brought about by the direct volition of provinces, as in the case of Holland, Switzerland and Belgium; or again, by a general sentiment, the tardy conqueror of the freaks of feudalism, as in the case of Italy and Germany. At all times such formations have been guided by the urge of some deep-seated reason. In such cases, principles burst out with the most unexpected surprises. In our own times we have seen Italy unified by its defeats and Turkey demolished by its victories. Every defeat advanced the Italian cause, while every victory served to ruin Turkey, since Italy is a nation, and Turkey, apart from Asia Minor, is not. It is to the glory of France that, by the French Revolution, she proclaimed that a nation exists of itself. It is not for us to disapprove of imitators. The principle of nations is our principle. But what, then, is a nation? Why is Holland a nation, while Hanover and the Grand

Duchy of Parma are not? How is it that France persists in being a nation, when the principle that created her has vanished? Why is Switzerland, with its three languages, its two religions and three or four races, a nation, when Tuscany, for example, which is so homogeneous, is not? Why is Austria a state and not a nation? In what does the principle of nations differ from that of races? These are points on which thoughtful men require, for their own peace of mind, to come to some conclusion. Although the affairs of the world are rarely settled by arguments of this nature, yet studious men like to bring reason to bear on these questions, and to unravel the skein of confusion that entangles the superficial mind.

II

We are told by certain political theorists that a nation is, above all, a dynasty representing a former conquest that has been at first accepted, and then forgotten, by the mass of the people. According to these politicians, the grouping of provinces effected by a dynasty, its wars, marriages and treaties, ends with the dynasty that has formed it. It is quite true that most modern nations have been made by a family of feudal origin, which has married into the country and provided some sort of centralizing nucleus. The boundaries of France in 1789 were in no way natural or necessary. The large area that the House of Capet had added to the narrow strip accorded by the Treaty of Verdun was indeed the personal acquisition of that family. At the time when the annexations were made no one thought about natural limits, the right of nations or the wishes of provinces. Similarly, the union of England, Ireland and Scotland was a dynastic performance. The only reason Italy took so long to become a nation was that, until the present century, none of her numerous reigning families became a centre of union. It is an odd fact that she derives the royal * title from the obscure island of Sardinia, a land which is scarcely Italian. Holland, self-created by an act of heroic resolution, has none the less entered into a close bond of marriage with the House of Orange, and would run serious risks, should this union ever be endangered.

Is, however, such a law absolute? Doubtless, it is not. Switzerland and the United States which have been formed, like conglomerates, by successive additions, are based on no dynasty. I will not discuss the question in so far as it concerns France. One would have to be able to read the future in order to do so. Let us merely observe that this great French line of kings had become so thoroughly identified with the national life

---

* The House of Savoy owes its royal title solely to the possession of Sardinia (1720).

that, on the morrow of its downfall, the nation was able to subsist without it. Furthermore, the eighteenth century had entirely changed the situation. After centuries of humiliation, man had recovered his ancient spirit, his self-respect and the idea of his rights. The words "mother country" and "citizen" had regained their meaning. Thus it was possible to carry out the boldest operation ever performed in history — an operation that may be compared to what, in physiology, would be an attempt to bring back to its former life a body from which brain and heart had been removed.

It must, therefore, be admitted that a nation can exist without any dynastic principle, and even that nations formed by dynasties can be separated from them without thereby ceasing to exist. The old principle, which takes into account only the right of princes, can no longer be maintained: and, besides dynastic right, there exists also national right. On what criterion is this national right to be based? By what sign is it to be known? And from what tangible fact is it properly to be derived?

1. Many will boldly reply, from race. The artificial divisions, they say, the results of feudalism, royal marriages and diplomatic congresses, have broken down. Race is what remains stable and fixed; and this it is that constitutes a right and a lawful title. The Germanic race, for example, according to this theory, has the right to retake the scattered members of the Germanic family, even when these members do not ask for reunion. The right of the Germanic family over such-and-such a province is better than the right of its inhabitants over themselves. A sort of primordial right is thus created analogous to the divine right of kings; and the principle of ethnography is substituted for that of nations. This is a very grave error, and if it should prevail, it would spell the ruin of European civilization. The principle of the primordial right of race is as narrow and as fraught with danger for true progress as the principle of nations is just and legitimate.

We admit that, among the tribes and cities of the ancient world, the fact of race was of capital importance. The ancient tribe and city were but an extension of the family. In Sparta and Athens all citizens were related more or less closely to each other. It was the same among the Beni-Israel; and it is still so among the Arab tribes. But let us leave Athens, Sparta and the Jewish tribe and turn to the Roman Empire. Here we have quite a different state of affairs. This great agglomeration of completely diverse towns and provinces, formed in the first place by violence and then held together by common interests, cuts at the very root of the racial idea. Christianity, characteristically universal and absolute, works even more effectively in the same direction. It contracts a close alliance with the Roman Empire, and, under the influence of these two incomparable unifying agents, the ethnographic argument is for centuries dismissed from the government of human affairs.

In spite of appearances, the barbarian invasions were a step further on this road. The barbarian kingdoms which were then cut out have nothing ethnographic about them; they were decided by the forces or whims of the conquerors, who were completely indifferent with regard to the race of the peoples whom they subjugated. Charlemagne reconstructed in his own way what Rome had already built, viz., a single empire composed of the most diverse races. The authors of the Treaty of Verdun, calmly drawing their two long lines from north to south, did not pay the slightest attention to the race of the peoples to right or left of them. The frontier changes which took place in the later Middle Ages were also devoid of all ethnographic tendencies. Let it be granted that the consistent policy of the Capets managed more or less to gather together, under the name of France, the territories of ancient Gaul; yet this was by no means the consequence of any tendency on the part of their inhabitants to unite themselves with their kindred. Dauphiné, Bresse, Provence and Franche-Comté no longer remembered any common origin. The consciousness of Gallic race had been lost since the second century A.D., and it is only in modern times, and retrospectively, that the erudite have unearthed the peculiarities of the Gallic character.

Ethnographic considerations have, therefore, played no part in the formation of modern nations. France is Celtic, Iberic and Germanic. Germany is Germanic, Celtic and Slav. Italy is the country in which ethnography finds its greatest difficulties. Here Gauls, Etruscans, Pelasgians and Greeks are crossed in an unintelligible medley. The British Isles, taken as a whole, exhibit a mixture of Celtic and Germanic blood, the proportions of which are particularly difficult to define.

The truth is that no race is pure, and that to base politics on ethnographic analysis is tantamount to basing it on a chimera. The noblest countries, England, France and Italy, are those where breeds are most mixed. Is Germany an exception in this respect? Is she a purely Germanic country? What a delusion to suppose it! All the South was Gallic; and all the East, starting from the Elbe, is Slav. And as for those areas which are said to be really pure from the racial point of view, are they in fact so? Here we touch on one of those problems concerning which it is most important to have clear ideas and to prevent misunderstandings.

Discussions on race are endless, because the word "race" is taken by historians who are philologists and by anthropologists with physiological leanings in two quite different senses. For the anthropologists race has the same meaning as it has in zoology: it connotes real descent—blood relationship. Now the study of languages and history does not lead to the same divisions as physiology. The words "brachycephalic" and "dolichocephalic" find no place either in history or philology. Within the human group that created the Aryan tongues and the Aryan rules of life there were already brachycephalics and dolichocephalics; and the same must be said of the primitive group that created the languages and institutions termed Semitic. In other words, the zoological origins of the human race are vastly anterior to the origins of culture, civilization and language. The primitive Aryan, Semitic and Turanian groups were joined in no physiological unity. These groupings are historical facts which took place at a certain period, let us say fifteen or twenty thousand years ago; whereas the zoological origin of the human race is lost in impenetrable darkness. What the sciences of philology and history call the Germanic race is assuredly a quite distinct family among human kind. But is it a family in the anthropological sense? Certainly not. The distinctive German character appears in history only a very few centuries before Jesus Christ. Obviously the Germans did not emerge from the earth at that period. Before that time, when mingled with the Slavs in the great shadowy mass of Scythians, they possessed no distinctive character. An Englishman is certainly a type in the whole sum of human kind. Now the type of what is very incorrectly termed the Anglo-Saxon race * is neither the Briton of the time of Caesar, nor the Anglo-Saxon of Hengist, nor the Dane of Canute, nor the Norman of William the Conqueror: it is the sum total of all these. The Frenchman is neither a Gaul, nor a Frank, nor a Burgundian. He is that which has emerged from the great cauldron in which, under the eye of the king of France, the most diverse elements have been simmering. As regards his origin, an inhabitant of Jersey or Guernsey differs in no way from the Norman population of the neighbouring coast. In the eleventh century the most piercing gaze would

---

* Germanic elements are not much more important in the United Kingdom than they were in France at the time when she possessed Alsace and Metz. The Germanic language prevailed in the British Isles solely because Latin had not completely ousted the Celtic forms of speech there, as was the case with the Gauls.

not have perceived the slightest difference on either side of the strait. Trifling circumstances decided Philip Augustus not to take these islands together with the rest of Normandy. Separated from each other for nearly seven hundred years, the two peoples have become not only foreign to each other, but entirely dissimilar. Race, then, as we historians understand it, is something that is made and unmade. The study of race is of prime importance for the man of learning engaged on the history of human kind. It is not applicable to politics. The instinctive consciousness which has presided over the drawing of the map of Europe has held race to be no account, and the leading nations of Europe are those of essentially mixed breed.

The fact of race, therefore, while vitally important at the outset, tends always to become less so. There is an essential difference between human history and zoology. Here race is not everything, as it is with the rodents and the cats; and one has no right to go about feeling people's heads, and then taking them by the throat and saying "You are related to us; you belong to us!" Apart from anthropological characteristics, there are such things as reason, justice, truth and beauty, which are the same for all. For another thing, this ethnographic policy is not safe. To-day you may exploit it against others; and then you see it turned against yourself. Is it certain that the Germans, who have so boldly hoisted the banner of ethnography, will not see the Slavs arrive and, in their turn, analyse village names in Saxony and Lusatia; or seek out the traces of the Wiltzes or the Obotrites; or say that they have come to settle accounts arising out of the massacres and wholesale enslavements inflicted upon their ancestors by the Ottos? It is an excellent thing for us all to know how to forget.

I like ethnography very much, and find it a peculiarly interesting science. But as I wish it to be free, I do not wish it to be applied to politics. In ethnography, as in all branches of learning, systems change. It is the law of progress. Should nations then also change together with the systems? The boundaries of states would follow the fluctuations of the science; and patriotism would depend on a more or less paradoxical dissertation. The patriot would be told: "You were mistaken: you shed your blood in such-and-such a cause; you thought you were a Celt; no, you are a German." And then, ten years later, they will come and tell you that you are a Slav. Lest we put too great a strain upon Science, let us excuse the lady from giving an opinion on problems in which so many interests are involved. For you may be sure that, if you make her the handmaid of diplomacy, you will often catch her in the very act of granting other favours. She has better things to do: so let us ask her just to tell the truth.

2. What we have said about race, applies also to language. Language invites union, without, however, compelling it. The United States and England, as also Spanish America and Spain, speak the same language without forming a single nation. Switzerland, on the contrary, whose foundations are solid because they are based on the assent of the various parties, contains three or four languages. There exists in man a something which is above language: and that is his will. The will of Switzerland to be united, in spite of the variety of these forms of speech, is a much more important fact than a similarity of language, often attained by vexatious measures. It is to the honour of France that she has never tried to attain unity of language by the use of coercion. Is it impossible to cherish the same feelings and thoughts and to love the same things in different languages? We were talking just now of the objections to making international politics dependent on ethnography. It would be no less objectionable to make them depend on comparative philology. Let us allow full liberty of discussion to these interesting branches of learning, and not mix them up with what would disturb their serenity. The political importance ascribed to languages comes from regarding them as tokens of race. Nothing could be more unsound. In Prussia, where nothing but German is now spoken, Russian was spoken a few centuries ago; in Wales, English is spoken; in Gaul and Spain, the original speech of Alba Longa; in Egypt, Arabic; and we could cite any number of other examples. Even in the beginning of things, similarity of language did not imply that of race. Take the proto-Aryan or proto-Semitic tribe. It contained slaves speaking the same language as their masters, whereas the slave very often differed from his master in race. We must repeat that these divisions into Indo-European, Semitic and other languages, which have been laid down by comparative philologists with such admirable acumen, do not coincide with those laid down by anthropology. Languages are historical formations which afford little clue to the descent of those who speak them and which, in any case, cannot be permitted to fetter human liberty, when it is a question of deciding with what family one is to be linked for life and death.

This exclusive importance attributed to language has, like the exaggerated attention paid to race, its dangers and its objections. If you overdo it, you shut yourself up within a prescribed culture which you regard as the national culture. You are confined and immured, having left the open air of the great world outside to shut yourself up in a conventicle together with your compatriots. Nothing could be worse for the mind; and nothing could be more untoward for civilization. Let us not lose sight of this fundamental principle that man, apart from being penned up within the bounds of one language or another, apart from being a member of one race or another, or the follower of one culture or another, is above all a reasonable moral being. Above French, German or Italian culture, there stands human culture. Consider the great men of the Renaissance. They were neither French, nor Italian, nor German. By their intercourse with the ancient world, they had rediscovered the secret of the true education of the human mind, and to that they devoted themselves body and soul. How well they did!

3. Nor can religion provide a satisfactory basis for a modern nationality. In its origin, religion was connected with the very existence of the social group, which itself was an extension of the family. The rites of religion were family rites. The religion of Athens was the cult of Athens itself, of its mythical founders, its laws and customs. This religion, which did not involve any dogmatic theology, was, in the full sense of the words, a state religion. Those who refused to practice it were not Athenians. At bottom it was the cult of the personified Acropolis; and to swear on the altar of Aglauros * amounted to an oath to die for one's country. This religion was the equivalent of our drawing lots for military service or of our cult of the national flag. To refuse to participate in such cult would have been tantamount to a refusal nowadays to serve in the army, and to a declaration that one was not an Athenian. On the other hand, it is clear that such a cult as this meant nothing for those who were not Athenians; so there was no proselytising to compel foreigners to accept it, and the slaves of Athens did not practice it. The same was the case in certain small republics of the Middle Ages. No man was a good Venetian if he did not swear by St. Mark; nor a good citizen of Amalfi if he did not set St. Andrew above all the other saints in Paradise. In these small societies, acts, which in later times became the grounds for persecution and tyranny, were justifiable and were as trivial as it is with us to wish the father of the family many happy returns of his birthday or a happy new year.

What was true of Sparta and Athens was no longer so in the kingdoms that emerged from the conquests of Alexander, and still less so in the Roman Empire. The persecutions carried out by Antiochus Epiphanes to induce the Eastern world to worship the Olympian Jove, like those of the Roman Empire to maintain the farce of a state religion, were mis-

---

* Aglauros, who gave her life to save her country, represents the Acropolis itself.

taken, criminal and really absurd. Nowadays the situation is perfectly clear, since the masses no longer have any uniform belief. Every one believes and practices religion in his own way according to his capacities and wishes. State religion has ceased to exist; and a man can be a Frenchman, an Englishman or a German, and at the same time a Catholic, a Protestant or a Jew, or practice no form of worship at all. Religion has become a matter to be decided by the individual according to his conscience, and nations are no longer divided into Catholic and Protestant. Religion which, fifty-two years ago, was so important a factor in the formation of Belgium, is still equally so in the heart of every man; but it is now barely to be reckoned among the reasons that determine national frontiers.

4. Community of interest is certainly a powerful bond between men. But do interests suffice to make a nation? I do not believe it. Community of interest brings about commercial treaties. Nationality, which is body and soul both together, has its sentimental side: and a Customs Union is not a country.

5. Geography, and what we call natural frontiers, certainly plays a considerable part in the division of nations. Geography is one of the essential factors of history. Rivers have guided races: mountains have impeded them. The former have favoured, while the latter have restricted, historic movements. But can one say, as some people believe, that a nation's boundaries are to be found written on the map, and that it has the right to award itself as much as is necessary to round off certain outlines, or to reach such-and-such a mountain or river, which are regarded as in some way dispensing the frontier a priori? I know no doctrine more arbitrary or fatal than this, which can be used to justify all kinds of violence. In the first place, is it the mountains, or is it the rivers that constitute these alleged natural frontiers? It is indisputable that mountains separate; but rivers tend rather to bring together. Then again all mountains cannot divide states. Which are those that separate and those that do not? From Biarritz to Tornea there is not one estuary which is more like a boundary than another. If History had so decreed, then the Loire, the Seine, the Meuse, the Elbe and the Oder would have, as much as the Rhine has, this character of national frontier, which has been the cause of so many infringements of that fundamental right, which is the will of men. People talk of strategic grounds. Nothing is absolute; and it is evident that much must be conceded to necessity. But these concessions must not go too far. Otherwise, every one will demand what suits him from a military point of view and we shall have endless war-

fare. No; it is not the soil any more than the race which makes a nation. The soil provides the substratum, the field for struggle and labour: man provides the soul. Man is everything in the formation of this sacred thing that we call a people. Nothing that is material suffices here. A nation is a spiritual principle, the result of the intricate workings of history; a spiritual family and not a group determined by the configuration of the earth.

We have now seen those things which do not suffice to create such a spiritual principle. They are race, language, interests, religious affinity, geography and military necessity. What more then is required? In view of what I have already said, I shall not have to detain you very much longer.

III

A nation is a soul, a spiritual principle. Two things, which are really only one, go to make up this soul or spiritual principle. One of these things lies in the past, the other in the present. The one is the possession in common of a rich heritage of memories; and the other is actual agreement, the desire to live together, and the will to continue to make the most of the joint inheritance. Man cannot be improvised. The nation, like the individual, is the fruit of a long past spent in toil, sacrifice and devotion. Ancestor-worship is of all forms the most justifiable, since our ancestors have made us what we are. A heroic past, great men and glory — I mean real glory — these should be the capital of our company when we come to found a national idea. To share the glories of the past, and a common will in the present; to have done great deeds together, and to desire to do more — these are the essential conditions of a people's being. Love is in proportion to the sacrifices one has made and the evils one has borne. We love the house that we have built and that we hand down to our successors. The Spartan song "We are what ye were, and we shall be what ye are," is, in its simplicity, the abridged version of every national anthem.

In the past, a heritage of glory and of grief to be shared; in the future, one common plan to be realized; to have suffered, rejoiced and hoped together; these are things of greater value than identity of custom-houses and frontiers in accordance with strategic notions. These are things which are understood, in spite of differences in race and language. I said just now "to have suffered together," for indeed common suffering unites more strongly than common rejoicing. Among national memories, sorrows have greater value than victories; for they impose duties and demand common effort. Thus we see that a nation is a great solid unit, formed by the realization of sacrifices in the past, as well as of those one is prepared to make in the future. A nation implies a past; while, as regards the present, it is all contained in one tangible fact, viz., the agreement and clearly expressed desire to continue a life in common. The existence of a nation is (if you will forgive me the metaphor) a daily plebiscite, just as that of the individual is a continual affirmation of life. I am quite aware that this is less metaphysical than the doctrine of divine right, and smacks less of brute force than alleged historic right. According to the notions that I am expounding, a nation has no more right than a king to say to a province: "You belong to me; so I will take you." A province means to us its inhabitants; and if any one has a right to be consulted in the matter, it is the inhabitant. It is never to the true interest of a nation to annex or keep a country against its will. The people's wish is after all the only justifiable criterion, to which we must always come back.

We have excluded from politics the abstract principles of metaphysics and theology; and what remains? There remains man, with his desires and his needs. But you will tell me that the consequences of a system that puts these ancient fabrics at the mercy of the wishes of usually unenlightened minds, will be the secession and ultimate disintegration of nations. It is obvious that in such matters no principles should be pushed too far, and that truths of this nature are applicable only as a whole and in a very general sort of way. Human wishes change indeed: but what in this world does not? Nations are not eternal. They have had beginnings and will have ends; and will probably be replaced by a confederation of Europe. But such is not the law of the age in which we live. Nowadays it is a good, and even a necessary, thing that nations should exist. Their existence is the guarantee of liberty, which would be lost, if the world had but one law and one master.

By their various, and often contrasting, attainments, the nations serve the common task of humanity; and all play some instrument in that grand orchestral concert of mankind, which is, after all, the highest ideal reality that we attain. Taken separately, they all have their weak points; and I often tell myself that a man who should have the vices that are held to be virtues in nations, a man battening on empty glory, and so jealous, selfish and quarrelsome as to be ready to draw his sword at the slightest provocation, would be the most intolerable creature. But such discordant details vanish when all is taken together. What sufferings poor humanity has endured and what trials await it yet! May it be guided by the spirit of wisdom and preserved from the countless dangers that beset the path!

And now let me sum it all up. Man is the slave neither of his race, nor his language, nor his religion, nor of the windings of his rivers and mountain ranges. That moral consciousness which we call a nation is created by a great assemblage of men with warm hearts and healthy minds: and as long as this moral consciousness can prove its strength by the sacrifices demanded from the individual for the benefit of the community, it is justifiable and has the right to exist. If doubts arise concerning its frontiers, let the population in dispute be consulted: for surely they have a right to a say in the matter. This will bring a smile to the lips of the transcendental politicians, those infallible beings who spend their lives in self-deception and who, from the summit of their superior principles, cast a pitying eye upon our commonplaces. "Consult the population! Stuff and nonsense! This is only another of these feeble French ideas that aim at replacing diplomacy and war by methods of infantile simplicity." Well, let us wait a while. Let the kingdom of the transcendentalists endure for its season; and let us learn to submit to the scorn of the mighty. It may be, that after many fruitless fumblings, the world will come back to our modest empirical solutions. The art of being right in the future is, at certain times, the art of resigning oneself to being old-fashioned.

THE DUTIES OF MAN

by Joseph Mazzini *

Your first Duties — first, at least, in importance — are . . . to Humanity. You are *men* before you are *citizens* or *fathers.* . . .

But what can *each* of you, with his isolated powers, *do* for the moral improvement, for the progress of Humanity? You can, from time to time,

* As translated by Thomas Okey in *Essays by Joseph Mazzini*, London, 1894, and reprinted in Joseph Mazzini, *The Duties of Man and Other Essays*, Everyman's Library, J. M. Dent and Sons, Ltd., London and Toronto, E. P. Dutton and Company, New York (1915). By permission of E. P. Dutton and Company, Inc.

give sterile expression to your belief; you may, on some rare occasion, perform an act of *charity* to a brother not belonging to your own land, no more. Now, *charity* is not the watchword of the future faith. The watchword of the future faith is *association*, fraternal co-operation towards a common aim, and this is as much superior to *charity* as the work of many uniting to raise with one accord a building for the habitation of all together would be superior to that which you would accomplish by raising a separate hut each for himself, and only helping one another by exchanging stones and bricks and mortar. But divided as you are in language, tendencies, habits, and capacities, you cannot attempt this common work. The *individual* is too weak, and Humanity too vast. *My God*, prays the Breton mariner as he puts out to sea, *protect me, my ship is so little, and Thy ocean so great!* And this prayer sums up the condition of each of you, if no means is found of multiplying your forces and your powers of action indefinitely. But God gave you this means when he gave you a Country, when, like a wise overseer of labour, who distributes the different parts of the work according to the capacity of the workmen, he divided Humanity into distinct groups upon the face of our globe, and thus planted the seeds of nations. Bad governments have disfigured the design of God, which you may see clearly marked out, as far, at least, as regards Europe, by the courses of the great rivers, by the lines of the lofty mountains, and by other geographical conditions; they have disfigured it by conquest, by greed, by jealousy of the just sovereignty of others; disfigured it so much that to-day there is perhaps no nation except England and France whose confines correspond to this design. They did not, and they do not, recognise any country except their own families and dynasties, the egoism of caste. But the divine design will infallibly be fulfilled. Natural divisions, the innate spontaneous tendencies of the peoples will replace the arbitrary divisions sanctioned by bad governments. The map of Europe will be remade. The Countries of the People will rise, defined by the voice of the free, upon the ruins of the Countries of Kings and privileged castes. Between these Countries there will be harmony and brotherhood. And then the work of Humanity for the general amelioration, for the discovery and application of the real law of life, carried on in association and distributed according to local capacities, will be accomplished by peaceful and progressive development; then each of you, strong in the affections and in the aid of many millions of men speaking the same language, endowed with the same tendencies, and educated by the same historic tradition, may hope by your personal effort to benefit the whole of Humanity.

To you, who have been born in Italy, God has allotted, as if favouring you specially, the best-defined country in Europe. In other lands, marked by more uncertain or more interrupted limits, questions may arise which the pacific vote of all will one day solve, but which have cost, and will yet perhaps cost, tears and blood; in yours, no. God has stretched round you sublime and indisputable boundaries; on one side the highest mountains of Europe, the Alps; on the other the sea, the immeasurable sea. Take a map of Europe and place one point of a pair of compasses in the north of Italy on Parma; point the other to the mouth of the Var, and describe a semicircle with it in the direction of the Alps; this point, which will fall, when the semicircle is completed, upon the mouth of the Isonzo, will have marked the frontier which God has given you. As far as this frontier your language is spoken and understood; beyond this you have no rights. Sicily, Sardinia, Corsica, and the smaller islands between them and the mainland of Italy belong undeniably to you. Brute force may for a little while contest these frontiers with you, but they have been recognised from of old by the tacit general consent of the peoples; and the day when, rising with one accord for the final trial, you plant your tri-coloured flag upon that frontier, the whole of Europe will acclaim rerisen Italy, and receive her into the community of the nations. To this final trial all your efforts must be directed.

Without Country you have neither name, token, voice, nor rights, no admission as brothers into the fellowship of the Peoples. You are the bastards of Humanity. Soldiers without a banner, Israelites among the nations, you will find neither faith nor protection; none will be sureties for you. Do not beguile yourselves with the hope of emancipation from unjust social conditions if you do not first conquer a Country for yourselves; where there is no Country there is no common agreement to which you can appeal; the egoism of self-interest rules alone, and he who has the upper hand keeps it, since there is no common safeguard for the interests of all. Do not be led away by the idea of improving your material conditions without first solving the national question. You cannot do it. Your industrial associations and mutual help societies are useful as a means of educating and disciplining yourselves; as an economic fact they will remain barren until you have an Italy. The economic problem demands, first and foremost, an increase of capital and production; and while your Country is dismembered into separate fragments — while shut off by the barrier of customs and artificial difficulties of every sort, you have only restricted markets open to you — you cannot hope for this increase. To-day — do not delude yourselves — you are not the working-class of

Italy; you are only fractions of that class; powerless, unequal to the great task which you propose to yourselves. Your emancipation can have no practical beginning until a National Government, understanding the signs of the times, shall, seated in Rome, formulate a Declaration of Principles to be the guide for Italian progress, and shall insert into it these words, *Labour is sacred, and is the source of the wealth of Italy.*

Do not be led astray, then, by hopes of material progress which in your present conditions can only be illusions. Your Country alone, the vast and rich Italian Country, which stretches from the Alps to the farthest limit of Sicily, can fulfil these hopes. You cannot obtain your *rights* except by obeying the commands of *Duty.* Be worthy of them, and you will have them. O my Brothers! love your Country. Our Country is our home, the home which God has given us, placing therein a numerous family which we love and are loved by, and with which we have a more intimate and quicker communion of feeling and thought than with others; a family which by its concentration upon a given spot, and by the homogeneous nature of its elements, is destined for a special kind of activity. Our Country is our field of labour; the products of our activity must go forth from it for the benefit of the whole earth; but the instruments of labour which we can use best and most effectively exist in it, and we may not reject them without being unfaithful to God's purpose and diminishing our own strength. In labouring according to true principles for our Country we are labouring for Humanity; our Country is the fulcrum of the lever which we have to wield for the common good. If we give up this fulcrum we run the risk of becoming useless to our Country and to Humanity. Before *associating* ourselves with the Nations which compose Humanity we must exist as a Nation. There can be no association except among equals; and you have no recognised collective existence.

Humanity is a great army moving to the conquest of unknown lands, against powerful and wary enemies. The Peoples are the different corps and divisions of that army. Each has a post entrusted to it; each a special operation to perform; and the common victory depends on the exactness with which the different operations are carried out. Do not disturb the order of the battle. Do not abandon the banner which God has given you. Wherever you may be, into the midst of whatever people circumstances may have driven you, fight for the liberty of that people if the moment calls for it; but fight as Italians, so that the blood which you shed may win honour and love, not for you only, but for your Country. And may the constant thought of your soul be for Italy, may all the acts of your life be worthy of her, and may the standard beneath which you range yourselves to work for Humanity be Italy's. Do not say *I*; say *we*. Be every one of you an incarnation of your Country, and feel himself and make himself responsible for his fellow-countrymen; let each one of you learn to act in such a way that in him men shall respect and love his Country.

Your Country is one and indivisible. As the members of a family cannot rejoice at the common table if one of their number is far away, snatched from the affection of his brothers, so you should have no joy or repose as long as a portion of the territory upon which your language is spoken is separated from the Nation.

Your Country is the token of the mission which God has given you to fulfil in Humanity. The faculties, the strength of *all* its sons should be united for the accomplishment of this mission. A certain number of common duties and rights belong to every man who answers to the *Who are you?* of the other peoples, *I am an Italian.* Those duties and those rights cannot be represented except by one *single* authority resulting from your votes. A Country must have, then, a single government. The politicians who call themselves federalists, and who would make Italy into a brotherhood of different states, would dismember the Country, not understanding the idea of Unity. The States into which Italy is divided to-day are not the creation of our own people; they are the result of the ambitions and calculations of princes or of foreign conquerors, and serve no purpose but to flatter the vanity of local aristocracies for which a narrower sphere than a great Country is necessary. What you, the people, have created, beautified, and consecrated with your affections, with your joys, with your sorrows, and with your blood, is the City and the Commune, not the Province or the State. In the City, in the Commune, where your fathers sleep and where your children will live, where you exercise your faculties and your personal rights, you live out your lives as *individuals*. It is of your City that each of you can say what the Venetians say of theirs: "Venice is our own: we have made her." In your City you have need of *liberty* as in your Country you have need of *association*. The Liberty of the Commune and the Unity of the Country — let that, then, be your faith. Do not say Rome and Tuscany, Rome and Lombardy, Rome and Sicily; say Rome and Florence, Rome and Siena, Rome and Leghorn, and so through all the Communes of Italy. Rome for all that represents Italian life; your Commune for whatever represents the *individual* life. All the other divisions are artificial, and are not confirmed by your national tradition.

A Country is a fellowship of free and equal men bound together in a brotherly concord of labour towards a single end. You must make it and maintain it such. A Country is not an aggregation, it is an *association*.

There is no true Country without a uniform right. There is no true Country where the uniformity of that right is violated by the existence of caste, privilege, and inequality — where the powers and faculties of a large number of individuals are suppressed or dormant — where there is no common principle accepted, recognised, and developed by all. In such a state of things there can be no Nation, no People, but only a multitude, a fortuitous agglomeration of men whom circumstances have brought together and different circumstances will separate. In the name of your love for your Country you must combat without truce the existence of every privilege, every inequality, upon the soil which has given you birth. One privilege only is lawful — the privilege of Genius when Genius reveals itself in brotherhood with Virtue; but it is a privilege conceded by God and not by men, and when you acknowledge it and follow its inspirations, you acknowledge it freely by the exercise of your own reason and your own choice. Whatever privilege claims your submission in virtue of force or heredity, or any right which is not a common right, is a usurpation and a tyranny, and you ought to combat it and annihilate it. Your Country should be your Temple. God at the summit, a People of equals at the base. Do not accept any other formula, any other moral law, if you do not want to dishonour your Country and yourselves. Let the secondary laws for the gradual regulation of your existence be the progressive application of this supreme law.

And in order that they should be so, it is necessary that *all* should contribute to the making of them. The laws made by one fraction of the citizens only can never by the nature of things and men do otherwise than reflect the thoughts and aspirations and desires of that fraction; they represent, not the whole country, but a third, a fourth part, a class, a zone of the country. The law must express the general aspiration, promote the good of all, respond to a beat of the nation's heart. The whole nation therefore should be, directly or indirectly, the legislator. By yielding this mission to a few men, you put the egoism of one class in the place of the Country, which is the union of *all* the classes.

A Country is not a mere territory; the particular territory is only its foundation. The Country is the idea which rises upon that foundation; it is the sentiment of love, the sense of fellowship which binds together all the sons of that territory. So long as a single one of your brothers is not represented by his own vote in the development of the national life — so long as a single one vegetates uneducated among the educated — so long as a single one able and willing to work languishes in poverty for want of work — you have not got a Country such as it ought to be, the

Country of all and for all. *Votes, education, work* are the three main pillars of the nation; do not rest until your hands have solidly erected them.

And when they have been erected — when you have secured for every-one of you food for both body and soul — when freely united, entwining your right hands like brothers round a beloved mother, you advance in beautiful and holy concord towards the development of your faculties and the fulfilment of the Italian mission — remember that that mission is the moral unity of Europe; remember the immense duties which it imposes upon you. Italy is the only land that has twice uttered the great word of unification to the disjoined nations. Twice Rome has been the metropolis, the temple, of the European world; the first time when our conquering eagles traversed the known world from end to end and prepared it for union by introducing civilised institutions; the second time when, after the Northern conquerors had themselves been subdued by the potency of Nature, of great memories and of religious inspiration, the genius of Italy incarnated itself in the Papacy and undertook the solemn mission — abandoned four centuries ago — of preaching the union of souls to the peoples of the Christian world. To-day a third mission is dawning for our Italy; as much vaster than those of old as the Italian People, the free and united Country which you are going to found, will be greater and more powerful than Caesars or Popes. The presentiment of this mission agitates Europe and keeps the eye and the thought of the nations chained to Italy.

Your duties to your Country are proportioned to the loftiness of this mission. You have to keep it pure from egoism, uncontaminated by false-hood and by the arts of that political Jesuitism which they call diplomacy.

The government of the country will be based through your labours upon the worship of principles, not upon the idolatrous worship of interests and of opportunity. There are countries in Europe where Liberty is sacred within, but is systematically violated without; peoples who say, *Truth is one thing, utility another: theory is one thing, practice another.* Those countries will have inevitably to expiate their guilt in long isolation, oppression, and anarchy. But you know the mission of our Country, and will pursue another path. Through you Italy will have, with one only God in the heavens, one only truth, one only faith, one only rule of political life upon earth. Upon the edifice, sublimer than Capitol or Vatican, which the people of Italy will raise, you will plant the banner of Liberty and of Association, so that it shines in the sight of all the nations, nor will you lower it ever for terror of despots or lust for the gains of a day. You will have boldness as you have faith. You will speak out aloud to the world, and to those who call themselves the lords of the world, the thought which thrills in the heart of Italy. You will never deny the sister nations. The life of the Country shall grow through you in beauty and in strength, free from servile fears and the hesitations of doubt, keeping as its *foundation* the people, as its *rule* the consequences of its principles logically deduced and energetically applied, as its *strength* the strength of all, as its *outcome* the amelioration of all, as its *end* the fulfilment of the mission which God has given it. And because you will be ready to die for Humanity, the life of your Country will be immortal.

SELF-DETERMINATION AS THE BASIS FOR PEACE

by Woodrow Wilson *

"Self-Determination" is not a mere phase. It is an imperative principle of action, which statesmen will henceforth ignore at their peril. We cannot have general peace for the asking, or by the mere arrangements of a peace conference. It cannot be pieced together out of individual understandings between powerful states. All the parties to this war must join in the settlement of every issue anywhere involved in it; because what we are seeking is a peace that we can all unite to guarantee and maintain, and every item of it must be submitted to the common judgment whether it be right and fair, an act of justice, rather than a bargain between sovereigns.

The United States has no desire to interfere in European affairs or to act as arbiter in European territorial disputes. She would disdain to take advantage of any internal weakness or disorder to impose her own will upon another people.

She is quite ready to be shown that the settlements she has suggested are not the best or the most enduring. They are only her own provisional sketch of principles and of the way in which they should be applied. But

* Statement of February 11, 1918. The Fourteen Points, Articles VI–XIII of which follow, were presented to both houses of Congress on January 8, 1918.

she entered this war because she was made a partner, whether she would or not, in the sufferings and indignities inflicted by the military masters of Germany against the peace and security of mankind; and the conditions of peace will touch her as nearly as they will touch any other nation to which is intrusted a leading part in the maintenance of civilization.

She cannot see her way to peace until the causes of this war are removed, its renewal rendered, as nearly as may be, impossible.

This war had its roots in the disregard of the rights of small nations and of nationalities which lacked the union and the force to make good their claim to determine their own allegiances and their own form of political life. Covenants must now be entered into which will render such things impossible for the future; and those covenants must be backed by the united force of all the nations that love justice and are willing to maintain it at any cost.

The Fourteen Points

ARTICLES VI–XIII

VI

The evacuation of all Russian territory and such a settlement of all questions affecting Russia as will secure the best and freest cooperation of the other nations of the world in obtaining for her an unhampered and unembarrassed opportunity for the independent determination of her own political development and national policy and assure her of a sincere welcome into the society of free nations under institutions of her own choosing; and, more than a welcome, assistance also of every kind that she may need and may herself desire. The treatment accorded Russia by her sister nations in the months to come will be the acid test of their good will, of their comprehension of her needs as distinguished from their own interests, and of their intelligent and unselfish sympathy.

VII

Belgium, the whole world will agree, must be evacuated and restored, without any attempt to limit the sovereignty which she enjoys in common with all other free nations. No other single act will serve to restore confidence among the nations in the laws which they have themselves set and determined for the government of their relations with one another. Without this healing act the whole structure and validity of international law is forever impaired.

VIII

All French territory should be freed and the invaded portions restored, and the wrong done to France by Prussia in 1871 in the matter of Alsace-Lorraine, which has unsettled the peace of the world for nearly fifty years, should be righted, in order that peace may once more be made secure in the interest of all.

IX

A readjustment of the frontiers of Italy should be effected along clearly recognizable lines of nationality.

X

The peoples of Austria-Hungary, whose place among the nations we wish to see safeguarded and assured, should be accorded the freest opportunity of autonomous development.

XI

Rumania, Serbia, and Montenegro should be evacuated; occupied territories restored; Serbia accorded free and secure access to the sea; and the relations of the several Balkan states to one another determined by friendly counsel along historically established lines of allegiance and nationality; and international guarantees of the political and economic independence and territorial integrity of the several Balkan states should be entered into.

XII

The Turkish portions of the present Ottoman Empire should be assured a secure sovereignty, but the other nationalities which are now under Turkish rule should be assured an undoubted security of life and an absolutely unmolested opportunity of autonomous development, and the Dardanelles should be permanently opened as a free passage to the ships and commerce of all nations under international guarantees.

XIII

An independent Polish state should be erected which should include the territories inhabited by indisputably Polish populations, which should be assured a free and secure access to the sea, and whose political and economic independence and territorial integrity should be guaranteed by international covenant.

ISRAEL'S NATIONAL ASPIRATIONS

by David Ben Gurion *

Mr. Chairman and Gentlemen, I fully realise you have been on this enquiry for more than two months and you have already had a good deal of evidence, oral and in writing, and I cannot presume to tell you new things entirely. The reason for my statement is that up till now you have had only the view of Jews from abroad looking to this country. I will try to present to you the case as seen by those in their own country; by those who are no more American, British, Russian, Polish, German Jews, but just Jews. . . .

. . . On behalf of our community I tell you you are invited to see how we are living, what we are doing and you will be welcome everywhere.

Sir, our case it seems to us rather simple and compelling and it rests on two elementary principles; one, that we Jews are just like other human beings, entitled to the same rights as every human being in the world and we Jewish people are just like any other people entitled to the same equality of treatment as any free and independent people in the world. The second principle is, this is and will remain our country. We are here as of right. We are not here on the strength of the Balfour Declaration or the Palestine Mandate. We were here long before. I myself was here before. Many thousands were here before me, but we were here long before that. The Mandatory Power is here on the strength of the Mandate speaking legally from the legal point of view. Our case, and I think you will meet many such cases now in Europe, our case is that of one who builds a house for his family to live there who was expelled forcibly and the house was given to somebody else. It changed hands and then the owner comes back and wants to get his house again. In many cases the Jew is being kept out, it is occupied by somebody else. To make it more

* Statement of Mr. David Ben Gurion, appearing before the Anglo-American Committee of Inquiry, Hearing in Jerusalem, Palestine, Monday, 11th March, 1946. Printed by the Government Printing Office (Jerusalem: 1946). Mr. Ben Gurion was, at the time of these hearings, Chairman of the Executive, Jewish Agency.

exact I will say it this way. It is a large building, our building, of say 150 rooms. We were expelled from that house, our family was scattered, somebody else took it away and again it changed hands many times and then we had to come back and we found some five rooms are occupied by other people, the other rooms from neglect are destroyed and uninhabitable. We said to these occupants we do not want to remove you, please stay where you are, we are going back to these uninhabitable rooms, we will repair them, and we did repair some of them and settled there. Then some other members of the family are coming back and they want to repair some other uninhabitable rooms, but then these occupants say "no, we are here, we do not want you; we do not live in them, these rooms are no good for any human beings but we do not want you to repair them, to make them better," and again we do not say to them "leave, it is ours." We say "You stay, you are there but from yesterday, you may stay please and we will help you to repair your rooms too if you want; if not you can do it yourself." In the neighbourhood there are many big buildings half empty, we do not say to them "Please move over to that other big building." No, we say "Please stay here, we will be good neighbours." This is the case, this is what I say, it is simple and compelling, but I realise the intellectual difficulty of the case. There are other practical difficulties, but now I am talking of the intellectual difficulty of understanding our case because it is unique. There is no precedent, there is no example in the world's history of this problem of the Jews and their country. There is no example or precedent of such a people. It is a people and it is not. There is no example of the history of the Jewish people. There is no example of the fate of this country, no precedent to the significance of this country, to the position of this country. There is no example of the relations between the people of the country. It is unique and people usually when they are faced with a new phenomenon, if they cannot understand it, they simply deny it, but here it is. There is the unique case of the Jewish people in this old country. . . .

. . . It is true there is a Jewish people and there is a problem. They have been torn away from this country for many centuries, the greater part of them, and still it is their country, but it is not empty. There are people there, part of them have been there for many centuries, a great part of them also newcomers, but a part of them for many centuries, and from afar it is not easy really to get at the core of the problem, but I believe when you see things here it will become a little more easy to understand.

What I am going to do is simply to tell you what we Jews in our own country, who we are, what we are doing, what we are aiming at. Why are we here, for what purpose are we here? Perhaps this will explain things.

There are here now some 600,000, more than one-third are born in this country, some of them living here for many centuries, not only in the towns. There are Jewish fellaheen, peasants who are living here for centuries. They are living in Ramleh and in Galilee, but the majority of us were not born in this country; I am one of them. We came from all parts of the world, from all countries, and we came not only from countries where Jews were persecuted physically, exterminated, repressed as in Nazi Germany, as in Poland, as in the Yemen, as in Morocco, as in Tzarist Russia, as in Persia, as in Fascist Italy. Many of us came from free countries where Jews were treated like citizens, where there was no persecution as from England, from the United States of America, from Canada, from the Argentine, from pre-war Germany, from Imperial Germany, from Soviet Russia, from France, Egypt and other countries. Why did they come? They did not come because they were persecuted; what is the common denominator which brought all these people whether from Nazi Germany or from England, whether from Yemen or from Egypt. That is what I want to tell you.

The first thing which brought them over, all of them, was to escape from dependence and discrimination. I do not mean from anti-Semitism. There was a great deal of talk in your Commission about anti-Semitism and many of our people were asked to explain why is it. It is not for us. It is your baby, it is a Christian baby. It is for you Gentiles to explain why it is. Perhaps it would be necessary to set up a Jewish Commission, to make an enquiry of the Gentiles or perhaps a joint Jewish-Gentile Commission, one Chairman Jewish, one Chairman Gentile, to make an enquiry among leaders of the Church, teachers, educators, journalists, political parties as to what disease this is, what is the reason for it in the gentile world. To me it seems it is part of a larger phenomenon which does not concern only Jews. It is a general human phenomenon. Wherever you have two groups, one a strong group, powerful, and the other weak and helpless, there is bound to be mischief. The strong group will always take advantage of the weaker group, rightly or wrongly. You cannot expect human beings, human nature being what it is, people having power over other people, that they should not sometimes, not always, not necessarily always, abuse it. But I am not concerned with anti-Semitism, it is not our business. I am concerned with the question why Jews have to come to this country, and have come not only from countries where they were physically persecuted. They came because they felt it was unendurable for many of them that they are at the mercy of others. Sometimes the others are excellent people but not always, and there is a discrimination, not necessarily a legal one; or a political one or an economic one; sometimes merely a moral discrimination and they do not like it as human beings with human dignity, they do not like it, and they do not see how they can change the whole world. . . .

. . . Why this discrimination? There are many Jews who submitted; there are some Jews who refused and that is what brought them over here. There they were at the mercy of nice people, but nice people may sometimes become very nasty, when they have the power and are dealing with a minority. Why is there this discrimination. As I see it, it is for two reasons; because we happen to be different from others, and we happen to be a minority. We are not the only people who are different from others. In truth we are not different at all because difference is a term of relativity. If there was only one person in the world he would not be different. We are what we are. Others are different, but as they see us, we are different, but we are what we are and we like to be what we are. Is it a crime? Cannot a man be what he is? Cannot a people be what it is. I know on the Continent they consider British people very different and they are, but no Britisher will think he is different. He is, but he is not different, he is just what he is, but to the Continental people he looks different. He is just what he is and we are too; we are just what we are. We happen to be different because other people are different. For that our people suffer. The English people do not suffer because they are different. On the contrary, it is a great compliment, it is a great strength. They have their own individuality and people are brought to respect it. But with us, not only are we different we are in a minority. We are at the mercy of others in that people do not like us being different. It becomes most dangerous sometimes for us because other people want us to be like them and they want us to renounce from time to time either our being a people or our religion or our country or our language, and many of us did renounce, not all, but some of us do and did. You have perhaps met some of them. The Jewish people as a whole defy superior material power when asked by this superior material power to renounce spiritual values which are dear to us and which are ours. And we pay the price, sometimes a very high price for that because we stick to our spiritual values. It is a long long story. It goes back 2,300 years when the world became Hellenised, when Egypt, Syria, Persia became Hellenised. Judaea did not submit to that superior culture, and it was in many respects a superior culture, but the Jews preferred to be just what they were and they suffered. There was another clash when Rome became the dominant Power and we were asked to accept the divinity of the Caesars, and we refused; the most powerful rulers of the world, they were above all other people, recognised as divine persons but not by us and we suffered and fought and were defeated, but only materially, not spiritually. We defied that superior material power. Then it happened again with the rise of Christianity. I must be careful now in speaking. The whole of Europe was converted to Christianity many by force, we refused. We perhaps had more to do with it than other peoples; St. Paul was a Jew. We refused and we paid the price. We are still paying it, a very high price. I read some evidence of some Moslem people and I felt it was repeated again with the rise of another great religion. Here I prefer to be entirely silent. Then the French Revolution asked us to renounce our being a people. Some Jews did it. The Jewish people refused, and now the last phase, I am not going to speak about that. What has happened in the last few years, it is unspeakable, why should I burden you with Jewish feelings. It happened to us, not to anybody else. I will tell you only one feeling which I had, one of the feelings which I had when I knew of what happened, at least I am happy in my children that we belong to a people who is being slaughtered and not to those who are slaughtering us and not to those who are looking at it indifferently. I know many Christians in France, in Holland, in Belgium and other countries who risked their lives to save a Jew or a Jewish baby. We will never forget that, never, but there were other things, not what happened in Nazi Europe, they are outside the pale of humanity, I am not discussing them, but there was a conspiracy of silence in the entire world. . . .

In evidence given to you in America, an American Arab, I believe it was John Hassan said there was never known any Palestine as a political and geographical entity and another American Arab, a great Arab historian, Dr. Hitti, he went even further and said, and I am quoting him "There is no such thing as Palestine in history," absolutely not. And I agree with him. That is not the only thing in which I agree with Arabs. I agree with him entirely; there is no such thing in history as Palestine, absolutely, but when Dr. Hitti speaks of history it means Arab history, he is a specialist in Arab history and he knows his business. In Arab history there is no such thing as Palestine. Arab history was made in Arabia, Syria, Persia and in Spain and North Africa. You will not find Palestine in that history, nor was Arab history made in Palestine. There is not only however an Arab history; there is a world history and a Jewish history and in that history there is a country by name Judea or as we call it Eretz Israel, the Land of Israel. We have called it Israel since the days

of Joshua the son of Nun. There was such a country in history, there was
and it is still there. It is a little country, a very little country, but that
little country made a very deep impression on world history and on our
history because this country made us a people; our people made this
country. No other people in the world made this country; this country
made no other people in the world. Again they are beginning to make this
country and again this country is beginning to make us. It is unique; it
is a fact, and this country came into world history by many wars,
Egyptians, Babylonians, Assyrians, Persians, Greeks, Romans, Byzantines
and others, it gained a place in history and in world history for the same
reason, because our people created here, perhaps a limited, but a very
great civilization, and shaped our people, the Jewish people to make it as it
is from then until today; a very exclusive people on one side and a
universal people on the other; very national and very international.
Exclusive in its internal life and its attachment to its history, to its
national and religious tradition; very universal in its religious, social and
ethical ideas. We were told there is one God in the entire world, that
there is unity of the human race because every human being was created
in the image of God, that there ought to be and will be brotherhood and
social justice, peace between peoples. Those were our ideas; this was our
culture and this made history in this country and it took its place in world
history. We created here a book, many books; many were lost, many
remained only in translations, but a considerable number, some twenty
four remain in their original language, Hebrew, in the same language, Mr.
Chairman, in which I am thinking now when I am talking to you in
English and which the Jews in this country are speaking now. We went
into exile, we took that book with us and in that book which was more
to us than a book, it was us, we took with us our country in our hearts,
in our soul, and there is such a thing as a soul, as well as a body, and
these three, the land, the book and the people are one for us for ever. It
is an indissoluble bond. There is no material power which can dissolve it
except by destroying us physically.

. . . Sir, our rights and our attachment and our significance in this
country you will find in that book, in that book alone. That book is
binding upon us, only that book. It is binding on us. Whether or not it is
on anyone else is not for me to say. I know many Christian people which
believe it is binding upon them too, but it is binding upon us. You cannot
conceive of our people without this book, either in the far away past or in
the present, and it is my conviction in the future too. Somebody may tell
you, "All this is merely a mystical attachment to a mystical Zion, not of

this physical Zion." But now you will see 600,000 living human beings which the love of Zion has brought over and kept them here. They are attached to the living Zion. It has for them also a great and deep spiritual significance.

Then we are asked this question, which seems a very commonplace question: When the Arabs conquered Spain didn't they create there a magnificent civilization? And they did. They created a magnificent civilization in Spain and then they were driven out. Can they claim Spain for the Arabs? Have they a right to Spain? I know of no other objection which proves so forcibly our case as this one, and I am taking it up. Is there a single Arab in the Iraq or in Egypt or anywhere who knows the rivers and mountains of Spain more than he knows this country? Is there an Arab in the world who will give his money to Spain? What is Spain to him? Does he care about Spain?

There are many people who want to conquer countries and possess countries. I am speaking about love for their country. Is there a single Arab in the world who loves Spain? I know many peoples who would like to possess this country. They have tried it for many generations, not because of love for this country, but people who want power.

Here are Jews who are away for centuries, some of them many centuries, some of them thousands of years, as the Jews in Yemen, where they have always carried Zion in their hearts, and they came back and came back with love. You will find in no other country in the world people loving their country as the Jews love this country. . . .

Why? What is it? A man can change many things, even his religion, even his wife, even his name. There is one thing which a man cannot change, his parents. There is no means of changing that. The parents of our people is this country. It is unique, but it is there. . . .

There was a third reason why we came, and this is the crux of the problem. We came over here with an urge for Jewish independence, what you call a Jewish State. I want to explain to you, since this is the center of the entire programme, what is meant by that. When people talk outside in the world about a state, it means power, it means domination. I want to tell you what it means for us.

We came here to be free Jews. I mean in the full sense of the word, 100 percent free and 100 percent Jews, which we couldn't be anywhere, couldn't be in the full sense Jews, we couldn't be free, in no country in the world, and we believe we are entitled to be Jews, to live a full Jewish life as an Englishman lives an English life and an American lives an American life, and to be free from fear, from dependence, not to be an object of pity and sympathy, of philanthropy and justice by others. We believe we are entitled to that as human beings and as a people.

We are the freest Jews in the world. Not in a legal sense. On the contrary, here we are deprived even from equality before the law. We are living in a most arbitrary regime. I know no other regime in the entire world as arbitrary as here, as the regime of the White Paper administration. But it is not what I want to emphasize here.

Freedom begins at home, it begins in the human mind and the human spirit, and here we built our Jewish freedom more than any Jew in the entire world. Why? Why do we feel freer than any Jew? Because we are self-made Jews, made by our country, making our country. We are a Jewish community which is, in fact, a Jewish commonwealth in the making.

I will tell you in a few words how we are making it. When we say "Jewish independence" and "a Jewish state" we mean Jewish country, and I will say what it is. We mean Jewish soil, we mean Jewish labour, we mean Jewish colony, Jewish agriculture, Jewish industry, Jewish seed. We mean Jewish language, schools, culture. We mean Jewish safety, security, independence, complete independence as for any other free people.

I will begin from the foundation. You heard already from Dr. Hitti that there is no such thing as Palestine, absolutely nothing. We are not coming to Palestine; we are coming to a country which we are recreating. When we came here as newcomers, what you call immigrants, we found hundreds of Arab villages, Moslem Arabs, and Christians. We didn't take them away; we didn't settle there. Not a single Jew settled in all these villages. We established hundreds of new Jewish villages on a new soil. We didn't produce soil, it is made by God, but what nature left to people is not enough, they must work. We didn't merely buy the land, we recreated the land. It was rocky hills. You will find a description in the Royal Commission's report. In Hedera hundreds of Jews died, and they refused to leave that place because of love of Zion, because of the need to create their own soil. It was the sand dunes of Rishon-le-Zion, and with our toil, our sweat, and with our love and devotion we are re-making the soil to enable us to settle there, not at the expense of anybody else.

Now you are here and you may visit, and you are cordially invited to visit these villages. You will find the land was reclaimed by our own toil. It was uncultivable, it was certainly uncultivated. We made it cultivable and we cultivated it. Land for us is not an object of trade. We bought and sold. We considered it for the whole world, as the foundation for humanity; everything comes from there. It is a sacred trust to human beings. They shouldn't spoil it. We shouldn't neglect it. We should fortify it, fertilize it, keep it. This is what we are trying to do to the best of our ability, and we did not entirely fail in our endeavours, although we are for many centuries living in the towns and we are told there is a law, this time not a legal law. It was not an illegal act in our sight, but it was a scientific law that people from the country go to the town, but not people in the town go to the country. We didn't like that law because it was contrary to our existence, because we believed we had to go back to the land and we went back to the land and we brought that law. I hope it was not illegal. We did it and will continue to do it.

You heard the evidence presented from an Arab state about this country, that more than 60 percent of this country is uncultivable. It is certainly uncultivated. These lands which are uninhabitable, we want to make them cultivable, perhaps all of them, perhaps all of them, I don't know. We will make an effort. Is there a crime in making this effort? We don't consider manual work as a curse. It is a bitter necessity. It is a means of making a living. We consider it as a high human function, as the basis of human life, the most dignified thing in life of the human being which ought to be free, creative. Man ought to be proud of it.

Our boys and girls, middle-class boys and girls, before they finish high school they are encouraged to go out and work on the land, if they cannot find land to work somewhere else. The Jewish commonwealth means Jewish work. You cannot buy a commonwealth; you cannot conquer a commonwealth. You have to create it by your own work. We are trying to do it, and you will find Jews working here in such trades as you will find anywhere else in the entire world, in fields and factories, in quarries, and everywhere. I mean outside, in the country.

By Jewish commonwealth we mean the Jewish economy, Jewish agriculture, industry, seafaring trades, fishing. Independence means first of all you created yourself, you made yourself independent by your labour and by your economy and by your culture. We don't want to say that this is our country because we conquered it, but because we made it. We remade it; we recreated it. That is what we are trying to do, and you will see it wherever you go. You cannot have a Jewish commonwealth without a great, continuous, constructive effort on land, on sea, in fields and factories, and a Jewish commonwealth means Jewish culture and Jewish language.

If you would come here, not now, but 40 years ago and I would tell you that we are going to revive the Hebrew language and make it a spoken language and a language of work and of trades and of industry and of schools, of universities and science and art, you would say we were mad, it couldn't be done, it is a dead language, it is an old language, it hasn't got all the modern words. Well, it was done, and those Jews came from America and England and Canada and Russia and Poland and Persia and Yemen. With all their many languages they speak now their Hebrew. We have educated their children in Hebrew, and this is now the modern tongue of our children and of our grandchildren.

We don't believe that men live only on bread, and we are creating a Jewish society and we are trying to base it on high intellectual, scientific, cultural and artistic values. . . .

It means Jewish independence to be our own masters, not to depend, to make our own laws, to live according to our own needs, desires, and ideas of life, and we have ideals of life. We have Jewish ideals and we have human ideals. They are not contrary; they are complementing each other.

We are trying to build up a new society, a free society based on justice, and human justice, and based on the highest human intellectual and moral endeavour. If you will have time to visit our agricultural settlement you will find some of that spirit there. Therefore, and for another reason which I will give you, we want Jewish independence. We don't conceive of being independent and being ruled by somebody else. We are building a Jewish state for these two reasons. . . . One is in order to enable us to live our own lives, and the other is to help the solution of their tragic problem, the great tragic historic problem of the Jewish people in the world. Because, sir, only a Jewish state will be able to build a Jewish National Home. We need the state in order to continue building the National Home for the Jewish people, for those Jews who for one reason or another will have need, even if his fate is death, to come out here just as we come out here, and only the Jewish state can do it. . . .

. . . the Jewish state is a historical necessity. It is a moral, political and economic necessity. . . .

. . . we are not strangers to this land. It always has been and remains forever a historic hamlet. History has decreed that we should return to our country and re-establish here a Jewish State, and a Jewish State will be established. . . .

THE PHILOSOPHY OF THE EGYPTIAN
REVOLUTION

by Gamal Abdul Nasser *

. . . an exposition of the philosophy of the July 23 Revolution would require the deep investigations of scholars into its roots and origins, striking to the depths of the history of our people. Because there are no discontinuities in the story of national struggles; things don't just leap into existence without introductions. The struggle of any people, generation after generation, is a structure rising stone upon stone. And as each stone finds in the stone beneath its firm support, so too the episodes in the struggles of a people. Each new episode derives from the one preceding, and becomes in turn the basis for a new one still to come. . . .

I don't want to claim for myself the role of a history professor; nothing could be farther from my mind. All the same, were I, like any elementary school student, to attempt a study of the struggles of our people, I would

* Gamal Abdul Nasser, *The Philosophy of the Egyptian Revolution* (New York: 1954). Translated and annotated by Richard H. Nolte. By permission of Institute of Current World Affairs, Inc.

"Gamal Abdul Nasser is the son of a post-office clerk. As a schoolboy in Alexandria, his political career began when he was jailed for a few days 'for political reasons.' Released, he led a demonstration against the Government and the British, and was wounded in the head by a police bullet. In 1937, he dropped out of law school to enter the Egyptian Military Academy and was commissioned in 1938. After serving in the Sudan for two years, he returned to Cairo in time to participate in an attempt to spring Aly Maher, the perennial premier, from house arrest which was imposed on him by the British. . . . [on 4 February] 1942 when Rommel was approaching, when the pro-Axis Maher was the King's choice for premier, and when the British used tanks to convince the King to appoint Nahas instead. He participated in the Palestine war. . . .

"This statement was published originally in the Egyptian weekly *Akher Sa'a* in three installments in 1953 and written by Colonel Nasser 'apparently to commemorate the first year of the Revolution,' which took place on July 23, 1952. At that time the regime of King Farouk was replaced by the Revolutionary Council. At the time of writing Colonel Nasser was serving as Vice-Premier in the Cabinet of President-Premier General Neguib; he has, since then, risen to the Presidency of the United Arab Republic of Egypt and Syria — a development which might not have been totally surprising to those who considered the views expressed by him in these articles."

say for one thing that the Revolution of 23 July marks the realization of the hope held by the people of Egypt since the beginning of modern times: self-government and sovereign independence. . . .

WHENCE THE REVOLUTION?

Let me now try, after all that has happened and after the long years that have gone by since the idea of revolt began, to go back into memory and recall the first moment I discovered within myself the seeds of this idea. . . .

The seeds of the Revolution were present within me long before Palestine, even before the episode of 4 February, 1942, a day after which I wrote to a friend, saying: "What is to be done now? After our acceptance of what happened on our knees in surrender and disgrace? As a matter of fact, I believe that the Imperialism was playing with only a single card in his hand, with the object of threatening us only. And if only the Imperialism had been shown that Egyptians were prepared to shed their blood and oppose force with force, it would have given way like any prostitute."

. . . the Revolution of 23 July marked the realization of a great hope felt by the people of Egypt since the beginning of modern times: self-government and sovereign independence. But if that is so, and if what happened on the 23rd of July was neither a military mutiny nor a popular uprising, why then was it given to the army instead of some other force to bring about this Revolution? . . .

Our real crisis in my view is that we are going through two revolutions, not merely one. Every people on earth goes through two revolutions — a political revolution by which it wrests the right to govern itself from the hand of tyranny or from the army stationed upon its soil against its will; and a social revolution involving the conflict of the classes which settles down when justice is secured to the inhabitants of the united nation.

Peoples preceding us on the path of human progress have passed through two revolutions, but they have not had to face both at once; their revolutions in fact were a century apart in time. But as for us, the terrible experience through which our people is going is that we are having both revolutions at once.

BETWEEN THE MILLSTONES

The terrible experience is the result of the fact that both revolutions have attendant factors which clash and contradict violently. The political revolution, to be successful, must attain the objective of uniting all the elements of the nation, binding them together solidly, and instilling the ideal of self-abnegation for the sake of the country as a whole. But the social revolution, from the moment of its first appearance, shakes values and loosens principles, and sets the citizenry as individuals and as classes to fighting each other. It gives free rein to corruption, doubt, hatred . . . and egotism.

We are caught between the millstones of the two revolutions we are fated now to be going through. One revolution makes it obligatory for us to unite and love one another and fight side by side to the death; the other forces dissension upon us in spite of our desires, we are blackened by hatreds, and each of us thinks only of himself. . . .

There was no escaping the fact that we were going through two revolutions at once. When, for example, we moved along the path of the political revolution and removed Farouk from his throne, we took a similar step on the path of the social revolution by deciding to limit property.

I have continued to believe right up to the present time in the necessity for the Revolution of 23 July to maintain its ability to move swiftly and its initiative in order to be able to perform the miracle of traveling through two revolutions at the same time, however contradictory our resulting actions might at times appear to be. . . .

It would have been easy at the time — and it has been easy right along — to spill the blood of ten people, or twenty, or thirty, and thus instill fear in many hesitant persons, forcing them to swallow their greeds and hatreds and passions.

But what results could we gain from such a course? I have been accustomed to think that the method to overcome a difficulty was to go to the root of the matter and try to discover the causes.

It would be unjust to institute a rule of blood without examining the historical circumstances through which our people have passed and which have left in us all these tendencies and made of us what we are today. . . .

Fate decreed that we should be at the crossroads of the world. Many times we have been the channel for invasion and the prize of adventurers; and we have passed through so many vicissitudes that it is impossible to analyze the underlying factors in the souls of our people without giving them due respect and consideration.

In my view, we cannot shrug off the history of Pharaonic Egypt, nor the subsequent inmixing of the Hellenistic spirit. We cannot neglect the Roman invasion, or the penetration of Islam and the waves of Arab immigration that followed. Moreover, we must dwell at length on our history during the Middle Ages, for it was the vicissitudes of this period which chiefly made us what we are today.

If the Crusades were the beginning of the Renaissance in Europe, they were the beginning of the Dark Ages for our country. Our people alone bore most of the burden of the Crusades. We emerged from them poor, destitute, and exhausted. And at the same time that Egypt had been forced to her knees by this long struggle, she was fated to suffer further indignity under the hooves of the cavalry of the early Mongol tyrants. They came to Egypt as slaves, then murdered their rulers and became rulers themselves. They came as slaves; but in no time at all, they were kings in our good and peaceful land.

Tyranny, oppression, and ruin were the hallmark of rule in their time, during which Egypt lived for long centuries in ignorance. Our country became a wilderness ruled by carnivorous beasts, the Mamelukes regarding it as their prey, their easy booty for which they struggle ferociously among themselves. Our wealth and land and spirit — they were the booty. . . .

European society went through an orderly development, crossing the bridge between the period of the Renaissance at the end of the Middle Ages and the 19th century step by step, in gradual connecting stages.

But as for us, everything came at once. We had been living behind an iron curtain, and suddenly it collapsed. We had been cut off from the world and had withdrawn from its affairs, especially after commercial traffic with the East began to use the sea route around the Cape of Good Hope. And then suddenly, we became the object of European ambition and the springboard for European colonization to the east and south.

Waves of ideas were loosed upon us without our having made the journey which would have brought us up to the point where we were ready to receive them. Our spirits continued to live in the captivity of the 13th century even though here and there appeared manifestations of the 19th, and then the 20th, century. Our mentalities tried to overtake the caravan of human progress from our starting point five centuries and more behind. The long journey is exhausting and the race is frightening and fearful. . . .

These, then, are the origins from which our present circumstances emanate; they are the sources from which our present crises flow. If you add in the problems of the economic revolution we are going through, and those of the political revolution for the sake of which we removed Farouk and for which we need the freedom of our country from all foreign troops; if you put all this together, you get a clearer conception of our position — exposed to every wind that blows, the victim of storms, lightning, and thunder. On top of all this, it would be monstrous to impose a rule of blood. . . .

Our role has been defined for us by the history of our nation; we cannot avoid playing it no matter what price we may have to pay. We make no mistake in our understanding of this role, or in the nature of the duties it imposes upon us. We removed the former king without consulting anyone because he was an obstacle to the progress of the caravan. We began our plans for expelling the English from Egypt because their existence here blocks our progress and leads many of us astray from the path. These are steps for the reform of the legacy of the past and its misfortunes, steps which we have made and for the sake of which we have endured everything. . . .

In simpler terms, if we cannot now deny the facts of history and return to the 10th century and wear its clothes that now seem strange and ludicrous and be misled by its ideas which appear today to be those of a dark and ignorant age devoid of light, we equally cannot behave as if we were a piece of Alaska in the most distant regions of the north, or a Wake Island remote and alone in the wilderness of the Pacific. As time imposes its developments upon us, so does geography impose *its* realities. Twice I have tried to deal with the time factor; this time, I will turn to the geographical factors of place.

GEOGRAPHICAL LIMITS

Before we can proceed with this discussion, there is something we must get clear; and that is what we mean by place in relation to our people. If someone were to say to me that place applies only to this capital city we live in, I would disagree. If someone were to say that it means Egypt within its political borders, I would also disagree.

Because if the matter were to be confined within the city limits of Cairo, or the political boundaries of our country, things would be simple. We could lock all the doors behind us and live in our ivory tower, staying as far aloof as possible from the world and its problems and wars and crises. Instead of which we find problems hammering at the gates of our country and exerting their influence inside it in spite of all we can do.

For the time of isolation is past. Gone are the days when lines of barbed wire could mark the real as well as the political boundaries of nations. They can no longer provide a line of defense around a country.

Nowadays, nations have to keep a sharp lookout outside the boundaries in order to know from which direction come the currents that influence the interior and to learn how to get along with other countries, and so on.

No state can neglect to glance around itself to get an idea of its geographical context and to discover what opportunities are open to it in the surrounding area, what constitutes its living space and the field of its growth, and what its positive role in this troubled world is to be.

Sometimes, sitting in a room of my office, I direct my thoughts to this very subject and ask myself: what is *our* positive role in this troubled world, and what is the zone in which we must play it? I ask myself about the area around us, and find certain zones toward which we must turn for our activity and in which we must act with all our ability.

All this is not just a matter of chance. Fate does not jest; things are not just conjured into existence for nothing. We cannot look at the map of the world without comprehension, without realizing Egypt's position on the map and her role by the logic of that position. Can we fail to see that there is an Arab zone surrounding us? That this zone is part of us and we part of it, our history being inextricably part of its history and our interests linked closely with its interests? That this is fact, and not just talk?

Can we possibly ignore the fact that there is an African continent which we have been made part of by fate, and that the terrible contention now going on about its future will have its influence on us whether we will or no?

Can we ignore the fact that there is an Islamic world with which we are united by bonds of religious principle reinforced by historical realities? As I remarked just now, the dispositions of fate are not to be taken lightly; fate does not jest.

Nor is it lacking in significance that our country is located in south-western Asia in contiguity with the Arab nations with whose existence our own is intermixed. It is not to be shrugged off that our country lies in northeastern Africa overlooking the Dark Continent wherein rages a harsh struggle between the white colonizers and its black inhabitants for control of its unlimited resources.

It is important, too, that when the Mongols swept away the cities of ancient Islam, Islamic civilization and the Islamic heritage fell back on Egypt and took shelter there. Egypt protected them and nourished them. . . .

All these are fundamental realities having a profound bearing on our existence; however we may try, we cannot overlook them or avoid them.

A PART IN SEARCH OF AN ACTOR

I don't know why, but when I reach this point in my thinking as I sit daydreaming alone in my room, I'm always reminded of the famous tale . . . "Six Characters in Search of an Author."

The vicissitudes of history are full of heroes who create for themselves roles of great glory and heroism, playing them at decisive moments on the stage of history. And certainly the vicissitudes of history are also full of heroic and glorious roles which never find heroes to perform them. For some reason, it always strikes me that in this area in which we live is a role running around aimlessly looking for a hero to give it being. For some reason, it seems to me that this role, exhausted by its wanderings in the vast spaces around us, has collapsed on the borders of our country and is beckoning to us to stir ourselves, to go to it, take it up, put on its costume, and give it life. And indeed, we are the only ones who can do so.

Here, let me hasten to say that the role is not one of leadership or domination. It is rather a role of interaction with and response to all the factors mentioned above, which involves making use of the tremendous latent strength in the region surrounding us to create a great power in this area which will then rise up to a level of dignity and undertake a positive part in building the future of mankind.

THE FIRST ZONE

There can be no doubt that the Arab zone is the most important and the one with which we are most closely linked. For it is intertwined with us by history. We have suffered together, we have gone through the same crises, and when we fell beneath the hooves of invaders, it was with us under the same hooves.

This zone is intermixed with us also by virtue of religion. The center of Islamic learning has been synonymous with several Arab capital cities, first Mecca, then shifting to Kufa, then to Damascus, next to Baghdad, and finally to Cairo.

Lastly, mutual contiguity joins us all together in a geographical framework which is made solid by all these historical, material, and spiritual factors.

So far as I can recall, the first glimmers of Arab awareness began to steal into my consciousness when I was a student in secondary school. I used to go out on a general strike with my comrades every year on the second of December because of the Balfour Declaration which Britain made on behalf of the Jews, giving them thereby the populated land of Palestine, tyrannously wresting it from its rightful owners.* And at that time, when I asked myself why I went out on strike with such zeal and why I was angry about a country I'd never even seen, I could find no answer except the ties of sentiment.

Then a kind of understanding began to develop when I became a student in the Military Academy where I studied in particular the history of military campaigns in Palestine, and in general the history of the area and its surroundings which have made of it during the past hundred years an easy prey for the allied fangs of hungry beasts! Things grew still more clear, and the underlying realities became apparent when, in the General Staff College, I began to study the Palestine offensive and the problems of the Mediterranean Sea in detail.

The result was that when the Palestine crisis began, I was utterly convinced that the fighting in Palestine was not taking place on foreign soil, nor was our participation a going beyond the requirements of simple friendship. It was a duty made obligatory by the necessity of self-defense.

Positive Efforts in the Arab Zone

· I remember that just after the announcement of the decision to partition Palestine in September 1947, the Free Officers agreed on the necessity of supporting the resistance in Palestine. Next day, I knocked on the door of Hajj Amin al-Husseini, Mufti of Palestine, who was then living in Zaitoun.† I said to him, You have need of officers to lead in the struggle and to train volunteers. In the Egyptian Army there are a large number of officers who wish to offer their services. They are at your command at any time you wish! He said that he was pleased with this spirit, but that he thought the permission of the Egyptian Government would be necessary. Then he said: I will give you my answer after asking permission. A few days later, I went back, and he told me: the Government's reply was negative! We didn't let this stop us, however.

* In 1919, the population of Palestine was about 700,000: 570,000 Arabs, 58,000 Jews, a ratio of about 10 to 1. In 1948, the total was about 1,900,000; Arabs about 1,250,000, Jews about 650,000, a ratio of 2 to 1. Occupying ⅔ of the old Palestine, Israel has now a population of about 1½ million. There remains in Israel a nine or ten per cent Arab minority.

† In 1936, "the Arab Higher Committee, drawn from leaders of various Arab states, was formed under the chairmanship of the Mufti (meaning 'religious juris-consult') of Jerusalem, Hajj Amin al-Husseini, to prosecute the Arab cause — mostly as it turned out, by sporadic violence . . ." Zaitoun is a "suburb of Cairo."

Some time later, the artillery of Ahmad Abdul Aziz began to hit the Jewish colonizers south of Jerusalem. The c. o. of the artillery was Kemal ed-Din Hussein, a member of the Central Committee of the Free Officers which has since become the Council of the Revolution. . . .

For the present, I don't wish to dwell on the details of that war. It is a subject about which accounts differ, and it would involve much effort. What concerns me is the important lesson it teaches.

All the Arab peoples entered Palestine in a single wave of enthusiasm. They did so on the basis of common feelings and a common estimation shared by all as to the borders of their security. All the Arab peoples emerged from Palestine with the same bitterness and disappointment, and then each in its own internal affairs encountered the same factors, the same ruling forces that had brought about their defeat and forced them to bow their heads in humbleness and shame. . . .

Then, over there, you see the forces of our brothers-in-arms, our brother Arabs, brothers in the common enterprise and in the common urge that hastened us all to rescue the land of Palestine. There are the armies of our brothers, army after army, each one surrounded by circumstances which have equally surrounded their governments.

They all, armies and governments, seemed to be pawns, devoid of power and self-motivation, moved only by the hands of the players. And behind the lines, all our peoples seemed to be the victims of a well-knit conspiracy which deliberately suppressed the realities of what was happening, the facts of the actual situation. . . .

When the struggle was over in Palestine and the siege lifted, and I had returned to Egypt, the Arab zone in my eyes had become a single whole. The events that have taken place since have confirmed my belief. I have followed developments in the Arab countries and find they match point for point. What happens in Cairo has its counterpart in Damascus the next day, and Beirut, Amman, Baghdad, and elsewhere. This all fits in with the picture drawn by long experience. It is a single region, with the same circumstances affecting each part of it, the same factors, the same forces united in opposition. And it was clear that the foremost of these forces was Imperialism. Even Israel itself is nothing but one of the results of Imperialism. For if Palestine had not fallen under the British Mandate, Zionism would never have been able to get the support necessary for realization of the idea of a national state in Palestine. The idea would have remained a mad impossible dream. . . .

Let me now go back to what I was saying — that Imperialism is the great force which is imposing a murderous invisible blockade on the whole region. . . .

When all these truths had impressed themselves on me, I began to believe in the need for a common struggle. I said to myself, so long as the region continues to be one region; existing in the same circumstances; with the same problems and the same future . . . and, however he tries to change his disguise, the same enemy; so long as this goes on, why should we divide up our efforts to escape?

The experiences which followed the Revolution of 23 July have increased my conviction in the efficacy and necessity of this common struggle. And now, the hidden parts of the long-developing picture in my mind began to be disclosed, the obscuring shadows to disappear.

I admit that in the process, I also began to see the great obstacles which block the path to the common struggle; but I began to believe that these obstacles themselves had to be removed, being the creation of the same enemy.

Finally, I began to make political contacts for the sake of unifying the struggle by whatever means. After a month of such contacts, I emerged with the important conclusion that the first obstacle on our path is "doubt." And it was clear that the roots of this doubt were planted in us by that same common enemy in order to prevent our embarking on the common struggle! . . .

I don't want to minimize the obstacles between us and unity in the common struggle. There is no doubt that in part these obstacles have their roots in the nature of the situation and in the historical and geographical circumstances of our people. But it is also certain that with a little flexibility based on insight, not on neglect, it will be possible to call into being a plan upon which everyone will be able to agree without strife and constraint, a plan for mounting the common struggle.

NUMERICAL BALANCE SHEET OF POWER

I do not doubt for a moment that our common struggle will achieve for us and our peoples everything we desire and long for. For I shall always maintain we are strong. The only trouble is, we do not realize just how strong we are.

We make the wrong definition of strength. It is not strength to shout at the top of our lungs; real strength is to act positively with all the means at our command. When I try to analyze the elements of our strength, there are three main sources which must go down first in the ledger.

The first of these sources is that we are a community of neighboring peoples linked by all the material and moral ties possible, and that our peoples have characteristics and abilities and a civilization which have given rise to three high holy religions — which absolutely cannot be neglected in the effort to build a secure and peaceful world. This is the first source.

As for the second source of strength, it is our land itself and its position on the map of the world — that important strategic position which embraces the crossroads of the world, the thoroughfare of its traders and passageway of its armies.

There remains the third source: oil, a sinew of material civilization without which all its machines would cease to function. The great factories producing every kind of goods; all the instruments of land, sea, and air communication; all the weapons of war, from the mechanical bird above the clouds to the submarines beneath the waves — all would cease to function, and rust would overcome every iron part beyond hope of motion or life.

I would like to pause for a moment on oil. Perhaps its existence as a material reality demonstrable by facts and figures will provide a useful model for our analysis of the importance of the sources of strength in our country.

I read recently an article published by the University of Chicago on the oil situation. It would be a good thing if every Arab could read it, grasp its implications, and see the great meaning concealed behind the statistics and figures.

The article points out, for example, that the effort to extract oil in the Arab countries requires comparatively little capital. The oil companies spent $60 million in Colombia from 1917 without discovering a drop of oil until 1939. They spent $44 million in Venezuela and didn't get a drop of oil for 15 years. They spent $39 million in Indonesia and only recently discovered oil. According to the article, it all adds up to the fact that the cost of producing a barrel of oil in America is 78¢, in South America 43¢, but in the Arab countries, only 10¢.

The article further says that the center of world oil production has shifted — from the U.S. where wells are going dry, the cost of land is going up, and the wages of construction workers have risen — to the Arab area where the wells are still virgin, where land over vast spaces continues to cost nothing, and where the worker continues to receive less than a subsistence wage. Half the proven reserves of oil in the world lie beneath Arab soil, the remainder being divided between the U.S., Russia, the Caribbean, and other parts of the world.

It is a fact too that the average daily production per well is 11 barrels in the United States, 20 barrels in Venezuela, and 4,000 barrels in the

Arab area. Have I made clear how great the importance of this element of strength is? I hope so.

So we are strong. Strong not in the loudness of our voices when we wail or shout or cry for help but rather when we remain silent and measure the extent of our ability to act in a situation, when we really understand the strength resulting from the tie binding us together and making our land a single region from which no part can withdraw and of which no part, like an isolated island, can be protected without protection of the whole.

THE INTERIOR OF THE DARK CONTINENT

So much for the first zone to which we must turn and in which we must act with all our ability — the Arab zone.

If next we turn to the second zone, the continent of Africa, I may say without exaggeration that we cannot under any circumstances, however much we might wish, remain aloof from the terrible and sanguinary struggle going on in Africa today between 5 million whites and 200 million Africans. We cannot do so for an important and obvious reason: we are in Africa. The peoples of Africa will continue to look to us, who guard the northern gate and who constitute their link with all the outside world. We will never in any circumstances be able to vacate our responsibility to support with all our ability the spread of enlightenment and civilization to the remotest depths of the jungle.

There remains an important reason, which is that the Nile is the artery of life for our country, bringing water from the heart of the continent. As a final reason, the boundaries of our beloved brother, the Sudan, extend far into the core of Africa, bringing into contiguity the sensitive regions in that area.

The Dark Continent is now the scene of a strange and excited turbulence; the white man, representing various European nations, is again trying to carve up the map of Africa. We shall not, in any circumstances, be able to stand idly by in the face of what is going on in Africa in the belief that it will not affect or concern us.

I will continue to dream of the day when I will find in Cairo a great African Institute dedicated to opening up the regions of the continent to view, to creating in our minds an enlightened African consciousness, and to sharing with others from all over the world in the work of advancing the peoples of the continent and their welfare.

ISLAMIC PARLIAMENT

There remains a third zone — a zone which stretches across continents and oceans and which is the domain of our brothers in faith who all, wherever under the sun they may be, turn as we do in the direction of Mecca and whose devout lips speak the same prayers.

When I went with the Egyptian delegation to the Kingdom of Sa'udi Arabia to offer condolences on the death of its sovereign, my belief in the possibility of extending the effectiveness of the Pilgrimage, building upon the strength of the Islamic tie linking all Muslims, grew very strong. I stood in front of the Ka'ba, and was aware of the circling round of all the regions of the earth reached by Islam. Then I found myself saying: our view of the Pilgrimage must change. It should not only be regarded as a ticket of admission into Paradise after a long life, or as a mere seeking for forgiveness after a merry one. It should become an institution of great political power and significance. The press of the world should hasten to cover the Pilgrimage, not because it is a traditional ritual affording entertaining pictures for the reading public, but because of its function as a periodic political conference in which the leaders of the Islamic states, their leaders of thought, their learned men in every branch of knowledge, their writers, captains of industry, merchants, and their youth can meet in order to lay down in this Islamic world parliament the broad lines of their national policies and their mutual cooperation until the next time of meeting the following year.

Pious and humble, but strong, they assemble; stripped of greed, but active; weak before God, but mighty against their problems and their enemies; solicitous of the rights of others, but sure of their own appointed place in the sun.

I remember that I mentioned some of these thoughts to H. M. King Sa'ud, and he replied to me: "It is indeed the real *raison d'être* of the Pilgrimage." To tell the truth, I myself am unable to imagine any other *raison d'être*.

When I consider the 80 million Muslims in Indonesia, and the 50 million in China, and the millions in Malaya, Siam, and Burma, and the close-to-100 million in the Middle East, and the 40 million inside the Soviet Union, and the other millions in far-flung parts of the world — when I consider these hundreds of millions united by a single creed, I emerge with a sense of tremendous possibilities which we may realize through the cooperation of all these Muslims, a cooperation not going beyond the bounds of their natural loyalty to their own countries, but which will enable them and their brothers in faith to wield a power without limit.

And now I go back to the wandering role looking for a hero to play it. The role is there. Its characteristics have been described. This is the stage. By the laws of geographical circumstance, we alone are able to play it.

TOWARD FREEDOM

by Jawaharlal Nehru *

It was natural and inevitable that Indian nationalism should resent alien rule. And yet it was curious how large numbers of our intelligentsia, to the end of the nineteenth century, accepted, consciously or unconsciously, the British ideology of empire. They built their own arguments on this, and only ventured to criticize some of its outward manifestations. History and economics and other subjects that were taught in the schools and colleges were written entirely from the British imperial viewpoint, and laid stress on our numerous failings in the past and present, and the virtues and high destiny of the British. We accepted to some extent this distorted version, and, even when we resisted it instinctively, we were influenced by it. At first there was no intellectual escape from it, for we knew no other facts or arguments, and so we sought relief in religious nationalism, in the thought that at least in the sphere of religion and philosophy we were second to no other people. We comforted ourselves in our misfortune and degradation with the notion that though we did not possess the outward show and glitter of the West we had the real inner article, which was far more valuable and worth having. Vivekananda and others, as well as the interest of Western scholars in our old philosophies, gave us a measure of self-respect again and roused up our dormant pride in our past.

Gradually we began to suspect and examine critically British statements

* Jawaharlal Nehru, *Toward Freedom* (New York: 1941). Copyright 1941, 1942, The John Day Company. Reprinted by permission of The John Day Company, Inc.

about our past and present conditions, but still we thought and worked within the framework of British ideology. If a thing was bad, it would be called "un-British"; if a Britisher in India misbehaved, the fault was his, not that of the system. But the collection of this critical material of British rule in India, in spite of the moderate outlook of the authors, served a revolutionary purpose and gave a political and economic foundation to our nationalism. Dadabhai Naoroji's *Poverty and Un-British Rule in India*, and books by Romesh Dutt and William Digby and others, thus played a revolutionary role in the development of our nationalist thought. Further researches in ancient Indian history revealed brilliant and highly civilized periods in the remote past, and we read of these with great satisfaction. We also discovered that the British record in India was very different from what we had been led to believe from their history books.

Our challenge to the British version of history, economics, and administration in India grew, and yet we continued to function within the orbit of their ideology. That was the position of Indian nationalism as a whole at the turn of the century. . . . Dominion status within the Empire. . . . is a naïve notion impossible of achievement, for the price of British protection is Indian subjection. We cannot have it both ways, even if that was not degrading to the self-respect of a great country. . . . The complete withdrawal of British control of India will be the beginning of Indian freedom.

It is not surprising that the Indian intelligentsia in the nineteenth century should have succumbed to British ideology; what is surprising is that some people should continue to suffer that delusion even after the stirring events and changes of the twentieth century. In the nineteenth century the British ruling classes were the aristocrats of the world, with a long record of wealth and success and power behind them. This long record and training gave them some of the virtues as well as failings of aristocracy. We in India can comfort ourselves with the thought that we helped substantially during the last century and three-quarters in providing the wherewithal and the training for this superior state. They began to think themselves — as so many races and nations have done — the chosen of God, and their Empire an earthly Kingdom of Heaven. If their special position was acknowledged and their superiority not challenged, they were gracious and obliging, provided that this did them no harm. But opposition to them became opposition to the divine order, and as such was a deadly sin which must be suppressed. . . .

Yet India with all her poverty and degradation had enough of nobility and greatness about her; and, though she was overburdened with ancient tradition and present misery and her eyelids were a little weary, she had "a beauty wrought out from within upon the flesh, the deposit, little cell by cell, of strange thoughts and fantastic reveries and exquisite passions." Behind and within her battered body one could still glimpse a majesty of soul. Through long ages she had traveled and gathered much wisdom on the way, and trafficked with strangers and added them to her own big family, and witnessed days of glory and decay, and suffered humiliation and terrible sorrow, and seen many a strange sight; but throughout her long journey she had clung to her immemorial culture, drawn strength and vitality from it, and shared it with other lands. Like a pendulum she had swung up and down; she had ventured with the daring of her thought to reach up to the heavens and unravel their mystery, and she had also had bitter experience of the pit of hell. . . .

Though often broken up politically, her spirit always guarded a common heritage, and in her diversity there was ever an amazing unity. Like all ancient lands she was a curious mixture of the good and bad, but the good was hidden and had to be sought after, while the odor of decay was evident, and her hot, pitiless sun gave full publicity to the bad.

There is some similarity between Italy and India. Both are ancient countries with long traditions of culture behind them, though Italy is a newcomer compared to India, and India is a much vaster country. Both were split up politically, and yet the conception of Italia, like that of India, never died, and in all their diversity the unity was predominant. In Italy the unity was largely a Roman unity, for that great city had dominated the country and been the fount and symbol of unity. In India there was no such single center or dominant city, although Benares might well be called the Eternal City of the East, not only for India but also for Eastern Asia. But, unlike Rome, Benares never dabbled in empire or thought of temporal power. Indian culture was so widespread all over India that no part of the country could be called the heart of that culture. From Cape Comorin to Amaranath and Badrinath in the Himalayas, from Dwarka to Puri, the same ideas coursed; and, if there was a clash of ideas in one place, the noise of it soon reached distant parts of the country.

Just as Italy gave the gift of culture and religion to Western Europe, India did so to Eastern Asia, though China was as old and venerable as India. And even when Italy was lying prostrate politically, her life coursed through the veins of Europe.

It was Metternich who called Italy a "geographical expression," and many a would-be Metternich has used that phrase for India; strangely enough, there is a similarity even in their geographical positions in the two continents. More interesting is the comparison of England with Austria, for has not England of the twentieth century been compared to Austria of the nineteenth, proud and haughty and imposing still, but with the roots that gave strength shriveling up and decay eating its way into the mighty fabric?

It is curious how one cannot resist the tendency to give an anthropomorphic form to a country. Such is the force of habit and early associations. India becomes *Bharat Mata*, Mother India, a beautiful lady, very old but ever youthful in appearance, sad-eyed and forlorn, cruelly treated by aliens and outsiders, and calling upon her children to protect her. Some such picture rouses the emotions of hundreds of thousands and drives them to action and sacrifice. And yet India is in the main the peasant and the worker, not beautiful to look at, for poverty is not beautiful. Does the beautiful lady of our imaginations represent the bare-bodied and bent workers in the fields and factories? Or the small group of those who have from ages past crushed the masses and exploited them, imposed cruel customs on them and made many of them even untouchable? We seek to cover truth by the creatures of our imaginations and endeavor to escape from reality to a world of dreams.

And yet, despite these different classes and their mutual conflicts, there was a common bond which united them in India, and one is amazed at its persistence and tenacity and enduring vitality. What was this strength due to? Not merely the passive strength and weight of inertia and tradition, great as these always are. There was an active sustaining principle, for it resisted successfully powerful outside influences and absorbed internal forces that rose to combat it. And yet with all its strength it could not preserve political freedom or endeavor to bring about political unity. These latter do not appear to have been considered worth much trouble; their importance was very foolishly ignored, and we have suffered for this neglect. Right through history the old Indian ideal did not glorify political and military triumph, and it looked down upon money and the professional money-making class. Honor and wealth did not go together, and honor was meant to go, at least in theory, to the men who served the community with little in the shape of financial reward.

The old culture managed to live through many a fierce storm and tempest, but, though it kept its outer form, it lost its real content. Today it is fighting silently and desperately against a new and all-powerful opponent — the *bania* [merchant] civilization of the capitalist West. It will succumb to this newcomer, for the West brings science, and science brings food for the hungry millions. But the West also brings an antidote to the evils of this cut-throat civilization — the principles of socialism, of co-operation, and service to the community for the common good. This is not so unlike the old Brahman ideal of service, but it means the brahmanization (not in the religious sense, of course) of all classes and groups and the abolition of class distinctions. It may be that when India puts on her new garment, as she must, for the old is torn and tattered, she will have it cut in this fashion, so as to make it conform both to present conditions and her old thought. The ideas she adopts must become racy to her soil.

RAISING A CRY FOR SECESSION

by Phillips Talbot *

NATIONALISTIC ASPIRATIONS OF THE DRAVIDIAN PROGRESSIVE FEDERATION

Among independent India's many problems I would rate highly the competing pulls of national versus regional loyalties. Before 1947 articulate elements of the country as a whole (excepting the All India Muslim League with its demand for Pakistan) were broadly united in the freedom struggle led by Mahatma Gandhi against British rule. Since victory on that front Jawaharlal Nehru and his associates have waged a new struggle for the emotional integration of the Indian people as a nation. With no external foe (again excepting the Pakistan forces), the task of welding India with its many races and languages into a united whole becomes a search for unity in diversity. How far Nehru has succeeded can be judged by comparing India's present national stability with conditions in most other newly-free countries on the rim of Asia. How far the true nationalists have yet to go, however, has become increasingly clear in political developments during the past year. Thus it seems worth while to take a look at what is, at least verbally, the extreme example to date of politically fis-

* Phillips Talbot, Executive Director, American Universities Field Staff, Notes from a Tamilnad Tour, A Letter from Phillips Talbot. Copyright 1957 by American Universities Field Staff, Inc. and reprinted with their permission.

siparous tendencies in free India — the first legislative party to raise a cry for secession.

Several well-informed persons in South India have assured me that the Dravida Munnetra Kazhagam which means Dravidian Progressive Federation — is not seriously demanding that the four southern states (Madras, Andhra Pradesh, Mysore and Kerala) secede from the rest of the country. This is just a gimmick, they argue, by which the D.M.K. hopes to build up an effective opposition to the governing Congress party in Madras and to advance the cause of states' rights against the overriding powers of the central government.

I have myself found that party wheelhorses quickly go vague when pressed on the implications of separate nationhood for Dravidian South India.

Dravidian sentiments have ancient roots. Not only were Dravidians uppermost in India before the Aryan invasions that started about 5,000 years ago, but in recent millenia the Dravidians have kept their cultural distinctiveness and developed their principal languages (Tamil, Telugu, Kannada and Malayalam) in the South even while becoming fitted into the elaborate Hindu social system. Dravidians can also remember great ancient empires. Among the Tamils the race-memory goes back unerringly to the Chola kings (A.D. 907–1310), who not only dominated South India but also spread Tamil culture to Ceylon and across Southeast Asia.

"That's one trouble with India," a Madrasi Brahman said the other day as we were discussing the present-day political Dravidians. "Each part of the country not only has its separate language and literature but also its great royal tradition. These help feed the fire of regionalism under our new democratic system. Each group wants to recreate its past greatness. As most empires included territories that belonged to other empires in other ages, some of the current regional movements conflict with others."

In Tamilnad (land of the Tamils), now virtually conterminous with Madras State, the Dravida Munnetra Kazhagam is the third political organization in a generation to trade mainly on cultural sentiment. The Justice party blazed the way before World War II as an anti-British political movement whose chief concern was to win opportunities for non-Brahmans in government service and the professions. Then came the Dravida Kazhagam (D.K., or Dravidian Federation) from which, as the name indicated, the D.M.K. is an offshoot. . . .

The fullest program statement of the D.M.K. that I have seen is its 1957 election manifesto, a brew of vague egalitarianism and states'-rights regionalism. The flavor of the appeal can be judged from its main points:

> Each state should have full freedom to secede from the Indian Union if it desires and should be given full and equal representation in parliament so that the large states do not dominate the others. The central government's taxing powers in the states must be limited.
>
> The South must have heavy industries to develop, but the Five Year Plans have been formulated mainly to improve the wealth and raise the living standards of the North. The majority of the irrigation and hydroelectric projects and new industries have been concentrated in the North; Dravida Nad (the land of the Dravidians) has been completely neglected.
>
> The medium of instruction at all stages must be in the students' mother tongue (e.g. Tamil rather than English or Hindi). The fanaticism with which Hindi is being imposed in the South is to be deplored. English, being an international language, should be given due encouragement and should be treated on a par with the mother tongue to facilitate the spread of technological and scientific knowledge. To concede Hindi in our State would be dangerous.
>
> Uniform wage scales should be established for employees of the central and state government. . . .
>
> Only Tamil diplomats should be appointed as envoys to countries with many Tamil settlers (e.g., Ceylon, Malaya).
>
> Tamilnad must not be joined in any bilingual or trilingual state but must include all Tamil-speaking areas such as Devikulam, Peermede and Tiruthani. (N.B.: Major Tamil-speaking areas outside Madras state were joined to it by the States Reorganization Act last November. The places named are mixed estate areas in Kerala where Tamil labor has penetrated Malayali country.) Madras state should be renamed Tamilnad. . . .

To try to learn what this mélange of proposals and demands means, I hunted out the D.M.K. headquarters in a far northern ward of Madras city . . .

As for the party itself, the secretary specified that "our main aim is a separate and independent Dravidian state to be composed of the four southern states in federation. The four languages will be recognized equally and federally, just as the Swiss manage their languages."

Why should there be a separate state in South India? The reply came easily, drawing in part on the manifesto. "Between the Northerners and the Southerners there are great cultural differences. The two are fundamentally different. We want to live our way and let them live their way." (Shades of the old Muslim League!) Furthermore, "the South is being dominated by the imposition of Hindi. The Central Government's taxing power is being used to discriminate against the South. Constitutionally the states have no power — they are no stronger than municipalities." In short, "we want to liberate ourselves from the Northern shackles."

Is the proposal for a Dravidian state practical? "It would have nearly 100,000,000 people — more than any European country except Russia. Ceylon, Malaya, Jordan, Israel and Luxembourg are very small nations but they want to be independent despite all difficulties. That is our position too. The Dravidian state would have two major ports (Madras and Cochin) and several lesser ports along 1,700 miles of coastline. It would get the revenues and foreign exchange that now go to the New Delhi government for exports of hides and skins, pepper, groundnuts, cashews, and other Southern products. With a fair partitioning of the Indian merchant marine, Navy, Army and Air Force it could manage its maritime and defence needs. It is definitely practical."

Again I was reminded of the Muslim League's arguments of 20 years ago, when the politicians assumed that statehood would bring solutions to all the difficulties and discriminations against which they complained. Like Pakistan, the South lacks not only heavy industries but also some quite important natural resources for an industrial base, such as coal. Furthermore, I have heard independent economists express doubt that with comparable taxation the South by itself could generate more development funds than it is now allocated from New Delhi. But just as the Pakistan debate was never settled on economic grounds, I would assume that the quality of its economic analysis does not measure the appeal of the D.M.K. . . .

"For the present and even in the future we want to attain our aspiration in a constitutional way. The constitution provides that any area can secede from India if it gets two-thirds majority of the whole parliament. Under that provision, it is true, we cannot get our goal. Even if our party should get a cent per cent perfect victory in the next elections, the Congress party at the center won't yield. Then we will have to choose some other course — civil disobedience or picketing, perhaps. I can't say what it will be. But we are not like the Pakistanis; we hate violence and will not use violent methods."

This seems vague and even contradictory, I commented. How do you really see the future of India? "We feel that after Nehru India will not be one," came the blunt reply. "He is the only factor that is holding India together. After Nehru there will be no leader who will be able to command the support of all the people of India. Each and every state is going to demand self-determination: Bengal, Maharashtra, and others as well as ourselves. And this is not so bad. There is the United Nations: what is its purpose if not to protect small nations? Europe has 32 nations. Why should not we? A big India means nothing to us. Bigness or smallness has nothing to do with safeguarding the peace of the world. . . ." And so forth. . . .

The D.M.K. has recently acquired an unexpected ally in its struggle for power, the former governor general of India and chief minister of Madras, C. Rajagopalachari, a Brahman. The party secretary has told me that "Rajaji" who in 1943 or 1944 was the first prominent personality in the Congress party to accept the idea of Pakistan, was "moving toward support of a separate state in the south." When I saw the former governor general he turned my question on that point by saying that the D.M.K. itself does not really want separation but greater states' rights. In "Rajaji's" estimation the D.M.K., whatever its ultimate ambitions, could become an important influence in the constitutional government of Madras by developing an effective opposition to the Congress. "I am advising them along these lines," he said, "but whether they will take my advice I don't know."

India's elder statesman may be right about the Dravida Munnetra Kazhagam. It may never evolve into an effective threat to India's unity. It is still too young, too unformed and too untried to be judged. But there can be no question of the continuing force of regional feelings in the South, nor any doubt that whatever influence the D.M.K. may generate will be thrown on the side of regional as against national loyalties. Its activities can only add difficulties for the other influences — the all-India political parties, the films, rapidly improving communications, the spread of literacy and education, etc. — whose net effect is presumably to weave the strands of Indian life into a national fabric.

THE AUTHORS

DAVID BEN-GURION (1880–   ), Prime Minister of Israel since its creation
except for a brief period of retirement. Leader of Mapai, the Israeli Labor
party. Born in Poland, he emigrated to Palestine, where he soon became a
Zionist leader. A collection of his essays has been published in English
translation under the title *Rebirth and Destiny of Israel.*

HOUSTON STEWART CHAMBERLAIN (1855–1927), English by birth, he lived on
the Continent most of his adult life, at Dresden, Vienna, and Bayreuth. At
the height of World War I, in 1916, he became a naturalized German
citizen. He was the son-in-law of the composer Richard Wagner. *The
Foundations of the Nineteenth Century* was his most significant work, although he wrote a great deal on World War I, on Wagner and philosophy.

G. D. H. COLE (1889–1959), an English Fabian socialist and Professor of
Political Theory at Oxford University, who served as president of the
Fabian Society after World War II. In addition to *World Socialism Restated,* he was also the author of *The World of Labour, Socialist Economics, An Intelligent Man's Guide to the Post-War World,* and more
than a score of Fabian tracts.

JOHN DEWEY (1859–1952), American philosopher and educator, best known
for his modification of pragmatism into what he termed instrumentalism.
A liberal in politics as well as education, his broad mind and prolific pen
touched upon a vast variety of subjects. In addition to *Freedom and Culture,* his most relevant political works include *The Public and Its Problems, Individualism Old and New,* and his essays in *Characters and Events.*

MILOVAN DJILAS (1911–   ), Yugoslav writer and former Communist party
official. Once thought to be the likely successor to President Tito, his
gradual ideological break culminated in imprisonment in 1956 when an
article sharply critical of the regime was smuggled out of the country and
appeared in the American press. In addition to *The New Class,* he is the
author of *Land Without Justice,* an autobiographical account of his early
years in Montenegro, *Anatomy of a Moral,* and *Conversations with Stalin.*

FRIEDRICH ENGELS (1820–1895), Anglo-German social philosopher and businessman. A life-long collaborator of Marx, he attempted to apply Marx's

ideas to evolutionary and anthropological theory. His editing of the incomplete manuscripts of *Das Kapital* represented a major contribution to Marxism. His best-known works are *Anti-Duhring, Origin of the Family, Private Property and the State,* and *Dialectics of Nature,* from which "The Part Played by Labor in the Transition from Ape to Man" is taken.

JOHANN GOTTLIEB FICHTE (1762–1814), German philosopher and patriot. As a student in Switzerland he was impressed by the philosophy of Immanuel Kant, whose recognition Fichte achieved when he published his *Critique of Revelation* in 1792. Part of his career was devoted to solving some fundamental problems of Kant's philosophy. In his latter years in Berlin he wrote on practical politics and the German movement for national independence.

GEORGE GALLUP (1901–   ), American pioneer in public opinion sampling. Founder and director of the American Institute of Public Opinion and founder of the British Institute of Public Opinion. In addition to the published results of his polls, Gallup is the author of *A Guide to Public Opinion Polls* and the editor of *The Political Almanac.* SAUL FORBES RAE, Canadian sociologist and co-author of *The Pulse of Democracy* worked with the British Institute of Public Opinion as well as with the American Institute.

CORRADO GINI (1884–   ), Italian statistician, sociologist, and economist, and Professor of Statistics at the University of Rome, he has been president of the Italian Society of Statistics since 1941. He has also presided over the Italian Sociological Society since 1937 and over the Italian Society of Genetics and Eugenics since 1924.

FRIEDRICH A. HAYEK (1899–   ), Austrian by birth, British by naturalization, and American by profession, this cosmopolitan professor of economics has produced in *The Road to Serfdom* one of the most widely read books on political economy in recent years. Hayek is the author also of *Collectivist Economic Planning* and *Individualism and Economic Order.*

ADOLF HITLER (1889–1945), Führer of Nazi Germany from 1933 until his death near the end of World War II. Founder of the Nazi party in 1919–1920, Hitler led an unsuccessful revolt in Munich. He was sentenced for nine months to prison, and it was there that he dictated *Mein Kampf,* a virulently anti-Jewish and anti-democratic tract.

JOHN MAYNARD KEYNES (1883–1946), English economist, philosopher, Cambridge University lecturer, and a director of the Bank of England. He first made his mark on world politics with his critique of the Paris Peace Conference of 1919 entitled *The Economic Consequences of the Peace.* In addition to *The General Theory of Employment, Interest, and Money,* Keynes wrote *The End of Laissez Faire,* and *Essays in Persuasion,* and numerous other works.

NIKITA S. KHRUSHCHEV (1894–   ), First Secretary of the Soviet Communist party since 1953 and Soviet Premier since 1958. A high party functionary for many years, he became its foremost agricultural spokesman after World War II. His 1956 address, "The Crimes of the Stalin Era," marked a major pronouncement in the program of "de-Stalinization."

VLADIMIR ILYICH LENIN (1870–1924), a founder of Russian Communism, leader of the Bolshevik revolution of October 1917, and chairman of the Soviet government from 1917 until his death in 1924. Lenin attempted to adapt Marxism to twentieth-century conditions and to Russia's backwardness by means of his theory of imperialism, his view of the peasants' role in revolution, and his elevation of the party to a position of central importance.

A. D. LINDSAY (1879–1952), English scholar and socialist, for many years Master of Balliol College, as well as an active participant in the Workers Education Movement in England. Besides *The Modern Democratic State*, Lindsay is noted for his study of *Kant* and the *Essentials of Democracy*.

WALTER LIPPMANN (1889–   ), political scientist, journalist, and one of the most respected American political commentators. His many books include *A Preface to Politics, Public Opinion, The Good Society*, as well as *Essays in the Public Philosophy*.

JOHN LOCKE (1632–1704), English philosopher, Oxford tutor, and assistant to the Earl of Shaftesbury, who was an important spokesman for the Whig party. Locke is noted for his *Letters Concerning Toleration* and *Essay Concerning Human Understanding* as well as for his classic formulation of democratic ideology as presented in the second of his *Two Treatises of Government*.

KARL MARX (1818–1883), German social philosopher, economist, publicist, and one of the founders of the international Communist movement. Among his major works are *A Contribution to the Critique of Political Economy, Capital, Critique of the Gotha Program*, and *The German Ideology*.

JOSEPH [GIUSEPPE] MAZZINI (1805–1872), an Italian patriot who formed *La Giovine Italia* (Young Italy), in the 1830s. This organization aimed to liberate Italy from the foreign yoke and domestic tyranny and to achieve its unification under a republican form of government. Mazzini was the theoretician of Italian unification, but when the great dream of his life was realized in 1860 by Garibaldi's armies, his disappointment over the establishment of the monarchy led him to spend his latter years attempting to organize the working class on a democratic basis.

JOHN STUART MILL (1806–1873), English philosopher and economist. While he is best remembered for his magnificent essay *On Liberty*, his other major works are *Representative Government, Utilitarianism*, and *Principles of Political Economy*. The last was the standard textbook on economics for many years in the United States.

BENITO MUSSOLINI (1883–1945), Italian dictator from 1922 to 1943. He formed the black-shirted Fascist movement shortly after World War I, and on attaining power, he established a secret police and reorganized the state economy into what he called the Corporate State. He joined with Hitler to form the Rome-Berlin Axis in 1937. He was executed by Italian Partisans after the allied liberation in 1945.

GAMAL ABDUL NASSER (1918–   ), President of the United Arab Republic. An outspoken opponent of colonialism and British influence in Egypt since his high-school days, he planned for ten years the 1952 coup against King Farouk's regime. Within a few years after seizing power, he began to carry out a program of land reform and nationalized the Suez Canal. The leading spokesman of the Pan-Arab movement, he united Egypt and Syria into one nation in 1958, but this union was short-lived.

JAWAHARLAL NEHRU (1889–   ), the first Prime Minister of India after independence, Nehru was educated in England. He succeeded his father as President of the Indian National Congress in 1929 and was, next to Gandhi, the major political leader of the Congress party, which he heads today. In addition to his numerous speeches and occasional political writings, such as *The Tragic Paradox of Our Age*, he is the author of *Independence and After, Autobiography, Glimpses of World History*, and *Toward Freedom*.

MORDECAI NESAHAHU (1929–   ), Professor of Sociology and Political Science at the Mapai Educational Institute, Bet-Berel, at Zofit, Israel. Nesahahu is one of the leading theoreticians of the Mapai party.

FRIEDRICH WILHELM NIETZSCHE (1844–1900), a German philosopher who began a brilliant teaching and literary career at age 25 when he was appointed to the faculty of the University of Basel. Among his most important works are *Thus Spake Zarathustra, Beyond Good and Evil*, and *The Genealogy of Morals*.

NICOLAAS J. J. OLIVIER (1919–   ), Vice-Chairman of the South African Bureau of Racial Affairs. Born at Pearston, Olivier was graduated a Bachelor of Law and admitted to the Cape Bar, but he has never practised as a barrister. He remained at Stellenbosch University, where he has been a Professor of Native Administration in the Department of Bantu Studies.

ERNEST RENAN (1823–1892), French philosopher and Orientalist. Studied Catholic theology before he turned to metaphysical inquiries and underwent an intellectual struggle between the two. Turning to politics in *The*

Future of Science, he tried to reconcile his belief in the need for an aristocracy of knowledge with the utilitarian doctrine of the greatest good of the greatest number. His more mature thought broke with the latter ideas. He also carried on research in Semitic philology and Phoenician archaeology.

JEAN JACQUES ROUSSEAU (1712–1778), French encyclopedist and philosopher. In addition to *The Social Contract,* Rousseau is well known for his self-appraisal in his *Confessions,* his *Discourses on Political Economy, The Arts and Sciences,* and *On the Origin of Inequality.* In *Émile* he set forth his famous and influential theory of education.

HERBERT RAVENEL SASS (1884–1958), American author, a native of Charleston, South Carolina, where he spent his life. His articles and stories appeared in numerous periodicals. Among his novels were *War Drums, Look Back to Glory,* and *Emperor Brims.*

CARLO SCHMID (1896–   ), German lawyer, intellectual and political leader of the Social Democratic party, in which he has served as a member of the Central Committee since 1947. He has been Minister of State in Württemberg, a member of the Diet, a member of the Parliament Council in Bonn, and, since 1949, a member and Vice-President of the Federal Parliament.

ADAM SMITH (1723–1790), British economist and philosopher, Professor of Moral Science in the University of Glasgow. His famous *Wealth of Nations* went through five editions in his own lifetime and has appeared in numerous editions and translations since then. He was also the author of *Theory of Moral Sentiments* and *Lectures on Justice, Police, Revenue, and Arms.*

JOSEPH STALIN (1879–1953), General Secretary of the Central Committee of the Soviet Communist party from 1922 until his death, Soviet Premier from 1941. Under Stalin, the U.S.S.R. developed modern technology through a series of Five-Year Plans which provided for the development of basic industries and collectivization of agriculture. In the 1930s, Stalin carried out purges of party and military officials in the course of which an estimated seven million people died or disappeared. One of the "Big Three" allied leaders in World War II, his postwar foreign policy break with his former allies led to the Cold War.

JOSIAH STRONG (1847–1916), American Congregational minister and secretary of the Home Missionary Society for Ohio, Kentucky, West Virginia, and western Pennsylvania. In addition to his highly popular *Our Country,* his writings include *Expansion, The Challenge of the City,* and *Our World: The New World Religion.*

PHILLIPS TALBOT (1915–   ), for many years the Executive Director of the American Universities Field Staff, a team of professors who since 1951 have served as foreign correspondents. Originally a Chicago newspaperman, Talbot obtained his doctorate in International Relations at the University of Chicago, where he specialized in relations between India and Pakistan. He has spent several years in India and is a co-author of *India and America: A Study of Their Relations*.

SIDNEY WEBB (1859–1947), and BEATRICE WEBB (1858–1943), famous English husband and wife team of non-Marxian socialists, who for many years were the most prolific writers for the Fabian Society (which was founded in large part through the efforts of Sidney Webb in 1884). Their lengthy list of joint authorships includes *The Decay of Capitalist Civilization*, *A Constitution for the Socialist Commonwealth of Great Britain*, a fifteen-volume study of English local government, and numerous Fabian tracts.

THOMAS WOODROW WILSON (1856–1924), Twenty-eighth President of the United States. A political scientist, president of Princeton University, and governor of New Jersey before becoming Chief Executive, he sought neutrality in World War I, but Germany's submarine activity against American shipping forced a declaration of war. His Fourteen Points, including the League of Nations proposal, were the basis for the armistice, but America did not join the League, for Wilson rejected compromise with a hostile Senate that refused to ratify the peace treaty. His Johns Hopkins Ph.D. thesis, *Congressional Government*, is a classic of American political science.

DAVID McCORD WRIGHT (1909–   ), American lawyer and professor of economics and political science who has taught at numerous colleges in the United States and abroad. He is presently serving at McGill University, Canada. In addition to *Democracy and Progress*, his other major works include *The Economics of Disturbance*, *Capitalism*, and *A Key to Modern Economics*.